MW00534481

Verification and Validation of Modern Software-Intensive Systems

G. Gordon Schulmeyer, CDP

Garth R. MacKenzie

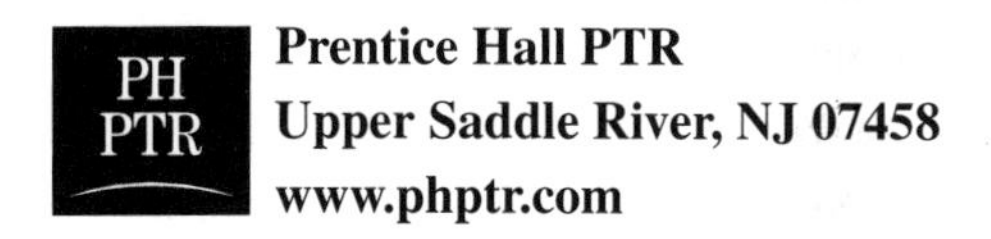
Prentice Hall PTR
Upper Saddle River, NJ 07458
www.phptr.com

Library of Congress Cataloging-in-Publication Data

Schulmeyer, G. Gordon
Verification and validation of modern software-intensive systems /
G. Gordon Schulmeyer, Garth R. MacKenzie
p. cm.
Includes bibliographical references and index.
ISBN 0-13-020584-2 (hardcover)
1. Computer software--Verification. 2. Computer software--Validation. I. MacKenzie, Garth R. II. Title.
QA76.76.V47S38 1999
005.1'4--dc21 98-53297
CIP

Editorial/Production Supervision: *MetroVoice Publishing Services*
Acquisitions Editor: *Paul Petralia*
Marketing Manager: *Bryan Gambrel*
Cover Design: *Anthony Gemmellaro*
Cover Design Direction: *Jerry Votta*
Manufacturing Manager: *Alexis R. Heydt*

Prentice-Hall, Inc.
Upper Saddle River, NJ 07458

Prentice Hall books are widely used by corporations and government agencies for training, marketing, and resale.

The publisher offers discounts on this book when ordered in bulk quantities.
For more information, contact Corporate Sales Department, phone: 800-382-3419;
fax: 201-236-7141; e-mail: corpsales@prenhall.com
Or write: Prentice Hall PTR
Corporate Sales Department
One Lake Street
Upper Saddle River, NJ 07458

Printed in the United States of America
10 9 8 7 6 5 4 3 2 1

ISBN 0-13-020584-2

Prentice-Hall International (UK) Limited, **London**
Prentice-Hall of Australia Pty. Limited, **Sydney**
Prentice-Hall Canada Inc., **Toronto**
Prentice-Hall Hispanoamericana, S.A., **Mexico**
Prentice-Hall of India Private Limited, **New Delhi**
Prentice-Hall of Japan, Inc., **Tokyo**
Pearson Education Asia Pte. Ltd.
Editora Prentice-Hall do Brasil, Ltda., **Rio de Janeiro**

For Jane

and

For Nancy

Contents

	Foreword	**ix**
	Dr. John Callahan	
	Preface	**xi**
	Organization of Book	*xi*
	Acknowledgments	*xvii*
	References	*xvii*
1	Introduction	**1**
	Definitions/Benefits	*1*
	Traditional V&V Methods	*3*
	Responsibility/Organization	*5*
	Multidimensional Model	*7*
	Basic Tenets of V&V	*11*
	Summary	*15*
	References	*16*
2	Processes, Models and Standards	**17**
	Multidimensional Model	*17*
	Processes	*18*
	Models	*28*
	Standards	*46*
	Summary	*48*
	References	*49*
3	Tools and Methodologies	**51**
	Introduction	*51*
	Multidimensional Model	*56*
	Traditional V&V	*56*
	Contemporary V&V	*70*
	Summary	*81*
	References	*82*
	Appendix A	*84*
	Appendix B	*91*
4	Documentation	**93**
	Introduction	*93*
	Multidimensional Model	*94*
	Documentation Process	*94*
	Requirements and Design Specification V&V	*98*

Functional and Test Specification V&V 106
Documentation Review Methods 113
Summary 115
References 116
General References 117

5 Metrics **119**

Introduction 119
Multidimensional Model 119
Traditional V&V 120
Contemporary V&V 132
Summary 140
References 140

6 Object Oriented (OO) Methods **141**

Introduction 141
Multidimensional Model 147
Traditional V&V 148
Contemporary V&V 154
Summary 162
References 164
General References 166
Appendix 166

7 Rapid Application Development (RAD) **169**

Introduction 169
Multidimensional Model 172
Traditional V&V 172
Contemporary V&V 177
Summary 197
References 198

8 Graphical User Interface (GUI) Development—Usability **201**

Introduction 201
Multidimensional Model 205
Traditional V&V 206
Contemporary V&V 209
Summary 230
References 231
General References 232
Appendix 232

9 Client / Server Networks **237**

Introduction 237
Multidimensional Model 245

Traditional V&V 245
Contemporary V&V 254
Summary 259
References 261
General Reference 262

10 Knowledge Based Systems (KBS) **263**

Introduction 263
Multidimensional Model 264
Traditional V&V 264
Contemporary V&V 267
Summary 283
References 284
General References 284

11 Internet and Intranet **287**

Introduction 287
Multidimensional Model 291
Traditional V&V 291
Contemporary V&V 297
Summary 310
References 311
General References 312

12 Data Warehousing **313**

Introduction 313
Multidimensional Model 316
Traditional V&V 316
Contemporary V&V 320
Internet/Intranet 332
Summary 336
References 336
General References 337
Appendix 337

13 Project Management **341**

Introduction 341
Multidimensional Model 344
Traditional V&V 345
Contemporary V&V 350
Summary 362
References 363
General Reference 364
Appendix 364

14 Risk Management **373**

Introduction 373
Multidimensional Model 374
Traditional V&V 374
Contemporary V&V 382
Summary 399
References 400

15 Integrated Product Teams (IPTs) **401**

Introduction 401
Multidimensional Model 404
V&V Aspects of IPTs 405
Summary 427
References 429
General References 429

16 Conclusion / Future Trends **431**

Introduction 431
Conclusion/Trends 432
Summary 451
References 451

Appendices

A Case Studies **453**

Introduction 453
Case Study 1: MAPS Information System 453
Case Study 2: Formal Methods for Verification and Validation of Partial Specifications 468
References 484

B Acronyms **485**

Index **489**

Foreword

John R. Callahan

This is a book for ALL software developers—not just software quality assurance personnel. Software quality is an integral part of our jobs as developers. Software quality is fundamental to software development—not simply the job of an add-on task, some other corporate division or an external reviewer.

The construction of any complex system involves two fundamental, complementary activities: design and analysis. After analysis of a problem, we propose the design of a solution. Given a solution, we test whether or not it solves our problem. If we determine that our solution is deficient or that we have misunderstood the problem, we revise the design. And so on. As software developers, we cycle between these activities to construct and refine our solutions through an improved understanding of the problem and our proposed solutions.

From this perspective, analysis is a fundamental and inseparable activity that occurs naturally during the development of any software system. Verification and validation (V&V) is a collection of analysis methods from which analysts can choose to accomplish their goal of finding deficiencies and potential risks in proposed solutions. Verification methods involve determining if the product is being built properly. Validation methods involve determining if the proper product is being built. The goal of finding deficiencies and risks in the processes and products of a project is not to punish the designers of a solution, but to focus improvements in the next version of the solution.

The development of a solution through iterative cycles of design and analysis is not a simple process. Failure to identify important deficiencies and risks as early as possible can lead to disaster. Without the effective use of proper analysis methods, poor designs will not reveal their weaknesses. The products of a software development effort—documents, designs, code, and test cases—can be properly analyzed to reveal problems and potential improvements, but the selection and application of methods and tools must be done by skillful analysts. Finally, these tools and methods must be applied to selected critical subsystems to economize analysis efforts, AND they must be applied to the entire, integrated system to stress critical dependencies between components. Indeed, it has been demonstrated empirically that most critical failures occur at the system level between "correct" components that have been incorrectly integrated.

In the cases of safety-critical systems, it is necessary that analysis be performed by an independent entity. Independent verification and validation (IV&V) is used during the development and maintenance of large-scale, high-cost, and high-assurance systems. This does not exempt the designers from their analysis tasks. Analysis can be performed independently of a design organization to provide a unique perspective on a problem. It has been shown that having "another set of eyes" looking at a system often finds more problems because the independent analysts do not have a vested interest in building the system, but rather they are charged with trying to break the system. The design side is concerned with demonstrating that the system does what it is supposed to do under nominal conditions. The analysis side is concerned with the flip side of the coin: demonstrating that the system does not do what it is not supposed to do under off-nominal conditions.

This dichotomy of builders and breakers on either side of a fence in a development project is a paradigm currently employed at organizations such as Microsoft, NASA, Motorola, Intel and Internet security firms. The Space Shuttle project, for example, relies on IV&V to find critical flaws and potential risks in successive operational increments (OIs) of the Shuttle's flight software. In such projects that integrate V&V activities, it is the dialogue between the builders and breakers that embodies software development. Neither side of the fence is more or less important than the other. It has been my experience that in large projects, analysis performed by the designers tends to focus on nominal behaviors. But my observation is not unique. Glenford Myers said much of this over 20 years ago in his book, *The Art of Software Testing*, when he stated that "developers should not test their own code."

It is not enough to find an error or risk in a proposed design. The errors and risks must be tracked from their initial identification to their eventual resolution or acceptance. Many errors and risks on a project will never be resolved, but may be accepted as low priority, non-critical flaws. Some of these flaws will be fixed in subsequent release, or work-arounds will be issued as corrective actions. Nevertheless, it is important to manage these risks and errors by recognizing and tracking their existence. If such problems are not identified and tracked, then these unknown risks can develop into unexpected failures.

This book presents a compendium of V&V methods within a structured framework that allows developers (designers and analysts) to determine the methods most applicable to their processes and products. The framework organizes the techniques so that designers and analysts can apply methods that have the largest return on investment (ROI) for finding errors and risks in designs at the earliest possible phase during development. This book serves as an important catalog of V&V methods used during all phases of software development. It also reports on the effectiveness of various techniques and discusses future trends and promising approaches.

We must seek a balance between our cultural biases of optimism and pessimism in software development. We must strive towards an acceptance of identifying flaws and potential risks. Instead of judging problems as abject failures, we should instead view an error as an opportunity to better understand the problem and the refine our solutions. In some cases, problems can guide us to redirect and re-scope our solution completely. As you read this book, I hope that you will view verification and validation (V&V) as an aid to software design and not an impediment. Better analysis can lead to improved understanding and better design.

—Fairmont, WV

Preface

Modern software-intensive systems surround us. These modern systems include banks, investment institutions, weapons systems, automobiles, medical systems and even environmental systems, as well as most of the systems that touch our lives. A fundamental question is: Can we trust the software-intensive system? There have been failures reported in the press, such as the long distance telephone failure that tied up transactions for nearly a day. These failures are significant enough to make us pause and consider the consequences. What can we do about it?

One approach that has been successful in the past for these software-intensive systems has been the use of independent verification and validation (V&V) to ensure the successful implementation of these systems. Past experience with independent V&V was mostly confined to Department of Defense (DoD) weapons systems and NASA manned space systems.

Today, the modern software-intensive systems pervade our society. This book attempts to provide V&V material so that today's modern software-intensive systems can be trusted. Many of these modern systems are described in this book, such as client/server networks, data warehousing, knowledge-based systems, graphical user interface (GUI) development, Internet/intranet, etc.

The prior successful application of V&V to previous system is updated to be applied to modern systems. There has been significant success in the application of V&V to these areas already. What is happening in modern methods of V&V and how it is being successfully applied is discussed throughout the book.

Organization of Book

Many projects, which ought not be attempted, nonetheless are attempted and with bad results. Many of them proceed because of the Abilene Paradox discovered and named by Jerry Harvey in 1988. The Abilene Paradox occurs when one decision maker suggests a project, but has no good reason for it except to see what others will say about it. As it often happens, the others have no real reason to object and they assume the suggester is highly motivated, so they go along with the suggested project. As a result, the project gets started and nobody really wants it. Jerry Harvey noticed that sometimes "organization members make collective decisions that lead them to take actions contrary to what they want to do, and thereby arrive at results that are counterproductive to the organization's intent and purposes." He gives several symptoms, but they add up to the notion that "you go along to get along"[1] (pp. 36, 92, 93).

As the reader takes a trip through this book, some points need to be made to prevent a "trip to Abilene" that no one really wants to take. The main point is that there is a wide-ranging scope of subjects in this book, such as knowledge-based systems (KBS), object oriented (OO) methods, graphical user interfaces (GUI)—usability, data warehousing, etc. The authors do not claim to be experts in these numerous areas, but have done sufficient research and have sufficient experience to approach these subjects, especially in limiting their scope to the perspective of V&V, in a useful manner for the reader.

Another point is that within each of the subject areas of each chapter there are numerous, world-wide V&V tools, techniques, and methods discussed to provide the reader with a sense of the V&V activities going on in that area. Although the authors have not utilized all of the V&V tools, techniques, and methods discussed in each chapter, the reader is focused on the most pervasive and most successful of these in use for V&V in that area.

In this book, the authors tried to maintain a balance of recognized books, standards, technical magazines, and Internet resources as a research basis, recognizing that some academics have condemned the use of the Internet for scholarly or technical research. Without the Internet resource the authors believe that the timeliness of the book's contents would have greatly suffered because publication lag time would have precluded including the use of the latest V&V information. While discussing the Internet references it should be pointed out that the Internet references were accurate and active at the time of publication, but are subject to change.

With these points in mind the organization of the book is provided with a brief summary of each chapter.

Chapter 1 gives an introduction to the book and establishes the basis for the multidimensional model that flows throughout the book. Details of the multidimensional model are given in this chapter. The basic traditional concepts related to software verification and validation are covered in Chapter 1.

Chapter 2 discusses software development processes; analyzes V&V in the context of the various life-cycle models, and looks at the standards related to V&V. The purpose of process is to provide a clear description of what is intended to be done. The idea that a process package is a set of documents and training material that communicates everything about the technology is set forth in Chapter 2. Inspections as process are also discussed. The most pervasive model for software development is the Software Engineering Institute's Capability Maturity Model (CMM[sm*]) for Software, which is discussed in this chapter with the emphasis on model. A brief overview of the most prevalent life cycle models used for software—waterfall, modified waterfall, build, ISO 12207, spiral, model-based, and fourth-generation model—is given because they provide the foundation in which V&V personnel operate with software development. The Product Maturity Model

* CMM is registered in the U.S. Patent and trademark Office. Capability Maturity Model is a registered service mark of the Carnegie Mellon University.

and the product validation model are discussed in this chapter. The standards that apply to V&V are covered.

Chapter 3 covers specific tools and methodologies to be used in the V&V process. When requirements are analyzed in association with an initial set of V&V tasks, various tool categories for the V&V tasks are discussed. Testing, as the basic tool to aid validation, is covered. V&V methods covered include a release method, regression testing, program verification, peer reviews, and traceability. The need for a V&V Tool Management Plan is covered in the chapter. Because of Microsoft Corporation's forefront position on the world stage, what they do in regard to tools and methods for V&V has special significance, and is covered in this chapter.

Chapter 4 discusses the V&V aspects of documentation. The V&V of specifications is covered, including: completeness, consistency, feasibility, and testability. Document reviews are a mainstay of any V&V effort. The interim products of a software development effort are documents, and they must be analyzed to ensure the right product is being developed in an efficient manner. Documentation review levels include:

Level 1: Document completeness—individual document.

Level 2: Compatibility with standards.

Level 3: First-level consistency check—internal.

Level 4: Second-level consistency check—requirements check, external, minimal CASE (computer aided software engineering) tool usage.

Level 5: Major review—review code logic, algorithms, full use of CASE tools.

The importance of certifying specifications is covered next. How to verify and validate test specifications is discussed.

Measurement and metrics associated with the V&V process is the focus of Chapter 5. Metrics can be collected throughout software development. These metrics can be plotted using bar graphs, histograms, and Pareto charts as part of statistical process control (SPC). The plots can be analyzed by software management as well as V&V persons. Some generic procedures for estimating software reliability are discussed. The Goal/Question/Metric (GQM) paradigm, which helps managers establish the appropriate metrics and helps the V&V person to monitor the level of risk in a software development project, is covered.

Chapter 6 provides a brief definition of object oriented (OO) methods. The Esprit Project called AVAL (automated validation) to improve the V&V process in OO is discussed. Also covered is OO database verification using a system that automates proving correctness of database transactions.

The VOCAL Method, which is built around information encapsulation to apply the benefits of multiperspective methodologies to V&V, is covered. This chapter also covers dynamic verification, which works on C++ to help find errors not easily found by debugging & testing. OVID (Object View Interaction Design), which focuses on objects that the user is aware of, a view of objects, and the interaction (or interfaces) between user and objects, is discussed. Correctness verification and an object oriented design (OOD) verifier are also covered in Chapter 6.

Chapter 7 is a discussion of V&V for rapid application development (RAD). Just in Time (JIT) inspections are used for RAD development V&V at the Jet Propulsion Laboratory. ObjectGEODE, a major toolset dedicated to analysis, design and V&V through simulation, code generation and test of real time, and distributed applications, is covered. DSDM (dynamic systems development method) is a consortium-developed, de facto UK standard for RAD. Within DSDM are concepts applied to V&V, such as scope management through time boxing and testing concepts that shift to validation throughout. These important concepts are discussed in Chapter 7. VV&A (verification, validation and accreditation) is covered for RAD, and a "SMART"* response to VV&A is discussed.

Chapter 8 covers the V&V of graphical user interfaces (GUI) with the emphasis on usability. The concept of a User Validation Plan that describes project objectives, what the user will do, how to validate, critical success factors, and user validation methods is discussed. Formative testing for defect removal, questionnaires and interviews, and SUMI (Software Usability Measurement Inventory), providing an internationally standardized questionnaire, are all part of this usability chapter. Usability inspections, where evaluators inspect or examine usability-related aspects of user interface, are covered for many different aspects. A mathematically based technique for describing system properties called formal methods is covered. MUSiC (Measuring Usability of Systems in Context), another ESPRIT Project that analyzes performance measurement, is discussed in this chapter. Context analysis of usability composed of users, tasks, and work environments is also discussed.

Chapter 9 defines client/server networks as characterized by division of application into components processed on different network computers, made up of client (request information) and server (process request, perform service, and return requested information to client). Expanded V&V considerations beyond the mainframe are discussed. Caching and cache coherency issues are covered in this chapter. What V&V needs to take into account for load testing and scalability are considered. How distributed component platforms and advanced distributed simulations impact on V&V of client/server networks is covered. When processes continue to operate in disconnected components, they might perform incompatible operations, causing network partitioning faults, of which the V&V person must be aware. How client/server networks move towards the Web browser as a client and the server as the DBMS (database management system) is discussed in relationship to the V&V aspects.

Chapter 10 covers V&V aspects of knowledge-based systems (KBS), which are described as the manipulation of data or knowledge structures using artificial intelligence, while attempting to mimic "expert" performance (formerly expert systems). Discussed is that V&V must determine knowledge base structure, find knowledge base partitions, and completeness and consistency of expert systems. To satisfy the specification V&V must validate underlying knowledge (logical validation and semantic consistency). V&V gets help by using the described decision tree for V&V. V&V must focus on human interaction with intelligent agents.

---

* Susceptibility Model Assessment and Range Test

Chapter 11 discusses V&V of the Internet/intranet. VDTs (Verifiable Development Techniques) used on the NASA FACADE project demonstrate changes to development where V&V cannot be performed due to inappropriate or unavailable information from development. However, what V&V can do is discussed. When development efforts are predictable and measurable and highly amenable to V&V, they are called VDTs, which are amenable to Internet/intranet V&V. This chapter covers V&V constraints on the Internet/intranet, such as language (Java) issues, security considerations, and standards.

Chapter 12 defines data warehousing as an electronic means to store large amounts of data and to support decision-making needs. Data considerations are the keys to V&V here; data acquisition and storage and data quality are covered, as well as how the Internet/intranet affect V&V and implementation of data warehousing is covered.

Chapter 13 covers project management for V&V. Items covered in this chapter are V&V planning, phase audits to be conducted by the V&V person, scheduling of the V&V activities, and various strategies for choosing V&V techniques. How the Software Engineering Institute's CMM key process areas of Software Project Planning and Software Project Tracking and Oversight affect V&V management is discussed. Because of the continuing importance of process to software development the V&V person is provided information about project management process methods and process variability.

Chapter 14 covers risk management, a subject that many consider to be the essence of V&V. A V&V approach to the GQM (goal, question, metric) approach is covered. A GQM predictive function method is discussed in which the characteristic certainty and confidence functions associated with goals and questions can be based on many existing methods. These methods have evolved from experiences on large numbers of actual projects. The V&V GQM model simply tries to relate the calculation of risk to the analysis these methods provide in order to help identify areas of a project that need attention. A formalized methodology for criticality and risk assessments is called CARA methodology. This is a systematic procedure for rank-ordering program elements with respect to well-defined scoring factors associated with criticality areas and risk drivers of importance to a project. CARA provides V&V project management with the capability to efficiently develop appropriate and realistic V&V plans. V&V product/process risk maturity provides a measurement method for determining V&V project risks. A particularly unique aspect of risk assessment is covered with a discussion of V&V of expert systems.

Chapter 15 covers the V&V aspects associated with having successful integrated product teams (IPTs) on a project. The main thrust of the chapter relates the elements of IPTs to a picture puzzle and shows how to assemble the pieces correctly for a successful IPT from a V&V perspective. The puzzle elements covered are:

- Customer
- Systems
- Software Development
- Program Management

- Quality Assurance (QA)
- Configuration Management (CM)
- Verification and Validation (V&V)
- Other Groups (within an IPT)
- Other IPTs

The benefit of this approach is that in a true IPT application, the V&V agents are participating members of the IPTs and are provided information readily so that the process can be maximally effected. Team effectiveness methods are briefly covered. An integrated product development (IPD) CMM and assessment method is discussed in relationship to V&V aspects of IPTs.

Chapter 16 starts with a discussion of the Testing Maturity Model because of the importance of testing to the essence of validation. A mature testing process requires the expanded definition of testing to include reviews, audits, walkthroughs, and inspections activities considered to be a part of V&V processes. A continuous improvement program is discussed in this chapter as important to a project's V&V methodology, where performance assurance collected metrics on V&V performance can be used to mold and improve V&V methods, tools, and procedures. Analyzing software products after each major development stage to ensure that the product agrees with the specification established prior to that stage for V&V, is discussed. How the SEI's CMM for software maturity level of an organization affects V&V is considered in this chapter. A truly exciting future trend is the use of KBS to perform the V&V activities as an automated aid to the V&V person. How V&V helps to provide for the future safety at the Federal Drug Administration is covered. The most practical and effective way to enhance software system safety is to apply safety-enhancing techniques throughout software development and maintenance. A V&V matrix for the future is provided that provides a cross reference between the future trends for V&V and the items of concern to modern V&V.

The appendices contain some case studies that bring together concepts from multiple chapters for a V&V practical solution and a glossary of acronyms used in this book.

The structure used for most of the chapters in this book is:

- Introduction to the technology area (usually providing a short definition)
- Multidimensional model aspects of this chapter's subject
- Traditional V&V (what is the same)
- Contemporary aspects of V&V
- Summary
- References

Chapters 3, 4, 5, 13, 14, and 16 lend themselves to the introduction of special comparison tables. These tables focus on specific V&V elements that the V&V person may use as a concise method for reviewing what needs to be done.

Acknowledgments

Many of the principles, concepts and tools discussed throughout this book are built upon the concepts covered in Lewis' 1992 book, *Independent Verification and Validation.*[2] The Lewis book provides a way to perform V&V in a large development environment. An earlier book, *Software Verification and Validation: Realistic Project Approaches,*[3] by Michael S. Deutsch, provides a framework based on a toolset generically called *automated verification system* (AVS) for performance of V&V on a large, real time project.

James J. Holden, III essentially wrote the chapter on IPTs and developed the unique puzzle pieces concept for bringing the elements together in a coherent manner. Special thanks for reviewing and commenting on the book are in order for John Callahan and Raymond Schulmeyer. The Prentice Hall, Inc. editor-in-chief, Jeffrey Pepper, made this book possible. The Prentice Hall Inc. copy editor, Sharon Jehlen, and project manager Scott Suckling helped to make this a readable book.

References

1 DeGrace, Peter and Stahl, Leslie Hulet, *Wicked Problems, Righteous Solutions* (Englewood Cliffs, NJ: Prentice Hall, 1990).

2 Lewis, Robert O., *Independent Verification and Validation* (New York: John Wiley & Sons, Inc., 1992). Copyright © 1992 John Wiley & Sons, Inc., Adapted by permission of John Wiley & Sons, Inc.

3 Deutsch, Michael S., *Software Verification and Validation: Realistic Project Approaches* (Englewood Cliffs, NJ: Prentice Hall, 1982).

CHAPTER 1

Introduction

Definitions/Benefits

Verification and validation (V&V) can be and is being effectively applied to modern software-intensive systems. This book covers many aspects of V&V in relationship to the challenging field of system development involving a significant amount of software. Simply because of the nature of the evolution of software-related systems development, it is not necessary that the computer be embedded into the system for this book to apply to the V&V of the system. Many modern systems that require V&V include client/server and an intranet where the computer is far from being embedded into the system. Any significant quantity of software in a system whether the computer is embedded or not is appropriate for the application of the V&V concepts discussed in this book.

Why perform V&V on software-intensive systems? Perhaps one answer lies in Edward Yourdon's (1992) book, *Decline and Fall of the American Programmer.*[1] Yourdon, in his introduction, discusses major issues facing the production of software, particularly in the United States:

> It doesn't do much good to write lots and lots of software if it doesn't work, or if it can't be trusted, or if it can't be easily modified and maintained. The quality of software is just as important (if not more important) than the productivity with which it is generated. This, I think, is going to be the key issue of the 1990s. (p. 6)

Can V&V improve software quality? The theoretical answer is "yes," and this is substantiated by many cases where empirical data is available. Then why is it not more widely practiced? While on one side of the spectrum there are large organizations like NASA that have set up entire facilities dedicated to the theory and practice of V&V, on the other side there are a large body of software producers who not only do not practice it, but are largely ignorant in the entire subject. On the surface, the basic premise of V&V is very simple. Verification is the assurance that the products of a particular phase in the development process are consistent with the requirements of that phase and the preceding phase. Validation is the assurance that the final product satisfies the system requirements. Robert O. Lewis[2] gives the following definition, specifically of *independent* V&V:

> Independent verification and validation (IV&V) is a series of technical and management activities performed by someone other than the developer of a system to improve the quality and reliability of that system and to assure that the delivered product satisfies the user's operational needs. (p. 7)

This definition covers the essence of V&V, but this book does not give the emphasis to "independent" that Lewis does.

Another perspective of V&V modified from Air Force Instruction 16-1001 (1996), *Verification, Validation and Accreditation,* focuses on the software-intensive aspects of V&V. Verification is the process of determining that a system accurately represents the developer's conceptual description and specifications. This is accomplished by identifying and eliminating mistakes in logic, mathematics, or programming. This process establishes that the system's code and logic correctly perform the intended functions, and to what extent the development activities conform to state-of-the-practice software engineering techniques. Validation is the process of determining the degree to which a system accurately represents the user's requirements.

The authors, however, began to believe that V&V is one of the most misunderstood and misappreciated subdisciplines in systems and software development, while instructing a graduate-level course on the subject. We found that even our combined 60-plus years of experience as programmers, software developers, engineering managers, project managers, consultants, and teachers did not fully prepare us to answer our students when they asked, "How does V&V work in the context of modern software development?"

This book answers the question—by (a) investigating the historical and theoretical underpinnings of V&V, (b) explaining why V&V remains an important part of the development process, and (c) discussing how many traditional V&V methodologies are reengineered for modern software-intensive systems.

The concept of traditional V&V is based on several primary assumptions:

- There is—or should be—a predefined process with predefined phases by which a system is developed. (V&V can appropriately interact with software development when this is done.)
- These development phases result in physical products that can be reviewed or tested against defined requirements. (Product artifacts are important for V&V persons to verify the system.)
- It is better to detect and fix product errors earlier in the development process than later. (V&V significantly aids in detecting errors and reducing overall development costs.)

Twenty-five years ago when V&V first started to become a "hot topic," there was little reason to question these assumptions. Even today, most practitioners would agree that these points are still valid. What has gotten murkier are the definitions, and that is because the domain of software intensive systems, and in turn of V&V, has greatly expanded since the 1970s.

Benefits of V&V

Software V&V is a systems engineering discipline which evaluates the software in a systems context, relative to all system elements of hardware, users, and other software. Like systems engineering, V&V uses a structured approach to analyze and test the software against all system functions and all hardware, user, and other software interfaces. Software quality depends on many attributes (e.g., correctness, completeness, accuracy, consistency, testability, safety, maintainability, security, reusability). Each organization, including V&V, involved in the software development process contributes to the building of quality of the software.

When performed in parallel with software development, Wallace and Fujii state that V&V yields several benefits:[4]

- It uncovers high risk errors early, giving the design team time to evolve a comprehensive solution rather than forcing them into a makeshift fix to accommodate software deadlines.
- It evaluates the products against system requirements.
- It provides management with visibility into the quality and progress of the development effort that is continuous and comprehensive, not just at major review milestones (which may occur infrequently).
- It gives the user an incremental preview of system performance with the chance to make early adjustments.
- It provides decision criteria for whether or not to proceed to the next development phase. (pp. 2–3)

Traditional V&V Methods

Traditional V&V methods are important to the readers of this book because they provide a foundation. That foundation involves what needs to be done from both a technical and managerial perspective. Robert O. Lewis (1992) in *Independent Verification and Validation* provides a framework for traditional V&V. He covers support functions, management functions, and technical aspects. This section summarizes the four major V&V aspects from Lewis' book:

1. requirements verification
2. design verification
3. implementation verification
4. validation.

Lewis reviews the following significant elements for each V&V phase: assessment activities, products reviewed/analyzed, and the tools related to the phase.

Requirements Verification:

1. Assess Requirements:

a. for criticality and risk (user interface, I/O data, system trade studies, test strategy);
b. review (meetings and reviews participation, problem reports produced)

2. Products Covered: system specification, software requirements specification, requirements tracing, interface requirements specification, hardware prime item specification, software development plan (SDP)

3. Acquire Tools: perform verification with V&V and developer's tools, simulation and modeling

Design Verification:

1. Assess Design:

a. design risk;

b. timing & sizing analysis;

c. adherence to SDP;

d. review (meetings and reviews participation, problem reports produced)

2. Products Covered: critical algorithms, software design document, interface design document, software test plan, requirements tracing to design, user interface, I/O data at detailed level

3. Acquire Tools: perform verification with software analysis tools, simulation or rapid prototyping, design reviews

Implementation Verification:

1. Assess Code (standards followed, structure and syntax, cyclomatic complexity, library contents, version control adequacy):

a. review (meetings and reviews participation, problem reports produced);

b. release procedures

2. Products Covered: data dictionary terms, I/O data, algorithms, compiler, OS and utilities versions, software development files (SDFs)

3. Run static analysis tools

Validation:

1. Assess Test Readiness/Testing:

a. interfaces, especially with hardware;

b. actual to simulated results on key algorithms;

c. monitoring contractor testing;

d. review (meetings and reviews participation, problem reports produced);

e. track configuration control board (CCB) actions;

f. perform independent V&V tests, perform independent analysis

2. Products Covered: software test plan, test coverage by mapping software requirements specification into software test description, actual tests vs. software test description, user and operator manuals, software design document readiness as product specification

3. Run Dynamic Analysis Tools

One needs to be aware that this summary is exactly that—not enough to perform contemporary V&V, but enough to provide what basically is performed in the traditional environment. It is certainly important to note that validation in contemporary V&V is much more than testing as is divulged throughout the book.

Responsibility/Organization

This entire section on the responsibility and organization of V&V is derived from Dolores R. Wallace and Roger U. Fujii, *Software Verification and Validation: Its Role in Computer Assurance and Its Relationship with Software Project Management Standards*[4] (p. 4–6). While the techniques of V&V may be applied by anyone involved in software development and maintenance, a comprehensive V&V effort is often administered by a specific group. Similarly a project may have developers who are from the end-user organization or who may be contractors or subcontractors. Other groups may be software quality assurance (SQA), configuration management, and data management. The organizational structure of a project depends on many characteristics (e.g., size, complexity, purpose of the software, corporate culture, project standards, contractual requirements). Often these groups are separate, but in many instances, especially for small projects, the structure is not as diverse.

A functional view of V&V and other groups demonstrates how they complement software quality responsibilities. The software development group builds the software product to satisfy the established quality and performance requirements and relies on its SQA group, configuration management specialists, documentation specialists, and many others. The SQA group verifies that the development process and products conform to established standards and procedures. Through the use of reviews, audits, inspections, and walkthroughs, it acts as a formal check and balance to monitor and evaluate software as it is being built. The software systems group ensures that the software product satisfies system requirements and objectives. It uses techniques such as simulations to gain reasonable assurance that system requirements are satisfied.

The configuration and data management groups monitor and control the software program versions and data during their development using such techniques as formal audits, change control records, traceability of requirements, and sign-off records. The user group must provide assurance that the software product satisfies user requirements and operational needs. Typically, it uses techniques such as formal design reviews and acceptance testing.

The V&V group is responsible for verifying that the software product at each life-cycle phase satisfies software quality attributes and that the software product at each phase satisfies the requirements of the previous phase; this is discussed in detail in Chapter 2. In addition, V&V is responsible for validating that the software satisfies overall system requirements and objectives. It is also V&V's job in relation to requirements to validate that the system does not perform as not required, which is a safety consideration. The activities are directed at the software, but V&V must consider how the software interacts with the rest of the system—including hardware, users, other software—and with other external systems. V&V maintains its own configuration and data management functions on programs, data, and documentation received from the development organization to ensure that V&V discrepancy reports are against controlled documents and to be able to repeat V&V tests against controlled software releases. V&V responsibilities may vary for different projects.

V&V documentation evaluation and testing may be different from those conducted by other groups. The SQA group reviews documents for compliance to standards and performs a check on the technical correctness of the document contents. V&V may perform in-depth evaluation by such activities as re-deriving the algorithms from basic principles, computing timing data to verify response time requirements, and developing control flow diagrams to identify missing and erroneous requirements. V&V may suggest, if appropriate, alternative approaches. V&V testing is usually separate from the development group's testing. In some cases, V&V may use development test plans and results and supplement them with additional tests.

A major influence on the responsibilities of V&V, and its relationship to other groups, is to whom V&V reports: whether it is independent, embedded in the development system group, embedded in the SQA group, or embedded in the user group. The traditional approach is that the V&V group is independent of the development group and is called independent V&V or IV&V. In this relationship the V&V organization establishes formal procedures for receiving software releases and documentation from the development team. V&V sends all evaluation reports and discrepancy reports to both the user (or higher level management agency in charge of the development responsibility) and development group. To maintain an unbiased technical viewpoint, V&V does not use any results or procedures from the SQA or systems group.

The V&V tasks are oriented toward analysis (i.e., algorithm analysis control/data flow analysis) and comprehensive testing (i.e., simulation). The objective is to develop an independent assessment of the software quality and to determine whether the software satisfies critical system requirements. Advantages of this approach are detailed analysis and test of software requirements, an independent determination of how well the software performs, and early detection of high-risk software and system errors. Disadvantages may be short term higher cost to the project and additional development interfaces. Later discussions in this book demonstrate that V&V pays for itself and then some in the long term.

When the V&V group is embedded in the developer's systems group, the V&V tasks are to review the group's analyses (e.g., algorithm development, sizing/timing) and testing (e.g., test evaluation or review of the adequacy of the development test planning document). In some instances, the V&V organization may be the independent test team for the system group. The results of V&V are reviewed and monitored by the systems and SQA groups. An independent V&V group reporting to the systems group is another alternative. Advantages to using systems personnel in the V&V tasks are minimum cost impact to the project, no system learning for the staff, and no additional development interfaces. A disadvantage is the loss of engineering analysis objectivity.

When the V&V group is embedded in the developer's SQA group, its tasks take on a monitoring, auditing, and reviewing content (e.g., audit performance, audit support, test witnessing, inspection support, documentation review). In these tasks, the V&V group is part of SQA and maintains its relationship to systems and other development groups in the same manner as SQA. The main advantages of embedding V&V as part of SQA are low cost to the project and bringing V&V analysis capabilities into reviews, audits, and inspections. A disadvantage is the loss of an independent software systems analysis and test capability.

When the V&V group is embedded in the user group its tasks are an extension of the user responsibilities. The tasks consist of configuration management support of development products, support of formal reviews, user documentation evaluation, test witnessing, test evaluation of the development test planning documents, and user testing support (i.e., user acceptance testing and installation and checkout testing). As an extension of the user group, the V&V group would receive formal software product deliverables and provide comments and data to the development project management that distributes the information to its own development team. An advantage of this approach is the strong systems and user perspective that can be brought to bear on the software product during development. The main disadvantages are loss of detailed analysis and test of incremental software products (since these typically are not formal deliverables); also, error detection and feedback to the development team are constrained by the frequency of formal product deliverables. If the user group has an IV&V group reporting to it, then the disadvantages can be overcome. However, in this instance, the project incurs the disadvantage of having an additional development interface.

Multidimensional Model

Figure 1.1 illustrates the multidimensional model for V&V. It is the set of various parameters that define and influence both the problems with which V&V must contend and the tools and methodologies that V&V has at its disposal to perform its function.

Figure 1.1 Domain of software V&V

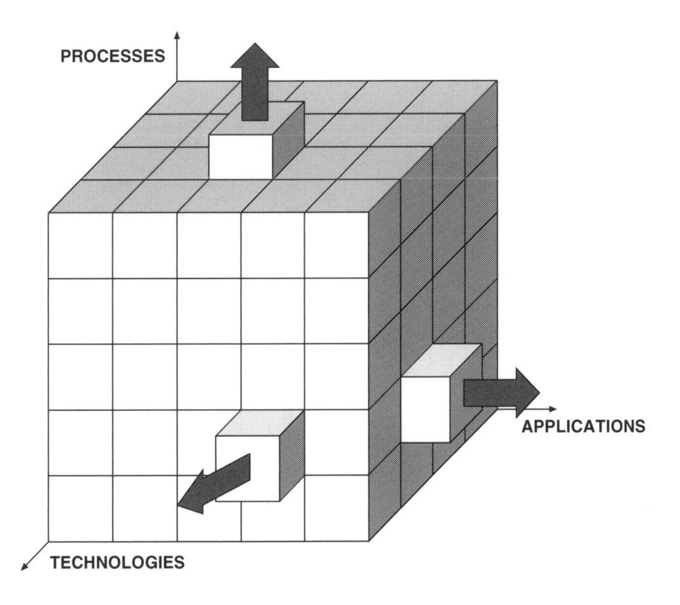

On one axis, we encounter processes—life-cycle models, development methodologies, protocols, and standards. These represent the techniques and paradigms that systems and software developers, as well as V&V personnel, have at their disposal. The history of software engineering management over the past thirty years has focused primarily on this process axis. The classical waterfall model for the software life cycle and its later derivatives (see Chapter 2), such as the incremental build, spiral, and model-based models, are evolutionary steps along the process axis. Similarly, programming methodologies have evolved—from top-down structured programming in the 1970s to object-oriented techniques in the 1990s (Figure 1.2).

On the next axis in Figure 1.1, we look at the effect of applications. When V&V was first systematically applied as a discipline, the major focus was on large, complex software programs as mission critical or safety related—largely in areas of aerospace, military, or nuclear safety. A timeline of computer applications is given in Figure 1.3. Since computer and software-based systems were much less pervasive than today, V&V for other, more mundane applications was largely ignored. But today, how do we define "complex" and "mission critical"? It is fairly safe to say that the average PC-based word processing program today contains more functionality and more "lines of code" than all the software running the on-board computers in NASA's SATURN program when the moon landing occurred in 1969. While a word processor might not fit the exact definition of mission critical, what about the software that tracks your accounts and runs the automated teller machines at your local bank? So in effect, the very fact that software-intensive systems have become such a part of our daily businesses and lives raises the question as to why V&V should not be viewed as equally important, if not more important, than it was thirty years ago.

Figure 1.2 Timeline of processes

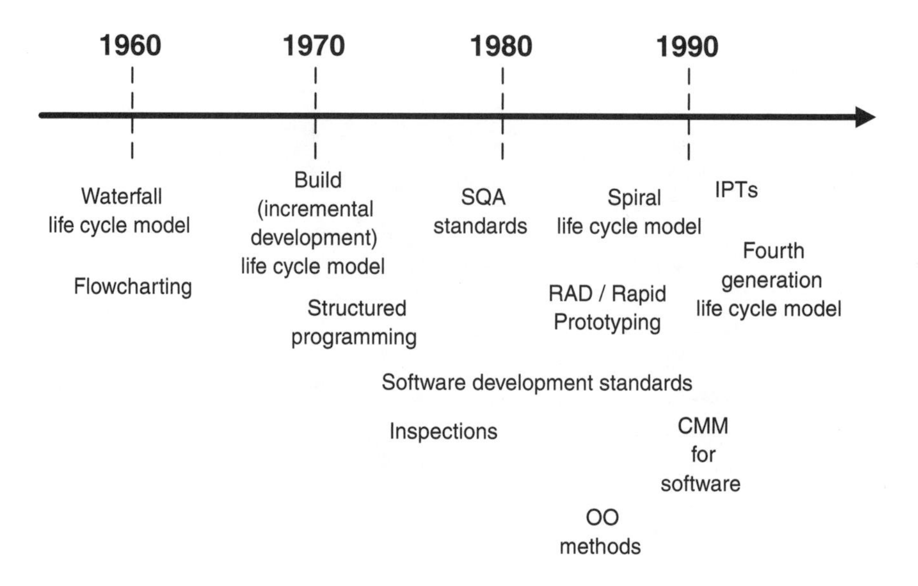

Figure 1.3 Timeline of applications

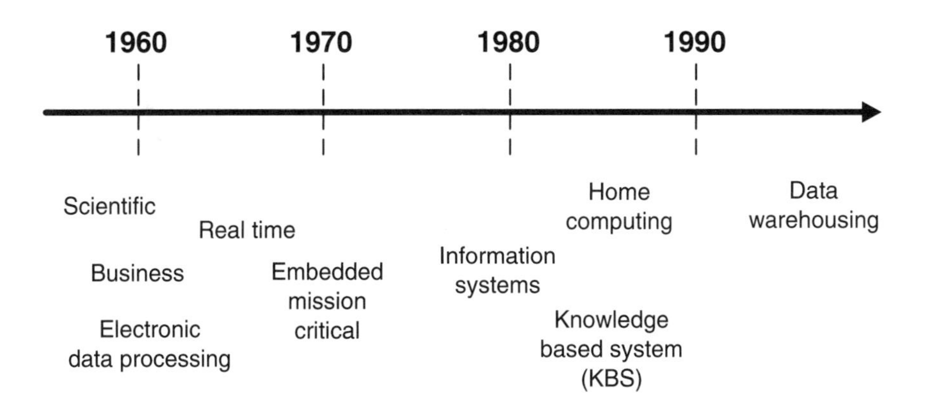

Figure 1.4 Timeline of computer hardware

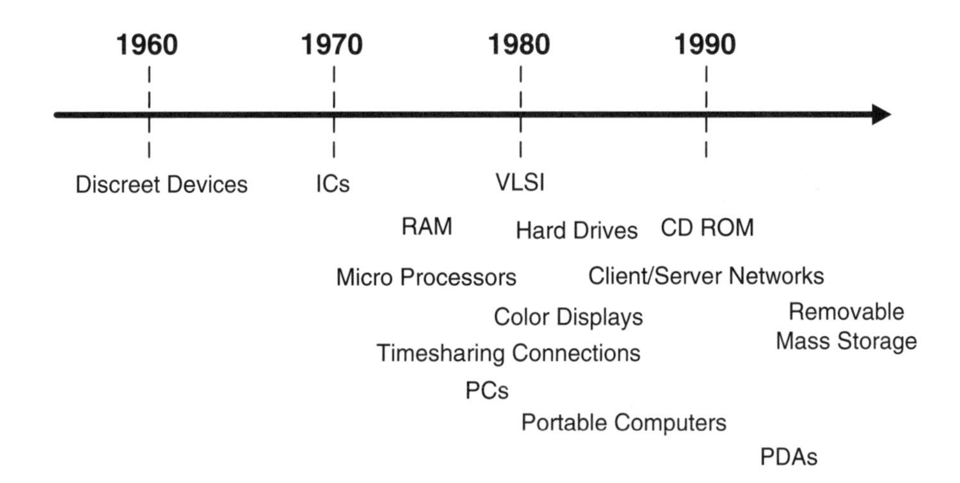

The enabler of the software "explosion" has been technology, represented by the third axis. The surge in stand-alone and networked PCs, and even advanced mini and mainframe computers has been made possible by low-cost, high-performance processors, memory devices, and permanent storage units (Figure 1.4). As a result, it would probably be a safe bet to say that the average mid-sized American company today has in its possession more raw computing capacity than existed in the entire world in 1950. Maybe even 1960!

Along with the remarkable advancements in computer hardware has been progress (not as pronounced) in software technology. By that is meant languages, toolsets, educational processes, and all

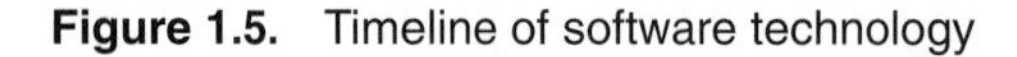

Figure 1.5. Timeline of software technology

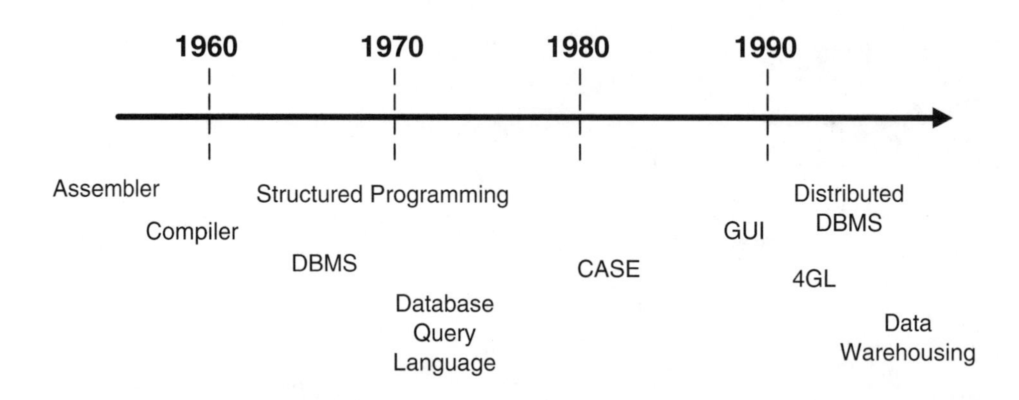

the underlying theory that supports modern software development (Figure 1.5). It is possible today for a small group of software developers, even a single individual using CASE (computer aided software engineering) tools, to build products with far more capability than could have been built by large project teams two decades ago.

Naturally the three domains' axes (summarized in Table 1.1) are not "orthogonal." They interact. As history progresses along any axis we observe trends, changes, and events that are caused, complemented, reinforced, and occasionally contradicted by similar movement along the other axes. The availability of low-cost desktop computers created a huge demand for applications, which in turn, forced changes in software technology that made even more advanced applications possible, which in turn, created a demand for even more powerful hardware. This "push-pull" effect between technology and applications has forced change along the process axis. This change is because many of the older development models and methodologies are no longer responsive to the needs of customers who demand, and developers who must produce, high-quality, advanced computer programs.

The professional who practices V&V in today's environment, whose primary goal is the production of high-quality software that satisfies the user's expectations, is therefore caught in a whirlwind of change, often dealing with conflicting priorities, objectives, and methods. Simultaneously, this professional must also constantly answer the question posed by developers, managers, and even customers, "Where is the added value of V&V?"

Table 1.1 Contents of the multidimensional model

Processes	*Applications*	*Technology*
life cycle models	embedded mission critical	ICs
• waterfall	business operations	PCs
• modified waterfall	product lines	ASICs
• build (incremental development)	data warehousing	architectures
• ISO 12207	KBS	software architectures
• spiral	intelligent/autonomous systems	software languages
• model-based	information services	object oriented languages
• fourth generation	real time	internet/intranet
RAD/prototyping		client/server networks
standards		CASE
protocols		workstations
methodologies		GUI (usability)
CMM for software		storage methods
project management		
risk management		
documentation		
metrics		
object oriented methods		
integrated product teams		

Basic Tenets of V&V

Gravitz and Waite[5] in "A VV&A Strategy for Legacy Models, Simulations, Algorithms and Software Components" describe verification, validation, and accreditation (VV&A) tenets. Seven of their tenets that generically apply to V&V are summarized below:

Tenet 1 (Using Object Oriented Analysis)

There is substantial value in using a point-of-view that is object oriented in planning a V&V program. Evaluation of components considers the degree of correctness or acceptability of the values of object attributes.

Tenet 2 (Employing a V&V Evaluation Activity Space)

The V&V evaluation activity space (Figure 1.6) is the system's multidimensional view of the V&V enterprise, whose dimensions exhaust the important attributes of the conceptual space. The points or cells in this evaluation activity space represent the V&V data products that are produced when a V&V agent carries out a V&V activity in evaluating a particular element. This representation of the evaluation space (i.e., the space projected onto the activities) is (a) a valuable representation of V&V program activity, (b) a convenient medium to support the balancing of "investment" in V&V activity, and (c) a simple form from which to generate estimates required for executing the proposed program. Using this V&V evaluation activity space assures a systematic, complete (not exhaustive)

Figure 1.6 V&V evaluation activity space[5]

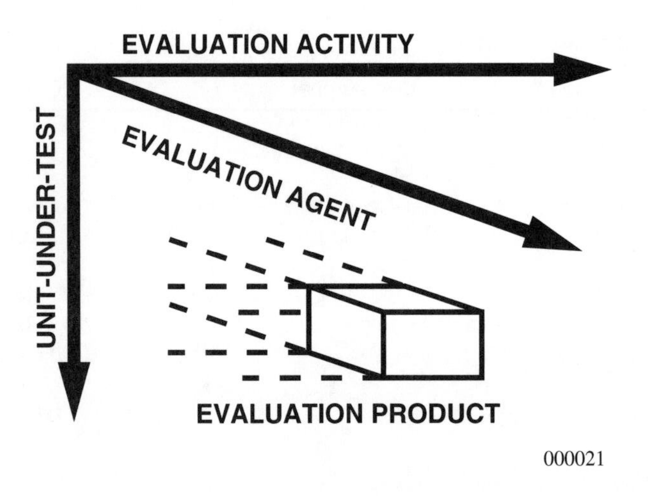

Figure 1.7 V&V evaluation kernel process model[5]

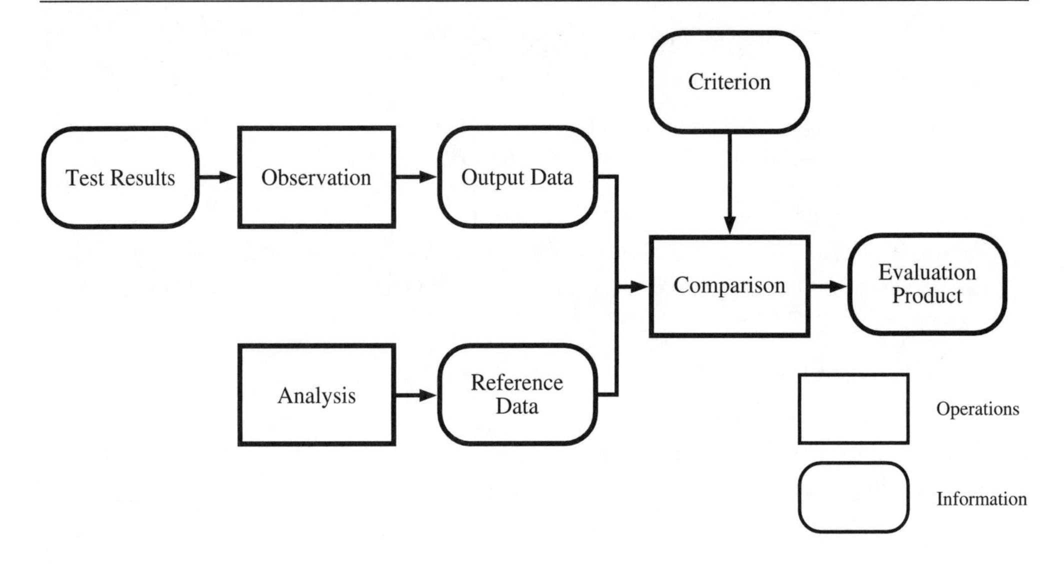

basis for description and revision of a proposed V&V Program, thereby defining enough of the V&V project to aid in estimating the cost.

Tenet 3 (Applying a V&V Evaluation Kernel Process Model)

The V&V evaluation kernel process model (Figure 1.7) serves as a template for V&V evaluation activity planning. V&V products are defined in terms of analysis and testing, an evaluation activity, and an evaluation agent.

Tenet 4 (Using a Systems and Requirements Flow-Down)

Requirements for a V&V program should be driven from the top down. The goal of all V&V activity is to achieve the appropriately performing system for a particular customer. It makes sense to start by identifying the basis of such a judgmental decision, infer the forms of evidence sufficient to support a positive outcome, and derive the means to generate such evidence as necessary and sufficient. V&V program execution is from the bottom up (Figure 1.8). V&V agents execute a suite of assessment activities to generate the V&V data products and information.

Tenet 5 (Applying a Managed Investment Strategy)

Managed investment is the execution, from all the possible candidate V&V activities (Figure 1.9), of a carefully selected subset of V&V activities that (a) offer the "best return on investment" by providing the essential information necessary for V&V reports findings, and (b) provide the evidence required to support successful V&V. Cost as an independent variable is considered during the selection and execution of the V&V activities, as well the realities of the program and fixed resources

Figure 1.8 Systems and requirements flow down[5]

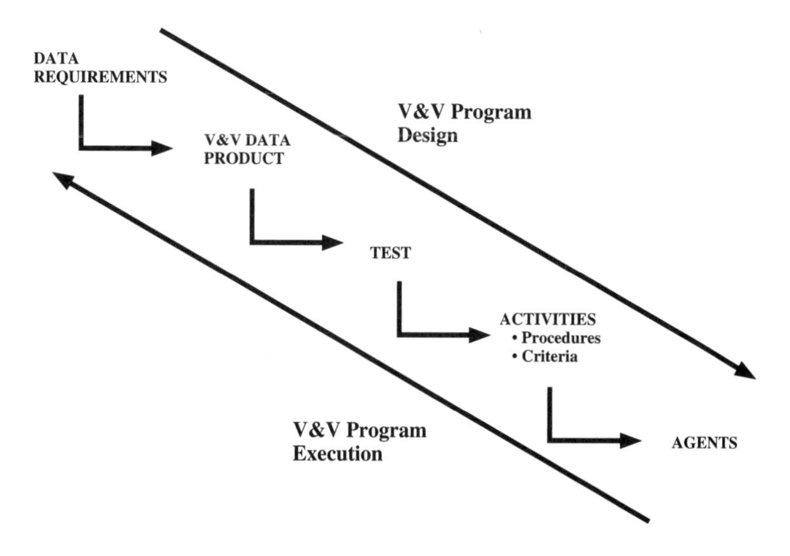

Figure 1.9 Managed V&V investment strategy[5]

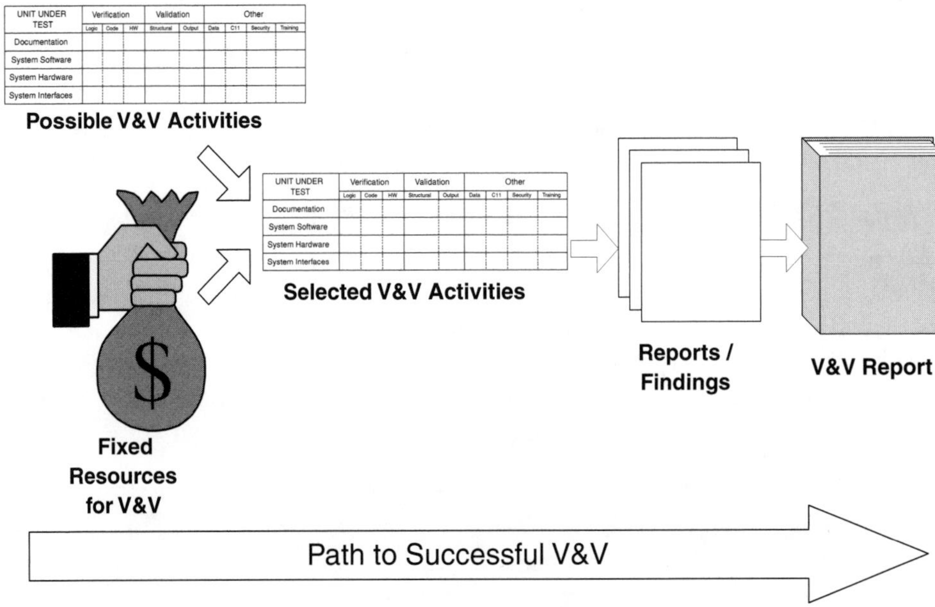

UNIT UNDER TEST	Verification			Validation		Other			
	Logic	Code	HW	Structural	Output	Data	C11	Security	Training
Documentation									
System Software									
System Hardware									
System Interfaces									

Possible V&V Activities

Fixed Resources for V&V

Selected V&V Activities

Reports / Findings

V&V Report

Path to Successful V&V

available for V&V. As the most cost-effective set of possible activities, the actual V&V evaluation suite subset of V&V activities chosen should constitute an optimal investment in V&V.

Tenet 6 (Developing an Audit Trail)

Configuration Management (CM) is integral to the V&V process (Figure 1.10). Generally, CM is defined as the meticulous control of code, documentation, change history, and usage of the test resource. Good CM precludes unauthorized modifications to the reference version of the test resource, which would invalidate previous V&V efforts. The CM process documents significant events in the life cycle, thus providing a consistent audit trail. Of primary concern for the V&V program is maintaining configuration identification, establishing configuration status accounting, and having change control. The goals for CM procedures put in place as they affect V&V should include (a) *ensuring* integrity of the code by version control management; (b) *recording* the history of its development by archiving code and documentation changes, as well as change requests, and its documented usage as a test resource; (c) *providing* a process by which users can input to the enhancement process; and (d) *establishing* a CM baseline for each V&V assessment activity.

Tenet 7 (Using an Integrated Product Team (IPT))

IPTs and their role in the V&V process in modern software development are so important that an entire chapter (15) is devoted to them. IPTs provide the foundation for the V&V planning process; help to reduce cost, schedule, and performance risk; and integrate customer and developer efforts to address and resolve cost, schedule, and performance issues.

Figure 1.10 Documentation and configuration management (CM) reinforce V&V[5]

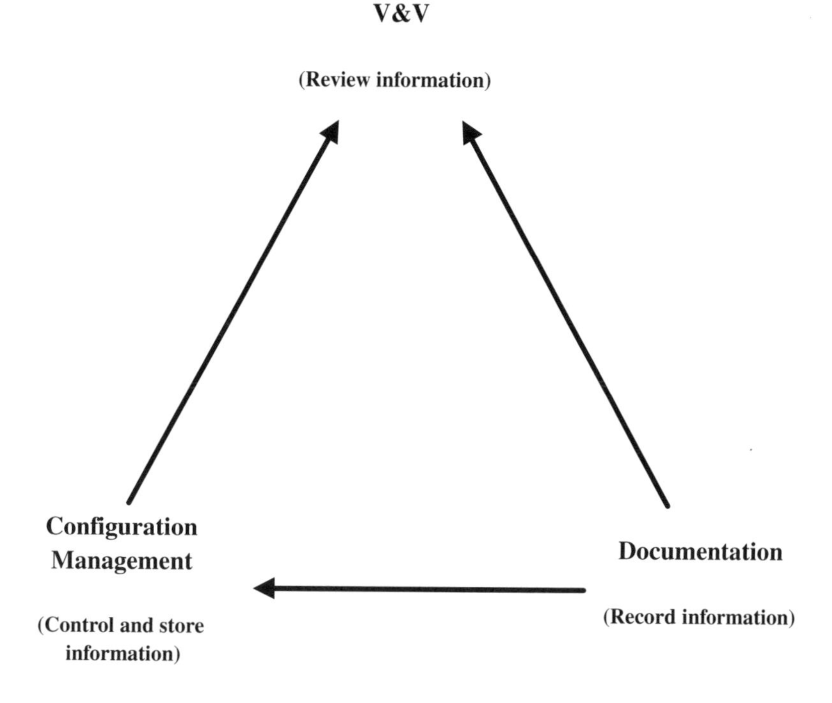

Summary

This introduction covered the responsibilities and organization for V&V. According to Wallace and Fujii (1989) the main benefits of V&V are that it:

1. uncovers high risk errors early;
2. evaluates the products against system requirements;
3. provides management with visibility into the quality and progress of the development effort that is continuous and comprehensive;
4. gives the user an incremental preview of system performance with the chance to make early adjustments; and
5. provides decision criteria for whether or not to proceed to the next development phase.[4]

Traditional V&V concepts are introduced. The multidimensional model of V&V containing processes, applications and technologies is discussed. Gravitz and Waite's (1997) seven tenets of V&V are covered:

Tenet 1 (Using Object-Oriented Analysis)

Tenet 2 (Employing a V&V Evaluation Activity Space)

Tenet 3 (Applying a V&V Evaluation Kernel Process Model)

Tenet 4 (Using a Systems and Requirements Flow-Down)

Tenet 5 (Applying a Managed Investment Strategy)

Tenet 6 (Developing an Audit Trail)

Tenet 7 (Using an Integrated Product Team (IPT)[5]

The following Bertrand Meyer[6] thought provoker is appropriate to close out this introduction:

> It does not have to be either/or! To say that careful, formal design removes the need for testing is just as absurd as to think that with enough V&V, imperfect software technology can be made up for. Especially in mission critical systems (and how many developments these days are not?), both are required. The best *a priori* efforts, managerial (simulation, careful design) and technological (the most sophisticated method, tools, hardware, languages) are needed. And *a posteriori* checks; an independent QA team, extensive testing, and V&V are needed. The motto should be: "Build it so you can trust it, then don't trust it." (p. 103)

References

1 Yourdon, Edward, *Decline and Fall of the American Programmer* (Englewood Cliffs, NJ: Prentice Hall Publishing Co., 1992).

2 Lewis, Robert O., *Independent Verification and Validation: A Life Cycle Engineering Process for Quality Software* (New York: John Wiley & Sons, Inc., 1992). Copyright © 1992 John Wiley & Sons, Inc., Adapted by permission of John Wiley & Sons, Inc.

3 Air Force Instruction 16-1001, *Verification, Validation and Accreditation (VV&A)*, June 1, 1996.

4 Wallace, Dolores R. and Fujii, Roger U., *Software Verification and Validation: Its Role in Computer Assurance and Its Relationship with Software Project Management Standards*, National Institute of Standards and Technology Special Publication 500-165, May 1989.

5 Gravitz, Robert M. and Waite, William F., "A VV&A Strategy for Legacy Models, Simulations, Algorithms and Software Components," *Proceedings of the Spring 1997 Simulation Interoperability Workshop*, Simulation Interoperability Standards Organization, Inc., March 1997, www.aegisrc.com

6 Meyer, Bertrand, "Practice to Perfect: The Quality First Model," *IEEE Computer*, (© May 1997 IEEE), pp. 102–106.

CHAPTER 2

Processes, Models and Standards

This chapter and the next on tools and methodologies establish an environment within which V&V functions. An explanation is given in this chapter of what process, model, and standard are. The process section elaborates on the purpose and packaging of processes. The systems engineering and the inspections processes are highlighted for insight into processes that are helpful to the V&V person. Methods of developing a model and modeling a process are discussed to tie together some of the concepts in this chapter. Life cycle models are very important to the V&V person and are given much coverage in this chapter. A model for product maturity is presented to aid the V&V person in understanding when a product is complete. A list of V&V standards is provided, and there is a brief discussion of V&V standards registry.

Software developers may employ processes such as software quality assurance, the Defect Detection Process (DDP), the Defect Prevention Process (DPP), and models, such as a specific life-cycle model, a product maturity model, or a capability maturity model with a focus on nominal requirements. This means that that they are demonstrating that the specifications and code implement customer requirements. V&V, however, focuses on off-nominal behavior; that is, their avoidance, safety, etc. This chapter, therefore, covers software development processes, models, and standards, so as to identify interface points for V&V processes.

Multidimensional Model

Processes, models, and standards all are on the process axis of the multidimensional model. In fact, processes is one of the axes. Table 1.1 lists of the contents associated with processes. As the technology advances, the processes are rethought and extended to respond to the advances to technology. One prime example is how life cycle models have evolved over time to meet the technological needs of software development.

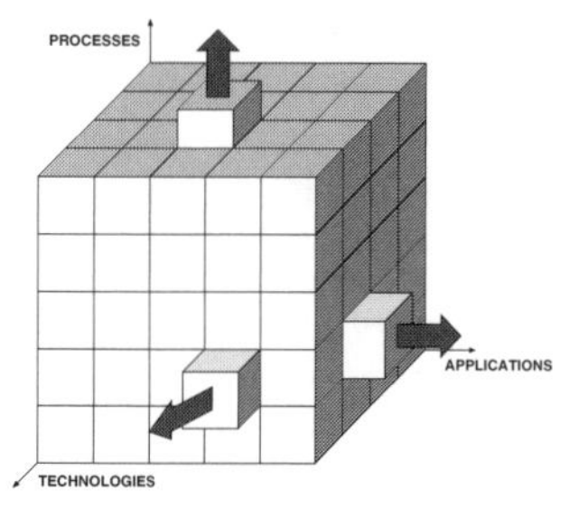

Models include life cycle models as a prime example for software development and the concomitant activities for V&V. As the initial software development and V&V thereof, expanded in complexity and size, the models to support that development and V&V also allowed for the complexities. Life cycle models have grown from the must complete all activities in a phase (waterfall) to the overlapping of activities within any phase (build—incremental development). Even what type of model to use for an aspect of the development project occurs in the model-based life cycle model.

Standards are on the processes axis of the multidimensional model simply because they are implementations of a way of doing software development. Standards provide generally accepted ways to develop, assure and V&V the software-intensive system product and process.

Processes

The following paragraphs describing a process comes from Mohamed Fayad's "Software Development Process: The Necessary Evil?"[1]

> A process…defines specifically who does what, when, and how. Webster's dictionary says it is "a particular method of doing something generally involving a number of steps or operations." … A process implements one part of a method, such as OMT [Object Modeling Technique], in sufficient detail such that the results are repeatable by any number of similarly trained individuals following the steps of the process. However, processes are generally locally documented implementations of methods. Processes usually tell which tools will be used to implement a method.
>
> Processes generally define "what" needs to be done, but they are only one part of what a method defines. They may define a set of "high-level" or "low-level" activities that need to be performed during the software development effort. They are usually partially ordered by time (e.g., activity A must precede activities B and C, and activities B and C must be done concurrently). Software processes may define a set of reviews or they may define how a review is to be conducted. Any complete set of processes will list the deliverables that result from each process. Processes can put object-oriented techniques to work.
>
> Where a method or a technique defines the theory behind an approach, a process addresses the practicalities of using the method in a given development environment. A technique explains the ideas that are to be applied, whereas a process lays out the concrete actions that have to take place. A technique can only predict results, while a process might define the metrics to be used to verify the result. [Figure 2.1] illustrates the differences between a method and a process.…
>
> Remember that a process is a description of the steps required to implement some goal, usually part or all of a method. Processes transform textbook theories and method descriptions into real action steps. Documented processes enable the development team to consistently apply and benefit from the application of techniques. It is essential to realize that processes are codified steps that describe a particular organization's way of achieving development goals. This means that processes cannot be acquired off the shelf, but must rather be developed over time.
>
> Management must support the move to process-based development. This means that process must not be abandoned when schedule pressures loom or process costs initially slow some development phases. Processes are especially important for new development teams. Even in a well-organized group, new methods and tools introduce confusion. Individuals will often perceive themselves as less skilled than before and the routines they had established with others

Figure 2.1 The differences between a method and a process[1] (p. 102)

METHOD	PROCESS
• Theoretical	• Practical Tools
• Ideas	• Concrete Actions
• Predictions	• Metrics

will certainly change. Management must make sure that establishing process-oriented development will allow team members to contribute positively. It is management's job to show how processes will help achieve the overalls goals of the organization and how each team and its members fit into the big picture. But perhaps the hardest challenge that management has in promoting processes is to make sure that people do not view processes as weapons against them, but rather as avenues for personal career, skill, and team growth. This requires a change in management's thinking from the individual as the basic unit to the team, and from individual performance measurement to process measurement. Process measurement will highlight problems and errors in the process. If these measurements are used for performance reviews rather than process improvement indicators, the process is doomed to fail.

Process orientation is hard to adopt. Processes are commonly seen as extra bureaucracy that only serves to make a project less effective. In far too many cases this perception is correct, and process adoption is resisted. Even if the organization is sincerely committed to adopting a process-oriented approach, many excuses are offered at first…

1. "My team is smart; they've been programming for years." This excuse shows a fundamental misunderstanding of what a process is. Experienced teams benefit as much or more from repeatable processes as do new teams. While an experienced group may have a perfectly acceptable approach in doing certain tasks, the approach is dependent on the particular knowledge of particular people. The approach is not scaleable, transferable, or measurable. Environmental changes can cause undue difficulty to the team without an explicit process.

2. "We're too busy. No time for processes." This might be true, but implementing processes will reduce the time it takes to perform some tasks. On a larger scale, process improvement often shortens the development cycle.

3. "Maybe on a new start, but my program has been around for years." What better opportunity can there be? For a team that knows its goals, implementing processes is easier. The team understands what must be done and how to do it. Documenting new methods and techniques is considerably harder.

4. "Processes are busywork that no one ever reads." This is unfortunately true in far too many organizations. If the only purpose of the process documentation is to sit on a shelf, then do not bother implementing processes. But if the team understands that the processes are for

> them, the measurements they make will mostly be for process improvement. If the team realizes processes allow them to improve their own work, then processes are not busywork.
>
> 5. "Software is a creative process, not an assembly line." This is one of the hardest excuses to overcome because it requires substantial re-education throughout the organization. At its core is the misconception that techniques such as software development that involve creativity cannot be documented. However, without defined processes the development team cannot consistently apply any development approach. Without the process, developers freely apply their own unique version of software development. This approach becomes especially risky when implementing a new technique. Core development processes should exist before starting a project, and should be continuously tuned as the program matures.
>
> Very few organizations have established a set of defined processes for software development. Those groups having processes often have not spent the time and money to do real process assessment and improvement. It is common to see "processes" that are merely lists of rules in a somewhat arbitrary order. In many organizations, especially those trying to conform to the Software Engineering Institute's Capability Maturity Model (SEI/CMM), turning everything into a process has become a goal in itself. [Fayad believes] this is the wrong approach. Software development organizations exist to develop software rather than processes. The intent of the SEI/CMM and other process improvement programs, such as Bootstrap, and SPICE [Software Process Improvement and Capability dEtermination], is not to change focus from developing software to developing processes, but instead to use processes and process improvement to better develop software.
>
> Because of the pressure to improve processes, it is easy to move into "process paralysis." Process paralysis, as defined by Yourdon, is when the project team can become thoroughly overwhelmed by the new technology and gradually end up spending all of its time (a) trying to understand the new technology, (b) arguing about the merits of the new technology, or (c) trying to make it work. At the...detailed process level, this paralysis can cause groups to forget that they are developing software rather than processes. Part of these problems can be attributed to a misunderstanding of what a process is. (pp. 102–103)

Yamamura and Wigle[2] provide a specific example of the benefits of process based on Boeing's long history of software process improvements for its STS (Space Transportation Systems) business unit (Figure 2.2). Boeing's STS has recently achieved a SEI CMM Level 5, indicating a high level of software process maturity that very few organizations have achieved.

> Long before the SEI CMM, STS had strong process champions motivated to manage with facts and data. In the early 1980s, the organization first documented its software processes, a first step in defect analysis and prevention. The core set of metrics was defined to measure status. STS participated with other Boeing organizations and the central software group to develop a company-wide embedded software development standard. Training in these standards was developed and made available to all software employees.
>
> In the late 1980s, an organization-wide process improvement effort was initiated that used a six-step method for software. At this time, all documented processes were evaluated and updated accordingly. Defect data was used as a basis to institute a formal design- and code-inspection process that significantly reduced defects found beyond designer testing...

In the early 1990s, continuous quality improvement...methods were implemented throughout the organization. [Continuous quality improvement] teams were formed and, again, all software processes were evaluated and updated accordingly. The focus of this effort was on productivity increase and cycle-time reduction; some processes realized a 50% reduction in cycle-time. The [continuous quality improvement] methods provided a more formal structure for process improvement than the previous six-step method.

[In the mid 1990s, at Boeing's STS], the SEI CMM had been used as a framework to support process improvement. This framework, specifically designed for software, provides a more complete set of criteria to assess progress. Much of the activity has been to correlate the existing STS processes to the CMM framework, though most of the practices at CMM Levels 2 through 5 were already institutionalized in STS. The [Software Engineering Process Group] SEPG activities were expanded and formalized during this time to include the evaluation and implementation of new processes, maintenance of existing processes, training, defect prevention, and technology insertion. Members of the SEPG include the STS software engineering manager, all program software managers and leads, key domain experts, and the process focal points. A process focal point leads the weekly SEPG meetings; all members, including managers, take on action items and implement team decisions.

One major savings from managing most of the processes at the organization level rather than the program level is that new-start programs can use an existing set of common processes with trained personnel. Instead of being a new set of measures, metrics become just another data

Figure 2.2 History of process improvement[2] (p. 4)

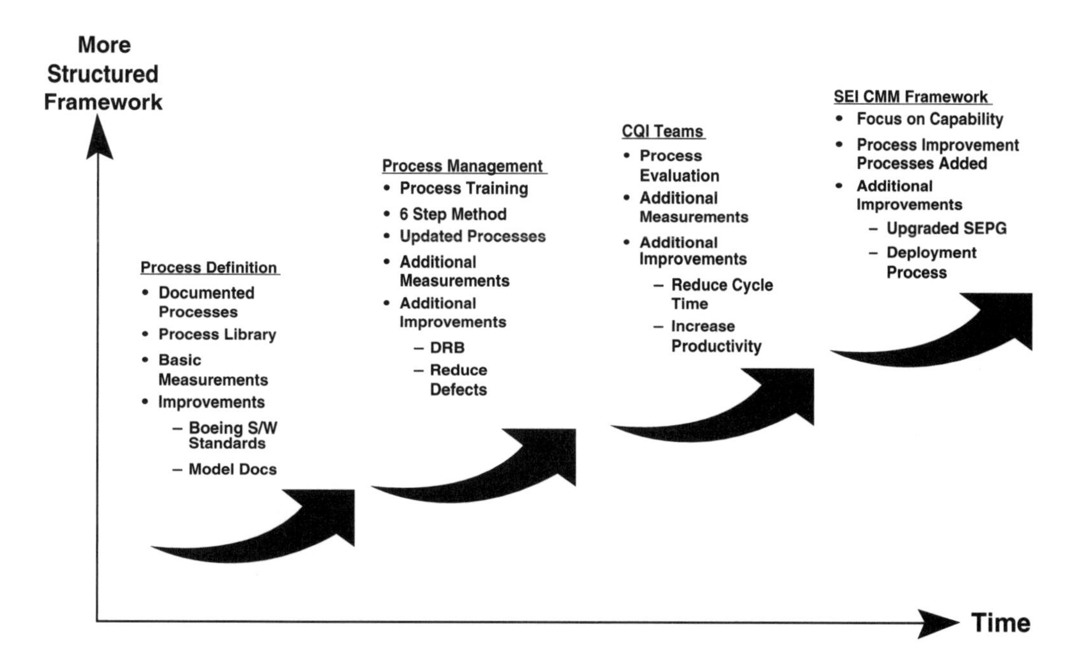

point added to the profile, and the lessons learned are fed back into the processes for use on the next program.

[Figure 2.2] should not be viewed as a road map to Level 5; it simply shows that process improvement had been occurring over many years and that the best practices were used during each period. Each framework provided more structure and knowledge to the process improvement activities than the previous one. [It is likely that] a program that starts out today will now use the SEI CMM as its framework for assessment and achieve similar improvements in a much shorter time. (p. 3–4)

Purpose of Process

The purpose of process is to provide a clear and succinct description of what is intended to be done. There are several language and modeling methods to represent processes. Sophisticated techniques are sometimes appropriate, but remember that programs are enacted by machines, while processes are principally enacted by people. The objective should be to make the process understandable and usable. So, do not use some advanced method unless it clearly supports your needs. One such method is called information mapping (Horn, 1990) shown in Table 2.1. Much like software development, process definition is a skill that one can learn and practice. As one gains experience in defining and using processes, one soon sees what tools and methods work best.[3]

Table 2.1 Principles of Information Mapping® [Horn][3]

Chunking	Group information into manageable chunks.
Relevance	• Place "like things" together. • Exclude unrelated items from each chunk.
Consistency	Use consistent: • terms within each chunk of information, • terms in the chunk and label, • organization, and • formats.
Integrated graphics	Use tables, illustrations, and diagrams as an integral part of the writing
Accessible detail	Write at the level of detail that will make the document usable for all readers.
Hierarchy of chunking and labeling	• Group small chunks around a single relevant topic. • Provide the group with a label.

Information Mapping® is a registered trademark of Information Mapping, Inc., Waltham, MA.

Process Packaging

A process package is a set of documents and training material that communicates everything about the technology. A process package includes an overview of what to expect, how to use the information, references to other corporate efforts and process packages, guidelines for using the process, training aids targeted to different user groups, a set of slides for conducting training workshops, and data and lessons learned.

As Figure 2.3 shows, a process package evolves over time as experience is gained and feedback is incorporated. The approach builds on the Quality Improvement Paradigm's three phases: planning, execution, and analysis (and packaging), much like the Boeing's STS experience just discussed. Within these three phases, Basili and colleagues[4] define seven steps that unfold much as they did practically for Boeing's STS:

1. Characterize and evaluate the organization's current environment and technology.
2. Set organizational goals and refine them into quantifiable questions and metrics. Choose the processes that have the best chance of paying off if technology improvements are made.
3. Create documents, targeted to different audiences, that define new technology or improvements to existing technology in those high-payoff areas.
4. Pilot the technology in sample projects, analyze the data, refine the technology, and create a lessons learned document.
5. Enhance the process package by targeting the training materials and consulting support to a particular audience.
6. Deploy the technology within a business unit, monitor its use carefully, and learn from the organization's progress.
7. Analyze data from using the process package, evaluate the practices, and improve the process package. Proceed to step 1 and, armed with the recorded, structured experience gained from this and previous cycles, start the cycle again. Package this experience to make it accessible to others involved in creating process packages. (p. 71)

Systems Engineering Process

In "The Role of Independent V&V in Upstream Software Development Processes" Easterbrook[5] states:

> The distinction between the terms verification and validation has largely to do with the role of specifications. Validation is the process of checking whether the specification captures the customer's needs, while verification is the process of checking that the software meets the specification. Verification includes all the activities associated with producing high quality software: inspection, design analysis, specification analysis, and so on. It is a relatively objective process, in that if the various products and documents are expressed precisely enough, no subjective judgments should be needed in order to verify software.

Figure 2.3 Evolution of a process package[4] (p. 74)

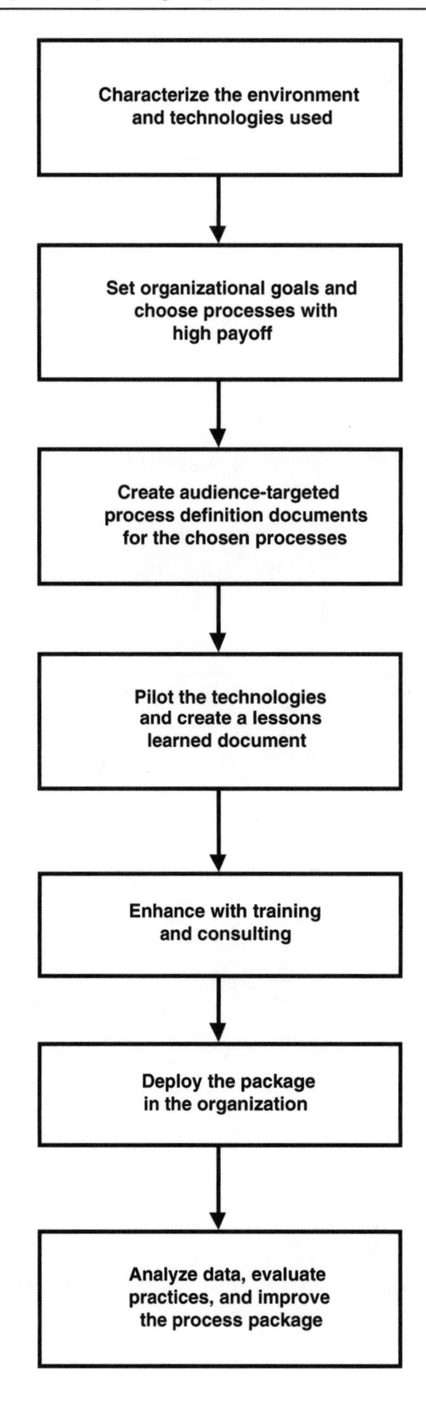

In contrast, validation can be an extremely subjective process. It involves judgments of how well the (proposed) system addresses a real-world need. Validation includes activities such as requirements modeling, prototyping and user evaluation. In a traditional phased software life cycle, verification is often taken to mean checking that the products of each phase satisfy the requirements set in the previous phase. Validation is relegated to just the beginning and ending of the project: requirements analysis and acceptance testing. This view is common in many software engineering textbooks, and is misguided. It assumes that the customer's needs can be captured completely at the start of a project, and that those needs will not change while the software is being developed. In practice, requirements change throughout a project, partly in reaction to the project itself: The development of new software makes new things possible. Therefore, both validation and verification are needed throughout the life cycle. For practical purposes, the distinction is not important. V&V is now regarded as a coherent discipline: Software V&V is a systems engineering process which evaluates the software in a systems context, relative to all system elements of hardware, users, and other software.

Figure 2.4 The Systems Engineering Process[6] (p. 8)

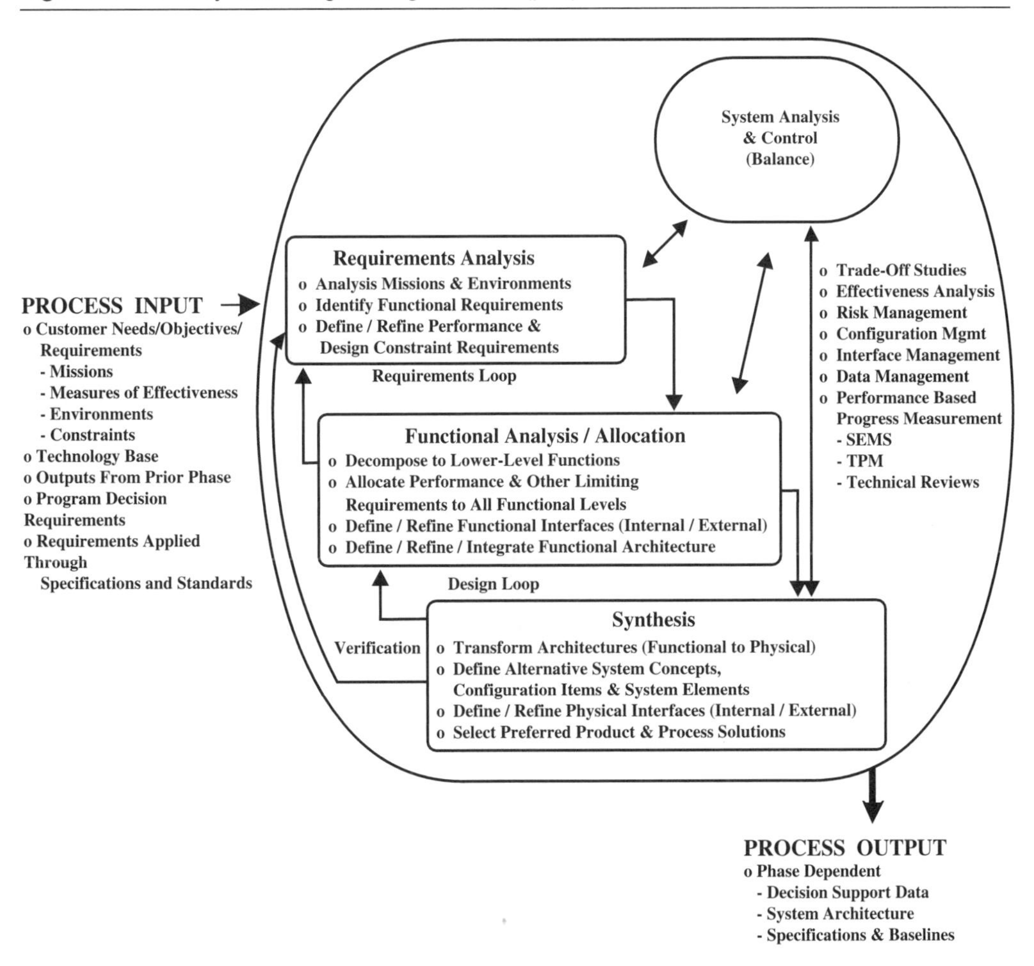

The generic systems engineering process (Figure 2.4) discussed in the next few paragraphs is extracted from the Systems Engineering[6] (pp. 7–10) military standard. This systems engineering process is applied for product and process development, engineering changes, modifications, and improvements. The systems engineering process activities of requirements analysis and allocation, synthesis, and systems analysis and control commensurate with contractual objectives are executed for the definition of the system products and processes and their verification.

The customer must provide the required systems engineering inputs to this systems engineering process. Any additional information required to conduct the systems engineering effort should be included in the proposal—items such as:

1. New or updated customer needs, requirements, and/or objectives in terms of missions, measures of effectiveness, utilization environments, and constraints.
2. Technology-based data including identification of key technologies, performance, maturity, cost, and risks.
3. Non-functional requirements from contractually cited standardization documents and specifications for the system and its configuration items.

Systems engineering generates system and configuration item unique specifications. Specifications are formalized in configuration baselines commensurate with the contracted effort. These configuration baselines are documented, controlled, and audited in accordance with configuration management practices. The V&V person should be able to verify the requirements included in specifications. These specification requirements will not be approved until:

1. The completeness of the specifications and its design attainability have been verified.
2. The costs of the item have been determined and that costs satisfy established design-to-cost requirements or other prescribed affordability limits.
3. The cost, schedule, and performance risks associated with the item and its processes have been determined and the risk levels are acceptable.

System and configuration item processes to be included in item specifications are: manufacturing, verification, deployment, operations, support, training, and disposal. System functional and configuration item development specifications need to be performance based. All these points reinforce software V&V's role as being a systems engineering process.

Technical objectives are a method to define the major characteristics of the system (customer needs in a proof of concept phase), when it is too early to formulate all of the contractual requirements. When used in this fashion, technical objectives provide a basis for defining relationships among need, urgency, risks, and worth. Technical objectives may also be defined for capabilities beyond established requirements when opportunities have been identified for substantial increases in effectiveness, decreases in cost, or added flexibility in product and process utilization in likely environments that vary from baseline conditions. Technical objectives identified should assist in converging on a system solution, focus on factors critical to success, and offer substantive capability payoffs for resources expended. Technical objectives should be proposed for customer consideration, and because requirements are affected, the V&V person must be kept informed. Metrics and success criteria must be developed to ensure that the increase in system capabilities is cost-effective when technical objectives are established for capabilities beyond established requirements.

Example: Inspections as Process

Inspection, as Tom Gilb defines it (shown with a capital "I") in *Software Inspections*[7], consists of two main processes: the Defect Detection Process (DDP) and the Defect Prevention Process (DPP). Continuing from Gilb,[7] a major defect is one that, if it is not dealt with at the requirements or design stage, will probably have an order-of-magnitude or larger cost to find and fix when it reaches the testing or operational stages. On average, the find-and-fix cost for a major defect is one work hour upstream, but nine work hours downstream. When DDP is applied, 88% of existing major defects in a document are found on a single pass. This alone is important, but DDP actually achieves greater benefit by teaching software developers. They go through a rapid, individual learning process, which typically reduces the number of defects they make in their subsequent work by two orders of magnitude.

In addition, DDP can and should be extended to support continuous process improvement. This is achieved by including the associated DPP, which is capable of at least 50% (first year, and first project used on) to 70% (second or third year) defect cause reduction, and over 90% in the longer term. It has also shown at least a 13-to-1 ratio return on investment, and is used as a key process in the SEI CMM Level 5.

Gilb[7] provides a good case study from Raytheon. In six years (1988 to 1994), using DDP combined with DPP, Raytheon reduced rework costs (costs of dealing with preventable errors) from about 45 percent to between 5 percent and 10 percent, and had a 7.7-to-1 return on investment. They improved software productivity by a factor of 2.7-to-1, reduced negative deviation from budget and deadlines from 40% to near zero, and reduced error density by about a factor of three.

Following are some key tips about how to improve the Inspection process and how to begin to achieve the kind of results that Raytheon achieved. According to Gilb[7]:

- know your purpose for using Inspection
- measure Inspection benefits
- make intelligent decisions on what you choose to inspect
- focus on finding the major defects
- apply good practice when leading Inspections
- decide whether to log minor defects, continue checking, and vary checking rates to achieve optimum
- ensure you have provided adequate training and follow-up

- give visibility to your Inspection statistics and support documentation
- continuously improve your Inspection process.

Models

Approach to Model Development

The most pervasive model for software development is the SEI's Capability Maturity Model (CMM) for Software,[8] which is discussed below with particular emphasis on the model. Although software engineers and managers often know their problems in great detail, they may disagree on which improvements are most important. Without an organized strategy for improvement, it is difficult to achieve consensus between management and the professional staff on what improvement activities to undertake first. To achieve lasting results from process improvement efforts, it is necessary to design an evolutionary path that increases an organization's software process maturity in stages. The software process maturity framework orders these stages so that improvements at each stage provide the foundation on which to build improvements undertaken at the next stage. Thus, an improvement strategy drawn from a software process maturity framework provides a model for continuous process improvement. It guides advancement and identifies deficiencies in the organization; it is not intended to provide a quick fix for projects in trouble.

The CMM provides software organizations with guidance on how to gain control of their processes for developing and maintaining software and how to evolve toward a culture of software engineering and management excellence. The CMM was designed to guide software organizations in selecting process improvement strategies by determining current process maturity and identifying the few issues most critical to software quality and process improvement. By focusing on a limited set of activities and working aggressively to achieve them, an organization can steadily improve its organization-wide software process to enable continuous and lasting gains in software process capability.

The maturity framework into which established quality principles have been adapted was first inspired by Philip Crosby (1979) in his book *Quality is Free*.[9] Crosby modeled a quality management maturity grid that describes five evolutionary stages in adopting quality practices, which Watts Humphrey brought to the SEI in 1986. He used Crosby's model and his management and process experience from IBM as a basis and added the concept of maturity levels, and developed the foundation for the Software CMM.

The CMM is a descriptive model in the sense that it describes essential (or key) attributes that would be expected to characterize an organization at a particular maturity level. It is a normative model in the sense that the detailed practices characterize the normal types of behavior that would be expected in an organization doing large-scale projects. The intent is that the CMM is at a sufficient level of abstraction that it does not unduly constrain how the software process is implemented by an organization; it simply describes what the essential attributes of a software process would normally be expected to be. The CMM is not prescriptive; it does not tell an organization how to improve. The CMM describes an organization at each maturity level without prescribing the specific means for getting there.

The CMM establishes a yardstick against which it is possible to judge, in a repeatable way, the maturity of an organization's software process and compare it to the state of the practice of the industry. The CMM can also be used by an organization to plan improvements to its software process. Since 1990, the SEI, with the help of many people from government and industry, has further expanded and refined the model based on several years of experience in its application to software process improvement.

Life Cycle

This section covers a brief overview of the most prevalent life cycle models used for software: ***waterfall, modified waterfall, build, ISO 12207, spiral, model-based, and fourth generation model***. Life-cycle models exhibit variability with respect to how the phases are labeled, what specific activities are included in a particular phase, and how the phases overlap during transitions.[10] In the respective areas, an emphasis is placed on the implications to V&V. When a particular life cycle model is relevant to the V&V person for a forthcoming chapter in this book, that model is so noted.

Waterfall model (Figure 2.5)

All activities and work products are to be completed in a life cycle phase before moving into the next phase. The V&V person has the opportunity to verify as a phase is completed. Validation should be performed also at the end of each phase by assuring the requirements are being met at that phase by traceability and analysis. A brief description of each phase taken from AverStar's

Figure 2.5 Waterfall life cycle model[11]

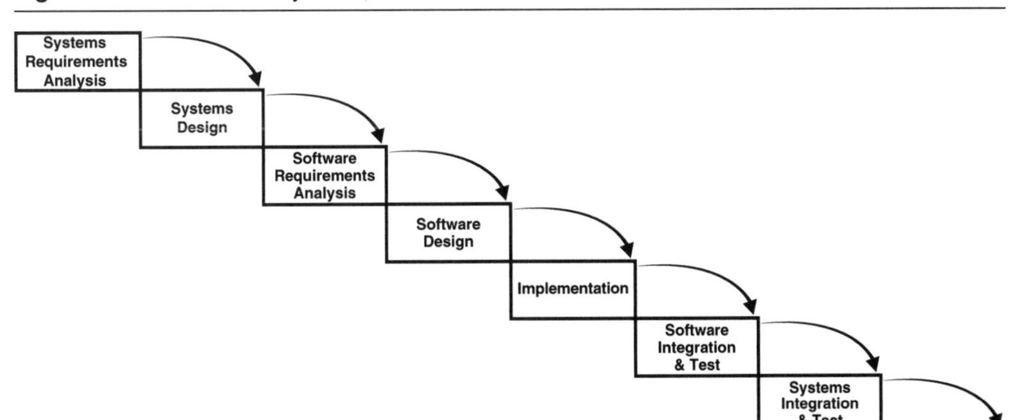

(1994) *Independent System Verification and Validation Plan*[10] follows along with classic V&V activities during that phase.

Systems requirements analysis discovers and communicates the problem needed to be solved by the system. V&V objectives during the systems requirements analysis are to ensure the establishment of the requirements hierarchy and linkages, to verify the soundness of the results of the developer's requirements process, and to identify requirements that are likely to represent challenges or problems for the developers.

Requirements are analyzed for technical integrity, criticality, risk, and conflict with programmatic constraints (e.g., need dates, operational environment considerations, etc.). The allocation of requirements to a release is verified to ensure a complete set of requirements, consistent with the intended use of the release. A requirements tracking database provides the baseline needed to keep the requirements under control.

Systems design generates the high-level design of the system, including hardware, software, and manual operations. V&V objectives associated with the systems design are to assess the functionality of the design and the correctness of its interfaces. V&V examines the system interfaces, including analysis of the structure, data content, and functionality. Also, traceability from the systems requirements to the systems design is closely examined.

Software requirements analysis is concerned with the proper representation of the software requirements for use by the software developers. V&V objectives during the software requirements analysis are to ensure the establishment of the software requirements, to verify the testability of these software requirements, and to identify problem software requirements. Requirements are analyzed for appropriateness through requirements traceability verification. Ensure the effective use of the requirements tracking database as the requirements are flowed down to software.

Software design defines the high-level software architecture that is fleshed out by the detailed design to provide the "blueprints" for software implementation. V&V objectives associated with the software design are to assess the functionality of the design, the soundness of its expression in tool output or documentation, and the viability of its interfaces. The design is assessed with respect to well-defined criteria associated with its functionality, with its tool output or documentation, and with its ability to support evolution and growth requirements. Attention is given to both the design expression and its compliance with standards, because these are the foundation for software coding, and experience shows confusion and misinterpretations during the hand-off from design to implementation to be a major source of errors.

Standard V&V practices treat the interfaces as one element of the design. This includes full analysis of the structure, data content and functionality of the interfaces and includes provisions for assessing consistency across multiple (chained or sequentially linked) interfaces. Also, during this phase, traceability is extended from the requirements to the design elements satisfying the requirements.

Implementation includes the coding and the unit testing of units/modules implemented according to the detailed design. Objectives of implementation V&V are to verify that developed code mechanizes the design, and to assess the sufficiency of the testing process to which code is subjected during the developer's software development process. Traceability is extended to the code structure level, and test cases are linked to the requirements during this phase.

The code verification effort includes analysis of the code structure versus the design, analysis of the databases and assessment of the listings. All aspects of the code implementation are subject to scrutiny during this phase, including the procedures employed as specified in the Software Development Plan and the technical details reflected in the contents of the Software Development Files (SDFs), formerly called folders.

V&V serves as a monitor and watchdog over the development contractor's testing: reviewing plans and procedures for completeness and appropriateness, watching tests to ensure proper conduct and recording, and reviewing results documentation for accuracy and scope of coverage provided by the test program. The principal objectives of software unit testing are to validate that the various elements within each component are compatible with each other, and that each component complies with its allocated functional and performance requirements.

Software integration and test consists of the incremental assembly (integration) and test of a progressively larger and larger sub-set of all software units/modules. Objectives of the testing phase V&V are to certify that functional and performance requirements allocated to a release are satisfied, and to certify that all components and key interfaces function together correctly to yield desired operability. V&V testing is conducted in-line, as part of the overall development effort. Software integration and testing begins with evaluations of single interfaces, followed by evaluations of progressively more complex combinations of interfaces, leading up to end-to-end testing of software threads/strings. Objectives include validation that each interface meets its functional and performance requirements, supports operational scenarios requiring transmission of data across that interface, and works in concert with other interfaces without any degradation in performance.

Systems integration and test consists of the progressive integration and test of all components (hardware and software) comprising the system, which leads to the ultimate construction of the system. System integration and testing is a natural continuation of software integration and testing using representative mission scenarios and data throughput rates to validate that the fully integrated system meets the functional and performance requirements.

Maintenance involves the continuous evolution of the software system after initial delivery to the customer. It involves both correction of the problems uncovered after fielding the system and modifications implemented based on new user requirements. The objective of maintenance phase V&V is to provide life-cycle support for on-going operation. V&V activities during the maintenance phase constitute a microcosm of the software development life cycle, focused on changes to the baselined system. This life cycle includes all the traditional phases just discussed with a compressed time frame. The basic V&V methodologies used are de-scoped variations on the standard methodologies employed during initial development, and include maintenance of the traceability matrices. These matrices are essential inputs during this phase. They are used to assess impacts of proposed requirements and engineering changes, and as a means for determining what testing is required to evaluate changes at the test case level.

Modified waterfall model (Figure 2.6)

Like the waterfall model, the modified waterfall model has not only the activities and work products completed in a phase, but also allow latitude to iterate back to a prior phase. The V&V person needs to be aware of any iterations so that the activities or work products can be reviewed again.

Build model (Figure 2.7)

Because activities and work products are being generated for various phases simultaneously, the V&V person must be able to handle verification activities of differing complexity, while simultaneously supporting the testing aspect of validation. In the build model each "build" is defined to demonstrate a certain capability that is available for demonstration. Often, the first build contains the supporting software architecture of the system, so that other applications may added to it. Usually each build is demonstrated to the customer to obtain feedback and demonstrate feasibility and completion. The build model is most closely associated with Rapid Application Development (RAD).

Figure 2.6 Modified waterfall life cycle model[12]

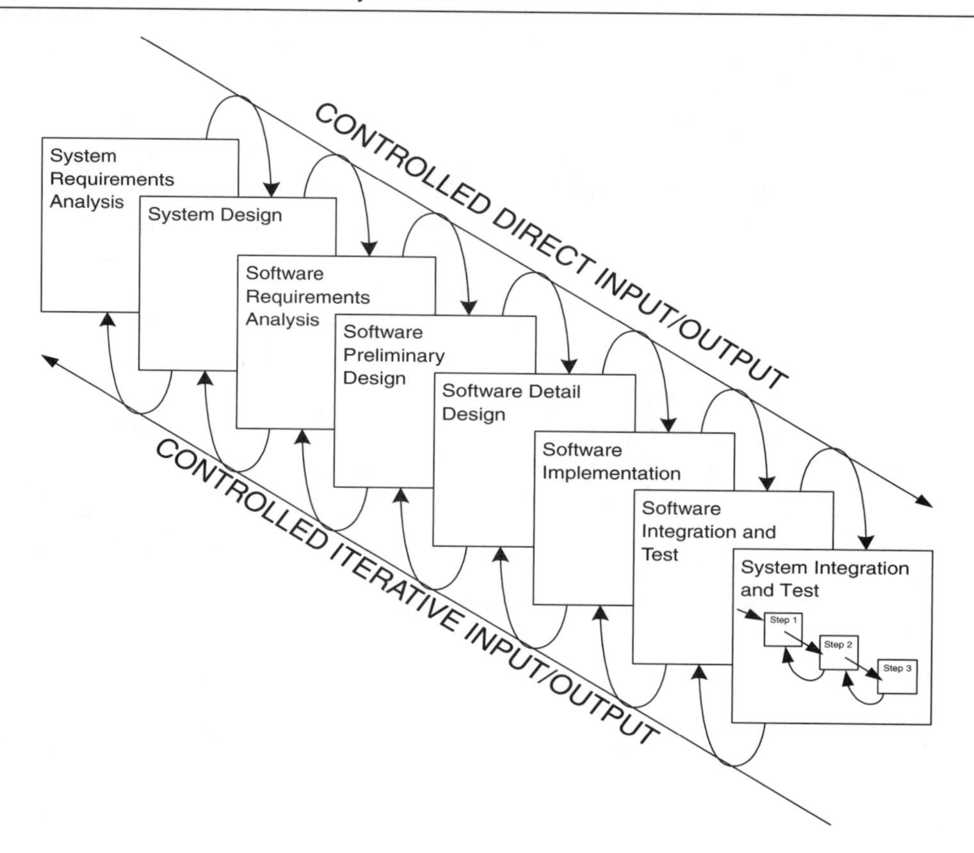

Figure 2.7 Build life cycle model[12]

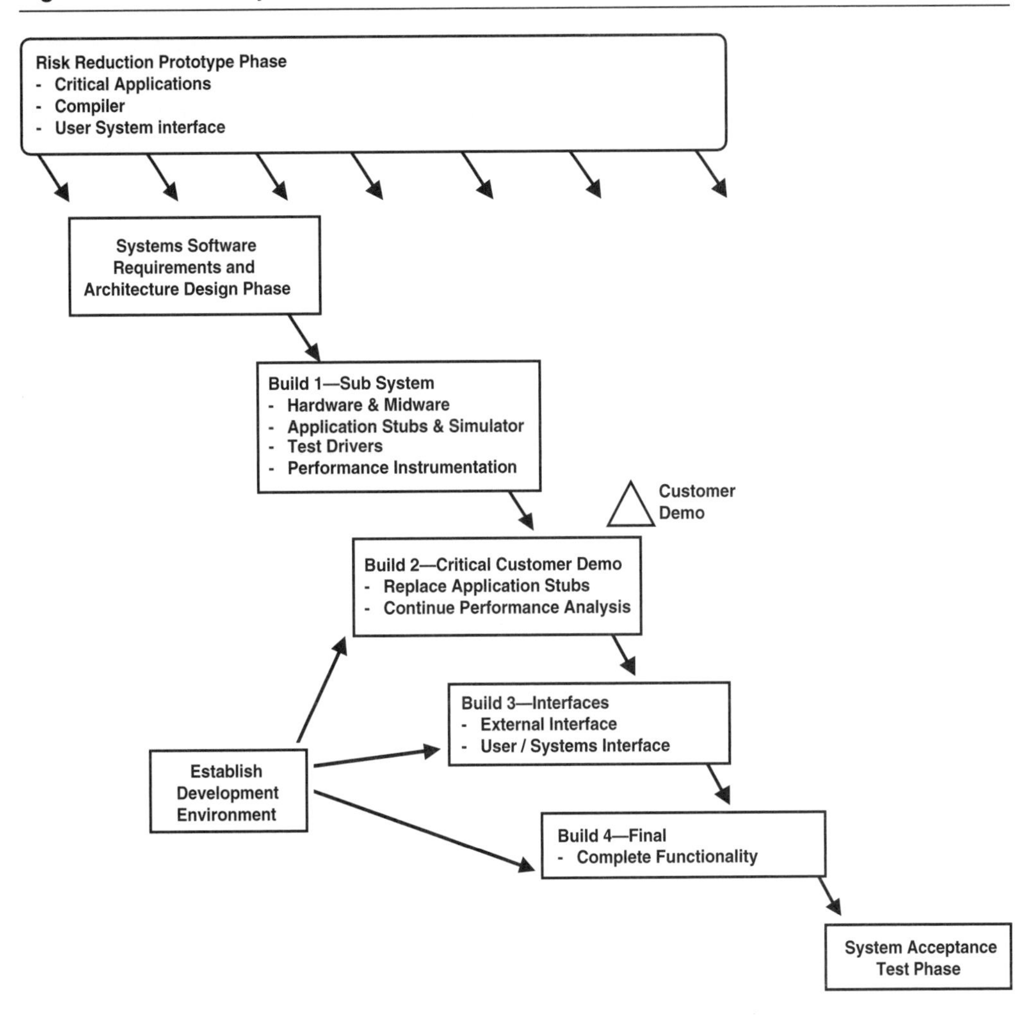

ISO 12207 model (Figure 2.8)

In this unique life-cycle model, V&V exists as part of the supporting life cycle process. So, the V&V person can go to the standard and understand her performance requirements. The V&V person must perform V&V on the primary processes (acquisition process, supply process, development process, operation process, and maintenance process), as well as on the organizational life cycle processes (management process, infrastructure process, improvement process, and training process). This model lists processes without tying down a life-cycle model for software development.

Figure 2.8 ISO 12207 model[13] (p. 7)

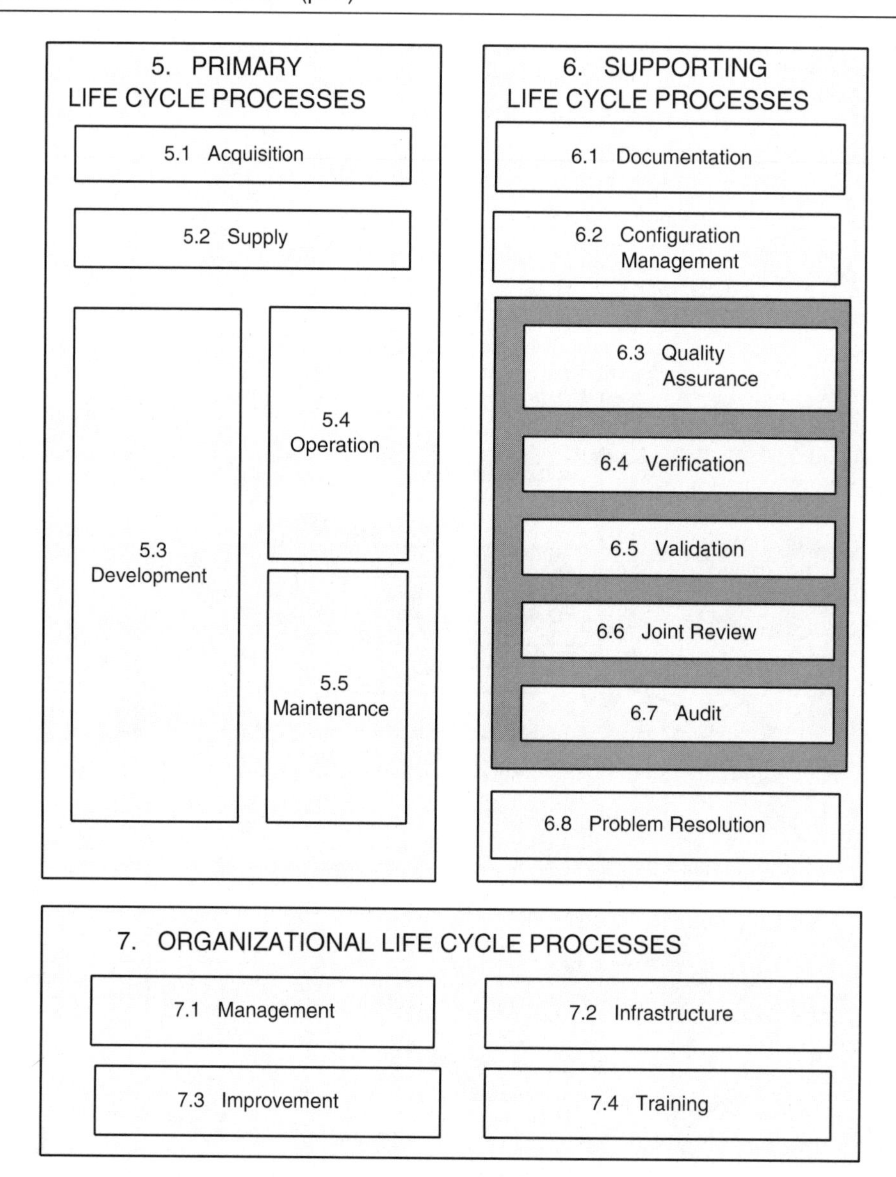

Spiral model (Figure 2.9)

Much emphasis is placed on prototyping, models, and simulation with the spiral model as described by Barry Boehm (1996). That emphasis requires the V&V person to be able to react quickly to prototypes available and assure they perform satisfactorily by representing the user. The model stresses requirements validation early in the spiral, with design validation and verification flowing shortly thereafter. Note also that the V&V person needs to be involved in the continuing risk analysis unfolding around the spiral.

Figure 2.9 Spiral life cycle model[14]

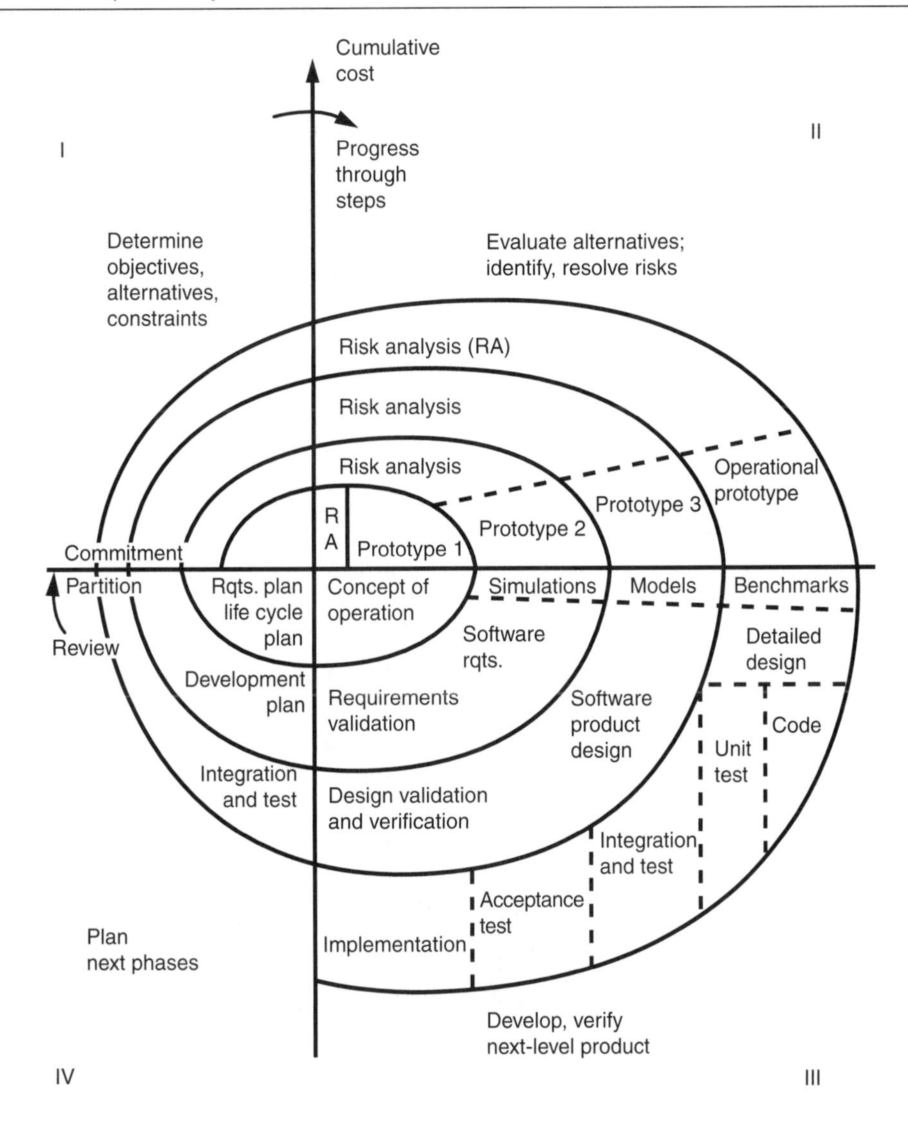

Model-based model (Figure 2.10)

This model supports a development approach that helps design and implement client/server applications and applications based on a GUI (graphical user interface). It is applicable to a wide range of business and information systems (Rakitin, 1997). This approach helps the V&V person when implementation is for client/server applications and GUI developments because of its great advantage for that type of development. The phase structure of the model is lacking, making it much more challenging for the V&V person to get a handle on phase-produced activities and work products.

Fourth generation model (Figure 2.11)

The fourth generation model is a hybrid model that includes aspects of multiple models, and is based on fourth generation techniques (4GT), which consist of a wide variety of tools that enable software developers to depict software characteristics at a very high level of abstraction. For well known requirements, the relatively standard waterfall portion on the left is followed. Where requirements are not well known the prototyping path is followed. The confusion that such a model may cause for a V&V person is that is the correct path must be discerned. When that is accomplished, if the 4GT path is followed, then a particular focus is needed. A key element of the fourth generation model is automatic code generation which means the focus for the V&V person is what goes into the automatic code generator. The tool requires specific inputs, so the tool and its requirements are where appropriate V&V emphasis should be placed.

The IEEE 1012-1986 *Standard for Software Verification and Validation Plans*[16] (p. 6) standard requires V&V management tasks spanning the entire life cycle and V&V tasks for maintenance. Table 2.2 lists some optional V&V tasks in the life cycle phase, where they most likely can

Figure 2.10 Model-based life cycle model[15] (p. 24)

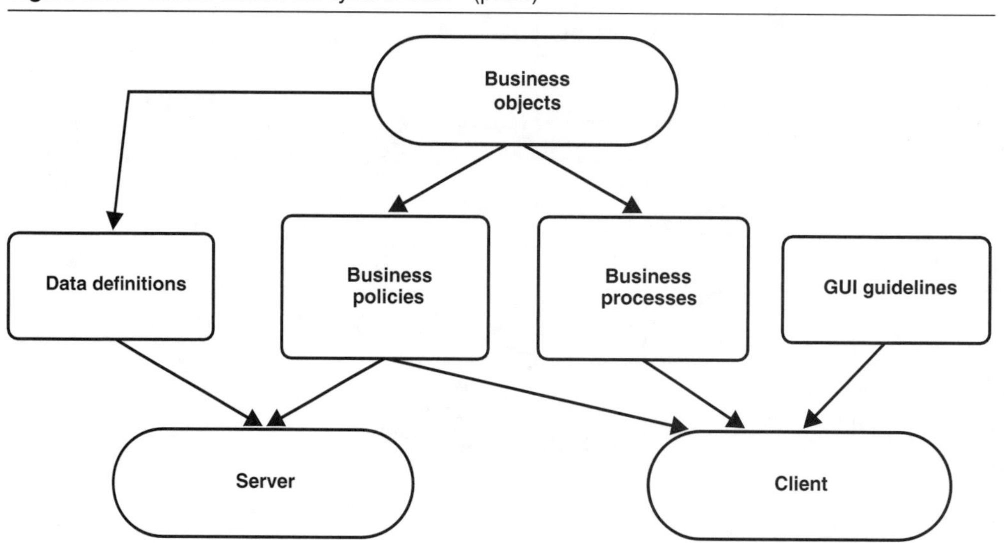

Figure 2.11 Fourth generation life cycle model[15] (p. 23)

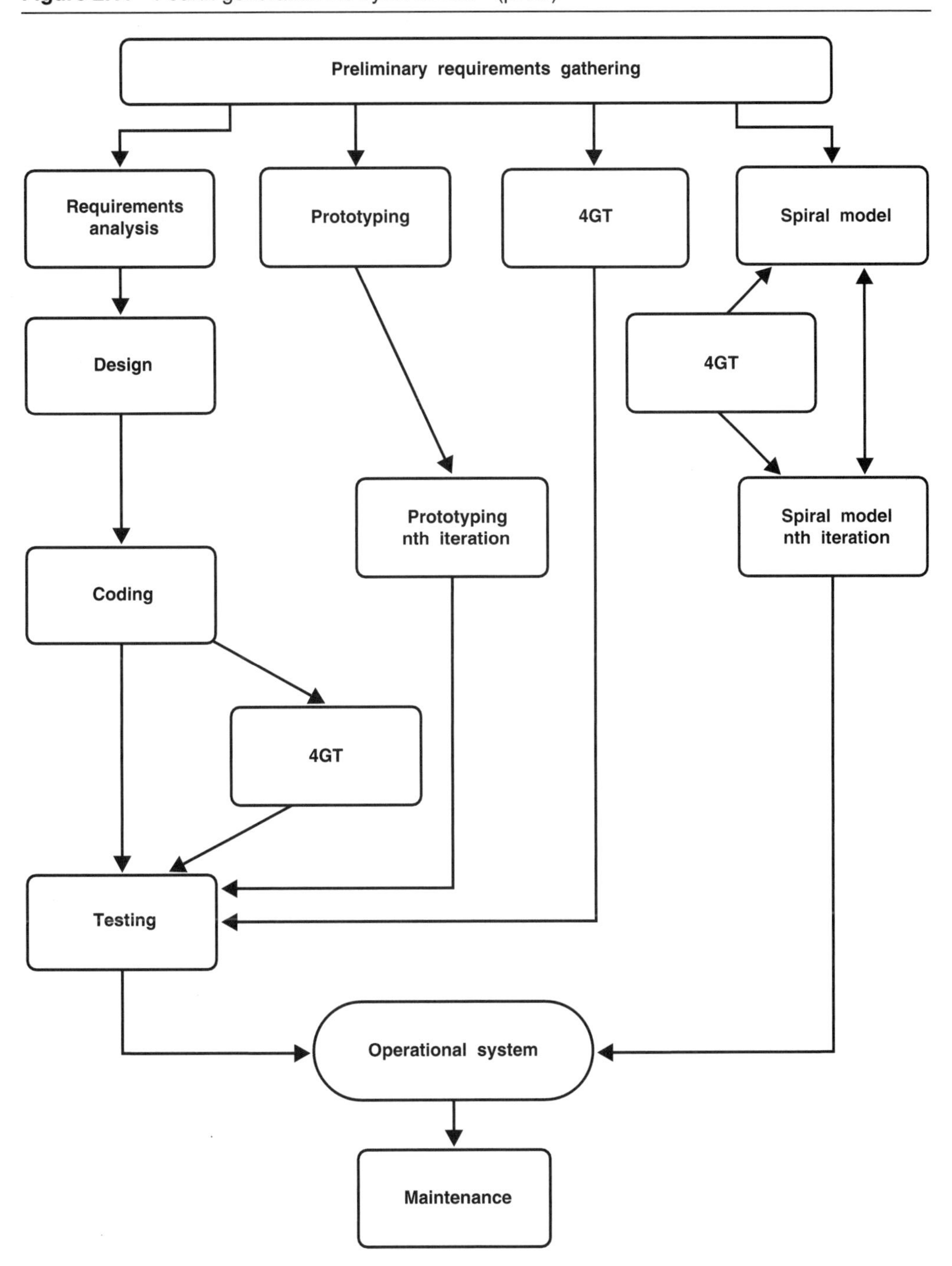

Table 2.2 Optional V&V tasks and suggested application[17] (p. 8)

Optional V&V Tasks	Management	Concept	Requirements	Design	Implementation	Test	Installation & Checkout	Operations & Maintenance	Considerations for Selecting Optional V&V Tasks
	Life Cycle Phases								
Algorithm Analysis			☐	☐	☐	☐		☐	Numerical and scientific software using critical equations or models
Audit Performance									When V&V is part of SQA or the user organization; for large software development to help SQA or user staff audits
Configuration Control					☐	☐	☐	☐	
Functional					☐	☐	☐	☐	
In Process			☐	☐	☐	☐	☐	☐	
Physical						☐	☐	☐	
Audit Support									When V&V is part of systems engineering or independent; for large software development
Configuration Control					☐	☐	☐	☐	
Functional					☐	☐	☐	☐	
In Process			☐	☐	☐	☐	☐	☐	
Physical						☐	☐	☐	
Configuration Management	☐	☐	☐	☐	☐	☐	☐	☐	When V&V is part of the user organization
Database Analysis			☐	☐	☐	☐		☐	Large database application; if logic stored as parameters (Data Warehousing)
Data Flow Analysis			☐	☐	☐			☐	Data driven, real time systems (Data Warehousing)
Control Flow Analysis			☐	☐	☐			☐	Complex, real time software
Feasibility Study Evaluation		☐							High risk software using new technology or concepts
Inspections/Walkthroughs									When V&V is part of SQA or systems; for large software developments to staff inspections/walkthroughs
Requirements			☐					☐	
Design				☐				☐	
Source Code					☐			☐	
Test					☐	☐	☐	☐	
Installation and Checkout Testing*			☐	☐	☐	☐	☐	☐	When part of the user organization, SQA, or systems
Performance Monitoring								☐	Software with changeable interfaces (GUI/Usability)
Qualification testing*			☐	☐	☐	☐	☐	☐	When V&V is part of the user organization or systems
Regression Analysis and Testing			☐	☐	☐	☐	☐	☐	Large, complex systems
Reviews Support									When V&V is part of user organization or systems
Operational Readiness							☐	☐	
Test Readiness					☐	☐	☐	☐	
Simulation Analysis			☐	☐	☐	☐	☐	☐	Unavailable system test capability or need to preview concept for feasibility or requirements for accuracy (RAD)
Sizing and Timing Analysis				☐	☐	☐		☐	Software contained by memory or response time (Internet/Intranet)
Test Certification						☐	☐	☐	For critical software
Test Evaluation			☐	☐	☐	☐	☐	☐	When V&V is part of user organization or SQA
Test Witnessing						☐	☐	☐	When V&V is part of user organization, SQA or systems
User Documentation Evaluation		☐	☐	☐	☐	☐	☐	☐	Interactive software requiring user inputs (KBS)
V&V Tool Plan Generation	☐							☐	When acquiring or building V&V analysis/test tools

* Test plan, test design, test cases, test procedures, and test execution

be applied, and considerations that one might use to assign the tasks to V&V. These optional V&V tasks can be applied to different life-cycle models simply by mapping traditional phases to models such as those described above. The *Software Verification and Validation Plans* standard specifies minimum input and output requirements for each V&V task. A V&V task may not begin without specific inputs, and is not completed until specific outputs are completed. Table 2.2 is modified to accommodate some notes about the latest techniques described in this book.

Two tables provide some special considerations for the V&V person in relationship to the life cycle models just discussed. First, there is a high-level comparison of the life cycle models in Table 2.3. The opportunities and risks associated with these life cycle models are listed in Table 2.4. Opportunities are potential benefits from using that model, and risks are potential problems that might occur with the use of that model.

Table 2.3 Life cycle model comparisons

Model	All Rqmts Defined First?	Multiple Builds?	Use Interim Products?	Remarks
Waterfall	Yes	No	No	Recursion/Iteration, As Needed
Modified Waterfall	Yes	No	No	
Build	No	Yes	Yes	Build N = Build (N-1) + More Capabilities. Recursion/Iteration, As Needed
ISO 12207	No	No	No	Recursion/Iteration, As Needed
Spiral	No	Yes	Yes	Build N = Build (N-1) + More Capabilities. Recursion/Iteration, As Needed
Model-Based	No	No	Yes	Recursion/Iteration, As Needed
Fourth Generation	No	Yes	Yes	Build N = Build (N-1) + More Capabilities. Recursion/Iteration, As Needed

Table 2.4 Life cycle model opportunities and risks

Factors	Opportunity	Risk
1. Requirements not well defined.	3, 5	1, 2, 4, 6, 7
2. System too large to do once.	3, 5, 7	1, 2, 6
3. Full capability needed at once.	1, 2, 6, 7	3, 5
4. Part capability needed early.	3, 5	1, 2, 6, 7
5. Phase out of old system to be gradual.	3, 5	1, 2
6. Rapid changes in requirements anticipated.		ALL
7. Rapid changes in technology anticipated.	6, 7	1, 2, 3, 4, 5
8. Long run staff/funds commitment doubtful.	3, 5, 7	1, 2

Legend Models:

1 = Waterfall; 2 = Modified Waterfall; 3 = Build; 4 = ISO 12207; 5 = Spiral; 6 = Model-Based; 7 = Fourth Generation

Example: Modeling a Process

The use of the STATEMATE modeling tool resulted from an earlier SEI effort to develop, refine, and apply a technology-based method for modeling software processes. The tool is intended to help organizations manage and improve those processes. Previous application experience with this modeling approach includes modeling and analyzing 5 large-scale, real-world software processes, plus various small examples. Results have been described in over 12 published papers from the SEI dealing with aspects of this modeling work.

Discussed briefly here are certain quality-related activities that were selected from IEEE Std 1074 *IEEE Standard for Developing Software Life-cycle Processes*[18] for consideration in their prototyping exercise. More specifically, the intention was to focus on those IEEE 1074 activities which cover the CMM Level 2 Key Process Area (KPA) on Software Quality Assurance (SQA). Two major processes were identified from IEEE 1074 which met the selection criteria:

- Software Quality Management Process
- Verification and Validation Process

Modeling of the selected components of IEEE 1074 resulted in four diagrams, supplemented with textual forms. The model includes activity charts—depicting the functional perspective, and statecharts—depicting the behavioral perspective. No organizational perspective was developed for the model, since no such information was available in the source document. An activity chart and statechart pair represents the reused process element named "Execute Verification and Validation Tasks" fragment (included in Figure 2.12). The remainder of the modeled processes are repre-

Figure 2.12 Fragment of STATEMATE modeling tool (Modified from IEEE, 1992)

DICTIONARY
IEEE Std 1074—1991

Small sample statecharts?:
Activity EXEC_V_AND_V
Type: INTERNAL
Defined in chart: SQA_FCT_MONO
Description: 7.1.4 Execute Verification and Validation Tasks

State EXEC_V_AND_V
Type: BASIC
Defined in chart: SQA_BHV_MONO

State EXEC_V_AND_V_CTRL
Type: OR—COMPONENT
Defined in chart: SQA_BHV_MONO

---

sented in a second pair of charts; this portion includes 7 invocations of the "Execute Verification and Validation Tasks" process element.

Product Maturity Model

The CMM focuses on the processes involved in the creation of software products. However, it seems to de-emphasize the end product. In response, John Nastro[19] has presented the concept of a Product Maturity Model:

> With the rapidly changing technology of software development, what was considered standard software practice 20 years ago is no longer viable. The credit goes to the advent of new development life cycles, methods, languages, and high-speed processors as is covered throughout this book in the multi-dimensional model sections. Long faded are the days of traditional waterfall life cycle software development that produced executable software products. Spiral, incremental build and evolutionary life cycles—much more dynamic and flexible for software developers and V&V personnel—have replaced the old ways. As a result of these changes, there need to be new methods to evaluate and track executable software products during development. A software product maturity model could satisfy this need....
>
> ***Process vs. Product Maturity***. Unlike software process maturity, product maturity is concerned solely with the final product, the executable software, and not necessarily with how the software was developed. However, process and product maturity are not mutually exclusive; the product maturity model should work in conjunction with the process maturity.
>
> Software process maturity has passed through extensive analysis and modeling. The...CMM continues to be the benchmark to which many organizations aspire in their process improvement efforts. That model consists of five maturity levels that range from the initial ad hoc Level 1 to the repeatable Level 2, up to the optimized Level 5. Many consider strong, process-driven software development vital to a successful project; however, there are a few caveats to remember with respect to the CMM. Software process maturity deals exclusively with the development of the software. It provides no guarantees as to the quality of the final product, nor does it directly address other key variables in software development, such as people and technology....
>
> A shared thread that runs through all software organizations is that they try to produce a quality software product that pleases the customer. To measure this product with a standardized model lends more confidence toward its quality. That is the motivation of product maturity. Product maturity is defined as "a quantifiable estimate of the maturity of a software product based on readily measurable, key project indicators." The salient words in this definition are "quantifiable," "estimate," and "readily measurable." Product maturity must be quantifiable to achieve its goal. It is not sufficient to state that "the product is coming along" or that it is "more mature than I had hoped." The term "estimate" provides latitude in measurement, which avoids an over dependence on figures: a product maturity figure of 0.5432 would be just as useless as the non-quantified example. Similarly, the measurement of product maturity must come from those metrics that are readily measurable and accessible, especially to a company that employs CMM Level 2 metrics in its software development. A software engineer may rightfully state, "I develop my software in accordance with the SEI CMM. My executable product is subject to a rigorous formal qualification test...that ensures the maturity of the software. Why do I need another model?"

The answer to this questions is twofold:

1. A product maturity measurement provides a more thorough analysis of a software product than a qualification test alone. Qualification testing focuses on compliance to the requirements derived from the specification, the statement of work... or equivalent. It does not address items that are not in the specification, nor does it address important software evaluation requirements that are not in the product specification. Even when software passes a [formal qualification test], it may still be extremely immature.
2. Product maturity provides management and the V&V person with insight into the software development effort. Product maturity may be an essential tool to track the development of a life cycle when an executable product is available early in the process, as in the case of the spiral or incremental life cycles. Previously, it was relatively uncomplicated to track software development with a traditional waterfall life cycle. A well-defined task, such as detailed design, would culminate with a design review, and interim milestones that lead to that baseline would be monitored weekly or monthly.

Since the arrival of the dynamic life cycles just discussed, however, development phases, such as requirement analysis, design, code, and test, occur concurrently and seamlessly. Nevertheless, management can still use the product as a defining benchmark to track the progress of the development. If the product can be measured, it can be tracked. To measure the product at regular intervals or at key milestones provides necessary management insight, which obviates the need to classify a development phase as a tracking item when the development phase cannot be clearly defined; that is even if software developers cannot tell you when the requirements phase will end, they or a V&V person can still determine the maturity level of their product.

A product maturity measurement can also be used to track and compute technical risk. Most risk models involve the probability of failure and the consequence of failure. Product maturity can be factored in to both parts of the equation. As maturity increases, the probability and consequence of failure decrease....

The Product Maturity Model. To compute product maturity first requires a model. The model provided here describes a core set of elements that constitute the basis of a product maturity calculation. Product maturity measurements should be maintained independently from life cycle, development methods, and language used. Each of the core elements the model describes can be applied to an individual development effort. However, their importance or weight may vary from project to project. Sub-elements, though not part of the product maturity core, may apply to specific software applications.

Determination of the maturity of individual elements should be based on common, readily available metrics taken during program development. These metrics should then be interpolated against industry standards, historical data, or a statement of work specifications to develop the relative maturity of each element. The product maturity model has three core elements: product capability, product stability, and product maintainability. Two sub-elements, product repeatability and product compatibility, are not universal to every software product. Product maturity can be measured from the individual elements according to the following equation:

Product Maturity = PC * (PS + PR + PM)/3
where
PC = Product Capability
PS = Product Stability
PR = Product Repeatability
PM = Product Maintainability

Product Capability. Product capability, the quintessence of product maturity, refers to the performance of the product against the specification. It can be measured by examining the success or failure of the product against the applicable qualification tests. These tests represent the validation of the derived requirements as stated in the software requirements specification or equivalent. This value can be weighted against the percentage of software developed at the time of measurement by calculating the product of the two; that is, if 50% of the software were developed and 50% of the qualification tests were successful, software capability would be 0.25....

Product Stability. Product stability refers to the impact of modifications to a baseline software product over a specified period. These modifications are usually indicated as software problem or change reports. Product stability can be measured by interpreting the software changes per period, then weighting the changes by impact or severity. The results can then be interpreted through evaluation against a previously established benchmark that may be the result of an industry standard, a project specification, or historical data of a similar project....

Product Maintainability. Product maintainability refers to the ability of a software organization to understand, maintain, use, and upgrade software. Therefore, a software product may be quite stable and fully capable, but if it is not usable or upgradeable, it is immature and, more important, useless. Maintainability can be measured through examination of the documentation and code status of the product and through comparison to the standards described in the statement of work (SOW) or from internal company policies and procedures. This measurement, which may be the most difficult metric to obtain, can range from a fairly simple estimate of code compliance (the percentage of code that is not compliant would be considered immature) to a full analysis of code quality. Currently, there is a concerted effort in the software community to measure code quality through use of key indicators such as module cohesion, coupling, and complexity. The quantification of this metric would aid greatly in the computation of product maintainability....

Product Repeatability. Product repeatability refers to the ability of a software product to provide consistent results from execution to execution. This element is important when discussing real-time systems or those that have strong algorithmic dependencies. If this were not the case, this sub-element could be folded under product stability. Product repeatability can be measured by examining two sub-elements: the first is derived from the number of open problems against the software product that affect consistent measurements, and the second from analysis of a general baseline test (or tests) that encompasses a large percentage of the software functionality. The open problems in the first sub-element are usually intermittent and have not been isolated sufficiently so that they may be solved. These problems can be weighted by their severity similar to the product stability calculation....

Product Compatibility. Product compatibility refers to the performance of the software product against the interface specification (internal or external). This sub-element can be used in

> conjunction with multiple software configuration item...systems or a singular [software configuration item] that has extensive hardware interfaces. If this is not the case for the system under evaluation, product compatibility can be folded into product capability. Product compatibility can be measured through examination of the performance of that subset of qualification tests that deal with interface issues. Measurement is then similar to the capability element.
>
> The concept of product maturity addresses the most important element of any software effort—the deliverable product. Product maturity should become a key metric in the ability of a software manager to track and report software development efforts for emerging software life cycles. It also allows the V&V team to quantify the "goodness" of the product throughout the development life-cycle. It can provide benefits when integrated with a software process improvement effort or as a stand-alone activity. It should be based on readily available metrics so that it can be easily calculated. (pp. 21–24)

Product V&V

With a basic understanding of a product maturity model established, what are the elements of product specific V&V? Northrop Grumman's *Product Verification/Validation*[20] provides some of the answers discussed in this section. Program management has a responsibility that the product V&V process (Figure 2.13) is scheduled and included in the project.

Product verification

A systems level requirements verification matrix (RVM) is generated and updated during the product development plan phase. It contains requirements based on the customer's design specifications and notes on program standards obtained from the SOW and placed in the requirements specification. If no methods of verification are included in the qualification section of the design specification, it is the responsibility of the systems organization to derive this information with inputs from the customer and other affected groups.

In addition, during this phase, the system test and evaluation organization develops a master test plan and attaches the RVM to this product. An RVM is generated at the systems level to correlate requirements and verification methods used to verify that the product meets requirements. This test plan includes, as a minimum, information regarding the test and evaluation process within the program, program test documentation, methods of test and evaluation, test/simulation trade studies required, development test programs, (such as demonstration test programs and data collection activities and system development requirements), and requested customer and internal facilities. This plan precedes any detailed test plans and procedures required on the project.

At the start of the preliminary design phase, a design requirements document is generated to specify the requirements for the test platform and other support facilities for the program. Both design verification and design validation practices may be integrated into the processes for product development. Determination of design verification methods is agreed to by an internal systems requirements review and presented to the customer through a program system design review. Test software requirements specifications are generated to begin development of the test software for system integration and qualification test. As the product requirements are verified through inspec-

Figure 2.13 Product verification and validation elements[20]

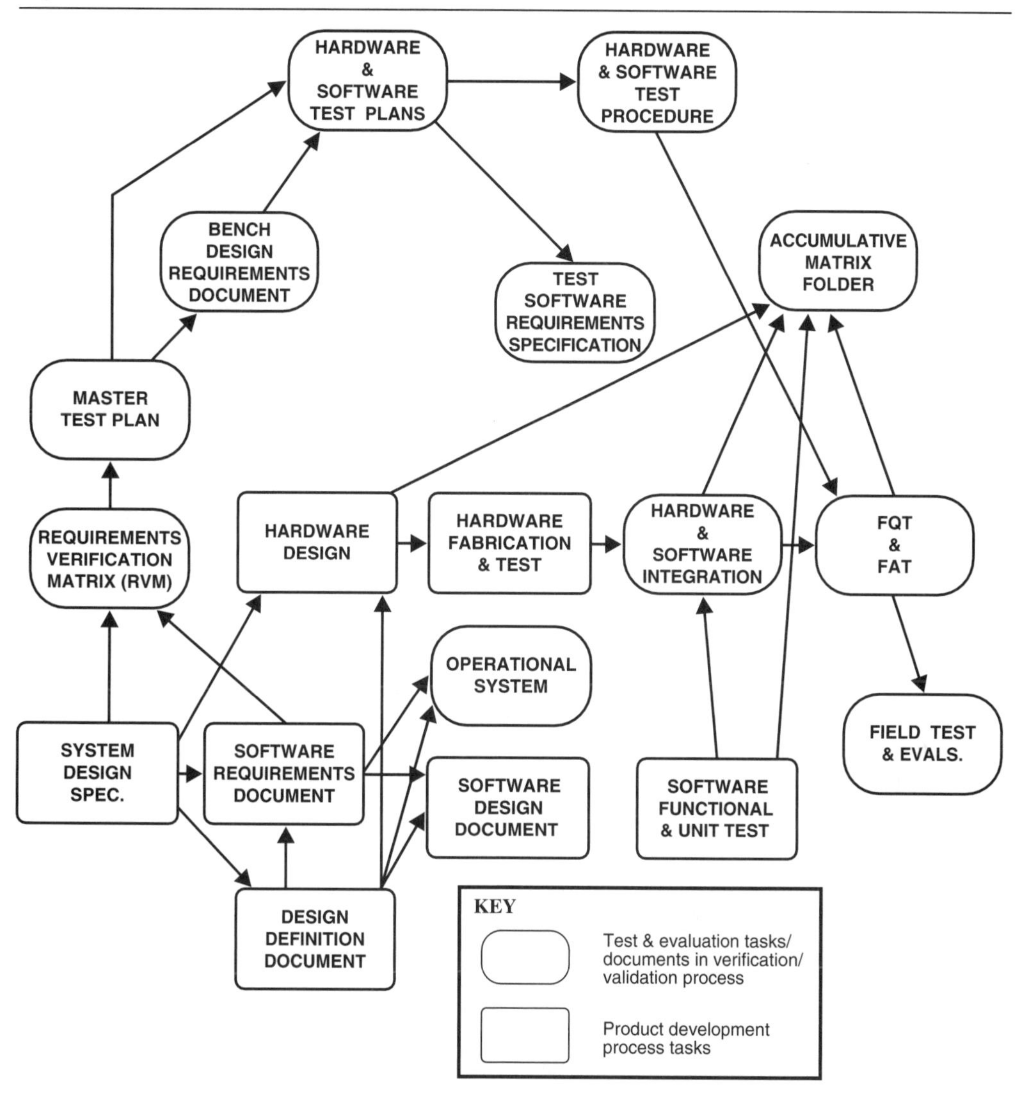

tion, analysis, demonstration, and test, this information is collected and linked into an accumulative matrix folder with the final copy of the RVM. Once verification is over, the accumulative matrix folder is configured and placed under configuration control.

Product validation

Product validation is determined by the program contract and ensures that the product performs to customer specifications within the contractually specified conditions. In the event that there are no specific contractual specifications, it is recommended that validation practices ensure that the product meets its intended use. Based on information within the master test plan, a set of detailed qualification test plans and procedures are written according to the program requirements documented in the SOW and design specifications.

Standards

Software standards are mandatory requirements employed and enforced to prescribe a disciplined uniform approach to software development[8] (p. 367). Many software developers have said, "You cannot apply standards or controls to something as creative as developing software." There are some people still falsely saying this.

According to Dr. Raghu Singh (1998), editor of ISO/IEC 12207, this international standard on software life cycle processes was created to establish a common international framework to acquire, supply, develop, operate and maintain software. ISO/IEC 12207 was proposed in 1988 and published in August 1995. Now, IEEE/EIA (1998) 12207.0-1996—*Software Life Cycle Processes* describes the major component processes of a complete software life cycle, their influences with one another, and the high-level relations that govern their interactions. ISO 12207 is expected to become an important standard for international commerce in software because it provides a common framework of terminology and process structure for acquirers and suppliers in different countries. Many countries are moving toward the adoption of 12207 as a national standard.

There are two complementary standards to IEEE/EIA 12207.0-1996: (1) Draft IEEE/EIA P12207.1 *Guide for information technology:—Software life cycle processes,—Life cycle data;* and (2) IEEE/EIA 12207.2-1997 *Software life cycle processes—Implementation considerations*. The 12207.1 Guide provides recommendations for data; that is, specifications and plans. The 12207.2 Guide, implementation considerations, provides suggested methods for primary life cycle, supporting and organizational life cycle processes. Nevertheless, there is an obstacle to use, particularly in the United States, in that the standard provides no way for an organization to assert that its own internally institutionalized software development methods conform to 12207. These standards differ from the military standards in that these standards are properly applied through voluntary adoption rather than contractual imposition.[21]

This section addresses not those standards specifically, but the standardization of V&V, which ensures that there is discipline and control in the software development process via continuous evaluation. Table 2.5 contains a collection of standards relevant to a V&V person. Most of these standards are discussed throughout this book.

If any organization wants a successful standardization program, standardization authorities must recognize that they have two objectives: (1) develop or adopt usable standards, and (2) convince users and developers that the standards are usable. If the first objective is not realized, the second will not be, either. Without the second objective, the first is useless. Usable standards development requires the participation of developers. It must be system requirements-based. Simply, if you cannot state a specific use for a piece of information, you cannot consider it usable for standardization. Development of usable standards means cooperation and teamwork with actual devel-

Table 2.5 Sample V&V standards list

AFSC/AFLCP 800-5—*Software Independent Verification and Validation.*

Air Force Instruction 16-1001, *Verification, Validation And Accreditation (VV&A)*, 1 June 1996.

ANS 10.4—*Guidelines for the Verification and Validation of Scientific and Engineering Computer Programs for the Nuclear Industry*, 1987.

DI-M-2051A *Technical Manual Quality Assurance Data*, Navy, 8 Sept. 1976.

DI-MCCR-80770, *Software Independent Verification and Validation Plan*, 21 Feb. 1989.

FHWA Handbook, Wentworth, James A., Knaus, Rodger, and Aougab, Hamid, *Verification, Validation, and Evaluation of Expert Systems: An FHWA Handbook,* Version 1.2—1st Edition (McLean: Federal Highway Administration, Jan. 1997).

FIPSPUB 101—*Guideline for Life cycle Validation, Verification, and Testing of Computer Software.*

FIPSPUB 132—*Guideline for Software Verification and Validation Plans*, 19 Nov. 1987.

IEEE 1012 *Standard for Software Verification and Validation Plans*, 1986.

IEEE Standard 1074, *Software Quality Management Process and Verification and Validation Process*, 30 Oct. 1992.

IEEE/EIA 12207.0-1996—*Software Life Cycle Processes*, March 1998.

IEEE/EIA P12207.1 (Draft) *Guide for information technology:—Software life cycle processes,—Life cycle data*, 11 February 1997.

IEEE/EIA 12207.2-1997 *Software life cycle processes—Implementation considerations*, April 1998.

ISO 9001, *Quality Systems—Model for Quality Assurance in Design, Development, Production, Installation, and Servicing*, (Geneva, International Organization for Standardization, 1994).

ISO 9000-3, *Quality management and quality assurance standards—Part 3: Guidelines for the application of ISO 9001 to the development, supply and maintenance of software*, (Geneva, International Organization for Standardization, 1991).

JPL D 576—*Independent Verification and Validation of Computer Software Methodology*, 1983.

MIL-M-81203, *Validation/Verification Plan.*

MIL-STD-499B, *Systems Engineering Management Plan* (SEMP).

NASA-GB-002-95, *Formal Methods Specification and Verification Guidebook for Software and Computer Systems*, Volume I: Planning and Technology Insertion, Release 1.0, kemp@ivv.nasa.gov.NBS.

NBS Special Publication 500-93, *Software Validation, Verification, and Testing Technique and Tool Reference Guide*, National Bureau of Standards, Computer Science and Technology, Washington, DC, Sept., 1982.

NIST Special Publication 500-234, Wallace, Dolores R., Ippolito, Laura M. and Cuthill, Barbara, *Reference Information for the Software Verification and Validation Process*, National Institute of Standards and Technology, Computer Systems Laboratory, Gaithersburg, MD 20899, 29 March 1996.

UDI-M-23928 *Validation and Verification Plan, Navy*-SH, 2 Jan. 1973.

opment systems. These concepts of standards and those following concerning registries thereof come from Ham and Mann[22] (pp. 27–29) "If Nobody Uses It, It Ain't* a Standard."

Adoption of usable standards implies that the standards are already in use somewhere. They may be industry, government, or standards-organization sponsored. Usability is a function of quality, but the real measure of usability is widespread acceptance and implementation. Standardiza-

* "Ain't" is a well-understood, generalized representation for a concept whose preferred representations are "am not," "are not," and "is not." As a generalization, ain't is a more "standard" term than any of its substitutes.

tion may require compromise where the most widespread standard is "not as good" as its less widely used competitor or the one developed in-house.

There may be no one standard for any particular concept or representation of that concept. Instead, there may be several. The best standardization programs choose the "best" standards by reviewing them all against mission activity and system development and V&V requirements. It is conceivable that more than one representation of the same concept could be adopted to meet differing mission requirements.

In the marketplace, there is no "standard" set of standards. There are, however, multiple standard-setting organizations that offer their goods to the world. A standards registry can be used as a tool to provide an effective marketplace for these standards. Standard-setting organizations act as registration authorities, entering their adopted standards to their own space on the registry. Other organizations can then adopt standards from the registry for their own use or put up competing standards of their own in their own space.

Several organizations are developing registries based upon ISO and ANSI standards. The U.S. Environmental Protection Agency has the Environmental Data Registry. The Australian Institute of Health and Welfare has developed a health-care-related registry. The U.S. Census Bureau is about to release its registry. All these meet the international standard for registries. It may be time, if not for a V&V standards registry, then for a software standards registry.

A change toward competitive registration of standards in software and V&V and bottom-up standards model development, and away from dictated single models, would result in a standardization program that makes sense. Standards would be defined in usable form. Standards could be traced to mission-based requirements. Most important, standards would be used to enhance communication between systems without the side effects of retarded development and increased cost.

Summary

This chapter ties V&V concepts to processes, models, and standards. A process is a description of the steps required to implement some goal, usually part or all of a method. A process transforms textbook theories and method descriptions into real action steps. A process focuses on the practical, with concrete actions, and related measurements. The purpose of a process is to provide a clear and succinct description of what is intended to be done. How Boeing's STS process enhancements resulted in significant process improvement is discussed. The systems engineering process is highlighted to show an example process approach that is particularly relevant to the V&V person.

The development of the CMM for software is traced from Philip Crosby's book, *Quality is Free*. It establishes an approach to model development useful for understanding software development models and their applicability to V&V. The implications to V&V of the popular software life cycle models is covered. A software product maturity model is provided to give the V&V person another method to evaluate the "quality" of the software product.

A software standard is a mandatory requirement employed and enforced to prescribe a disciplined uniform approach to software development. A table of standards that relate to the V&V field is given. The case for a V&V standards registry is provided.

References

[1] Fayad, Mohamed E., "Software Development Process: The Necessary Evil?," In *Communications of the ACM*, Sept. 1997, Vol. 40, No. 9.

[2] Yamamura, George and Wigle, Gary B., "SEI CMM Level 5: For the Right Reasons," In *CrossTalk*, Software Technology Support Center, Ogden: Hill AFB, Vol. 10, No. 8, August 1997, pp. 3–6.

[3] Horn, Robert E., Developing Procedures, Policies, and Documentation (Waltham, MA: Information Mapping, Inc., 1990).

[4] Basili, Victor R., Daskalantonakis, Michael K. & Yacobellis, Robert H., "Technology Transfer At Motorola," *IEEE Software*, (© March 1994 IEEE), pp. 70–78.

[5] Easterbrook, Steve, "The Role Of Independent V&V In Upstream Software Development Processes," *Proceedings of 2nd World Conference on Integrated Design and Process Technology*, 1996, NASA/WVU Software Research Lab, NASA IV&V Facility, 100 University Drive, Fairmont, WV 26554, URL: steve@atlantis.ivv.nasa.gov.

[6] MIL-STD-499B, *Systems Engineering*, ASD Directorate of Systems Engineering (ASD/ENS) and DSMC Systems Engineering Department (DSMC/FD-SE), 6 May 1992.

[7] Gilb, Tom, "Optimizing Software Inspections." published in DoD "Crosstalk," March 1998. Web available at: www.STSC.hill.af.mil/crosstalk/1998/mar/optimizing.html.

[8] *Key Practices of the Capability Maturity Model for Software*, Version 1.1, SEI-93-TR-25; and *The Capability Maturity Model for Software*, Version 1.1, SEI-93-TR-24, Carnegie Mellon University, Software Engineering Institute, Carnegie Mellon University, Software Engineering Institute, 1993.

[9] Crosby, Philip, *Quality is Free* (New York: New American Library, Inc., 1979).

[10] *Independent System Verification and Validation Plan (ISVVP),* AverStar, 6301 Ivy Lane, Suite 200, Greenbelt, Maryland 20770 for Goddard Space Flight Center, December 15, 1994.

[11] Winston Royce first formalized the concept. Permission for use from Northrop Grumman Corporation, Melbourne, FL.

[12] Permission for use from Northrop Grumman Corporation, Melbourne, FL.

[13] IEEE/EIA 12207.0-1996—*Software Life Cycle Processes*, March 1998

[14] Boehm, Barry, "A Spiral Model of Software Development and Enhancement," In *ACM SIGSOFT*, Vol. 11, August 1996, pp. 14–24.

[15] Rakitin, Steven R., *Software Verification and Validation—A Practitioner's Guide*, (Boston: Artech House, 1997), Reprinted from permission from Artech House, Inc., Norwood, MA, USA, http:\\www.artech-house.com.

[16] IEEE 1012-1986. *Standard for Software Verification and Validation Plans.*

[17] Wallace, Dolores R. and Fuji, Roger U., *Software Verification and Validation: Its Role in Computer Assurance and Its Relationship with Software Project Management Standards*, National Institute of Standards and Technology Special Publication 500-165, May, 1989.

[18] IEEE Standard 1074, *Software Quality Management Process and Verification and Validation Process*, October 30, 1992.

[19] Nastro, John, "A Software Product Maturity Model," In *CrossTalk*, Software Technology Support Center, Ogden: Hill AFB, Vol. 10, No. 8, August 1997, pp. 21–24.

[20] Northrop Grumman ESSD Command Media, ESSD No. E109, *Product Verification/Validation*, October 1, 1997.

[21] Singh, Raghu as quoted in Schulmeyer, G. Gordon, "Standardization of Software Quality Assurance," in Schulmeyer, G. & McManus, J., *Handbook of Software Quality Assurance* (3rd edition), (Upper Saddle River, NJ: Prentice Hall Inc., 1998).

[22] Ham, Gary A. and Mann, Douglas D., "If Nobody Uses It, It Ain't a Standard: Thoughts on Retooling DoD Data Standardization Efforts," In *CrossTalk*, Software Technology Support Center, Ogden: Hill AFB, Vol. 11, No. 6, June 1998, pp. 26–30.

CHAPTER 3

Tools and Methodologies

Introduction

There are many tools and methods available generally for software development and specifically for software V&V. In fact, many of the software development tools are also software V&V tools. This chapter addresses the fact that the explosive growth of applications involves many dichotomies. There is a constant search for the best match between application domain, application development methodology, V&V requirements, and V&V tools. Specific tool names are not listed because available tools change so frequently, but occasional tools are discussed as representative examples. An attempt is made to categorize and describe basic functions performed by tools that are in use today. V&V practitioners who are interested in up-to-date information will find the Internet to be an invaluable resource.

It should be recalled from Chapter 2 that a process is more narrow than a methodology. The methodology is the theoretical underpinning, whereas the process defines practical step-by-step ways of accomplishing something. The values to a V&V person of understanding this distinction and how models, tools, and standards fit into the big picture are: (a) knowledge categorization for better adoption, (b) awareness of various levels of formality of methods and tools, (c) access to various software-related maturity models, and (d) introductory awareness of many contemporary standards affecting software development.

Tool Categories

When requirements are analyzed in association with an initial set of V&V tasks, the following list of tool categories for the V&V from *EOSDIS Independent Verification and Validation (V&V) Management Plan* may be appropriate:

- Office Automation Tools
  - Word Processing
  - Graphics

- Spreadsheets
- Presentations

- Management Tools
  - Project Tracking
  - Configuration Management Tools (Hardware and Software)

- Network/Communication Tools
  - E-Mail
  - File Transfer Tool

- Information Tracking Tools
  - Requirements Traceability Management Tool
  - Discrepancy Tracking System

- Data Base Tools
  - Relational Database Management System
  - Groupware

- Interface Analysis Tools
  - Interface Data Consistency/Analyzer
  - Graphic Communications Interface Analyzer

- Language Environment Tools

- Test Tools (usually shared with developers and other test agencies)
  - Automated Test System
  - Regression Test Suite
  - Capture/Replay Tools[1] (p. 26).

This list covers the initial V&V tasks, and is discussed later in the chapter in relation to an V&V integrated support environment.

V&V Tools and Methods Selection

The *Software Validation, Verification, and Testing Technique and Tool Reference Guide*[2] provides the background for this section on selecting tools and methods. This selection which follows, modifed from the *Guide* begins with the determination of a goal—a specific, measurable outcome. For example, 90% statement execution is a goal. Once a goal is determined, the selection matrices (Appendix A: Tables 3A.1, 3A.2 and 3A.3) are utilized to see if a tool or method is applicable to the selected goal. For the statement coverage example, the coverage is checked during code execution. Referencing the code selection matrix (Appendix A: Table 3A.3), one finds statement coverage. Next, the alphabetized keyword table (Appendix A: Table 3A.4) is searched for the appropriate keyword(s). For the example, the tool for statement coverage is found to be test coverage analyzers. The last step is to reference the tool and method descriptions (Appendix A: Table 3A.5) and confirm that the tool or method does accomplish the desired goal. For the example under test coverage analyzers, the statement "Completeness is measured in terms of the branches, statements or other elementary constructs which are used during the execution of the program over the tests," confirms that a statement coverage analyzer measures the completeness of statement execution.

To aid in the V&V tools and methods selection see Appendix A: Tables 3A.1, 3A.2 and 3A.3, which separate tools and methods into the broadly defined software development phases: requirements, design, and code. The purpose of a selection matrix is to suggest possible tools or methods for a goal in a development phase. The goal is stated (directly or indirectly) in terms of the form or content of a development product (requirements, design, code). The matrices list V&V tools and methods applicable to analyzing the form or content of a product. Specifically, manual and automated static analysis tools and methods aid in analyzing the form and the semantic content of each of the three products.

Appendix A: Table 3A.4 lists, alphabetically, the keywords and the associated tool or method. It may be used to identify characteristics of the tool or method from one of the three matrices in Appendix A: Tables 3A.1, 3A.2 or 3A.3. Appendix A: Table 3A.5 lists each tool or method with applicable keywords. It may also be used to identify the characteristics of a tool or method.

Tester's Workbench

Having introduced tool categories and tool and method selection criteria, one may ask what would be a basic set of tools to aid validation (i.e., testing). In order to achieve testing process (validation) maturity growth, the support of automated tools is essential. The following "Tester's Workbench" should provide that support. The workbench may be built from a basic set of testing tools for use at the lower testing maturity levels. Then, more sophisticated tools may be added as the organization progresses through the testing maturity levels. Below, a group of tools suggested by Burnstein, Suwannasart, and Calson (1996) in "Developing a Testing Maturity Model[sm*]"[3] are described for an organization. The tools support basic goals, such as test planning, incorporation of basic testing techniques, testing as an execution-based activity, and the separation of testing and debugging.

Project Planning Tools

Testing should be a planned activity. This implies a commitment to completion of testing activities. A project planning tool will aid the project manager in defining test activities and allocating time, money, resources, and personnel to the testing process.

Capture and Replay Tools

These tools automatically record test inputs from a keyboard or other device and replay them for subsequent testing when changes are made to the software. The tool user is able to prepare test

* Testing Maturity Model and TMM are service marks of Illinois Institute of Technology.

scripts and use them with the recorded inputs to replay the tests under automated control. Program errors can be detected by using an associated comparator tool that can compare current screens, dialogs, and files with results recorded from previous tests. This type of tool is invaluable for regression testing and has a positive effect on productivity.

Simulators and Emulators

These are hardware or software components that can substitute for missing, unavailable, or valued systems components during the testing process.

Syntax and Semantic Analyzers

These tools are useful for detecting code anomalies when code reviews are not a planned activity. Use of these tools before the execution of test cases will reduce errors and test time.

Debugging Tools

Because testing and debugging are recognized as separate activities, simple tools can be purchased to support debugging. Staff responsible for debugging duties can be trained to use these tools. A useful debugging tool allows the user to set breakpoints, examine memory during execution, and step through a set of instructions. Other suggested tool support includes test generation tools; metrics collection tools such as complexity and size measurers, coverage and frequency analyzers, defect and change trackers; and statistical tools for defect analysis and defect prevention.

V&V Methods

This chapter deals with tools and methods. This discussion of methodology is from The Object Agency[4] whose URL on the Internet provided in reference 4 includes an extensive bibliography on methodology and object-oriented methods. The Object Agency[4] relates that "methodology" literally means "the study of methods," however, in the software community, methodology is taken to mean "an approach to accomplishing a task," spoken of as analysis methodologies, design methodologies, etc. When a methodology is thorough or complete, it provides a relatively complete set of tasks, deliverables, roles and responsibilities, and heuristics. Although the most emphasis is placed on tools, Wallace, Ippolito, and Cuthill (1996) provide a brief introduction to a set of V&V methods from the National Institute of Science and Technology (NIST) *Reference Information for the Software Verification and Validation Process*[5] paper. It provides much useful information, and the methods are shown in Table 3.1.

Table 3.1 Software V&V Methods[5] (p. 25)

TECHNIQUE	REQ	DSGN	CODE	UNIT	INTEGR	SYS	INSTALL	OPER	MAINT
Algorithm Analysis	X	X	X	X					X
Analytic Modeling		X	X						
Back-to-Back Testing				X	X	X			
Boundary Value Analysis				X	X	X			
Code Reading			X						
Control Flow Analysis	X	X	X						
Coverage Analysis				X	X	X			
Critical Timing/Flow Analysis		X							
Database Analysis	X	X	X						X
Data Flow Analysis	X	X	X						X
Decision (Truth) Tables	X		X						
Desk Checking		X	X						
Error Seeding				X	X	X			
Event Tree Analysis	X	X	X						
Finite State Machines	X								
Functional Testing				X	X	X			
Inspections	X	X	X						
Interface Analysis	X	X	X	X	X	X			
Interface Testing			X	X	X	X			
Mutation Analysis				X	X	X			
Performance Testing				X	X	X			
Petri-Nets		X	X						
Proof of Correctness			X						
Prototyping	X	X							
Regression Analysis & Testing	X	X	X	X	X	X	X		X
Requirements Parsing	X								
Reviews	X	X	X	X	X	X	X	X	X
Sensitivity Analysis				X	X				
Simulation	X	X	X	X			X		
Sizing and Timing Analysis		X	X	X	X				
Slicing			X						
SFMECA[1]	X	X	X						
Software Fault Tree Analysis	X	X	X						
Stress Testing				X	X	X			
Structural Testing				X					
Symbolic Execution			X						
Test Certification				X	X	X	X		
Walkthroughs	X	X	X	O	O	O[2]	X		
			Reuse-Specific						
Consistency Analysis	X								
			KBS-Specific						
Alternative Model	X							X	
Control Groups				X					
Credibility Analysis				X					
Field Testing								X	
Illegal Attribute Testing			X						

Table 3.1 continued

TECHNIQUE	REQ	DSGN	CODE	UNIT	INTEGR	SYS	INSTALL	OPER	MAINT
Logical Verification	X								
Meta Models				X					
Partition Testing	X	X	X						
Rule Verification	X								
Statistical Validation				X					
Turing Tests				X					
Weight Analysis				X					

[1] Software Failure Mode, Effects and Criticality Analysis
[2] indicates that it is a walkthrough of the test code

Multidimensional Model

How do tools and methods interface with our multidimensional model? V&V tools are basic software technology innovations that are part of the CASE explosion. These CASE tools have been improving over the years. Initially, the stand-alone tool assisted software development and V&V, but soon the benefits of combining the toolset became obvious. So, not only was there a tool for test data generation and a tool for test input scenarios, but they were combined for more efficient interaction and use. More recently, the CASE suite of tools has combined and packaged configuration management tools with defect tracking and software quality analysis.

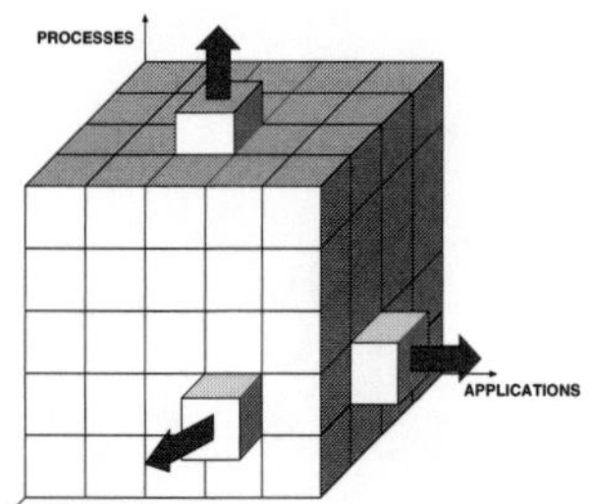

V&V methods fit within the process axis of the multidimensional model. Initially, there was the "spaghetti" (complex, no structure) development, followed by structured methods, and more recently OO methods. Other methods on this axis discussed later in this book are integrated product teams (IPTs), project management, and risk management.

Traditional V & V

Traditionally, a project produces a V&V Project Plan. Pushing that concept to the next level, certain large projects, such as Intermetrics' Earth Observing System Data and Information System (EOSDIS), have produced an entire set of V&V plans, such as a V&V Tool Management Plan.[6] The suggested contents of a V&V Tool Management Plan from the EOSDIS project follow:

1 Tool Management Approach
  1.1 Tool Infrastructure
  1.2 Tool Management Overview
2 Requirements Definition Process
  2.1 Needs Assessment

- 2.2 Tool Requirements Identification
- 2.3 Tool Assessment Criteria

3 Tool Identification Process
- 3.1 Tool Survey
- 3.2 Vendor Product Evaluations
- 3.3 Tool Demonstration

4 Tool Selection Process
- 4.1 Cost Benefit/Schedule Constraints Analysis
- 4.2 Tool Evaluation Exercise
- 4.3 Final Tool Recommendations
- 4.4 Tool Selection by Management

5 Tool Development/Procurement Process
- 5.1 Tool Development/Procurement Plans
- 5.2 Tool Environment Preparation and Integration Plan
- 5.3 Test Plans & Procedures

6 Tool Configuration Management (CM) Process
- 6.1 Configuration and Data Management Control
  - 6.1.1 Data Management Control
  - 6.1.2 Configuration Management Control
- 6.2 Acceptance/Validation Testing
- 6.3 Tool Validation and Post Test Analysis

7 Training and Operation
- 7.1 User Training
- 7.2 Tool Implementation/Utilization

8 Life Cycle Maintenance
- 8.1 Tool Maintenance Improvement Process
- 8.2 Tool Modification/Upgrade/Substitution

9 Glossary and List of Acronyms/Abbreviations
- 9.1 Glossary
- 9.2 List of Acronyms/Abbreviations

10 References[6] (pp. A-i, A-ii)

A quick perusal of this table of contents shows that it clearly covers important considerations for any V&V tool effort—items such as the identification, selection, development, purchase, control, and importantly, training and maintenance of the V&V tools. Moreover, McCabe[7] says that most successful tool applications happen when the particular tool is a piece of a larger project plan (such as we have here) that specifies the domain of the tool, who uses the outputs, when the outputs are available, etc. Even when the benefits are very clear, it still takes a planned, disciplined approach to apply tools. Only planning will bring this about.

Many commercial tools are available to help organize V&V activities—from Khodabandeh and Palazzi[8] there are those that detect memory access errors and memory leaks in C and C++ programs, and similarly, those that can visualize which part of the code has been executed during test (test coverage).

Paul Herzlich in "A Quick Win for Testing"[9] relates that static code analysers perform code inspection almost for free. By eliminating the wait for third party verification, a project can move forward more quickly. Since it is likely that more formal test designs will be missing for a large part of the testing, dynamic analysis tools like array bounds checkers, memory leakage detectors, profilers, etc., should be used. These will detect errors during demonstrations of software that might otherwise be missed.

Herzlich continues that:

> Capture/replay tools can be used to great advantage to help build up and repeat tests. As the software is being continually modified, the old tests can be rerun to ensure that stable functionality has not been affected by changes.... Properly developed and maintained, automated tests can be run every night. This helps reduce the built system testing at the end of the DSDM process.
>
> A capture/replay tool can also be employed to document tests. In the absence of test scripts, the quickest way to document tests ... is to record them as they are performed, using the capture facility of the capture/replay tool. The recorded scripts might or might not be repeatable, but more importantly they can be archived as a record of what testing has taken place.

Paliotta and McCaffrey state that:

> Computer software technology has been used to successfully automate time-consuming and repetitive engineering tasks with a goal of improving quality and productivity. For instance, Computer-Aided Design and Computer-Aided Manufacturing programs have dramatically transformed electrical engineering by increasing productivity and quality in the development of computer hardware components. The development and implementation of Computer-Aided Software Engineering (CASE) tools have attempted to achieve the same results for software engineering. Computer-Aided Software Test (CAST) is a subdiscipline of CASE. This area of technology is only now gaining a foothold within some software engineering organizations.... First we will provide an overview of the unit test process, a description of and the common problems encountered in unit testing software. Then we will suggest how CAST solutions that are specific to unit test can provide significant improvements to the software development process. Although most of the concepts are applicable to all software languages, the focus is with the Ada programming language.[10]

Organizations sometimes create project-specific tools that can help with some part of the process, but few organizations implement a complete CAST solution. Paliotta and McCaffrey relate that the current environment is ripe for the broad adoption of CAST technology for three reasons. First, the constantly expanding selection of commercial off-the-shelf software dedicated to test is currently robust enough to support all phases of the unit test process. Second, software organizations are re-evaluating their software processes in an attempt to increase productivity. Third, software tools are an important mechanism that can dramatically increase productivity.[10]

Dorothy Graham in "Software Testing Tools" tells us that the most popular category of CAST is test running (including capture/replay). Descending order of popularity of CAST tools are comparison tools, performance tools, static analysis, test data/database preparation, and debugging tools independent of the compiler. Next are test coverage tools, test design tools, and simulation tools. Finally, there are test management tools.[11] In Appendix B of this chapter are twenty helpful questions to ask of CAST tool users.

Below, Graham provides recommendations that help an organization gain benefits from CAST:

- Appoint a champion to oversee the evaluation and implementation of the tool.
- Investigate and evaluate candidate tools properly.
- Make sure the tool addresses real needs.
- Make sure the tool fits your hardware and software environment.
- Take usability factors into account.
- Provide training in tool use for all tool users.
- Use simple metrics to evaluate the benefits from using the tool.
- Don't expect miracles.[11]

It should be noted that many V&V projects build specific tools for their tasks from general templates. This is not only a way to perform V&V, but also it helps formalize information in a project (for software development). That is, software developers formalize the structure of information in the process of communicating it to V&V.

Regression Testing

In the complex development and testing environment of today, the use of tools is an essential element for the V&V person to be able to perform or assure appropriate regression testing. A multilevel regression testing framework abstracted in this Regression Testing section from Onoma and colleagues "Regression Testing in an Industrial Environment"[12] can be easily adapted into a software development and maintenance process in which regression testing can play a key role in improving and ensuring consistent software quality. Regression testing is used extensively. In fact, other than functional testing (or black box testing) and software inspection, regression testing is probably the most commonly used software testing technique. The frequent and extensive use of regression testing has led to several companies to develop in house regression testing tools to automate the process. In some instances, all existing test cases are rerun in regression testing. In other words, minimizing test cases for rerun has not been a critical issue for these companies.

Large programs are usually developed in stages by teams of developers, testers and managers using a development model such as waterfall or prototyping. Each large program is decomposed into components, and each component can be further decomposed. During the process, the software is being tested or inspected at various stages, such as at requirements stage or design stage. Testing is divided into unit testing, multiple levels of integration testing, functional testing, reliability testing, usage testing, stress testing, acceptance testing, and field testing.

Regression testing should be used whenever there is any change in the software, and it should be embedded in the software development and maintenance process. It should not be an independent stage of a software development and maintenance process; instead regression testing should be performed at each stage whenever there is a change. For example, if a module has been changed, it must be submitted to unit regression testing before it is submitted for integration with other modules. This is simply an application of divide-and-conquer strategy commonly used in software development. It is called multilevel regression testing.

In multilevel regression testing, test cases may be run multiple times during the process because a test case designed for unit testing may be rerun again at an integration level. This is so because at the time the concerned module is linked with other modules its faults may be detected using exactly the same test cases for unit testing. Thus, some test cases may be rerun as a quality assurance procedure.

Multilevel regression testing has many advantages. First, test suites can be attached to each software component at different levels of granularity. At the module level, test cases for unit testing will be attached. This helps in configuration control. Also, multiple components can be tested concurrently by different groups of programmers, reducing the time required to perform regression testing.

Another major reason for practicing multilevel regression testing is that the delay in detecting faults is minimized. If a software component is submitted for integration with other components without thorough testing (including new functional tetsing and regression testing), its error may be detected several weeks later by integration testing. If a fault is found during integration testing, the effort to correct the fault may have increased tremendously (pp. 81–86).

If a software group or V&V person is interested in using regression testing, concluding from "Regression Testing in an Industrial Environment"[12] the following tools are recommended:

- *Test execution tool:* This tool is a must because the number of test cases required to be run is enormous and it will be impossible without an automated test execution tool.
- *Test result comparator:* This tool is helpful in identifying test failures and can save significant time and effort in regression testing.
- *Configuration tool:* This tool will prove to be useful if it can track both software modules and their associated test cases, as well as software versions and software architecture.
- *Test management tool:* This tool should keep track of status of testing including the failures identified so far, the faults identified so far, actions taken for those identified failures and faults, test case dependency, and modification dependency (p. 96).

Program Verification

Often as a supplement, rather than as a distinct alternative, to testing is the technique of program verification. It is noted in the *Encyclopedia of Computer Science* that to verify a program means to demonstrate via a mathematical proof that the program is consistent with its specifications. It may be quite useful just to prove limited properties, such as that the program terminates (and without undefined operations) or that certain variables remain unchanged. The criterion of success requires a sufficiently believable proof, as do all mathematical proofs. Failure to complete the proof may be due to a problem with either the program or the specification, as well as because of insufficient information about the problem domain or even actually inability to prove a true theorem[13] (p. 1111).

The *Encyclopedia* states that a major aim of program verification is to provide techniques for actually verifying programs in order to eliminate the defects in programs and to know that this has been done in particular instances, thereby significantly decreasing the incidence of unreliable program behavior. The discipline of program verification also provides an important viewpoint that affects program construction, program specification, program decomposition, and language design[13] (p. 1113).

In program verification, the *Encyclopedia* concludes that a specification is the statement against which a program is proved correct. Verification is the process of showing the consistency between a program and its specification. In program validation, a specification can be used to generate test cases for black box testing. Together with the program, it can be used for path testing, unit testing, and integration testing. Finally, a specification serves as a kind of program documentation since it is an alternative, usually more abstract description of a program's behavior[13] (p. 1108).

The program verification work of Mellergaard and Staunstrup[14] described here involves the common object request broker architecture (CORBA) protocol:

> The objective of Work Package 1 Specification (CORBA-WP1) is to investigate, evaluate and refine existing techniques, especially VHDL [very high definition language], for performing integrated modeling and verification of hardware and software, this is called co-specification. VHDL as a standard hardware design and description language is in wide use in industry and, in addition to having many strong features, e.g., packages, data typing, encapsulation, componentiation, and instantiation, VHDL exhibits well-defined mechanisms for describing communication, sequential and parallel behavior, and structure. Methods for using formal methods (via Synchronized Transitions) together with VHDL is investigated to utilize the strong features of both. The Synchronized Transitions approach brings parallel, provable behavioral descriptions available to VHDL users, while providing those using formal methods with the support of advanced features and design environments of VHDL.
>
> Verification aims at checking properties, e.g., functionality, timing, and resource requirements of a design prior to the realization. It is highly desirable to base as much as possible of the verification on high-level abstract descriptions (cospecifications), for example, verifying that hardware and software components have a consistent interpretation of common interfaces. The aim of Work Package 4: Verification (CORBA-WP4) is to provide the designer with verification tools that supplement other CAD/CASE tools. Such verification tools range from timing simulators to theorem provers. These could become a valuable supplement to the low-level tools that are in widespread use today. Considerable theoretical work has been done on formal verification techniques supporting the specification level. Furthermore, prototype tools have been constructed to support such verification. However, most previous work has concentrated on verifying well-defined and self-contained designs. In this project of Mellergaard and Staunstrup (1996), verification of interfaces between components will play a key role. Designers must have tools that allow them to check whether a component complies with the specification of an interface. This is particularly important when the different components can be realized in different technolo-

gies and by different designers. The protocol concept of Synchronized Transitions is the starting point for interface verification. In connection with the work on co-specification done in Work Package 1: Specification (CORBA-WP1), verification tools and methods should be developed or modified to handle the VHDL-oriented co-specification notation developed as part of CORBA-WP1. This would allow a single description to be both formally verified using mechanical verification tools and simulated using VHDL simulators.

Inspections

The formal reviews constitute a thorough inspection mechanism used to detect errors in system components and documentation. Several inspections are generally conducted for each item as it progresses through the life cycle. The most commonly recognized inspections are conducted during the design and programming stages and are referred to as design inspections and code inspections. However, the inspection concept may be applied to any functionally complete part of a system during any or all phases of the life cycle and are typified by utilization of checklists and status reports. Another unique feature of an inspection is the use of data from past inspections to stimulate future detection of categories of errors.

A complete description of inspection methods and personnel is covered by James Dobbins (1998) in "Inspection as an Up-Front Quality Technique" in *Handbook of Software Quality Assurance* (3rd ed). An example from the NBS's (1982) *Software Validation, Verification, and Testing Technique and Tool Reference Guide* follows of a design inspection of a software component or item which defines the roles and responsibilities of the inspection team members. Upon decision of management to conduct a design inspection, the selected leader initiates process planning by identifying team members and their roles and responsibilities. If this is the first inspection for this item (i.e., there has been no requirements inspection), the leader next schedules an overview presentation. The project and backup documentation (i.e., functions specification, system flow charts, etc.) is distributed and the item designer leads the team through a high-level description of the item.

After the presentation each team member reads and reviews the documentation and lists any questions. This list of prepared distributed questions is often given to the leader and/or designer prior to the inspection meeting. At the designer inspection meeting the implementer leads the team through a detailed description of the design of the item being inspected. Backup documentation facilitates the description and clarifies points that may be brought up. The checklist is used by each team member to help identify errors and enforce standards. The problem definition sheet is prepared by the team leader at the end of the inspection. The item design will either be approved as-is, approved with modifications, or rejected. In the last two cases, the problem definition sheet is given to the designer and the correction process begins.

The *Software Validation, Verification, and Testing Technique and Tool Reference Guide*[2] states that at the start of this rework process an estimate is made by the leader and designer specifying time required for correction. This estimate is provided to management, who can then make a judgment as to whether their project schedule will be affected. Necessary changes to the item are made and the item is either re-inspected or submitted to follow-up procedures. During follow-up, the estimate provided to management is used as a checklist for the leader and designer to verify that all errors have been analyzed and corrected. The reader then fills out the appropriate reports and submits them to management (p. 70).

Since the cost to correct an error increases rapidly as the development process progresses, detection of errors by early use of inspections is an attractive prospect. Studies have been carried out that indicate that inspections are an effective method of increasing product quality (reliability, usability and maintainability). Experience with the technique indicates that it is effective on projects of all sizes. The best results are generally achieved when the inspection leader is experienced in the inspection process.

Some of the best quantitative results of the use of inspections have been provided by IBM, which has been studying the use of the technique. Their comparison of the benefits of inspections and walkthroughs indicated 23% higher programmer productivity with inspections than with walkthroughs. Some qualitative benefits attributable to the use of inspections from the *Software Validation, Verification, and Testing Technique and Tool Reference Guide* are also available:

- Programs are less complex.
- Subprograms are written in a consistent style, complying with established standards.
- Highly visible systems development.
- Estimating and scheduling are more reliable.
- Education and experience of all individuals involved in the inspection process are increased.
- User satisfaction is increased.
- Documentation is improved.
- There is less dependence on key personnel for critical skills.[2] (p. 71)

As pointed out by Steven Rakitin's *Software Verification and Validation: A Practitioner's Guide*,[16] it is very important to make inspections part of a company's culture because it is a leading aid to the verification process, but it can be a difficult task (pp. 68–69). Management may question the cost savings that can be realized by judicious use of inspections and may ask for an economic justification. Surprisingly, some software engineers and project managers may be reluctant to accept inspections. Some software engineers fear peer reviews and have legitimate concerns regarding the use of such reviews as part of performance evaluations. Some project managers may be reluctant to incorporate inspections into project schedules because they do not understand the benefits and tend to focus on short-term objectives (e.g., meeting a schedule) at the expense of long-term goals (e.g., increasing customer satisfaction). Understanding the root causes of this reluctance is essential to overcoming resistance to institutionalization inspections. Some key management issues that Rakitin[16] says need to be addressed are:

- Does management understand and support the objectives of the inspection process?
- Is management willing to commit the resources necessary to train inspectors?
- Is management willing to include inspections in project schedules?

Rakitin[16] identifies issues related to the software development process:

- Is there a written software development process? If not, could one be developed?
- Is there management support for a software development process?
- If a software development process exists, can it be modified to include inspections at appropriate points in the process?
- Is the software development process being actively managed?
- Does the software engineering group support the inspection process?
- Are resources available to train people in the inspection process? Is there a commitment to provide training over time as new employees are hired?
- Issues pertaining to inspection metrics are:
- Are the product and process metrics that will be collected from inspections defined? How will those data be used?
- Is there a continuous improvement process that would drive improvement to the inspection process based on collected data? (p. 69).

Earl Lee's (1997) article in *CrossTalk* concerning software inspections is discussed:

> The use of formal inspections is nothing new to the software industry. Begun in the 1970s by Michael Fagan at IBM, inspections continue to be the most effective and efficient method to find defects during software development. As a key process area of the SEI CMM, formal inspection is the most powerful of all peer review techniques. On projects such as Lockheed Martin's space shuttle onboard software project, formal inspections form the cornerstone of the quality program.
>
> As low-technology solutions to quality problems in a high-technology world, inspection concepts remain straightforward and easily understood by any software engineer. Yet attempts to use inspections yield remarkably varied results. Many, such as the space shuttle onboard software project, embrace inspections and garner error detection rates of 85% to 90%. Other projects find inspections useful enough to become a standard part of their development process, but defect detection rates fail to achieve optimum levels. Still others fritter away the inspection opportunity through poorly planned or executed attempts to institute inspection. The most frustrating situation of all, however, occurs when inspections become highly effective, but then performance declines to pre-inspection levels....
>
> Fortunately, there are methods to monitor the effectiveness of inspections. Unlike most software development activities, inspections provide an early indication of the quality of the product, sometimes months before delivery. This allows quality deficiencies to be addressed while there is still time to act. The key is to collect measurements and use the data to manage the process. Measurement data often comes after delivery, when it is too late to change the outcome. The use of statistical process control techniques provides the opportunity to identify problem inspections or high-defect concentrations, and to take appropriate action while production is still in progress. (pp. 10, 13)

Peer Review

This section on peer reviews is from *Software Validation, Verification, and Testing Technique and Tool Reference Guide.*[2]

> A peer review is a process by which project personnel perform a detailed study and evaluation of code, documentation, or specification. The term peer review refers to product evaluations which are conducted by individuals of equal rank, responsibility, or of similar experience and skill. There are a number of review techniques that fall into the overall category of a peer review. Code reading, round-robin reviews, walkthroughs and inspections are examples of peer reviews that differ in formality, participant roles and responsibilities, output produced, and input required. (p. 84)

Outline of method of the peer review methodology and participants of reviews

Continuing from the *Software Validation, Verification, and Testing Technique and Tool Reference Guide:*[2]

> Most peer reviews are not attended by management. (An exception is made in circumstances where the project manager is also a designer, coder, or tester—usually on very small projects.) The presence of management tends to inhibit participants, since they feel that they are personally being evaluated. This would be contrary to the intent of peer reviews—that of studying the product itself. Another common feature is the assembly and distribution of project review materials prior to the conduct of the peer review. This allows participants to spend some amount of time reviewing the data to become better prepared for the review. At the end of most peer reviews, the group arrives at a decision about the status of the review product. This decision is usually communicated to management.
>
> Most reviews are conducted in a group organization as opposed to individually by participants or by the project team itself. While this may seem an obvious feature, it bears some discussion. Most organizations doing software development and/or maintenance employ some variation of a team approach. Some team organizations are described as follows:
>
> - Conventional Team—A senior programmer directs the efforts of one or more less experienced programmers.
> - Egoless Team—Programmers who are of about equal experience share product responsibilities.
> - Chief Programmer Team—A highly qualified senior programmer leads the efforts of other team members for whom specific roles and responsibilities have been assigned (i.e., backup programmer, secretary, librarian, etc.).
>
> The group that participates in the peer review is not necessarily the same as the team organized to manage and complete the software product. The review group is likely to be composed of a subset of the project team plus other individuals as required by the form of review being held and the stage of the life cycle in process. The benefits of peer reviews are unlikely to be attained if the group acts separately, without some designated responsibilities. Some roles commonly used in review groups are described below [not all of the roles are employed in any one review but represent a list of potential roles]:

- Group/Review leader—the individual designated by management with planning, detecting, organizing and coordinating responsibilities. Usually has responsibilities after the review to ensure that recommendations are implemented.
- Designer—the individual responsible for the specification of the product and a plan for its implementation.
- Implementer—the individual responsible for developing the product according to the plan detailed by the designer.
- Tester—the individual responsible for testing the product as developed by the implementer.
- Coordinator—the individual designated with planning, directing, organizing and coordinating responsibilities.
- Producer—the individual whose product is under review.
- Recorder—the individual responsible for documenting the review activities during the review.
- User Representative—the individual responsible for ensuring that the user's requirements are addressed.
- Standards Representative—the individual responsible for ensuring that product standards are conformed to.
- Maintenance Representative—the individual who will be responsible for updates or corrections to the installed product.
- Others—individuals with specialized skills or responsibilities which contribute during the peer review.

While the forms of peer reviews have some similarities and generally involve designation of participant roles and responsibilities, they are different in application. The remainder of this section will summarize the application methods associated with the forms of peer reviews previously introduced.

a. Code Reading Review. Code reading is a line-by-line study and evaluation of program source code. It is generally performed on source code that has been compiled and is free of syntax errors. However, some organizations practice code reading on uncompiled source listings or handwritten code on coding sheets in order to remove syntax and logic errors prior to code entry. Code reading is commonly practiced on top-down, structured code and becomes cost ineffective when performed on unstructured code.

The optimum size of the code reading review team is three to four. The producer sets up the review and is responsible for team leadership. Two or three programmer/analysts are selected by the producer based upon their experience, responsibilities with interfacing programs, or other specialized skill.

The producer distributes the review input about two days in advance. During the review the producer and the reviewers go through each line of code checking for features that will make the program more readable, usable, reliable, and maintainable. Two types of code reading may be performed: reading for understanding and reading for verification. Reading for understanding is performed when the reader desires an overall appreciation of how the program module works, its structure, what functions it performs, and whether it follows established standards. Assuming that [Figure 3.1] depicts the structure of a program component, a reviewer reading for understanding would review the modules in the following order: 1.0, 2.0, 2.1, 2.2, 3.0, 3.1, 3.2, 3.3.

Figure 3.1 A Program Structure[2] (p. 87)

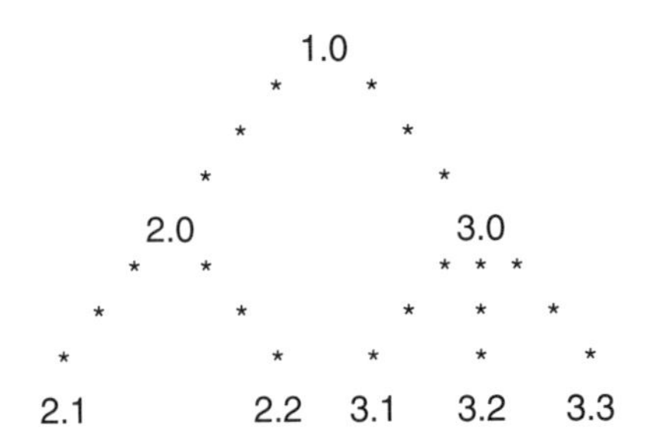

In contrast to this top-to-bottom approach, reading for verification implies a bottom-up review of the code. The component depicted above would be perused in the following order: 3.3, 3.2, 3.1, 3.0, 2.2, 2.1, 2.0, 1.0. In this manner it is possible to produce a dependency list detailing parameters, control switches, table pointers, and internal and external variables used by the component. The list can then be used to ensure hierarchical consistency, data availability, variable initiation, etc. Reviewers point out any problems or errors detected while reading for understanding or verification during the review.

The team then makes an informal decision about the acceptability of the code product and may recommend changes. The producer notes suggested modifications and is responsible for all changes to the source code. Suggested changes are evaluated by the producer and need not be implemented if the producer determines that they are invalid. There is no mechanism to ensure that change is implemented or to follow up on the review.

b. Round-Robin Review. A round-robin review is a peer review where each participant is given an equal and similar share of the reviewed to study, present, and lead in its evaluation. A round-robin review can be given during any phase of the product life cycle and is also useful for documentation review. In addition, there are variations of the round-robin review that incorporate some of the best features from other peer review forms but continue to use the alternating review leader approach. For example, during a round-robin inspection, each item on the inspection checklist is made the responsibility of alternating participants.

The common number of people involved in this type of peer review is four to six. The meeting is scheduled by the producer, who also distributes some high-level documentation as described at the beginning of this Peer Review section. The producer will either be the first review leader or will assign this responsibility to another participant. The temporary leader will guide the other participants (who may be implementers, designers, testers, users, maintenance representatives, etc.) through the first unit of work. This unit may be a module, paragraph, line of code, inspection item, or other unit of manageable size. Will participants (including the leader) have the opportunity to comment on the unit before the next leader begins the evaluation of the next unit? The leaders are responsible for noting major comments raised about their piece of work. At the end of the review all the major comments are summarized and the group decides whether or not to approve the product. No formal mechanism for review follow-up is used.

c. Walkthroughs. This type of peer review is more formal than the code-reading review or round-robin review. Distinct roles and responsibilities are assigned prior to review. Pre-review preparation is greater, and a more formal approach to problem documentation is stressed. Another key feature of this review is that it is presented by the producer. The most common walkthroughs are those held during design and code, yet recently they are being applied to specifications documentation and test results.

The producer schedules the review and assembles and distributes input.... In most cases the producer selects the walkthrough participants (although sometimes this is done by management) and notifies them of their roles and responsibilities. The walkthrough is usually conducted with fewer than seven participants and lasts not more than two hours. If more time is needed a break must be given or the product should be reduced in size. Roles usually included in a walkthrough are producer, coordinator, recorder, and representatives of user, maintenance, and standards organizations.

The review is opened by the coordinator, yet the producer is responsible for leading the group through the product. In the case of design and code walkthrough, the producer simulates the operation of the component, allowing each participant to comment based upon his area of specialization. A list of problems is kept, and at the end of the review each participant signs the list or other walkthrough form indicating whether the product is accepted as-is, accepted with recommended changes, or rejected. Suggested changes are made at the discretion of the producer. There is no formal means of follow-up on the review comments. However, if the walkthrough review is used for products as they evolve during the life cycle (i.e., specification, design, code, and test walkthrough), comments from past reviews can be discussed at the start of the next review.

d. Inspections. Inspections are the most formal, commonly used form of peer review. The key feature of an inspection is that it is driven by the use of checklists to facilitate error detection. These checklists are updated as statistics indicate that certain types of error are occurring more or less frequently than in the past. The most commonly held types of inspections are conducted on the product design and code, although inspections may be used during any life cycle phase. Inspections should be short since they are often quite intensive. This means that the product component to be reviewed must be of small size. Specifications or design that will result in 50–100 lines of code are normally manageable. This translates into an inspection of 15 minutes to 1 hour, although complex components may require as much as 2 hours. In any event, inspections of more than 2 hours are generally less effective and should be avoided. Two or three days prior to the inspection the producer assembles input as described here in the Peer Review Section and gives it to the coordinator for distribution. Participants are expected to study and make comments on the materials prior to the review.

The review is led by a participant other than the producer. Generally, the individual who will have the greatest involvement in the next phase of the product life cycle is designated as reader. For example, a requirements inspection would likely be lead by a designer, a design review by an implementer, and so forth. The exception to this occurs for a code inspection which is lead by the designer. The inspection is organized and coordinated by an individual designated as the group leader or coordinator.

The reader goes through the product component, using the checklist as a means to identify common types of errors as well as standards violations. A primary goal of an inspection is to identify items which can be modified to make the component more understandable, maintainable, or usable. Participants (identified earlier in this section) discuss any issues which they identified in pre-inspection study.

At the end of the inspection an accept/reject decision is made by the group and the coordinator summarizes all the errors and problems detected and provides this list to all participants. The individual whose work was under review (designer, implementer, tester, etc.) uses the list to make revisions to the component. When revisions are implemented, the coordinator and producer go through a mini-review using the problem list as a checklist. The coordinator then completes Management and Summary Reports, which are used to update checklists for subsequent inspections. (pp. 85–90)

The NBS *Software Validation, Verification, and Testing Technique and Tool Reference Guide*[2] tells us that:

Studies have been conducted which identify the following qualitative benefits from peer reviews:

- higher status visibility
- decreased debugging time
- early detection of design and analysis errors which would be much more costly to correct in later development phases
- identification of design or code inefficiencies
- ensuring adherence to standards
- increased program readability
- increased user satisfaction
- communication of new ideas or technology
- increased maintainability.

Little data is available which identifies the quantitative benefits attributable to the use of a particular form of peer review. However, one source estimates that the number of errors in production programs was reduced by a factor of ten by utilizing walkthroughs. Another source estimates that a project employing inspections achieved 23% higher programmer productivity than with walkthroughs. No data was available indicating the amount of increased programmer productivity attributable to the inspections alone. (p. 91)

Sunita Menon in "Defect Prevention"[18] mentions that other types of reviews, besides the peer reviews and inspections, are *preview meetings* (discusses problems anticipated and possible workarounds) and *post mortem* meetings (focus on lessons learned, so that past mistakes can be avoided especially in upcoming phases of this project) that serve valuable V&V functions.

Contemporary V & V

Formality of Methods and Tools

Methods and tools useful in the V&V environment are listed in order of increasing formality and effort suggested from *Formal Methods Specification and Verification Guidebook for Software and Computer Systems:*[19]

1. Use of manual review and inspection (e.g., "structured walkthroughs" and "formal inspections"), relying on documents written in a natural language, pseudocode, or programming language, possibly augmented with diagrams and equations, and validated with conventional testing techniques. Methods at this level are not "formal" in a strict sense, but serve as a baseline of discipline and structure necessary to support the additional methods/tools at higher levels of formality.
2. Use of notations and concepts derived from logic and discrete math to develop more precise requirements statements and specifications. Proof, if any, is informal. This level typically augments existing processes without imposing wholesale revisions. Examples include various CASE and object oriented modeling techniques and cleanroom methodology, although the latter is an exception in that it supplants rather than augments existing processes.
3. Use of formalized specification languages with mechanized support tools ranging from syntax checkers and pretty printers to type checkers. This level usually includes support for modern software engineering constructs (e.g., modules, abstract data types, and objects, all with explicit interfaces), but has not historically offered mechanized theorem proving.
4. Use of fully formal specification languages with rigorous semantics and correspondingly formal proof methods that support mechanization. Examples include state exploration, model checking, and language inclusion technologies. These technologies are highly specialized, automatic theorem provers that are limited to checking properties of finite-state systems. (pp. 10, 11)

Traceability

A major V&V review method is traceability. "The importance of the traceability activity lies in the uses to which the resultant traceability databases can be put. These databases can be searched, traced, and analyzed to enable" (p. 14):

- Management of cross-release requirements allocation
- Identification of dangling requirements (i.e., requirements not implemented) and extraneous code (i.e., code not driven by a defined requirement)
- Identification of common-requirement code coupling (a common source of maintenance coding errors)
- Scope/impact of proposed changes to the requirements base (valuable during requirements scrubs prompted by program redefinition/redirection)
- Determination of test program coverage
- Assessment of validation and/or regression testing needs.

In theory, the traceability methodology can be applied either manually or automatically; in practice, the number of requirements to be managed on any large project can only be effectively tracked via an automated process.[1] (p. 14)

Environments

Elaine Fedchak's "An Introduction to Software Engineering Environments."[20] says:

A software engineering environment is a name given to a set of tools, structures, rules and procedures that together provide a framework for software development and support.... The systems, capabilities and approaches presented in the literature as environments cover a wide range. To some, an environment is simply a terminal, its physical surroundings, and one or more tools. To others, an environment contains a complete set of integrated tools that support software development, automatic documentation, configuration management, project management, user orientation, and quality assurance, according to some specified methodology and for some specified language. To many, an environment implies the existence of a database that captures and makes available all relevant information for a project.

In the case of software engineering environment development, the users are software engineers. But software engineers are still in the process of defining software engineering, and therefore do not yet know exactly what they need or would like their software development and support systems to do for them....

One of the distinguishing features between differing views of environments is methodology-dependent versus methodology-independent. A methodology dependent environment is designed so that the user of the environment can only conform to a specific methodology as the tools are used. A methodology independent environment may contain similar tools, but the way the tools are used is left to the user to decide. As new methodologies are developed and become common, environments will be developed to support them. As existing methodologies are replaced, existing support environments may falter and disappear as well.

Designers of environments must be sensitive to the needs and attention span of users. The purpose of integrating individual tools into environments was to shield the user from all the interworkings and to provide a consistent interface. Even though the intended user audience for many software engineering environments is software engineers, this should not preclude designing them for ease of use. (p. 456–459)

From the EOSDIS *IV&V Tool Management Plan*,[6] the concepts from Averstar are provided below of an integrated support environment for IV&V tools. These paragraphs detail the approach for managing the integrated support environment IV&V toolset. Think in terms of V&V for every occurrence of IV&V.

The purpose of the integrated support environment is to provide consistent, accessible, and controlled use and availability of tools and information to the ISE [integrated support environment] user community, independent of user location or source of information. The [integrated support environment] ISE provides visibility to EOSDIS system development and integration and to associated IV&V products. The environment provides real-time remote site testing, plus the flexibility to keep pace with technology. The ISE consists of an Integrated Information Repository (IIR), a Toolbox, and a Test Buddy. The ISE supports a user community consisting of ISE

> support staff, IV&V task teams, project level users, EOSDIS developers, and the scientific user community. The hub of the ISE is the IIR that holds IV&V project data and EOSDIS development information. The Toolbox supplies the user community access to the IIR with an array of front end access tools. The Test Buddy is a self-contained, portable platform that has direct access to the IIR and is used to test related information. [Table 3.2 lists basic requirements that would support the foundation of an integrated support environment.] (p. A1–2)

The integrated support environment is the backbone of the V&V effort. It enables visibility into system development as reflected in V&V products, provides the capability to perform remote site testing, and, most importantly, ensures the flexibility needed to keep pace with technology—a major thrust of this book.

The IIR is at the center of the integrated support environment, and should hold all the V&V project data and results, as well as the software development information. This repository is accessible to a customer via front-end tools provided by the tool box. Along with the front-end tools, the toolbox also contains all of the V&V tools necessary for the V&V team to complete their task activities. Output products as well as data generated by the tools are stored in the IIR. The tools also retrieve data and products from the IIR when necessary.

The toolbox compartmentalizes the tools needed to access the IIR, support the V&V effort, and establish and maintain the integrated support environment. Front-end tools provide user access to data and products stored in the IIR. The V&V effort is supported by a wide variety of electronic office and technical analysis tools, which are integrated to facilitate data sharing. It is important that data storage is separate from tool software, because that allows tools to be plugged in and out. As long as a tool can access the IIR, it should be able to get needed data. This concept supports technology migration over a project's life span.

The Test Buddy is a self-contained, portable test support tool that can also access the IIR. It can be taken to remote, customer test sites and electronically linked to the IIR to download test data sets, test plans, test procedures, and test case definitions. After completion of tests, the test logs,

Table 3.2 System level integrated support environment operational requirements[6]

Operational Requirement Number	ISE Requirement (ISE=integrated support environment)
ISE-0010	The ISE shall be accessible to geographically dispersed users via modem or Wide Area Network (WAN).
ISE-0020	The ISE shall provide capabilities for the establishment of user accounts
ISE-0030	The ISE shall perform user authentication upon user login.
ISE-0040	The ISE shall implement user access control based upon user login.
ISE-0050	The ISE shall provide a tailored Graphical User Interface (GUI) for accessing tools and data that is based upon user login information.
ISE-0060	The ISE shall allow data transfer to geographically dispersed users.

discrepancies, and recorded test data can be ported to the IIR via the Test Buddy. All of this provides a validation suite for the V&V team to use.[6]

Formalized Specification

Moving to the more formal level that introduced this Contemporary V&V section, an example is CACI's VeriSpec tool that provides a drawing environment enabling one to put together a requirements analysis of the system based on the Hatley/Pirbhai Requirements and Architecture Methods or the method of choice. This includes state transition diagrams, process activation tables, textural process specifications, and timing specifications. In addition, the developer can define various 'Use Case' scenarios, enter timing requirements, and execute the whole specification over time. Execution reflects the state changes that occur in the system and the dynamic conditions that trigger different parts of the specification. One may identify anomalous and inconsistent responses, and discover parts of the specification that may never be reached (because of a fault in the specification).[21]

With VeriSpec, one begins by developing the requirements specification of the system, and probably a prototype of a user interface representation. The output of this is a validated specification of the functionality of the proposed system. The next step is to think about how the system is divided into subsystems, and how to implement these as physical modules. In other words, how will the specified system be realized in practice? There are many design choices, each with their relative merits and each placing constraints on the performance of the finished system.

VeriSpec allows one to model several proposed architectures for the finished system and to map the requirements specification onto various parts of any particular design. The developer can specify the performance characteristics of the equipment, so when the model is executed, resource contention is identified and overall performance is predicted. Message sequence charts and timing diagrams are the principle outputs.[21]

There are symbolic verification methods that use a symbolic representation of the transition relation, such as:

- boolean expressions represented by BDDs (Binary Decision Diagrams)
- linear constraints represented by convex polyhedra

These symbolic representations are used in different tools, such as the one previously mentioned. In that tool are implemented alternative methods for the comparison of systems modulo behavioral equivalences and pre-orders based on symbolic representations. Also an algorithm for the generation of a minimal model with respect to strong and weak bi-simulation based on symbolic representations has been implemented. This algorithm avoids, in many cases, the state explosion due to the fact that there are many equivalent states in the "initially generated" model.[22]

There are also verification methods based on deductive methods. In case the verification problem cannot be expressed in a decidable theory (or the decision procedure for the theory is too expensive), it can be interesting to use deductive methods, even if it is impossible to have at once a complete method and complete automatization. Work done in this domain aims more for maximal automation than for completeness. Tools are available that, given a program (a parallel composition of sequential components) and a safety property (an invariance property):

- compute in a compositional way a set of "structural invariants" obtained by static analysis from the control graphs of each parallel component.
- try to compute in an iterative way the greatest assertion that:
  - is implied by the predicate representing the set of initial states
  - is stable for the transition relation
  - implies the predicate representing the invariance property to be verified.

The structural invariants found in the first step very often allow a significant decrease in the number of iterations necessary in order to find the required predicate. Each time a tool needs to know the validity of a predicate, it may submit this predicate to a theorem prover, in which may be implemented tactics allowing to automatize most "simple" proofs (including some very simple tactics doing automatic inductions).[22]

Formal Proofs

The reason for going into these unique, though difficult, V&V tools and methods at the formal level is that there are substantial benefits of formal methods. The remainder of this section is from NASA's *Formal Methods Specification and Verification Guidebook for Software and Computer Systems*.[19]

> Formal specifications feature a high degree of logical precision, which eliminates much of the ambiguity that is found inevitably in informal specifications. This precision translates into a higher likelihood that all requirements writers and readers have a consistent understanding of the requirements and a higher likelihood that the requirements will be implemented correctly. Since formal specifications support abstract descriptions, they help engineers focus on what they want to accomplish instead of how to accomplish it. This may reduce the amount of detail needed in a requirements document, [which is a major help to V&V team].
>
> Formal proofs eliminate ambiguity and subjectivity from requirements analysis by providing a logical and precise argument for the behavior of the requirements. This enhances the analysis performed in informal reviews and inspections [by developers and V&V personnel].
>
> The use of formal specifications and formal proofs provides a systematic, repeatable approach to analysis. This translates into more consistent analysis and a process that is less dependent on the skill and perseverance of a particular analyst. [This is particularly beneficial today when such persons are in very high demand.]
>
> The use of formal specifications and proofs is not an all-or-nothing approach. It can be tailored to the level of rigor appropriate to a given budget, schedule, and technical need. [With that understanding the V&V team may help the project by giving guidelines for scaling to match the needs of a project.]

Formal specifications and proofs can be applied at any life cycle phase, including early in the life cycle where better analysis approaches are currently most needed. Detecting and fixing defects earlier in the process is far cheaper than finding them later in the process. For example, [the V&V person] could tailor the use of specifications and proofs to focus on the verification of critical properties early in the life cycle.

Formal specification and proofs can be supported by computer-based tools. This provides automation for tasks such as consistency checking and the preparation of proofs. These tools are analogous to the use of automatic calculators (and computers) in the analysis of engineering equations, but rather than "plugging in" numbers into a formal specification, one "plugs in" symbolic variables and calculates the equivalent of a closed form solution. This is an important benefit that provides an additional level of assurance as well as reducing the cost of certain aspects of the analysis. These tools greatly enhance the repeatability of the analysis by allowing proofs to be re-executed. This also allows quick answers to the consequences of "What if…" questions [by the development and/or the V&V team] early in the developmental life cycle.

Formal specifications and proofs complement the existing testing approach, but they go beyond what testing can accomplish. They complement testing by providing a precise specification from which better test plans can be derived. They go beyond testing because they have the unique capability to show that key properties are satisfied in entire classes of scenarios.

There is hard evidence that formal systems can increase the quality of real systems as well as solve historically difficult problems in computer science. This evidence comes from demonstrations of formal methods on several NASA projects as well as from increasing use in commercial systems and other government programs. Formal methods have been used by V&V personnel to find issues in mature requirements and to improve the understanding of complex systems.

In summary, formal methods [see Appendix B to this chapter for a guide to formal methods and tools available on the Internet] enable defects in requirements to be detected earlier than otherwise, and can greatly reduce the incidence of mistakes in interpreting, formalizing, and implementing correct requirements. Furthermore, used early in the life cycle, formal methods yield formalized statements that can be analyzed and their consequences calculated in a repeatable manner. In addition to these generic benefits attributable to the full spectrum of formal methods, the most rigorous and fully formal versions of formal methods cause more defects to be detected than would otherwise be the case and, in certain circumstances, subject to certain caveats, guarantee the absence of certain defects. When used judiciously and skillfully on suitable applications by V&V, or even development personnel, formal methods provide compelling evidence of correctness early enough to be useful, cheaply enough to be feasible, and on the basis of modeling that is simple enough to be credible.[19] (pp. 27, 28)

Data Quality

The V&V of data warehousing brings some unique problems, which are discussed in Chapter 12. Myles[23] tells us that project management tools are typically limited in their ability to check data quality. Process enactment audits enhance the typical project management tools, for V&V persons monitoring data quality in the data warehouse, to ensure that:

- activity identifiers follow an enterprise-defined pattern prescribed for that specific organizational entity,
- all required fields are completed,
- data in specified fields is limited to specified values, and
- time-now dates are within a specified range.

"Process enactment ensures that data quality problems are identified and corrected in the earliest stages of the processes"[23] (p. 21).

A toolset that cuts across the life cycle phases would be very beneficial for the V&V effort. The *ObjectGEODE Toolset Overview*[24] relates that there are such toolsets dedicated to analysis, design, verification, and validation through simulation, code generation, and testing of real-time and distributed applications, for use in many fields such as telecommunications, aerospace, defense, process control, or medical systems. These toolsets support a coherent integration of complementary approaches based on standards, which are:

- Rumbaugh's OMT (Object Modeling Technique)
- SDL (Specification and Description Language) issued from an international standard organization
- ITU-T (former CCITT)
- MSC (Message Sequence Chart) also issued from ITU-T.

These toolsets consist of graphical editors, a powerful interactive random and exhaustive simulator, a C/C++ code generator, targeting popular real-time operating systems and network protocols, and a design-level debugger. Complete traceability is ensured by such toolsets from requirement to code. Various editors provide for intuitive means of creating, modifying, and viewing the diagrams of a toolset description:

- Class
- Instance
- Scenario
- Architecture
- Interconnection and Message Sequence diagrams.

Consistency and compliance with notation rules is controlled by the checker part of such toolsets. These toolsets also provide graphical representation to professional documentation standards. There are powerful multi-user features available for large, distributed projects.

Most important for the V&V personnel is a powerful simulation and formal verification and validation tool provided to graphically detect, before coding starts, any pathological behavior pattern or show proof that the toolset description complies with requirements.[24]

Discussed here from the *V&V Research Quarterly*[25] are new tools for software development that allow improved application of V&V analysis. One tool, called WISE (Web-Integrated Software Environment), is a metrics tool that permits continuous tracking of the progress of a software project. Another, called FACADE (FAst CAse Development Environment), is a set of tools for rapid software development that tries to unify many different aspects of software development. The FACADE project is an experiment to explore V&V methods related to the goal of verifiable development techniques. These verifiable development techniques provide the V&V analyst with a capability to help at the level of requirements statement proof.

Both WISE and FACADE incorporate commercial off-the-shelf (COTS) software and build upon other widely available software tools. WISE and FACADE techniques are being used in the implementation of several software efforts including the development and V&V of a multicasting protocol program. As part of this effort, formal methods are being used to explore the efficacy of such approaches on safety-critical software projects. So far, the multicasting protocol program is serving well as an exemplary testbed for research of verifiable development techniques.[25]

Documentation V&V

Sorensen[26] relates that documentation tools that focus on the publishing task (producing a document) provide a better-looking document than was produced years ago using typewriters. This is one reason that word processors and desktop publishers are so pervasive in the workplace.

Documentation tools that focus on the management of documents have the potential to further improve documents, and perhaps of more significance, have the potential to improve the process that produces documents, which is where the V&V team may step in. But two areas where current document management tools fall short of providing all the needed functionality are in (a) change control and in (b) linking changes in software documentation to the software. In a work group situation, a technical writer should receive an automatic electronic notification that changes have been made to critical files indicating a probable need for a documentation update. And the V&V person must also be kept informed electronically.[26]

There are connections between verification and task control and between validation and testing, states Robert Dunn.[27] Assuming that the V&V contractor has been able to engage staff with the ability to do all this, the development contractor can use the V&V's findings as a check on the effectiveness of its own phase exit control evaluations. Given the arm's-length learning process inherent in V&V, the results of the independent evaluations are rarely timely enough for effective task control. In the operational model, direct products of development are verified, rather than documents prepared at some time removed from actual development[27] (p. 138). This places us back to the point just made that to avoid this time lost, the documents need to be electronically available to the developers and V&V team as soon as possible. Chapter 4 covers V&V of documentation in some detail.

Microsoft V&V

Because of the forefront position on the world stage of the Microsoft Corporation, what they do in regard to tools and methods for V&V has special significance. This section discusses issues from Roger Sherman's 1994 article, "Shipping the Right Product at the Right Time: A View of Development and Testing at Microsoft."[28]

> Microsoft uses an internal groupware product called Source Library Manager (SLM) to control source code. Each developer has all the code necessary to build the project on his or her own machine. After developing new code and unit testing it, the developer builds the product and runs a suite of automated test cases against it. The cases are often provided by the testing group. The purpose of the "quick test" is to demonstrate whether the new code breaks functionality in the product.
>
> If the new code passes this test, the developer does a "check-in," and his or her code is included in the daily build of the project. If the developer checks in code that breaks the daily build, he or she most likely will be given daily build responsibilities until another developer commits a similar transgression. Teams also employ other playful forms of stigma.
>
> Development teams at Microsoft work closely with test engineers to make products testable. Development includes many "asserts" in the "debug" version of its code. The asserts test the value of data structures while the code is executed, often reporting a problem before it manifests itself through the user interface. Most products also include an invisible menu that can be activated manually or through an automated script. This menu activates code within the application to simulate resource failures (low memory, low disk space, etc.), to "shake the heap" (i.e., to test the use of pointers), to verify the integrity of data structures, to fill memory with assigned values, and so on.
>
> The most common automation tools at Microsoft are C or C++ (for testing API layers), MS-Test (testing through user interfaces or managing test drivers), Visual Basic for Applications (or VBA, for inter-application testing), or the macro language that ships with the product (Microsoft Excel's macro language, Word-Basic for Word, Access-Basic for Access, etc.). Testers perform verification using a variety of means: smart file comparisons, direct queries to the application, direct queries to the operating system, and as a last resort, screen dumps and comparisons. There are also a number of test case execution managers in use at Microsoft. Among the most interesting is "Teacher/Pupil." When testers leave for the night, they enroll their machines as "pupils" in school. The teacher (server machine) downloads an automated suite and the pupil machine executes it, reporting test results back to the teacher machine. The teacher can determine whether a machine has frozen and can reboot it if necessary. Automated cases are used in a variety of ways at Microsoft. Groups that have to test APIs make heavy use of automation, since that is the only way to test them. The Windows NT test group wrote over 4 million lines of test code (50% of the total lines of source code for the shipping product).
>
> Most application groups have not found it cost effective to automate everything. Other groups achieve nearly 100% statement coverage with their automated tests, but they have found that this never tests the code completely; therefore, automation is used for particular tasks. The most efficient use of automation is regression testing. Regression suites are made up for breadth-testing nightly builds of the product and are enhanced and augmented as the project develops. Since regression tests are rerun more than any other kind of test, automating these tests has the greatest

payback for the time invested. Another application of automated tools is the use of "monkeys." A monkey is a tool that drives an application in random fashion, sending keystrokes that the product designer or developer may or may not have intended. Monkeys of this type are used in an informal way to determine how robust a product is. Further up the evolutionary chain is the "intelligent monkey." This kind of automated tool understands the user interface and sends valid user input to the application under test. An intelligent monkey can be calibrated to imitate customer usage, if such a profile is known. When imitating a statistically valid customer profile, the intelligent monkey can be used to determine a true mean time to failure. Most intelligent monkeys in use at Microsoft allow tracing when a fault occurs, to determine the set of keystrokes that caused the failure.

There are several types of beta testing at Microsoft. Marketing runs beta tests that have very little to do with testing the product for defects. Marketing betas are quite useful for getting customer feedback on the way the features have been implemented, and sometimes adjustments are possible before release to the general public.

Technical betas, as they are called at Microsoft, are for the purpose of finding bugs. Internal betas (called alpha testing elsewhere) are popular and effective. For many Microsoft products, internal betas have been far more useful for finding bugs than external beta tests. Beta versions of products are posted on internal servers, and everyone in the company is invited to download them and try them. Anomalies are reported via e-mail. Some developers are so proud of their code that they offer "bug bounties"—cash—for anyone who can find a bona fide bug in their product. External betas can be quite large and are run by a centralized group that has developed expertise in managing beta sites. The internal beta group can put together a beta site list that duplicates the user profile of any product's target market.

External betas are most important to the Systems group, since it writes code that is most likely to be affected by hardware configuration. In spite of the large number of beta sites and the length of beta tests, bugs from external beta testing account for less than 5% of all bugs found in most products, including operating systems. While some groups find those remaining 5% important enough to continue such testing, other groups have abandoned external beta tests. For these groups, internal testing has been effective enough.

An internally developed tracking tool called the Reporting And Information Database (RAID) enforces a procedure for resolution of problem reports and bugs. Originally developed for testers and developers for tracking defects, RAID databases have become complete "to do" lists for shipping projects, because resolution of each issue is enforced and tracked. Once an issue has been opened in the database, it is assigned to a developer or a program manager for resolution. The developer may fix a problem if it is a defect or assign it back to the tester if he or she cannot reproduce the problem. The developer may also assign the issue to a committee of the test lead, development lead, program manager, and product support lead for resolution. Typically, the committee members will choose to fix it if they believe it is a defect, postpone it if necessary, or do nothing if the product behaves as they intend. Once resolved, issues are closed. Test engineers are the only people who can close an issue, thereby assuring that every issue is completely fixed or appropriately reviewed.

Issues in RAID are ranked by severity and priority, and they are tracked by status (ACTIVE, RESOLVED, CLOSED), assignee, product area, open date, change date, closed date, version number, and how the issue was resolved. Product teams add additional fields to track other

> items—such as how an issue could have been avoided in the first place. RAID provides data for most of the metrics used in the company. Because everyone uses the same tool, conclusions using these metrics are widely applicable. Data from RAID databases are our primary source for analyzing process improvements and comparing best practices between groups. Because individual teams can add their own fields to issue reports in RAID, test engineers also use RAID to test hypotheses on the causes of bugs and ways to improve development efficiency. RAID is an important tool for improving our capability to deliver world-class products on time.
>
> From its start 19 years ago, Microsoft has gone through many stages of evolution in its capability for producing the right software at the right time. From small teams developing software for early adopters, through the use of more defined processes today, Microsoft still embodies the organizational values that made it successful: small, empowered, focused teams, producing the best product that they can for their customers.[28] (pp. 8–9)

Maturity Goals at the Test Maturity Model (TMM) Levels

Based upon the Software Capability Maturity Model defined by the Software Engineering Institute, a team concerned with improving testing (i.e., validation) has devised a Testing Maturity Model. The operational framework of the TMM provides a sequence of hierarchical levels that contain the maturity goals, subgoals, activities and tasks, and responsibilities that define the testing capabilities of an organization at a particular level. They identify the areas where an organization must focus to improve its testing process. The hierarchy of testing maturity goals is shown in Figure 3.2. Details of the TMM are found in Developing a Testing Maturity Model in September, 1996 *CrossTalk*.[3]

With the TMM a V&V person or team may evaluate the level at which the organization being V&V'ed is operating. With that knowledge, a much better V&V program may be laid out. The testing capability is exceedingly important, so this innovation will provide a help for the V&V team.

Figure 3.2 TMM maturity goals by level (Redrawn from Burnstein et al in reference 3)

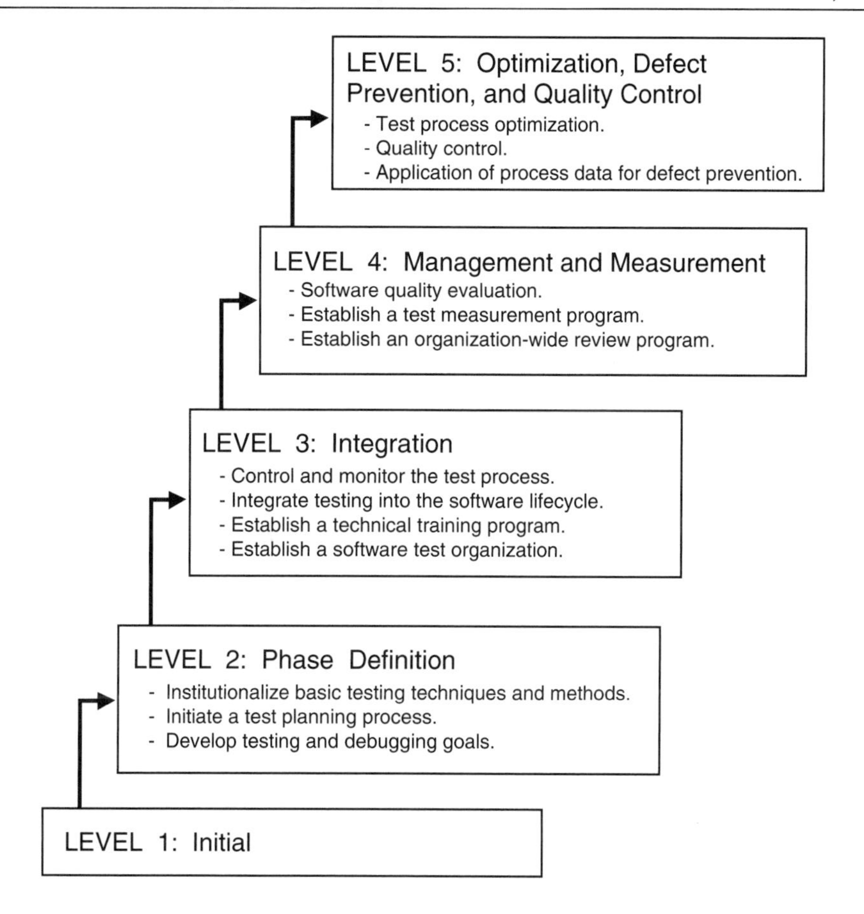

Summary

The conduct of software V&V tasks to fulfill the requirements of the V&V activities generally involves static, dynamic, and formal analysis methodologies. Static analysis methods are those which directly analyze the form and structure of a product without executing the product. Reviews and inspections are examples discussed in this chapter of static analysis methods. Static analysis methods are traditionally applied to software requirements, software design, and source code. They may also be applied to test documentation, especially test cases, to verify their traceability to the software requirements, their adequacy to fulfill test requirements, and their accuracy.

Dynamic analysis methods covered in this chapter involve execution of a development activity product to detect errors by analyzing the response of a product to sets of input data. For these methods, the output values, or ranges of values, must be known. Testing is the most frequent dynamic analysis method. Prototyping, especially during the software requirements V&V activity, can be considered a dynamic analysis method. In this case the exact output is not always known, but enough knowledge exists to determine whether the system response to the input stimuli meets system requirements. Formal analysis is the use of rigorous mathematical techniques to analyze the algorithms of a solution.[5]

In this chapter a wide variety of example tools and methods for V&V have been discussed. However, due to the explosion occurring in the field, this is just an introduction to the subject.

For application areas, such as those covered in this book and others not yet defined, these tools and methods provide a basic trend. The trend to be garnered is that tools and methods for V&V are for full automation and available over networks for use by the V&V team.

References

1. *EOSDIS Independent Verification And Validation (V&V) Management Plan* (Deliverable 0301), Prepared By: AverStar, 6301 Ivy Lane, Suite 200, Greenbelt, Maryland 20770; Prepared For: NASA Goddard Space Flight Center, EOSDIS Project, Code 505, Greenbelt, Maryland 20770; December 2, 1994.
2. *Software Validation, Verification, and Testing Technique and Tool Reference Guide* (NBS Special Publication 500-93), National Bureau of Standards, Computer Science and Technology, Washington, DC, September, 1982.
3. Burnstein, Ilene, Suwannasart, Taratip and Carlson, C.R., "Developing a Testing Maturity Model, Part II," In *CrossTalk*, Software Technology Support Center, Ogden: Hill AFB, Vol. 9, No. 9, September 1996, pp. 19–26.
4. www.toa.com, The Object Agency, 843-G Quince Orchard Boulevard, Gaithersburg, Maryland 20878-1626, (301) 977-8800, 1997.
5. Wallace, Dolores R., Ippolito, Laura M. and Cuthill, Barbara, *Reference Information for the Software Verification and Validation Process*, NIST SP500-234, Gaithersburg, MD 20899, April, 1996.
6. *IVVMP Appendix A: EOSDIS IV&V TOOL MANAGEMENT PLAN (Deliverable 0301 App A)* prepared for: NASA Goddard Space Flight Center, EOSDIS Project, Code 505, Greenbelt, Maryland 20770, prepared by: AverStar, WVU/NASA Software IV&V Facility, 100 University Drive, Fairmont, West Virginia 26554, December 2, 1994.
7. McCabe, Tom, *Successful Tool Usage*, SQM issue 21, © 1994 Tom McCabe, Web presentation © 1996 Tesseract Publishing, February 11, 1996, http://www.avnet.co.uk/tesseract/QiC/articles/McCabe/21.html.
8. Khodabandeh, A. & Palazzi, P., *Software Development: People, Process, Technology*, CERN (European Laboratory for Particle Physics)—ECP Division—Programming Techniques Group, http://www.cern.ch/PTGroup/Papers/Sopron94/CSCproceedings_19.html, web.office@cern.ch, 1994.
9. Herzlich, Paul, *A Quick Win for Testing*, SQM issue 25, © 1995 Paul Herzlich, Web presentation © 1996 Tesseract Publishing, March 11, 1996, http://www.avnet.co.uk/tesseract/QiC/articles/Herzlich/25.html.
10. Paliotta, John J. and McCaffrey, William K., "Computer-Aided Software Test Tools for Unit Level Test," In *CrossTalk*, Software Technology Support Center, Ogden: Hill AFB, Vol. 7, No. 12, December 1994, pp. 17–28.
11. Graham, Dorothy, *Software Testing Tools*, SQM issue 24, © 1994 Dorothy Graham, Web presentation © 1996 Tesseract Publishing, February 15, 1996, http://www.avnet.co.uk/tesseract/QiC/articles/Graham/21.html.
12. Onoma, Akira K., et al, "Regression Testing in an Industrial Environment," *Communications of the ACM*, ACM, New York, Vol. 41, No. 5, May, 1998, pp. 81–86.
13. Ralston, Anthony & Reilly, Edwin (editors), *Encyclopedia of Computer Science* (New York: Van Nostrand Reinhold, 1993).

[14] *CORBA: Work Package 4: Verification*, Niels Mellergaard, Jorgen Staunstrup, May 31, 1996.

[15] Dobbins, James, "Inspections as an Up-Front Quality Technique," In Schulmeyer, Gordon and McManus, James, *Handbook of Software Quality Assurance* (3rd ed.), (Upper Saddle River, NJ: Prentice Hall Inc., 1998).

[16] Rakitin, Steven R., *Software Verification and Validation—A Practitioner's Guide*, (Boston: Artech House, 1997), Reprinted from permission from Artech House, Inc., Norwood, MA, USA, http://www.artech-house.com.

[17] Lee, Earl, "Software Inspections: How to Diagnose Problems and Improve the Odds of Organizational Acceptance," In *CrossTalk*, Software Technology Support Center, Ogden: Hill AFB, Vol. 10, No. 8, August 1997, pp. 10–14.

[18] Menon, Sunita, "Defect Prevention," *Society for Software Quality*, Spring 1996 Grant Winner, Sept. 1996, http://www.ssq.org.

[19] *Formal Methods Specification and Verification Guidebook for Software and Computer Systems*, Volume I: Planning and Technology Insertion, NASA-GB-002-95, Release 1.0. http://www.ivv.nasa.gov

[20] Fedchak, Elaine, "An Introduction to Software Engineering Environments," *IEEE 0730-3157/86/0000/0456*, (© 1986 IEEE), pp. 456–463.

[21] Gorman, Paul, *CACI Design & Validation Tools—VeriSpec*, CACI Products Company.

[22] http://www.imag.fr/VERIMAG/VERIF/methodes-english.html

[23] Myles, Jr., David T., "Project Management Systems Featuring Process Enactment," In *CrossTalk*, Software Technology Support Center, Ogden: Hill AFB, Vol. 8, No. 3, March 1995, pp. 17–28.

[24] *ObjectGEODE Toolset Overview*, © 1996 VERILOG SA—All rights reserved, <webmaster@ verilog.fr>, November 1, 1996.

[25] *V & V Research Quarterly* Issue 2, Web Curators: Bob Burkhard and Rick C. Cavanaugh on webmaster@ ivv.nasa.gov, Independent Software Validation and Verification Facility, Fairmont, West Virginia, April 14, 1995.

[26] Sorensen, Reed, "Documentation Management Awareness is Increasing," In *CrossTalk*, Software Technology Support Center, Ogden: Hill AFB, Vol. 7, No. 2, February 1994, pp. 20–25.

[27] Dunn, Robert H., *Software Quality: Concepts and Plans* (Englewood Cliffs, NJ: Prentice Hall Publishing Co., 1990)

[28] Sherman, Roger W., "Shipping the Right Products at the Right Time: A View of Development and Testing at Microsoft," In *CrossTalk*, Software Technology Support Center, Ogden: Hill AFB, Vol. 8, No. 10, October 1995, pp. 6–9.

Appendix A

Table 3A.1 Selection Matrix I—Requirement Specification[2]

ANALYSIS TYPE	AUTOMATED TOOLS	MANUAL TECHNIQUES	REVIEWS
Static	Requirements tracing aids (Note 1) Cross-reference Data flow analyzer	Requirements tracing aids (Notes 1&2) Inspections • Selected manual application of techniques listed in column one (Note 3)	Inspections Peer review Formal reviews
Dynamic	Requirements analysis Cause-effect graphing Assertion generation Data flow analyzer	Assertion generation (Note 4) Specification-based functional testing (Note 5) Cause-effect graphing (Note 5) Walkthroughs	Walkthroughs Formal reviews
Formal	Assertion generation	Formal verification (Note 6)	

NOTES

[1] The requirements indexing and cross-referencing schemes are established and documented as part of the requirements specification.

[2] Requirements tracing may be performed through a totally manual process.

[3] Certain techniques may be manually applied to small applications or on selected portions of a given specification. This requires planning and preparation. The larger the amount of information being analyzed, the greater the probability of error.

[4] Assertion generation is performed either for later analysis using an assertion processing tool, or for manual analysis as an adjunct to testing.

[5] This is a test data generation technique/tool.

[6] Axiomatic specification is necessary to support analysis.

Table 3A.2 Selection Matrix II—Design Specifications[2]

ANALYSIS TYPE	AUTOMATED TOOLS	MANUAL TECHNIQUES	REVIEWS
Static	Requirements tracing aids Cross-reference Data flow analyzer	Requirements tracing (Note 1) Inspections • Selected manual application of techniques listed in column one (Note 2)	Inspections Peer review Formal reviews
Dynamic	Cause-effect graphing	Assertion generation (Note 3) Specification-based functional testing (Note 4) Cause-effect graphing (Note 4) Walkthroughs	Walkthroughs Formal reviews
Formal	Analytical modeling of software designs (Note 6) Global roundoff analysis of algebraic processes (Note 5) Formal verification (Note 8)	Algorithm analysis Formal verification (Notes 7 & 8)	

NOTES

[1] Requirements tracing may be performed through a totally manual process.

[2] Certain techniques may be manually applied to small applications or on selected portions of a given specification. This requires planning and preparation. The larger the amount of information being analyzed, the greater the probability of error.

[3] Assertion generation is performed either for later analysis using an assertion processing tool, or for manual analysis as an adjunct to testing.

[4] This is a test data generation technique/tool.

[5] Analyzes an algebraic algorithm, independent of a given level of specification and therefore is applicable to a design or code level specification.

[6] Requires the manual development of a model, which is then run.

[7] Axiomatic specification is necessary to support analysis.

[8] Formal verification is a primarily manual exercise though supporting tools have been developed.

Table 3A.3 Selection Matrix III—Code[2]

ANALYSIS TYPE	AUTOMATED TOOLS	MANUAL TECHNIQUES	REVIEWS
Static	Requirements tracing Cross-reference Data flow analyzer Control structure analyzer Interface checker Physical units checking Code auditor Comparator Test data generator	Requirements tracing aids (Note 1) Inspections • Selected manual application of techniques listed in column one (Note 2)	Inspections Peer review Formal reviews
Dynamic	Assertion processing Test data generators Test support facilities Test coverage analysis Mutation analysis (Note 4) Interactive test aids Execution time estimator/analyzer (Note 5) Software monitor (Note 5) Statement coverage Symbolic evaluation	Assertion generation (Note 3) Regression testing (Note 6) Walkthroughs	Walkthroughs Formal reviews
Formal	Formal verification (Note 7)	Formal verification (Note 7)	

NOTES

[1] Requirements tracing may be performed through a totally manual process.

[2] Certain techniques may be manually applied to small applications or on selected portions of a given specification. This requires planning and preparation, the larger the amount of information being analyzed, the greater the probability of error.

[3] Assertion generation is performed either for later analysis using an assertion processing tool, or for manual analysis as an adjunct to testing.

[4] This is a test data generation technique/tool.

[5] Assist in testing the satisfaction of performance related requirements.

[6] Testing after modification of tested software, i.e., re-testing.

[7] Formal verification is a primarily manual exercise though supporting tools have been developed.

Table 3A.4 V&V Tool And Method Keywords[2]

KEYWORDS	TOOL/METHOD
accuracy analysis	algorithm analysis
algorithm efficiency	algorithm analysis
amount of space (memory, disk, etc.) used	algorithm analysis
amount of work (CPU operations) done	algorithm analysis
assertion violations	assertion processing
bottlenecks	analytical modeling of software designs
boundary test cases	specification based functional testing
branch and path identification	control structure analyzer
branch testing	test coverage analyzers
call graph	control structure analyzer
check list	inspections
code reading	peer review
completeness of test data	mutation analysis
computational upper bound, how fast	algorithm analysis
consistency in computations	physical units testing
correspondence between actual & formal parameters	interface checker
data characteristics	assertion generation
dynamic testing of assertions	assertion processing
environment simulation	test support facilities
evaluation along program paths	symbolic execution
execution monitoring	software monitors
execution sampling	software monitors
execution support	test support facilities
expected inputs, outputs, and intermediate results	assertion generation
expected versus actual results	comparator
file (or other event) sequence errors	data flow analyzer
formal specifications	assertion generation
functional interrelationships	requirements analyzer
global information flow	interface checker
go/no go decisions	formal reviews
hierarchical interrelationships of modules	control structure analyzer
information flow consistency	requirements analyzer
inspections	peer reviews
inter-module structure	cross reference generators
loop invariants	assertion generation
manual simulation	walkthroughs
module invocation	control structure analyzer
numerical stability	global round-off analysis of algebraic processes
path testing	test coverage analyzers
performance analysis	requirements analyzer
physical units	assertion generation
portability analyzer	code auditor
program execution characteristics	execution time estimator/analyzer
	software monitors
proof of correctness	formal verification
regression testing	comparator
requirements indexing	requirements tracing
requirements specification analysis	cause–effect graphing
requirements to design correlation	requirements tracing

Table 3A.4 continued

requirements walkthrough	requirements analyzer
re-testing after changes	regression testing
round—robin reviews	peer reviews
rounding error propagation	global round-off analysis of algebraic processes
selective program execution	interactive test aids
standards checker	code auditor
statement coverage	test coverage analyzers
statement testing	test coverage analyzers
status reviews	formal reviews
system performance prediction	analytical modeling of software designs
technical reviews	peer reviews
test case preparation (definition and specification)	test data generators
test data generators	mutation analysis
	specification—based functional testing
test harness	test support facilities
testing thoroughness	test coverage analyzers
type checking	interface checker
uninitialized variables	data flow analyzer
unused variables	cross—reference generators
variable snapshot/tracing	symbolic execution
walkthroughs	peer reviews

Table 3A.5 V&V Tool/Method with Keywords[2]

TOOL/METHOD	KEYWORDS
algorithm analysis	accuracy analysis algorithm efficiency amount of space (memory, disk, etc.) used amount of work (CPU operations) done computational upper bound, how fast
analytical modeling of software designs	system performance prediction bottlenecks
assertion generation	data characteristics loop invariants physical units expected inputs, outputs, and intermediate results formal specifications
assertion processing	assertion violations dynamic testing of assertions
cause–effect graphing	test case design using formal specification requirements specification analysis
code auditor	portability analyzer standards checker
comparator	regression testing expected versus actual results
control structure analyzer	call graph hierarchical interrelationships of modules module invocation branch and path identification
cross reference generators	inter-module structure variable references
data flow analyzer	uninitialized variables unused variables file (or other event) sequence errors
execution time estimator/analyzer	program execution characteristics
formal reviews	go/no-go decisions status reviews
formal verification	proof of correctness
global round-off analysis of algebraic processes	numerical stability rounding error propagation
inspections	check list
interactive test aids	selective program execution variable snapshot/tracing
interface checker	correspondence between actual & formal parameters type checking global information flow

Table 3A.5 continued

mutation analysis	test data generators completeness of test data
peer reviews	technical reviews code reading round-robin reviews walkthroughs inspections
physical units testing	consistency in computations
regression testing	re-testing after changes
requirements analyzer	functional interrelationships information flow consistency performance analysis requirements walkthrough
requirements tracing	requirements indexing requirements to design correlation
software monitors	execution monitoring execution sampling program execution characteristics
specification based functional testing	test data generation boundary test cases
symbolic execution	evaluation along program paths verification of algebraic computation
test support facilities	environment simulation execution support test harness
test coverage analyzers	branch testing statement testing statement coverage path testing testing thoroughness
test data generators	test case preparation (definition and specification)
walkthroughs	manual simulation

Appendix B

From *Software Testing Tools*[11] are:

Twenty Questions to ask other CAST tool users:

1. How long have you been using this tool?
2. How many copies/licenses do you have?
3. How many users can be supported?
4. How many users actually use the tool?
5. What other tools did you consider when purchasing this tool?
6. How did you evaluate and decide on this tool?
7. What is your impression of the vendor (commercial professionalism, on-going level of support, documentation and training)?
8. What is your assessment of the quality of your own internal testing practices prior to acquiring the tool?
9. How did the use of the tool affect the quality of the testing? Were there any problems in your organization from introducing the tool, and how were they overcome?
10. Is the tool now integrated into your work processes and standard procedures? How much effort did this take?
11. What were your objectives or success criteria when buying the tool? (e.g., improved quality of software, improved quality of testing, improvement in meeting release deadlines, improved productivity, capacity planning, performance assessment)
12. Have your objectives been achieved?
13. Were they the right objectives? If not, what should they have been?
14. Were there any other benefits or problems in using the tool, which were not anticipated?
15. Have you saved any money by using this tool?
16. Can you quantify the savings or improvements? If so, what was your Return on Investment?
17. Do you feel the tool gives you value for money?
18. How long did it take you achieve real benefits? What are the critical factors for achieving payback?
19. What improvements are needed in the tool? Is the vendor responsive to requested enhancements?
20. If you were doing it over again now, would you still purchase this tool? What would you do differently?[11]

Formal Methods and Tools

The following from *Formal Methods Specification and Verification Guidebook for Software and Computer Systems*[19] is a list of URLs that lead to lists of formal method tools:

http://www.comlab.ox.ac.uk/archive/formal-methods.html by Jonathan Bowen.

file://chopwell.ncl.ac.uk/pub/fm_tools/fm_tools_db by The Formal Methods Tools Database maintained by Tim Denvir.

ftp://sail.stanford.edu/pub/clt/ARS/README by The Database of Automated Reasoning Systems maintained by Carolyn Talcott.

Nearly all are available electronically and come free of charge. This selection is not intended to be an endorsement of any of these tools, but serves to highlight tools that are better known, better supported, and have been subjected to more widespread use.[19]

CHAPTER 4

Documentation

Introduction

Documents are a convenient medium to share ideas. Throughout the 1980s the DoD with DOD-STD-2167 (Software Development) standard and its related Data Item Descriptions (format of documents) perpetuated a document-centric software development process. Because of the previous lack of discipline in much software development this "write-it-down" discipline was most beneficial to better product development. It probably was, however, overkill that caused some projects to get bogged down in format, rather than content.

As CASE tools became more sophisticated and reliable, software developers have been able to use the tool output to communicate with others on the development team. In fact, with shared development networked environments, other team members had instant access to the tool output themselves. The flow and speed of information sharing across the project was greatly enhanced. The wait for document updates became a burden on moving the project forward. Software developers depended on the development environment for their information.

With the growth of wide area networks (WANs), intranets, and the Internet it became easier for the customer to access the CASE tool outputs. These technological advances decreased the need for the formal documentation of the past.

Having related that history, documents are still important to software development and are a mainstay for the V&V specialist to perform her verification activities. Many of the concepts related in this chapter will assist the V&V specialist, whether the information is captured in a "formal" document or captured as the output of a CASE tool. It is the content that the V&V specialist needs to deal with in verifying adequacy, correctness, etc., of the on-going development.

This chapter has sections concerning the documentation process itself, requirements and design specification V&V, functional and test specification V&V, and document review methods.

Multidimensional Model

The multidimensions of processes, applications, and technologies have significant impact on the V&V of software documentation. It is widely recognized that software documents are used regularly as the exit criteria for a life cycle phase, so which process life cycle model is used effects this. Also, when using reduced life cycle processes, the quantity of software documentation is questioned. To achieve a quick software product it must be accompanied with smaller, more concise documents.

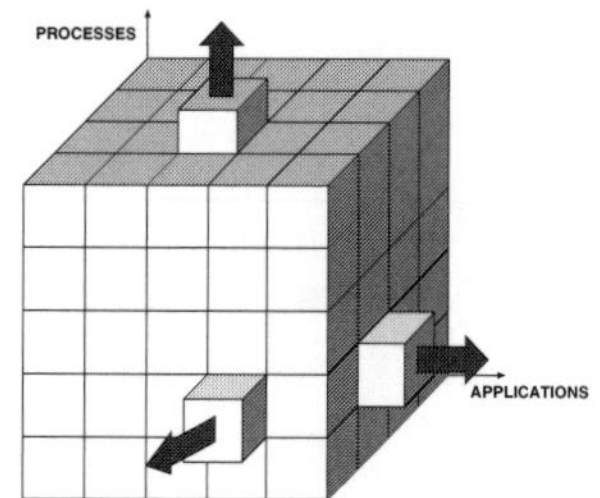

Another process element of development methods and tools impacts software documents very strongly. Levels of V&V associated with different methods and tools are discussed in this chapter with specific reference to the use of tools for document production. There is a table comparing manual and automated methods according to eight criteria; such as, completeness, traceability, etc.

Technological impacts on document production—and consequently, document V&V—include the word processing software. However, that software has been greatly enhanced to allow multiple reviewers to uniquely highlight their comments so that the document owner may easily update the document. The intranet also has had significant impact on document production and V&V because people in remote locations have easy access to the document for markup—but not necessarily official change.

Which application the software documents are written for has a minor impact on the differences. The criticality of the application drives the quantity of the documents. It is important to determine whether the documents are describing transactions involving the access to money or if they are just descriptions of games.

Documentation Process

As with the software itself, documentation has a development process that is described here as adapted from Atkinson and Sorensen's *Documentation Technology Report.*[1]

> The documentation process that produced a document is reflected in the quality of the document. If the process is well defined and well understood, the documentation quality tends to be higher than if the process is nebulous. Process implementation has many benefits, the greatest of which is that predictable high-quality output is consistently produced. This consistency is made possible because cooperative relationships are established, proper feedback mechanisms are in place to monitor the process, unnecessary and time-consuming rechecking is eliminated, and work activities are well defined. While each organization's documentation process will be different, there should be some common denominators to a successful process. Those common denominators are described here....
>
> A team must be assembled that is capable of performing the documentation tasks. The team may include a contractor and contracting agency, since they may select the documentation types. Besides selecting documentation types, other tasks to be considered are managing,

editing, writing, illustrating, page layout, and liaison between the technical expertise and the documentation team. Note that, depending on the size of the effort, one or two people may perform all these functions or several persons may share any one of the tasks.

Selecting the documentation types consists of … deciding what documents need to be produced. A decision on which documents are needed is driven by the software's complexity, software users' requirements, the possible consequence of software errors, and project resources. For example, the operational software for a major weapon system involving nuclear safety issues will require some document types that will not be required for the graphical user interface for supply depot applications software.

The scope and content of each software document must be determined. [If a project is tailored based upon military standards, then that tailoring defines much of this, including the content outline, depth and breadth.] The plan also addresses the source of data, the use of graphics, and audience guidelines. The documentation plan is prepared by the managing and editing members of the documentation team with input from the writers who will be following the plan. The writers prepare the software documentation based on the document plan.

Documentation standards apply to the structure and content of the documentation.… The software development organization also needs documentation standards that address document format, readability, typography, and punctuation. Excellent style guides that cover these details are available commercially.… Documentation standards are a set of rules and examples that writers can following in creating new documentation.

[The document management] plan consists of the schedule (when) and the mechanics (how) of developing the documentation. A PERT, Gantt chart, or both are developed to show when the various drafts are created and how the documentation schedule relates to the software development schedule. Some of the tasks that could appear on the schedule [are shown in Table 4.1].

The [document management] plan also outlines the facilities needed for document creation, such as documentation tools, technical support, working prototype of the software, and access to classified information. The dependencies of the documentation schedule on this support are identified in the PERT or Gantt charts.

The mechanics of creating software documentation may mean keyboarding on a word processor or desktop publisher to create text and using a drawing or flowchart package to

Table 4.1 Document development tasks.[1]

TASK	ASSIGNEE
write first draft	writer
create rough graphics	writer
internal review	writer and editor
create working draft	writer and editor
create working graphics	illustrator
technical review	V&V specialist
create formal review draft	writer and editor
formal customer/user review	customer/user
produce final baseline document	writer and editor

> generate graphics. More automated approaches involve the use of CASE tools that generate documentation based on user inputs. The user inputs specify the software development methodology (e.g., Shlaer-Mellor, Booch), software language (e.g., Ada, COBOL) and the desired format of the output file. The CASE tools provide data from a requirements/design repository that can be imported to a publishing product for final formatting as a document.
>
> The technical liaison function coordinates and [the V&V specialist may coordinate] this review with the creators of the software. The technical liaison and the [role of V&V specialist] is most effectively performed by a member of the group that creates the software since (a) they can answer some technical questions directly and (b) they may have more influence with the analysts and programmers who create the software than documentation specialist do. The reviewers are formally notified of the amount of their required time to support the review and of the deadline for comment submission. Corrections based on the comments are made. This process may be repeated as needed until the document is technically complete and correct.

Atkinson and Sorensen continue with the concept that the review of the document occurs in conjunction with the appropriate software review as outlined in the Software Development Plan and highlighted in the document management plan. These reviews may include the Preliminary Design Review, Critical Design Review, etc.

> The end-user and V&V specialists, when appropriate, are able to make corrections through these reviews. Again note that reviews may be an iterative process that continue until the document is correct.
>
> The last step is the incorporation of comments and corrections. The document is then submitted to configuration management personnel and baselined. Any possible updates to the baselined document are submitted as change requests that must pass a formal change process. Updates may take the form of change pages, or they may be a complete new version of the document depending on the scope of the changes. The changes are provided to personnel appearing on a formally maintained distribution list. If the document is being published on CD-ROM, changes may be distributed as a new CD. (pp. 14–16)

Al-Rawas and Easterbrook in "Communication Problems In Requirements Engineering: A Field Study,"[2] say:

> Documents are a poor substitute for interpersonal communication. This we attributed to the inherent restrictions of the available notations. While we appreciate the role of meetings such as design reviews in clarifying ambiguities and resolving conflicts in the specification documents, we feel that more can be done to make these documents into a more effective means of communication. A pressing and practical problem is to find out more about the communicational weaknesses of current notations and methods so we can accommodate for their weaknesses. For each concern, we need to determine what types of questions that concern may wish to make of a description produced in a notation. This can only be achieved by observing the meetings and conversations in which descriptions are referred to.
>
> There are a number of pitfalls in trying to make effective use of restricted communication channels. One of the dangers is that each community interprets things in the light of its own background assumptions. This is especially problematic with non-interactive communication, such as

specification documents, where there is no opportunity to check that the reader has interpreted them as was intended. McDermid [1993] points out a fundamental problem to do with the communication of abstract concepts, in that requirements specifications "document what it is that the analyst thought it was that the problem owner said he thought he might want." The uncertainties that McDermid describes propagate and multiply at each exchange of information. Robinson and Bannon [1991] use the term "Ontological Drift" to describe the change in meaning of abstract terms as they are passed between different communities.[2]

In the *Documentation Technology Report*,[1] is reported:

Eighty percent of software errors in large real-time systems are requirements and design errors due to ambiguity, incompleteness, or faulty assumptions. The idea that better documentation can solve a big percentage of maintenance problems seems to be suggested by most, but not all of the data. When process and modeling staffs do not document the reasons why they have reached certain conclusions, this causes problems during the product life cycle. From the early days of computing it has been recognized that some information other than the code is needed to maintain a program.

A good documentation system has several important characteristics:

- It helps the developer uncover and understand the problem, and encourages the thinking process needed to solve the problem.
- It provides easy access to various levels of documentation, then quickly delivers proper information to the appropriate audience.
- It helps the maintainer by providing subject matter with expert information and by demonstrating how the application satisfies requirements.

Documentation has at least the following limitations:

- documentation requires resources to be produced and maintained
- it may be inaccurate
- it may not be read
- it may not be understandable
- it may not be maintained. (pp. 17, 18)

The V&V person working with the documentation specialist should be able to respond to these limitations in the software development arena. Major resources are required in the production of the documents, but is the payoff there? Since software development is a mainly invisible activity to management, the production of the specifications describing what is being produced is an essential element to the project.

The inaccuracies that may appear in the documents are greatly minimized by the activities of the V&V team and the documentation specialist. It is a major focus of the V&V team and the documentation specialist to remove inaccuracies from the software documents. Remember that most specifications are not written to be read in the classic sense. They are there to provide a description of what is being developed and to guide that development. It is only while the development flows, the specifications are used to move through the details of development.

Understandability of documents, again, should be greatly enhanced by the V&V team. As technical experts, the V&V team and the documentation specialist can provide insight into clarification of technical points that may otherwise remain obscure. Understandability is also enhanced by the V&V team and the documentation specialist ensuring that the documents are consistent and the technical points are traceable up and down.

The maintenance of the documents comes about as the software is changed. It is only then that an effort needs to be expended to keep the document(s) in synchronization with the software. It is a task of the V&V person and the documentation specialist to ensure that this document maintenance takes place when these changes are made to the software.

Requirements and Design Specification V & V

This section is modified from Dr. Barry Boehm's article "Verifying and Validating Software Requirements and Design Specifications"* from IEEE Software.[3] The four basic V&V criteria for requirements and design specifications are completeness, consistency, feasibility, and testability. A taxonomy of satisfactory software specifications is shown in Figure 4.1, and each of the basic V&V criteria is discussed below.

Completeness

A specification is complete to the extent that all of its parts are present and each part is fully developed. A software specification must exhibit several properties to assure its completeness.

No TBDs

TBDs are places in the specification where decisions have been postponed by writing "To be determined" or "TBD." For example:

- "The system shall handle a peak load of (TBD) transactions per second."
- "Update records coming from the personnel information system shall be in the following format: (TBD)."

No nonexistent references

These are references in the specification to functions, inputs, or outputs (including databases) not defined in the specification. For example:

- "Function 3.1.2.3 Output

  3.1.2.3.a Inputs

  1. Output option flags obtained from the User Output Options functions...," which is undefined in the specification.
- "A record of all transactions is retained in the Transaction File," which is undefined.

* Portions reprinted, with permission, from IEEE Software, January 1984, pp. 75–88, © 1984 IEEE

Figure 4.1 Taxonomy of satisfactory software specification.[3] (© 1984 IEEE)

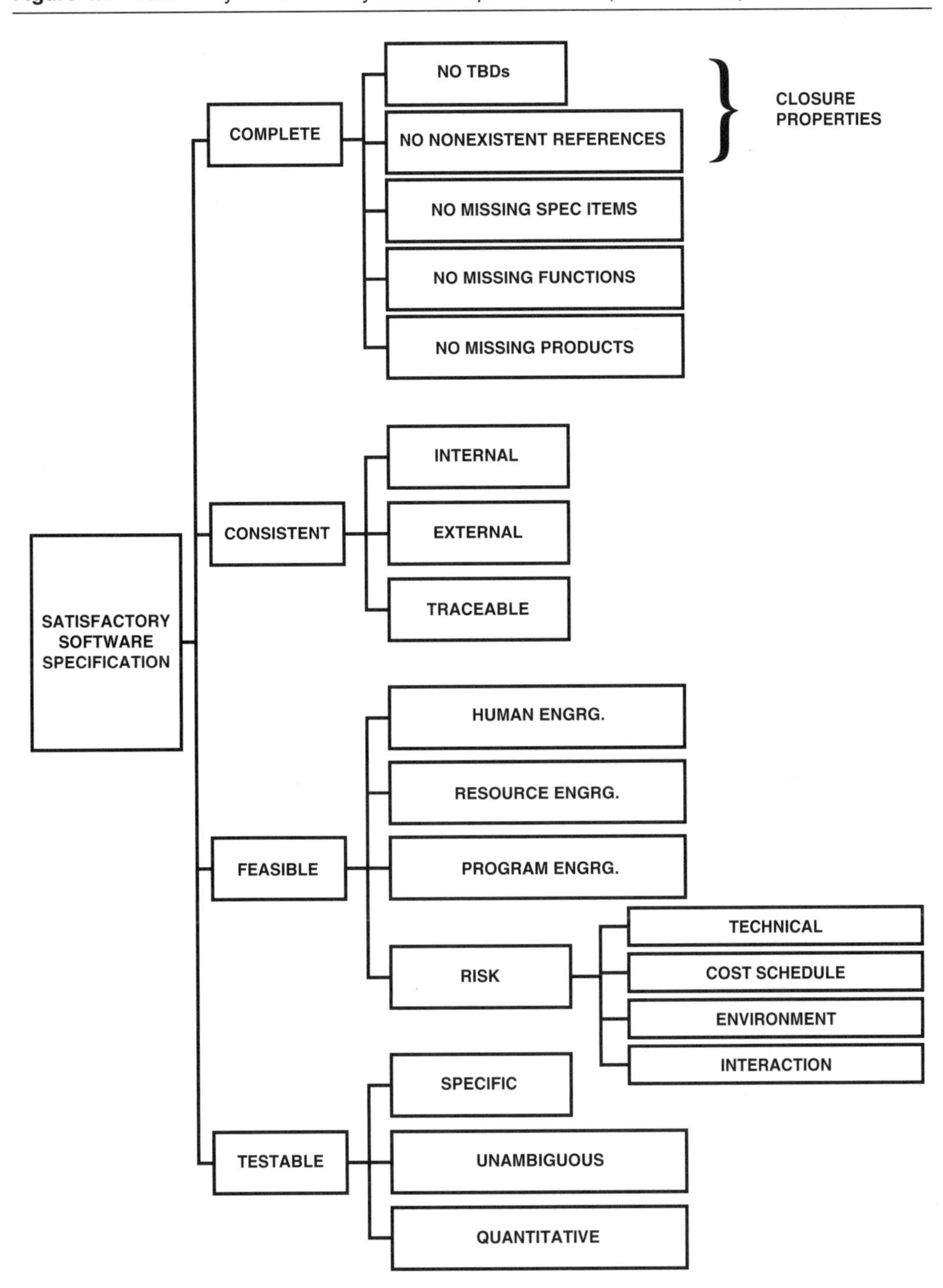

No missing specification items

These are items that should be present as part of the standard format of the specification, but are not present. For example:

- No verification provisions
- No interface specifications

Note that verification of this property often involves a human judgment call: a small, stand-alone system may have no interfaces to specify.

No missing functions

These are functions that should be part of the software product, but are not called for in the specification. For example:

- No backup functions
- No recovery functions[3] (p. 75–88)

Whenever possible, Watts Humphrey says that there should be

> a precise specification for the design's intended function. This specification permits the definition of the preconditions and ensures that the logic properly handles every case. In many cases, however, there is not a precise specification and so work must be done with a less formal understanding of what the program is intended to do. Regardless of the methods and notations in use, consider all possible logic cases and verify that they are correctly handled. Use whatever method that is found to be most effective, but be sure to review all possible conditions comprehensively.[4] (pp. 436, 437)

In *Testing Computer Software*[5] the point is made to verify a program by checking it against the most closely related design document(s) or specification(s). If there is an external specification, the function test verifies the program against it (p. 52).

Continuing from Dr. Boehm:

No missing products

These are products that should be part of the delivered software but are not called for in the specification. For example:

- Test tools
- Output post-processors

The first two properties—"no TBDs" and "no nonexistent references"—form a subset of the completeness properties called closure properties. Closure is distinguished by the fact that it can be verified by mechanical means; the last three properties generally require some human intuition to verify or validate.

Consistency

A specification is consistent to the extent that its provisions do not conflict with each other or with governing specifications and objectives. Specifications require consistency in several ways.

Internal consistency

Items within the specification do not conflict with each other, unlike the following counter-examples:

- "Function *x*
  (1) Inputs: A 4 × 4 matrix z of reals.

  .
  .
  .

  Function *y*

  .
  .
  .

  (3) Outputs: A 3 × 3 matrix z of integers."
- Page 14: "Master real-time control interrupts shall have top priority at all times."
  Page 37: "A critical-level interrupt from the security subsystem shall take precedence over all other processes and interrupts."

External consistency

Items in the specification do not conflict with external specifications or entities, unlike the following counter-example:

- "Spec: All safety parameters are provided by the preprocessor system, as follows…

"Preprocessor system spec: The preprocessor initializes all safety parameters except for real-time control safety parameters, which are self-initialized.

Al-Rawas and Easterbrook[2] point out that:

standard software development cycles rely heavily on documentation as an exit condition in moving from stage to stage. Documents are also used as the medium for communicating ideas. Consequently, a colossal amount of paper work is generated. The nature, the domain complexity, the variety of methods and notations, and the interdependency of partial requirement make it very difficult to establish total consistency. For example,… the recipient of the services provided… was referred to as client, customer, applicant, candidate, and land owner by different participants who contributed to the production of the specification documents. All these names were used to describe the same entity. The names used reflected the concern of each stakeholder.

Continuing with Dr. Boehm's V&V criteria:

Traceability

Items in the specification have clear antecedents in earlier specifications or statements of system objectives. Particularly on large specifications, each item should indicate the item or items in earlier specifications from which it is derived to prevent

- misinterpretations, such as assuming that "on-line" storage implies a requirement for random access storage (a dedicated on-line tape unit might be preferable); and

- embellishments, such as adding exotic displays, natural language processing, or adaptive control features that are not needed for the job to be done (and may not work as reliably as simpler approaches).

Feasibility

A specification is feasible to the extent that the life cycle benefits of the system specified exceed its life cycle costs. Thus, feasibility involves more than verifying that a system satisfies functional and performance requirements. It also implies validating that the specified system will be sufficiently maintainable, reliable, and human-engineered to keep a positive life cycle balance sheet.

Further, and most importantly, feasibility implies identifying and resolving any high-risk issues before committing a large group of people to detailed development.

Human engineering

Verifying and validating feasibility from a human engineering standpoint involves answering the following questions:

- Will the specified system provide a satisfactory way for users to perform their operational functions?
- Will the system satisfy human needs at various levels?

Examples of human engineering considerations are given in [Shneiderman]* and in [Smith and Aucella].

Resource engineering

This involves the following V&V questions:

- Can a system be developed that satisfies the specified requirements (at an acceptable cost in resources)?
- Will the specified system cost-effectively accommodate expected growth in operational requirements over its life cycle?

Examples of resource engineering considerations are given in [Boehm] and [Ferrari].

Program engineering

This addresses the following questions regarding a specified system:

- Will it be cost-effective to maintain?
- Will it be cost-effective from a portability standpoint?
- Will it have sufficient accuracy, reliability, and availability to cost-effectively satisfy operational needs over its life cycle?

Examples of these program engineering considerations are given in [Lipow, White, and Boehm's] checklists on maintainability and portability.

* Detailed citations of the bracketed references may be found in the General References section at the end of this chapter.

Risk

If the life-cycle cost-effectiveness of a specified system is extremely sensitive to some system aspect that is not well known or understood, there is a high risk involved in the system. If such high-risk issues are not identified and resolved in advance, there is a strong likelihood of disaster if or when this aspect of the system is not realized as expected.

Four major sources of risk in software requirements and design specifications are technical, cost-schedule, environmental, and interaction effects. Technical risk, for example, can involve:

- achievable levels of overhead in a multiprocessor operating system
- achievable levels of computer security protection
- achievable speed and accuracy of new algorithms
- achievable performance in "artificial intelligence" domains (e.g., pattern recognition, natural language processing)
- achievable levels of man-machine performance (e.g., air traffic control).

Cost-schedule risks include the sensitivity to cost and schedule constraints of such items as

- availability and reliability of the underlying virtual machine (hardware, operating system, database management system, compiler) upon which the specified software will be built
- stability of the underlying virtual machine
- availability of key personnel
- strain on available main memory and execution time.

Some environmental risk issues are

- expected volume and quality of input data
- availability and performance of interfacing systems
- expected sophistication, flexibility, and degree of cooperation of system users.

A particular concern here is the assessment of second-order effects caused by introduction of the new system. For example, several airline reservation systems experienced overloads because new capabilities stimulated additional customer requests and transactions. Of course, this sort of reaction can't be predicted precisely. The important thing is to determine where system performance is highly sensitive and to concentrate risk-avoidance efforts in those areas.

If the development is high-risk in several areas, the risks tend to interact exponentially. Unless high-risk issues are resolved in advance, you may find yourself in the company of some of the supreme disasters in the software business. For example, one large government agency attempted to build a huge real-time inventory control system involving a nationwide network of supercomputers with:

- extremely ambitious real-time performance requirements
- a lack of qualified techniques for the operating system and networking aspects
- integration of huge, incompatible databases
- continually changing external interfaces
- a lack of qualified development personnel.

Although some of these were pointed out as high-risk items early, they were not resolved in advance. After spending roughly seven years and $250 million, the project failed to provide any significant operational capability and was cut off by Congress.

Testability

A specification is testable to the extent that one can identify an economically feasible technique for determining whether or not the developed software will satisfy the specification. To be testable, specifications must be specific, unambiguous, and quantitative wherever possible. Below are some examples of specifications which are not testable:

- The software shall provide interfaces with the appropriate subsystems.
- The software shall degrade gracefully under stress.
- The software shall be developed in accordance with good development standards.
- The software shall provide the necessary processing under all modes of operation.
- Computer memory utilization shall be optimized to accommodate future growth.
- The software shall provide a 99.9999% assurance of information privacy (or "reliability," "availability," or "human safety," when these terms are undefined).
- The software shall provide accuracy sufficient to support effective flight control.
- The software shall provide real-time response to sales activity queries.

These statements are good as goals and objectives, but they are not precise enough to serve as the basis of a pass–fail acceptance test. Below are some more testable versions of the last two requirements:

- The software shall compute aircraft position within the following accuracy:

  ± 50 feet in the horizontal;

  ± 20 feet in the vertical.
- The system shall respond to:

  Type A queries in ≤ 2 seconds;

  Type B queries in ≤ 10 seconds;

  Type C queries in ≤ 2 minutes;

  where Type A, B, and C queries are defined in detail in the specification.

In many cases, even these versions will not be sufficiently testable without further definition. For example:

- Do the terms "± 50 feet" or "≤ 2 seconds" refer to root-mean-square performance, 90% confidence limits, or never-to-exceed constraints?
- Does "response" time include terminal delays, communications delays, or just the time involved in computer processing?

Thus, it often requires a good deal of added effort to eliminate a specification's vagueness and ambiguity and make it testable. But such effort is generally well worthwhile. It would have to be done eventually for the test phase anyway, and doing it early eliminates a great deal of expense, controversy, and possible bitterness in later stages. (pp. 75–88)

Roger Pressman[6] notes that validation criteria are probably the most important, and ironically, the most often neglected section of the Software Requirements Specification. How do we recognize a successful implementation? What classes of tests must be conducted to validate function, performance, and constraints? We neglect this section because completing it demands a thorough understanding of software requirements—something that we often do not have at this stage. Yet, specification of validation criteria acts as an implicit review of all other requirements. It is essential that time and attention be given to the validation criteria section (p. 200).

If there is an external specification, testing the program against it is only part of the task. *Testing Computer Software*[5] reminds the V&V person to validate a program by checking it against the published user or system requirements. The testing phase includes both function and system testing. System testing and integrity testing are validation tests. Integrity testing is a more thorough release test that is seen later to involve the use of the company's marketing material as an element of its success. It provides a last chance to rethink things before the product goes out the door. The integrity tester tries to anticipate every major criticism that will appear in product reviews, or, for contract work, every major complaint the customer will raise for the next few months. The integrity tester should be a senior tester who was not involved in the development or testing of this product, who may work for an independent testing agency. The integrity tester assumes that function and system testing were thorough, and does not deliberately set out to find errors. The integrity tester may carefully compare the program, the user documentation, and early requirements. The integrity tester may also make comparisons with competing products. An integrity test should also include all marketing support materials. The product must live up to all claims made in the advertisements. Test the ad copy and sales materials before they are published (p. 53).

Barry Boehm[3] continues to point out that there are differences in how different sized systems are handled as related to their documents. Those differences are covered in relation to small, medium, and large systems, and also who in the project has what responsibilities.

For the small system, to V&V a small specification:

- customer and/or project manager should:
  - outline the specification before opening
  - read the specification for critical issues, interview the specification developer(s)
  - determine the best allocation of V&V resources
  - coordinate efforts and resolve conflicts.
- V&V agent should:
  - read the specification
  - use checklists and manual cross-referencing
  - use simple models if accuracy or real-time performance are critical
  - use simple scenarios if the user interface is critical
  - use mathematical proofs on portions where reliability is extremely critical.

- users should:
  - read the specification from the user's point of view
  - use a human engineering check-list.
- maintainers should:
  - read the specification from the maintainer's point of view
  - use maintainability and reliability/availability checklists
  - use a portability checklist if portability is a consideration.
- Those responsible for interfacing the system should:
  - read the specification
  - perform manual cross-referencing with respect to the interfaces.

> To V&V a medium specification, use the same general approach as with small systems, with the following differences:
>
> - use automated cross-referencing if a suitable aid is available
> - use simple-to-medium manual and automated models for critical performance analyses
> - use simple-to-medium scenarios for critical user interfaces
> - prototype high-risk items that cannot be adequately verified and validated by other techniques.
>
> To V&V large systems, use the same general approach for large specifications as for medium systems, but use simple to detailed instead of simple to medium models and scenarios.
>
> For special situations, of course, you will have to tailor your own best mix of V&V methods. But in general, these recommendations will provide you with a good starting point for identifying and resolving your software problems. (pp. 75–88)

Table 4.2 provides a way to determine the best mix of V&V methods for the requirements and design documentation on a project. It evaluates the methods discussed above with respect to their ability to help V&V specifications and even provides a distinction between different size systems as just discussed above. The evaluation is done in terms of the basic V&V criteria discussed earlier.

Functional and Test Specification V&V

Focus is now directed to some concepts about the V&V of functional and test specifications extracted from *Verification, Validation and Evaluation of Expert Systems.*[9]

> Specifications are important for V&V.... Verification determines if a system meets its specifications, which is meaningless if there are no specifications. Validation determines if a system does what is needed; this is only possible if it has been decided what a system is supposed to do. The results of these decisions are specifications.

Table 4.2 V&V techniques rated according to eight criteria. (© 1984 IEEE)[3]

	Completeness		Consistency		Traceability		Human	Resource	Maintainability,		Relative Economics	
	Small	Large	Small	Large	Small	Large	Engrg.	Engrg.	Reliability	Accuracy	Small	Large
Simple Manual Techniques												
Reading	**	—	**	—	**	—	**	—	**	—	***	*
Manual Cross-Referencing	***	*	***	*	***	*	*	—	*	—	**	*
Interviews	*	*a	*	*a	**	**a	**a	—	**a	—	***	***
Checklists	*	*	—	—	—	—	***	*	***	*	**	*
Manual Models	—	—	—	—	—	—	—	*b	—	*b	**	**
Simple Scenarios	*	—	*	—	**	*	***c	—	—	—	**	**
Simple Automated Techniques												
Automated Cross-Referencing	***	***	***	***	***	***	—	—	—	—	*d	*d
Simple Automated Models	—	—	—	—	—	—	—	**b	—	**b	*	**
Detailed Manual Techniques												
Detailed Scenarios	*	*	*	*	**	**	***	—	—	—	—	*
Mathematical Proofs	***c	—	***c	—	***c	—	—	—	—	—	—	—
Detailed Automated Techniques												
Detailed Automated Models	**	**	**	**	**	**	—	***	—	**	—	*
Prototypes	**	**	**	**	**	**	***	***	*	***	—	*

Ratings:
- *** Very strong
- ** Strong
- * Moderate
- — Weak

Notes:

a. Interviews are good for identifying potential large-scale problems but not so good for detail.
b. Simple models are good for full analysis of small systems & top-level analysis of large systems
c. Simple scenarios are very strong for small-system and strong for large-system user aspects.
d. Economy rating for automated cross-referencing is strong for medium systems.
   If the cross-reference tool needs to be developed, reduce the rating to weak.
e. Proofs provide near-certain correctness for the finite-mathematics aspects of soflware.

At the specification stage the emphasis is on producing a clear identification of:

- What is to be produced?
- When should it be produced?
- What are the resources required?

The issue is to find a trade-off between the requirements specification (client) and the resources (time and money). The use of formal approaches (such as Structured Analysis, Software Requirements Engineering Methodology [SREM], and Structured Analysis and Design Technique [SADT; a trademark of SofTech]) prove to be very useful in this process. This is especially important to the V&V task because of the clarification provided by the use of these methods. (p. 18)

There are the functional specification and the test specification. The functional specification specifies the functions to be performed by the system and the constraints within which it must work. The test specification provides the test definition, by answering the following questions:

- Who will perform the test(s)?
- When (at what point) will they be performed?
- How do we ensure that the system behaves according to the functional specification?
- What V&V techniques are to be used, and when (at which time)? (p. 18)

In addition to the above-mentioned items, the following items should also be addressed in the test specification:

- A clear definition of the population of problems the system is supposed to solve.
- A provision of test and development samples.
- The required level of performance.
- A clear definition of what constitutes a correct problem solution verification:
  - Is it possible to collect inputs that could solve the problem?
  - Is it possible to compute the proposed output from the input validation?
- Can the V&V team certify that the specifications, if properly implemented, would solve the problem?
  - Can V&V team judge that the system is worth the probable cost?
  - Can V&V team judge that the system would be useful in practice?
  - Is it possible to build a system that could be integrated with other components as necessary?

It is particularly important to define specifications for the critical cases a system may encounter. A critical case for a system is a set or range of input data on which failure of the system to perform correctly causes an unacceptable, perhaps catastrophic, failure of the system.

There are several steps in defining and verifying specifications for a system:

1. Gather informal requirements from the systems experts, with particular attention to defining the critical cases.

2. Obtain V&V team certification of the specifications.
3. Validate informal descriptions of the specifications.
4. Validate the translation of informal specifications into the formal notation.
5. [When using formal statements], validate the formal statement of the requirements using symbolic evaluation.

Each step is detailed below, with particular attention to critical cases.

The first step in verifying specifications is to gather a complete set of requirements. Only the domain expert(s) can provide this list. Ideally, during the original acquisition phase for the system, the critical cases were gathered, documented, and validated. If the informally stated requirements are not available, however, gathering them is the first necessary step in verifying the correctness of a system.

Typically, to gather the critical cases, the domain expert(s) should list critical cases and keep a careful record of them. As with most acquisition tasks, it is important to ask for the following information:

- General principles: for example, "What are the critical performance requirements for this system?"
- Specific projects, and the critical performance requirements found in those projects: To get this information, a technical person should ask the expert(s) to tell him about their projects and experiences that are within the scope of the project. The purpose of this is that by reviewing the specific projects the expert's memory will be spurred. This process will help the technical person to decide what the critical cases really are.

In gathering a set of critical cases, it is important to let the experts describe critical cases in their own words and notation, not in any special notation. This is because the system may have missed a critical variable that may be needed to recognize a critical case. If the technical person asks the expert to verify requirement's gobbledygook, the expert may become too distracted to think of a critical case not described with the incomplete set of variables used in the incomplete baseline.

[Next], it is important... to certify the specifications, especially those concerning the critical cases. This is a vital step in the process because the system will be built to meet and tested against the specifications. If the specifications are in error, the system will almost surely fail to perform properly.

In order to obtain meaningful certification of the specifications, [the V&V team must] focus on a careful review of the specifications. Among the ways to obtain this focus are:

- Have a group of systems experts [from the V&V team] reach consensus on the specifications, with one of them functioning as a moderator. In this role, the moderator will:
  - Be familiar with the ongoing discussion, and in addition, will be in a position to solicit important issues that must be resolved.
  - Ensure that the [systems] experts [from the V&V team] address those issues and reach an agreement.
- Have the [V&V team] sign off on the specifications. (p. 17–20)

For systems where correct performance is critical, the next step in validating specifications of the system is to validate the informal descriptions of critical cases. A basic method for validation may be cultural consensus, in which the V&V team of systems experts are used to validate the correctness of those specifications. Continuing from *Verification, Validation and Evalustion of Expert Systems:*

> There are two questions that should be asked concerning the informal list of critical cases to validate:
>
> - Is the set of critical cases complete?
> - Are the critical cases correct?
>
> To validate completeness, the [V&V team] should conduct interviews with [systems] experts who have not contributed to the critical case list. This interview is similar to the one used to gather the list of critical cases, with one additional step: At the end of the interview, ask the systems expert to certify not just the critical cases proposed, but the entire list of critical cases gathered so far, including those that were added during the interview. After additional systems experts no longer provide new critical cases, the entire list gathered has been validated to a confidence level depending on the number of systems experts who certify the list.... (p. 20)
>
> To validate the critical cases, the informal descriptions should be translated into formal statements in a more formal language. The goal of this translation is to produce statements of the form:
>
> $$\text{if } I_1 \text{ and } I_2 \ldots \text{ and } I_n \text{ then } C_1 \text{ and } C_2 \ldots \text{ and } C_n.$$
>
> The I's should be stated in terms of input variables of the system, and the C's should be possible conclusions of the system. (p. 21)

The translation into a formalized language is a process that can introduce errors. So, the translation of critical cases need to be validated by the V&V team. When the V&V team validates the translation of critical cases, it is important to:

- Have an independent V&V team.
- Have the V&V team familiarize themselves with the formal language before examining the individual items.

In translating the informal requirements into formal statements, there are some typical kinds of errors, such as false negatives in the input variables. One problem in translation results from the fact that a symptom is often used in a base to stand for an underlying condition. If a single symptom is used to test for a condition, a false negative of that symptom will produce an error in what the system does.

In *Verification, Validation and Evaluation of Expert Systems* is stated:

> The solution to the false negative problem is to separate symptoms and underlying conditions. If C is a condition, a rule should be used of the form:
>
> $$\text{if } S_1 \text{ or } S_2 \text{ or } \ldots S_n \text{ then C} \quad \text{(Rule C).}$$

Where S_1 through S_n are a set of symptoms such that the probability of false negatives in all the S's is less than some agreed-on threshold. Outside of Rule C, and similar condition-inferring rules, the S's should not appear when a condition (i.e., C) is intended. Therefore, every occurrence of an S outside of a condition-inferring rule should be validated by the [V&V team].

In the case where a single symptom has such low false negatives that it identifies C by itself below the acceptable error threshold, it is unnecessary to separate the symptom and condition in the knowledge base:

> **Missing input variables:** ...An expert system may use only a small number of variables. Whether the small number of variables is adequate is a matter that [the V&V team] must validate. It is important to ask [systems] experts what data they gather in looking at problems covered. If the [systems] expert looks beyond the system, for example variable X, then: Can the [systems] expert get along without <variable X> as an item that should be validated? (p. 22)

Figure 4.2 outlines the steps to be considered at this specification stage.

Figure 4.2 Specification flow.[9]

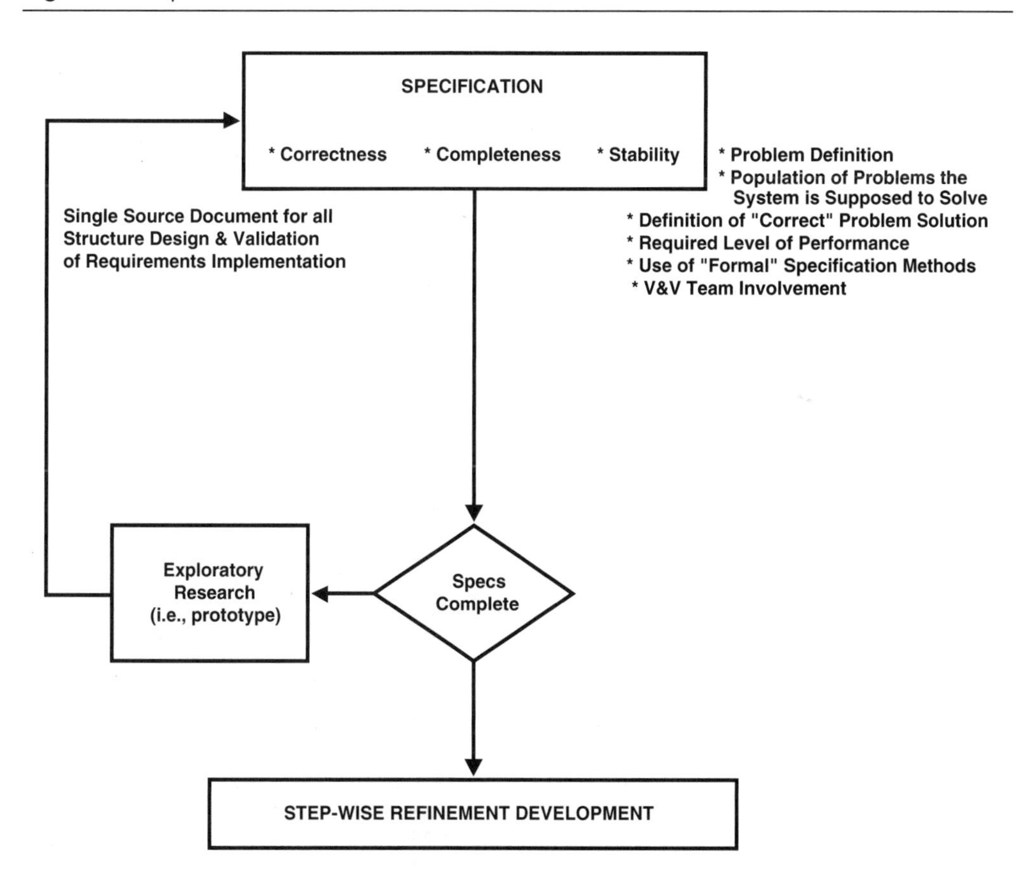

Following is a discussion of test specifications modified from the *Encyclopedia of Computer Science.*[10] The critical elements of software test revolve around the specification of testing:

1. specifications of validation or verification products to be tested
2. goals and thresholds for the tests
3. specifications of test activities and data
4. evaluations.

A V&V product is any engineering product analyzed during the test. An example of an early V&V product is a prototype graphical interface for validating ease-of-use by end-users. An intermediate V&V product is a detailed design specification that is used to verify that elaboration of high-level design has been carried out correctly. A very late V&V product is a partially integrated software system. A goal or threshold for the test is a specification of what it means to pass or fail the test. Ideally, these are quantitative specifications that correspond to direct measurements of a V&V product.

Examples of such specifications include observed failure rates, coverage criteria for correctness tests, and independent estimates of test data quality. A typical threshold requirement is that the input/output behavior of a given program unit must conform to its detailed design specification on at least k test points chosen randomly from a specified probability distribution. The specification of test activities and data refer to the procedures and conditions under which the test will be carried out. The evaluations comprise the important results of the test. The principle question answered by the evaluation is: Does this test demonstrate that the specified goal or threshold has been achieved? These elements are frequently formalized in a series of test plans. The design, management, and use of an effective test plan is sometimes an engineering process as complex and costly as the software product development itself. Frequently, the term "testing" is reserved for dynamic analysis (i.e., for those activities that involve running programs and observing outputs). Even in this restricted usage, however, intermediate V&V products may be involved and used for either validation or verification.

Remember that the level of formality of testing must be reduced in those life-cycle methodologies (the process dimension) that shorten development time. To see how this is achieved, consider from *A Quick Win for Testing*[11] that the formality of testing manifests itself in several ways:

- documentation of tests
- formality of the techniques used to design or choose tests
- control over the test environment and running of tests.

For one of those formalities, with a shortened life-cycle methodology, there is less documentation of tests. A list of conditions to test is all that is needed—to identify test coverage and to prioritize testing to focus on the areas that are most responsible for delivering the benefits. The same list is used to track test pass/fails. Prediction of expected results will, in many cases, not be documented, but will be based on the judgment of the testers at the time a test is run. A capture/replay tool as discussed in Chapter 13 can be used to enhance this basic level of documentation (p. 1246).

Documentation Review Methods

Document reviews are a mainstay of any V&V effort. AverStar's *EOSDIS Independent Verification and Validation (V&V) Management Plan*[7] concepts are discussed in this section. The interim products of a software development effort are documents, and they must be analyzed to ensure that the right product is being developed in an efficient manner. Life-cycle verification requires that the outputs of each phase be complete, consistent with the input requirements, and capable of ready incorporation in the next phase (i.e., be unambiguous). These general criteria are employed when reviewing any document. More specific criteria related to both the life-cycle phase the project is in and the type of document being reviewed are also employed.

Document reviews verify completeness, accuracy, and consistency of development documents. Selecting the appropriate reviewers is probably the most important element in successful document reviews. The reviewers needed for the requirements documents are probably not the same individuals selected to review a design phase audit report. For many documents during a reduced life-cycle (the process dimension), it is a cost saver for formal notes to be entered into a review form. Such formal notes allow each action item to be assigned and a place for initials for resolution and verification of the action item. When these kinds of review documents are utilized, the defects found in the document review process do not need to be entered into the defect tracking system. Looking over these completed review forms is done during the phase audit. Any outstanding document defect can be added to the defect tracking system at that time.

A document review methodology for V&V is depicted in Figure 4.3. As documents are received, they are prioritized for review and analysis. This prioritization serves to establish both the order in which the documents will be assessed and the level (depth) of that assessment. The results of risk analyses are fundamental to the prioritization which ensures that the document review process is continually aligned with the project goals and constraints.

A two-pass review methodology is utilized according to the *EOSDIS Independent Verification and Validation Management Plan*. On the first pass, the reviewer makes margin notes in the document and flags areas that may require further analysis, or that may represent a deficiency serious enough to warrant issuance of a discrepancy report. Areas so identified are discussed with the development lead personnel for disposition, and to establish the need for possible analytic studies or impact analyses beyond the scope of the document review task. Analyses within scope of the document review (essentially short pen-and-paper studies) are completed, and the second pass review of the document initiated. On this second pass, the reviewer applies the results of analyses performed, and formulates the review comments to be issued in the document review special report. The entire documentation review process is scaleable (by using the software documentation review levels concepts provided below) to workload, time availability, and dollar limitation constraints, thus ensuring that the document review process does not become an end to itself and consume inordinate amounts of project resources.

Figure 4.3 Document review activity network (Modified from *AverStar's EOSDIS Independent Verification And Validation (V&V) Management Plan*).[7]

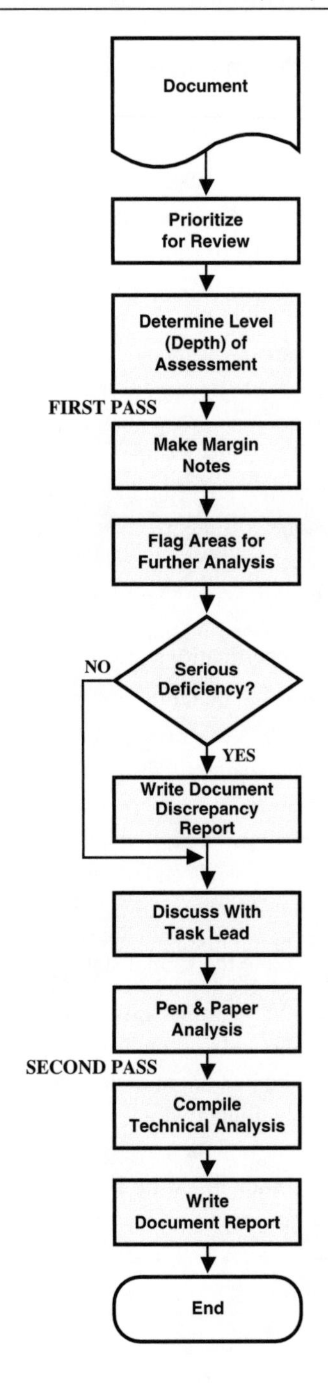

It has been suggested by Clayton[8] that there should be five levels involved in the review of documentation:

Level 1: Documentation completeness—individual document.
Level 2: Compatibility with standards.
Level 3: First-level consistency check—internal.
Level 4: Second-level consistency check—requirements check, external, minimal CASE tool usage.
Level 5: Major review—review code logic, algorithms, full use of CASE tools.

Utilizing these levels provides a guidline for the V&V specialist involved in document reviews.

Summary

A description of the documentation process itself to focus the V&V person on what to expect in the production of documentation leads off this chapter. The V&V of requirements and design specifications described by Dr. Barry Boehm has held up over many years. It is a detailed description of the elements for a V&V specialist to have available for this important task. The four basic criteria for requirements and design specifications (completeness, consistency, feasibility, and testability) are discussed.

The V&V of functional and test specifications are covered. The steps from *Verification, Validation and Evaluation of Expert Systems* in defining and verifying specifications for a system are:

1. Gather informal requirements from the systems experts, with particular attention to defining the critical cases.
2. Obtain V&V team certification of the specifications.
3. Validate informal descriptions of the specifications.
4. Validate the translation of informal specifications into the formal notation.
5. When using formal statements, validate the formal statement of the requirements using symbolic evaluation.

The V&V person must remember from the *Encyclopedia of Computer Science* that the critical elements of software test revolve around the following specifications of testing:

1. specifications of validation or verification products to be tested
2. goals and thresholds for the tests
3. specifications of test activities and data
4. evaluations.

Documentation review methods are described by Connie Clayton in terms of a two-pass review. In the first pass the V&V person concentrates on the seriousness of any deficiencies. If not serious, then a quick feedback is established with the developer to fix the shortfalls. For the more serious deficiencies, the second pass is for the V&V person to compile a technical analysis and write a documentation report.

Five levels are established for a V&V specialist to accomplish a systematic review of documents:

Level 1: Document completeness—individual document.

Level 2: Compatibility with standards.

Level 3: First-level consistency check—internal.

Level 4: Second-level consistency check—requirements check, external, minimal CASE tool usage.

Level 5: Major review—review code logic, algorithms, full use of CASE tools.

References

1 Atkinson, Shane and Sorensen, Reed, *Documentation Technology Report* (Ogden,UT: Hill AFB—Software Technology Support Center, April, 1994).

2 Al-Rawas, Amer and Easterbrook, Steve, "Communication Problems In Requirements Engineering: A Field Study," Proceedings of the First Westminster Conference on Professional Awareness in Software Engineering, Royal Society, London, February 1–2, 1996.

3 Boehm, Barry W., "Verifying and Validating Software Requirements and Design Specifications," IEEE Software, (© January 1984 IEEE), pp. 75–88.

4 Humphrey, Watts S., *A Discipline for Software Engineering* © 1995 Addison Wesley Publishing Co., Reprinted by permission of Addison Wesley Longman.

5 Kaner, Cem, Falk, Jack and Nguyen, Hung Quoc, *Testing Computer Software* (2nd edition) (Boston: International Thomson Computer Press, 1993), permission to duplicate this information provided by the copyright owner, The Coriolis Group.

6 Pressman, Roger S., *Software Engineering: A Practitioner's Approach* (New York: McGraw Hill Book Company, 1992).

7 EOSDIS *Independent Verification And Validation (V&V) Management Plan* (Deliverable 0301), Prepared by AverStar, 6301 Ivy Lane, Suite 200, Greenbelt, Maryland 20770; Prepared For: NASA Goddard Space Flight Center, EOSDIS Project, Code 505, Greenbelt, Maryland 20770; 2 December 1994.

8 Clayton, Connie, "Defining Review Levels for Software Documentation," *Journal of Society for Software Quality,* June 1997, pp. 11–13.

9 Wentworth, James A., Knaus, Rodger, and Aougab, Hamid, *Verification, Validation, and Evaluation of Expert Systems: An FHWA Handbook, Version 1.2—1st Edition* (McLean, VA: Federal Highway Administration, January 1997).

10 Ralston, Anthony & Reilly, Edwin (editors), *Encyclopedia of Computer Science* (New York: Van Nostrand Reinhold, 1993).

11 Herzlich, Paul, "A Quick Win for Testing," *SQM* issue 25, © 1995 Paul Herzlich, Web presentation © 1996 Tesseract Publishing, March 11, 1996, http://www.avnet.co.uk/tesseract/QiC/articles/Herzlich/25.html.

General References

Boehm, B. W., *Software Engineering Economics* (Englewood Cliffs, NJ: Prentice-Hall, 1981).

Shneiderman, B., *Software Psychology: Human Factors in Computer and Information Systems,* (Cambridge, MA: Winthrop Press, 1980).

Smith, S. L. and Aucella, A. F., "Design Guidelines for the User Interface to Computer-Based Information Systems," ESD-TR-83-122, USAF Electronic Systems Division, Bedford, MA, March,1983.

Ferrari, D., *Computer Systems Performance Evaluation* (2nd ed.), (Englewood Cliffs, NJ: Prentice-Hall, 1983).

Lipow, M., White, B. B., and Boehm, B. W., "Software Quality Assurance: An Acquisition Guidebook," TRW-SS-77-07, November, 1977.

CHAPTER 5

Metrics

Introduction

Software metrics, generally, have proved an enigma. At an ASQ (American Society for Quality) lecture on September 10, 1997, Dr. Boris Biezer[1] discussed the difficulties with software metrics. An apocryphal example he relates is that the correlation is so high between lines of code and weight of a listing, that size could be adequately measured with weight of listings. We laugh at one and accept the other as a serious measure.

If the state of software metrics is judged to be so weak, what may be expected of the closely related V&V metrics? Unfortunately, the level and understanding of the V&V metrics are also in a poor state. To address this basic shortfall in this chapter the focus is on alleviating the shortfall. For traditional metrics there is a review of the appropriate software metrics in use and their relationship to V&V of software. But, in the contemporary V&V section, that "shopping list" of software metrics and other specific V&V metrics are related to their use with the special modern applications discussed in this book. There is also an introduction to the testing measurements from the Testing Maturity Model (see Chapter 3), as another validation measurement method.

However, there is a problem in the state of measurement validation. David Card and Robert Glass[2] point out that for every positive validation, there is a negative validation (p. 23–24). This ambiguity about measurement evaluation means that the store of software measurement ideas increases daily. Measures persist even when challenged by evidence and experience. As we move through this chapter on V&V metrics, that point will unfortunately be illustrated again.

Multidimensional Model

V&V metrics are an aspect of the processes axis in the multidimensional model. V&V metrics may be applied equally to all life-cycle models (the process dimension), but remember, for a shortened process, such as rapid application development, the V&V metrics are greatly condensed. That is, for specifications quickly developed, the V&V metrics also must be quickly captured.

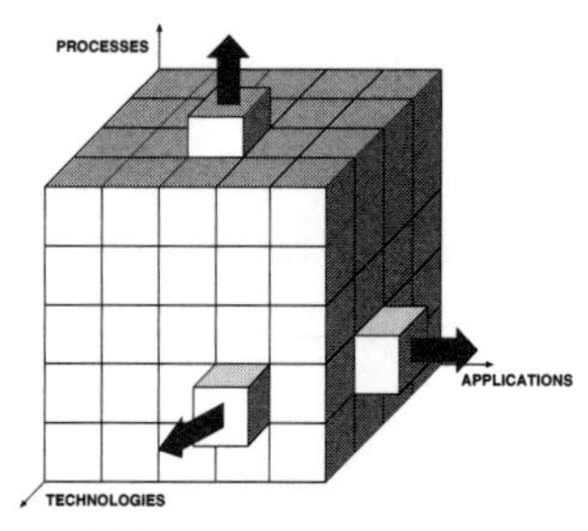

How V&V metrics are calculated and collected varies with the different dimensions to which the metrics apply. For instance, there are differences for an Internet development versus a knowledge-based system (KBS) development. The KBS, which resides on the technology axis, requires that V&V measure the knowledge database, whereas the Internet development, which resides on the technology axis, requires special V&V measurement of the security level of the application on the network. It is necessary for the V&V person to consider the axis of performance from the multidimensional model when determining the what and how of V&V metrics to collect on the project.

Traditional V & V

This section on traditional metrics useful for software developers and V&V personnel is extracted from an extensive work by Wallace, Ippolito, and Cuthill entitled *Reference Information for the Software Verification and Validation Process*[3] (pp. 36–46).

Metrics are used to assess the product or process and to aid the V&V team in the evaluation of the status of the software. SPC (statistical process control) techniques are used to monitor a project by observing trends and help to locate major problems in the software development process, the V&V processes, and the product itself. Software reliability estimation models provide information about the predicted performance of the software. Error data from the V&V activities can be collected over the entire project and stored in an organizational database, for use with the current project or future projects. An organizational database may also play an important role in reaching a Software Engineering Institute's Capability Maturity Model (CMM) Level 3. This is because the CMM Level 3 requires an organizational process definition that includes an organizational database. The database could provide data on the reliability or other quality attributes to help determine how much additional work is needed to increase the quality of the database element to the desired level.

In this section, a metric is defined to be the mathematical definition, algorithm, or function used to obtain a quantitative assessment of a product or process. The actual numerical value produced by a metric is a measure. Thus, for example, cyclomatic complexity is a metric, but the value of this metric is the cyclomatic complexity measure. Two general classes of metrics include the following:

- management metrics, which assist in the management of the software development process
- quality metrics, which are predictors or indicators of the product qualities for V&V use

Management metrics can be used for controlling any industrial production or manufacturing activity. They are used to assess resources, cost, and task completion. Quality metrics are used to estimate characteristics or qualities of a software product. Some metrics may be both management metrics and quality metrics; that is, they can be used for both project control and V&V assessment.

A disadvantage of some metrics is that they do not have an interpretation scale that allows for consistent interpretation, as with measuring temperature (in degrees Celsius) or length (in meters). This is particularly true of metrics for software quality characteristics (e.g., maintainability, reliability, usability). Measures must be interpreted *relatively,* through comparison with plans and expectations, comparison with similar past projects, or comparison with similar components within the current project. While some metrics are mathematically based, most, including reliability models, have not been proven. Since there is virtually an infinite number of possible metrics, users must have some criteria for choosing which metrics to apply to their particular projects.

Ideally, a metric should possess all of the following characteristics:

- simplicity—definition and use of the metric is simple
- objectivity—different people will give identical values; allows for consistency, and prevents individual bias
- ease of collection—the cost and effort to obtain the measure is reasonable
- robustness—metric is insensitive to irrelevant changes; allows for useful comparison
- validity—metric measures what it is supposed to; this promotes trustworthiness of the measure

Primitive metrics such as those listed in Table 5.1 can be collected throughout software development. These metrics can be plotted using bar graphs, histograms, and Pareto charts as part of SPC. The plots can be analyzed by management to identify the activities that are most error prone, to suggest steps to prevent the recurrence of similar errors, to suggest procedures for earlier detection of faults, and, through the V&V team, to make general improvements to the software development process.

Where specific items from Table 5.1 require further explanation, that is now provided. Software requirements metrics are collected because the main reason to measure software requirements specifications is to provide early warnings of quality problems, to enable more accurate project predictions, and to help improve the specifications. Large components are assumed to have a larger number of residual errors, and are more difficult to understand than small components; as a result, their reliability and extendibility may be affected.

Requirements traceability is used to assess the degree of traceability by measuring the percentage of requirements that has been implemented in the software design. It is also used to identify requirements that are either missing from or in addition to the original requirements. The measure is computed using the equation:

$$R_T = R_1 / R_2 \times 100\%$$

where R_1 is the number of requirements met by the architecture (software design), and R_2 is the number of original requirements.

Completeness is used to determine the completeness of the software specification during requirements activity. This metric uses 18 primitives (e.g., number of functions not satisfactorily

Table 5.1 Metrics applied to Software Development and V&V (Adapted from *Reference Information for the Software Verification and Validation Process*[3])

Although all these metrics apply to software development, they are not all X'ed because there are some cases when the most benefit to be gained is their use as a V&V metric.

METRICS	Software Development	V&V
Primitive problem metrics		
Number of problem reports per activity, priority, category, or cause	X	X
Number of reported problems per time period	X	
Number of open real problems per time period	X	
Number of closed real problems per time period	X	
Number of unevaluated problem reports	X	X
Age of open real problem reports	X	
Age of unevaluated problem reports	X	
Age of real closed problem reports	X	
Time when errors are discovered	X	
Rate of error discovery	X	X
Primitive cost and effort metrics		
Time spent	X	X
Elapsed time	X	X
Staff hours, months, years	X	X
Primitive change metrics		
Number of revisions, additions, deletions, or modifications	X	X
Number of requests to change the software requirements specification and/or software design	X	
Primitive fault metrics		
Number of unresolved faults at planned end of activity	X	X
Number of faults that have not been corrected, and number of outstanding change requests	X	
Number of software requirements and design faults detected during reviews, walkthroughs, and inspections	X	X
Software Requirements Metrics		
Number of pages or words	X	
Number of requirements	X	X
Number of functions	X	
Requirements traceability		X
Completeness		X
Fault-days number		
Activity, date, or time that the fault was introduced	X	
Activity, date, or time that the fault was removed.	X	
Function points	X	X
Software Design Metrics		
High cohesion of modules		X
Low coupling of modules		X
Effective modularity		X
Primitive size metrics		
Number of pages or words	X	X
Number of modules	X	X
Number of functions/objects	X	
Number of inputs and outputs	X	
Number of interfaces	X	

Table 5.1 (continued)

Primitive fault metrics		
Number of faults associated with each module	X	X
Number of requirements faults and structural design faults detected during detailed design		X
Primitive complexity metrics		
Number of parameters per module	X	X
Number of states or data partitions per parameter	X	X
Number of branches in each module	X	X
Coupling	X	
Cohesion	X	
(Structural) fan-in/fan-out	X	
Information flow metric	X	
Staff hours per major defect detected	X	X
Defect Density (DD)	X	X
Test related primitives		
Number of software integration test cases planned/executed involving each module		X
Number of black box test cases planned/executed per module		X
Number of requirements faults detected (and re-assesses quality of requirements specification)		X
Code Metrics		
Lines of Code (LOC)	X	X
Halstead software science metrics		X
Cyclomatic complexity		X
Amount of data.	X	
Live variables	X	
Variable scope	X	
Variable span	X	
Test Metrics		
Number of faults detected in each module	X	X
Number of requirements, design, and coding faults found during unit and integration testing	X	X
Number of errors by type (e.g., logic, computational, interface, documentation)		X
Number of errors by cause or origin		X
Number of errors by severity (e.g., critical, major, cosmetic)		X
Fault density		X
Defect age	X	
Defect cost	X	
Defect removal efficiency	X	X
Statement coverage		X
Branch coverage		X
Path coverage		X
Data flow coverage	X	
Test coverage		X
Mean time to failure (MTTF)		X
Failure rate		X

defined, number of functions, number of defined functions, number of defined functions not used, number of referenced functions, and number of decision points). It then uses 10 derivatives (e.g., functions satisfactorily defined, data references having an origin, defined functions used, reference functions defined), which are derived from the primitives. The metric is the weighted sum of the 10 derivatives expressed as $CM = w_i D_i$, where the summation is from $i = 1$ to $i = 10$, each weight w_i has a value between 0 and 1, the sum of the weights is 1, and each D_i is a derivative with a value between 1 and 0. The values of the primitives also can be used to identify problem areas within the software requirements specification.

The fault-days number (FD) metric specifies the number of days that faults spend in the software product from its creation to their removal. This measure uses two primitives: the activity, date, or time that the fault was introduced, and the activity, date, or time that the fault was removed. The fault days for the *i*th fault, (FD*i*), is the number of days from the creation of the fault to its removal. The measure is calculated as follows:

$$FD = \sum_{i=1}^{n} FD_i$$

This measure is an indicator of the quality of the software design and software development process. A high value may be indicative of untimely removal of faults and/or existence of many faults, due to an ineffective software development process.

The function points metric uses a weighted sum of the number of inputs, outputs, master files, and inquiries in a product to predict development size. To count function points:

1. Classify each component by using standard guides to rate each component as having low, average, or high complexity.
2. Tabulate function component counts. This is done by entering the appropriate counts in the Function Counting Form, multiplying by the weights on the form, and summing up the totals for each component type to obtain the Unadjusted Function Point Count.
3. Rate each application characteristic from 0 to 5 using a rating guide, and then adding all the ratings together to obtain the Characteristic Influence Rating.
4. Calculate number of function points is calculated using the equation:

$$FP = \text{Unadjusted Function} \times (0.65 + 0.01 \times \text{Character Influence Rating})$$

The software design metric gives early indication of project status; enables selection of alternative designs; identifies potential problems early in the software development process; limits complexity; and helps in deciding how to modularize so the resulting modules are both testable and maintainable. In general, good design practices involve high cohesion of modules, low coupling of modules, and effective modularity.

Primitive size metrics are used to estimate the size of the software design or software design documents. This metric provides measure of product size, against which the completeness of subsequent module-based activities can be assessed. The estimate for the number of modules is given by $NM = S / M$, where S is the estimated size in lines of code, M is the median module size found in similar projects. The estimate *NM* can be compared to the median number of modules for other projects.

Primitive fault metrics identify potentially fault-prone modules. This metric focuses on the collection and analysis of inspection data. Primitive complexity metrics identify modules which are complex or hard to test. The V&V person looks at the number of parameters and the number of branches per module when considering primitive complexity metrics.

Coupling is the manner and degree of interdependence between software modules. Module coupling is rated based on the type of coupling, using a standard rating chart. According to the chart, data coupling is the best type of coupling, and content coupling is the worst. The better the coupling, the lower the rating.

Cohesion is the degree to which the tasks performed within a single software module are related to the module's purpose. The module cohesion value for a module is assigned using a standard rating chart. According to the chart, the best cohesion level is functional, and the worst is coincidental, with the better levels having lower values. Case studies have shown that fault rate correlates highly with cohesion strength.

Structural fan-in/fan-out represents the number of modules that call or are called by a given module. It identifies whether the system decomposition is adequate (e.g., no modules which cause bottlenecks, no missing levels in the hierarchical decomposition, no unused modules ["dead" code], identification of critical modules). May be useful to compute maximum, average, and total fan-in/fan-out.

The information flow metric represents the total number of combinations of an input source to an output destination.

Staff hours per major defect detected is used to evaluate the efficiency of the design inspection. Primitives are time expended in preparation for inspection meeting, conduct of inspection meeting, number of major defects detected during the *i*th inspection, and total number of inspections to date. The staff hours per major defect detected is applied to new code, and should fall between three and five. If there is significant deviation from this range, then the matter should be investigated (may be adapted for code inspections).

Defect density is used after design inspections of new development or large block modifications in order to assess the inspection process. Primitives are total number of unique defects detected during the *i*th inspection or *i*th software development activity, total number of inspections to date, and number of source lines of design statements in thousands (KSLOD). The measure is calculated by the ratio:

$$\frac{\sum_{i=1}^{n} D_i}{\text{KSLOD}}$$

This measure can also be used in the implementation activity, in which case the number of source lines of executable code in thousands (KSLOC) should be substituted for KSLOD.

Test-related metrics check that each module will be or has been adequately tested, or assesses the effectiveness of early testing activities. A point made from *Software Quality Assurance and Measurement: A Worldwide Perspective*[4] is that a major aim of program testing is to uncover errors, so that a measure of program correctness can be made by considering the number and condition of errors in the program. One method is to invoke the concept of eight different verification levels, where the higher the position of a program in the verification level, the better its quality is considered to be. Another method of measuring program correctness is by assigning an appropriate weight to each of the activities in the testing process, and the result of each activity is evaluated and a score is given (p. 160).

Lines of Code is one of the most popular metrics, but it has no standard definition. Returning for the remainer of this section to the NIST publication, *Reference Information for the Software Verification and Validation Process,*[3] the predominant definition for Lines of Code is "any line of a program text that is not a comment or blank line, regardless of the number of statements or fragments of statements on the line" (p. TK). It is an indication of size, which allows for estimation of effort, time scale, and total number of faults. For the same application, the length of a program partly depends on the language the code is written in, thus making comparison using Lines of Code difficult. However, Lines of Code can be a useful measure if the projects being compared are consistent in their development methods (e.g., use the same language, coding style). Because of its disadvantages, the use of Lines of Code as a management metric (e.g., for project sizing beginning from the software requirements activity) is controversial, but there are uses for this metric in error analysis, such as to estimate the values of other metrics. The advantages of this metric are that it is conceptually simple, easily automated, and inexpensive.

Halstead software science metrics claim to evaluate the mental effort and time required to create a program, and how compactly a program is expressed. These metrics are based on four primitives:

1. number of unique operators
2. number of unique operands
3. $N1$ = total occurrences of operators
4. $N2$ = total occurrences of operands.

The program length measures $N = N1 + N2$. Other software science metrics are listed below.

Cyclomatic complexity determines the structural complexity of a coded module in order to limit its complexity, thus promoting understandability. In general, high complexity leads to a high number of defects and maintenance costs. This metric is also used to identify minimum number of test paths to assure test coverage. The primitives include the number of nodes (N), and the number of edges (E), which can be determined from the graph representing the module. The measure can then be computed with the formula, $C = E–N + 1$.

Amount of data can be determined by primitive metrics, which can be obtained from a compiler cross reference.

For each line in a section of code, determine the number of live variables (i.e., variables whose values could change during execution of that section of code). The average number of live variables per line of code is the sum of the number of live variables for each line, divided by the number of lines of code.

Variable scope is the number of source statements between the first and last reference of the variable. For example, if variable A is first referenced on line 10, and last referenced on line 20, then the variable scope for A is 9. To determine the average variable scope for variables in a particular section of code, first determine the variable scope for each variable, add up these values, and divide by the number of variables. With large scopes, the understandability and readability of the code is reduced.

Variable spans is the number of source statements between successive references of the variable. For each variable, the average span can be computed. For example, if the variable X is referenced on lines 13, 18, 20, 21, and 23, the average span would be the sum of all the spans divided by the number of spans—that is, (4+1+0+1) / 4 = 1.5. With large spans, it is more likely that a far back reference will be forgotten.

Test metrics include primitives (i.e., defect/error/fault metrics) that can be used effectively with SPC techniques, such as bar charts and Pareto diagrams. These metrics can also be used to form percentages (e.g., percentage of logic errors = number of logic errors/total number of errors).

Fault density is computed by dividing the number of faults by the size (usually in thousands of lines of code). It may be weighted by severity using the equation

$$FD_w = (W_1\, S / N + W_2\, A / N + W_3\, M / N) / \text{Size}$$

where
N = total number of faults
S = number of severe faults
A = number of average severity faults
M = number of minor faults
W_i = weighting factors (defaults are 10, 3, and 1)

Fault density can be used to:

- predict remaining faults by comparison with expected fault density
- determine if sufficient testing has been completed based on predetermined goals
- establish standard fault densities for comparison and prediction.

Defect age is the time between when a defect is introduced to when it is detected or fixed. Assign the numbers 1 through 6 to each of the software development activities from software requirements to software operation and maintenance. The defect age is computed as shown:

$$\text{Defect Age} = \frac{(\text{Activity Detected—Activity Introduced})}{\text{Number Defects}}$$

Defect cost may be a sum of the cost to analyze the defect, the cost to fix it, and the cost of failures already incurred due to the defect.

Defect removal efficiency is the percentage of defects that have been removed during an activity. The defect removal efficiency can also be computed for each software development activity and plotted on a bar graph to show the relative defect removal efficiencies for each activity. Or, the defect removal efficiency may be computed for a specific task or technique (e.g., design inspection, code walkthrough, unit test, 6-month operation, etc.).

Statement coverage measures the percentage of statements executed (to assure that each statement has been tested at least once).

Branch coverage measures the percentage of branches executed.

Path coverage measures the percentage of program paths executed. It is generally impractical and inefficient to test all the paths in a program. The count of the number of paths may be reduced by treating all possible loop iterations as one path. Path coverage may be used to ensure 100% coverage of critical (safety or security related) paths.

Data flow coverage measures the definition and use of variables and data structures.

Test coverage measures the completeness of the testing activity. It is the percentage of requirements implemented (in the form of defined test cases or functional capabilities) multiplied by the percentage of the software structure (in units, segments, statements, branches, or path test results) tested.

Mean time to failure (MTTF) gives an estimate of the mean time to the next failure, by accurately recording failure times t_i, the elapsed time between the ith and the $(i-1)$st failures, and computing the average of all the failure times. This metric is the basic parameter required by most software reliability models. High values imply good reliability.

Failure rate is used to indicate the growth in the software reliability as a function of test time and is usually used with reliability models.

Statistical Process Control Techniques

Statistical process control (SPC) is the application of statistical methods to provide the information necessary to continuously control or improve activities throughout the entire development and V&V of a product.

SPC techniques help to locate trends, cycles, and irregularities within the software development process and provide clues about how well the process meets specifications or requirements. They are tools for measuring and understanding process variation and distinguishing between random inherent variations and significant deviations so that correct decisions can be made about whether to make changes to the process or product. To fully understand a process, it is necessary to determine how the process changes over time. To do this, one can plot error data (e.g., total number of errors, counts of specific types of errors) over a period of time (e.g., days, weeks) and then interpret the resulting pattern. If, for instance, a large number of errors are found in a particular software development activity, an investigation of the tasks by the V&V team in that activity or preceding ones may reveal that necessary development tasks were omitted (e.g., code reviews were not conducted during the code activity).

A plot of the number of specific types of errors may show that many errors are related to incorrect or unclear software requirements specifications (e.g., software requirements are written in a way that consistently causes misinterpretations, or they fail to list enough conditions and restrictions). This would indicate to the V&V specialist that the software requirements activity needs to be modified. There are several advantages to using SPC techniques:

1. Errors may be detected earlier or prevented altogether. By monitoring the software development process, the cause of the error (e.g., inadequate standards, insufficient training, incompatible hardware) may be detected before additional errors are created.
2. Using SPC techniques is cost-effective, because less effort may be required to ensure that processes are operating correctly than is required to perform detailed checks on all the outputs of that process. Thus, higher quality may be achieved at a lower development expense.
3. Use of SPC techniques provides quantitative measures of progress and of problems, so less guesswork is required.

Control Charts

The primary statistical technique for use by the V&V specialist to assess process variation is the control chart. The control chart displays sequential process measurements relative to the overall process average and control limits. The upper and lower control limits establish the boundaries of normal variation for the process being measured. Variation within control limits is attributable to random or chance causes, while variation beyond control limits indicates a process change due to causes other than chance—a condition that may require investigation.

The upper control limit and lower control limit give the boundaries within which observed fluctuations are typical and acceptable. They are usually set, respectively, at three standard deviations above and below the mean of all observations. There are many different types of control charts (np, p, c, etc.), which are described in Table 5.2. The list of steps below should be followed:

- Identify the purpose and the characteristics of the process to be monitored.
- Select the appropriate type of control chart based on the type of characteristic measured, the data available, and the purpose of the application.
- Determine the sampling method (e.g., number of samples (n), size of samples, time frame).
- Collect the data.
- Calculate the sample statistics: average, standard deviation, upper and lower control limits.
- Construct the control chart based on sample statistics.
- Monitor the process by observing pattern of the data points and whether they fall within control limits.

When the V&V person interprets the meaning of the control charts, there is a pay-off for the software development process. The existence of outliers, or data points beyond control limits, indicates that non-typical circumstances exist. A run, or consecutive points on one side of the average line (8 in a row, or 11 of 12, etc.) indicates a shift in process average. A sawtooth pattern, which is a successive up-and-down trend with no data points near the average line, indicates over-adjustment or the existence of two processes. A trend, or steady inclining or declining progression of data points, represents gradual change in the process. A hug, in which all data points fall near the aver-

Table 5.2 Types of control charts.[3]

TYPE	DESCRIPTION	IMPLEMENTATION
np	number of nonconforming units (e.g., number of defective units)	The number of units in each sample with the selected characteristic is plotted; sample size is constant.
p	fraction of nonconforming units (e.g., fraction of defective units)	For each sample, the fraction nonconforming, obtained by dividing the number nonconforming by the total number of units observed, is plotted; sample size is constant.
c	number of nonconformities (e.g., number of errors)	For each sample, the number of occurrences of the characteristic in a group is plotted; sample size is constant.
u	number of nonconformities per unit (e.g., number of errors per unit)	For each sample, the number of nonconformities per unit, obtained by dividing the number of nonconformities by the number of units observed, is plotted; sample size can change.
x	single observed value	The value for each sample of size 1 is plotted.
xB	X-Bar	For each sample, the mean of 2 to 10 observations (4 or 5 are optimal) is plotted.
r	range	The difference between the largest and smallest values in each sample is plotted.
xM	median	The median of each sample is plotted
MR	moving range	The difference between adjacent measurements in each sample is plotted.

age line, may indicate unreliable data. A cycle, or a series of data points that is repeated to form a pattern, indicates a cycling process.

Bar Graph

A bar graph is a frequency distribution diagram in which each bar represents a characteristic, and the height of the bar represents the frequency of that characteristic. The horizontal axis may represent a continuous numerical scale, or a discrete non-numerical scale. Generally, numerical-scale bar charts in which the bars have equal widths are more useful for comparison purposes; numerical-scale bar charts with unequal intervals can be misleading because the characteristics with the largest bars (in terms of area) do not necessarily have the highest frequency.

In a simple bar graph in which the characteristics being measured are discrete and non-numerical, or if each bar has the same width, the measures for each characteristic can be compared simply by comparing the heights of the bars. For numerical-scale graphs with unequal widths, one should remember not to interpret large bars as necessarily meaning that a large proportion of the entire population falls in that range.

Pareto Diagram

A Pareto diagram is a bar graph in which the bars are arranged in descending order of magnitude. The purpose of Pareto analysis is to identify the major problems in a product or process, or to identify the most significant causes for a given effect. This allows a V&V person to prioritize problems and decide which problem area has the greatest potential impact on software quality.

Scatter Diagram

A scatter diagram is a plot of the values of one variable against those of another variable to determine the relationship between them. Scatter diagrams are used during analysis to understand the cause and effect relationship between two variables.

If the data points in a scatter diagram fall approximately in a straight line, this indicates that there is a linear relationship, which is positive or negative depending on whether the slope of the line is positive or negative. Further analysis using the method of least squares can be performed. If the data points form a curve, then there is a nonlinear relationship. If there is no apparent pattern, this may indicate no relationship. However, another sample should be taken before making such a conclusion.

Software Reliability

The following is a generic procedure for estimating software reliability. It can be tailored to a specific project or software development activity; thus some steps may not be used in some applications.

Identify the application. The description of the application should include, at a minimum, the identification of the application, the characteristics of the application domain that may affect reliability, and details of the intended operation of the application system.

Specify the requirement. The reliability requirement should be specific enough to serve as a goal (e.g., failure rate of 10–9 per hour).

Allocate the requirement. The reliability requirement may be distributed over several components, which should be identified.

Define failure. A specific failure definition is usually agreed upon by testers, developers, and users prior to the beginning of testing. The definition should be consistent over the life of the project.

Classification of failures (e.g., by severity) is continuously negotiated.

Characterize the operational environment. The operational environment should be described in terms of the system configuration (arrangement of the system's components), system evolution, and system operational profile (how the system will be used).

Select tests. The test team selects the most appropriate tests for exposing faults. Two approaches to testing can be taken: Testing duplicates actual operational environments as closely as possible, or testing is conducted under more severe conditions than expected in normal operational environments, so that failures can occur in less time.

Select the models. The user should compare the models prior to selection based on the following criteria: predictive validity, ease of parameter measurement, quality of the model's assumptions, capability, applicability, simplicity, insensitivity to noise, and sensitivity to parameter variations.

Collect data.

Determine the parameters. There are three common methods of estimating the parameters from the data: method of moments, least squares, and maximum likelihood. Each of these methods has useful attributes, but maximum likelihood estimation is the most commonly used approach. As stated previously, some data sets may cause the numerical methods not to converge. There exist automated software reliability engineering tools that are capable of performing parameter estimation.

Validate the model. The model should be continuously checked to verify that it fits the data, by using a predictive validity criteria or a traditional statistical goodness-of-fit test (e.g., Chi-square).

Perform analysis. The results of software reliability estimation may be used for several purposes, including, but not limited to, estimating current reliability, forecasting achievement of a reliability goal, establishing conformance with acceptance criteria, managing entry of new software features or new technology into an existing system, or supporting safety certification.

Contemporary V & V

In Robert O. Lewis' *Independent Verification and Validation: A Life Cycle Engineering Process for Quality Software,*[5] specific V&V metrics are addressed. A review of those V&V metrics are given in Table 5.3. Each measure is applied to each requirement or design statement in the systems specification, software requirements specification, and design document.

Table 5.3 V&V document metrics (Adapted from *Independent Verification and Validation*).[5]

MEASURE	SCORING BASIS
UNDERSTANDABILITY	0 = Well Expressed
1. Will the requirements lead to satisfactory implementation?	– 1 = Poorly Expressed, but Usable
2. Is the language appropriate and acceptable?	– 2 = Ambiguous or Vague
3. Is it adequate?	– 3 = Impossible
QUANTIFIABILITY	0 = Accurate to Desired Level
1. Ranges	– 1 = Requires Refinement
2. Rates and limits	– 2 = Missing Sign or Inaccurate
3. Accuracies	– 3 = Incorrect Value
4. Contraints	
5. Capabilities	
6. Performance	
DATA FLOW COMPLETENESS*	0 = Adequate
1. Is input fully specified and matched to interfaces?	– 1 = Fails One Question
2. Is process described in algorithmic or logic expressions?	– 2 = Fails Two Questions
3. Is output fully specified and matched to interfaces?	– 3 = Fails All Three
TRACEABILITY	0 = 1 : 1 Correspondence
1. Does it match discrete data found elsewhere?	– 1 = Vague or Inadequate
2. Are footnotes, cross-references, and indexes provided?	– 2 = Nonexistent
3. Can all outside requirements be traced to appropriate areas herein?	

Table 5.3 continued

Criterion	Score
TESTABILITY 1. Can capabilities be tested? 2. Is an appropriate form of testing recommended?	0 = Adequate – 1 = Fails One Question – 2 = Fails Both Questions
COMPLIANCE 1. Does document meet all standards and specifications?	0 = Satisfactory – 1 = Unsatisfactory
CONSISTENCY 1. Coherence (Do all parts belong together?) 2. Uniformity (Is there parallel depth of coverage throughout?)	0 = Adequate – 1 = Inadequate
LEGIBILITY 1. Are figures, tables, text impossible to read for any reason?	0 = Readable – 1 = Unreadable
EFFICIENCY+ 1. Is planned implementation efficient in terms of algorithm selected? 2. Is approach optimized?	0 = Adequate – 1 = Inadequate
ROBUSTNESS+ 1. Is error detection handling provided in the code at key points? 2. Is error tolerant design included?	0 = Adequate – 1 = Inadequate
MAINTAINABILITY+ 1. Is code sufficiently modular to support minimum change impact? 2. Are comments and identifiers sufficient to support maintenance?	0 = Adequate – 1 = Inadequate
PERSPECTIVE+ 1. Are system functions tailored to environment? 2. Does design match internal hierarchy?	0 = Adequate – 1 = Inadequate

* applies only to software requirements specification and design document
+ applies only to design document

The perfect score for the systems specification is 13, for the software requirements specification 16, and for the design document 20. The score is calculated for each requirement and for each design statement. After the total is determined, then it is divided by the total perfect score for the document giving a relative percent excellence of the document.

A principal focus of V&V specialists is to accurately measure the testing process. The proposed testing maturity model from *Developing a Testing Maturity Model,*[6] covered in Chapter 3, defines some practices elaborated upon here that help to better measure the test activities and work products. Monitoring test functions should be supported by an established test measurement program. Software work products as well as test-related work products, such as test plans, test designs, and test procedures, are all reviewed. This definition of testing covers activities typically categorized as V&V activities. The primary goal of this broadened set of testing operations is to uncover defects occurring in all phases of the life-cycle (the process dimension) and to uncover them as early as possible. Test cases and procedures are stored for reuse and regression testing.

Burnstein and colleagues[6] define three maturity goals for Level 4 of the Testing Maturity Model. Two that are relevant to V&V follow:

1. Establish an Organization-Wide Review Program. At Testing Maturity Model Level 3, an organization integrates testing activities into the software life-cycle. At Level 4, this integration is augmented by the establishment of a review program. Reviews are conducted at all phases of the life-cycle to identify, catalog, and remove defects from software work products and to test work products early and effectively. Maturity sub-goals that support this goal include:
   - Upper management must develop review policies, support the review process, and take responsibility for integrating them into the organizational culture.
   - The test group and the software quality assurance group must develop and document goals, plans, follow-up procedures, and recording mechanisms for reviews throughout the software life-cycle.
   - Items for review must be specified by the above bodies.
   - Personnel must be trained so that they understand and follow proper review policies, practices, and procedures.
2. Establish a Test Measurement Program. A test measurement program is essential in the evaluation of the quality of the testing process, to assess the productivity of the testing personnel and the effectiveness of the testing process, and for test process improvement. Test measurements are vital in the monitoring and controlling of the testing process. A test measurement program must be carefully planned and managed. Test data to be collected must be identified: how they are to be used and by whom must be decided. Measurement data for every test life-cycle phase must be specified. Measurements include those related to test progress, test costs, data on errors and defects, and product measures such as software reliability. Maturity sub-goals that support this goal include:
   - Organization-wide test measurement policies and goals must be defined.
   - A test measurement plan must be developed with mechanisms for data collection, analysis, and application.
   - Action plans that apply measurement results to test process improvements must be developed and documented. (p. 22)

Goal/Question/Metric Paradigm

There is an approach using the Goal/Question/Metric (GQM) paradigm that allows managers to monitor the level of risk in a software development project. This section reviews the IV&V GQM model from Callahan, Zhou and Wood's *Software Risk Management Through Independent Verification and Validation.*[7] (Note: In the following quotation, V&V replaces IV&V and GQM replaces IGQM.)

> Using a V&V GQM method, managers can use past projects as "yardsticks" against which to measure present projects. They can also assess the potential impact of their decisions about resource allocations, schedules, costs, and tradeoffs. Managers of large, complex software projects often rely on [V&V specialists to verify and validate the computer software produced by the development team]. [A V&V team] helps identify, manage, and reduce the potential risk of

> failures to meet intended requirements in a software project at all phases of development. While some level of risk will always remain in a software development effort, it is through this V&V GQM method that risks may be identified, then mitigated.
>
> The V&V GQM method provides continuous reporting of the status of a project in terms of what areas are at risk of failure. The method represents a formal interface between the V&V team, the software development team, and the customer. It summarizes the analysis work performed by the V&V team in terms of what project goals are at risk of failure and allows managers to make informed decisions about why problems are occurring.
>
> As a software development process progresses, events are triggered in the V&V process. The V&V team must analyze changes in the development process and publish its findings in the form of a V&V report. This report is generated using the V&V GQM method by a tool that is integrated into a CASE environment. The reporting tool collects and summarizes analysis results (i.e., metrics) from other V&V CASE tools in an incremental fashion. When a change occurs in the development process, the project measurements and risk are updated incrementally as values and formulas in a spreadsheet. The risk impact of each change is assessed immediately relative to the project goals.
>
> Unlike existing metric-based models, this V&V GQM approach does not emphasize any specific set of metrics or functions for assessing risk. The model allows for use of other assessment models. The V&V GQM model is used to collect and summarize the metrics and relate them directly to project goals. Although the approach to V&V relies on metrics from past projects as baselines, the model can be "primed" with informal estimates or external project databases. Results from pilot projects are then used as feedback to provide continuous improvement to the model itself in order to improve its predictive accuracy.
>
> The V&V GQM approach to software V&V focuses on the quantification, identification, management, and reduction of risk in software development projects based on objective metrics taken during the software development life-cycle. Metrics include process measures (i.e., whether or not a particular procedure has been performed at this phase) as well as artifact measures (i.e., quantitative measurements of documents, code, tests, and other products). The V&V GQM method defines the impact of such measures on the failure or success in meeting project goals. The V&V GQM model can accommodate several existing software estimation and tracking methods, including such as the COCOMO method and Software Equation for estimating cost, size, and effort. (pp. 1–2)

The V&V GQM method follows the basic paradigm of GQM, described next, but applies it to the V&V of software. A project must completely satisfy a set of goals to be implemented successfully. Goals include requirements, but are much broader and can include ambiguous statements like "the system must be highly reliable." Each goal is satisfied by answering a set of related questions. The questions define the features needed to satisfy a particular goal. Questions are answered true or false, but can be parameterized with limits: for example, "does the system have a 10,000 hour mean time between failures?" Each question is answered based on a set of quantifiable project metrics. A metric might be "lines of code" or "estimated mean time between failures" or any other discrete value.

The GQM approach is used as a dialogue between customers and development organizations for agreeing on the details of a project. In this fashion, it should be clear to the developer exactly what is expected of the final product and the criteria for its acceptance:

- Low cost
- Medium effort
- Use of prototyping
- High reliability

The questions related to each goal in the V&V GQM model will determine exactly what is meant by each goal.

An example from the authors for the V&V GQM method is appropriate here. A goal should be established for the project, such as "Perform an optimal V&V effort." Some questions that support that goal for the project include:

1. How many V&V personnel are required?
2. How many estimated defects are allowed when ready to deliver the product to the customer?
3. What is the expected rate of error discovery during the software development process?

Supporting metric(s) for each of those questions are:

1. a. Estimating method results of V&V personnel required
   b. V&V persons estimated versus actual over time
2. a. Defect count during development
   b. Domain analysis of prior defects delivered for this type of project
   c. Error seeding to project the amount of defects left in the software product
3. a. Number of errors uncovered per unit of time
   b. Domain analysis of prior error discovery rate for this type of project
   c. Projection of actual errors uncovered per unit of time to projected errors uncovered per unit of time.

Metrics for V&V Applications

In the traditional V&V section of this chapter, Table 5.1 contains an extended list of metrics with an indication of their applicability to V&V. An extension of that list of metrics is provided in Table 5.4 to indicate the strongest applicability of those metrics (and others) to the specific new application areas discussed within this book. Highlighted are object oriented methods, rapid application development, usability (GUI interface), client/server networks, knowledge based systems, Internet/intranet, and data warehousing.

Specific V&V metrics added to the bottom of Table 5.4 that do not appear in Table 5.1 include Lewis' document effectiveness metrics, knowledge database metrics, and server database metrics. The Lewis document effectiveness metrics are described above in the Traditional V&V section.

Table 5.4 Metrics applied to new V&V applications (Adapted from *Reference Information for the Software Verification and Validation Process*[3])

METRICS V&V APPLICATIONS	Object Oriented (OO) Methods	Rapid Application Dev. (RAD)	Usability (GUI I/F)	Client/Server Networks	Knowledge Based Systems (KBS)	Internet/Intranet	Data Warehousing
Primitive problem metrics							
Number of problem reports per activity, priority, category, or cause	X	X	X	X	X	X	X
Number of reported problems per time period	X		X	X	X	X	X
Number of open real problems per time period	X		X	X	X	X	X
Number of closed real problems per time period	X		X	X	X	X	X
Number of unevaluated problem reports	X		X	X	X	X	X
Age of open real problem reports	X		X	X	X		X
Age of unevaluated problem reports	X		X	X	X		X
Age of real closed problem reports	X		X	X	X		X
Time when errors are discovered	X		X	X	X	X	X
Rate of error discovery	X	X	X	X	X	X	X
Primitive cost and effort metrics							
Time spent	X	X	X	X	X	X	X
Elapsed time	X	X	X	X	X	X	X
Staff hours, months, years	X	X	X	X	X	X	X
Primitive change metrics							
Number of revisions, additions, deletions, or modifications	X		X	X	X	X	X
Number of requests to change the software requirements specification and/or software design	X		X	X	X		
Primitive fault metrics							
Number of unresolved faults at planned end of activity	X		X	X	X	X	X
Number of faults that have not been corrected, and number of outstanding change requests	X		X	X	X		X
Number of software requirements and design faults detected during reviews, walkthroughs and inspections	X	X	X	X	X	X	X
Software Requirements Metrics							
Number of pages or words	X		X	X	X		
Number of requirements	X	X	X	X	X	X	X
Number of functions	X	X	X	X	X		
Requirements traceability	X	X	X	X	X	X	X
Completeness	X	X	X	X	X	X	X
Fault-days number							
Activity, date, or time that the fault was introduced	X		X	X	X		X
Activity, date, or time that the fault was removed.	X		X	X	X		X
Function points	X		X	X		X	

Table 5.4 continued

METRICS / V&V APPLICATIONS	Object Oriented (OO) Methods	Rapid Application Dev. (RAD)	Usability (GUI I/F)	Client/Server Networks	Knowledge Based Systems (KBS)	Internet/Intranet	Data Warehousing
Software Design Metrics							
High cohesion of modules	X	X	X	X	X	X	
Low coupling of modules	X	X	X	X	X	X	
Effective modularity	X	X	X	X	X	X	
Primitive size metrics							
Number of pages or words	X		X	X	X		
Number of modules		X	X	X		X	
Number of functions/objects	X						
Number of inputs and outputs							X
Number of interfaces	X	X	X	X	X	X	X
Primitive fault metrics							
Number of faults associated with each module		X	X	X	X	X	X
Number of requirements faults and structural design faults detected during detailed design	X	X	X	X	X	X	X
Primitive complexity metrics							
Number of parameters per module		X	X	X	X	X	X
Number of states or data partitions per parameter		X	X	X	X	X	X
Number of branches in each module		X	X	X	X	X	X
Coupling	X	X	X	X	X	X	
Cohesion	X	X	X	X	X	X	
(Structural) fan-in/fan-out	X		X	X	X	X	
Information flow metric							X
Staff hours per major defect detected	X		X	X	X	X	X
Defect Density (DD)	X		X	X	X	X	X
Test related primitives							
Number of software integration test cases planned/executed involving each module			X	X	X	X	X
Number of black box test cases planned/executed per module		X	X	X	X	X	X
Number of requirements faults detected (and re-assesses quality of requirements specification)	X	X	X	X	X	X	X
Code Metrics							
Lines of Code (LOC)	X		X	X		X	
Halstead software science metrics	X		X	X		X	
Cyclomatic complexity	X		X	X		X	
Amount of data							X
Live variables	X		X	X		X	
Variable scope	X		X	X		X	
Variable span	X		X	X		X	

Table 5.4 continued

METRICS / V&V APPLICATIONS	Object Oriented (OO) Methods	Rapid Application Dev. (RAD)	Usability (GUI I/F)	Client/Server Networks	Knowledge Based Systems (KBS)	Internet/Intranet	Data Warehousing
Test Metrics							
Number of faults detected in each module			X	X	X	X	X
Number of requirements, design, and coding faults found during unit and integration testing			X	X	X	X	X
Number of errors by type (e.g., logic, computational, interface, documentation)	X		X	X	X	X	X
Number of errors by cause or origin	X		X	X	X	X	X
Number of errors by severity (e.g., critical, major, cosmetic)	X		X	X	X	X	X
Fault density	X		X	X	X	X	X
Defect age	X		X	X	X		X
Defect cost	X		X	X	X		X
Defect removal efficiency	X		X	X	X		X
Statement coverage	X	X	X	X		X	
Branch coverage	X	X	X	X		X	
Path coverage	X	X	X	X		X	
Data flow coverage							X
Test coverage	X	X	X	X	X	X	X
Mean time to failure (MTTF)	X		X	X	X	X	X
Failure rate	X	X	X	X	X	X	X
Lewis V&V Metrics							
Systems Spec. % effectiveness	X		X	X	X	X	
Software Requirements Spec. % effectiveness	X		X	X	X	X	
Design Spec. % effectiveness	X		X	X	X	X	
Knowledge Database							
Completeness					X		
Accuracy					X		
Consistent					X		
Server Database							
Completeness				X		X	X
Accuracy				X		X	X
Consistent				X		X	X
Secure				X		X	X

The knowledge database metrics tie in with Chapter 10 on KBSs. For knowledge databases it is very important that they be verified and validated for completeness, accuracy, and consistency. The rationale for this conclusion is covered in some detail in Chapter 10. Server databases relates to elements discussed especially in Chapter 9 on client/server methods, but also relate well to Chapter 11 on the Internet/intranet. For server databases it is very important that they be verified and validated for completeness, accuracy, consistency, and security. The security issue is discussed in some detail in Chapter 11, and is important for V&V personnel to be very sensitive to.

Summary

There are many metrics being used in the software development arena. There is a great deal of dissatisfaction with these metrics. Most of the same metrics that software development uses are applicable for use by the V&V team. A general statement concerning all of these metrics is that they provide value when used for comparison with each other in an organization's domain. The troubles usually start when domains or organizations are crossed. The question becomes: Are these metrics that are published relevant to your own environment? Also, the V&V specialist needs to inquire whether the metrics that software development has collected are meaningful for a V&V analysis. This chapter addressed some of these issues, but there are still major questions open in this critical area for V&V.

A table of traditional software-related metrics is provided with their application to the V&V effort checked off. Also, Lewis' classic V&V document metrics are reviewed. In the Contemporary V&V section there is a discussion of the testing maturity models application to validation measurements. A special implementation of the goal–question–metric paradigm applied to V&V is covered with a specific goal covered of "Perform an optimal V&V effort." Lastly, the use of the traditional software metrics list to new V&V applications covered in this book is supplied.

References

[1] Biezer, Boris, Ph.D., "Why Hardware Quality and Software Quality are Different," American Society for Quality presentation, September 10, 1997.

[2] Card, David N. and Glass, Robert L., *Measuring Software Design Quality* (Englewood Cliffs, NJ: Prentice Hall Publishing Co. 1990).

[3] Wallace, Dolores R., Ippolito, Laura M. and Cuthill, Barbara, *Reference Information for the Software Verification and Validation Process,* NIST SP500-234, Gaithersburg, MD 20899, April, 1996.

[4] Fenton, Norman, Whitty, Robin and Iizuka, Yoshinori, editors, *Software Quality Assurance and Measurement: A Worldwide Perspective* (Boston: International Thomson Computer Press, 1995).

[5] Lewis, Robert O., *Independent Verification and Validation: A Life Cycle Engineering Process for Quality Software* (New York: John Wiley & Sons, Inc., 1992). Copyright © 1992 John Wiley & Sons, Inc., Adapted by permission of John Wiley & Sons, Inc.

[6] Burnstein, Ilene, Suwannasart, Taratip and Carlson, C.R., *Developing a Testing Maturity Model, Part II, In CrossTalk,* Software Technology Support Center, Ogden: Hill AFB, Vol. 9, No. 9, September 1996, pp. 19–26.

[7] Callahan, John R., Zhou, Tong C. and Wood, Ralph; *Software Risk Management Through Independent Verification and Validation,* Department of Statistics & Computer Science, Concurrent Engineering Research Center, West Virginia University, 1994.

CHAPTER 6

Object Oriented (OO) Methods

Introduction

Possibly the union of OO (object oriented) methods with distributed computing is the most compelling aspect of OO methods and its use in client/server networks (Chapter 9). There are other important OO methods applications, but with that one use alone, the V&V of OO systems is extremely topical. Both from the traditional V&V and contemporary V&V aspects discussed in this chapter, it is clear that specific methods or tools have been made available for the V&V person in this OO methodology. Such techniques as VOCAL, dynamic verification methods, and OVID (Object View Interaction Design) are covered. Some object oriented (OO) definitions (Table 6.1) set the stage for this chapter.

Schach[1] represents the properties of objects in the form of a hierarchy, as shown in Figure 6.1. Modules might represent classic subprograms. In order for modules to have the properties of true objects, they must not only use encapsulation, data abstraction, and information hiding in their construction, but they should also have high cohesion (well-bounded functionality) and low coupling (limited functional interdependency). The V&V person must be sensitive to these qualitative aspects of good object oriented design.

Bruce Webster[2] tells us that OO is popular because people realize many of the following major benefits:

- Faster development: the real benefit of faster development comes with ensuing projects—either revisions to a given project or creation of new projects that can reuse software form existing ones.
- Reuse of previous work: the greatest potential is here with the concomitant greatest difficulties.
- Modular architecture—OO systems have a natural structure for modular design: objects, subsystems, frameworks, etc.
- Management of complexity: just as difficult in OO systems for large projects as any other projects.

Table 6.1 General object terminology.[2, 3*]

Term	Definition
Object	An entity combining behavior with relevant attributes and states. In terms of software, a collection of data with the relevant instructions to do something with or to that data.
Class	The general declaration and definition of a collection of identical objects. The class specifies the data required for a given instance of itself; it presents the interface, giving the list of available operations; and it contains the implementation of those operations.
Message	A command to an object.
Instance	An actual copy of an object, with memory allocated for the data specified by the class. A class is instantiated to create an instance.
Abstraction	Focusing on what needs to be represented and eliminating does not.
Type checking	Determining which class an object belongs to. Strong or static type checking is done at compile time; weak, or dynamic checking is done at run time.
Specialization	When a new object class is a refinement of an existing one; defines the "is-a" relationship.
Composition	Having an object be built out of other objects; defines the "has-a" relationship.
Containment	Having an object be a container for other objects; defines the "holds-a" relationship.
Association	One object being able to refer to another; may be bi-directional; defines the "knows-about" relationship.
Encapsulation+	An object generally has two parts: Data—information that describes the object's state; and methods—software that can operate on the object's data or otherwise carry out the object's function. For example, an object describing a bank account might include data such as the account balance and owner name. The account's methods might include mechanisms to read and modify the owner, credit and debit the balance, or just read the balance. The only way to access or modify account data—balance and owner—is via the methods. A user of an object is presented with a well-defined interface, and everything else is encapsulated within. Hiding information in this way is essential to object orientation.
Inheritance+	Inheritance provides the potential for reuse of existing code, making the implementation of new objects much easier. For example, an object representing a checking account—a very specific type of bank account—might "inherit" all the data and methods of a generic account object, together with a few additions of its own.
Polymorphism+	Polymorphism: This refers to the ability to treat different things as if they were the same. As seen by a user, two objects may both provide the same method, but each may implement that method differently. For example, the method that implements debiting a withdrawal from a generic account object may simply be to check that the balance is sufficient. The same method in a checking account object might also take into account an automatic loan for which the customer has been pre-approved. To users of the objects, this difference is invisible.

+ Most agree that a method requires these three things to be objected oriented.

* This table is from "Pitfalls of Object-Oriented Development: A Guide for the Wary and the Enthusiastic"[2] and the last three term from "CORBA (Common Object Request Broker Architecture) and Distributed Onject Technology Evolution."[3]

Figure 6.1 Properties of objects.[1] (p. 172)

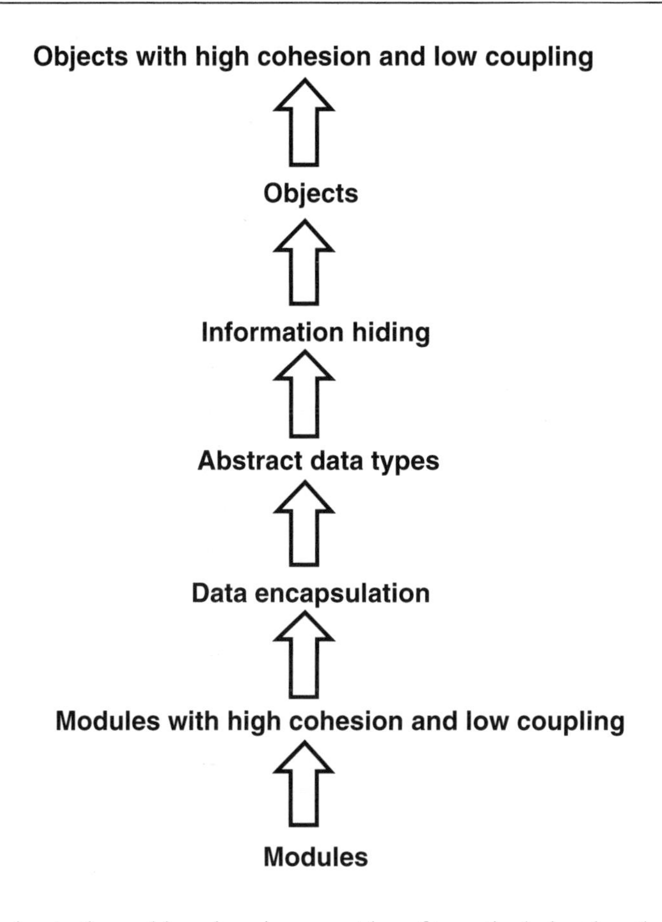

- Better mapping to the problem domain: a great benefit, particularly when the project maps to the real world.
- Client/server applications: the object—message metaphor of OO meshes nicely with the concept of sending messages back and forth over a network.
- Compound documents: the use of compound document architectures (OLE 2.0, OpenDoc, etc.) center on an object or object-like implementation. It follows directly from the **has-a** and **holds-a** relationships fundamental to object design (p. 21–23).

The V&V person dealing with OO technology must be aware of different standards—variations in symbology and methodology proposed by various authors and practitioners over the years. While the differences are not major in the context of the flow of activities between object oriented analysis, object oriented design, and object oriented programming, they can be confusing. The Unified Modeling Language (UML) designed by Booch, Rumbaugh, and Jacobson is one recent attempt

Figure 6.2 The views in UML[4] (p. 15).

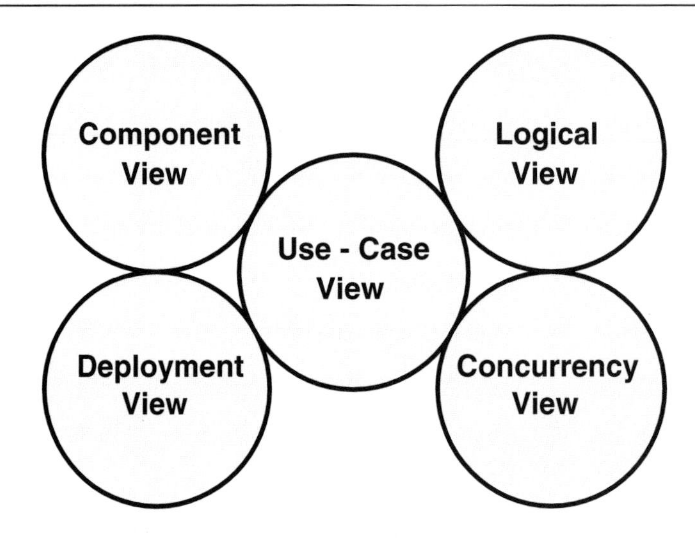

to resolve these differences and is gaining support among the OO community. From the *UML Toolkit*[4] the UML models a complex system with five views, as illustrated in Figure 6.2 (p. 15).

The V&V person using a black-box testing approach can initially focus on the Use-Case View, because it describes the functionality the system should deliver, as perceived by external actors.

Standards are especially important to the V&V person when OO concepts are joined with client/server systems. David Chappell[4] relates that a major player in creating standards for object technology is the Object Management Group (OMG) of Framingham, Massachusetts. The group has several hundred members—both users and vendors—and its most significant outputs thus far all relate to CORBA. CORBA (Common Object Request Broker Architecture) is a vendor-neutral standard aimed at describing and accessing objects in a distributed environment. Most major vendors—the significant exception being Microsoft, which has its own competing technology—currently offer or are about to release products that implement this standard.

The Microsoft approach is called the Component Object Model (COM). Roger Sessions[5] says that COM is gaining support among many software engineers who develop client/server and Internet-based applications. COM is an important Microsoft technology, and the following discussion about it is abstracted from "Modern Languages and Microsoft's Component Object Model."[6] Not surprisingly, it receives extensive support from the programming tools provided by Microsoft. In COM, software components communicate by means of interfaces, objects that are implemented by a server component and used by a client component. An interface is actually a pointer to a block of memory in which, like a C++ class, the first word is a pointer to a table of function addresses (called a virtual function table or *v*-table—see Figure 6.3). The client uses the interface by calling

Figure 6.3 COM interface representation. (Gray, ©1998 ACM)[6]

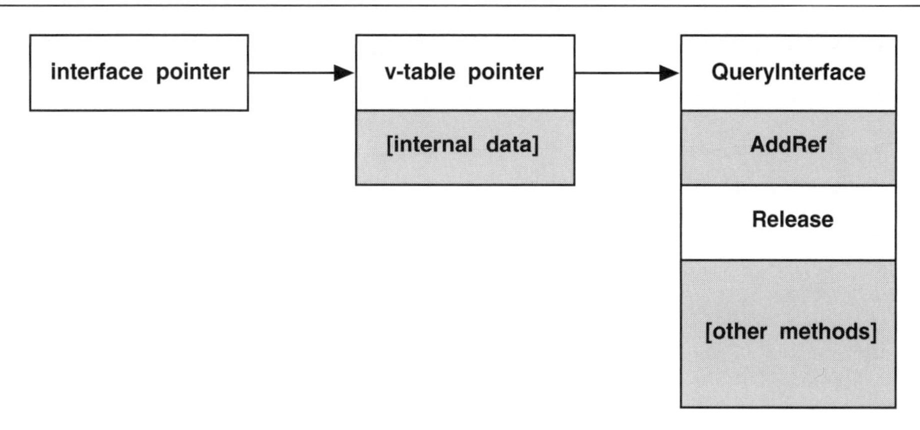

the functions from the table (referred to as methods of the interface) and passing the interface pointer itself as the first argument, with additional arguments depending on the particular function.

The client uses the interface only through its *v*-table, not by directly accessing any of the memory locations beyond the *v*-table pointer. This is necessary because the object may actually be nothing more than a proxy whose functions forward the argument values to the real object in another process. While the fundamental mechanisms described previously sound simple, the complexity of COM-based systems lies mainly in the various COM protocols—many kinds of interfaces, each with a number of methods, often using awkward structures for passing data. Constructing connections to these interfaces can be a very complex task.

David Chappell[3] goes on relating that traditionally, objects have been used in the creation of standalone applications, but merging them with client/server computing brings us to contend with distributed objects. V&V personnel need to understand that distributed object computing requires two fundamental things:

1. a way to describe objects to one another
2. a mechanism to communicate between distributed objects.

OMG's work has concentrated on the first and has also focused on specifying the basic interface to an object-to-object communication service, but the CORBA specification says essentially nothing about how communication between objects should occur. Chappell[3] notes the following:

> Perhaps the most important part of the CORBA specification is its definition of an Interface Definition Language (IDL). Every object in the CORBA world, and even few things that are not really objects, has an interface defined in IDL. This interface consists primarily of operations, definitions of how to invoke the object's methods, and attributes, which are essentially shorthand ways to define simple operations. An interface provides a complete definition of what an object provides to the outside world; that is, it provides encapsulation.

IDL interfaces also support inheritance. A new interface can be defined that inherits all of the operations and attributes of an existing one, but also adds a few of its own. It is worth noting that CORBA IDL provides direct support only for inheriting an object's interface, not its actual implementation. While the potential for reuse of existing code is present, reusability is not automatically provided with CORBA.

Using IDL to describe the interface to an object is essential, but it is not enough. There also must be some way for one object to invoke operations of another, analogous to the way that a program invokes a subroutine. In CORBA, objects do not perform these interactions directly with one another. Instead, all object-to-object communication services are provided by an intermediary—the Object Request Broker (ORB). According to the CORBA specification, an ORB is a software component that provides the mechanisms for objects to transparently make requests and receive responses. The ORB relieves objects of the responsibility for locating and communicating with other objects. Instead, all objects talk to the ORB and the ORB finds all other objects.

A major part of the CORBA specification is devoted to defining the interfaces that objects use to access the ORB's services, but since how one is to implement an ORB is not specified, vendors have used a variety of approaches. In some CORBA-based products, an ORB exists as a separate software component, and all communication between objects is literally passed through this component. In others, there might not be any particular piece of software that can be identified as the ORB and, instead, its functionality is spread among different parts of the application and its supporting platform. In this case, it is common for objects to communicate directly with one another without going through some software intermediary. The ORB still exists, but in a somewhat more abstract, theoretical way.

Distributed objects can benefit from various services: for example, a directory for locating object references, a way to exchange asynchronous events between objects, or some way to store an object's data. Although CORBA-based objects would like some standard way to access these kinds of services, different distributed environments provide them in different ways. [However], OMG is defining a group of object services. Each will define a particular distributed service as one or more objects, then specify appropriate IDL interfaces to access those objects. These interfaces, however, do not specify how to actually implement the objects, and each vendor is free to support the defined operations as it sees fit. To the object using them, all of these directory services look the same.

There is an obvious problem here that is of concern to a V&V person. In defining an interface common to heterogeneous services, one is all but forced to include only those features that are common to all. For example, the directory interfaces defined by OMG provide a basic service, but they do not allow access to the unique (and arguably the most powerful) features of the underlying a platform's directory services. In addition, OMG's consensus-oriented approach can lead to interface definitions that are almost breathtaking in their generality. For example, the primary operations for one OMG-defined object service contain two parameters: the first is optional, and the second is undefined. This makes it difficult to see how having a standard helps at all in this case.

To unite distributed computing and object technology is a worthy goal, and to do so in an open, vendor-neutral way is even more desirable. The difficulties in reaching this goal are substantial. Still, the problems being solved are important, and the demand for effective, multivendor solutions is great. If CORBA and its related technologies can provide the answer, [many will benefit]. If CORBA cannot provide a truly multivendor solution, it will quickly become irrelevant, since other vendors are eager to lead the way in distributed object technology.

Appendix A to this chapter compares the ORB implementation in CORBA by Sun's Java and in DCOM (Distributed Component Object Model) by Microsoft. This discussion about objects is extracted from Soren Lauesen's "Real-Life Object oriented Systems:"[7]

> OO development starts with OO analysis, in which the problem domain is modeled as a collection of objects. During design and implementation, these objects are transformed into other objects of slightly different shape that make up the actual computerized system. An object contains data and operations that operate on that data. Objects cooperate by calling operations in each other, that is, by sending messages. The data in an object are accessible only through the operations; no object can access another object's data directly.
>
> In a true OO system, data and functions exist only in the form of objects. We can distinguish two kinds of degenerate objects: an object without any data, which is the same as a traditional subroutine library, and an object with only trivial create, retrieve, update, and delete operations. The latter corresponds to a traditional data structure in which the data is visible to the entire system. A system composed of degenerate objects is not a true OO system; however, most business applications consist mainly of degenerate objects.
>
> Expanding on the benefits of OO listed above, specifically for business applications, the expected advantages of OO systems relative to traditional systems include:
>
> - a development process understandable to users in that the objects model the real world
> - a seamless transition from analysis to final implementation
> - a graphical user interface where objects correspond to the user's objects
> - easier maintenance as objects are modified without changing the entire system
> - reuse of objects in other applications, because objects encapsulate data and provide a service useful in other contexts. (p. 77)

Multidimensional Model

OO methods are process elements from the multidimensional model. The introduction to this chapter states that OO methods are in a state of flux because of the standards issues. Therefore, the V&V person needs to understand the OO processes and stay aware of the standards and their impact on OO.

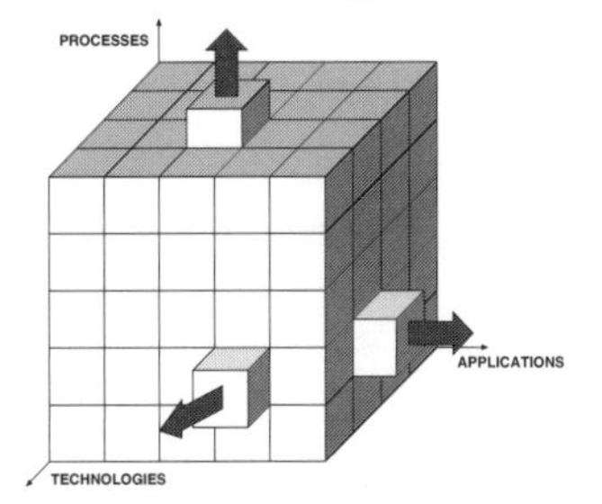

Technologies of major significance to the OO process are the client/server network technology, Internet/intranet, and GUI (usability). Each of these three technologies is so significant that a chapter of this book is devoted to it.

The applications dimension associated with the OO process include business applications, embedded mission critical, technical development, RAD (rapid application development), data warehousing, and especially KBS (knowledge-based systems).

Traditional V & V

The challenges are great for the V&V person in OO development. There is a great opportunity for V&V in OO development as the software is being built, instead of having to wait until everything is finished before becoming involved. Some in-process problem situations of OO development, along with recommended preventions available for V&V from Bruce Webster's *Pitfalls of Object-Oriented Development: A Guide for the Wary and the Enthusiastic*[2] are listed:

1. *Problem:* The number of possible message links among objects increases geometrically as the number of objects increases.

   Prevention: Find ways to reduce the combinatorial factors. This process may not be easy or even possible, given the current design, but should be tried anyway. Here are the factors for the V&V person to work on:

   - Work to make objects less visible to each other.
   - For every sender–receiver object pair, $A \rightarrow B$, do the following:
     - Reduce the number of different messages that *A* sends to *B*.
     - Reduce the number of times *A* calls a given method of *B*.
     - Reduce the range of parameter values *A* sends to *B* for a given method.

   - For each method *M* of a given receiver object *B*, do the following:
     - Where possible, make *M*'s behavior more state-invariant with regard to *B*; make the consequences of calling *M* less dependent or even independent of *B*'s state at the time of the call.
     - Work to make *M*'s behavior more source-invariant—independent of or less dependent on the object calling *M*.
     - Do proper conditioning of input parameters to reduce the number of possible outcomes (including new states for *B*).

   - For each sender Object *A*, sending method *M* to Object *B*, do the following:
     - Ensure that *B* is in the proper state to receive *M*.
     - Condition any parameters being passed to *M* to ensure that they fall within legal and desirable bounds.

2. *Problem:* Given the potential complexity of object oriented systems, classic procedures probably will not be adequate for an object oriented project of any size.

Prevention: Institute a simple white box testing process, picking key (troublesome) objects to start with. See that the tester goes through the source code method-by-method and does a code review, devising a test plan for each method as the test proceeds. This action alone will probably be helpful to flush out any number of defects. Then have the tester carry out the test plan for each method, getting help as needed from the software developer in charge of that object. Although this is only a small step, it tends to establish the concept of component testing and sends many software developers scrambling to clean up the code before white box testing starts.

3. *Problem:* It is often the case that testing—and thinking about testing—does not begin until the project reaches the alpha (feature complete) or beta (fully functional) stage.

   Prevention: When the project begins, the V&V person should ensure that there is a plan for constant, ongoing testing. This should include the following recommendations:

   - Plan for a component white or black box test plan for every object and subsystem created.
   - Treat component design reviews as a form of testing.
   - Have the software developers embed the appropriate trace, dump, and assert commands into their code.
   - Have the project architecture support (if possible) logging all method calls, including sender, receiver, method name, parameter list, and receiver state before and after the call.
   - Have the software developers build workbenches—mini-programs that can be used to drive object and subsystem components for white box and black box testing.
   - How new versions of components undergo white and black box testing before they are released into the general project.

This process involves a lot of testing, but the V&V person knows that it will pay off significantly in code stability and correctness, and probably reducing total time-to-completion.

4. *Problem:* Project testing and support are often treated as an afterthought, both in terms of planning and in terms of financial budgeting. The usually unspoken idea is this: develop the project, let some testers pound on it for a week or two, fix a few defects, release it, and forget about it.

   Prevention: The V&V person should recommend that the majority of the time spent in object oriented development should be focused on two activities: design and testing. Actual implementation tends to be a very small part of the project cycle, especially because of the nature of object oriented design and the support tools available. If the V&V person insists on a focus on design-and-test, it will help to shift the mindset of the software developers and testers. (pp. 203–211)

AVAL (Automated VALidation)

This subsection is abstracted from Esprit Project 21362—"AVAL, Improvement of Validation and Verification Practices."[8] On the Esprit Project, a decision was taken to improve the V&V process and especially for high interactive, client/server applications developed with OO techniques. An objective is to get at least the same level of maturity for V&V as for the requirements and design process. This means:

- decrease by 20% the number of remaining defects when the software is delivered
- avoid the risk of regressing from one version to the next one
- optimize the effort dedicated to V&V by 20%
- reduce time to deliver the product with the same level of quality.

This improvement is based on three aspects:

1. definition of the V&V process itself
2. technology to support and monitor the process
3. training to facilitate teams' adoption.

The ami® (Application of Metrics in Industry) method was selected for this experiment, and the AVAL project implements one iteration of the ami® loop. ami® results from a collaborative European research project involving 9 centers of excellence, with many years of experience in implementing measurement in software industry. The aim of the project, which ran from 1990 to 1992, was to make the European software industry aware of the benefits of using measurements. The goal was to provide a practical and validated approach to installing and using quantitative approaches to control and improve software production. Validated in more than 20 different industrial contexts, the ami® method that resulted from the project, was largely disseminated in the world and experimented by many organizations. Users' group, created in 1993, helps to capture and analyze various experiences and continuously improve the method.

This AVAL experiment was divided into 3 phases:

1. Status and overall framework definition phase: set quantitative improvement goals for the V&V process, both for defining improvement goals and for measurement plan production.
2. Set up and formalizing phase: through strategies and scenarios developed from the project specification, prepare how practitioners of the baseline project will implement standard V&V techniques and tools on the baseline project.
3. Final synthesis phase: evaluate cost/efficiency analysis, lessons learned, introduction of successful practices.

Phase 1: The objective of this preliminary analysis was to be able to quantitatively define improvement goals for the V&V process (e.g., number of remaining bugs that could be accepted within the first six months after delivery, minimum percentage of operations to be covered by V&V—normal conditions and/or stressed conditions—before delivery to match the reliability target, effort profile and efficiency figure).

Phase 2: The second phase was based on these results and focused on the project data and improvement areas identified for the V&V process. The V&V process, strategies, and procedures to build testing scenarios, derived from the object oriented specifications, were defined. Then this process was instansiated in a V&V plan, tailored for the baseline project (testing strategy definition, review, and V&V planning). The measurement plan started during first step was now modified to take into account V&V plan particularities so that it could be easily adopted and used by the project team.

Phase 3: The last stage was an improvement project review, a tentative generalization of results, and a dissemination phase. During this step, new projects were selected to adopt the process, required training, and possible internal—or external—awareness actions.

The AVAL experiment established a baseline application, based on a client/server architecture using object oriented methods. This baseline application has been developed using object oriented methods for specification and design. The AVAL experiment expects short-term lessons from this improvement effort: (a) a measurement framework for progress monitoring, (b) cost/benefit analysis, and (c)V&V process definition according to existing standards. As part of the AVAL experiment procedures to plan, measure, document and control the validation process will be established. The commercial impact of such a repeatable and well-documented validation process will be in several directions:

- increased confidence in the baseline project and the V&V process and culture
- opportunity to share practical results from the baseline application
- measures related to tool implementation and usage costs
- suggested tool functions evolution and improvements.

The conclusions of the AVAL experiment follow:

- V&V process and testing application is an asset for the company, transferable to other projects, and well sustained by practical and real examples of documents; it can be a great help in ISO9001 certification success.
- More control of subcontractors is attained by focusing on the procedures and joint reviews. Subcontracting should be based on step-by-step progress in order to adapt to new project conditions and common understanding.
- Dissemination is under way to increase awareness and interest in the application of V&V in projects. But dissemination in itself is not the goal, it is good technical results that convince internal practitioners and external customers.

Reviews & Audits

This subsection on reviews and audits is extracted from Ivar Jacobson et al.'s *Object-Oriented Software Engineering.*[9] The characteristics for high quality in a product are not exhaustive and not even independent of each other. Additionally, they often tend to conflict in a development. Therefore, when starting a development, it is often a good idea to decide which characteristics are the most important for this specific project and then focus on these throughout the development. Often, in OO software development, the focus is on maintainability characteristics, where the maintenance of the product is the major objective when developing the structure of the system. However, this will have effects on the suitability criteria. If it is easy to introduce changes to the system, it will also decrease the number of faults introduced when the system is modified and thus give the product a higher reliability. Therefore, OO software development that focuses on maintainability gives a good platform for carrying out quality assurance in an accurate way.

The main tools for verification occur in the development process itself, reviews and audits, testing, and metrics. Here, the integration of reviews in OO software development is discussed. A formal review's objective is to decide whether or not to proceed to the next phase, and is held at every major project milestone. The V&V person needs to understand that in OO software development, when to use the different kinds of reviews depends on the size and criticality of the project. In a small-to-medium sized project, typical formal review points are between the main activities—that is, each model when it has reached its first version. Informal reviews may be used after each subprocess, possibly grouping some subprocesses in one review.

A quite large review team is often involved, and customers usually also participate. An informal review's objective is to discover errors that have been made. These reviews can be held at any time during development, such as when something is completed that ought to be checked before continuing the development. Informal reviews often have a quite limited participation, typically involving some of the developers. Shlaer and Mellor[10] tell us that both review types are just as beneficial to V&V of OO software development as they are to most software development. A particular example of an information model should be subjected to intensive critical review to ensure that it represents an accurate reflection of the world problem (p. 89). The review can be formal or informal; to be effective, it is necessary that people other than those who constructed the model be involved (p. 464).

Design & Testing

Because of the special emphasis on design and testing of OO systems following are some recommendations for the V&V person to look for during this critical OO phases. Booch[11] describes several metrics suggested by Chidamber and Kemerer[12] that are of potential use to the V&V person reviewing the design aspects of an OO-based implementation from quality and complexity points of view:

- weighted methods per class
- depth of inheritance tree

• number of children
• coupling between objects
• response for a class
• lack of cohesion in methods

The following discussion is extracted from *Designing Object-Oriented Software:*[13]

It is difficult to evaluate a design with neither a basis for comparison, nor knowledge of the problem domain. The specifics of the problem domain will differ in every case. However, for a given problem, [the V&V person] can make the following comparisons for two or more designs that solve the problem:

- How many classes does it have?

  An application with more classes means that each class encapsulates relatively less of the overall system intelligence. Thus, more knowledge is required of anyone trying to understand the application. This is another indicator of complexity. Fewer numbers of relatively more intelligent classes typically means a simpler overall design.

  There are, however, tradeoffs here. The more intelligence a class encapsulates, the harder it is to reuse the class in other software. Ideally, then, classes should be exactly as intelligent as required to make them generally useful, and applications should have exactly as many classes at this intelligence level as is required for them to function meaningfully. The judgment of the V&V person should be applied to make these nebulous statements mean something in a specific context.

- How many sub-systems does it have?

  Does the design have a lot of sub-systems, and relatively few classes not within any sub-system? Or does it instead have a lot of discrete classes, and relatively fewer classes encapsulated within systems? Fewer sub-systems and more discrete application specific classes means greater complexity. In general, the V&V person should be aware that the more sub-systems encapsulate application functionality, the better.

- How many contracts are there per class?

  The average number of contracts per class is another rough indicator of complexity. In general, the more contracts per class, the harder it will be to maintain the application.

- How many abstract classes does it have?

  Are the inheritance hierarchies deep, making use of a lot of abstract super-classes to capture generally useful behavior? Or are the hierarchies shallow, with few abstractions defined?

  The depth of an inheritance hierarchy is an indicator of how much effort was spent to refine the design. Other things being equal, a relatively larger number of abstract classes is better. Deeper hierarchies mean more reusable code (pp. 189–190).

As OO design progresses, Derek Coleman[14] tells us that there are two basic checks that need to be carried out by the V&V person once the developer is satisfied with the initial designs. In the case where object interaction graphs are developed for each schema in the operation model, these checks are:

1. *Consistency with the system specification.* Check that each of the classes in the system object model is represented in at least one object interaction graph. A class not represented is irrelevant to the defined system behavior, and should not be considered part of the system object model unless it exists for other reasons, such as reuse. Note that new classes may be introduced during design, for example, to deal with events to agents of the system. These classes will not be shown on the system object model developed during analysis.

2. *Verification of functional effect.* Check that the functional effect of each object interaction graph satisfies the specification of the system operation given in the operation model (pp. 77–78).

To enhance the validation of an OO system, a V&V person should address anomalies and multiplicity testing. Anomalies and multiplicity testing may be combined to enhance the validation of an OO system. Details concerning these tests are available in Robert Binder's "Verifying Class Associations."[15]

In object oriented testing, Paul Herzlich[16] relates that there are numbers of low level techniques for integration testing of objects which is quite different than integration of non-object oriented software. Most of these methods are based on the life histories of the messages as they pass from object to object. The V&V person should use validation tests of behind-the-scenes functionality, recognizing that they are driven via the user interface, which kicks off a chain of events that tests integration through to the server and back (pp. 18–20).

Contemporary V & V

OO Database Verification

Herman Balsters' "Verification of Transactions in Object Oriented Databases"[17] tells us that transactions on a database can change the state of a database in the case of an update. After invocation of such a transaction it is always the question whether the integrity constraints of the database have remained in tact. What is of concern is how to verify (i.e. prove) that an update operation on a database state results in a new state that still satisfies the set of (static) constraints of the database. Moreover, this very process is performed irrespective of any particular input state, and support needs to be automated in the process. In doing so, compile-time verification of update operations can be written as part of the schema of an object oriented database. In Balster's research, the TM language was used for describing the OO database schema, TM was developed at the University of Twente. TM is a strongly typed functional database language used for specification of OO database schemas. Operations methods on TM database states are part of the database schema and can operate on different levels, namely on the object, class, and database levels.

The Isabelle interactive proof development system was used to provide automatic support for proving correctness of database transactions. Based on this action, this project coded the formal specification language (TM) into the Isabelle proof checker. First, the proof tool can find a minimal precondition for any given database update method, such that if the input state satisfies this condition then invariance of the integrity constraints is guaranteed. Secondly, the proof tool can, as an alternative, generate so-called compensating actions; that is, by altering the output state (after invoking the update method) according to this minimal set of compensating actions, it is again guaranteed that invariance is satisfied. A large benefit in OO design gained by the V&V person using such a proof tool is that, given some method *M*, it determined which constraints have to be satisfied that are as local as possible to *M*, such that the global integrity constraints are guaranteed to be satisfied after invokement of *M*.

VOCAL

This subsection is abstracted from "VOCAL: A Framework for Test Identification & Deployment."[18] Companies know that they must be first to market with a new product, or the first to release an enhanced version mirroring a competitor's product, to retain their existing customer base. Furthermore, it is not only tight deadlines that pose problems, but also the notion that the finished product must be

- reliable
- responsive
- easy to learn and use, while providing customer satisfaction through use of the product
- in possession of any other relevant quality attributes selected according to product type, and customer base.

"Testing, therefore, is not just the process of looking for defects, but also that of judging quality, and validating products with customers' personal requirements."[18] Testing (validation) practice must change concomitant with development practices.

"Testing needs to embrace reuse by the capture and creation of distributable, reusable test specifications. Releasing a product ahead of competition, meeting customer requirements, and ensuring that code is reliable requires a carefully structured V&V approach."[18] The VOCAL method is based around a life-cycle set of test process perspectives, guiding expertise, and test identification, to help to achieve these goals. Typically, three perspectives can be observed during V&V:

- A development perspective, that focuses on defect detection and removal, system performance, and reliability.
- A customer perspective, focusing on robustness, usability, and conformance with real requirements.
- An organizational perspective, dealing with schedule, cost, standards, and conformance with the captured specification. (pp. 249)

Perspectives can be reflected in this set of test process perspectives to capture and record information derived from each view, so that every aspect of the product complies with the requirements.

William Hetzel's* definition of software testing is "the process of establishing confidence that a program or system does what it is supposed to do." "This implies that tests take into account user requirements," which is correct. Glenford Myers, however, says that tests should be designed and executed to find errors. "There have been some previous attempts to define testing as a life-cycle activity, such as the approach proposed by [William E.] Perry. Other work in the area of testing maturity assessment has come some way to characterizing the goals, and objectives required for life-cycle testing, though without defining a framework to implement this."

VOCAL addresses these problems through the construction of an integrated testing and quality control process applicable throughout software development. This achieves test process maturity and moves away from the ad hoc nature of traditional testing. A testing process model should be acceptable to the software development community and based around agreed software engineering principles and practices, while remaining industrially practicable. The whole view of testing (validation) needs to be redefined to change the classical process model's conception from an execution only based activity, to a test life-cycle integrated with the software development life-cycle. VOCAL assists the creation of well planned and clearly defined test life-cycle policies that can be used and reused throughout an organization.

Utilization of this set of test process perspectives in software development acknowledges the roles played by the many individuals in the software process. Test process perspectives have developed from a requirements elicitation technique to a method for V&V. The VOCAL framework is built around information encapsulation, to apply the benefits of multiperspective methodologies to V&V. The specific exclusion of imposing prespecified methods for testing should help to aid workability of the method in specific company working practices.

> The objective of VOCAL is to look at testing from a different standpoint. VOCAL guides and identifies V&V throughout the life-cycle, providing an organizational framework for controlled distribution and activity assignment among participants. This was deemed a more appropriate route to follow rather than trying to convey an unwieldy test strategy that constricts the applicability and real-life value of the method. Using VOCAL should lead to much greater test coverage, where it matters in a system. Traditional test methods fail to identify and verify attributes of a system that not only does its job correctly, but in a manner the customer wants. VOCAL addresses this problem directly by including stakeholders in the process wherever possible throughout development. Stakeholders are in regular contact through front-end reviewing and operational product validation.
>
> Emphasis has been given to the importance of the three types of traceability (inter, intra, and temporal traceability) for conflict management and resolution of product attributes. Conflicts should be detected as early as possible in development to save later correction effort and unnecessary cost. The importance of specifying correct viewpoint granularity is discussed, and trade-offs between viewpoint domain size and management are highlighted. Novel process models in the area of user interface evolution and combined system and integration testing were introduced. Such strategies arise predominantly through the application of viewpoint structuring and

* Hetzel, Myers, and Perry references are contained in General References at the end of this chapter.

> encapsulation. The potential benefits of structured validation activities via scenarios has also been discussed. VOCAL approaches quality assurance, and how this integrates with V&V process activities, by using test process perspective stakeholder structuring methods. Attribute identification, conflict resolution, and sample quality viewpoint templates have been described to aid this process. Stakeholder quality structuring assists nonfunctional requirements verification, or if the requirement is not feasible, its resolution to a satisfactory level. The importance of making quality attributes quantifiable is also stressed.... Weaknesses of the method that need to be addressed arise from the information overhead created by viewpoint encapsulation. This, coupled with defining full traceability, can place a greater focus on information management than traditional techniques. A prototype tool supporting VOCAL has been implemented to aid efficient application of the technique... and relieve some of the information management overhead. Implementing a well-defined test management model helps administer resources to areas of the project requiring most effort to keep the product on schedule. Process management information collection is... integrated to give visual indications of problematic areas in the test plan. Defect tracking is also an integral part of test management. Current investigation is being undertaken using tool-generated defect tracking information as a test exit criterion to determine the point where test costs outweigh the benefits... of continuing to test.... This is obviously crucial if the approach is to be taken up in favor of more established and mature methods. It is therefore hoped that in the near future the tool and technique will be used to aid development of a large-scale system. This will help [the evolution] into a potentially indispensable approach for structured test identification and deployment[18] (p. 249).

Dynamic Verification

Wang and Musser's "Dynamic Verification of C++ Generic Algorithms"[19] presents a new approach to formal verification, called dynamic verification, as applied to C++ template-based generic algorithms.

> The method employs Hoare-style pre/post condition specifications, symbolic execution based on forward assignment axioms (rather than the usual backward substitution), and a while-loop inference rule based on sub-goal induction. The symbolic execution mechanism includes multiple run-time analysis oracles, each of which provides a C++ interface to one or more rule-based inference engines. (p. 321)

> Many aspects of the dynamic verification method are based in part on previous work on symbolic execution, formal specification of abstract data types and generic concepts, and axiomatic treatments of imperative programming languages. In each case, previous methods have been adapted to make it possible to use them without transforming source code. (p. 315)

> The purpose of dynamic verification is to help developers find bugs that cannot easily be found by debugging or testing. It differs from conventional formal verification by leaving the handling of language constructs to the compiler and only formalizing higher-level application concepts, which are more prone to errors than built-in language constructs. Since a dynamic verification system is built upon a conventional debugger already familiar to many programmers, it may assist in spreading the use of symbolic execution and formal verification technologies whose use has hitherto been limited to a few research projects. (p. 315)

> [There is] a specification technique developed for dynamic verification that allows specifications to be defined by a set of high-level formal rules, yet also can be directly evaluated in the same execution environment as that of the program being verified. In [the] dynamic verification system, a program (segment) is specified by describing its precondition state and postcondition state.... Specifications for dynamic verification are two-tiered and must be written by the user. The interface specifications, which consist of assertions about program states, make up one tier. The abstract concept specifications that define the semantics of symbolic values and primitive concepts, on which the assertions depend, constitute the other tier. (p. 317)

Wang and Muser[19] describe the MEta-Level program Analysis System (MELAS), which supports the dynamic verification method. MELAS extends a conventional debugging system with additional commands for formal verification, normal and symbolic testing, and rapid prototyping using executable specifications. Since MELAS is an extension of debugging tools many programmers are already familiar with, and it can be applied selectively to small program segments, it should assist in achieving more widespread use of symbolic execution and formal verification technology.

MELAS is implemented using a debugging system, which needs to:

1. Set (conditional) breakpoints.
2. Attach expressions and/or function calls to breakpoints such that they can be evaluated automatically whenever the breakpoints are encountered.
3. Disable and enable breakpoints. A breakpoint is set at a program line; the same line can appear on different execution paths. This feature allows a breakpoint to be effective only on a specified path.
4. Set a variable. This allows the program state to be changed by executing specifications instead of the original code. This is needed for inductive verification of while-loops.
5. Operate from a user-supplied script, as needed for fully automatic verification.

OVID

This subsection on Object View Interaction Design (OVID) is extracted from Roberts and colleagues, "Developing Software Using OVID."[20]

> OVID focuses the design and implementation phases, using information about the users' tasks to create a designer's model. It then prepares this model for transfer to the team's implementers. OVID takes task analysis information as input. You can use any type of task analysis, but because better input results in better output, a more complete and rigorous analysis will result in a better application. At a minimum, the analysis should have proper English sentences describing each task. OVID focuses on three design elements: the objects that the user is aware of, views of the objects, and interactions between the user and the objects. OVID produces a set of documented tasks that detail how the objects and views are used to accomplish things.
>
> First, an initial set of objects is generated by examining the task analysis. Next, views are defined so users can see appropriate aspects of each object; tasks are described in terms of the new objects and views; and details of the interactive behavior of each object are recorded. [Fig-

ure 6.4] shows the main flow of these activities, which occur iteratively until the design is complete. There may be several iterations of this process, depending on team experience and problem complexity. Work from any stage can impact that in any other. (p. 53)

In interface design, we call the model in users' heads the "user's model." We try to take advantage of how users employ this model in our designs. We also use two other models in product design: the designer's model and the implementation model. The designer's model is what users are supposed to see when they use the product (the specification). The implementation model is what the programmers really build (the code).

As [Figure 6.5] shows, [the design process can be summed up] in terms of these three models. In the discovery phase, the designers try to understand the users' mental models. In the design phase, the designers develop a designer's model to complement the user models that are thus easier to learn. During implementation, programmers try to develop a product that matches the designer's model. Finally, in the learning phase, users launch the application, try to understand the designer's model, and adapt their own model to accommodate it.

Object View Interaction Design [was developed] to convert user needs into a solution and thus help prevent breakdowns. OVID is a structured design methodology that helps the design team create a good, object-based user interface design. Because OVID uses a structured process and appropriate tools, the design progresses more quickly with fewer cycles of iteration. OVID's output documents the interface design and feeds directly into tools and methods commonly used for code design, reducing the risk of introducing interface errors later in development. (p. 52)

Figure 6.4 OVID iterative process flow (© 1997 IEEE).[20] (p. 53)

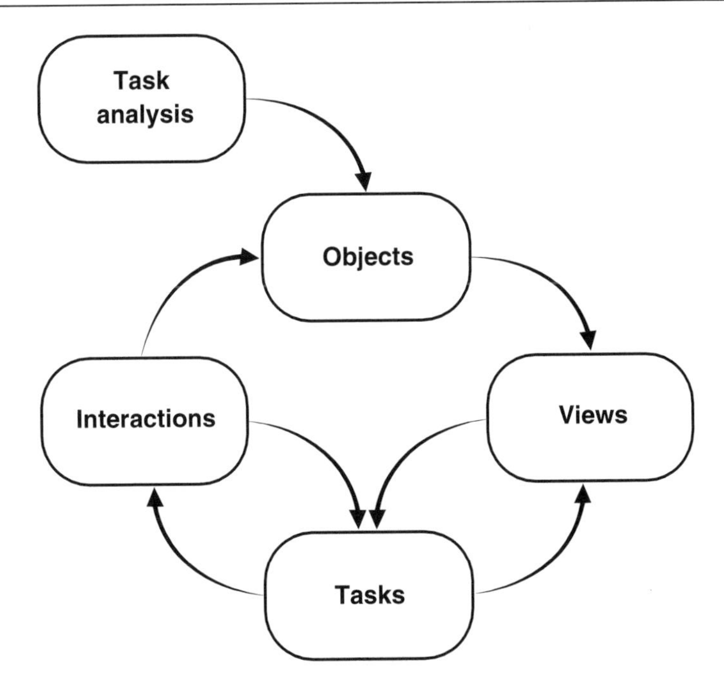

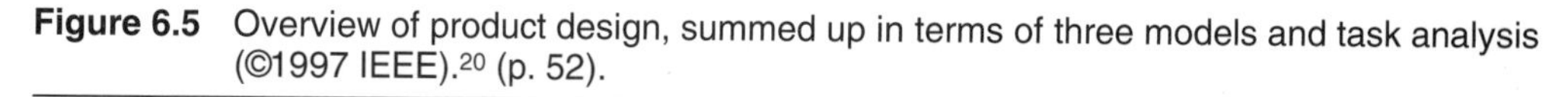

Figure 6.5 Overview of product design, summed up in terms of three models and task analysis (©1997 IEEE).[20] (p. 52).

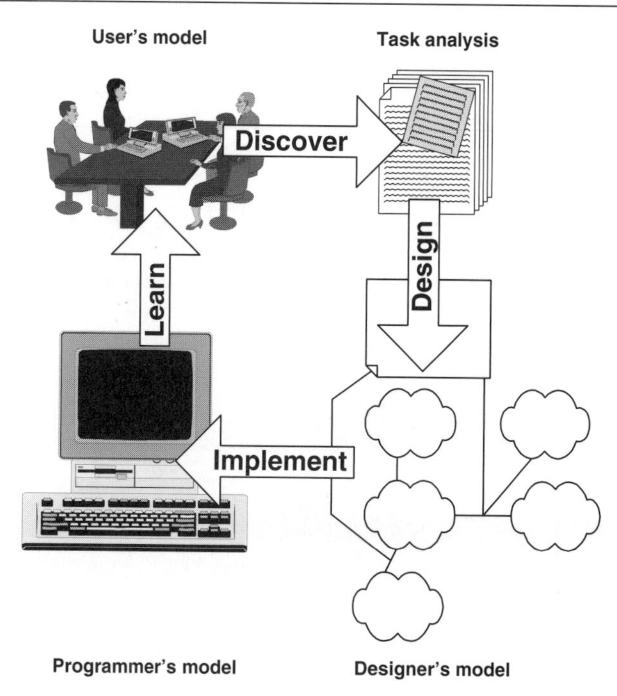

User interface design should be an iterative process. It is hard work to design a usable interface, and it is not usually exactly right the first time. Derek Coleman[14] says to plan to prototype the interface—or at least significant portions of it—and conduct usability tests (Chapter 8) (p. 6). These tests will help identify functionality needed to support tasks that may have been missed in the initial task analysis, to identify mismatches between the user and designer models, and find other usability problems resulting in errors or dissatisfaction.

There are numerous design hints for objects, views, and interactions that may be derived from OVID (Table 6.2).

Syntactical Checking OO Tool

This subsection is abstracted from Periyasamy and Baluta's "A Verifier for Objected-Oriented Designs."[21]

> Many object oriented design methods such as Rumbaugh's, Booch's and Coad and Yourdon's methods use graphical notations which enable a software designer to describe a design more precisely and in an easily comprehensible manner. Tools supporting such object oriented design methods generally provide a graphical user interface (GUI). The GUI will display a list of symbols corresponding to object oriented design primitives and a working area. A designer using

Table 6.2 Design hints derived from OVID (© 1997 IEEE).[20] (p. 56).

Hints for Objects

- Underline each noun in the task analysis; double-underline the names of real, physical objects.
- Write a one-sentence description of each object. Each sentence should have only one clause: no "ifs," "ands," or "buts." If you cannot write such a sentence for an object, you have probably bundled several objects into one. Split that object until the descriptions fit the rules.
- Record the number of times a particular object occurs in each task and weight these counts according to the frequency of the task. Work on the objects with a higher score first.
- Exclude objects that are in the task descriptions only because of the present method of performing the task. These will clutter analysis; if you really need them you'll find out during task design.

Hints for Views

- Every object must have at least one view. If an object is seen only as part of another object's view, make it an attribute of that object.
- Refer to the style guide for the system where your application will run. Use as many of the standard recipes as you can for elements of each view.

Hints for interactions

- Circle all the verbs in the task analysis. Check them against the transitions for an object. Each verb that does not have a corresponding transition should be carefully considered. There should be a reasonable explanation for the absence.
- On occasion, "islands" of states may be observed in a Harel diagram. These are clusters of states that have no transitions connecting them to other states. This pattern indicates that two objects have been merged. In such cases, a new object should be added and named to hold the states from one of the "islands." The new object becomes a property of the object in which it was found.
- Whenever there is a "can't happen" condition for a state, all transitions to that state must disable any controls that could cause that event.

> such a tool will develop object oriented designs by selecting appropriate symbols from those provided by the GUI and by connecting them in a meaningful way.
>
> One of the problems with existing tools for object oriented design methods is that they merely act as drawing tools with minimal syntax checking. For example, OMTool, which implements Rumbaugh's method, ensures that no two classes in a single class diagram have the same name. However, it is possible to develop a design diagram using OMTool in which two classes, *A* and *B*, inherit each other (i.e., *A* inherits *B* and *B* inherits *A*). Such cyclic inheritance is semantically invalid according to principles of object orientation. A possible remedy for these problems is to embed verification strategies in the tool itself. This process requires the development of formal semantics of the modeling notations used by the tool.

Periyasamy and Baluta describe axiomatic semantics for the modeling notations used by the Object Modeling Technique (OMT) proposed by Rumbaugh* and others and the verifier that implements the semantics:

> The modeling notations, [for which the formal semantics are developed], include class structure, its components (such as attributes and operations), relationships among classes (such as association and aggregation), object states, transitions between states and events. Most of these notations

* Rumbaugh reference is contained in General References at the end of the chapter.

are also available in the UML. The Z (pronounced "zed," see Chapter 10) normal notation was used to develop the semantics; the specification has been type checked using the fuzz type checker. The implementation of the semantics was carried out using a rule-based approach; CLIPS was used, an industrially approved tool for developing knowledge-based systems for this purpose. The axioms in Z have been implemented as rules in CLIPS. All the rules have been constructed using templates with slots for generic parameters. When verifying a particular design, the design elements are substituted for the parameters of appropriate rules and the rules are fired.

The CLIPS tool was developed by NASA at its Johnson Space Center. CLIPS is a rule based system that uses a dialect of LISP. It supports three types of knowledge representations: ordered facts (expressed as tuples and relations), structured facts (expressed as frames and templates), and objects (described using object oriented approach) Only ordered facts and structured facts are used for this implementation.

A rule in CLIPS contains two parts: left-hand side and right-hand side. The left-hand side is represented by a pattern of symbols, and the right-hand side is represented by a network of patterns of symbols. If the left-hand side of a rule matches with the input, the rule will be placed on the agenda. An agenda is a sequence of rules to be fired. The inference engine in CLIPS selects and fires rules from the agenda based on the priority of each rule. The priority may be based on the conflict resolution strategy implemented in CLIPS or it may be a user identified priority.

The V&V person could use the verifier to support both online and off-line verification. During online verification, every step in the design process is verified immediately after the step is completed. For example, as soon as the designer enters the name of a class, the verifier attempts to check whether there exists another class with the same name in the current module. In most cases, a designer prefers off-line verification mainly because it provides flexibility to change the design until the time of verification. In the verifier, online verification is limited to primitive checks such as checking duplication of names, checking multiple inconsistent relationships between the same pair of classes (aggregation and generalization), and so on.

Summary

General object terminology is presented for the V&V specialist at the start of this chapter. Both common interfaces and the difference between two kinds of objects—an object without any data and an object with only trivial create, retrieve, update, and delete operations—are discussed.

Typical problems and preventions concerning OO methods are listed. The Esprit Project AVAL is focused to improvement of V&V of OO systems. AVAL is based upon three aspects:

1. definition of the V&V process itself
2. technology to support and monitor the process
3. training to facilitate teams' adoption.

The reviews and audits of OO systems are important for V&V considerations. Key questions of OO design and testing include:

- How many classes does it have?
- How many subsystems does it have?
- How many contracts are there per class?
- How many abstract classes does it have?

The V&V person needs to remember that anomalies and multiplicity testing may be combined to enhance the validation of an OO system. OO database verification techniques are aided by the use of TM (strongly typed functional database language). Three perspectives can be observed during V&V using the VOCAL method:

- a development perspective that focuses on defect detection and removal, system performance, and reliability.
- a customer perspective, focusing on robustness, usability, and conformance with real requirements.
- an organizational perspective, dealing with schedule, cost, standards, and conformance with the captured specification.

Dynamic verification using the MELAS system is an approach to formal verification of specifications and tests. OVID (Object View Interaction Design) is a structured design methodology that helps the design team create a good, object-based user interface design. The V&V person can review OVID to assure that the design is satisfactory for the user.

The V&V person must consider some special attributes for "Managing OO Projects Better,"[22] that are provided as follows from Paolo Nesi's several years of managing OO projects:

> Traditional methods are inadequate for managing OO projects for several reasons:
>
> - There is a sizable gap between OO software development methodologies and diffuse managing approaches.
> - The life-cycles that are usually adopted focus too much on single-task projects and structured or functional methodologies.
> - Managers lack prior experience in the adoption of OO indicators for controlling system development at both project and task levels.
> - Organizations share a deeply ingrained tradition of allocating and disallocating human resources among different projects.
> - Projects and subsystem managers lack the technical expertise necessary to profitably manage OO projects. Thus, to be effective the OO approach… proposed must be introduced throughout the whole organization (pp. 50–60).

The key points for better OO project management that Nesi has captured are indicated as follows:

The hierarchical organization of a team can be successfully applied to OO projects [see Chapter 15]. The main subsystems are re-extracted* from the general collection of classes by identifying branches related to the most important classes, usually called key classes. These new versions of subsystems are reassigned to subsystem managers.... The number of identified key classes multiplied by a factor, *K*, gives an approximate measure of the final dimension of each system or subsystem in terms of classes. *K* is equal to 2 for subsystems without a user interface and communication with devices, and 4 for subsystems that include the relationships with a complex user interface. The hypothesis for the number of system classes is used to predict the effort needed for each task by considering the typical person-hours needed to analyze, design, and implement a class....

The effort spent in documenting and assessing depends quite linearly on the number of classes, while testing depends on time for testing classes and their relationships. The first factor is linear, and the second takes time that depends more than quadratically on type number of classes, since interactions among classes exploiting relationships of is-part-of and is-referred-by are frequently made concrete with several method calls....

During [the test] phase each subsystem manager may meet with other subsystem managers and the project manager, depending on task relationships, to:

1. identify new detailed requirements for generalizing classes and clusters developed so that they can be used in the whole system.
2. provide other teams with the current version of software developed in the corresponding task or subtask, along with its documentation, test, and assessment reports.
3. discuss with the project manager how to correct problems identified by the assessment activity....

Periodic meetings avoid class duplication and facilitate the adoption notations in the project database's quality manual for the selection of class, method, and attribute names; for compiling documentation; for preparing test scripts; and so on.... The project manager can profitably manage the project only if she directly knows how the problem domain has been covered in terms of classes and class relationships. Moreover, the subsystem manager must participate actively in the task and subtask development by analyzing details and designing and implementing specific parts, or parts related to other tasks.... Because no clear separation exists between the life-cycle phases of OO methodologies, allocating a constant number of people to the task team is consistent with the OO approach, letting the same people who perform the analysis work on all other phases. This leads to a reduction of effort and less risk of misunderstanding. The lack of clear separation stems mainly from the impossibility, in many cases, of separating the development phases—for example, whether to include or exclude object and class specialization and relationship identification for the analysis phase (pp. 50–60).

References

1 Schach, Stephen R., *Classical and Object-Oriented Software Engineering,* (3rd ed.) (Chicago: Irwin, 1996).
2 Webster, Bruce F., *Pitfalls of Object-Oriented Development: A Guide for the Wary and the Enthusiastic* (New York: MIS Press, Inc., 1995), Copyright © 1995. All rights reserved. Reproduced here by permission of IDG Books Worldwide, Inc., (800)762-2974, www.idgbooks.com.

* Passive voice replaces the use of the personal pronoun throughout the quote.

[3] Chappell, David, "CORBA (Common Object Request Broker Architecture) and Distributed Object Technology Evolution," *Business Communications Review,* July, 1994, Vol. 24, No. 7, p. 62–66.

[4] Eriksson, Hans-Erik and Penker, Magnus, *UML Toolkit* (New York: John Wiley & Sons, Inc., 1998). Copyright © 1998 John Wiley & Sons, Inc., Adapted by permission of John Wiley & Sons, Inc.

[5] Sessions, Roger, *COM and DCOM: Microsoft's Vision for Distributed Objects* (New York: John Wiley & Sons, Inc., 1998). Copyright © 1998 John Wiley & Sons, Inc., Adapted by permission of John Wiley & Sons, Inc.

[6] Gray, David N. et al, "Modern Languages and Microsoft's Component Object Model," *Communications of the ACM,* Vol. 41, No. 5, May 1998, pp. 55–65

[7] Lauesen, Soren, "Real-Life Object-Oriented Systems," *IEEE Software,* (© March/April 1998 IEEE), pp. 76–83.

[8] Esprit Project 21362—AVAL, *Improvement of Validation and Verification Practices,* Objectif Technologie, +33-1-49085800, http://www.objectif.fr, 01/01/96.

[9] Jacobson, Ivar et al., *Object-Oriented Software Engineering* (New York: Addison Wesley Publishing Co., 1992), Reprinted by permission of Addison Wesley Longman Ltd.

[10] Shlaer, Sally & Mellor, Stephen J., *Object-Oriented Systems Analysis: Modeling the World in Data* (Englewood Cliffs, NJ: Prentice Hall Publishing Co., 1988).

[11] Booch, Grady, *Object-Oriented Analysis and Design,* (2nd ed.) © 1994 Benjamin Cummings Publishing Company Inc., Reprinted by permission of Addison Wesley Longman Ltd..

[12] Chidamber, S. and Kemerer, C., *A Metrics Suite for Object-Oriented Design* (Cambridge, MA: MIT Sloan School of Management, 1993).

[13] Wirfs-Brock, Rebecca, Wilkerson, Brian and Wiener, Lauren, *Designing Object-Oriented Software* (Englewood Cliffs, NJ: Prentice Hall Publishing Co., 1990).

[14] Coleman, Derek et al., *Object-Oriented Development: The Fusion Method* (Englewood Cliffs, NJ: Prentice Hall Publishing Co., 1994).

[15] Binder, Robert, "Verifying Class Associations," *Object Magazine,* November 1997, pp. 18, 20.

[16] Herzlich, Paul, "A Quick Win for Testing," *SQM* issue 25, © 1995 Paul Herzlich, Web presentation © 1996 Tesseract Publishing, March 11, 1996, http://www.avnet.co.uk/tesseract/QiC/articles/Herzlich/25.html.

[17] Balsters, Herman, "Verification of Transactions in Object Oriented Databases," *New Trends in Database Languages,* University of Toronto, March 4–8, 1996, http://wwwis.cs.utwente.nl:8080/oodm.html.

[18] Pemberton, Duncan & Sommerville, Ian, "VOCAL: A Framework For Test Identification & Deployment," IEEE Proceedings—Software Engineering, Vol. 144, Issue 5–6, (© Oct-Dec 1997 IEEE), p. 249.

[19] Wang, Changqing and Musser, David R., "Dynamic Verification of C++ Generic Algorithms," *IEEE Transactions on Software Engineering,* Vol. 23, No. 5, (© May 1997 IEEE), pp. 314–322.

[20] Roberts, David, Berry, Dick, Isensee, Scott and Mullaly, John, "Developing Software Using OVID," *IEEE Software,* (© July/August 1997 IEEE), pp. 51–57.

[21] Periyasamy, K. and Baluta, W., "A Verifier for Objected-Oriented Designs," Proceedings of the Twenty-Second Annual Software Engineering Workshop, Goddard Space Flight Center, Greenbelt, Maryland, December 1997, pp. 303–336.

[22] Nesi, Paolo, "Managing OO Projects Better," *IEEE Software,* (© July/August 1998 IEEE), pp. 50–60.

[23] Horowitz, Ellis, "Migrating Software to the World Wide Web," *IEEE Software,* (© May/June 1998 IEEE), pp. 18–21.

General References

Hetzel, William C., *The Complete Guide to Software Testing,* 2nd ed. (Wellesley, MA: QED Information Sciences, 1988).

Myers, Glenford J., *The Art of Software Testing* (New York: John Wiley & Sons, Inc., 1979).

Perry, William E., *Effective Methods for Software Testing* (New York: John Wiley & Sons, Inc., 1995).

Rumbaugh, J., Blaha, M., Premerlani, W., and Lorensen, W., *Object-Oriented Modeling and Design* (Englewood Cliffs, NJ: Prentice Hall Inc., 1991).

Appendix

The appendix is abstracted from Ellis Horowitz's "Migrating Software to the World Wide Web:"[23]

> The object request broker is an essential concept in CORBA. Given a network of clients and servers on different computers, ORB support means that a client program, which is treated as an object, can request services from a server program or from another object without having to understand where the server is in the network or what the interface to the server program actually is. As with all client/server programs, ORBs assume there is a server that waits for a request, receives it, and responds.
>
> The interface they use, the General Inter-ORB Protocol (GIOP), is implemented across several layers of the Open Systems Interconnect protocol. The most important, mapping of GIOP is IIOP; an object oriented protocol that enables distributed programs written in different programming languages to communicate over the Internet using the Transmission Control Protocol. Besides TCP, other possible transport layers include IBM's Systems Network Architecture and Novell's IPX, and implementation for all of these exist.
>
> When a client makes a request to a server in the network, it must have an address for the server (a URL, for example). In CORBA this address is known as the Interoperable Object Reference, or IOR. Using IIOR, part of the address is based on the server's port number and Internet Protocol (IP) address. In the client's computer, a table can be created to map IORs to easier-to-use proxy names. The GIOP lets the program connect with an IOR and then send requests to it. When appropriate, servers send replies. A common data representation provides a way to encode and decode data so that it can be exchanged in a standard way.
>
> A competing vision of distributed objects and their intercommunication comes from Microsoft in its Distributed Component Object Model (DCOM). Figure 6A.1 shows the major elements of Microsoft and Sun JavaSoft solutions for distributed objects[23] (p. 20).

Figure 6A.1 Distributed object solutions: Sun Java versus Microsoft's DCOM (© 1998 IEEE).[23]

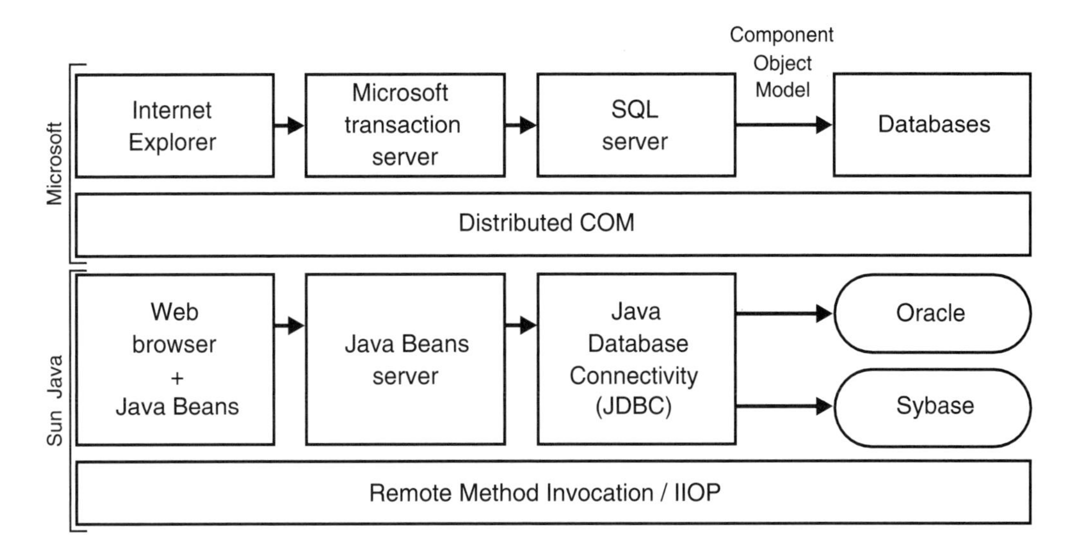

CHAPTER 7

Rapid Application Development (RAD)/Prototyping

Introduction

Rapid Application Development (RAD) is a process designed for high-speed application development as defined by Mark Trescowthick.[1] RAD products tend to be complete—and relatively small, non-complex systems. RAD is not a new concept; as introduced in 1989 by James Martin, it represents a methodology for small, focused teams that produce systems quickly. This approach relied on team dynamics and the use of tools to produce the desired reduction in development schedules. A RAD process is schedule-driven, recognizing that project scope must be flexible to accommodate a fixed schedule. The article "Achieving Software Quality in a RAD Process"[2] notes that changes in scope, also known as scope creep, cannot be tolerated in a RAD process. Project management must keep the customer involved to control creeping scope and forever prototyping.[3]

In *Wicked Problems, Righteous Solutions,*[4] the authors discuss three primary prototyping models:

1. prototyping to achieve better requirements
2. simulation, which also attempts to achieve better requirements
3. prototyping as the application development itself.

They say that RAD is mostly considered to be item 3; however, to "broaden" V&V coverage in this chapter, the RAD issues include prototyping and simulating. It has been noted that prototyping reduces the cost and time to develop software, improves communications between developers and users, and improves communications among developers themselves (pp. 3, 146).

Roger Pressman[5] says

> for software prototyping to be effective, a prototype must be developed rapidly so that the customer may assess results and recommend changes. To conduct rapid prototyping, three generic

classes of methods and tools are available: fourth-generation techniques, reusable software components, formal specification, and prototyping environments. Fourth-generation techniques encompass a broad array of database query and reporting languages, program and application generators, and other very high-level nonprocedural languages. Because fourth-generation techniques enable the developer to generate executable code quickly, they are ideal for rapid prototyping. (pp. 192–193)

Pressman further asserts:

another approach to rapid prototyping is to assemble, rather than build, the prototype by using a set of existing software components. A software component may be a data structure (or database), a software architectural component (i.e., a program), or a procedural component (i.e., a module). In each case the software component must be designed in a manner that enables it to be reused without detailed knowledge of its internal workings. Melding prototyping and program component reuse will work only if a library system is developed so that components that do exist can be catalogued and then retrieved. Although a number of tools have been developed to meet this need, much work remains to be done in the area. It should be noted that an existing software product can be used as a prototype for a "new, improved" competitive product. In a way, this is a form of reusability for software prototyping. (p. 193)

Pressman also says:

a number of formal specification languages and tools have been developed as a replacement for natural language specification techniques.... Developers of these formal languages are in the process of developing interactive environments that (a) enable an analyst to interactively create a language-based specification of a system or software, (b) invoke automated tools that translate the language-based specification into executable code, and (c) enable the customer to use the prototype executable code to refine formal requirements. (p. 193)

Using this prototyping or RAD methodology enables organizations to develop strategically important systems faster, while reducing development costs and maintaining quality. This is achieved by using a series of proven application development techniques within a well-defined methodology. These techniques from SystemHouse's RAD methodology[6] include the use of (a) small, well-trained development teams, (b) evolutionary prototypes, (c) integrated power tools that support modeling, prototyping, and component re-usability, (d) a central repository, (e) interactive requirements and design workshops, and (f) rigid limits on development time frames. Later, these techniques are examined in relation to V&V.

At the highest level, Robert Lewis[7] explains that:

prototyping tools allow the developer to begin defining the system, usually on a CRT screen with a series of symbols and interconnections. The more sophisticated tools allow the user to define icons (symbols that look a little like the thing it is portraying). As the model grows, it can have attributes such as behavior and physical properties associated with the icons and can be made to execute the model in a specified order. More and more detail can be added until the system architecture is pretty well laid out and confirmed to be reasonable. V&V, then, works with the rapid prototype to determine its completeness and how well it solves the system problem. The major shortcoming with the current tools of this type is that none of them produce a traditional specification, so someone has to interpret the graphical specifica-

> tion and then write the system and software specifications based on this prototype and perform verification using simulations and modeling. (p. 74)

Lewis goes on to say simulations and modeling should not be attempted unless a framework already exists from another similar project. Rapid prototyping tools can also be used in place of simulations to assess system architecture. Even then it is recommended that the effort be focused only on critical parts of the system. These efforts take a significant investment in computer resources, manpower, and time. Another alternative is to build an elaborate benchmark program that is representative of the types of processing that the new system will be expected to perform and have the manufacturers run it while it is being witnessed.

Mark Trescowthick[1] believes that Steve McConnell's book, *Code Complete,*[8] may be the bible on programming in the RAD environment. Others have mentioned McConnell's *Rapid Development: Taming Wild Software Schedules*[9] as another premier book in this RAD area. Steve McConnell[8] uses the term "evolutionary delivery" to describe an approach to software development that fairly quickly releases operational capabilities that are a subset of the customer's requirements. The term often used to describe this is "builds." McConnell asks "Is evolutionary delivery a form of prototyping?" No. It is different in several ways. Prototyping is always exploratory. Its goal might be to determine the functionality that the customer really wants. The point might be to explore the user interface or to refine the feature set, or some other function of the software (pp. 671–672).

McConnell's ideas continue to cover the point of evolutionary delivery as being less exploratory. Each version of the product is supposed to be acceptable, and each version is supposed to be a step toward a final product. One might or might not plan to respond to the customer's requests for changes. The point might simply be to get an initial version of the software into the customer's hands more quickly.

"Much RAD/prototyping is in line with Fred Brook's suggestion of build one to throw away," continues McConnell.[8] "The idea is to build a cheap version to refine the software concept and then build the fast, small, robust version using a traditional development cycle. With evolutionary delivery, one does not build one to throw away. One simply sequences the construction tasks so that a part of the system is available sooner rather than later. Some forms of prototyping include a plan to keep the prototype, eventually evolving it into finished software. Such an approach can be tantamount to an evolutionary delivery approach. However, in general, prototyping can occur without evolutionary delivery and evolutionary delivery can occur without prototyping" (p. 671). There are prototypes and simulations that fall within the elements of this chapter (i.e., development that is RAD).

Paul Herzlich[10] relates that the skeptical are sure that RAD can only mean a license to hack, whereas the experienced quickly realize that a three letter acronym is not a panacea. One may ask how RAD can be different from making it up as one goes along. One company's standard states "The simulation and models not only provide a means to predict performance, but also are an essential item in the verification and validation of performance"[11] (p. 5). Herzlich continues that when the focus is on almost any other aspect of software development except prototypes, models, or simulations, these items are the V&V tools and methods. This chapter, however, is looking at the details of performing V&V on RAD, often as instantiated as prototypes, models, or simulations.

The challenge of RAD from "Achieving Software Quality in a RAD Process"[2] is the focus on development speed, which places the following pressures on the development team and the V&V of the development:

- Steps are omitted to reduce cycle times.
- Scope is improperly defined and managed in relation to the delivery time frame.
- System design and development are initiated with an incomplete understanding of the requirements.

In this chapter, these pressures are covered with an emphasis on their relationship to V&V.

Multidimensional Model

RAD/prototyping falls on the process axis of the multidimensional model for V&V. It is an alternative life-cycle/development model, not a design methodology; it is certainly not on the application axis, even though application is a part of its name.

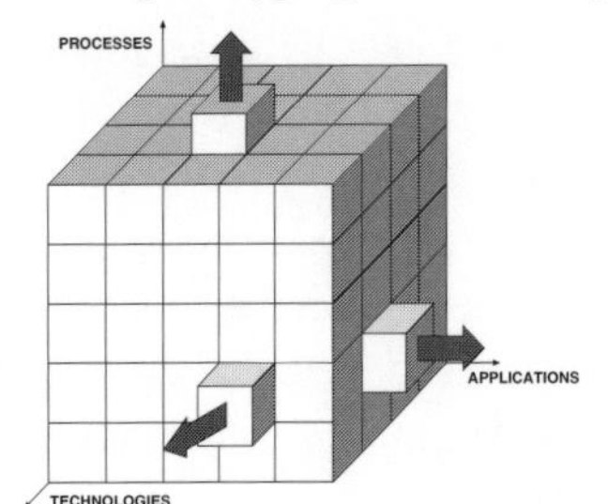

The processes that impact on RAD are methodologies as mentioned in this chapter, such as OO, inspections, and documentation. These processes can be significant contributors to the success or failure of a RAD. For example, documentation of the system is critical, but is the time for proper documentation in a RAD? This type of issue is addressed in this chapter.

The interaction with the technology axis is strong, because of the very high use of tools in the V&V of RAD. CASE tools are essential in this area because of the speed of development. A number of these toolsets are discussed in this chapter for the V&V of RAD. Other "technology" impacts on RAD include client/server networks, Internet/intranet, and GUI. All of these require a quick response to market, and RAD provides the solution. Often, it is too tempting to ignore the V&V of RAD to meet these market pressures. This chapter focuses back on that V&V of RAD, so that the development is rapid, but the product receives adequate V&V.

Traditional V & V

In this section, the concepts introduced above of fourth-generation techniques and prototyping are covered from their traditional V&V perspective. Supporting concepts are also discussed, such as contrasting development approaches for different application scopes, joint application development (JAD) used with RAD, and just-in-time (JIT) development (implying RAD).

Fourth-Generation Techniques

Fourth-generation techniques, introduced above as a viable technique for RAD, have become a rather traditional method. Their presence and use are pervasive. Because they are automated code producers, it is especially important for the V&V person to be involved as the analysis and design are being accomplished. A significant change for verification of fourth-generation techniques is the imposition of a design expert to interpret the adequacy of what is going into the fourth-generation language that results in code. Of course, the validation of the results of the fourth-generation language is appropriate if a V&V or test person tests the results of what was automatically generated.

Prototyping

Prototyping of the user interface is the most effective way to elicit user requirements and to improve usability of applications (see Chapter 8). The concepts that follow are abstracted from Anthony Wasserman's "Toward a Discipline of Software Engineering:"[12]

> Over the past few years, prototyping of graphical user interfaces has become a central component of RAD. This step is supported by a wide variety of GUI builders and user interface management systems, including both stand-alone and RAD tools. User interface prototyping is traditionally associated with the development of interactive information systems. However, such prototyping also plays an important role in many embedded systems: Copy machines, automated teller machines, and aircraft all contain software with an important user interface component. [This method] combines prototyping of the user interface, a systematic approach to software development, and a set of supporting tools; it also introduced a three-part architecture for such systems, separating the user interface from system operations and the database, which allowed interface design to be treated independently. (This same architectural structure is now common in client/server systems [See chapter 9].) Experience with such prototyping approaches has shown that the user interface is a key determinant of system usability and user satisfaction and that users working with the prototype were better able to contribute to the analysis process. [The V&V lesson here is that prototyping involves the users earlier, giving a higher probability of delivering the right product.]
>
> Over the past decade, GUIs have become nearly universal. It quickly became clear that the skills needed for designing good user interfaces are quite different from those needed for other aspects of software development. The needed expertise is likely to increase as new forms of interactivity, such as speech and gesturing, become more common. Many software product teams now include user interface experts and conduct extensive usability tests on their interfaces at an early stage of the development process. Applications for simulation, visualization, and charting are user-interface intensive, with half or more of the finished code related to the GUI. The same is true for games, where video, sound, and 3D graphics are a key part of the interactive experience.
>
> Repeated prototyping of the user interface is a natural step when following a spiral* approach to application development. For large projects this prototyping activity should be treated as a V&V part of the analysis and design process, not as a shortcut to rapid system deployment.

* See Chapter 2 for a picture of the spiral model of software development.

> Different types of software need differing degrees of development infrastructure. [Figure 7.1] shows the contrast between enterprise-wide applications, for which controlled development is needed, and individual and department-level applications, for which RAD methods may suffice. (pp. 25–30)

Recent improvements to the software engineering process include the widespread acceptance of object oriented techniques, and the demand for application programming interfaces (APIs) draws from the fundamental ideas of abstraction and modularity. These concepts underlie the Internet and the World Wide Web. Similarly, today's RAD tools came into existence because their creators recognized the value of reusable components and standard architectures and incorporated them into a visual tool. Claude Bauer, in *The Washington Post,*[13] noted that the Magic tool from Magic Software Enterprises allows software developers to work with database tables through dialog boxes, rather than writing code. It uses a totally table-driven approach to client/server application development. Java is particularly interesting because it facilitates large-scale reuse through its built-in class libraries and provides machine independence through a layer of abstraction (the Java virtual machine). Bauer[13] also noted that the Sun Microsystem's Java Studio tool has many RAD aspects to it, because developers can assemble Java applets by stringing together Java Beans. Collectively, such tools help to reduce the time needed to build and to modify systems, thereby requiring V&V to be closely involved up-front, so that RAD development is assured to be correct.

"During the development of a complex conceptual application, specifying the end-users' needs could be difficult because they often do not know exactly what they want until they can see

Figure 7.1 Contrasting development approaches for different application scopes (© 1996 IEEE).[12], (p. 28)

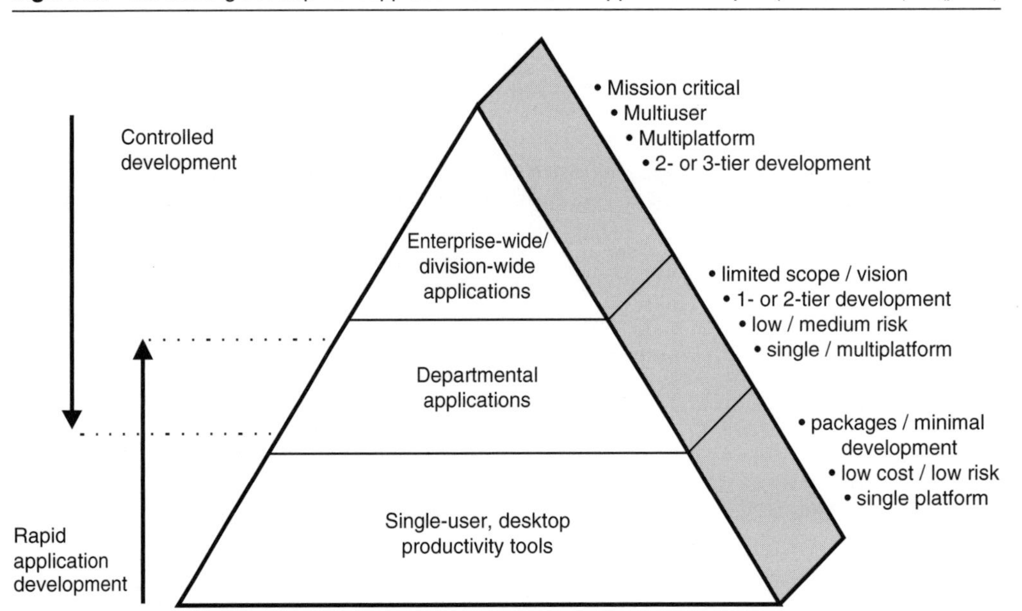

or use a prototype (working model of the product). Even if they have a working model of the product, very often major misunderstandings among the end-users surface, and inconsistencies may be uncovered." Olu Omolayole[14] of Grambling State University provides the concepts related:

> One thing to remember is that different end-users have different interpretations of the same data. They sometimes may find parts of the software product confusing, especially the screens. Thus, operating a system for a few weeks may change their perceptions of what they really want. What is recommended is an incremental development step in which the product development staff works with the end-users to create the first prototype of the product. Then the prototype is tested by the end-users, modifications are made if necessary, and the prototype is tested again. The cycle, which consists mainly of modifying and testing and is commonly referred to as prototype development life-cycle (PDLC), continues until the end-users are satisfied with the product. Then the final product is built from the final modification. The end-user's perception of quality is very important in the final determination of what constitutes a quality software product; hence, a PDLC should be used in the engineering process of a software product. (p. 3.11-2)

Although the PDLC is again traditional development, unless maturing prototypes are each sufficiently verified the final product will not be as expected. Each prototype cycle may be thought of as a RAD. PDLC combined with Joint Application Development (JAD) and management participation of the end-users is depicted in the software prototyping process management flowchart (Figure 7.2). Omolayole says, "The process starts by constructing the first prototype from the product specification. Then the end-users are given the opportunity to interact and test the prototype. An Eu-GSSJAD session is held to resolve open or conflicting issues relating to the prototype. The management is consulted about the modifications to be made to the prototype. Then the prototype is modified and the end-users are again given the opportunity to interact and test the modified prototype. The cycle continues until the end-users are satisfied with the prototype" (p. 3.11–5). This addresses one of the challenges of RAD, "steps omitted to reduce cycle times," mentioned in the Introduction to this chapter.

Mark McDonald[2] tells us that JAD along with quality function deployment (QFD) facilitate the identification and analysis of the requirements. V&V should assure that this analysis effort produces a requirement's specification containing the system's event, data and process models, functional requirements and quality attributes (p. 3.2-6).

Steven R. Rakitin in *Software Verification and Validation: A Practitioner's Guide*[15] makes us aware that there are significant advantages and disadvantages to RAD/prototyping. Advantages of RAD/prototyping are:

1. Users own the requirements, which reduces the likelihood of misunderstanding or misinterpretation
2. The developers are confident that they are building the right product
3. For those situations in which customers do not know exactly what they need, RAD/prototyping provides a means of requirements discovery.

Figure 7.2 An end-user-oriented prototype development process management.[14] (p. 3.11-5)

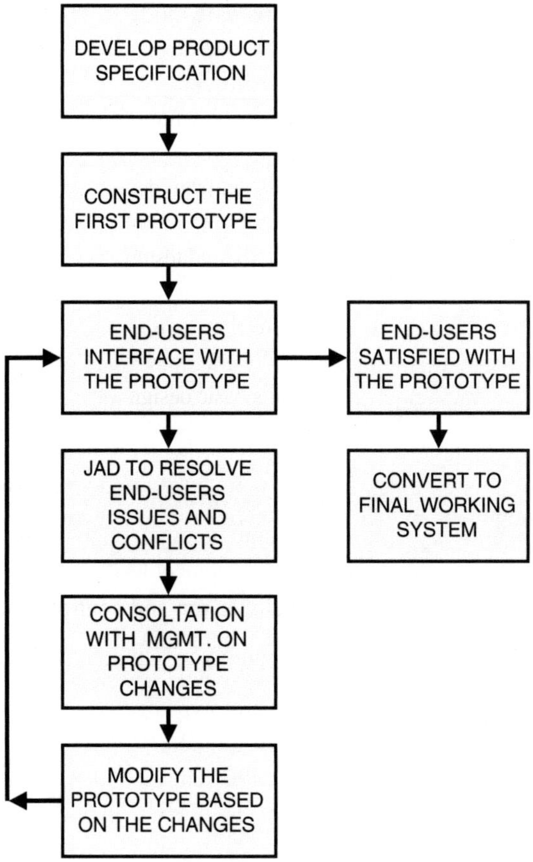

DEVELOP PRODUCT SPECIFICATION
CONSTRUCT THE FIRST PROTOTYPE
END-USERS INTERFACE WITH THE PROTOTYPE
END-USERS SATISFIED WITH THE PROTOTYPE
CONVERT TO FINAL WORKING SYSTEM
JAD TO RESOLVE END-USERS ISSUES AND CONFLICTS
CONSOLTATION WITH MGMT. ON PROTOTYPE CHANGES
MODIFY THE PROTOTYPE BASED ON THE CHANGES

Disadvantages of RAD/prototyping are:

1. Major problems for long term support and maintenance of the product can occur depending on how the prototype was developed
2. Extensive participation and involvement of the customer is required, which is not always possible
3. Software validation is difficult because requirements usually are not well documented
4. Because of the short time frame, the developers often act as the testers (pp. 2–19).

The following ideas of verification and validation testing are from Robert Lewis.[16] With testers acting as developers, the only source of independent testing is likely to be relegated to V&V. This is an acceptable practice, if it is incorporated into the proper plans. Ignored, it will definitely cause big problems. Verification tests typically examine and confirm functional performance and configuration integrity, while validation tests examine operation and behavior in the context of the real world and the real system being modeled. A real-life example of this situation is related by Selby and Cusumano in *Microsoft Secrets: How the World's Most Powerful Software Company Creates Technology, Shapes Markets, and Manages People.*[17] Their example relates how V&V personnel became the only testers, which led to a condition of infinite testing on poor prototype releases.

Lewis[16] tells us that verification is distinguished from development testing, in that (a) development tests support the process of compatibility analysis between components and the test control center, allow the network to be brought online incrementally and tested, and support component-to-environment testing, and (b) verification tests typically continue this process by testing the pieces of an operational node, examining major functions to ensure that requirements… are met, and that specified capabilities and performance are provided. Verification tests ask the question, "Did the developer build that node correctly, and does the component meet its basic design criteria and specifications?…" (p. 6).

Lewis[16] continues that validation testing occurs once testers begin to observe and measure interactions, behaviors, and effectiveness of components in a realistic operational setting. A realistic operational setting means that V&V focuses on off-nominal conditions. Under tight schedule constraints in RAD, developers focus only on nominal testing to mostly demonstrate functionality, rather than for errors. The difference between development tests (developer-initiated and run) and validation tests (V&V-initiated and often developer-run and controlled, although it is clear that V&V require resources) needs to be delineated. These validation tests should not interfere with development testing; in fact, it is just an extension of it. Using this concept, everyone knows from the beginning what it will take to ensure that the prototype performs as required.

Another aspect of validation is the reference model. To what is the performance of the prototype compared, while asserting that we have a "sufficiently" valid model? The real system issues, other known simulations with known performance, in-depth analysis and evaluation, other real-world sources, and subject matter experts are all used for comparison.

The Jet Propulsion Laboratory (JPL) has begun using multiple deliveries and a strong verification technique of modified Fagan inspections to shorten software development life cycle time. Griesel and Welz[18] share that these modified Fagan inspections can be tailored to effectively support RAD, and help to make RAD a rigorous development process.

Contemporary V & V

In this contemporary V&V of RAD section, the special concepts associated with the following are covered, Verilog's ObjectGEODE toolset, Dynamic Systems Development Method (DSDM), Models and Simulations, and SMART (Susceptibility Model Assessment and Range Test), which is a particular version of V&V and accreditation. Each of these tools and methods, although relatively new, have a proven track record in industry and government.

Callahan and Easterbrook's experiences with "Verification and Validation in a Rapid Software Development Process"[20] lead off this section as abstracted from Dr. Callahan's GSFC Software Engineering Workshop presentation. "Many RAD organizations are composed of two distinct and complementary subgroups: (a) Design ('the builder')—responsible for system requirements, design, implementation, and testing of nominal functionality; (b) Analysis ('the breakers')—responsible for analysis of requirements, design, implementation, and testing of nominal and off-nominal behaviors; [they also] play a constructively critical role in development (not adversarial)."

The focus of the Design group becomes myopic with regard to nominal behaviors of the system under construction as schedules compress. An independent advocate/analyst of off-nominal behaviors (e.g., faults, unexpected conditions) is needed to complement this bias. In a rapid development environment the use of issue reports can become a major way for V&V to be able to provide timely response to Design. Figure 7.3 shows the flow of the issue report between V&V and Design teams.

"An issue report contains details of an inconsistency identified during the development process. An issue report contains information such as:

- description of the problem
- phase in which the problem was found
- criticality of the problem
- proposed solutions and options.

Issues are best reported directly to the Design group (not through management unless necessary). Issue databases must be managed, tracked, and statistically analyzed for trends."

A brief case study from the International Space Station project was presented to illustrate V&V's role and the value of issue reports. An issue report was submitted by V&V involving the use of the MatrixX CASE tool concerning unit testing through simulation, instead of Ada-based

Figure 7.3 Issue reports from V&V to design team.[20] (p. 422)

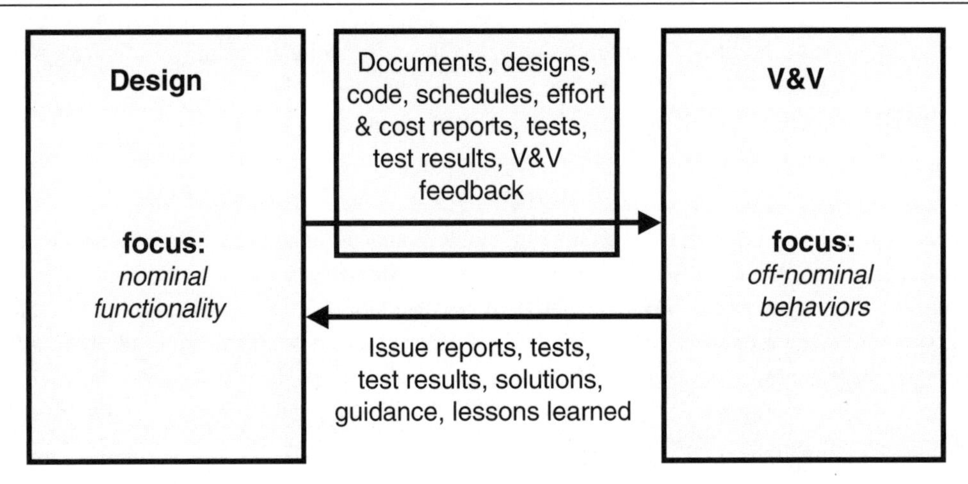

direct unit testing. "The issue was contested by the Design group, who claimed that unit testing within the [MatrixX CASE] design tool (through simulation) was adequate. [Because of] the high criticality and conflict of opinion management became involved. A research team was asked to examine the issue in detail."

There were three sub-issues:

1. Unit testing of... components is necessary to reduce the amount of system level testing to maintain release schedule.
2. Errors found during testing and mission operations are difficult to isolate and debug.
3. The generated code does not comply with Ada coding standards.

The solutions provided by the research team were "(a) use modularization mechanisms in MatrixX tool to control generation of code and preserve unit boundaries, [which may] lead to some [acceptable] inefficiencies in code size and CPU usage; (b) limit feature development in releases to help offset code bloat and processor overhead caused by modularization; (c) work with tool vendor to improve code generation and test support mechanisms. These solutions reduced turnaround time for V&V analysis by reducing system level tests on generated... code and enabling unit testing."

The conclusions of this case study are:

- High-level design and simulation are beneficial to productivity and quality.
- V&V is an essential part of rapid development itself.
- V&V is not just an add-on "insurance."
- Rapid development processes need some form of iterative analysis to guide system design evolution.
- More empirical studies of the dialectic between design and analysis are needed.
- Collection of issues made easier through automated tools and e-mail.

ObjectGEODE Toolset

There are some RAD tools and toolsets that provide an aid in the V&V of RAD. An example of such a toolset is Verilog's ObjectGEODE; the information provided here was retrieved from the Verilog Web pages.[21 & 22] ObjectGEODE is a tool set dedicated to analysis, design, verification, and validation through simulation, code generation, and testing of real-time and distributed applications. Such applications are used in many fields such as telecommunications, aerospace, defense, process control, or medical systems. ObjectGEODE supports a coherent integration of complementary approaches based on standards. These standards are (a) Rumbaugh's OMT (Object Modeling Technique), (b) SDL (Specification and Description Language) issued from an international standard organization, ITU-T (formerly CCITT), and (c) MSC (Message Sequence Chart) also issued from ITU-T. ObjectGEODE includes a formal verification and validation tool to graphically detect before coding starts, any pathological behavior pattern or show proof that the ObjectGEODE description complies with requirements.

Features of ObjectGEODE for RAD development are rather extensive, and include:

- RAD and V&V techniques
- ObjectGEODE simulator presentation
- Interactive simulation
- Random simulation for verification purpose
- Validation and observation techniques
- Exhaustive simulation
- Simulation strategy
- Test generation
- Integration of external code and openness
- Restrictions and extensions to SDL
- Advanced features, such as creation of script files.

Verification of the models is achieved by enabling the V&V specialist to view the behavior of the system and access all the dynamic information, such as current values of the variables. Errors such as deadlocks, live locks, or dead code are highlighted, if encountered. Because of its focus on simulations, this toolset is particularly useful in the V&V of RAD.

DSDM

The Dynamic Systems Development Method (DSDM) was launched in February, 1995. It is a non-proprietary RAD method which has been developed through capturing the experiences of a large consortium of vendor and user organizations. The consortium includes companies such as IBM, ICL, British Airways, BT, Logica, Data Sciences, and many others with an interest in contributing to a common understanding of how to conduct, manage, and control RAD projects. The beginning of this DSDM section is extracted from articles by Jennifer Stapleton: "A Quality Approach to Rapid Application Development"[23] and "DSDM in a TickIT Environment."[24]

> Since the focus of DSDM is on producing quality software to tight time scales, it is fast becoming the de facto standard for all RAD projects in the U.K. DSDM supplies a set of criteria that should be checked every time its use is considered on a project. There should be evidence that this check has been made. Given that the emphasis of controls are very different for rapid development, if problems arise, disaster can ensue if DSDM is chosen for the wrong reason (i.e., "we want the system now and we do not care about the rest of the selection criteria"). The converse is also true. If traditional controls are applied to RAD, the project will probably not succeed in delivering quality software to the business when it wants it.
>
> The RAD approach to development is viewed by many skeptics as a license to return to the uncontrolled practices of the early days of computing. The aim of DSDM is to build quality into this approach. The method is certainly designed to deliver systems in tight time scales, but such systems will also meet the quality criterion of being fit for purpose. A fundamental assumption of the DSDM approach is that nothing is built perfectly the first time, but that a usable and useful 80% of the solution can be produced in 20% of the time it would have taken

to produce the total solution. A key principle of DSDM is that satisfying the business requirements has a higher priority than the quality of the system's operational characteristics—build the right system before you build it right!—which is an interesting paraphrase of Barry Boehm's succinct definition of validation—"build the right product." (p. 18)

Stapleton[23] continues,

DSDM is a framework of controls for rapid and responsive delivery of software systems. It provides a generic process that has to be tailored for use in a particular organization depending on the business and technical constraints. The method outlines a five-stage process (Figure 7.4): feasibility study, business study, functional modeling, design and build, and finally, implementation in the working environment. Each stage of the process has a minimum set of products emanating from it. Each of the products has a defined purpose and a set of quality criteria by which achievement of that purpose can be assessed. The quality criteria are necessarily minimal to enable tailoring either on an organization-wide basis or on a project-by-project basis. For example, one product is a set of design prototyping review documents. Their stated purpose is to:

- record user feedback for all design prototypes
- help steer future DSDM developments clear of any pitfalls that have been encountered
- highlight any areas that should be implemented or tuned either during the building of the system or following delivery of the system.

Figure 7.4 DSDM 5-stage process.[24] (p. 18)

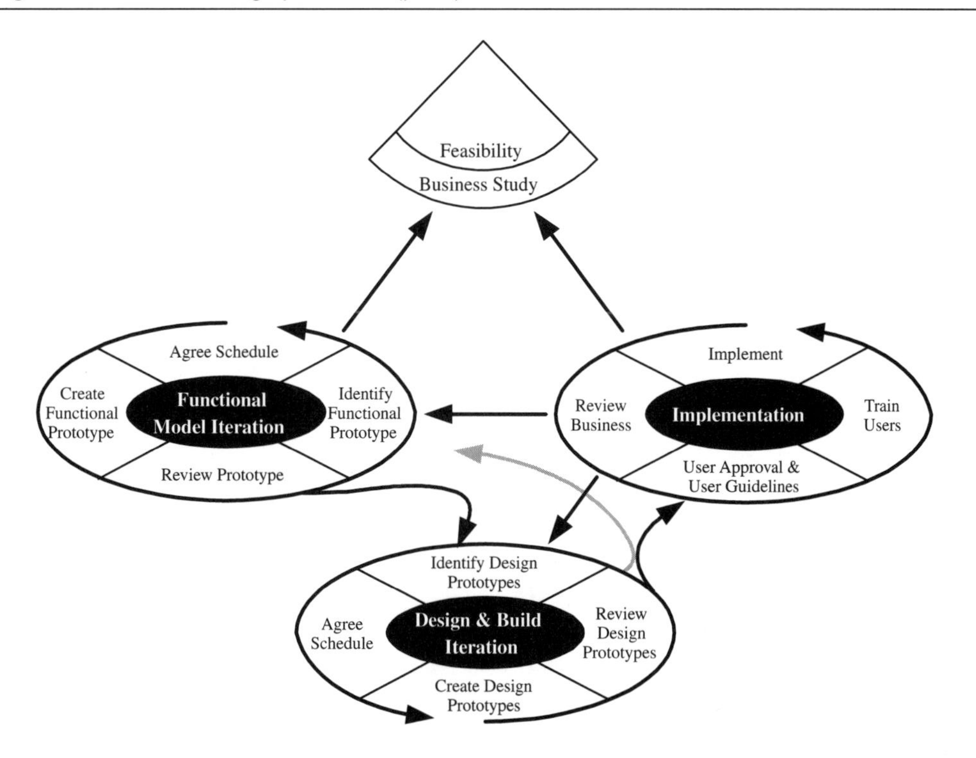

The associated quality criteria are:

- Do the review documents cover all design prototypes?
- Are all comments from users and/or developers recorded to their satisfaction?

The content and format of review documents are not defined, nor how they are produced or stored. Furthermore, DSDM does not define any method for recording review results nor for verifying any corrective actions. All these procedural aspects are left to the organization itself to define based on local practices.

The major difference between DSDM and traditional approaches to software development (Figure 7.5) is the shift away from fixing the requirements (and delivering software which satisfies all of them) while allowing time and resources to vary during development. In DSDM the exact opposite is true, time and resources are fixed for the life of a project, but requirements are allowed to change. (p. 18)

A further examination of the DSDM five-stage life cycle is beneficial. Stapleton[23] says:

To ensure a controlled transition between stages, preconditions for entry into each stage are defined. The preconditions are both management-based and product-related. The feasibility study assesses the suitability of the application for prototyping against criteria defined by DSDM and checks that certain technical and managerial conditions are likely to be met. Once the short feasibility study is complete, the business study scopes the overall activity of the project. Again, this is a short stage. The bulk of development work is in the two iteration stages where prototypes are built incrementally towards the tested system, which is placed in the user environment during the implementation stage.

The prime focus of the functional stage is on prototyping to elicit requirements; for the design and build stage, the focus is on ensuring that the prototypes are sufficiently well engineered for production-quality software. Each iteration may be navigated a number of times, usually no more than three. It should be noted that the dividing line between these phases is not as clear cut as Figure 7.4 suggests. Some components of a system may well pass from the functional proto-

Figure 7.5 RAD vs. traditional development.[24, p. 19]

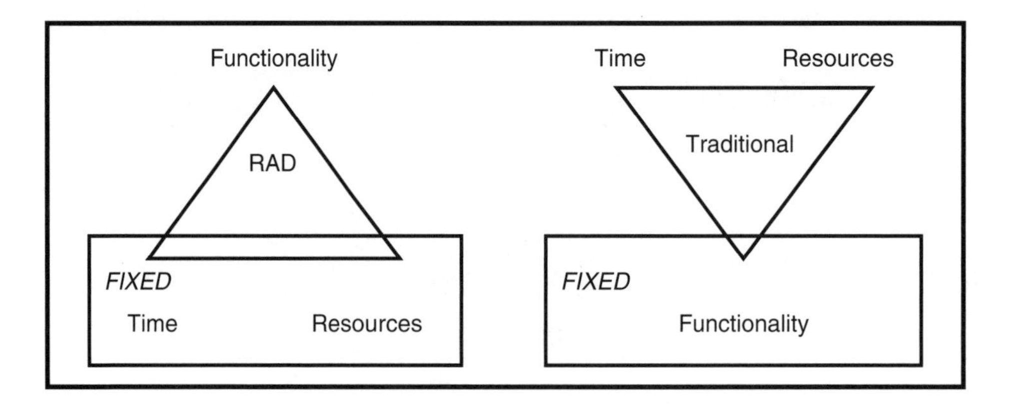

type iteration to the design-and-build iteration, while other components are still very sketchy or even nonexistent.

The preconditions for moving from functional modeling to system design-and-build include agreement of a functional prototype which may or may not be fully automated (depending on the application and on the development environment). The agreement of the functional prototype may be for only part of the functional model. This means that system design-and-build activities may happen concurrently with the functional prototyping activities. Similarly in a large DSDM development the implementation may be phased, so system design may be concurrent with some implementation.

This approach is not as chaotic as it might at first appear. Each cycle consists of four phases: identify the prototype to be built and define its objectives and quality criteria; agree on the time scale for the cycle; build or enhance the prototype focusing on the objectives of the cycle; and finally, review the prototype in its current state against the objectives set out at the beginning of the cycle. This approach is perfectly in line with the best tenets of quality control: Say what you are going to do, do it, and then check that you did it. The results of reviews feed into the setting of objectives for the next cycle. This addresses another of the challenges of RAD; that is, system design and development initiated with an incomplete understanding of the requirements. (pp. 3–4)

Stapleton[23] continues:

In line with its philosophy of ensuring a controlled approach to RAD, DSDM also describes how configuration management should be carried out. The dynamic nature of DSDM renders good configuration management essential. In a development project using DSDM, there are more things happening at once and products being delivered at a faster rate per week than would occur during traditional development of a system of a similar size. Therefore it is imperative that strict control is kept on the products as they achieve completion (whether partial or otherwise).

During prototyping activities, developers may well be working on the same product. This is particularly true of the data structures that are common to all. It is therefore necessary for all developers to know that they are working with information that is controlled and in a known state, and that they can resolve clashes or prevent the possibility of them occurring. Also, a prototype may go down a blind alley. When this occurs, the ability to return to a known, safe state before setting off again is essential.

The control of products must be an integral part of the development team activities. Using the more "standard" approach of having a librarian who is not part of the team or a configuration management manager who is an organization-wide administrator will endanger the speed of the development process. In DSDM the control of configuration items rests with the development team. In this way the possibility of bottlenecks that can arise through using a third party who has different priorities from those of the developers will be eliminated.

It is the developers who must make the decisions as to what impact a particular change will have. It is they who decide what the configuration items are and when a product they are working on is to become a configuration item. Guidance is provided within the method as to what should be considered suitable as a configuration item. For instance, during development of a database, each field should be a configuration item to ensure that all team members are using the same data definitions. One high-level configuration item is a prototype. This should never be placed under configuration management on its own, but should be bundled together with all relevant tests, test results, and comments resulting from demonstrations. This allows verification of the status of a prototype if backtracking is required and demonstrates that the appropriate checks have been performed before moving on to further development. (p. 2)

Prototyping is something of a misnomer for the activity undertaken in a DSDM project; more correctly, this is a RAD. It is not experimental, as suggested by the name. It is really the development of small increments of software to meet short-term objectives based on the high-level requirements for the system. However, since prototyping is [the industry-accepted terminology], DSDM has somewhat reluctantly kept the name while ensuring that the supporting controls will remove the possibly negative image that the term might imply in quality-conscious quarters.... (p. 2)

The best way of showing a user what the developers are doing is through demonstration of a working model—a prototype. The normal problems of visualization evaporate with the strong use of incremental prototyping in DSDM. Many organizations may feel uncomfortable with using prototypes as system models rather than the more conventional paper-based models, but if prototyping activity is properly controlled, such worries are unnecessary. (p. 3)

This shift in emphasis has a number of implications. The first implication is the need for prototyping in close collaboration with knowledgeable users who have been empowered to make decisions. Only by seeing a demonstration of how the system will work can the users be sure it is the right system. The second implication is the need for iterative development. As soon as the users see the system they will want to make changes and create a further prototype. Thirdly, planning focuses on the high-priority components of the system before worrying about developing the less important aspects of the system. This differs from the "normal" approach to project planning where the assumption is that everything in a specification will be delivered. (p. 1–2)

McDonald[2] tells us that a RAD process requires a robust approach to managing scope. Time-boxing is used by many RAD processes as the tool to meet this challenge. A time-box is a fixed set of resources (people and time) assigned to a specific set of activities. The time-box acts as a limit on the systems development resource, with this limit being the primary weapon in combating scope creep. However, the time-box approach is a blunt means of managing scope, as it uses a binary set of priorities that do not provide sufficient guidance to deal with the legitimate scope issues. Every priority in a time-box is expressed in binary terms: the requirement is either in scope (and therefore in the time-box) or out of scope (and therefore out of the time-box).[2]

Stapleton[23] continues,

Requirements are baselined early in the project at a high-level to allow their refinement through prototyping activity, but more importantly in a RAD project, they have to be clearly prioritized. All activity is time-boxed. During a time-box a particular set of mandatory requirements will be dealt with, and any time left at the end of the time-box will be used to add in some or all of the associated "nice to haves." Any of the lesser requirements which cannot be fit into the time available are either considered for inclusion in the next cycle or they may be left to later enhancement work after the project is over. If during a time-box new requirements are discovered, their relative priorities are discussed and recorded. Since time-boxed activity has a clear cut-off date, the introduction of new requirements means that the possibility of dropping existing requirements to a lower priority to allow their implementation is negotiated. In a DSDM project, desirable features may not always be provided, but time constraints are always met.

Stapleton[24] relates that:

A time-box lasts typically between two and six weeks and will produce something visible in order for progress and quality to be assessed. Each time-box should be kicked off with a meeting to decide the relative priorities of the work to be undertaken based on previous completion of work and to assign the acceptance criteria to each of the requirements. These decisions are left until the time-box starts since it would be pointless to attempt work that depends on requirements which were supposed to have been addressed in an earlier time-box but which have had to be dropped due to time pressures. Each time-box will be subdivided into three parts: investigation (a quick pass to see whether the team is taking the right direction), refinement (to build on the comments resulting from the review at the end of investigation), and finally consolidation to tie up any loose ends. This format means that the acceptance criteria will be used at the end of refinement in order to decide what needs to be done to produce the deliverable which satisfies at least the minimum usable subset of requirements. (p. 19)

Reviews are a key element with the use of the time-box in RAD. All reviews should have their comments recorded. Reviews are usually informally run, but they should be formally documented. Most importantly, reviews do not consist of putting a large document out for comment over a period of, say, two weeks. If the total length of the project is three months, then waiting two weeks for comments is unacceptable. Review comments are key documents in controlling the direction and quality of a DSDM project.

If the time-box is producing working software, the acceptance criteria should be defined as test cases at the start of the time-box, but detailed test scripts should not be produced until testing takes place: There is little point in producing detailed test scripts against optional requirements that may not be satisfied by the delivered software. The preferred approach is to document, at the time of applying a particular test case, the actions that were taken, the data that were used, and the system responses that resulted. DSDM advocates the use of capture-and-replay tools in order to alleviate the burden of documentation that this could put on the team. Such tools will also facilitate regression testing, which is an important feature of the iterative and incremental approach to development that DSDM takes. DSDM also recommends the use of other testing tools in order to alleviate the human burden wherever it can he automated. For instance, static code analyzers provide a degree of inspections almost for free and eliminate the need to wait for other verification. Also, dynamic analysis tools can be used during demonstrations and functional tests to detect errors that might otherwise be missed. (pp. 19–20)

This addresses another of the challenges of RAD: scope improperly defined and managed in relation to the delivery time frame. Stapleton[23] asserts:

The acceptability of the tested system is assessed against the agreed minimum useful set of requirements rather than all the requirements. By allowing secondary requirements, rather than time, to slip, the project is meeting its quality objective of delivering a usable system to the business when it is required rather than delivering all the bells and whistles too late to gain maximum business benefit. (p. 4)

The remainder of this DSDM section is abstracted from Paul Herzlich's "A Quick Win for Testing."[10]

> For testers, the short time scales are initially the most discouraging aspect of RAD. Even in the best of circumstances in waterfall-based development projects, testing is squeezed—used as contingency for development slippages. How will there ever be enough time to test in RAD? Even more importantly, the lack of a complete specification shakes the theoretical foundations of formal testing. Deterministic testing is based on comparing the results of a test against a specification that allows you to predict the result expected. How can you test, if you do not have a specification? Before we condemn RAD on this point, we should question whether waterfall-based developments provide adequate specifications for testing. They should in theory, but they often do not in practice. In the RAD life-cycle [PDLC] it is expected that testing must cope with both tight time scales and incomplete specifications. Because we expect and accommodate these constraints in DSDM, and for other reasons that are structural to the RAD life-cycle, we may actually attain a higher standard of testing than we can in waterfall-based projects.
>
> The DSDM testing model is based on seven stated principles and one implicit principle. The Table 7.1 lists the principles and indicates how they relate to traditional ideas about testing. Some principles are unchanged. Others are entirely new to DSDM. In between, there are aspects of testing that are either facilitated by DSDM or are more critical than ever.
>
> DSDM does not change how a test works. Testing cannot prove there are no errors; it can only demonstrate that you have not discovered errors with the tests you have run. Testing is still error-centric, and if there is to be any control over the testing process at all, the tests that have been run must be documented. This becomes even more essential given the need to repeat tests as a prototype grows.

Table 7.1 Testing principles.[10] (p. 2)

Unchanged	
Error-centric	A good test is one that finds an error that would not be found by any other existing test.
Documented	To control testing and to make a test repeatable, it needs to be documented.
DSDM Facilities	
Testing throughout the life-cycle	Testing must be performed on software products at all stages of the life-cycle.
Independent testing	Tests should be performed by someone other than the software's author.
More Critical in DSDM	
Repeatable testing	Tests need to be repeatable as prototypes are extended, or it becomes necessary to fall back to an earlier prototype.
Automated	The only way to achieve the level of testing required is through test execution tools, dynamic analysis, and static analysis tools.
New to DSDM	
Validation	The overriding objective of testing at all stages is validation that a system meets the real business requirements.
Benefit-directed	Testing of the parts of a system that deliver the key business benefits is the highest priority.

A key feature of DSDM is that a few things are produced in the initial phases that are not destined to become part of the built, delivered product. This permits starting testing at an early stage in the life-cycle—something that has been relatively thwarted in waterfall-based developments. There is no escaping early testing in DSDM.

Independence of testing is another often unattainable ideal in waterfall-based development that is integral to the DSDM process. Users are part of the team and they are constantly in a position to test the software independently of the authors. DSDM also includes processes for demonstration and review of the product (throughout the development) to the wider user community.

Because of the iterative and incremental development of the software, repeatability of testing is more critical, and harder than ever, in DSDM. Automation has to be considered the most efficient means of achieving the repeatability. Because of the tight time scales and the complexity of software environments (like GUI and client/server), it is also essential that conventional test design techniques are supplemented with automated static and dynamic analysis. Test automation is rapidly improving in all respects, and it is genuinely feasible to keep our reliance on tools in line with the necessity for testing to keep pace with rapid code development.

Everything about the DSDM life-cycle is oriented towards ensuring that we deliver a system that meets the business requirements. The short time scales and the involvement of the user are mechanisms that keep the project on target and permit frequent, rapid course corrections. Do not reviews and testing do this in waterfall developments? Well, yes and no. In fact, most of our effort goes into verification that the output of one stage is fit to be used as the input to the next stage. Because of the number of translations (from requirements to logical design to physical design to code) and the extended time scales, verification activities are not that effective at catching the errors that eventually cause delivery of the wrong system. Validation that a system actually functions as the business requires is a very late cycle activity in the waterfall model. By the time the users do acceptance testing, too much has been invested to fix the real problems.

The focus in DSDM testing shifts away from verification and towards validation throughout. This is possible because software is available at an early stage and because the users are there to discover at an early stage whether it is fit for purpose. Tests (based on scenarios of user activities, rather than on program structure or system design) can be prepared and executed at an early stage.

The tight focus on meeting business requirements also affects how tests are prioritized in DSDM. In conventional testing, the overriding principle is risk. If you have limited testing resources (as is always the case), you must ensure that you test the areas of highest risk. It may be splitting hairs, but this is not entirely appropriate in DSDM. Rationing of test resources is guided not by risk, but by benefit. In other words, if you have limited testing resource, be sure to test those areas of the system most responsible for delivering the business benefits that justify the system's development. Sometimes the priorities arrived at by applying the risk and benefit principles will coincide, but not always.

Having set out the underlying principles, we can now examine how the test process is designed to work. DSDM is a product-based, rather than activity-based, method, so the test process is most easily understood by looking at which products undergo dynamic testing....

The dynamic testing of the built system and delivered system products should look familiar. Tests of those products may be conducted in separate stages (i.e., unit, integration, system), but this is optional, and the stages of testing should be chosen in light of the history of prototypes. Where the delivered system has evolved from earlier prototypes, the objectives of unit and integration testing will have been covered during the production of the prototypes. The main testing of the built software will normally be combined into a single test stage with system test-like flavor. In any event, DSDM does not have a "test phase" per se—testing is performed throughout the whole process. (pp. 1–4)

Herzlich, in "A Quick Win for Testing" continues:

The level of formality of testing must be reduced in DSDM because of the short time scales. To see how this is achieved, consider that the formality of testing manifests itself in several ways:

- the documentation of tests
- the formality of the techniques used to design or choose tests
- the control over the test environment and running of tests.

DSDM requires less documentation of tests. A list of conditions to test is all that is needed—to identify test coverage and to prioritize testing to focus on the areas that are most responsible for delivering the benefits. The same list is used to track test pass/fails. Prediction of expected results will not be documented in many cases, but will be based on the judgment of the testers at the time a test is run. In this type of situation, the V&V person must be closely involved to be able to evaluate test results accurately. As described below, a capture/replay tool can be used to enhance this basic level of documentation.

For most DSDM projects, testing will be a matter of designing tests from the end-user perspective via the visible user interface. User tests will be based on business scenarios. However, the developers must also ensure that the invisible functionality (e.g., database updates) and non-functional characteristics (e.g., performance) are tested. Conventional test techniques for performance testing, concurrent access, security, etc., still apply in DSDM.

When it comes to formal test case design techniques, DSDM projects are, in reality, no less rigorous than conventional projects in the commercial environment, which rarely employ formal test case design techniques. Furthermore, formal test techniques are not adequately addressed yet for testing within any life-cycle for the large body of systems now being produced that (a) have GUI front ends, (b) may be based on the client-server model, and (c) may include object oriented software. (p. 5)

The tests of the built system can be grouped into "test types" covering a class of technical or functional requirements, like business functionality, usability, performance, security, operability, and conversion. User and operator information (documentation, help, training materials) are tested in the context of one of the above tests, not as separate test types.

...Systems [usually] undergo business functionality testing. The various technical tests (such as performance, operability, etc.) are generally only required when a system will be implemented on a new platform whose technical characteristics are not already known. These tests may also be skipped or limited in scope if they have been tested earlier in a prototype.

One of the knottier problems faced in DSDM is how to test prototypes. A DSDM prototype serves two different functions:

- It is a partial build of the system that will be delivered.
- It is a technique for gathering information to clarify functional or technical requirements.

Different test criteria apply depending on the role the prototype is serving:

- Where the prototype represents the functionality of the built system, a test pass/fail can be based on whether the test result from the prototype matches an expected result based on the known requirements.
- Where the prototype is intended to clarify requirements, the criteria for test success or failure is whether the prototype generates the expected information.

A single prototype may serve in both roles and therefore be tested against a combination of both criteria. Prototypes have a mini-life-cycle with four phases, and the four phases iterate up to three times. The prototypes that are produced can fall within any of four categories. Prototypes of all categories can be tested against a mixture of "expected result" and "expected information" criteria. This iterative life-cycle is summarized in Table 7.2, which shows the categories of prototype, where in the life-cycle they are tested, and the type of criteria that will tend to apply. (p. 4)

The brief introduction to DSDM provides a basic understanding of the scope for RAD/prototyping and its power to focus V&V in such an environment.

Table 7.2 DSDM iterative life-cycle.[10] (p. 4)

	Iteration within Phase		
DSDM Phase	**Investigative**	**Refining**	**Consolidating**
Business	EI	EI/ER	ER
Usability	EI	EI/ER	ER
Performance	EI	EI	EI
Operability	EI	EI	EI

EI = expected information as test criterion
ER = expected results used as test criterion

Models and Simulations

As mentioned in the introduction to this chapter, RAD often results in a model simulation or prototype. The prototype aspect of RAD is discussed above. Below is a technique used by government and industry to focus on V&V of models and simulations. Dr. Paul Muessig, in "A 'SMART' Approach to VV&A,"[25] says a rise in the capabilities of computer model and simulation to replicate complex phenomena, coupled with a drop in defense outlays, has made model and simulation an extremely attractive alternative to costly testing in the weapons system acquisition process. Model and simulation are used in nearly all phases from concept development to operation and maintenance.

The *DoD Models and Simulations Master Plan*[26] states that recently, it has become conventional wisdom that the key elements of model and simulation credibility are V&V, configuration management, and accreditation. A few years ago, the workings of "V&V and accreditation," and the supporting functions of configuration management, were understood only by software developers, but today, the term is recognized by program managers as a valuable method. Accreditation is an official determination that a model is acceptable for a specific purpose.[26]

The *IEEE Recommended Practices Guide for the Verification, Validation, and Accreditation of Distributed Interactive Simulations,*[27] March 5, 1996 (Draft) provides the following guidance. V&V agents serve as a source of advice and expertise to the accreditation authority and accreditation agent concerning V&V issues. They develop a plan, including resource requirements, that addresses the V&V deficiencies identified by the accreditation agent while remaining within the accreditation authority-identified constraints. If this is not possible, the V&V agent(s) will work with the accreditation agent to develop risk reduction and V&V plans that together will meet accreditation authority models and simulation acceptance criteria and constraints. They perform all V&V activities and prepare the final V&V report for submission to the accreditation agent and the model and simulation V&V manager.

In the V&V and accreditation environment, special clarification of these terms is in order. Verification is the process of determining that the model and simulation accurately represent the developer's conceptual description and specifications. This is accomplished by identifying and eliminating mistakes in logic, mathematics, or programming. This process establishes that the model and simulation code and logic correctly perform the intended functions, and to what extent model and simulation development activities conform to state-of-the-practice software engineering techniques.

On the other hand, validation is the process of determining the degree to which a model is an accurate representation of the real world from the perspective of the intended uses of the model. The validation process can be used to identify model improvements, where necessary. The validation process has two main components: (a) structural validation, which includes an internal examination of model and simulation assumptions, architecture, and algorithms in the context of the intended use; and (b) output validation, which determines how well the model and simulation results compare with the perceived "real world."

In "The Development of VV&A,"[28] notice is taken that validation is often an afterthought to verification. Figure 7.6, adapted from "The Development of VV&A," provides a framework to bring validation to a higher level of usage in V&V and accreditation. The route from realization through verification to validation and then back to the problem space is added. The more usual validation process is depicted on the right of the figure where the product is validated directly to the requirements.

The Models and Simulations Master Plan, VV&A Recommended Practices Guide[26] discusses the continuum of current perceptions about V&V and accreditation. On one end of the continuum, there are those who are successfully doing V&V and accreditation. They understand that the credibility of a model is integral to the success with which it is used, and their application of model and simulation technology is, therefore, made more valuable to both their customers as well as to future users of that model who can leverage off of their V&V and accreditation accomplishments. At the other end of the continuum are those who do not know about V&V and accreditation, do not care about V&V and accreditation, argue that it is too resource intensive, and claim that V&V and accreditation do not provide added value. The majority fall in the center of the continuum. They know that they need to do V&V and accreditation, but are unsure as to what to do or how to go about it. The goal of the V&V and accreditation effort is to provide the information and tools necessary to those in the middle so that they successfully utilize V&V and accreditation.

Figure 7.6 Validation emphasis in VV&A (Adapted from "The Development of VV&A"[28])

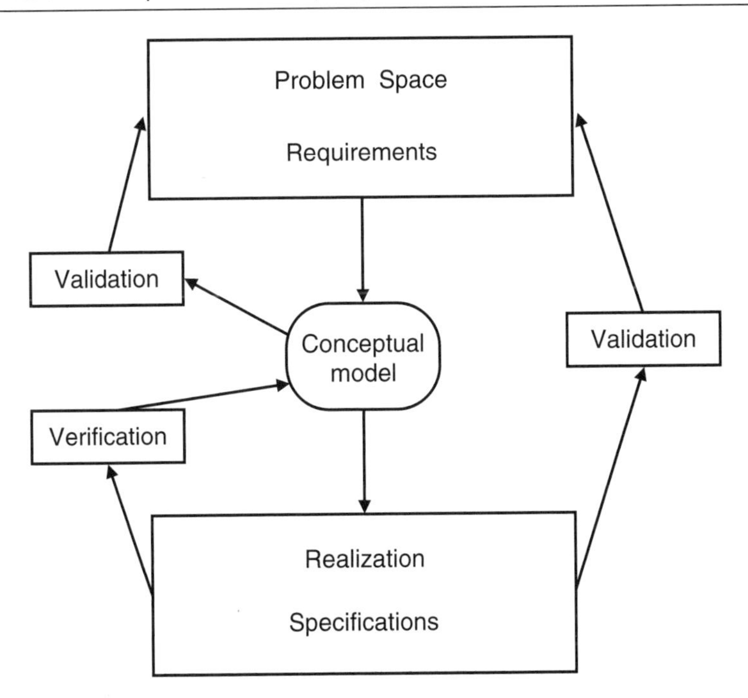

The V&V and accreditation effort recognizes that common misperceptions exist, particularly the concern among many that V&V and accreditation is too costly. There are also misunderstandings that fail to recognize that simply ensuring the V&V of the subsystems does not automatically guarantee the overall credibility of the system when everything is "connected." Conversely, V&V of a system does not imply that all of its component models are, by virtue of association, also sufficiently verified and validated for the purpose for which the system was developed.

The remainder of this section for models and simulations is abstracted from Dr. Muessig's "A 'SMART' Approach to VV&A."[25] For models and simulations Dr. Muessig relates that:

> verification establishes that software design specifications and requirements have been compared with their implementation in the code. This process flushes out design and coding errors early in the models and simulation development cycle, making them more cost-effective to repair. Verification provides documented confidence in code accuracy and in models and simulation design, assumptions, limitations, and constraints.
>
> Although reasonably straightforward for model and simulation in development, the attempt to develop a verification process for mature model and simulation, encountered four distinct challenges:
>
> 1. The codes for mature model and simulation were developed before detailed software design, coding, and verification standards were in place. The issue of which of the myriad current standards should apply, and how they should be applied, to mature model and simulation therefore became paramount.
> 2. Among model and simulation users, there was a poor understanding of the verification process in general, and no understanding of its technical elements. Developing consensus among users as to the technical constituents of verification, therefore, became difficult.
> 3. There was poor documentation of prior verification efforts, which made it difficult to avoid reinventing the wheel in some cases.
> 4. There was (and is) a profound fear of cost. This led to a tendency to avoid the verification problem altogether by redefining verification in such a way as to reduce its relevance to the problem of model and simulation credibility. (p. 1)

Dr. Muessig continues:

> The fundamental impetus for validation of models and simulations is a fiscal one; it is cheaper to compute than to test. Validation of model and simulation permits the replacement of a measurement (test) with a prediction about a measurement (computation). Validation provides confidence that a model behaves like the "real world" (assumed to be well-defined), at least within certain specified boundaries (also assumed to be well-defined). If the domain of conditions over which validation was performed is known, and the correlation between prediction and observation within that domain is known, [it can be] determined whether the model behaves enough like the "real world" for a given application by defining criteria for acceptable correlation. (p. 3)

Three distinct challenges in developing a validation process for mature model and simulation from Muessig are described below:

> 1. Functional redundancies across model and simulation were neither identified nor exploited. The resultant model-by-model validation paradigm meant that the same data

were being collected multiple times for validating the same functions of different models. If functional redundancies across model and simulation could be identified and exploited, a few well-focused data collection efforts could, in theory, collect enough data to validate large parts of multiple models over a reasonably broad domain.

2. Dedicated model-by-model validation testing was (and is) simply too costly (fear of cost again). A cost-efficient approach to model and simulation credibility across boundaries needed to be developed; it could not squander limited resources on massive, redundant data collection efforts and dedicated testing. The return on investment would be too low. An alternative, high-volume source of test data had to be found.
3. Documentation of prior validation efforts was sparse or nonexistent. Although many in the model and simulation community claimed they had been doing validation "for years," when pressed for documented results, it became apparent that years of work would be irretrievably lost with the retirement of the current generation of analysts. (p. 3)

Until recently, accreditation by acclaim (or fiat) was more or less the rule, but there are still challenges facing accreditation:

1. There are no consistent accreditation requirements or guidelines, making it hard to share models without repeating similar accreditation steps.
2. The application of stated accreditation guidelines is inconsistent, essentially leaving the meaning of accreditation to the eye of the beholder.

SMART (Susceptibility Model Assessment and Range Test)

In response to these verification, validation, and accreditation challenges, a SMART (Susceptibility Model Assessment and Range Test) approach was developed, and discussed adapted below from "A 'SMART' Approach to VV&A."[25] The SMART project was started to develop, test, and transition a proven and efficient credibility assessment process for aircraft survivability models and simulations. SMART integrates the key elements of models and simulations credibly into a process that provides essential information to decision makers and analysts to support accreditation decisions for survivability models and simulations. SMART pioneered the process of "verification in reverse," and tailored this process to mature survivability model and simulation by identifying reasonable verification standards and guidance from each model's developmental and V&V and accreditation history. Automated technologies to support the process, such as CASE tools, were also investigated and applied where appropriate.

The goal of reviewing existing standards was to seek guidance on the software verification process, to specify which verification steps were essential to the credibility of mature model and simulation, and to identify a minimum set of documentation that would establish the credibility of a mature model and simulation from the verification standpoint. Five pieces of documentation were identified as essential to model and simulation usage and verification:

- Software User's Manual (SUM),
- Software Programmer's Manual (SPM),
- Software Analyst's Manual (SAM),
- Software Design Document (SDD), and
- Verification Report (p. 2).

Of these, most models reviewed had the first three documents in some form or another. The SDD, however, without which detailed verification would be severely hampered, and did not exist for any model; likewise the Verification Report. SMART, therefore, pioneered a post-development substitute for the SDD, appropriately named the Post-Development Design Document (PDDD). The PDDD is the basis for all detailed verification of code. To capitalize on prior work and experience in verification, users and developers were surveyed to establish development, V&V, and configuration management statuses and histories. Dr. Muessig says:

> Experience confirmed what reason suggested: a dismal (but not wholly unanticipated) state of basic information relating to the history of model development and credibility assessment. This substantiated the need for SMART to do something about the lack of documentation supporting model and simulation credibility. Having identified what should be done and what had been done,... software quality [was assessed] using CASE tools. Factors such as use of standards, adherence to programming conventions, computational efficiency, and memory utilization were assessed in order to quantify the relationship between code quality and verification efficiency. With this last piece in place,... tailored verification plans [were developed].
>
> SMART has developed a set of accreditation information requirements based on emerging policies, procedures, and guidelines,... and has divided its V&V and configuration management processes into increments that produce the essential information elements that support accreditation. This incremental process reduces the cost required to accredit model and simulation by focusing V&V and configuration management efforts on identifiable information requirements, and by making the results available to the wider model and simulation community.
>
> SMART's accreditation requirements study led to four conclusions with broad ramifications for accreditation policy and practice:
>
> 1. Current and emerging accreditation policies are burdened with excessive administrative overhead, place artificial barriers between the Accreditation Agent and those performing the work, and tend to turn the accreditation process into a bureaucratic, process-oriented, "check the box" operation.
> 2. Current accreditation practices focus on the collection of essential information elements that relate to various facets of model and simulation credibility, and place the burden of proof squarely on the shoulders of those responsible for study results. The emphasis of accreditation practice is on information, not process.
> 3. SMART products satisfy the vast majority of information requirements that support current accreditation practices.
> 4. The SMART process can be incrementalized to produce these information elements in accordance with the definitions of "levels of accreditation" currently being formulated in policy directives across the services.

> Finally, to address fear of cost, SMART conducted a pilot verification study.… Using the tailored plans as a guide, the four highest priority common model functions (based on sensitivity analysis; see below) were verified. The goal was to identify the cost implications of performing "verification in reverse" and to investigate alternative methods of verification.
>
> In order to avoid costly, repetitive, dedicated data collection efforts, SMART decomposes model and simulation into functional elements, paying careful attention to identifying common functions across them. It then distills the results of the decomposition effort into hierarchical functional element templates, showing both the common and the unique functions of the models. These templates form the basis from which other models can be decomposed and functional similarities identified.
>
> For each functional element identified, a two-phase sensitivity analysis is conducted for each model. Phase I sensitivity analysis identifies those model functions that have the greatest impact on top-level model outputs (e.g., detection range for $Project_1$, probability of kill for $Project_2$, and probability of hit for $Project_3$). The purpose is to prioritize which functions need validation first. Functions with marginal impact on top-level outputs become candidates for "face validation" by a panel of subject matter experts, saving the trouble and cost of explicit data collection for validation of these functions. With data collection objectives specified and access to test data guaranteed, SMART developed an incremental approach to comparing test data with model predictions. Before detailed comparisons with test data are attempted, system characterization and calibration data from a test article (e.g., a radar or a missile) and system performance as modeled in the code are compared.
>
> Without a formal stamp of approval from an accrediting authority, model and simulation results in support of testing and analysis will always be suspect. One would think it axiomatic, therefore, given the prior discussion of the components of model and simulation credibility, that accreditation demands satisfaction of a well-defined set of acceptance criteria, criteria which would include the requirement for V&V and configuration management. This has not typically been the case, however. (pp. 3–5)

The steps of the V&V and accreditation process are discussed below and illustrated in the bottom box in Figure 7.7 from *The Models and Simulations Master Plan.*[26] As with the overall decision of how to solve a given problem and the tools that will be used, requirements are a first and necessary step. V&V and accreditation requirements are generated from a detailed analysis of the intended application of the model. This analysis reinforces the previously stated importance in the model and simulation life-cycle of clear problem definition, requirements, and criteria by which the model will be tested and accepted. V&V and accreditation requirements are also determined through identification of the most critical issues and relevant features of the model that will be used. Model functions and features that do not directly affect problem resolution will have less impact on the scope of the V&V and accreditation effort.

Initiating V&V and accreditation planning requires that a detailed plan be written that defines what level of effort will be accomplished, how it will be accomplished, by whom, by what date, and at what cost. Large-scale efforts often include a simulation plan in their documentation, and a V&V and accreditation plan is a natural and essential part of the simulation plan. It need not be extensive, but should provide a reasonable level of detail to inform the decision maker and other

Figure 7.7 V&V and accreditation process in the model and simulation life-cycle.[26]

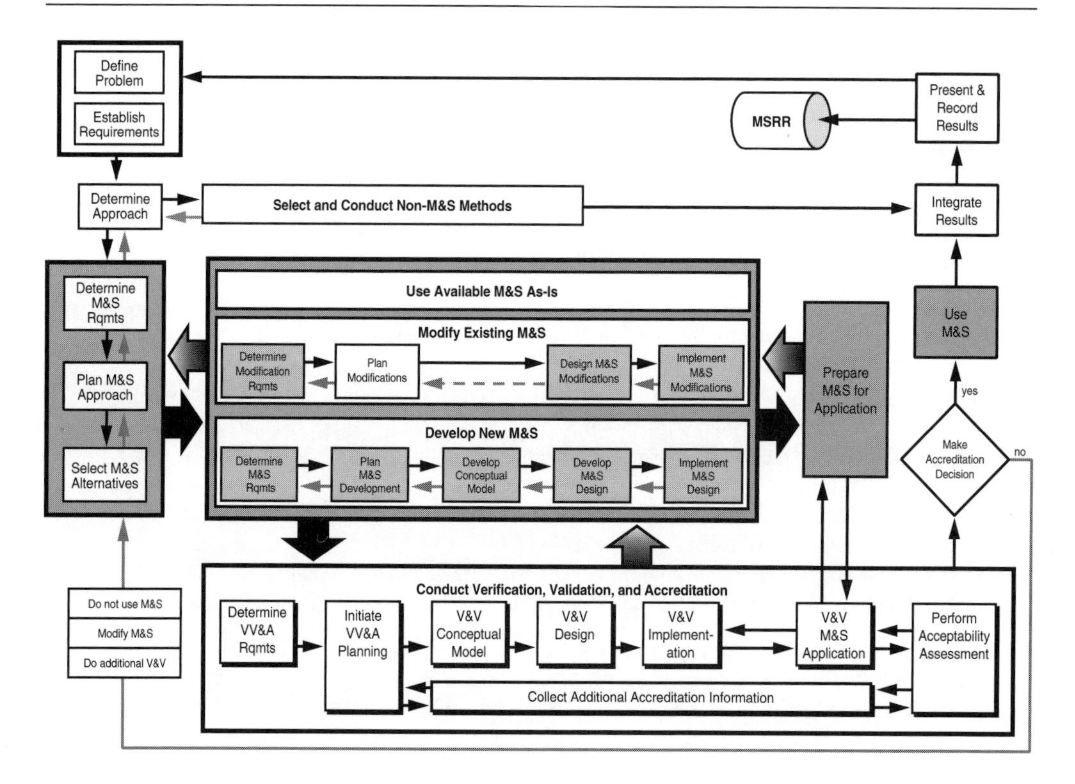

key team members what the V&V and accreditation effort is designed to achieve, how it will be achieved, and its overall contribution to the model and simulation application.

How much credibility comes from V&V and accreditation, and how much comes from the developer/tester team is a serious concern. To site a specific example, Robert Lewis[16] says of V&V and accreditation of advanced distributed simulations (ADS) that "the overarching goal is to make ADS testing realistic enough to accomplish the same level of evaluation that occurs if the test were live. In many cases, the ADS environment can actually create a much larger set of conditions and variations than live tests. Simulation is much more versatile than real life! It should be noted that sometimes too few live tests define the system baseline, which can (and almost always will) lead to skewed performance data. By using ADS and live tests in concert with each other, these biases can usually be removed" (p. 3).

Lewis goes on to report that the following examples help expand perspectives associated with V&V and accreditation of ADS. In this first case,

> V&V and accreditation is highly tailored and focused on achieving accreditation. The artifacts generated provide only essential information to convince the accreditation authority that product is acceptable. This results in a narrow "validation space" that is just sufficient to support the

> accreditation. The major risk in this approach is that small changes, such as varying the scenario even slightly, can throw the performance of the simulation into unexplored and unvalidated territory. Thus, we discourage using this approach unless the configuration is to be used once and then dismantled, never to be used again. Otherwise, it is too delimiting and constraining. It only costs a few percent more to broaden the scope of testing. (p. 5)

In this other case, "V&V and accreditation is either brought on the program late or is made to operate at a reduced level through early phases, with the idea that its contribution to adequate requirements and design is inconsequential. This approach ignores the requirements, conceptual model, and design verification, and many accreditation artifacts go unverified" (p. 5)
Lewis and Hanson[29] in discussing a Cost Estimating Tool (CET)[30] for VV&A state:

> In the past, cost estimating for Verification, Validation, and Accreditation (VV&A) programs has largely been based on coarse estimates of percentages of development cost, but this approach only works for new or recently completed modeling and simulation (M&S) efforts, and even then is not very accurate, primarily because each program has a unique development and execution environment and infrastructure. Percentage estimates also tend to ignore the unique attributes of each program.... These shortcomings provided the incentives to develop a much better cost estimating approach than has existed previously. This new approach has to be able to cope equally well with the various types of M&S and their uses. Thus, it has to support reuse of legacy M&S products with and without good VV&A history, legacy M&S with minor or major modifications, and new stand-alone M&S.... Because of the large number of variables and factors involved in the estimating process, the automated Cost Estimating Tool (CET) has been created to assist in the data capture, tailoring, and estimating process. Thus, the tool is referred to frequently as an integral part of the estimating process since it makes the task of calculating all of the necessary interim values much easier and more error free. It also makes replanning much quicker and more accurate. (p. 1)

Summary

The V&V of RAD contains many challenges and opportunities. The particular pressures associated with V&V challenges of RAD mentioned in the introduction are points worth re-emphasizing, with a brief statement from McDonald[2] of how to relieve those pressures:

1. Steps omitted to reduce cycle times—with a prototype development life-cycle, the steps are clearly defined, so that even in this rushed environment, no step is omitted.
2. Scope improperly defined and managed in relation to the delivery time frame—Time-boxing is used by many RAD processes as the tool to meet this challenge. A time-box is a fixed set of resources (people and time) assigned to a specific set of activities. The time-box acts as a limit on the systems development resource, with this limit being the primary weapon in combating scope creep.
3. System design and development initiated with an incomplete understanding of the requirements—With DSDM development the implementation may be phased, so each cycle consists of four phases: identify the prototype to be built and define its objectives and quality

criteria; agree on the time scale for the cycle; build or enhance the prototype focusing on the objectives of the cycle; and finally, review the prototype in its current state against the objectives set out at the beginning of the cycle. This approach is perfectly in line with the best tenets of quality control: knowing the requirements when building the prototype.

Two tool suites useful in RAD development are ObjectGEODE and Dynamic Systems Development Method (DSDM). ObjectGEODE includes verification of the models and validation and observation techniques. The major difference between DSDM and traditional approaches to software development is the shift away from fixing the requirements (and delivering software which satisfies all of them) while allowing time and resources to vary during development. In DSDM the exact opposite is true, time and resources are fixed for the life of a project, but requirements are allowed to change.

Models and simulations are used often in RAD environment, so that gave rise to a discussion of VV&A (verification, validation, and accreditation) of models and simulations. To address many challenges, a SMART (Susceptibility Model Assessment and Range Test) approach was developed. Dr. Muessig's presentation of the conclusions of the SMART's accreditation requirements study are:

1. Current accreditation policies are burdened with excessive administrative overhead.
2. Current accreditation practices emphasize information, not process.
3. SMART products satisfy the vast majority of information requirements that support current accreditation practices.
4. The SMART process can produce these information elements in accordance with the current definitions of "levels of accreditation."

References

[1] Trescowthick, Mark, "*Rapid Development* by Steve McConnell book review" [AVDF Article], GUI Computing, http://www.gui.com.au/avdf/may97/art_rapdev.html, May 1997.

[2] McDonald, Mark P., "Achieving Software Quality in a RAD Process," Andersen Consulting, *Proceedings of the Fourth International Conference on Software Quality (4ICSQ),* McLean, VA, October 3–5, 1994.

[3] SYS105 *Rapid Application Development and Joint Application Design* course, Center for the Application of Information Technology, Washington University in St. Louis, May 1997, http://www.cait.wustl.edu/catalog/software/sys105.html.

[4] DeGrace, Peter and Stahl, Leslie Hulet, *Wicked Problems, Righteous Solutions* (Englewood Cliffs, NJ: Prentice Hall Publishing Co., 1990).

[5] Pressman, Roger S., *Software Engineering: A Practitioner's Approach* (3rd edition), (New York: McGraw Hill Book Company, 1992).

[6] *Rapid Application Development Methodology,* SHL SystemHouse Homepage, www.systemhouse.com.

[7] Lewis, Robert O., *Independent Verification and Validation: A Life Cycle Engineering Process for Quality Software* (New York: John Wiley & Sons, Inc., 1992). Copyright © 1992 John Wiley & Sons, Inc., Adapted by permission of John Wiley & Sons, Inc.

[8] McConnell, Steve, Code Complete (Redmond, WA: Microsoft Press, 1993).

[9] McConnell, Steve, *Rapid Development: Taming Wild Software Schedules* (Redmond, WA: Microsoft Press, 1996).

[10] Herzlich, Paul, "A Quick Win for Testing," *SQM* issue 25, © 1995 Paul Herzlich, Web presentation © 1996 Tesseract Publishing, March 11, 1996, http://www.avnet.co.uk/tesseract/QiC/articles/Herzlich/25.html.

[11] Northrop Grumman ESSD Standard No. D170, November 4, 1997, p. 5.

[12] Wasserman, Anthony I., "Toward a Discipline of Software Engineering," *IEEE Software,* (© November, 1996 IEEE), pp. 23–31.

[13] Bauer, Claude J., "A New Generation of RAD Tools Boosts Productivity," *The Washington Post* Recruitment Supplement, April 26, 1998.

[14] Omolayole, J. O., "A model for quality software prototyping process management through Group Support System Technology-based Joint Application Design." *Proceedings of the Fourth International Conference on Software Quality (4ICSQ),* McLean, VA, October 3–5, 1994.

[15] Rakitin, Steven R., *Software Verification and Validation: A Practitioner's Guide,* (Boston: Artech House, 1997), Reprinted from permission from Artech House, Inc., Norwood, MA, USA, http://www.artech-house.com.

[16] Lewis, Robert O., "A Generic Model For Verification, Validation, And Accreditation (VV&A) of Advanced Distributed Simulations (ADS) Used for Test And Evaluation (T&E)," *Proceedings of the Spring 1997 Simulation Interoperability Workshop,* Simulation Interoperability Standards Organization, Inc., March 1997.

[17] Cusumano, Michael A. and Selby, Richard W. (Contributor), *Microsoft Secrets : How the World's Most Powerful Software Company Creates Technology, Shapes Markets, and Manages People* (Boston: Free Press, 1995)

[18] Griesel, Martha Ann Ph.D. and Welz, Linda L., "Using Modified Fagan Inspections To Control Rapid System Development," Jet Propulsion Laboratory, Pasadena, California.

[19] Fagan, Michael E., "Design and Code Inspections and Process Control in the Development of Programs," *IBM-TR-00.73,* June, 1976.

[20] Callahan, John R. and Easterbrook, Steve M., "Verification and Validation in a Rapid Software Development Process," *Proceedings of the Twenty-Second Annual Software Engineering Workshop,* Goddard Space Flight Center, Greenbelt, Maryland, December 1997, pp. 411–427.

[21] Verilog's ObjectGEODE, http://www.verilogusa.com/og/og.html; copyright © 1996 VERILOG SA, last updated: November 1, 1996.

[22] Verilog's ObjectGEODE, http://www.verilogusa.com/trn/trn.html; copyright © 1996 VERILOG SA, last updated: November 1, 1996.

[23] Stapleton, Jennifer, "A Quality Approach to Rapid Application Development," This article first appeared in SQM issue 25, http://www.avnet.co.uk/tesseract/QiC/articles/Stapleton/25.html, copyright © 1995 Jennifer Stapleton, Web presentation © 1996 Tesseract Publishing—Last updated 8th February 1996.

[24] Stapleton, Jennifer, "DSDM in a TickIT Environment" *TickIT,* March 1996, Tesseract Publishing, Cheshire, U.K., pp. 18-21.

[25] Muessig, Paul R., PhD., "A 'SMART' Approach to VV&A," Naval Air Warfare Center, Weapons Division Code C21806 (SMART Project Office), China Lake, California 93555-6001, 1993.

[26] *DoD M&S (Models and Simulations) Master Plan, DoD VV&A Recommended Practices Guide, DoD Modeling and Simulation Master Plan,* Common Technical Framework—Objective 5-2, 1996.

[27] *IEEE Recommended Practices Guide for the Verification, Validation, and Accreditation of Distributed Interactive Simulations* (Draft), March 5, 1996.

[28] Jacquart, Rene & Miller, Robin, "The Development of VV&A," CNERA-CERT and CDA, 1998.

[29] Lewis, Robert O., and Hanson, Jr., Anthony C., *Cost Estimating Tool (CET): An Automated Tool to Assist in VV&A Cost Estimating and Planning: Cost Estimating Tutorial and Rationale Guide,* Version 3.0—

February 25, 2000, Prepared on behalf of TRADOC Analysis Center (TRAC), Ft. Leavenworth, KS, and Development Test Command (DTC) Headquarters, Aberdeen, Maryland.

[30] The Cost Estimating Tool (CET) product is available free through the ASTARS website, TRAC (TRADOC Analysis Center at Ft. Leavenworth, Kansas); DTC (old TECOM Headquarters, Aberdeen, MD), and TecMaster, Inc. (blewis@tecmaster.com), at a minimum.

CHAPTER 8

Graphical User Interface (GUI) Development–Usability

Introduction

"Usability engineering is the discipline of supporting the entire development process of electronic information applications with user-centered design and user validation activities, in order to create applications that are fit for their intended use and are of added value to the intended users," Kirakowski[1] tells us.

The following initial concepts of usability are from "What is Usability?" by Bevan, Kirakowski and Maissel.[2]

> The term *usability* was coined [in the late 1980s] to replace the term *user-friendly,* which by the early 1980s had acquired a host of undesirably vague and subjective connotations. However, in the intervening years, the word usability itself has become almost as devalued as the term it was intended to supplant. There are still many different approaches to making a product usable, and there is no accepted definition of the term usability. The definitions that have been used derive from a number of views of what usability is. Three of the views relate to how usability should be measured:
>
> - the product-oriented view, that usability can be measured in terms of the ergonomic attributes of the product
> - the user-oriented view, that usability can be measured in terms of the mental effort and attitude of the user
> - the user performance view, that usability can be measured by examining how the user interacts with the product, with particular emphasis on either
>   - ease of use: how easy the product is to use, or
>   - acceptability: whether the product will be used in the real world.
>
> These views are complemented by the contextually oriented view, that usability of a product is a function of the particular user or class of users being studied, the task they perform, and envi-

> ronment in which they work. [Together these can be described as the "context of use" of the product.] For example, the definition given in the ISO standard for software quality (ISO 1991b) is product and user-oriented: "a set of attributes of software which bear on the effort needed for use and on the individual assessment of such use." (p. 1)

In the proposed ISO 9241-11—*Guidance on Usability,* ergonomics definition is usage, user, and contextually oriented: "the effectiveness, efficiency and satisfaction with which specified users can achieve specified goals in a particular environment," whereas Eason and Francis's definition is ease-of-use oriented: "the degree to which users are able to use the system with the skills, knowledge, stereotypes and experience they can bring to bear."[3]

Continuing from "What is Usability?":

> The position taken by the ESPRIT MUSiC (Measuring Usability of Systems in Context) project, [which is discussed in more detail later in this chapter], is that a complete definition of usability must encompass all these views. Usability is a function of the ease of use (including learnability when relevant) and the acceptability of the product and will determine the actual usage by a particular user for a particular task in a particular context. The current MUSiC definition of usability is: the ease of use and acceptability of a system or product for a particular class of users carrying out specific tasks in a specific environment, where "ease of use" affects user performance and satisfaction, and "acceptability" affects whether or not the product is used. (p. 1)
>
> Ease of use determines whether a product can be used; acceptability determines whether it will be used and how it will be used. Ease of use in a particular context is determined by the product attributes, and is measured by user performance and satisfaction. The context consists of the

Figure 8.1 Determinants of usability.[2] (p. 2)

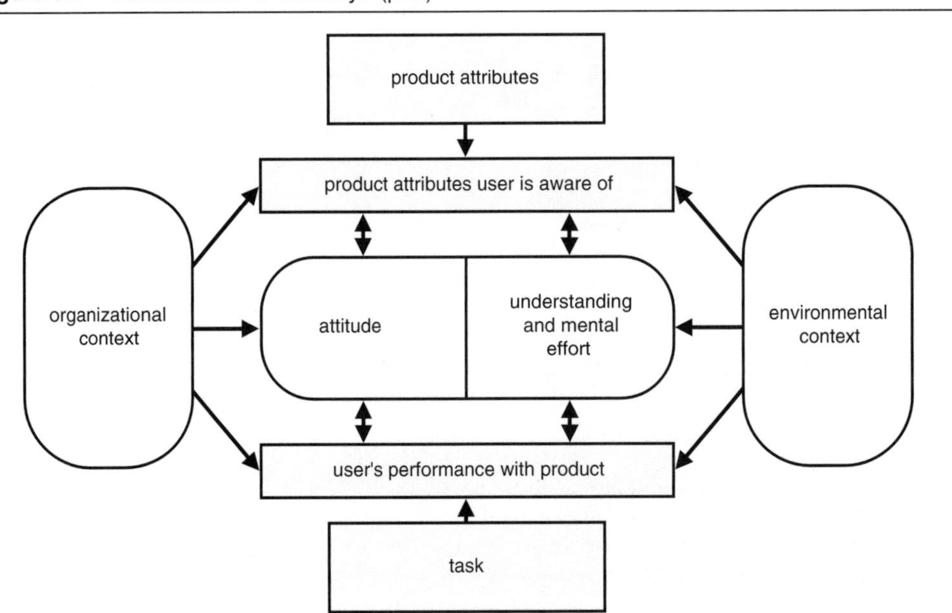

user, task, and physical and social environment. The relationship between these factors is shown in Figure 8.1.

> The product attributes that contribute to usability include the style and properties of the interface, the dialog structure, the nature of the functionality, and any other relevant properties such as system efficiency and reliability. Measures of attitude and performance provide the criteria that determine whether the design of the attributes is successful in achieving usability.... The distinction between product attributes and user performance leads to two very different approaches: (a) emphasis on the specification, design, and evaluation of product attributes that determine usability, or (b) concern with the specification and subsequent evaluation of criteria for the user's attitude and performance. (p. 1–2)

The V&V person needs to be cognizant of the ramifications of both approaches to thoroughly assess usability.

Finally, from "What is Usability?":

> [One issue surrounding usability] is to decide which performance should be assessed: performance determined by ease of use in a laboratory test, or actual usage in the real world. In many circumstances a user may have the discretion to choose not to use a system which has been shown to be perfectly easy to use in controlled conditions. To be used in the real world the system must be acceptable to the individual user (referred to as 'utility')—the user must judge the benefits of use to be greater than any alternative means of achieving the task. Acceptability will depend on the context of use and the characteristics of the user, and could be influenced by factors such as cost, convenience, availability, prerequisite training, dislike of computers, or organizational constraints.
>
> When evaluating usability, the performance of the user under controlled conditions will be determined by ease of use. If performance is measured in the laboratory, care must be taken that the context of use matches as closely as possible the intended context in the real world (types of users, tasks, and environment). A controlled measurement always masks some aspect of the real working environment, and an indication of how actual usage may differ as a consequence of acceptability can be obtained through interview or questionnaire techniques [covered in this chapter]. (p. 2)

Although developers would like to know what attributes to incorporate in the code to reduce the effort required for use, Bevan in "Quality and Usability: A New Framework"[4] tells us that:

> the presence or absence of predefined attributes cannot assure usability, as it is usually impossible to know how users will respond until they have actually experienced a prototype system. This is why, when defining usability in ISO 9241-11, the ISO software ergonomics committee took an approach to usability based on the degree of excellence of a product: usability is the extent to which a product can be used by specified users to achieve specified goals with effectiveness, efficiency, and satisfaction in a specified context of use. ISO 9241-11 explains how usability can be measured in terms of the degree of excellence in use: effectiveness (the extent to which the intended goals of use are achieved), efficiency (the resources that have to be expended to achieve the intended goals), and satisfaction (the extent to which the user finds the use of the product acceptable). ISO 9241-11 also emphasizes that usability is dependent on the context of use and that the level of usability achieved will depend on the specific circumstances in which a product is used. The context of use consists of the users, tasks, equipment (hardware, software, and materi-

als), and the physical and social environments that may influence the usability of a product in a work system. Measures of user performance and satisfaction thus assess the overall work system, and, when a product is the focus of concern, these measures provide information about the usability of that product in the particular context of use provided by the rest of the work system.

It is important to note that while this [ISO 9241-11] definition provides a practical way to measure usability, it is also measuring the consequences of other software quality characteristics such as the functionality, reliability and the efficiency of the computer system. Changes in these characteristics, or other components of the work system, such as the amount of user training, or improvement of the lighting, can also have an impact on user performance and satisfaction. (p. 2)

Bevan again tells us in "Usability Is Quality of Use"[5] that the V&V person must recognize that:

different people use the word usability in different ways.... Usability had its academic origins in psychology, human factors, and ergonomics. What makes usability different from the rest of design is that it focuses on the human issues. As a contribution to the design process it is most often interpreted by software developers as relating to skills in interface design which complement other design objectives such as functionality, efficiency (i.e., execution speed), and reliability. This is a narrow product-oriented view of usability, which suggests that usability can be designed into a product. In this sense usability is closely related to ease of use, which is probably the most common way the term is used and is consistent with Figure 8.2, which nests usability within usefulness, within practical acceptability, within system acceptability. It is also consistent with the limited responsibility of usability specialists* in many organizations.

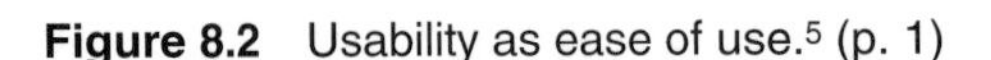

Figure 8.2 Usability as ease of use.[5] (p. 1)

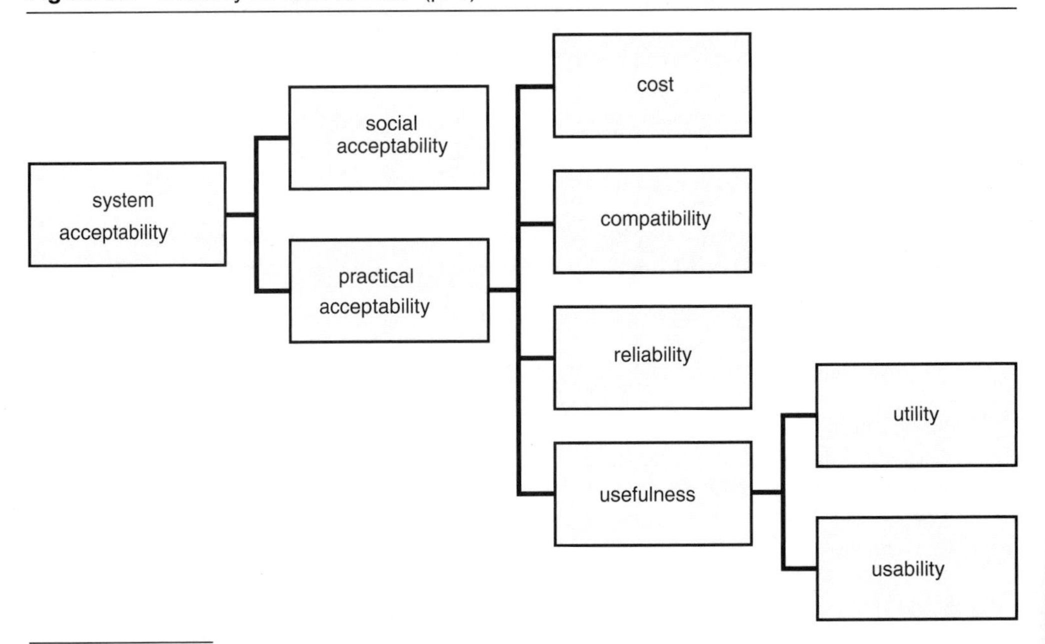

* Often called human factors specialists or human computer interface (HCI) specialists

> [As a design concept], one can talk about a system (with a well-designed user interface) that is usable, but not useful (i.e. has no utility). However, for this very reason, it is not a very good way to conceptualize usability. A system that is easy to use but useless will not sell. What really counts is whether users can achieve their intended goal when they use the product. This is also a "human" question: It immediately raises the issues of what users in what situations are carrying out what tasks (not typical software development concerns!). Unfortunately, the answer depends not only on usability as ease of use, but also utility (is the right functionality provided?), reliability (does the software crash and can you recover?), and computer efficiency (response time). In designing to enable users to achieve their goals, the V&V person needs to review the trade-offs made between these properties. (p. 1)

In "Usability: Practical Methods for Testing and Improvement,"[6] Macleod says,

> Usability professionals frequently meet people who think usability can be added to a system just by providing a specific style of interface. However, usability is much deeper than the superficial features of the user interface. While user interface features are important in helping shape the usability of the system, simply employing a good set of widgets does not guarantee usability—interface components are the building blocks for constructing parts of a system, with the aim of adequately presenting to the user clearly understandable information and feedback and providing an appropriate means of entering data and commands easily and efficiently. Adding, for example, a graphical interface—even one with easy-to-use objects—may not give a system an acceptable level of usability unless the design meets wider usability needs. Most style guides acknowledge this; for example, the Open Look™ graphical user interface application style guidelines (SUN Microsystems, 1990) states: "The presence of these graphical elements does not guarantee good application design; that depends on you."
>
> What then is usability? It can be thought of as "quality of use," a quality of the interaction between user and system. Now, this is where usability is more difficult to reason about than some other qualities of software products. Usability depends upon the characteristics of the user as well as the software. A system can have excellent quality of use for some people and poor quality of use for others. For example, a graphical user interface may have simple, well-structured menus—which novices can explore and use successfully and safely—but can be very frustrating for experienced, frequent users because it lacks keyboard short cuts. (p. 1)

Usability, then, should be thought of in terms of the quality of use of an interactive system by its (intended) users for achieving specific work goals and tasks in particular work environments.

Multidimensional Model

The graphical user interface (GUI) is on the technology axis of the multidimensional model. The GUI development is what represents usability to most projects. The GUI of today represented ubiquitously by Microsoft Windows is how most people use the computer. There are other interfaces on the horizon, described by Bill Gates[7] as "social user interfaces." These are to be much more "user friendly."

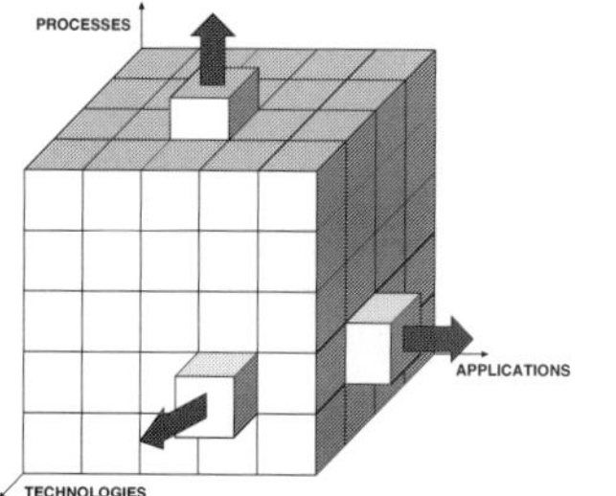

Also on the technology axis are tools like the useful and exciting Visual Basic™ and Visual C++™ compilers that shortcut the development of the GUI for the application under development. The "pre-canned" menus and icons aid both the designer and the implementers. The designer of the application knows the standards and protocols that are part of the compiler language, thereby limiting and focusing in on the easiest way to design for implementation. Any implementation that has broad acceptance in the user community.

The implementer does not have the burden of "programming" all the GUI details, but can use "point and click" to implement the GUI. This technology is a major step forward and one the V&V person should become proficient with in order to appropriately perform her activities during the development process.

Traditional V & V

The traditional V&V methods discussed in this section that have been used successfully in this relatively new area of usability are user validation plan, model-based development approach, and questionnaires and interviews.

User Validation Plan

An immediate, simple consideration for the V&V person is to consider what should happen first. A user validation plan that considers the end users' needs should be created. Kirakowski[1] says that such a plan should describe the:

- objectives, requirements, and constraints of the development project
- user groups—what they will do with the application, and the anticipated environments in which they will use it
- user validation scenario—how and when it is to be done
- critical success and quality factors for the application project from the point of view of both the developers and the users
- most appropriate user validation methods [many of which are included in this chapter].

Macleod[6] presents some underlying questions that could help to produce the user validation plan:

- How representative of real-world use is what is being evaluated?
- How safe is it to generalize from the limited scope of the evaluation to the wider use of the product in the workplace?
- Is the specific data being gathered relevant to usability and quality of use? (It is too easy to collect large quantities of data of little relevance to usability, this obscures relevant data and makes analysis difficult.)
- Is the data being analyzed appropriately, so that it may be used to reliably deliver valid indicators of usability? (p. 1)

Model-Based Development Approach

Several model-based development approaches have recently been introduced to help design and implement client/server applications and applications based on a GUI. The example of model-based development from Chapter 2 is shown in Figure 8.3, which is applicable to a wide variety of business and information systems software. There are several advantages to the model-based development approach, Rakitin tells us they are:

1. It is closely tied to specific business processes,
2. It clearly delineates client and server applications,
3. Tools are available to support the use of the models,
4. It includes a style guide for the GUI[8] (pp. 23, 24).

When performing V&V on model-based development, the usability verification is greatly aided by the GUI guidelines available. Since they are an integral part of the approach, V&V personnel can more easily perform their activities.

Figure 8.3 Model-Based development.[8] (p. 24)

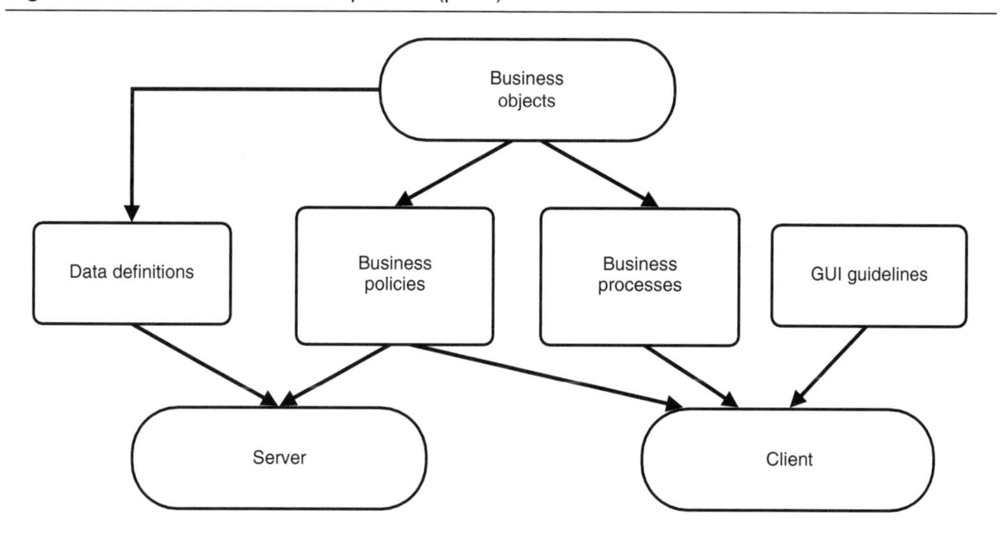

Questionnaires and Interviews

To understand how the user feels about a system, the V&V person should recommend the really basic approach taken from Jakob Nielsen, "Let's Ask the User."[9] Nielsen's ideas are presented in this section. Questionnaires and interviews are two methods that may be used to determine how people use a system and what features they particularly like or dislike. These methods do not study the interface itself, but rather the users' opinions about it. Studies indicate that users' statements cannot always be taken at face value. One example is that users said they never use certain commands, but made comments on it later in the survey. In another example, users were asked whether they understood cellular phone instructions, and most said they were not difficult, but missed about half the answers when questioned on the usage of the phone. The studies indicate that user behavior should receive precedence over user feedback.

Interviews are more flexible than questionnaires, but require more staff time. Follow-up questions may be asked when appropriate. Open questions provide significant benefits, but they have a downside. If a questionnaire rather than an interview is used, then closed questions are more appropriate because they are easier to understand. In an interview, users' responses may be evaluated, and questions clarified where appropriate. Questionnaires must stand on their own. It is therefore essential that all questionnaires be piloted and reworked as necessary before distribution.

Nielsen[9] says:

> As with all usability methods, you should know in advance what data is required and how it is to be used. This is especially important for questionnaires. To assess whether a question is really needed, try to imagine two drastically different reply statistics, then consider how the project would be changed in either case.
>
> Questionnaires are a great way of getting user feedback. You can repeat them at regular intervals to measure changes in user attitudes. They also are one of the cheapest ways to involve international users in decisions about interface design. Interviews are more time-consuming but can give deeper insights into each user's work environment and viewpoint. It is amazing how much time can be wasted in development projects by arguing over issues that could be resolved by simply asking the users. (pp. 110–111)

Many projects now have the users co-located with the development team so that the users are available to ask them. Some practical methods for questionnaires are presented here from Macleod's "Usability: Practical Methods for Testing and Improvement."[6]

> [The Software Usability Measurement Inventory], SUMI, is a fifty-item, internationally standardized questionnaire for quantitative measurement of how usable a product is in the view of the user. SUMI was developed within MUSiC by the Human Factors Research Group at University College, Cork, Ireland. It is available in Dutch, English, French, German, Italian, Spanish, and Swedish versions. SUMI gives a global measure of usability, together with measure of five relatively orthogonal factors: Efficiency, Affect, Helpfulness, Control, and Learnability, which have been empirically identified as dimensions of perceived usability. It also gives diagnostic data. The method is quick and straightforward to apply.

> The validity and reliability of SUMI have been established internationally, and it offers a convenient and inexpensive collection of trustworthy data about the usability of a product. A handbook guides the correct use of the questionnaire. SUMI can be used in two ways: by survey and by controlled study.... SUMI surveys measure the perceived usability of software systems already in use. For example, in response to the European Display Screens Directive, a company measured the perceived usability of software used by its employees—many hundreds of users. For several classes of software application, SUMI analysis gives a comparison with the expected level of usability for that particular class of application. [This is a particularly useful piece of knowledge for the V&V person.] SUMI is widely used in controlled studies, where performance is also measured and problems identified and analyzed. A minimum of about ten users is required. In usability evaluations, [users are given] SUMI after they have completed—or attempted—the selected representative tasks (see performance measurement, under the MUSiC subheading below).
>
> It generally takes users between five and ten minutes to complete the SUMI questionnaire. [Rapid analysis of data from the SUMI questionnaire is supported by the dedicated SUMISCO software.] Subsequent analysis using SUMISCO derives the measures and gives diagnostic information,... which identifies specific questions where the responses are unusually negative (or positive). This can be used to identify areas of difficulty and to guide the V&V person to follow up with those users about the nature of the difficulties. (pp. 4–5)

Contemporary V & V

There is much work going on in the usability arena. Everyone knows that the customer must be satisfied with how she uses a system. The emphasis on usability is covered in this section for the V&V specialist. Many contemporary V&V items included are usability testing, usability inspection, user interface correctness, usability and quality, MUSiC (Measuring Usability of Systems in Context), context analysis, and usability in Web sites. In the usability testing arena there is an expanded discussion of the usability testing concepts at Microsoft Corporation.

Usability Testing

To refine systems, to meet user needs and capabilities more fully requires user-based evaluation and testing. Macleod[6] reminds us that it is important for the V&V person to understand that:

> the specific goals of usability testing vary considerably, depending upon what is being tested and why. For a shrink-wrap stand-alone software product, the goals may be specified in terms of performance and user satisfaction for particular classes of users carrying out selected benchmark tasks. The target may be to equal or exceed the performance of competing products. For other IT (Information Technology) products, such as control systems, the targets may relate to the safe and efficient performance of specific critical tasks by operators of the system. For organizational information systems, targets typically relate to work using the system, compared with other ways of performing that work (e.g., an existing IT or paper-based system). For walk-up-and-use information systems and interactive consumer products, the concern is both initial usability for first-time users and efficiency and satisfaction for frequent users. Other systems assist in serving customers—for example, in sales, in counter transactions, and in answering

inquiries. Here the criteria relate to the efficiency and satisfaction with which the system supports an organization and its staff in serving the customer. (p.6)

From "UsAGE—User Graphing Effort"[10] the point is made that:

> Usability testing is a method of evaluating a user interface to determine where enhancements in the interface need to be made to improve the end-user's performance and satisfaction with the system. The testing involves observing a typical user performing predefined tasks with a system. Various types of information may be recorded, including the time it takes to perform the task, the number and types of errors made, and the user's rating of the system. Often video recordings of the user sessions are also made. This data is then analyzed to identify problem areas in the user interface. This analysis is largely a manual process and can be quite time-consuming. (p. 1)

Macleod[6] says that there are numerous constraints on usability testing:

- The work has to fit in with tight commercial development timescales.
- Prototype systems available for usability testing may have limited functionality and reliability.
- While some systems support tasks that are simple and frequently performed (and easy to assess), other tasks are highly complex and specialized, requiring substantial task expertise to enable their assessment.
- The availability of users with the required skills and other characteristics may be very limited.
- The specific methods employed in an evaluation must accommodate such constraints. (p. 6)

> As awareness of the benefits of usability evaluation and measurement has increased, [Macleod[6] tells us that] so has the demand for evaluation and for access to practical methods and tools. The development of MUSiC methods and tools and their refinement in commercial use—combined with training, support and evaluation services—have made available a flexible set of practical methods, which complement existing participative and expert usability methods. They are being adopted by organizations with existing human factors expertise and by [V&V personnel] where usability has previously only been informally addressed.... Current developments include establishing an accreditation scheme for their correct application, as part of quality management, and setting up support services.... As IT systems reach an ever-widening number of people, usability testing and improvement have increasing significance in helping to meet user needs.

Another aid to the V&V personnel performing in usability testing is an effort explained by the User Action Graphing Effort (UsAGE)[10] group:

> to develop a usability test tool that will automate detection of serious usability problems. The tool records the actions that a user makes while performing a predefined application task. Prior to a usability testing session, an "expert" user is recorded performing a task. This recording is used as a performance baseline. Later, during actual usability testing, a "novice" user is recorded performing the same task. The action recordings of the two users are then compared by the tool, and the comparison results are shown graphically as a series of nodes. The hypothesis is that by graphically comparing the actions of an expert to those of novice users, a usabil-

ity analyst can quickly determine where usability problems (e.g., confusion with menu choices) exist with the user interface.

This [usability test] tool is based on the scripting capability of the Transportable Applications Environment, a user interface development and management system, which has the capability to record user actions. The tool currently has the following features:

- record user actions
- record time-stamped comments made by a test administrator
- compare the actions of a novice user to those of an expert user using one of several matching algorithms and display the results graphically
- display various metrics about the matching
- replay all or a portion of the user's actions
- save and restore sessions
- change the node labels
- group nodes into "sub-tasks" (p. 1)

Access to these tools and methods should significantly help the V&V person during usability testing.

Another test that comes at the usability testing issue from a different perspective is PurePerformix, for example. The V&V person needs to be aware of PurePerformix and similar tools that capture user activities—including the actual keystrokes, mouse movements, and SQL requests that users generate while using an application—and creates emulation scripts. Remember, however, when using this "script-and-go technology," that it aids load testing.[11] To reflect its use in usability testing, the V&V person would observe the specific user on the system while the rest of the system is under load by the tool. This would provide a usability test for a specific user on a system that is under some stress.

A specific usability testing example with Application Programming Interface (API) is instructive for the V&V person. Here, the programmer is the user. From "Building More Usable APIs:"[12]

With examples, testing APIs up front can offer early indicators about usability to both API developers and API documentation specialists. In effect, they will see exactly if and how their application programmers will understand and use their APIs, in the same way that usability testing of user interface designs shows if and how users will work with these products. In particular, the results of such usability tests should lead to iterative API redesign and testing, where justified, so that API libraries are validated by the kind of programmers who will use them, and API reference manuals do not become repositories just for the deficiencies in API design. (p. 85)

Commented code examples, properly constructed, could help programmers learn very quickly the ins and outs of new API calls and their relationships in context. They also offer an opportunity to test and measure the usability of API designs early on. Usability, [for APIs], measures these product attributes:

- how easy the API is to learn
- how efficiently the API can be used for specified tasks
- how easy the API calls are to remember
- what misconceptions or errors programmers make using the API
- how programmers perceive the API. (p. 80)

Microsoft's Usability Testing

This section describes Microsoft's usability testing processes from Roger Sherman's "Shipping the Right Product at the Right Time: A View of Development and Testing at Microsoft:"[13]

> Users from the target market are given a prototype of a product under development [from Microsoft], with a task to accomplish using the prototype. Their actions are videotaped and annotated. This process provides product designers and V&V personnel concerned with usability with feedback on whether the design is easy to use or needs further refinement.
>
> Instrumented versions of [Microsoft] products are used in a similar way. These special versions record user actions, so designers can see how customers use a design to accomplish tasks. Designers used the data from instrumented versions of [Microsoft's] Office products to discover that users were not using the toolbar for common tasks but were going through menus instead. It was determined that many users could not remember what the icons on the toolbar meant, so the product design was changed so that an explanatory caption would appear whenever the mouse cursor passed over an icon. This solution was then tested in the Usability Lab to confirm that users naturally migrated toward the toolbar, which was quicker and easier to use than accessing the same functionality through menus.
>
> While these inputs help determine weaknesses in existing products, more is needed to create a product that exceeds customer expectations. Features of this type may come from extensive studies of customer behavior or shifts in available technology. Examples of the latter include OLE (Object Linking and Embedding), new Windows platforms, reusable code from other projects, or the presence of high-power processors in the target market. Groups often take retreats for creative brainstorming on product ideas. Once a product vision is defined, it is challenged by peer reviews and reviewed by the senior staff [a classic verification activity].
>
> The next step in defining the product is the product specification. This is a document that describes in detail how the product will work. The product specification receives line-by-line review from testers [acting as validation agents], developers, and user education staff. When the product specification is sufficiently detailed, the development team builds a schedule based on the specification. (p. 7)
>
> There are several types of beta testing at Microsoft. Marketing runs beta tests that have very little to do with testing the product for defects. Marketing betas are quite useful for getting customer feedback on the way the features have been implemented, and sometimes adjustments are possible before release to the general public.
>
> Technical betas, as they are called at Microsoft, are for the purpose of finding errors. Internal betas (called alpha testing elsewhere) are popular and effective. For many Microsoft products, internal betas have been far more useful for finding errors than external beta tests. Beta versions

of products are posted on internal servers, and everyone in the company is invited to download them and try them. Anomalies are reported via e-mail. Some developers are so proud of their code that they offer "bug bounties"—cash—for anyone who can find a bona fide error in their product. [Here, the entire company performs as validation testers.]

External betas can be quite large and are run by a centralized group that has developed expertise in managing beta sites. The internal beta group can put together a beta site list that duplicates the user profile of any product's target market. External betas are most important to the Systems group, since it writes code that is most likely to be affected by hardware configuration. In spite of the large number of beta sites and the length of beta tests, errors from external beta testing account for less than 5% of all errors found in most products, including operating systems. While some groups find those remaining 5% important enough to continue such testing, other groups have abandoned external beta tests. For these groups, internal testing has been effective enough. (p. 9)

According to *Testing Computer Software,*[14] something that the V&V person should consider is that a beta test may be considered an attempt to run a usability test cheaply (p. 54). However, since the problems are not seen as they arise, and the people's tasks are not seen, not as much will be learned from beta testing as would be from studying representative users in the laboratory. So usability testing does not equate with beta testing, although many similar lessons may be extracted from each.

Usability Inspection

"Usability inspection is the generic name for a set of methods based on having evaluators inspect or examine usability-related aspects of a user interface," (p. 2) defines *Usability Inspection Methods.*[15] This section on usability inspection is derived from Nielsen and Mack's book, *Usability Inspection Methods.*[15] Normally, usability inspection is intended as a way of evaluating user interface designs. There are numerous other kinds of evaluation methods and following is a brief contrast of them with usability inspection:

1. *automatic:* "usability measures computed by running a user interface specification through evaluation software"
2. *empirical:* "usability assessed by testing the interface with real users"
3. *formal:* "using exact models and formulas to calculate usability measures"
4. *informal:* "based on rules of thumb and the general skill, knowledge, and experience of the evaluators" (p. 2).

In this section of the contemporary V&V methods major subsections are explained for the V&V person, because usability inspections are conducted in various ways:

- heuristic evaluations
- cognitive walkthrough
- formal usability inspections

- perspective-based techniques
- usability inspection/usability testing.

Heuristic evaluations

Heuristic evaluation is a usability engineering method for finding the usability problems in a user interface design so that they can be attended to as part of an iterative design process. Heuristic evaluation involves having a small set of evaluators examine the interface and judge its compliance with recognized usability principles (the "heuristics").

The basic components of heuristic evaluations that are very easy to use are:

- Evaluators go through the interface twice, once to focus on its flow and once to focus on its individual dialog elements.
- The evaluators can inspect the interface with respect to whether it complies with a short list of basic usability heuristics and their general knowledge of usability principles.
- Three to five evaluators can combine their findings, although they work independently of each other.
- After the individual evaluations, the evaluators meet for a debriefing session, which is a most appropriate forum for V&V personnel involvement. Severity ratings are collected to help prioritize the fixing of the usability problems that were found.

It is important to re-emphasize that heuristic evaluation is performed by having each individual evaluator inspect the interface alone. Only after all evaluations have been completed are the evaluators allowed to communicate and have their findings aggregated. This procedure is important in order to ensure independent and unbiased evaluations from each evaluator.

A brief sampling of usability heuristics combined from tables in *Usability Inspection Methods*[15] is provided here:

- simple and natural dialog
- use of the users' language
- minimization of the users' memory load
- feedback
- clearly marked exits
- shortcuts
- precise and constructive error messages
- error prevention
- help for users to diagnose and recover from errors
- help and documentation
- user control and freedom
- consistency and standards

- recognition rather than recall
- flexibility and efficiency of use
- aesthetics and minimalist design
- match between system and the real world
- visibility of system status (pp. 29–30).

Cognitive walkthrough

Usability Inspection Method[15] says,

> The cognitive walkthrough is a usability method that focuses on evaluating a design for ease of learning, particularly by exploration. This focus is motivated by the observation that many users prefer to learn software by exploration. Instead of investing time for comprehensive formal training when a software package is first acquired, users prefer to learn about its functionality while they work at their usual tasks, acquiring knowledge of how to use new features only when their work actually requires them. This incremental approach to learning ensures that the cost of learning a new feature is in part determined by the feature's immediate benefit to the user. (p. 105)

Continuing from *Usability Inspection Method,*[15] the major steps that make up the cognitive walkthrough process are:

1. Define inputs to the walkthrough
   - Identification of the users
   - Sample tasks for evaluation
   - Action sequences for completing the task
   - Description or implementation of the interface
2. Convene the analysis
3. Walk through the action sequences for each task
   - Tell a credible story, considering...
   - Will the user try to achieve the right effect?
   - Will the user notice that the correct action is available?
   - Will the user associate the correct action with the effect that the user is trying to achieve?
   - If the correct action is performed, will the user see that progress is being made toward solution of the task?
4. Record critical information (this step is appropriate for the V&V person to perform)
   - User knowledge requirements
   - Assumptions about the user population
   - Notes about side issues and design changes
   - The credible success story
5. Revise the interface to fix the problems (p. 106)

Formal usability inspections

A formal usability inspection abstracted from *Usability Inspection Methods*[15] is a review of users' potential task performance with a product. It is completed by the product owner (i.e., the developer who is designing the product) and a team of peers, looking for defects. A formal usability inspection has the following characteristics:

1. A defect detection and description process: To detect defects, inspectors always use user profiles and step through task scenarios. While stepping these hypothetical users through tasks, inspectors apply task performance model and heuristics. Then, inspectors describe these defects in a user-centered manner as suggested by the task performance model and heuristics.
2. An inspection team: Inspectors represent various areas of knowledge, including, as appropriate, software, hardware, documentation, support, and human factors engineering. The method also defines the responsibilities that inspection team members have to the inspection process (i.e., a moderator, owner, inspectors, and a scribe).
3. A structure within the usability life-cycle: Defect detection is framed within a structure of six logistical steps. These six steps (Figure 8.4) provide an effective and efficient process and link the inspection into the usability life-cycle:
   a. Planning, consisting of:
      - Defining the inspection objectives
      - Choosing team members
      - Creating the inspection packet containing: inspection instructions, product description, supporting documents, user profiles, task scenarios, task performance model, heuristics, defect logging form, and logistics.

Figure 8.4 Six logical steps to a formal usability inspection.[15] (p. 153)

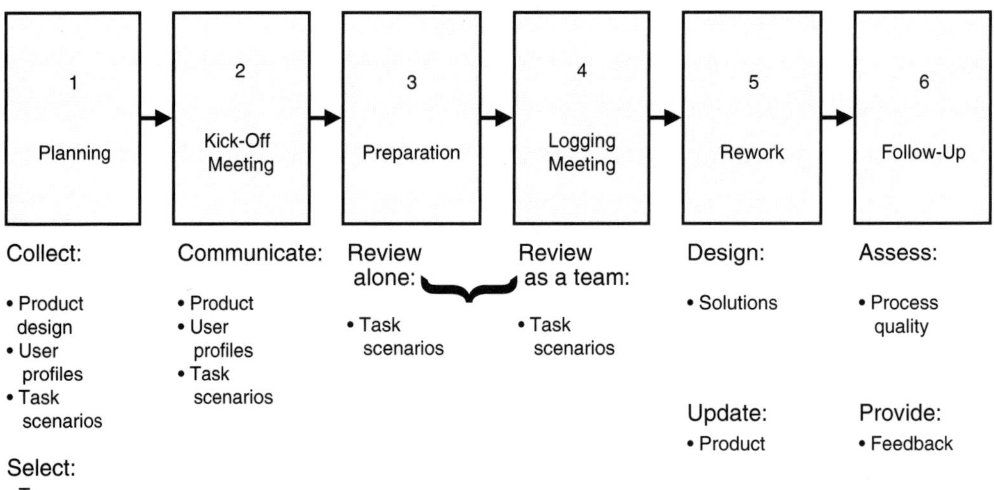

b. Kickoff meeting: Team comes together the first time, and the inspection packet is distributed
c. Preparation: Inspectors work alone, completing a particular scenario, and log defects when any task step cannot be done alone.
d. Logging meeting: Moderator manages meeting to step through each inspectors findings.
e. Rework: Solutions are found and implemented.
f. Follow-up: Measures of efficiency and effectiveness are provided to the team members.

Perspective-based technique

By applying some of the results from software inspection research to usability inspection, a more effective usability inspection technique can be achieved. The proposed perspective-based technique for usability inspection from Basili, Shneiderman, and Zhang[16] proposes that by applying some software inspection research to usability inspection, more effective usability inspections can be achieved:

1. Inspect from three perspectives. Each inspection session focuses on one of the three defined perspectives: novice use, expert use, and error handling.
2. Use task scenarios. This ensures that the inspection is from the user's point of view, which is what usability all about. A set of well-defined task scenarios will provide coverage of the inspection.
3. Achieve predictable inspection results through well-defined inspection process. Each task is decomposed into a canonical set of steps. Each canonical step is associated with a set of predefined inspection criteria.
4. Tailor and evolve the inspection criteria. The criteria should be tailored to fit the application domain and user interface artifacts. They should evolve according to the experience of the organization. (p. 1)

Separate defect detection and defect correction. Since defect detection is already a complex task, trying to solve the defects found will often reduce the effectiveness of defect detection. Achieve predictable inspection results through well-defined inspection process.

Usability inspection/usability testing

Now we return to Nielsen and Mack's *Usability Inspection Methods.*[15] Inspection methods are appropriate to use when the objectives of the study are:

- To find some of the major problems in the interface before user testing or implementation of the product is undertaken. It is less expensive to identify and remove some of the major problems at this early stage of product development rather than at a later stage. Also, if modifications are made as a result of the inspection test, then the user test can verify whether the modification was successful. The user test is then testing the solution rather than identifying the problem.
- To evaluate the usability on noncompliant products. If a company is choosing between two text editing packages for internal use, as opposed to developing a product to sell, then inspection methods may provide enough information to make an effective purchase

> decision. However, if a product is being designed for sale in the competitive market then user testing is probably needed to (1) provide the type of data necessary to convince management that the product will be successful in the competitive market, and (2) ensure product success. (p. 256)

To determine appropriate methods of testing *Usability Inspection Methods*[15] tells us to:

- Verify that customer demands have been met. Sometimes customers articulate a demand, such as "make the interface more consistent" or "comply with Motif standards." In these situations, experts are needed to verify compliance.
- Identify issues that need to be examined through user testing. Heuristic evaluation helps clarify usability issues so that the usability test can be designed to answer meaningful questions. Without this expert input, the user risks bringing back data that cannot impact the design decisions.
- Evaluate design alternatives on dimensions that are less important to users.

Inspection methods can be used effectively when the objectives of the study are to identify problems and choose from among the design alternatives in the early stages of the product development cycle.... When the risk is low and decisions are not being made on factors that are critical to the product success, then inspection methods are appropriate. There are, however, a range of issues in the design process that are difficult for an expert to address. The user is the best person to provide knowledge about important factors that impact the interface design, and user data is necessary to understand what correlates with product success in the market. (p. 257)

The following types of decisions extracted from section headings in *Usability Inspection Methods,*[15] made by the product design team and management require more information than inspection methods can effectively provide:

- Predicting the users' trade-off matrix
- Predicting the acceptability of the whole interface
- Predicting how acceptable the interface is relative to competitors' interfaces
- Predicting trade-offs with other aspects of the product
- Predicting user preferences
- Predicting differences in the interface trade-off matrix between users, choosers, and distributors
- Predicting usability in the global market.

User testing according to *Usability Inspection Methods*[15] in usability labs need to provide data that:

- Aid the development decisions being made by the product development team and management
- Indicate how acceptable the interface is: Will it delight users or cause returns?
- Indicate how the interface will perform in the competitive global market. (p. 258)

There are two major reasons for alternating between usability inspection and user testing. First, a usability inspection can eliminate a number of usability problems without the need to "waste users," who sometimes can be difficult to find and schedule in large numbers. Second, these categories of usability assessment methods (usability inspection and user testing) have been shown to find fairly distinct sets of usability problems; therefore, they supplement each other rather than lead to repetitive findings.

With these concepts in mind, the V&V person can review Table 8.1, which lists the relative strengths and weaknesses of usability testing and usability inspections methods.

User Interface Correctness

This section is concerned with the use of formal methods (not including formal inspections, just discussed) to increase confidence in the correctness of user interface software. Initially, consideration is given to notions of correctness and the means of achieving it. Formal methods are then introduced and how they can be used to increase confidence in the correctness of software is outlined. Finally, the application of formal methods to the development of user interface software is surveyed, and the potential for further work on specification-based testing of user interfaces is indicated. This section is derived from "User Interface Correctness"[17] by MacColl and Carrington from the University of Queensland, Australia.

> [When user interface correctness analysis is conducted], both validation and verification are important. Validation failure constitutes a breach of contract between the developer and the client for whom the software is being produced. Verification failure results in software containing potential faults or flaws. Clearly, neither is desirable.

Table 8.1 Strengths and weaknesses of usability testing and inspection methods[14, p. 220]

Issue		*Usability Testing*	*Inspection Method*
Ability to address evaluation objectives		+	–
Number and type of usability problems identified		+	–
Reliability of usability findings		+	+
Human factors involvement	In conducting method	–	+
	Data Analysis	+	–
Ability to facilitate acceptance of usability goals and activities		+	+
Appropriateness of method's use at different points in development cycle	For numerous lower-level design tradeoffs	–	+
	For high-level design guidance, full coverage of interface	+	–
Effectiveness of method in generating recommendations for change		+	–
Cost-effectiveness of method		+	+

Legend: + indicates a strength and – indicates a weakness

Correctness is particularly important for software that is critical in some way—for instance, when human lives are at risk. Correctness of all aspects of such software, including the user interface, should be strenuously pursued. The widely cited Therac-25 accidents, which resulted in deaths and injury, are partly attributed to enhancing usability of the user interface at the expense of the safety of the overall system.

Correctness is important for software in general, and is particularly important for user interface software. The user interface represents the aspect of the software which is directly perceived by a user. If the user interface is incorrect, the software will be perceived as incorrect, regardless of the correctness of the underlying functionality.

Confidence in the correctness of a user interface is usually achieved by prototyping or by testing. Prototyping can be used for validation and to verify that the user interface meets usability requirements. Testing can also be used for validation (acceptance test) and to evaluate usability. Traditional software testing (unit, integration, and system test) is still the major method for assessing the correctness of user interface software.

Although testing of user interface software, particularly graphical user interface software, has elements in common with other software testing, it also presents a number of challenges:

- The user interface is a large and complex component of a software system.
- Graphical and other presentations make it difficult to determine the expected result of an operation, particularly in the context of system-wide environment settings such as colors, desktop graphics, and default fonts.
- Input is derived from multiple, asynchronous devices, usually at least a mouse and a keyboard.
- Interaction styles are expected to be modeless with enabled actions permitted (and vice versa).
- Rapid semantic feedback on the results of operations is expected. (pp. 1–2)

MacColl and Carrington[17] say:

Formal methods are mathematically based techniques for describing system properties. [Formal methods are not specific to GUI development, but are used in many aspects of development.] They typically include a precise notation for constructing mathematical models of a (software) system. The notation is used for specifying (rather than designing or implementing) the required system, and is concerned with "what" is done by a system rather than "how" it is done. Two defining characteristics of formal methods are precision and abstraction.

Many formal methods use a notation with a mathematical appearance, but this is not a requirement. For example, programming languages with a sound semantic basis can be considered to be specification notations. These specification notations are precise notations for constructing (executable) models of a system (although they are not particularly abstract). Well-defined graphical notations such as Petri Nets and Harel's Statecharts are also specification notations.

Formal methods can be classified as model-, property-, or behavior-based. Model- and property-based methods are concerned with modeling underlying data structures and their operations, whereas behavior-based methods focus on externally observable behavior. Model-based methods define system behavior directly by constructing a model using mathematical structures such as sets. Model-based notations for sequential systems include Z (pronounced "Zed") and VDM [model-based notations for sequential systems]. Such notations are suited to specifying software involving complex data structures and simple operations, since the data types are modeled explicitly.

Property-based notations such as OBJ and Larch model data types implicitly by defining system behavior through a set of properties. Property-based methods can be further classified as axiomatic and algebraic: axiomatic methods are based on first-order predicate logic, and algebraic methods use equational axioms.

Behavior-based methods define systems in terms of possible sequences of states rather than data types and are commonly used to specify concurrent and distributed systems. Behavior-based notations include Petri Nets, Calculus of Communicating Systems (CCS), Communicating Sequential Processes (CSP), and Statecharts.

Formal methods can be used to increase confidence in the correctness of software by proof, refinement, and testing. Proof, sometimes called formal verification, involves a rigorous demonstration (usually involving deductive logic) that an implementation matches its specification. Refinement is the development of implementations that are correct by construction; a specification is rigorously transformed to derive an efficient implementation. Testing involves executing an implementation with some input and comparing the resulting output to output expected for that input. Specification-based testing uses a (formal) specification for determining appropriate inputs and expected outputs. (pp. 2–3)

"Formal methods can guarantee that software is perfect" amounts to a claim that formal methods can eliminate software testing, but the UsAGE[11] group points out that this is a myth. The fact is that some things can never be proved, and mistakes can be made in the proofs of those things that can be proved.

MacColl and Carrington[17] continue:

Much of the work applying formal methods to [human computer interface] (HCI) emphasizes reasoning and analysis rather than implementation. A project at The University of Queensland, [Australia], is concerned with formal notations for (object oriented) specifications of user interface software, and the development of designs by using relatively informal transformations based on software patterns. This project is using Object-Z, an object oriented extension of Z, for interactor specifications. Object-Z enhances the model-based capabilities of Z with encapsulation constructs, and includes operators for expressing dynamic aspects such as concurrency and communication between objects. (p. 5)

The Test Template Framework and the ClassBench methodology are testing techniques under investigation also at The University of Queensland. The Test Template Framework is a formal, abstract model of testing, used to derive a hierarchy of test information, including test inputs and outputs, from a formal specification. The ClassBench Methodology and the Test Template Framework provide an approach to automated testing of object oriented software. The Specification-Based Testing project, funded by the Australian Research Council and based at the Software Verification Research Center, involves researchers from University of Victoria, Canada, and aims to combine Test Templates and ClassBench to create methods and tools for testing object oriented software.

> The linguistic paradigm is based on the work of Foley and vanDam who distinguish lexical, syntactic, and semantic aspects of interactive command languages.... Agent-based architectures are an attempt to resolve the limitations of linguistic architectures as a basis for developing graphical user interfaces. The agent-based paradigm encapsulates data, functionality, and input and output within an "agent" such as a button, a screen, or an entire user interface. The encapsulation is consistent with abstract data type and object oriented software development.... Like object-oriented software development, formal approaches to development of agent-based user interfaces must address both static and dynamic aspects of the system. Model- and property-based notations are well suited to formalizing static aspects, whereas behavior-based notations are preferable for dynamic aspects. Many formal, agent-based approaches use multiple notations of different styles, or extend an existing notation to encompass capabilities of a different style.
>
> Behavior-based notations, such as Petri Nets, are useful for modeling external behavior but must be augmented to include static aspects of user interfaces. The Interactive Cooperative Objects (ICO) formalism [is used] to specify, verify, and implement user interfaces. ICO provides an object oriented framework for modeling static aspects of a system and uses Petri Nets for modeling dynamic aspects....
>
> The Esprit AMODEUS project has developed two formal models of interactors as encapsulations of a state, events that manipulate the state, and a mechanism to present the state to users. The first interactor model, developed at CNUCE in Pisa, Italy, uses the process algebra LOTOS, a property-based notation with behavioral capabilities. The CNUCE model is derived from work on graphics systems and input devices.
>
> The second AMODEUS interactor model was developed at University of York, UK. The York model uses model-based notations such as Z and VDM, augmented by [Communicating Sequential Processes] for behavioral aspects. The York model is a development of... extending Z to cover both static and dynamic aspects. The AMODEUS project has used interactor models for describing graphics systems and for analyzing interactive systems. [This] includes integration of formal descriptions of users and systems in an interactive framework, and investigation of scaling up formal development of user interface implementations.
>
> In addition to formally based development, testing was identified above as a means of improving confidence in the correctness of software. Researchers at Durham University, UK, developed a formal method to directly support testing user interface software that uses three notations to specify user interface software:
>
> 1. state-transition diagrams to express interaction sequences
> 2. a model-based notation similar to Z to define the state transitions
> 3. an algebraic notation for reasoning.
>
> Tests are derived from the state-transition diagrams, and the model-based specifications are used to determine expected outputs. (pp. 3–5)

The University of Queensland group has extended the Test Template Framework to accommodate specification-based testing of interactive systems. The extended framework accommodates model- and behavior-based notations and permits multiple test generation strategies.

Usability and Quality

Bevan's "Usability Is Quality of Use"[5] is returned to for the basis of this section on usability and quality. Remember that the definition of usability used in ISO 9241-11 and the MUSiC project is the extent to which a product can be used by specified users to achieve specified goals with effectiveness, efficiency, and satisfaction in a specified context of use.

> This broad definition of usability turns out to be synonymous with "quality of use"; that is, the higher level quality objective not only helps the product meet its specification, but also works in the real world! In software development, the conventional objective for quality is to build a software product that meets the specification. However, this alone is rarely sufficient to ensure quality of use—that is, that the product can be used for its intended purpose in the real world. The quality of a product in use can be measured by the extent to which the product can be used with effectiveness, efficiency and satisfaction in a particular context. (p. 2)

Bevan, in "Quality and Usability: A New Framework,"[4] relates that software product quality can be measured internally (typically by static measures of the code), or externally (typically by measuring the behavior of the code when executed). The objective is for the product to have the required effect in a particular context of use. Quality in use is the user's view of quality. Achieving quality in use is dependent on meeting criteria for external measures of the relevant quality subcharacteristics, which in turn is dependent on achieving related criteria for the associated internal measures.

Bevan in "Usability Is Quality of Use"[5] continues:

> The purpose of designing an interactive system is to meet the needs of users: to provide quality of use [see Figure 8.5, adapted from ISO/IEC 14598-1: Evaluation of Software Products].

Figure 8.5 Quality requirements in design.[5] (p. 3)

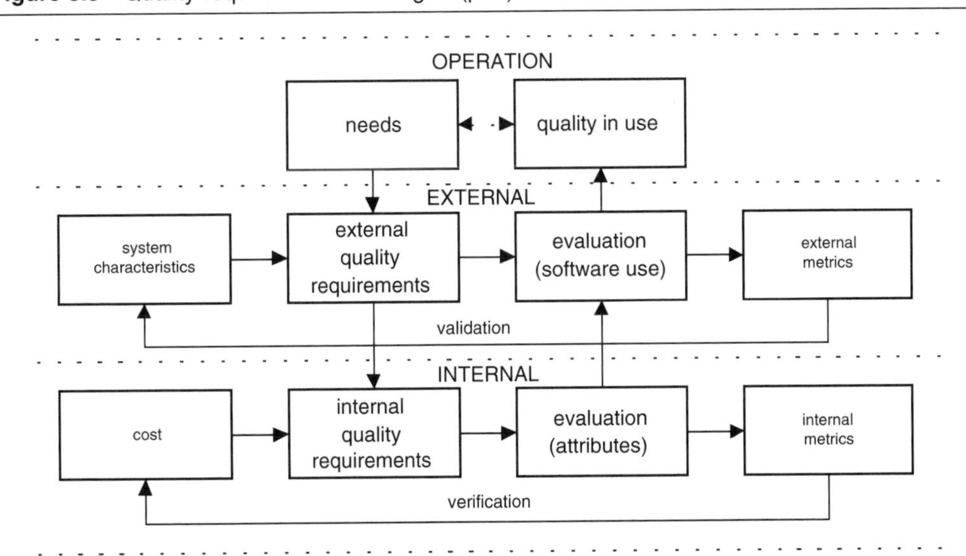

The users' needs can be expressed as a set of requirements for the behavior of the product in use (for a software product, the behavior of the software when it is executed). These requirements will depend on the characteristics of each part of the overall system, including hardware, software, and users.

The requirements should be expressed as metrics that can be measured when the system is used in its intended context—for instance, by measures of effectiveness, efficiency, and satisfaction. At this level, the required system characteristics could be minimum values for the effectiveness, efficiency, and satisfaction with which specified users can achieve specified goals in specified environments.

The required values of these external metrics provide goals for design. To achieve these goals, the internal attributes of the system can be specified as internal requirements. At this level, usability requirements may be in terms of general principles (e.g., provide consistency, support the user's task), specific interface details (e.g., icons and menu design), or use of style guides. These attributes of the software can be evaluated by the V&V person to produce internal metrics verifying how closely the internal requirements have been met. Although these attributes contribute to achieving quality of use, users and tasks vary so much that no set of interface guidelines alone can ensure that a product will be usable.

The usability attributes that contribute to quality of use will include the style and properties of the user interface, the dialog structure, and the nature of the functionality. Measures of quality of use provide the criteria that determine whether the design of the attributes is successful in achieving usability. There are a number of ways of evaluating the usability attributes of a product:

- Style guides such as Computer Users' Association (IBM) or Windows (Microsoft) can be used. These provide the raw material for an interface, although quality of use is dependent on the extent to which a dialog implemented in a particular style is successful in supporting the user's task.
- Detailed attributes of the user interface can be evaluated, for instance using ISO standards, such as ISO 9241-14 (Menu Dialogs).
- Individual features can be assessed, such as the presence of a help system or the use of a graphical interface. These are examples of functionality that generally contribute to usability, although particular aspects may not be required in every case.
- General usability principles can be used, such as the need to be consistent, to be self-explanatory, and to meet user expectations (e.g., those in ISO 9241-10 [Dialog Principles]). These are examples of useful guidelines for design, but they are difficult to use for evaluation by the V&V person, because guidelines are imprecise, are not universally applicable, and may conflict; and there is no way to weight the relative importance of the individual items for usability in any particular conditions.

There have been several attempts to use checklists as a basis for evaluating usability. Usability guidelines and checklists are useful aids for design and can be used to make quick expert assessments of user interface design, but they cannot provide a reliable means of assessing whether a product is usable.

Although the influence of usability professionals during design is often restricted to user interface issues, usability is frequently evaluated by testing a prototype of the product with users.

Table 8.2 Continual cycle of user-backed evaluation.[5] (p. 5)

	concept	*prototype*	*release*
understand context			
specify usability			
build solution			
evaluation by users			

> This leads to a number of problems. This type of user-based evaluation is often left till late in design when there is only scope to make minor changes to the user interface. If evaluation reveals deeper problems with the functionality or basic dialog design, this may be outside the responsibility of the usability professional. The best solution to these problems is to adopt a user-centered approach to design with a continual cycle of user-based evaluation. [Table 8.2 contains that recommended cycle from ISO 13407 (Human Centered Design).]
>
> At each stage of design it is important to understand the intended context of use, to specify usability requirements (preferably in terms of user performance and satisfaction), and then to construct design solutions that can be evaluated by users. If usability evaluation is left until just before release, there will be no chance to make any significant changes in design to correct deficiencies. In order to achieve a usable product, it is important to begin the cycle of understanding, specifying, and evaluating usability by using simple mock-ups at the earliest stages of design. For most cost-effective design feedback, repeated evaluation with 3 to 5 users is recommended, rather than less frequent evaluation with more users. However, to be confident that usability objectives have been achieved, a final evaluation with 10 or more users will be required.
>
> The objective of all usability, [including this user-centered approach], is to achieve quality of use. Usability requirements should be stated in terms of the effectiveness, efficiency, and satisfaction required in different contexts. User-based evaluation can be used by the V&V person to validate achievement of these requirements. Usability attributes provide a contribution to achieving quality of use. The presence or absence of these attributes can be verified early in design. In addition, frequent user-based evaluation of early mock-ups and prototypes is required to give feedback on the quality of use of potential solutions. (pp. 2–5)

Bevan, in "Quality and Usability: A New Framework,"[4] states that quality-in-use metrics measure the extent to which a product meets the needs of specified users to achieve specified goals with effectiveness, productivity, and satisfaction in a specified context of use. Evaluating quality in use helps the V&V person validate software quality in specific user–task scenarios. Quality in use is the user's view of the quality of a system containing software, and is measured in terms of the result of using the software, rather than properties of the software itself. Quality in use is the combined effect of the software quality characteristics for the user.

MUSiC (Measuring Usability of Systems in Context)

This section that covers the MUSiC concepts is derived from Macleod's "Usability: Practical Methods for Testing and Improvment."[6] The European MUSiC project has developed tools and techniques which enable usability to be specified and measured, implementing the principles of ISO 9241-11—Guidance on Usability. Macleod says:

> The need for practical, valid methods for the quantitative evaluation of usability in context—which can provide the usability measures required by management—underlay the work of MUSiC (ESPRIT Project 5429), a focus for European developments in this area from the [early 1990s]. The MUSiC consortium is continuing to work together and includes industrial and academic partners from six countries. After developing and verifying usability measures and evaluation methods, the major thrust of the MUSiC project's second phase was the use and refinement of the methods and tools in commercial contexts and the development of training packages and support services for companies adopting the methods. The MUSiC consortium has been marketing the resulting tools and services since mid-1993....
>
> MUSiC has produced a set of evaluation methods—analytic and user-based—from which evaluators can choose to adopt methods individually or in combination to measure those aspects which they (or the developers or [V&V specialists]) consider most important. Significant outputs of MUSiC include:
>
> - the usability context analysis method and guide
> - analytic measures supported by the SANe toolkit
> - a set of user-based methods for measuring usability, including the core factors (effectiveness, efficiency, and user satisfaction)
> - the cognitive workload imposed when using a system.
>
> MUSiC methods also enable measurement of the rate at which people can learn to use a system, and of its initial usability for first time users. As well as measures, the methods deliver diagnostic data which help identify usability problems and their causes.
>
> MUSiC user-based methods include performance measurement—supported by the Performance Measurement Handbook and a software tool, DRUM, the Diagnostic Recorder for Usability Measurement—and measurement of perceived usability supported by a fifty item questionnaire, Software Usability Measurement Inventory (SUMI) discussed above. Work at the Technical University of Delft, Netherlands, has advanced methods for measuring the cognitive workload (mental effort) imposed upon users. Objective measures are obtained by monitoring variations in heart rate, subjective measures by the use of questionnaires. All these user-based methods [need to be far enough along in the user-based evaluation cycle (such as prototype) (See Table 8.3)].
>
> An analytic [verification] method, applicable early in design, has been developed at Westfälische Wilhelms Universität, Münster, Germany. This enables analysis of the specification of an interactive system, before any design decisions are committed to code, in order to predict aspects of usability and identify areas where improvements can be made. It is supported by the SANe Toolkit, effectively a CASE tool that derives predictive analytic usability measures from device, task, and simple user models. As with any CASE tool, use of the SANe toolkit requires training in the underlying method; the software itself is relatively easy to use.

SANe has been successfully applied to early usability evaluation of designs in a range of major projects, including a complex workstation in the testbed for the European Space Agency Columbus Project.

The MUSiC Performance Measurement Method gives measures of core indicators of usability:

- Effectiveness: how correctly and completely goals are achieved in context
- Efficiency: which relates effectiveness to cost in terms of time
- Productive Period: the proportion of time spent not having problems
- Snag, Search and Help times: time spent overcoming problems, searching unproductively through a system, and seeking help.

These problem-related measures are valuable sources of diagnostic data and provide pointers to the causes of problems.

It is possible to tailor the method to individual evaluation need: for example, by choosing not to analyze the productive period—thus reducing analysis time—or by adding specific measures such as counts of errors. The Basic MUSiC Performance Measurement Method is a minimal version of the method, giving measures of effectiveness and efficiency without the use of video. It employs manual timing of task performance, together with assessment of task outputs. This takes less effort than the full method, but gives reduced diagnostic data. It relies on accurate observation in real time, plus analysis of task output. The basic method may be employed in quick, small scale evaluations, or where the budget is very constrained. [It is also a good starting tool in this complex area for the V&V person monitoring usability.]

A major focus of MUSiC was the development of tools to support the analysis of data, as well as the correct application of the methods. [One tool is SUMISCO, discussed above, and the other, discussed here, is DRUM.] There is a… need for support for analysis of observational data, to derive objective performance measures and diagnostic information. While observation can yield rich usability data, analysis solely in real time may lose valuable data. Video recordings preserve data, yet can be very time-consuming to analyze, conventionally taking ten or more hours to analyze a single hour of video. The Diagnostic Recorder for Usability Measurement, DRUM, helps reduce analysis time to 2 or 3 hours per hour of recording, and supports first-pass analysis in real time.

DRUM provides support for many aspects of evaluation, by assisting:

- management of data throughout evaluation
- task analysis
- video control
- creation of an interaction log of each evaluation session
- analysis of logged data
- derivation of the MUSiC performance measures and metrics, and user-defined measures.

DRUM also supports the identification of analyst-defined critical incidents and diagnosis of specific usability problems. Once logged, any observed event can be automatically found and reviewed on the video.… It should be emphasized that the validity of the MUSiC usability measures derived by DRUM in any evaluation depends upon the contextual validity of the evaluation, and on the evaluators applying the MUSiC performance measurement method for collecting and analyzing the data. (p. 6)

Context Analysis

Usability Context Analysis (UCA) helps developers and evaluators deal with contextual issues in usability. The UCA method and guide were developed in collaboration with industry as part of MUSiC by the UK National Physical Laboratory and HUSAT Research Institute, and so is also described here from Macleod's "Usability: Practical Methods for Testing and Improvement:"[6]

> It firstly provides a simple, structured method for describing key features of the users, tasks, and work environments for which a system is designed: the context of use. It secondly gives evaluators a method for characterizing the users, tasks, and environments appropriate for evaluation of the system, and for documenting how accurately this context of evaluation matches the intended context of use. UCA employs a questionnaire format. [To restate an important point], one of the simplest means of testing usability is to ask users—to sample their subjective views. This can be achieved in a structured way by using a questionnaire. Properly conducted and analyzed—with due consideration of contextual factors—this approach can provide valid and reliable measures of user satisfaction, which complement objective measures of performance. It is worth noting that user satisfaction is not necessarily closely correlated with performance: users may have positive perceptions of software applications that are not objectively particularly efficient to use, and vice versa. An evaluation that studies how well atypical users perform unrepresentative tasks in highly artificial circumstances is unlikely to give a worthwhile prediction of the usability of the implemented system....
>
> A less obvious aim of UCA is to increase understanding of user needs among people responsible for system development, and to establish a shared understanding of contextual factors. This is facilitated by applying UCA cooperatively. The need for increased user involvement in system development is widely recognized.... However, it is still commonplace for most IT development to be led from a software-centered perspective. Even where companies employ human factors engineers to help match products and systems to users' needs, the findings of human factors evaluations may be ignored or misunderstood by managers. Usability Context Analysis involves a range of people with a stake in the quality of use of the system. They may be drawn from product managers, project managers (procuring or developing systems), designers, quality managers, users, user support managers, documentation managers and technical writers, training managers, change management teams, work process analysts, [V&V people], people with responsibility for... health and safety, and human factors and usability professionals. Where UCA is applied cooperatively, much of the formal work is carried out in one or more group context meetings. The prerequisite is to identify and bring together a number of key people, typically six to ten.
>
> ...The formation of a usability team is encouraged, including stakeholders representing different interests, early in the development of an IT system. Members of the usability team participate in the context study and contribute to the planning and conduct of evaluations. They have a continuing role of liaison, informing and maintaining contact with other stakeholders throughout development.... The team should [at least] include someone with human factors knowledge, someone representing user interests [often the V&V person], and someone from the development team. We recommend a training course in the use of MUSiC methods, including

UCA. The usability team is responsible for arranging participation in the context meeting. Participants must be provided in advance with a copy of the Context Questionnaire, an adequate briefing about the aims of UCA, and the information they should have available at the meeting. The characterization of context of use can then be achieved cooperatively in a single group meeting. This involves working through the context questionnaire to record characteristics of users, tasks, and environments, and agreeing under each heading upon a fairly high-level description of that characteristic of the context of use.

The aim of the subsequent steps in UCA is to ensure that evaluation is carried out in a context, or in a specified subset of contexts, which fairly reflect real-life system use. This part of UCA is to be performed separately from recording context of use.... It requires at least one person with a background in human factors or HCI, working in consultation with other stakeholders and members of the usability team. The analyst considers each documented factor of the context of use and assesses its relevance to usability. For each contextual factor identified as possibly affecting usability, the usability team must decide how to control or monitor that factor in the evaluation, to achieve the specific objectives of the evaluation. Key issues are the choice of tasks for evaluation (e.g., critical or frequently performed tasks) and the profile of users. The result is a summary of the context of evaluation, which specifies the conditions under which the evaluation should take place. The team derives a user evaluation plan (discussed above) from this information, describing the practical details of how the evaluation will be carried out. (pp. 3–4)

Usability in Web-sites

Many users ask why so many web sites are frustratingly slow and complicated to use. Bevan, in "Usability Issues in Web Site Design,"[18] provides the reasons:

- Organizations often produce web sites with content and structure that mirrors the internal concerns of the organization rather than the needs of the users of the site.
- Web sites frequently contain material that would be appropriate in a printed form, but needs to be adapted for presentation on the web.
- Producing web pages is apparently so easy that it may not be subject to the same quality criteria that are used for other forms of publishing.

In short, web sites provide a unique opportunity for inexperienced information providers to create a new generation of difficult-to-use systems! Successful web development requires the combined skills of domain expertise, HTML, graphic design and web usability, [with a review by the V&V person]. (p. 1)

Planning for web-site usability should be inseparable from web-site development, say Nielsen and Spool in "Speaking with the Experts."[19] Again, a "usable product" is one that can be learned quickly and easily and then implemented to complete work effectively. Developers typically think of quality in terms of the product—it needs to be error-free, and it needs to run fast. Usability engineers, however, view the product from the users' perspective: Can they use this intuitively? Will the system stay up? How long do they have to wait? In essence, the difference is in the pronouns: Quality and usability are really two sides of the same coin. In advising companies on their fledgling web sites, the V&V person should emphasize the use of the pronoun "they" (the users). For example: How do they want to use it? What are they trying to do? These are the most important usability questions.

Bevan's "Usability Issues in Web Site Design"[18] re-enforces the idea that, "a web site will not meet the needs of the organization providing the site unless it meets the needs of the intended users and provides 'quality in use.' To implement a web site that users find effective, efficient, and satisfying requires a user-centered design process. A process that integrates existing empirical evidence and guidelines for web site design into a user-centered process that is consistent with ISO 13407 is needed." In the Appendix to this chapter, a listing of those guidelines is included for the V&V person, along with the references for the rationale for the individual design guidelines. It is essential to first define the business and usability objectives and to specify the intended contexts of use. These should drive an iterative process of design and evaluation by V&V personnel, starting with partial mock-ups and moving to functional prototypes. To assure continued usability, the V&V person must see to it that subsequent management and maintenance also takes place.

Summary

Figure 8.5 in this chapter gives a flow of verification and validation for usability. The verification of usability is highlighted in the chapter with usability inspections, questionnaires and interviews, and certain aspects of MUSiC. Usability testing, context analysis, user interface correctness, and much of MUSiC focus on usability.

Many tangible benefits are derived from improved usability of interactive systems. Macleod's "Usability: Practical Methods for Testing and Improvement"[6] says, "Work productivity and efficiency are higher when using IT systems with good usability, and there are fewer "user errors"; less training of staff is required to enable effective and efficient use the system, users are more satisfied, and there may be lower staff turnover. There are benefits both for users and producers in that less support and documentation is required. Such benefits can be quantified and incorporated into a business case for applying usability engineering in system development."

Bill Gates[7] states that graphical user interface is not easy enough for the users of future systems. Not enough guidance comes from the machine to make one feel comfortable. The use of an agent* (a capability programmed into your computer) simulates a dialog with an entity that behaves to some degree like a person. An agent that takes on a personality provides a *social user interface.* Agents will not replace the graphical user interface software, but rather will supplement it by providing a character of your choosing to assist you. If you hesitate or ask for help, the agent will reappear and offer assistance. You may even come to think of the agent as a collaborator built right into the software. It will remember what you are good at and what you have done in the past, try to anticipate problems, and suggest solutions. It will bring anything unusual to your attention. If you work on something for a few minutes and decide to discard the revision, the agent might ask if you are sure you want to throw the work away. But if you were to work for two hours and then give an instruction to delete what you have just done, the social interface would recognize that as unusual

* In Microsoft's Office 97™ there is an animated paper clip who provides helpful tips; this initiates the concepts of an agent.

and possibly a serious mistake on your part. The agent would say, "You've worked on this for two hours are you really, really sure you want to delete it?"[7] With the forthcoming social user interfaces, the V&V person must be prepared to verify and validate something new in the field of usability.

References

1 Kirakowski, Jurek et al., "A Quick Guide to Usability Engineering Resources," Human Factors Research Group, University College Cork, Ireland, www.ucc.ie/hfrg, March 5, 1998.

2 Bevan, Nigel, Kirakowski, Jurek and Maissel, Jonathan, "What Is Usability?" *Proceedings of the 4th International Conference on HCI,* Stuttgart, September 1991, National Physical Laboratory, DITC, Teddington, Middlesex, TW11 0LW, England.

3 Markus, M. L. & Robey, D., "Information Technology and Organizational Change: Causal Structure in Theory and Research," *Management Science,* Vol. 34, No. 5, May 1988, pp. 583-598.

4 Bevan, Nigel, "Quality and Usability: A New Framework," Usability Services, National Physical Laboratory, Teddington, Middlesex, In *Achieving Software Product Quality* edited by Nolthenius, T., Netherlands, 1997.

5 Bevan, Nigel, "Usability Is Quality of Use," *Proceedings of the 6th International Conference on Human Computer Interaction,* July 1995.

6 Macleod, Miles, "Usability: Practical Methods for Testing and Improvement," National Physical Laboratory, Teddington, Middlesex, *Norwegian Computer Society Software '94 Conference,* 1994.

7 Gates, Bill, *The Road Ahead* © 1996 Recorded Books, Inc. Tape 3, side 2, Prince Frederick, MD 20678.

8 Rakitin, Steven R., *Software Verification and Validation: A Practitioner's Guide,* (Boston: Artech House, 1997), Reprinted from permission from Artech House, Inc., Norwood, MA, USA, http:\\www.artech-house.com.

9 Nielsen, Jakob, "Let's Ask the Users," *IEEE Software,* (© May / June 1997 IEEE), pp. 110, 111.

10 Reprinted from "UsAGE: User Action Graphing Effort," *Computer-Human Interface (CHI) '95 Conference,* 1995, with permission from Elsevier Science.

11 Quinn, Stephen R. & Lucas, Kathie, "Get a Load of This," *InfoWorld* Vol. 18, No. 3, January 15, 1996, p. 55.

12 McLellan, Samuel G. et al., "Building More Usable APIs," *IEEE Software* (© May / June 1998 IEEE), pp. 78–86.

13 Sherman, Roger W., "Shipping the Right Products at the Right Time: A View of Development and Testing at Microsoft," In *CrossTalk,* Software Technology Support Center, Ogden: Hill AFB, Vol. 8, No. 10, October 1995, pp. 6–9.

14 Kaner, Cem, Falk, Jack and Nguyen, Hung Quoc, *Testing Computer Software* (2nd edition) (Boston: International Thomson Computer Press, 1993), permission to duplicate this information provided by the copyright owner, The Coriolis Group.

15 Nielsen, Jakob and Mack, Robert L. (editors), *Usability Inspection Methods* (New York: John Wiley & Sons, Inc., 1994). Copyright © 1994 John Wiley & Sons, Inc., Adapted by permission of John Wiley & Sons, Inc.

16 Basili, V., Shneiderman, B. and Zhang, Z., "A Perspective-Based Technique for Usability Inspection," Experimental Software Engineering Group at the University of Maryland, November 20, 1997.

17 MacColl, Ian (http://www.csee.uq.edu.au/~ianm) and Carrington, David (http://www.csee.uq.edu.au/~davec), "User Interface Correctness," *ACM Crossroads,* Spring 1997, 3.3, pp. 9–13.

18 Reprinted from Bevan, Nigel, "Usability Issues in Web Site Design," email: Nigel.Bevan@npl.co.uk, National Physical Laboratory, Usability Services, Teddington, Middx, TW11 0LW, UK. *Proceedings of the HCI International '97* San Francisco, Elsevier, 1997, with permission from Elsevier Science.

19 Nielsen, Jakob, PhD & Spool, Jared, "Speaking with the Experts," *Web Techniques Magazine,* April 1997 Volume 2, Issue 4; from "Interface '96," Conference.

General References

Cusumano, Michael A. and Selby, Richard W. (Contributor), *Microsoft Secrets : How the World's Most Powerful Software Company Creates Technology, Shapes Markets, and Manages People* (Boston: Free Press, 1995)

Appendix

This entire appendix is quoted from Nigel Bevan's "Usability Issues in Web Site Design."[18]

Planning

Define the business objectives of the site (provider requirements).

What is the purpose of the site? This could include disseminating information, positioning in the market, advertising services, demonstrating competency, or providing intranet services.

Who do you want to visit the site: what are the important user categories and what are their goals?

What type of pages and information will attract users and meet their needs? e.g. hierarchically structured information, a database, download of software/files, incentives to explore the site.

What are the quality and usability goals which can be evaluated? e.g., to demonstrate superiority of the organization to the competition, appropriateness of web site to user's needs, professionalism of web site, percentage of users who can find the information they need, ease with which users can locate information, number of accesses to key pages, percentage of users visiting the site who access key pages.

What is the budget for achieving these goals for different parts of the site?

Identify responsibilities for achieving quality and usability objectives, and estimate the resources and budget for these activities.

Specify in detail the intended contexts of use (user requirements).

Who are the important users?

What is their purpose for accessing the site?

How frequently will they visit the site?

What experience and expertise do they have? What nationality are they?

What type of information are they looking for?

How will they want to use the information: read it on the screen, print it or download it?

What type of browsers will they use? How fast will their communication links be?

How large a screen / window will they use with how many colors?

Define key scenarios of use.

Describe specific examples of people accessing the site, and what they want to achieve. These will help prioritize design, and should be the focus for evaluation.

Also identify any niche markets and interests which can be supported by the site without major additional investment (e.g. specialized information, access by users with special needs).

Site Structure and Content

Structure information so that it is meaningful to the user. The structure should make sense to the user, and will often differ from the structure used internally by the data provider.

What information content does the user need at what level of detail? Use terminology familiar to the user.

Interview users to establish the users' terminology and how they categorize information.

Produce a card (or post it note) for each anticipated page for the site,[i] and use card sorting techniques to design an appropriate structure.[ii]

Support navigation.

Help users find their way.[iii]

Show users where they are.

Use a consistent page layout.

Minimize the need to scroll while navigating.

The easiest to navigate pages have a high density of self-explanatory text links.[iv]

Try to make sure users can get to useful information in no more than four clicks.

Provide links to contents, map, index and home on each page; for large sites include search.[v]

Include navigational buttons at both the top and bottom of the page.

Use meaningful URLs and page titles. URLs should be exclusively lower case.

Plan that any page could be the first page for users reaching the site from a search engine.

Tell users what to expect.[vi]

Avoid concise menus: explain what each link contains.

Provide a site map or overview.

Distinguish between a contents list for a page, links to other pages, and links to other sites.

Do not change default link colors and style, otherwise users will not recognize the links.

Give sizes of files which can be downloaded.

Highlight important links.

The wording of links embedded in text should help users scan the contents of a page, and give prominence to links to key pages. (Highlight the topic—do not use "click here"!)

To keep users on your site, differentiate between on-site and off-site links.

Page Design

Design an effective home page.

This should establish the site identity and give a clear overview of the content.

It should fit on one screen, as many users will not bother to scroll the home page.[vii]

Design for efficiency.[viii]

Graphics add interest but are slow to load and can impede navigation.

Use the minimum number of colors to reduce the size of graphics.

Use the ALT tag to describe graphics, as many users do wait for graphics to load.

Use small images, use interlaced images, repeat images where possible.[ix, x]

Make text easy to read.

Never use flashing or animation, as users find this very distracting.

Avoid patterned backgrounds, as these make text difficult to read.

Support different browser environments.

Use a maximum 640 pixel width, or 560 pixels for pages to be printed in portrait mode.

Avoid frames—where possible use tables.[xi]

Test that your pages format correctly using the required browsers and platforms.

Support visually impaired users with text-only browsers.

Use a logical hierarchy of headings and use ALT tags which describe the function of images.[xii]

Evaluation Methods

Expert inspection.

Using a checklist to inspect pages for conformance with house style (consistency of layout) and with recommendations such as those in this paper.

Early mock-ups.

Early in design evaluate a partial mock up of the site with representative users performing representative tasks. Use first drafts of screens, either on-line or as color prints.[xiii]

Functional prototypes.

Produce a working version of a representative part of the site, taking account of the design principles and evaluation feedback.

Evaluate the working version with representative users performing representative tasks.[xiv]

Management and Maintenance

Ensure that new pages meet the quality and usability requirements.

What skills will be required of page developers?

What will be the criteria for approval of new pages? Is some automated checking possible?

Maintenance

Plan and review the site structure as it grows, to make sure it still meets user needs.

Monitor feedback from users.

Monitor the words used when searching the site.

Monitor where people first arrive on the site, and support these pages as entry points.

Check for broken links.

Compare your site to other comparable sites as web browsers and web design evolve.

As it is unlikely to be economic to test the usability of every page, it is important to establish a sound structure and style guide within which new pages can be developed, and for page developers to be aware of the business objectives and intended contexts of use. (pp. 1–4)

References

A version of this paper with live links can be found at http://www.npl.co.uk/npl/cise/us.

[i] http://www.sun.com/sun-on-net/uidesign/cardsort.html
[ii] http://info.med.yale.edu/caim/stylemanual/M_I_3.HTML
[iii] http://www.cybertech.apple.com/HI/web_design/find.html
[iv] UIETips 2/14/97. Jared Spool, User Interface Engineering (uie@uie.com)
[v] http://www6.nttlabs.com/HyperNews/get/PAPER180.html
[vi] http://www.cybertech.apple.com/HI/web_design/tell.html
[vii] http://www.sun.com/sun-on-net/uidesign/pagedesign.html
[viii] http://www.useit.com/alertbox/9703a.html
[ix] http://www.pantos.org/atw/35247.html
[x] http://www.pantos.org/atw/35247.html
[xi] http://www.useit.com/alertbox/9612.html
[xii] http://www.useit.com/alertbox/9610.html
[xiii] http://www.sun.com/sun-on-net/uidesign/papertest.html
[xiv] http://www.sun.com/sun-on-net/uidesign/screentest.html

CHAPTER 9

Client/Server Networks

Introduction

Verification and Validation for systems running on client/server networks presents unique challenges to the V&V practitioner who must not only contend with specific application software, but must also deal with a bewildering array of "off-the-shelf" operating systems, network hardware, and network management software. This introduction presents the underlying concepts of client/server networks and certain extensions. This is required to establish the setting for the traditional and contemporary V&V aspects associated with client/server networks.

Client/Server

From the "Overview of the Finance Standard Client/Server Guidelines,"[1] *clients* are defined as hardware, software, persons, or a combination that request services from servers. Servers are defined as hardware, software, or a combination that provides resources to one or more clients.

"Client/server is generally characterized by the division of an application into components processed on different networked computers. It is made up of two distinguishable entities: (a) a client, which requests a service or information from (b) a server, which processes the request, performs the service, and returns the requested information to the client" (A-1). The "Overview of the Finance Standard Client/Server Guidelines" goes on to relate that the client/server model has the following capabilities:

- The client and the server can interact seamlessly.
- Generally, the client and the server are located on separate platforms and are connected via a network.
- The client or the server can be upgraded individually.
- The server can serve multiple clients concurrently and, conversely, a client can access multiple servers.

> Applications based on the client/server model of computing provide great latitude in deploying application functionality across a network, consequently requiring a broad range of V&V methods and tools. This... enables the use of desktop and portable devices, which, when working in conjunction with high-power, low-cost servers, helps provide more cost-effective business solutions. The power of client/server is that it allows support to customers in making the transition from transaction-based processes to business-event and knowledge-based solutions. (A-1)

To support the client/server capabilities, four fundamental attributes from the "Overview of the Finance Standard Client/Server Guidelines," are associated with a client/server architecture:

- A many-to-many relationship exists between clients and servers. One server can support multiple clients at the same time and one client can access multiple servers at the same time.
- A server can in turn become a client to another server. A server can change roles depending on whether it is providing resources to a client or requesting resources from another server.
- Clients and servers can be, and usually are, replicated through the network.
- Request for servers are initiated by clients. Servers cannot initiate request to clients. (A-3)

This section draws its conclusions from Bernard H. Boar's *Implementing Client/Server Computing, A Strategic Perspective:*[2]

> Client/server computing is a processing model in which a single application is partitioned among multiple processors (front-end and back-end), and the processors cooperate (transparent to the end-user) to complete the processing as a single, unified task. A client/server bond product ties the processors together to provide a single-system image (illusion). Shareable resources are positioned as servers offering one or more services. Applications (requestors) are positioned as clients that access authorized services. The entire architecture is endlessly recursive; in turn, servers can become clients and request services of other servers on the network, and so on and so on. (p. 102)

Figure 9.1 illustrates the client/server concept and depicts many key attributes of the client/server environment from Boar[2] as follows:

- Multiple clients may access multiple servers.
- Multiple servers may be accessed by multiple clients.
- A server may provide multiple services.
- A service may be offered by multiple servers.
- The architecture is endlessly recursive; servers may, in turn, act as clients and request services from other servers.
- Because of the preceding attributes the architecture is understood to be a "many-to-many" architecture. This distinguishes it from the "one-to-many" architecture attribute of the traditional host-centered architecture. (p. 102)

Boar has developed a model to show why client/server computing has become so prevalent. As shown in Figure 9.2, enabling technologies and changing computer economics are just two of

Figure 9.1 Client/server concept.[2] (p. 6)

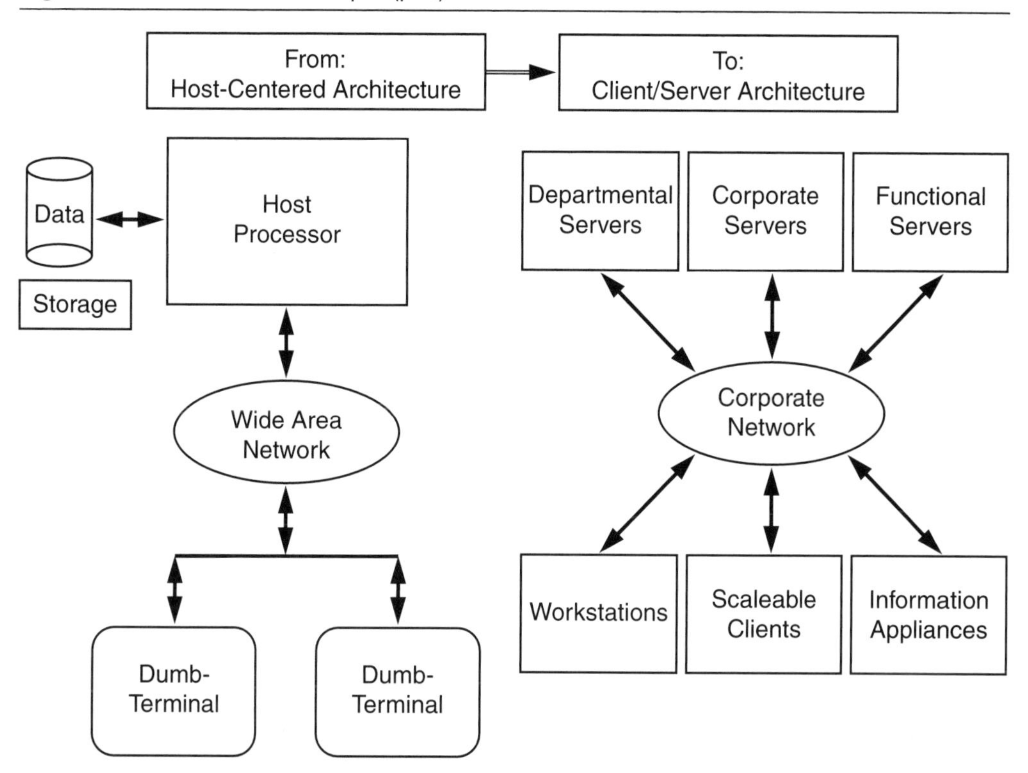

the factors. Others include an organization's need to be competitive in an environment where division of labor and the requirements for efficient information movement and management (IM&M) demand that powerful information processing capacity be placed in the hands of knowledge workers. He asserts that the "enabled technologies" for today's enterprise are best served by client/server architectures (pp. 110–111).

In discussing the "battle" between main-frame host based computing and client/server systems, Boar summarizes:

> Client/server computing has already won, and host-centered computing has already lost. The ascent of the client/server architecture as the predominant processing architecture of the 1990s is a *fait accompli.* It is a *fait accompli* because it better solves the enduring and foundational business requirement of competitive advantage with superior price/performance and new feature/functionality. It provides the business with the maximum reach and range to make business decisions operational.

Figure 9.2 Client/server forces.[2] (p. 110)

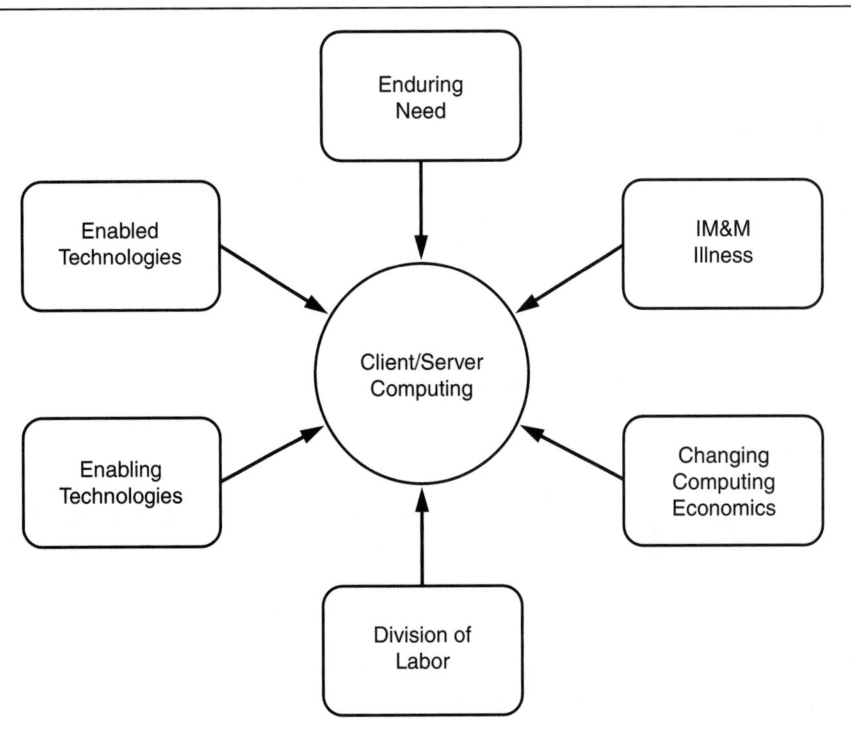

> Some analysts view client/server computing as the fourth wave of computing, which provides credence to the theory that postulates that technology progresses through major technology transformations. Client/server computing is the fourth subwave of the "Electronics and Information Technology" Wave, in which the advantages of the previous computing subwaves are consolidated by permitting all the previous computing models to interoperate. (p. 104)

Client/Server Communications

Boar[2] goes on to say that

> in client/server computing, the work is split between cooperating processors, where clients and servers may have the basic services of presentation, processing, and data partitioned across participating processors. The client may utilize shared resources from multiple servers to complete a unit of work. Servers may be general-purpose computers, specialized computers optimized for a specific task, or multitasking workstations or PCs. Although database access stands out as the most advantageous and obvious shared service, any activity is a server candidate that can be positioned as a general utility or reusable service (communication, numeric-intensive computing, electronic mail/fax, graphics, peripheral sharing, etc.) or could benefit from dedicated and/or specialized hardware/software. An enterprise-wide connectivity architecture consisting

of local area networking (LAN), metropolitan area networking (MAN), and wide area networking (WAN) interconnects the clients to the servers. Applications on appropriately scaled and functional clients perform part of the business function. Reusable and shareable resources required by the application are provided by an appropriate server. Servers, when required, take on the role of client to each other in order to avail themselves of each other's services.

Client/server computing is built upon a cooperative processing, or peer-to-peer, architecture. A cooperative processing architecture uses a peer-to-peer communications protocol (such as TCP/IP) to allow two programs to have an interactive conversation. In this model, each program executes an interactive verb set to carry on the conversation. Each participant in the interactive dialogue has to anticipate and handle all possible requests and replies. This includes error recovery. The client/server bonding software places a layer of software above the peer-to-peer protocol that vastly simplifies the application programming and hides the underlying protocol from both the clients and the servers. The application accesses the bonding software through an application programming interface (API). An API is provided on each side of the conversation, and it is through the hiding provided by the API that the illusion of a single system is created for both the clients and servers. The most common bonding software APIs are Remote Procedure Calls (RPCs) and Structured Query Language (SQL). (p. 104)

Multitiered Client/Server Architectures

Simple peer-to-peer networks, where one or more workstations communicates directly with other workstations, are being replaced by multitiered architectures as pictured by Boar in Figure 9.3. This section on multitiered client/server architectures is abstracted from Stan Schatt's *Linking LANs:*[3]

Figure 9.3 Multitiered client/server architectures.[2] (p. 103)

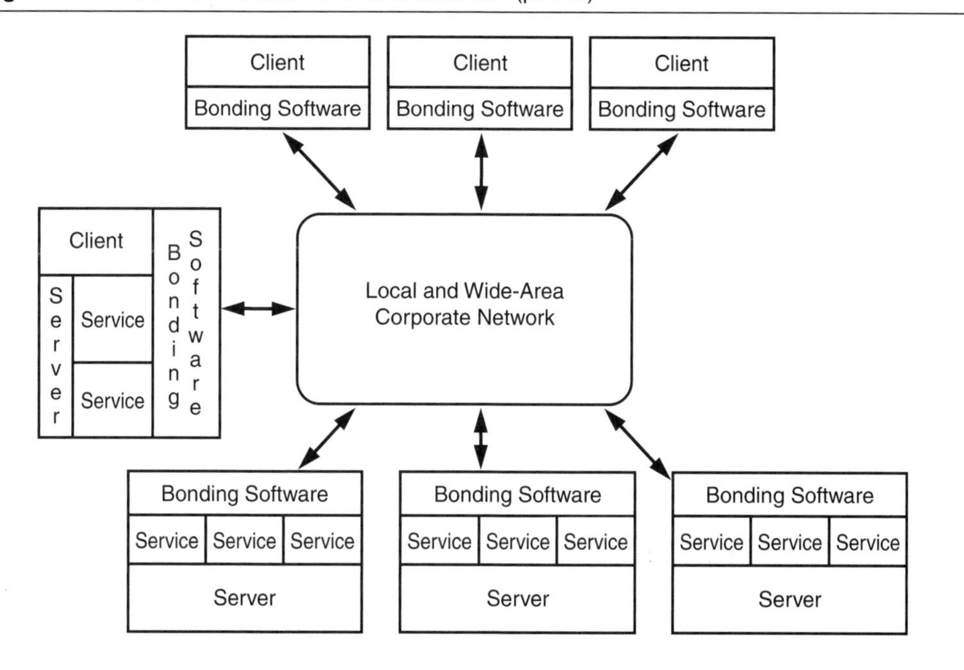

The presentation/users services tier is comprised of technology whose purpose is to service the presentational, connectivity, and other local needs of a client machine. Specific examples of services provided in this tier are graphical user interfaces (GUIs), remote procedure call (RPC) interfaces for sending requests to the application/object services tier, and logic needed to interact with the local operating system environment.

In a pure multitier client/server implementation, processing services are clearly separated from presentation tier applications. This supports IT efforts to reduce the cost of software maintenance and system administration. Furthermore, it provides an environment in which code reuse can become a reality rather than a distant wish of IT managers. The presentation tier is therefore committed only to maintaining resources needed to present information and processing to the client machines.

Andrew Tanenbaum[4] relates that there are two versions of client/server systems. In one version of a client/server system, "clients access their data by sending requests to the server, which carries out the work and sends back the replies. Communication always takes the form of request-reply pairs, always initiated by the clients, never by the server." In the other version of a client/server system, "the remote procedure call (RPC) school of thought approaches the client/server model* from a completely different perspective. In this view, a client sending a message to a server and getting a reply is like a program calling a procedure and getting a result. In both cases, the caller initiates an action and waits until it is completed and the results are available. Although in the ordinary (local) case, the procedure runs on the same machine as the caller, and with RPC it runs on a different machine, the caller need not be aware of this distinction."

---

* This client/server model is built on the OSI session layer. Tanenbaum[4] says:

OSI session primitives are best understood by dividing them into seven groups:

1. Connection establishment—contains four primitives, which specify a session identifier, the calling and called addresses, the quality of service, the initial synchronization number, the initial assignment of the tokens, some user data, and possibly various options.
2. Connection release—contains seven primitives concerned with releasing sessions, that are either ordinary or abrupt.
3. Data transfer—there are four independent data streams: (a) regular, (b) expedited, (c) typed, or (d) capability.
4. Token management—this has four tokens: (a) data token = data transfer in half-duplex mode; (b) release token = initiation of orderly release; (c) synchronize-minor token = insertion of minor sync points; (d) major/activity token = activity or major sync operations.
5. Synchronization—primitives are provided for major, minor or re-synchronization.
6. Activity management—activities can be started, interrupted, resumed, and discarded (abandoned).
7. Exception reporting—user or provider exceptions are handled.

The primary concern of the session layer is managing the dialog and dealing with errors occurring above the transport layer. In this OSI model, a connectionless session makes little sense. It has been assumed that the two processes of communicating over a session or transport connection are symmetric. This is frequently violated, as in the case of, a network of diskless personal computers or workstations, called clients, that are communicating over a network with a file server having a disk on which all the files are stored. In this system, clients access their data by sending requests to the server, which carries out the work and sends back the replies. Communication always takes the form of request-reply pairs, always initiated by the clients, never by the server.

Schatt[3] goes on to say that:

the application/object services tier is concerned with satisfying the application processing needs of end users. It does so by accepting requests from client machines and coordinating all data processing efforts needed to fulfill the user requests. Key technology components of this tier include transaction processing monitors and object request brokers based on CORBA and COM.

Use of transaction processing monitors can significantly improve the performance of multi-tier applications. This is due to the efficiency that transaction processing monitors have in coordinating application processing efforts such as two-phase commits and interprocess communication. In addition, most transaction processing monitors incorporate advanced multithreading control and task prioritization, which also add to their performance enhancements.

Like a transaction processing monitor, an object request broker is responsible for providing application processing to a client machine. An object request broker receives a message from the client machine and then manages the processing of the message by contacting the appropriate distributed object(s). These objects may exist anywhere on the network. The object request broker invokes the proper method (or logic) from the object and responds appropriately to the client machine.

There are several competing technologies for implementing multitier architectures based on distributed objects and object request brokers. Some of the more popular models include the Object Management Group's CORBA specification and Microsoft's COM specification. Both standards have gained industry acceptance. However, CORBA-based object technology has gained the widest acceptance.

The data services tier provides a robust, standard interface to an organization's enterprise data by managing data with relational and universal server databases. Organizations are increasingly finding it more important to create systems that share common databases. While one application may be the steward (or owner) of a particular data store, multiple end-user application may have a need to at least maintain read-only access to the data. This demands that databases be both accessible and compatible with multiple enterprise applications.

Local Area Networks (LAN)/Wide Area Networks (WAN)/ System Area Networks (SAN)

LANs are the network elements that hold the network together, but have distance limitations that vary depending upon the configuration. WANs, on the other hand, allow networks to expand by connection of LANs over vast distances. Figure 9.4 presents a representative view of the interconnection of LANs and WANs. SANs provide the network control for the environment where clusters, or multiple servers, are present.

Thin Clients/Network Computers

J.B. Miles[5] relates that elimination of most of the local peripherals, or other parts of network PCs (NetPC) result in network computers (NCs) or thin clients. Only monitors, mice, keyboards, fairly fast processors, graphics cards, and just enough memory to handle network input/output tasks are

Figure 9.4 Local Area Networks/Wide Area Networks.[2] (p. 109)

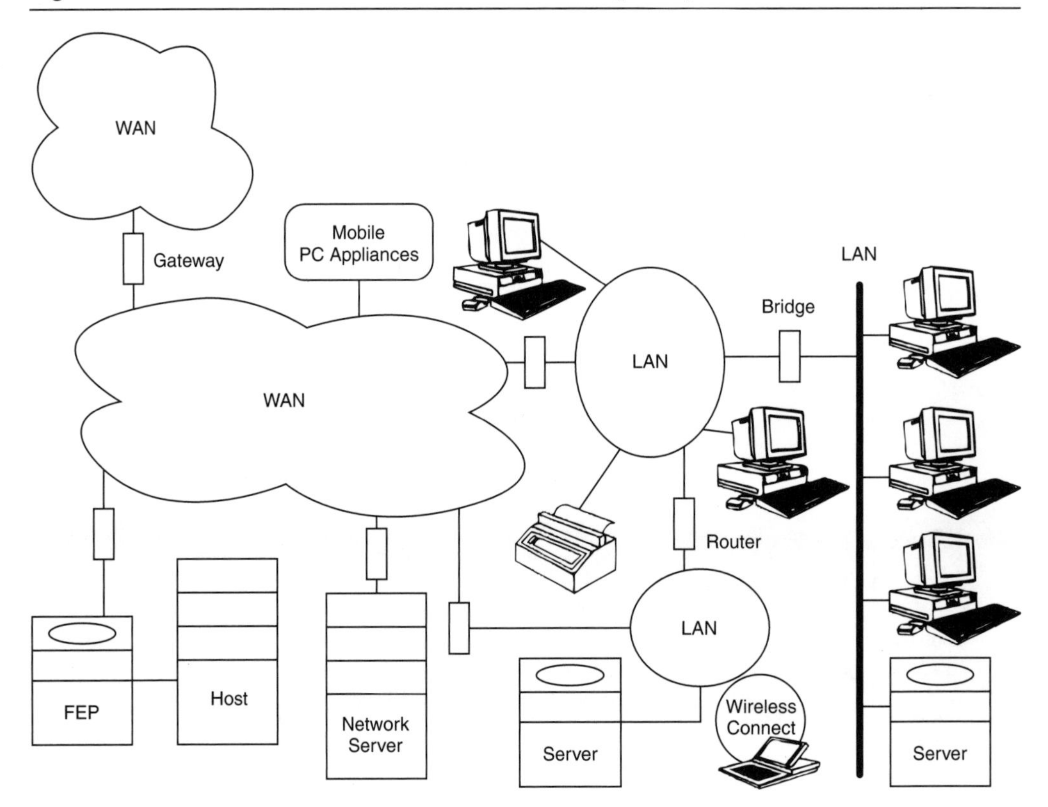

kept. The major pluses of NCs are: low initial purchase price and low total cost of ownership; and the major minuses of NCs are: more expensive than promised and limited expansion and storage capacity. The major pluses of NetPCs are: fast processors and mini-PC appearance; and the major minuses of NetPCs are: much pricier than NCs, some priced at more than $1,000 and higher maintenance costs. Hof[6] tells us that Microsoft's Windows Terminal Server lets terminals and PCs run Windows programs from a server, which is a major thrust in the establishment of NCs.

Server Clusters

Andy Marken[7] tells us that the benefits of moving to the client/server and network environments are faster service to users by placing a portion of the applications on the desktop and faster implementation. Rather than shifting to client/server and network environments, where there is less control over physical assets, a more flexible solution is the implementation of SAN [system area network] attached storage.

From the workgroup server under the desk to the large mainframes in the data center, these server clusters as described by Michael Cheek[8] are being implemented. "Although clustering can be done in many ways, simple failover has the broadest use because Microsoft Cluster Server is widely available in Microsoft Windows NT 5.0. In this failover setup, the two clustered servers connect to each other via dedicated network interface cards. If an application, resource, or server fails, an alert goes out for the other server to take over" (pp. 31–32).

Cheek[8] continues, as server clustering becomes more prevalent, load balancing will be the most requested feature. Load balancing means directing routines to individual processors. As more servers are clustered, both load balancing and the failover will be handled by the SAN, independent of the LAN or WAN.

Multidimensional Model

Client/server networks are clearly on the technology axis of the multidimensional model. The brief overview in the introduction to this chapter demonstrates that as usual, even the client/server network technology is in a state of significant change. So the V&V person has the burden of keeping up with technology innovations placed on top of the basic challenge of understanding the technology.

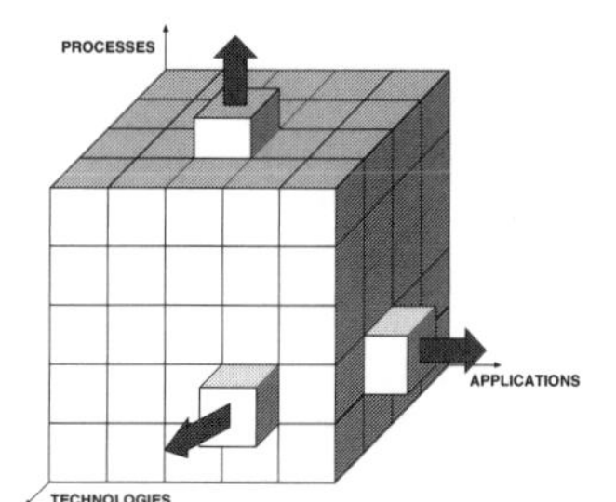

Processes of major significance to the client/server network technology are protocols in use and object oriented methods. Many protocols have been addressed in the introduction, such as OSI, RPC, TCP/IP, demonstrating that a V&V person involved with client/server networks requires a fundamental knowledge of these and related protocols.

In the client/server network environment the development process of choice is object oriented. Objects relate well to the implementation structure, often allowing the analyst to relate an object to a workstation, whereas the functional development method would complicate the mapping with multiple computers in the network.

The applications dimension has been almost any application type developed for client/server networks. For smaller data warehousing (Chapter 12), the client/server network is the appropriate technology, whereas large data warehouses are gravitating to an intranet or the Internet.

Traditional V & V

Major V&V considerations for client/server networks over and above the mainframe environment include:

1. System loads
   - Distribution of tasks
   - Architectural analysis

2. Transaction time
    - Distribution of tasks
3. Maintenance time
    - Recovery time
    - Recovery assurance of correctness (V&V)
    - Update time
    - Update assurance of correctness (V&V)
4. Data integrity
    - Data updates accuracy and completeness
    - Appropriate distribution of data
5. Ability to duplicate testing because of the complexity of the environment.

Each of these client/server V&V elements are addressed in this chapter.

In an "Overview of the Finance Standard Client/Server Guidelines"[1] we are reminded that:

> a number of influences must be considered when developing a client/server strategy. A strategy is a living, expandable plan that defines the scope of an operation and an approach for applying technology to solve business problems. It must respond to evolving customer requirements and advancing technology. [V&V personnel need to be involved in up-front decision making concerning client/server applicability, because] not all applications are suitable candidates for migration to a client/server architecture. The decision to migrate a system or application must be made in the setting of the business process the system or application is in. In other words, the decision should always consider the business process in which the system is embedded. (A-18)

Once the decision is made to use client/server architecture, the V&V person needs to understand some basic dynamics of the client/server environment. Paul Renaud in his *Introduction to Client/Server Systems*[9] provides these 25 rules of thumb:

1. Push as much processing as possible onto the client.
2. Do all compute-intensive activities on the client.
3. Separate per-user versus multi-user processing contexts.
4. Manage all shared resources with server processing.
5. Maintain a virtual view of servers during design.
6. Manage all data with server processing.
7. Avoid centralization of services.
8. Make sure local data is locally owned and managed.
9. Use tiered processing to achieve scalability.
10. Pull data transfers, instead of pushing them onto a server.
11. Minimize data transferred between clients and server.
12. Cache slowly changing or static data.
13. Compress large data transfers if possible.
14. Checkpoint large data transfers.

15. Use surrogate clients to implement multi-server data flows.
16. Use callbacks to hide server-to-server hand-offs.
17. Design for outages.
18. Centralize administration with distributed propagation.
19. Design for remote administration and monitoring.
20. Build security perimeters into systems and applications.
21. Analyze the reliability of your architecture.
22. Use the throughput chain to spot bottlenecks.
23. Use queuing models to spot hot spots.
24. Design for backward compatibility.
25. Measure demand independent of offered capacity (p. 308–314).

With these rules of thumb, a V&V person can better appreciate that client/server systems can fail in many ways, since many components are required for successful operation, as pointed out by Renaud. Figure 9.5 highlights some potential locations for failure. For example:

1. The client side of the application could fail due to a software defect.
2. The client system itself could fail due to a hardware failure.
3. The client's network card could fail.
4. High contention for the network could cause a client's connection to the server to time out.
5. Improper network administration could cause addressing conflicts, making it impossible to locate the server.
6. Key network elements (e.g., hubs, bridges) could fail due to hardware failures.
7. Messages get lost due to transmission errors.
8. The server could be using an incompatible vision of the network protocol.
9. The server system could fail due to hardware failure.
10. The server side of the application could experience a fault caused by a software defect.
11. The server's database could become corrupted due to a database fault.
12. The server's disk could be lost due to head crash.

These failure modes for client/server systems can be classified into the following categories:

1. Application software faults
2. Client hardware failures
3. Networking failures
4. Server hardware failures
5. Integration failures due to operational incompatibilities. (pp. 281–282)

Figure 9.5 Example failure locations.[9] (p. 271)

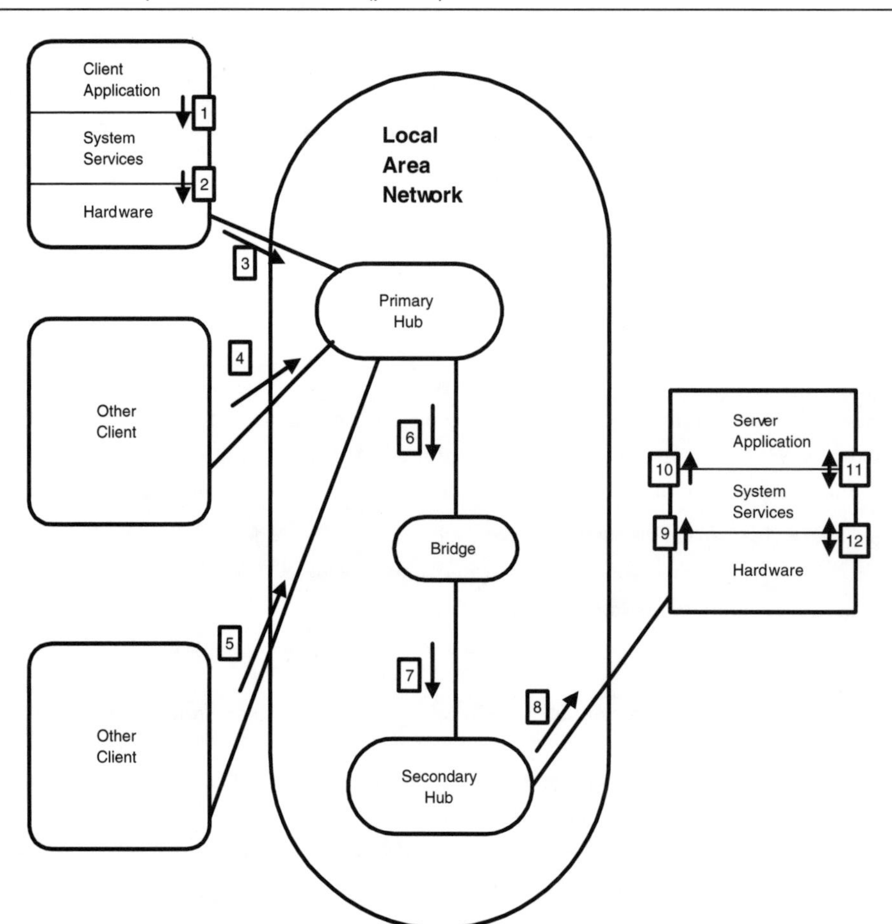

Concerning application software faults, the major V&V consideration for client/server networks that the V&V person must contend with is the ability to duplicate the faults because of the complexity of the environment.

For client and server hardware failures, the major V&V considerations for client/server networks that the V&V person must resolve are the assurance that the recovery is correct and that timing problems do not cause further hardware problems.

For networking failures, the major V&V considerations for client/server networks that the V&V person must consider are transaction times and concomitant distribution of tasks over the network. Also, the network system loads need to be evaluated.

Concerning integration failures due to operational incompatibilities, the major V&V considerations for client/server networks that the V&V person must resolve are primarily those of system loads and transaction time. However, the issues of data integrity and test repeatability are of concern in relation to operational incompatibilities.

Renaud goes on to say that the V&V person needs to be aware that:

> there are two views of performance in a client/server system: throughput and response time. Throughput is a measure of the amount of work done in a unit of time and is a view of the system's performance as seen by the server. It is measured in terms of the number of requests processed by the server per second. The definition of a transaction depends on the application, but it should include sending the results back to the client (i.e., a completed transaction). Response time, on the other hand, is a measure of the amount of time to do work and is the view of a system's performance as seen by the client. It is measured in terms of the time needed to complete a transaction. Generally, response time is estimated or measured over a number of transactions and is expressed in terms of the average time per transaction. The definition of a transaction again depends on the application, but response time is always measured from the time that a user initiates a request to the time the results are displayed to the user. (pp. 281–282)

The V&V person should especially be aware of the throughput linkage in a client/server network. Renaud[9] says:

> Since a client/server system is an end-to-end system, its throughput is throttled by the slowest throughput of the components used to process a transaction. In effect, a throughput chain is created by each of these components, as shown in [Figure 9.6]. The chain is only as strong as its weakest link! For example, suppose that:
>
> - Each client CPU can process 500 transactions per second
> - Network interface cards can handle 2400 packets per second
> - The LAN can carry 1200 packets per second before saturating
> - LAN/WAN routers can forward 7000 packets per second
> - The WAN can handle 650 packets per second
> - The server's CPU can handle 120 transactions per second
> - The server's only disk can perform 30 I/Os per second
>
> The fastest that this client/server system will work is 30 transactions per second (assuming that a transaction requires only one disk I/O), since it is bottlenecked by the server's disk throughput. (pp. 282–283)

V&V personnel need to ensure that several model-based development approaches are available to help design and implement client/server applications and applications based on a GUI.

Figure 9.6 Throughput chain.[9] (p. 282)

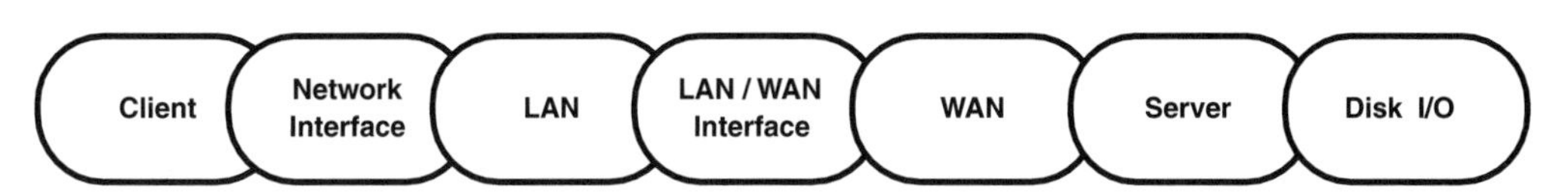

Figure 9.7 Model-based development.[10] (p. 24)

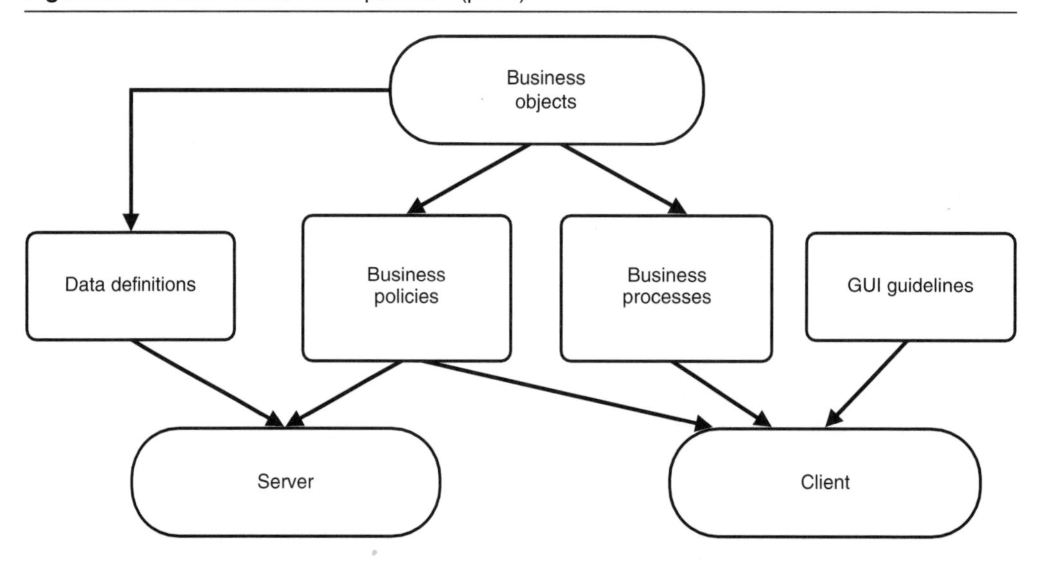

Such a model-based development example is shown in Figure 9.7. This approach is most applicable to a wide variety of business and IS software.

Steven Rakitin[10] points out that there are advantages and disadvantages to the model-based development approach. Advantages are: "(a) It is closely tied to specific business processes; (b) it clearly delineates client and server applications; (c) tools are available to support the use of the models; and (d) it includes a style guide for the GUI." Disadvantages are: "(a) It does not include a structured development approach; and (b) it does not reference specific documents, deliverables, or reviews" (pp. 23–24).

Design Verification

Some specific elements of object oriented design related to client/server networks are discussed here extracted from *Designing Object Oriented Software*[11] for the V&V person:

> Object oriented design seeks to model the world in terms of objects collaborating to discharge their responsibilities. These collaborations are viewed as one-way interactions: One object requests a service of another object. The object that makes the request is the client, and the object that receives the request and thereupon provides the service is the server.
>
> The ways in which a given client can interact with a given server are described by a contract. A contract is the list of requests that a client can make of a server. The V&V person assures that both fulfill the contract: the client by making only those requests the contract specifies, and the server by responding appropriately to those requests [Figure 9.8].

Figure 9.8 The Client/server contract.[11]

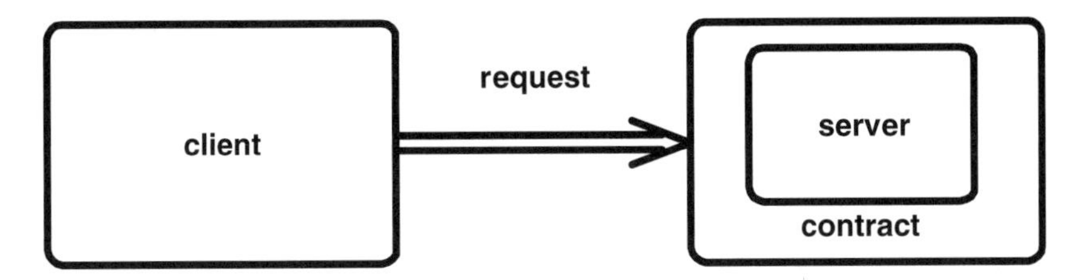

To model a design that performs this collaboration between clients and servers as a contract, the following must be done:

1. Find the objects
2. Determine their responsibilities
3. Determine collaborations

At the end of this process, [the V&V person verifies that] there is:

- a list of entities within the application to play the roles of clients and servers
- a list of collaborations between them to serve as the basis for contracts.

Caching

This discussion of caching is derived from the *Encyclopedia of Computer Science:*[12]

> Because files are accessed across a network, the performance of remote operations is generally lower than when accessing a local disk. To improve performance, systems are networked using caching techniques.... The client, server, or both maintain a cache of recently used file pages. Before the client forwards a request to the remote server, it checks to see if the request can be satisfied using information in the local cache. If the information resides in the cache, the file pages are retrieved from the cache, and the request need not be sent to the server at all, reducing latencies (access times...). Likewise, the server consults its local cache before issuing input/output commands to the disk device. Because file reference strings display similar locality to page reference strings in virtual memory systems, caching can greatly improve average access times.
>
> Although caching improves access time performance, the V&V person should be aware that it also raises cache coherency issues. For example, suppose that two machines have been accessing a file at the same time, and the contents of the file resides in both client caches. If a user on one machine deletes the file, a user on the other machine may find the file still exists because the client finds it in its local cache. To keep caches consistent, when a file on one machine is changed or deleted the caches on all other machines in the distributed network must be updated. Special protocols are used to solve such problems. For example, a server may specify that a file can be cached by only one client at a time, or disable caching completely for those files that are being shared.
>
> Another aspect of file server design that affects caching is whether the server should be "stateful" or "stateless." Upon machine reboots, a stateless server retains no knowledge about the

> files client machines are using. When a client makes a request, each request contains complete information needed to service it. For example, when reading a file sequentially, each request contains the starting and ending byte offsets of the desired information rather than requesting "the next 1,024 bytes." In contrast, stateful servers keep track of which clients are using files and in what ways. Such information is important for maintaining cache consistency and for providing such services as exclusive file flocks. The main drawback of stateful servers is that rebooting the server interrupts all client applications that were accessing files at the time the server went down. The server must reject all requests related to the accesses initiated before the server rebooted.
>
> File servers must also address the problem of authentication. That is, if a client requests the pages, how can the server be sure that the client is really who it claims to be? In a networked environment, an unauthorized client may masquerade as another in an attempt to access sensitive data stored on the file server. The V&V person must assure that authentication is handled by using cryptographic techniques.... Before authorizing access, the file server forwards the request to an authentication server. The messages exchanged by the file and authentication servers are encrypted using keys that only the two servers share, insuring that the authentication server can be trusted. The authentication server verifies access rights of the client (perhaps by exchanging messages directly with the client, using another set of private keys), and then returns its response to the file server. (pp. 554–555)

Load Testing

As we see adapted from "Continuous Testing Cures the Last Minute Crunch,"[13] "if one waits until after development of the client/server application to test it for defects and performance, one could be wasting thousands of dollars and hours of time. Fortunately, more corporations are listening to the V&V person telling them that after-the-fact testing just does not make sense" (p. 21). Testing may be very complete and good, but it often costs a lot of time and money. Testing can add months to the development of a client/server application. The problem usually is that developers turn over the application to testers only after development is complete. Since the test group is not involved in the initial plan, its role is unclear until it is time to test.

Client/server application development efforts should integrate sophisticated testing from day one of a project. They also should use automated testing tools. Improving the testing process requires hard work, and it may take two to three development cycles before the pay-off really becomes clear.

Quinn and Lucas[14] tell us that load testing, one of the major V&V considerations, is the process of simulating a large number of users running transactions against a server, which involves examining the performance of machines, networks, and databases under heavy user loads. Knowing that load testing is best at pinpointing software bottlenecks, the V&V person runs load tests to determine if the network connection is able to support the load, if the database server will fail, if the PC client front-end will break, or if the database configuration itself is tuned properly.

In "Beyond the Server,"[15] we learn that, "although the term 'load testing' suggests a measure of a database server's capability to handle many queries and updates, the 100Mbps Ethernet pipe (which makes up the lion's share of today's corporate networks) is often the bottleneck of performance. CACI Product Co.'s Comnet III and Systems and Network Inc.'s Bones products do LAN and WAN network simulations allowing the V&V person to do virtual load testing of the network itself, not database load testing."

"Strange as it sounds, but the 'toss 'em on the speeding treadmill' system," from "Getting Client/Server Off the Treadmill,"[16]

> is close to how client/server systems are often tested. A small (often, a really small) prototype and the individual system components are tested for load, but one never really knows what will happen until the application is running at full load on the actual network. Full load on a mission-critical application is the absolute least opportune time to determine that the system does not function properly.
>
> The basic idea is to provide an easy way to test corporate client/server implementations with a software package. The package does mark a departure from the testing tools in use today at most companies. Many companies do not stress test their client/server connection at all. Those that do usually do so after they notice a bottleneck. Most likely, companies will test their GUIs with a product such as Visual Test and then use a load testing tool to test the database alone. (p. 114)

Paul Herzlich[17] relates that for GUI and client/server, tests may be partitioned into various elements—user interface, communications, server-based, etc.—and each element treated as a separate concern for testing. The partitions often conveniently correspond to prototypes, which permit integration testing to be performed within the network. Tests of behind-the-scenes functionality are driven via the user interface, which kicks off a chain of events integrating through to the server and back, for example.

Scalability

The major V&V considerations for client/server networks of system loads and transaction timing are aided by the scalability of networks, Richard Martin tells us in "Scalability."[18] Furthermore, the client level and server level each scale differently, but extensively and independently. Items such as database performance, application logic, or user interface can be sped up as necessary.

Nik Sargent's[19] ideas are discussed in the remainder of this section. In the traditional V&V sense, his example of client/server network system steps were successful without being particularly exotic. The system he described was a modification to an existing system to perform complex network-based telecommunications tasks. Not only were the specification and new design features documents QA-reviewed in the customary fashion, but separate V&V reviews were held. He continues,

> these V&V reviews consisted of a rigorous formal inspection of documents against the requirements specification and included prepared criteria and guidance. Nearly 50% of all system defects were detected at these reviews. That is, when we came to testing, half the errors hadn't been introduced in the first place!
>
> To improve the review process, all the core system components were reviewed in a single session, thereby enabling developers to resolve inconsistencies with each other immediately

> so that the review did not stretch out unnecessarily. This process was then followed up with code walkthrough of the changed code, and this consistently detected nearly 100% of errors in the new functions. Taking metrics during these activities was essential for assessing their effectiveness.
>
> During the development phase it was necessary to try to detect and correct existing errors, as well as avoid new ones. Static analysis, as performed by the McCabe toolset, was found to be effective in allowing customized views of the behavior and structure of the code (important when the code is inherited), and in focusing on areas that were more error prone. Indeed, a striking correlation was found between the code where errors were located and the tool's indication of "problem" code.
>
> Automation of system testing is a key factor to its success, so bulk call generators were used to successfully load and stress test the system.... An essential of any system is its ability to archive its transactions. Combined with custom tools to extract, summarize, and recreate events on the platform, this forms an invaluable aid to debugging during the test phase and live service. It is an aim that the automated tester will take these logs as an input, and then accurately recreate the transactions on a model system, as an aid to debugging, in much the same way as can be done with a capture/replay tool.

Contemporary V & V

Distributed Component Platforms

In 1995, in the world of component software, several vendors and consortia independently developed standards that define the basic mechanics for building and interconnecting software components. This section is abstracted from Krieger and Adler's "The Emergence of Distributed Component Platforms."[20]

> Sun's JavaBeans has emerged as the leading rival to Microsoft's DCOM (Distributed Component Object Module), supplanting the OpenDoc standard. Component software is moving to enterprise applications that include distributed server components.
>
> The backers of competing standards are racing to capture market leadership by delivering the tangible benefits of component standards via distributed component platforms—integrated development and run-time environments that isolate much of the conceptual and technical complexity involved in building component-based applications. With distributed component platforms, businesses can assign their few highly skilled programmers to component construction and use less sophisticated developers to carry out the simpler assembly tasks. (p. 46)

The V&V person also needs to be aware of the major V&V considerations for client/server networks including the impacts of the distribution of tasks from the joint perspectives of the system loads and the effect of the transaction time. Krieger and Adler[20] continue:

> [These enterprise applications rely] on a robust set of services for accessing and managing services, information, and computing resources. To move beyond the desktop, components require five distributed services:

- Remote communications protocols, which enable interactions at the application layer among components distributed over a network. Protocols can be synchronous (e.g., remote procedure calls) or asynchronous (e.g., messaging services that enable an efficient, nonblocking store-and-forward model).
- Directory services, which provide a coherent global scheme for naming, organizing, and accessing shared services and resources.
- Security services, which protect shared resources by ensuring that communicating parties are properly authenticated and have suitable authorization and that third parties have not intercepted or tampered with their messages.
- Transaction services, which coordinate concurrent updates to enterprise-critical data, and ensure all updates leave data in correct and consistent states.
- System management services, which provide a unified set of facilities to monitor, manage, and administer services and resources across the enterprise.

[All of these services are included in Enterprise JavaBeans (EJB).]

Many distributed facilities are not services in the traditional client/server sense. Rather, they constitute part of a component's runtime environment. For example, a server component may obtain transactional persistence from its runtime context, rather than implementing it directly.... [Distributed component platforms] providers are attempting to generalize containment models to encompass the relationships between server components and their runtime hosts; like visual containers, transaction contexts provide runtime access to basic life-support and custodial services for their components. However, server components generally provide concurrent services to many users, whereas desktop components support single users.

Advanced Distributed Simulations

Robert O. Lewis presented a generic model for verification, validation and accreditation (VV&A) of advanced distributed simulation (ADS) used for test and evaluation (T&E) at the 1997 Simulation Interoperability Workshop. This presentation proposes a generic framework that addresses the use of ADS for T&E, and describes a process for VV&A to ensure the product is credible and acceptable to the users. Of particular interest and emphasis are ADS development strategies and alternative roles for the users of the ADS. This section is extracted from Lewis' presentation.[21]

The VV&A activity is immersed as a near-integral part of the development and checkout of the ADS. Two points about the differences among types of V&V are:

1. No matter what form V&V takes, it must do its own analysis and reports and brief the customer and the team.
2. Sharing data, tests, tools, software, resources, and test facilities with the developer may be the only sensible approach when replication is impractical. It saves time and a great deal of money, and it supports repeatability.

With the ADS, there is verification testing and validation testing, and the V&V person has a very specific role to play in each. Construction and Assembly (C&A) produces any new software required as glue code or for any specific application that needs to be modified to run in the ADS. There is some limited integration during this time, but no attempts are made to bring up the entire netted ADS as a system; that occurs in integration and test (I&T). At I&T, verification testing begins in earnest as components are brought on line, usually one at a time, with the control center to ensure compliance and basic compatibility. The test environment evaluates such discrete factors as—ability to share the common synthetic environment, to exchange data with a surrogate or another component in a realistic manner, and to perform basic interactions. The network, instrumentation, and proficiency of operators and players can be observed in manageable chunks.

Lewis[21] continues:

> Here, verification is distinguished from development testing. Development tests support the process of compatibility analysis between components and the test control center, allow the network to be brought on line incrementally and tested, and support component-to-environment testing. Verification tests typically continue this process by testing the pieces of an operational node, examining major functions to ensure that requirements and Measures of Performance (MOPs) are met, and that specified capabilities and performance are provided. Verification tests asks the question, "Did the developer build that node correctly, and does the component meet its basic design criteria and specifications, even when the ADS team is not responsible for the design?"
>
> V&V will also perform verification of any new software, as well as data developed to support the ADS configuration and testing, and analyze the instrumentation and data collection capabilities at the test control center and nodes. V&V may also perform other verification tests, such as those included in [Table 9.2] that depict various test levels. In this I&T phase, developer and V&V roles draw even closer together.
>
> [The assumption is that ADS integration is incremental.] Integration allows network performance measurement as components come on line and evaluates interactions in manageable chunks. When the teams are still examining the functional integrity and performance of pieces and components, that type of testing is called verification.
>
> Once testers begin to observe and measure interactions, behaviors, and effectiveness of components in a realistic operational setting, the term used is validation testing. The last significant hurdle in this phase is to delineate the difference between development tests (developer-initiated and run) and validation tests (V&V-initiated and probably developer run, since they likely control all the resources). The developer has an obligation to test the ADS to the level where all of the requirements are satisfied. Assume the test plan calls for a dozen test cases, with the first eight addressing incremental integration and testing of the components, network, and remote sites. V&V plays in the final end-point tests as monitors, analysts, or participants in a cooperative fashion with the developers.
>
> When these build-up tests are satisfactorily performed, a comprehensive "non-stressing" full-up integrated test is run. Once this test provides clean runs, the ADS is ready for its first major validation test(s). This test series should be designed by V&V jointly with the development team basically to cover all of the acceptability criteria, MOPs, MOEs, etc., needed for accreditation. One test case would perhaps be a maximum load test run by the developer with V&V to determine where ADS fails. Another test case might be boundary and/or sensitivity tests, where data are manipulated to see what happens. Finally, the last test series can be used

Table 9.2 V&V of networks.[21] (pp. 7, 8)

Type	Owner/Provider	ADS Developer	Runs for VV&A	ADS VV&A
ADS Verification Level				
Component Tests for ADS	Often Assists	Performs	Yes	Confirms rqmts tracing and MOPs
Compliance Tests	Performs or Assists	Assists or Performs	Yes	Confirms Confirms
Comm./ Network Tests	Assists	Performs	Yes	Monitors and Analyzes; Confirms MOPs
Data Certification /Authentication	Performs or N/A	Confirms or Performs		Confirms Confirms
Synthetic Environment Tests (and Compatibility with Components)	Performs or Confirms	Confirms or Performs		Confirms Confirms
Players and Users	Provides or Approves	Confirms or Provides		Confirms Confirms
ADS Validation Level				
Netted Interoperability of Components Tests	Observes	Performs	Yes	Confirms MOPs
Behavioral Analysis Tests	Observes	Performs	Yes	Confirms MOPs
Operational Effectiveness Tests	Observes	Performs	Yes	Confirms MOEs
Load Tests	Observes	Performs	No	Confirms Perf
Sensitivity Tests	Observes	Performs	Yes	Confirms MOPs
Boundary Tests	Observes	Performs	Yes	Confirms MOPs

MOP = Measure of Performance MOE = Measure of Effectiveness

as the accreditation run. This is an "everything normal" full-up case also used for performance benchmarking and regression testing.

Validation testing should not interfere with development testing; in fact, it is just an extension of it, with a specific criterion in mind—ensuring accreditation. This way, everyone knows from the beginning what it will take to get the ADS accredited, but that target is not the only goal; reasonable performance bounds also need to be ensured. The other aspect of validation is the reference model. To what is the performance of the ADS compared, when asserting that we have a "sufficiently" valid model? Typically the real system (best unless sample is small), other known accredited simulations, in-depth analysis and evaluation, other real-world sources, and SMEs (weak for T&E) are used. [For either type of testing the project can be aided by viewing the log files of transactions to see the results of tests. The DummyNet tool is such a view system.]

In summary, validation testing must be adequate to ensure first of all that the requirements, acceptability criteria, MOPs, MOEs, and any other test criteria are met; and, second, that the performance of the ADS is acceptable at some level beyond normal. Only then can we use the ADS with confidence to draw conclusions as to its utility for T&E. Remember, in T&E, the ADS developers are typically users as well. (p. 6)

Network Partitioning

This section is abstracted from "Surviving Network Partitions:"[22]

Applications implemented as distributed systems, particularly those distributed over a wide area, must withstand network partitioning faults, which split the system into two or more components. Though processes in the same component can communicate with each other, they cannot communicate with processes in other components. If processes continue to operate in the disconnected components, they might perform incompatible operations and make the application data inconsistent.…

Distributed systems are vulnerable to network partitioning faults, particularly over wide areas. Primary component methodologies that suspend operations in non-primary components are unacceptable to businesses, which need operations to continue in all components of a partitioned network. Fulfillment transactions allow continued operations, require little additional infrastructure, incur little additional overhead, and are programmed just like other types of transactions. The fulfillment transaction processing paradigm can be adapted easily to other programming paradigms. (pp. 62, 67)

Web-Based Client/Server

This section is from Mark LeBaron's "Web-Based Client/Server: Putting Database Management Systems on the Web:"[23]

In the simplest sense, web-based client/server computing fits the definition of client/server computing because it involves two or more pieces of software performing separate tasks in conjunction with one another to accomplish a common goal. The web browser, for example, can be thought of as a generic client that handles the display of information and processes the user interface events. As the server, the DBMS accepts and processes client requests for data and data manipulation.

Web-based client/server computing uses a typical web browser to access and manipulate dynamic information, stored in a centrally controlled DBMS, over the Internet. This is an alternative to the current client/server model, in which a custom-written GUI application accesses and manipulates dynamic information stored in a DBMS using proprietary communication software. Web-based client/server computing generates HyperText Mark-up Language (HTML) pages on the fly to provide the latest information via the WWW.

In its current state, web-based client/server applications cannot provide users with the fancy interfaces that are provided by applications constructed with other GUI development tools. Applications designed with these types of tools can be customized to complete complex transactions from a single screen. Although web-based client/server applications still do the job right, complex transactions may require the user to navigate several simple screens rather than use a single complex screen.

An example of this drawback is that HTML forms currently have no built-in method to perform input validation or masking. To the web browser, everything entered into HTML form is just text, which means a server-side process must perform data validation after the entry has already been submitted from the browser. If there is a validation error, the server-side process must send an HTML page back to the browser to inform the user of the error. This is not as efficient as having a client-side process perform the validations before the data is submitted.

Java, ActiveX, and other similar tools promise to allow development of more complex user interfaces for web-based client/server applications. Also, certain other proprietary browser "plug-ins" allow more complex client-side processing, as long as the HTML page has been designed to trigger the browser plug-in and instruct it how to operate. When deciding whether to use such proprietary client-side tools, a key consideration should be that using tools could nullify some of the major benefits of web-based client/server, such as platform-independent applications, easier software distribution, and a [less expensive] GUI. (pp. 8, 12, 13)

As with most client/server methods discussed in this chapter, web-based client/server computing has benefits and drawbacks elaborated from LeBaron[23] that the V&V person needs to be familiar with. The benefits include:

- better customer service
- platform-independent applications
- easier software distribution and configuration management (both upgrades and primary releases)
- reusable training
- cheaper GUI...

The drawbacks include:

- slow Internet speed
- limitations associated with HTML
- more complex security issues
- [need for a mature Internet staff]. (pp. 12, 13)

Summary

Major V&V considerations for client/server networks over and above the mainframe environment were introduced in this chapter. Each has been discussed in this chapter, and a highlight of the areas where those discussions occurred follow:

1. System loads
   - integration failures due to operational incompatibilities
   - scalability
   - distributed component platforms

2. Transaction time
   - integration failures due to operational incompatibilities
   - networking failures
   - scalability
   - distributed component platforms
3. Maintenance time
   - multitier client/server implementation
   - thin clients/network computers
4. Data integrity
   - integration failures due to operational incompatibilities
   - DBMS application development model
5. Ability to duplicate testing because of the complexity of the environment
   - load testing
   - scalability
   - advanced distributed simulations

With client/server networks, the V&V person needs to be aware of the large cost associated with being in maintenance. *The Washington Post*[24] reported in 1996 that it costs $8,140 a year to own and maintain a computer as part of a network. The cost elements that make that up are:

- hardware = $2,000
- software = $940
- training = $1,400
- network management $3,830.

The network management element that contains the "downtime" costs further decomposes to:

- desktop administrator = $1,278
- user downtime = $1,350
- co-worker time = $540
- disaster recovery = $470
- disaster prevention = $192.

However, from "Client/Server Benefits, Problems, Best Practices,"[25] we learn that:

> client/server applications can produce numerous valuable benefits, including improved integration of business information and system accessibility and reduced costs. Managers may have to struggle with several problems, including inadequate internal skills available, corporate politics, and inadequate security capabilities, that can diminish the benefits. Moreover, when companies introduce significant organizational change as part of their client/server implementation efforts, they exacerbate the problems. Managers can ease the transition to a client/server system by recogniz-

ing the potential benefits, deciding to move forward, and [implementing a V&V activity associated with the client/server system]. (p. 91)

References

1 "Overview of the Finance Standard Client/Server Guidelines," In *The CIM Help Disk* (CD-ROM), Functional Process Improvement, Vol. 2, (800)-TELL-CIM, January 1995.

2 Boar, Bernard H., *Implementing Client/Server Computing, A Strategic Perspective* (New York: McGraw Hill Book Company, 1993).

3 Schatt, Stan, *Linking LANs* (2nd ed.), (New York: McGraw Hill Book Company, 1995).

4 Tanenbaum, Andrew S., *Computer Networks* (2nd ed.), (Englewood Cliffs, NJ: Prentice Hall Publishing Co., 1989).

5 Miles, J. B., "Network Computers," *Government Computer News,* February 9, 1998, pp. 43–45.

6 Hof, Robert D., "How the 'PC Killer' Was Humbled," *Business Week,* April 13, 1998, p. 61.

7 Marken, Andy, "New Information Paradigm Impacts Network Storage," *Document Management,* January/February/March 1998, pp. 38,39.

8 Cheek, Michael, "Ride the Next Big Wave: Server Clusters," Technology Report section of *Government Computer News,* March 16, 1998, pp. 31, 32.

9 Renaud, Paul E., *Introduction to Client/Server Systems* (New York: John Wiley & Sons, Inc., 1993). Copyright © 1993 John Wiley & Sons, Inc., Adapted by permission of John Wiley & Sons, Inc.

10 Rakitin, Steven R., *Software Verification and Validation: A Practitioner's Guide,* (Boston: Artech House, 1997), Reprinted from permission from Artech House, Inc., Norwood, MA, USA, http:\\www.artech-house.com.

11 Wirfs-Brock, Rebecca, Wilkerson, Brian and Wiener, Lauren, *Designing Object-Oriented Software* (Englewood Cliffs, NJ: Prentice Hall Publishing Co., 1990).

12 Ralston, Anthony and Reilly, Edwin (editors), *Encyclopedia of Computer Science* (New York: Van Nostrand Reinhold, 1993).

13 Callaway, Erin, "Continuous Testing Cures the Last Minute Crunch," *PC Week,* March 25, 1996, Vol. 13, No. 12, p. 21.

14 Quinn, Stephen R. & Lucas, Kathie, "Get a Load of This," *InfoWorld* Jan. 15, 1996, Vol. 18, No. 3, p. 55.

15 "Beyond the Server," *InfoWorld,* Vol. 18, No. 3, Jan. 15, 1996.

16 Lundquist, Eric, "Getting Client/Server Off the Treadmill," *PC Week,* July 15, 1996, Vol. 13, No. 28, p. 114.

17 Herzlich, Paul, "A Quick Win for Testing," *SQM* issue 25, © 1995 Paul Herzlich, Web presentation © 1996 Tesseract Publishing, March 11, 1996, http://www.avnet.co.uk/tesseract/QiC/articles/Herzlich/25.html.

18 Martin, Richard J. "Scalability," *Journal of Systems Management,* May 1994, Vol. 45, No. 5, p. 26.

19 Sargent, Nik, "VV and T of a Complex Network-Based Telecom System," *SQM,* issue 26, Tesseract Publishing, Cheshire, U.K., http://www.avnet.co.uk/tesseract/SQM/articles/Sargent/26.html, 1997.

20 Krieger, David and Adler, Richard M., "The Emergence of Distributed Component Platforms," *IEEE Computer,* (© March 1998 IEEE), pp. 43–52.

21 Lewis, Robert O., "A Generic Model For Verification, Validation, And Accreditation (VV&A) of Advanced Distributed Simulations (ADS) Used for Test And Evaluation (T&E)," *Proceedings of the Spring 1997 Simulation Interoperability Workshop,* Simulation Interoperability Standards Organization, Inc., March 1997.

[22] Melliar-Smith, Peter and Moser, Louise, "Surviving Network Partitioning," *IEEE Computer,* (© March 1998 IEEE), pp. 62–68.

[23] LeBaron, Mark M., "Web-Based Client/Server: Putting Database Management Systems on the Web," In *CrossTalk,* Software Technology Support Center, Ogden: Hill AFB, Vol. 9, No. 12, December 1996, pp. 8–13.

[24] Forrester Research, *The Washington Post,* May 5, 1996.

[25] Duchessi, Peter and InduShobha, Chengalur-Smith, "Client/Server Benefits, Problems, Best Practices," *Communications of the ACM,* Vol. 41, No. 5, May 1998, pp. 87–94.

General Reference

Shaw, Mary and Garlan, David, Software Architecture: *Perspectives on an Emerging Discipline* (Englewood Cliffs, NJ: Prentice Hall Press, 1996).

CHAPTER 10

Knowledge-Based Systems (KBS)

Introduction

The definition of knowledge-based system (KBS) is supplied from the NIST publication, *Reference Information for Software Verification and Validation Process.*[1] It refers to systems that use or manipulate complex data or knowledge structures using artificial intelligence (AI) techniques. The goal of these systems is to apply specialized expertise to solving problems. KBSs typically incorporate a domain model and apply that model to new problems. The purpose of incorporating a KBS into a larger system is to improve the performance of the overall system for unanticipated situations (i.e., its robustness). KBS subsumes the older term "expert system," which typically refers to systems that encode an expert's knowledge as rules and apply those rules to solve problems (p. 26).

Playle and Beckman[2] tell us that:

> KBSs attempt to mimic the manner in which humans perform given tasks, especially to duplicate "expert" performance. They capture the knowledge and expertise, along with the rules used to apply the knowledge, and allow repeatable reapplication of the knowledge to problems. KBSs [are defined] as those "that attempt to perform at the same level of performance as a human expert over a given domain."... Their domains cannot be fully specified before the creation of the system and thus cannot be argued about in the formal styles available to the conventional software developer. (p. 17)

The National Institute of Standards and Technology (NIST)[1] publication relates that while many KBSs employ rules, the AI community has developed a variety of reasoning paradigms including case-based reasoning and the use of neural networks. Rules remain a popular, useful, well-understood approach to encoding an important subset of domain expertise. This subset is sometimes called a domain experts decision heuristics, or "rules of thumb" (p. 28).

The goals of KBSs are usually more ambitious than those of conventional or algorithmic programs. They frequently perform not only as problem solvers but also as intelligent assistants and training aids. This information is extracted from the Federal Highway Administration's *Verification, Validation, and Evaluation of Expert Systems.*[3] KBSs have great potential for capturing the knowledge and experience of current senior professionals and making it available to others in the form of training aids or technical support tools.

Daniel O'Leary[4] notes that an important aspect of KBSs is knowledge management, which entails formally managing knowledge resources in order to facilitate access and reuse of knowledge, typically by using advanced information technology:

> Historically, knowledge management has been aimed at a single group—managers—through what has been generally referred to as an executive information system (EIS). An EIS contains a portfolio of tools such as drill-down access to databases, news source alerts, and other information—all aimed at supporting managerial decision making.... [The fact is that] if executives need access to information and knowledge, their employees are also likely to have an interest in and need for [similar] information.
>
> In AI, knowledge bases are [generally] for consumption by so-called expert and knowledge-based experts, where computers use rule inference to answer user questions. Although knowledge acquisition for computer inferencing is still important, most recent knowledge management developments make knowledge available for direct human consumption or develop software that processes that knowledge. (p. 54)

Multidimensional Model

KBSs fall on the application axis of the multidimensional model. For instance, information services applications would be considered similar, but KBSs are more sophisticated. In the business environment, information systems that utilize a knowledge base are usually the EISs just discussed.

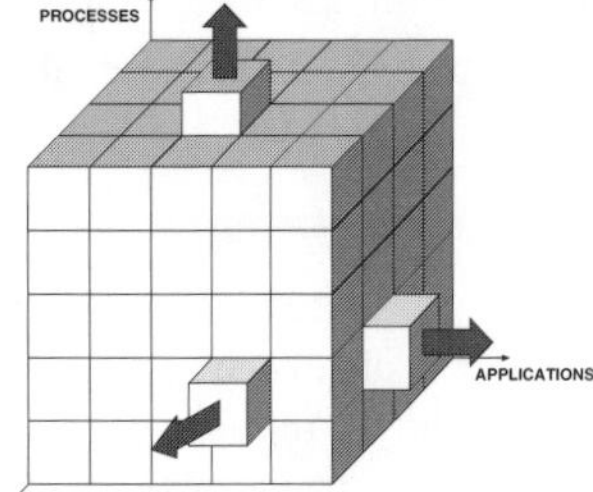

On the technology axis of the multidimensional model, the extensive storage and rapid response times available on today's computers provide an important aspect of the reason for the existence of KBSs. The storage allows a place to maintain the knowledge base, and the computer speed allows a reasonable response time to the user's queries.

The support to KBSs on the process axis comes from life-cycle models, particularly the model-based model that is specifically focused on the "model" under development—in this case, KBSs. It seems that project management is particularly more important to the success of KBS development than most other system developments. The reason is that related elements of the knowledge experts development and the software development are going on simultaneously. These multiple activities require more attention from management.

Traditional V & V

A KBS is "a computer program that includes a representation of the experience, knowledge, and reasoning processes of an expert" (pp. 1, 2). Wentworth et al., in *Verification, Validation, and Evaluation of Expert Systems,*[3] inform us that the difficulty of performing V&V on KBSs is one of the factors slowing the development and acceptance of KBSs. There is little agreement among experts on how to accomplish the V&V of KBSs. The complexity and uncertainty related to these tasks has led to the situation where most KBSs are not adequately tested. In some cases testing is ignored until late in the development cycle, leading to predictably poor results.

Wentworth et al.[3] go on to say that one of the impediments to a successful V&V effort for KBSs is the nature of expert systems themselves. KBSs are often employed for working with incomplete or uncertain information or "ill-structured" situations. Since KBS specifications often do not provide precise criteria against which to test, there is a problem in verifying and validating KBSs according to the definitions. Some vagueness in the specifications for KBSs is unavoidable; if there are precise enough specifications for a system, it may be more effective to design the system using conventional programming languages. Another problem in V&V for KBSs is that KBS languages (the technology dimension) are unstructured to accommodate the relatively unstructured applications (p. 4).

Verification of a KBS is the task of determining that the system is built according to its specifications. Validation of a KBS is the process of determining that the system actually fulfills the purpose for which it was intended. As a further extension, then, evaluation reflects the acceptance of the system by the end users and its performance in the field.

Dr. Eugene Santos[5] alerts us that V&V is important to the knowledge-base portion of a KBS.

> Traditional approaches to V&V have concentrated on the three "I"s of knowledge: Inconsistent, Incomplete, and Incorrect. Work in verification and validation alone has been mainly restricted to straightforward issues such as consistency and completeness for verification with little or no detail on validation. Verification is automatically performed during knowledge acquisition—an automated process itself. Validation automates the correcting of "incorrect" knowledge and the validation process interacts with the user to overcome any unacceptable levels of incompleteness.

Differences and Similarities between KBSs and Other Systems

The remainder of this traditional V&V section is abstracted from *Reference Information for Software Verification and Validation Process:*[1]

> There are critical differences between KBSs and traditional systems cited in the literature affecting V&V of KBSs:
>
> - A KBS is both a piece of software and a domain model.
> - There may not be a unique correct answer to a problem given to a KBS.
> - A KBS can adapt by modifying its behavior based on changes in its internal representation of the environment.
>
> These differences provide the flexibility and special capabilities of a KBS, but these differences make use of traditional V&V methods for KBSs difficult and require the introduction of new techniques.
>
> The key component of a KBS that distinguishes it from other types of software is its encoding of the domain model in a knowledge base. Elicitation, formulation, and encoding of this model

are major steps of KBS development. It is the knowledge base component that requires special emphasis during V&V. V&V of components other than the knowledge base (e.g., the inference engine, user interface) can rely on the same techniques as conventional systems.

With available KBS shells and tools, a new KBS may be able to reuse existing versions of these system components; however, reuse introduces new concerns. V&V of the knowledge base requires understanding how the KBS will use the knowledge base and how the KBS itself will be used. All the uses of the knowledge base and the KBS containing it may not be known at development time. A KBS may operate in a domain with unclear boundaries, without complete information, and with no unique correct answer to a given problem.

Complete enumeration of possible problems requiring the use of the domain model is unlikely. It is hard to predict what the range of problems are that any given model might apply to, or the enumeration of those problems might be prohibitively expensive. If the model is simple enough that experts could enumerate all of the possible problems that could be submitted to the KBS and all of the outcomes easily, a KBS would probably not be the best approach. One argument for using a KBS is that it can improve the robustness of a system by supporting problem solving under conditions that were not specifiable in advance. This can be through adaptation of the knowledge base from automatic knowledge acquisition.

Another area important to KBS usage and related to validation of the domain model is *establishing credibility* with KBS users. Even if the domain model is complete and accurate, a KBS user can lose confidence in the KBS if it appears to be using an obviously incorrect chain of reasoning. For example, the user may see this when the KBS is attempting to validate a chain of reasoning by asking for additional information that the user feels is unnecessary or inappropriate. Inappropriate questions can result from a failure to propagate knowledge generated from previous questions and asking redundant questions as the KBS tests new inference chains. Another source of inappropriate questions is incomplete specification of inference rules, resulting in the KBS asking questions that should be obvious. The classic example for medical diagnosis systems is the KBS asking if a male patient is pregnant. Obvious lapses of this type cause users to lose confidence in the system.

While there is no single "standard life-cycle" or development technique for KBSs, typical discussions of KBS development assume some form of rapid prototyping, evolutionary prototyping, or incremental development process. Because of the nature of the model-based development model [see Chapter 2], it has the most flexibility built in to accommodate most readily the rapid prototyping, etc., needed for KBS development. The assumptions underlying this choice are that experts and users cannot articulate expertise systematically and completely in one iteration, and that extensive tool support supplies parts of the system other than the knowledge base contents. There are many [KBS] shells and products supporting the rapid encoding of knowledge using particular styles of reasoning. While these shells and tools are helpful, they can also be deceptive since prototypes developed using these tools may not scale up or may require substantial further effort to become useable systems. Even with tools, the knowledge engineer must still work with the expert to formulate the expert's knowledge suitable for the [KBS]. There is no single set of rules for organizing this knowledge. (pp. 30–31)

Contemporary V & V

Many systems using the KB approach are no longer prototypes, but instead are complex, deployed systems. We will investigate V&V of these systems, whether they are KB systems themselves, or conventional systems supported by KB subsystems. Dr. Jim Schmolze[6] says that, "It is extremely difficult to perform V&V on KB systems for which V&V was never considered. Thus, methods for developing KB software that is more easily verified and validated are essential to the successful deployment of KB systems in critical applications" (p. 1).

More Differences between KBSs and Other Systems

Paul E. Janusz[7] tells us that,

> the V&V of KBSs poses some unique problems not typically faced with traditional software engineering. Some of the factors which may contribute to these problems include:
>
> 1. A modularized, top-down structured architecture may not be possible in all KBSs.
> 2. Defining testable requirements for KBSs is difficult.
> 3. KBSs tend to be more problem-oriented than process oriented. (p. 1)

Many KBSs acquire their information from a collection of experts who input knowledge into the knowledge database. This and the following information comes from *Verification, Validation, and Evaluation of Expert Systems.*[3] Since this often is not a structured approach, but is usually a parallel effort, it causes problems from the V&V perspective. This is because the data collection and structure follows availability, rather than the more formal architecture decomposition method of system/software development. When this occurs, the V&V person must maintain continuous involvement in the process, or important concepts or knowledge will not be appropriately evaluated.

When establishing the requirements for the KBS, there are myriad problems associated with the requirements that are being derived. Testability of a derived requirement is one such problem. This would assume that the path of inquiry used in the KBS would be known *a priori*; so that predicted response paths are encountered and thereby tested.

Since V&V focuses primarily on the process of software development, rather than the problem or application being developed, the V&V of KBSs is more difficult. V&V, to be effective for KBSs, must be involved in the problem set. This involvement allows the V&V person to verify that the knowledge base is correct and consistent. If this is not done, the KBS becomes effectively useless.

Basic Proof Method

The following extensive discussion is from the Federal Highway Administration Handbook, *Verification, Validation, and Evaluation of Expert Systems.*[3]

> An expert system is correct when it is complete, consistent, and satisfies the requirements that express expert knowledge about how the system should behave. For real-world knowledge bases containing hundreds of rules, however, these aspects of correctness are hard to establish.

There may be millions of distinct computational paths through an expert system, and each must be dealt with through testing or formal proof to establish correctness.

To reduce the size of the tests and proofs, one useful approach for some knowledge bases is to partition them into two or more interrelated knowledge bases. In this way the V&V problem can be minimized. The basic method of proving each of these aspects of correctness is basically the same. If the system is small, a technique designed for proving correctness of small systems should be used. If the system is large, a technique for partitioning the expert system must be applied and the required conditions for applying the partition to the system as a whole should be proven. In addition, the correctness of any subsystem required by the partition must be ensured. Once this has been accomplished, this basic proof method should be applied recursively to the subexpert systems.

To carry out a partitioning of an expert system, one generally requires expert knowledge to define the top-level problem-solving strategy of the expert system. A number of knowledge models follow that may be useful in formalizing the top-level structure of the knowledge base.

Knowledge models are high-level templates for expert knowledge. Examples of knowledge models are decision trees, flowcharts, and state diagrams. By organizing the knowledge, a knowledge model helps with V&V by suggesting strategies for proofs and partitions; in addition, some knowledge models have mathematical properties that help establish completeness, consistency, or specification satisfaction. More particularly:

- The knowledge model highlights the main points of a knowledge base, often obscured in the knowledge base.
- A knowledge model partitions a large KB into smaller, easier to verify, pieces.
- There are mathematical properties of the knowledge model that help establish the correctness of a knowledge base. (pp. 39, 54)

The steps in using a knowledge model in V&V from reference 3 are:

1. Collect the knowledge model from:
   - the domain expert(s) working on the project
   - standards documents in the domain
   - notes from knowledge acquisition at the time an existing system was built.
2. Validate the knowledge by logical and semantic completeness and consistency checks as discussed below. This step is to ensure that the knowledge going into the expert system represents correct expert knowledge.
3. Prove that the expert system using the knowledge model is complete, consistent, and satisfies its specifications; this section provides information on how to develop these proofs.

Through knowledge acquisition with one or more expert, the top-level structure of the knowledge base should be represented in a knowledge model. The correctness of this knowledge model should be validated with other experts or with standard reference materials in the target domain.

The basic method for validating a knowledge item is:

- Ask a panel of experts whether it is true or false.
- Tally the TRUE/FALSE answers.
- Analyze the results statistically. (p. 112)

The *Verification, Validation, and Evaluation of Expert Systems*[3] Handbook continues:

When the formalization of the top-level knowledge base has been so validated, the fact that the knowledge base has the validated structure can, from the standpoint of a formal proof, be assumed.

Once the top-level structure of the knowledge base has been validated, to show the correctness of the expert system, the following criteria must be accomplished:

- Show that the knowledge base and inference engine implement the top level structure.
- Prove any required relationships among sub-expert systems or parts of the top level knowledge representation.
- Prove any required properties of the sub-knowledge bases.

Discussed [above is] what exactly must be proved for various knowledge models and for various aspects of the correctness problem.

[For example], to illustrate the basic proof method, Knowledge Base 1 (Figure 10.1) will be proved correct. Although this knowledge base is small enough to verify by inspection, the proof will be carried out in detail to illustrate the proof method.

Figure 10.1 Knowledge Base 1.[3] (p. 40)

Knowledge Base 1

Rule 1: If "Risk tolerance" = high
AND "Discretionary income exists" = yes
then investment = "stocks."
Rule 2: If "Risk tolerance" = low
OR "Discretionary income exists" = no
then investment = "bank account."
Rule 3: If "Do you buy lottery tickets?" = yes
OR "Do you currently own stocks?" = yes
then "Risk tolerance" = high.
Rule 4: If "Do you buy lottery tickets?" = no
AND "Do you currently own stocks?" = no
then "Risk tolerance" = low.
Rule 5: If "Do you own a boat?" = yes
OR "Do you own a luxury car?" = yes
then "Discretionary income exists" = yes.
Rule 6: If "Do you own a boat?" = no
AND "Do you own a luxury car?" = no
then "Discretionary income exists" = no.

Illustrations of Knowledge Base 1

The knowledge base 1 (KB1) has six rules. There are seven variables which can take two possible values. It is therefore a seven-dimensional, binary problem. Let us focus on rule 3 to understand the illustrations of KB1. It has two hypotheses, and one conclusion. The hypotheses are "Do you buy lottery tickets?" = "yes," and "Do you currently own stock?" = "yes." They are associated with the logical operator "or." The consequent is "Risk Tolerance" = "low."

For the two variables of the hypotheses in rule 3, there are two possible values: "yes" or "no." The number of possible combinations of values for the variables is four. These four combinations appear in Figure 10.2 as four square regions defined by the closed boundary (defining the domain of the variables) and the line boundaries separating the possible values for each variable. Each square is [known as] a Hoffman region.

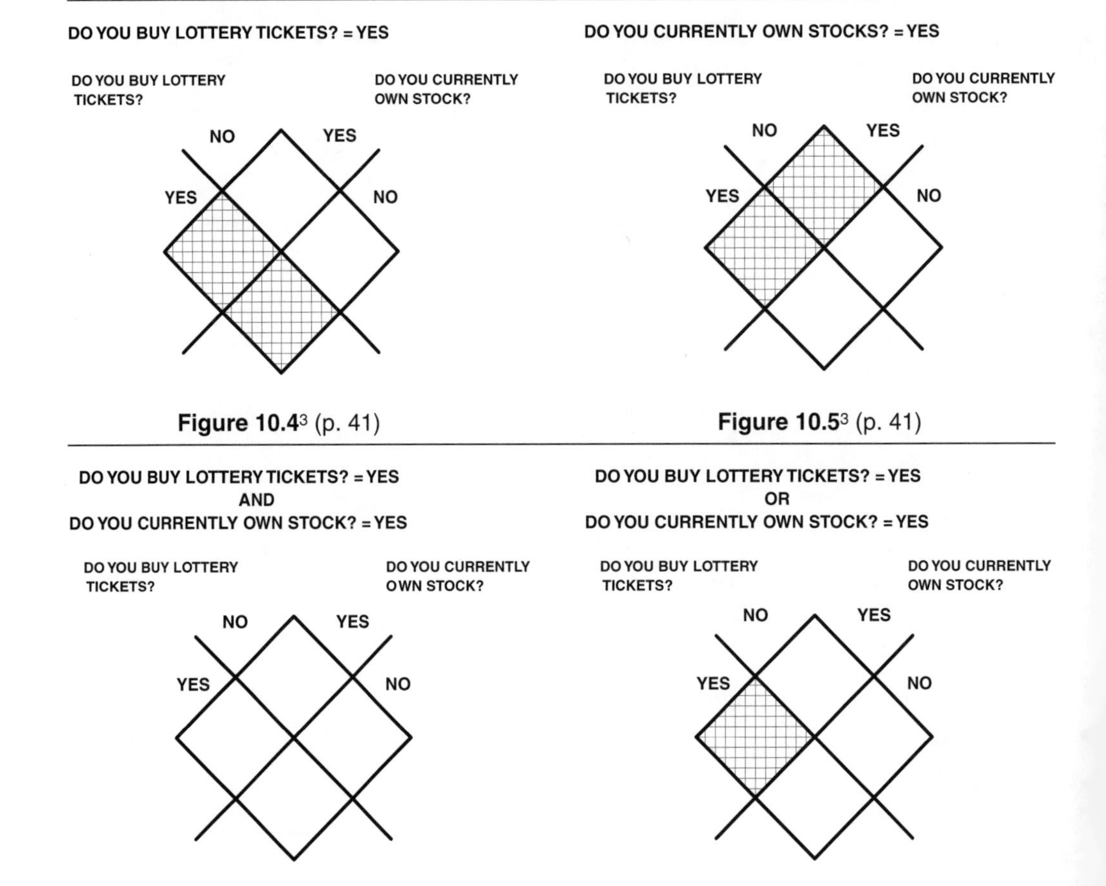

Figure 10.2[3] (p. 41)

Figure 10.3[3] (p. 41)

Figure 10.4[3] (p. 41)

Figure 10.5[3] (p. 41)

Figure 10.6[3] (p. 42)

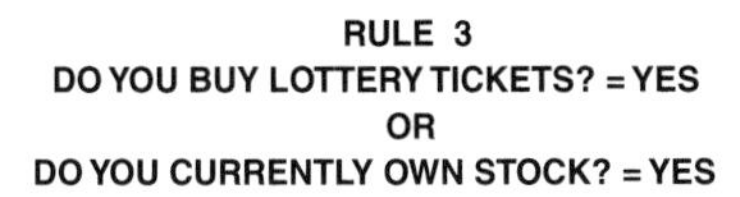

Figure 10.7[3] (p. 42)

RULE 3
DO YOU BUY LOTTERY TICKETS? = YES
OR
DO YOU CURRENTLY OWN STOCK? = YES

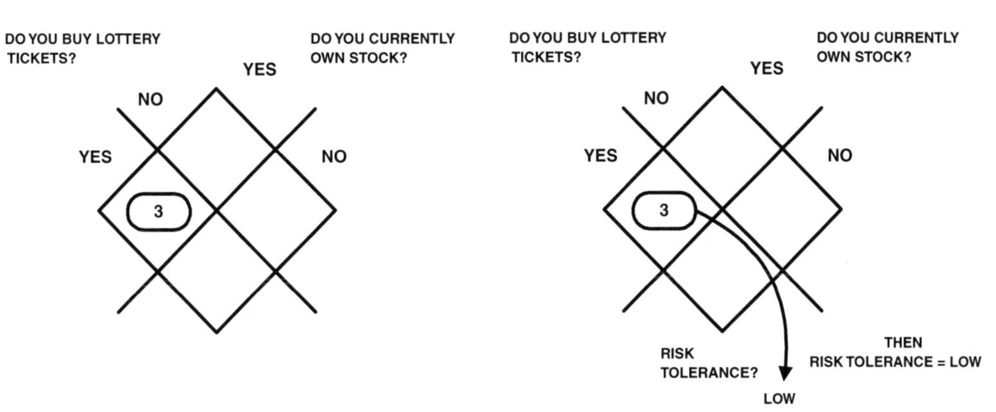

If variable "Do you buy lottery tickets?" is assigned a value "yes," then two of the four regions are relevant. In Figure 10.2, they are shown with a hatch. The two regions corresponding to hypothesis "Do you currently own stock?" = "yes" are hatched in Figure 10.3.

In Figures 10.2 and 10.3, the Hoffman regions corresponding to each hypothesis of rule 3 are hatched. When combined with an "and" logical operator, the intersection of the two sets of Hoffman regions demonstrates that logical expression. It is shown in Figure 10.4. The intersection in this case is a unique Hoffman region. In rule 3, an "or" logical operator connects the two hypotheses. In this case, the union of the two sets of Hoffman regions is taken, as shown in Figure 10.5.

Next, the region defined by the logical expression of hypotheses is labeled with its rule number. For rule 3, the three Hoffman regions are labeled with a circled 3, as shown in Figure 10.6. The consequent for the rule is linked to the label of the region of hypotheses. In Figure 10.7, a curved arrow starts at the circled 3, and ends at the value "low" of the variable "Risk Tolerance."

Step 1—Determine Knowledge Base Structure. To prove the correctness of Knowledge Base 1 (KB1), the expert knowledge can determine that the system represents a 2-step process:

1. Find the values of some important intermediate variables, such as risk tolerance and discretionary income.
2. Use these values to assign a type of investment.

KB1 was built using this knowledge; therefore, it can be partitioned into the following pieces:

- a subsystem to find risk tolerance (part of Step 1)
- a subsystem to find discretionary income (part of Step 1)
- a subsystem to find type of investment given this information (part of Step 2).

To prove the correctness of a multistep system, it must be proved that Step 1 satisfies the following criteria:

- For each set of inputs, all the outputs required by Step 2 are always produced by Step 1.
- For each set of inputs, all the outputs of Step 1 are single-valued.
- The correct outputs of Step 1 are assigned to each possible set of inputs.

It must also be proved for Step 2 that:

- For each set of inputs and computed Step 1 outputs, Step 2 produces some output.
- For each set of inputs and Step 1 outputs, all the outputs of Step 2 are single-valued.
- The correct outputs of Step 2 are assigned to each possible set of inputs and computed Step 2 outputs.

Step 2—Find Knowledge Base Partitions. To find each of the three subsystems of KB1, an iterative procedure can be followed:

1. Start with the variables that are goals for the subsystem, e.g., risk tolerance for the risk tolerance subsystem.
2. Include all the rules that set subsystem variables in their conclusions. For the risk tolerance subsystem, Rules 3 and 4 are included.
3. Include all variables that appeared in rules already in the subsystem and are not goals of another subsystem.
4. For the risk tolerance subsystem, include "Do you buy lottery tickets" and "Do you currently own stocks."
5. Quit if all rules setting subsystem variables are in the subsystem, or else go to Step 2. For the risk tolerance subsystem, there are no more rules to be added.

[Figure 10.8] shows the partitioning of KB1 using this method.

Step 3—Completeness of Expert Systems. *Completeness Step 1—Completeness of Subsystems:* The first step in proving the completeness of the entire expert system is to prove the completeness of each subsystem. To this end it must be shown that for all possible inputs there is an output; that is, the goal variables of the subsystem are set. This can be done by showing that the OR of the hypotheses of the rules that assign to a goal variable is true.

For example, the discretionary subsystem of KB1 will be shown to be complete. The discretionary subsystem consists of these rules:

Rule 5: If "Do you own a boat?" = yes
OR "Do you own a luxury car?" = yes
then "Discretionary income exists" = yes.

Rule 6: If "Do you own a boat?" = no
AND "Do you own a luxury car?" = no
then "Discretionary income exists" = no.

Figure 10.8 An example of knowledge base partitioning.[3] (p. 44)

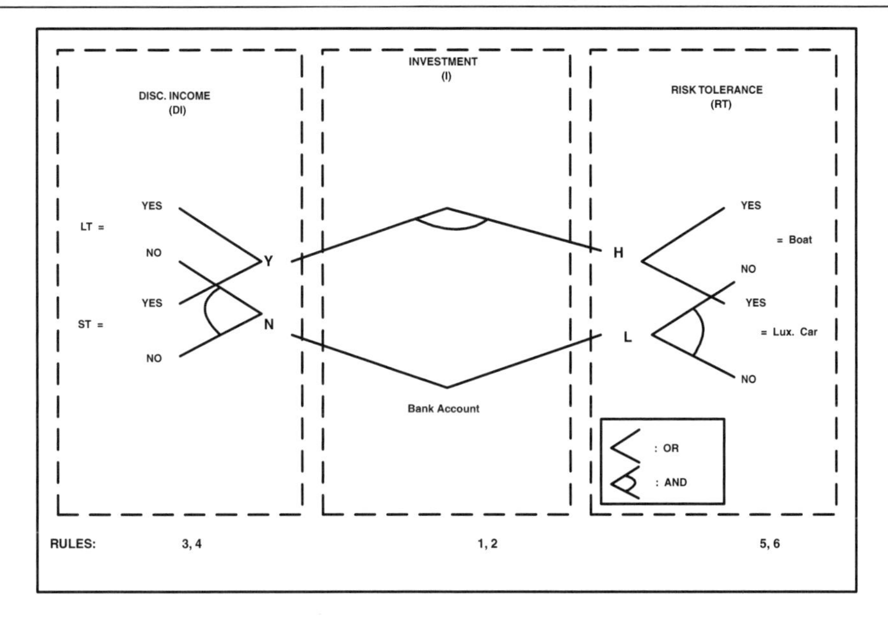

Step 3.1: The first step is to form the OR of the possible outputs of the system:

"Discretionary income exists" = yes (10.1)
OR "Discretionary income exists" = no

(10.1) expresses the condition under which some conclusion is reached.

Step 3.2: For each output condition in (10.1), the user substitutes the OR of rule hypotheses for rules that imply that condition. For example, for

"Discretionary income exists" = yes (10.2)

the only rule inferring (10.2) is Rule 5; its hypothesis is:

"Do you own a boat?" = yes (10.3)
OR "Do you own a luxury car?" = yes

Since this is the only rule concluding (10.2), (10.3) is the OR of rule hypotheses implying (10.2). Making the substitution of (10.3) for (10.2) in (10.1), and a similar substitution for:

"Discretionary income exists" = no (10.4)

the result is:

("Do you own a boat?" = yes (10.5)
OR "Do you own a luxury car?" = yes)
OR
("Do you own a boat?" = no
AND "Do you own a luxury car?" = no)

Step 3.3: Continue substitutions of the OR of rule hypotheses for inferred propositions (10.5) until the user obtains an expression where only input variables appear. In fact, (10.5) already contains only input variables, and no further substitutions are needed.

Step 3.4: Apply Boolean algebra to simplify the expression from Step 3; the goal is to show that the Step 3 expression always has the truth value TRUE.

Letting:

A = "Do you own a boat?" = yes
B = "Do you own a luxury car?" = yes

(10.5) can be rewritten as:

(A or B) or (Not A and Not B) (10.6)

Simplifying this gives:

(A or B) or (Not A and Not B)
= (A or B or Not A) and (A or B or Not B)
= true and true
= true

This means that the OR of conditions that imply some conclusion is true.

Completeness Step 2—Completeness of the Entire System: The results of subsystem completeness are used to establish the completeness of the entire system. The basic argument is to use results on subsystems to prove that successively larger subsystems are complete. At each stage of the proof there are some subsystems known to be complete; initially the subsystem that concludes overall goals of the expert system will be complete. At each stage of the proof, a subsystem that concludes some of the input variables of the currently-proved-complete subsystem is added to the currently complete subsystem. After a number of steps equal to the number of subsystems, the entire system can be shown to be complete.

When a complete subsystem that sets input variables of the currently complete subsystem is added to the latter, the augmented subsystem is complete. Any input to the augmented subsystem can be divided into a set *V1* of input variables for the unaugmented system and a set *V2* for the newly added subsystem. Note that some variables may be in both of these sets. Since the newly added subset is complete, given *V1,* that subsystem produces output *O1*. However, *O1 union V2* is an input for the unaugmented system, which, because of its completeness, produces an output showing that the augmented system is complete.

Since the number of subsystems is finite, the process of augmentation ceases after a finite number of steps. By mathematical induction, using a similar argument to that of the previous paragraph, it follows that the entire system is complete.

For KB1, this result can be applied, or alternatively the following specific argument can be made: Inputs to the system as a whole can be partitioned into inputs for the risk tolerance and the discretionary income subsystems. Each of these is complete, and so produces a risk tolerance and discretionary income respectively. These are inputs to the investment subsystem and are its only inputs. Since the investment subsystem is complete it produces an investment. So an output for the entire system exists for each input, and the system as a whole is complete.

Step 4—Consistency of the entire system. The first step in proving the consistency of the entire expert system is to prove the consistency of each subsystem. To do this, the user must show that for all possible inputs, the outputs are consistent; that is, that the AND of the conclusions can be satisfied.

For example, if an expert system concludes “temperature > 0” and “temperature < 100,” the AND of these conclusions can be satisfied. However, if the system concludes, “temperature < 0” and “temperature > 100,” the AND of these two conclusions has to be false. It is clear that based on the input that produced these two conclusions, it is not possible for all of the system's conclusions to be true at the same time, and thus the system producing these conclusions is inconsistent.

Consistency Step 1—Find the Mutually Inconsistent Conclusions: The first step in proving consistency is to identify those sets of mutually inconsistent conclusions for each of the subsystems identified in the “Find partitions” step above.

Some sets of conclusions are mathematically inconsistent. For example, if a system describes temperature, the set:

{“temperature < 0,”
“temperature > 100”}

is mathematically inconsistent.

However, other conclusion sets that are not mathematically inconsistent may be inconsistent based on domain expertise. For example, one investment advisor expert system could be designed to recommend several types of investments to each investor (probably not a bad idea). For such a system, “investment = stocks” AND “investment = bank account” are not inconsistent; stocks and bank accounts are just two of the investments recommended for some investor. However, if the system were designed to recommend only one investment per investor, “investment = stocks” AND “investment = bank account” would be interpreted as a contradiction, and the system recommending this would be inconsistent.

Because some sets of conclusions are inconsistent because of domain expertise, finding all sets of inconsistent conclusions generally requires expert knowledge.

Note that if there are no mutually inconsistent conclusions in the expert system as a whole, then consistency is true by default, and no further consistency proof is necessary.

Consistency Step 2—Prove Consistency of Subsystems: If there are inconsistent conclusions in the knowledge base as a whole, then the next step in proving consistency is to prove the subsystems consistent. This can be done by showing that no set of inputs to a subsystem can result in any of the sets of inconsistent conclusions. For each set of inconsistent conclusions, the user can construct, as detailed below, a Boolean expression B that represents all the conditions under which that set of inconsistent conclusions would be proved by the subsystem. If that Boolean expression can be shown to be FALSE, there are no such conditions.

Now the construction of the Boolean expression B to be proved false will be described. Let

$$S = \{C1, \ldots, Cn\}$$

be a set of potentially inconsistent conclusions for one of the subsystems.

B will be constructed by a backward chaining process, starting with

$B0 = C1$ AND ... AND Cn

Let *Ci* be one of the *C*s. For all rules that conclude *C*i, construct the OR of these rules initial conditions. Then substitute the resulting expression into *B0*.

Continue these substitutions until an expression results that has only the inputs to the expert subsystem. For each atomic Boolean expression *A* that is the conclusion of a rule in the subsystem, substitute the OR of the rule if parts of rules that conclude *A*. After at most a finite number of such substitutions, the user obtains an expression that states when all the *C*'s would be true in terms of the input variables of the subsystem.

For the risk subsystem, the only inconsistent set of rule conclusions is:

S = { "Risk tolerance" = high and "Risk tolerance" = low }

The only initial conditions for "Risk tolerance" = high are from Rule 3:

"Do you buy lottery tickets?" = yes
OR "Do you currently own stocks?" = yes

and the only initial conditions for "Risk tolerance" = low is from Rule 4:

"Do you buy lottery tickets?" = no
AND "Do you currently own stocks?" = no

Let:

*A*0 = ("Do you buy lottery tickets?" = yes)
*A*1 = ("Do you currently own stocks?" = yes).

This means:

not *A*0 = ("Do you buy lottery tickets?" = no)
not *A*1 = ("Do you currently own stocks?" = no).

Using this notation:

*B*0 = (*A*0 OR *A*1) AND (NOT *A*0 AND NOT *A*1)

For this small subsystem, *B*0 is actually expressed in terms of inputs to the subsystem (i.e., *B*0 is actually *B*). Distributing the top-level AND over the OR,

*B*0 = (*A*0 AND (NOT *A*0 AND NOT *A*1))
OR (*A*1 AND (NOT *A*0 AND NOT *A*1))

The first subexpression is FALSE because it contains *A*0 AND NOT *A*0. Likewise, the second is FALSE because it contains *A*1 AND NOT *A*1. Therefore, *B*0 is FALSE because it is the OR of only FALSE expressions.

Consistency Step 3—Consistency of the Entire System: The results of subsystem consistency are used to establish the consistency of the entire system. The basic argument is to use results on subsystems to prove that successively larger subsystems are consistent. At each stage of the proof, there are some subsystem known to be consistent; initially, this is the subsystem that concludes goals of the expert system as a whole. At each stage of the proof, a subsystem that concludes some of the input variables of the currently-proved-consistent subsystem is added to the currently consistent subsystem. After a number of steps equal to the number of subsystems, the entire system can be shown to be consistent.

When a consistent subsystem that sets input variables of the currently consistent subsystem is added to the currently consistent subsystem, the augmented subsystem is consistent. Any input to the augmented subsystem can be divided into a set *V1* of input variables for the unaugmented system and a set *V2* for the newly added subsystem. Note that some variables may be in both of these sets. Since the newly added subset is consistent, given *V1*, that subsystem produces and output *O1*. However, *O1 union V2* is an input for the unaugmented system producing output due to its consistency. This shows that the augmented system is consistent.

Since the number of subsystems is finite, the process of augmentation ceases after a finite number of steps. By mathematical induction, using the above mentioned argument, it follows that the entire system is consistent.

For KB1, one can apply the result, or alternatively make the following specific argument: Inputs to the system as a whole can be partitioned into inputs for the risk tolerance and the discretionary income subsystems. Each of these is consistent and so produces a consistent set of risk tolerance and discretionary incomes, respectively. These are inputs to the investment subsystem and are that system's only inputs. Since the investment subsystem is consistent, it produces a consistent investment. Thus an output for the entire system exists for each input, and the system as a whole is consistent. The other subsystems of KB1 can be proved consistent in the same way.

Step 5—Specification Satisfaction. In order to prove that KB1 satisfies its specifications, the user must actually know what its specifications are. This is a special case of the general truth that in order to verify and validate, the user must know what a system is supposed to do. Specifications should be defined in the planning stage of an expert system project.

To illustrate the proof of specifications it will be assumed that KB1 is supposed to satisfy:

> A financial advisor should only recommend investments that an investor can afford.

As with many other aspects of verification and validation, expert knowledge must be brought to bear on the proof process. For KB1, an expert might say that anyone can afford a savings account. Therefore, the user only has to look at the conditions under which stocks are recommended. However, that same expert would probably say that just having discretionary income does not mean that the user can afford stocks; that judgment should be made on more than one variable. Therefore, it would be reasonable to conclude that KB1 does not satisfy the above specification.

However, if the expert does agree that the expert system observes all necessary inputs, inputs must be used for the expert system to express a specification. For KB1, this means the specification is re-expressed as:

> KB1 recommends stocks only when there is discretionary income.

The user can prove this for the investment subsystem by assuming:

> NOT discretionary income

and proving:

NOT stocks

The only rule that concludes stocks has "discretionary income" = yes in an AND in its "if" part. Therefore, the investment system satisfies the specification.

To prove that the entire system satisfies the specifications, the user must look at the conditions under which "discretionary income" = yes is concluded from inputs for the system as a whole. A financial expert would surely say that owning a luxury car or boat does not mean that discretionary income actually exists, and the system as a whole fails the specification, an expected outcome of a small example system tackling a complex subject. (pp. 38–50)

Also, the proof steps just given only demonstrate partial correctness of the KBS system using completeness and consistency analysis, but it does not include any guarantee of termination. That is, the system could contain recursive constructs that are complete and consistent, but nonterminating.

Validating Underlying Knowledge

The *Verification, Validation, and Evaluation of Expert Systems*[3] Handbook continues:

If there are errors in the knowledge from which a knowledge base is built, there will usually be errors in the performance of the KBS. There are several ways that the KB can come to represent incorrect knowledge:

- The expert(s) provide incomplete or incorrect knowledge.
- The knowledge engineer fails to correctly understand or code the expert's knowledge.
- Formalizations of knowledge (e.g., using the range of a variable to test for some underlying condition) may fail to capture all instances of the underlying condition.

There are two kinds of validation that must occur on a knowledge base: logical and semantic. Logical validation checks how the rules and objects work together to reach logical conclusions.

In particular, logical validation checks for consistency (i.e., that all the conclusions of the knowledge base can be true at the same time) and completeness (i.e., that the knowledge base reaches a conclusion for all inputs). While the [Basic Proof Method section] focused on logical completeness and consistency, this section addresses semantic correctness and completeness.

Logical completeness and consistency are necessary for a knowledge base to be valid. However, logical completeness and consistency are not sufficient for knowledge base validity. For example, Knowledge Base 1 in [Figure 10.1] is logically complete and consistent; it contains no logical errors. However, KB1 makes investment decisions based only on risk tolerance and discretionary income. It uses no information about actual income, debt, fixed expenses, age, or other important inputs to good investment decisions. In other words, while KB1 is logically correct, it is seriously semantically incomplete. To be valid, a knowledge base must be semantically complete; that is, it must base its decisions on all information considered to be relevant by the expert.

An exception is that thorough testing... may show that some information can be left out without affecting performance. However, knowledge that the expert thinks is needed should be included until testing shows that an KBS performs correctly without that knowledge.

Similarly, a knowledge base can be logically consistent, but not semantically consistent for its intended application. Semantic consistency occurs when all facts, rules, and conclusions of the knowledge base are true for the application for which the KBS is intended. To illustrate the difference between logical and semantic consistency, consider ordinary Euclidean and spherical geometry. Both are logically consistent mathematical systems from which logically consistent KBSs can be built. However, for everyday life, Euclidean geometry is consistent and spherical geometry is inconsistent with observed facts, while for long distance navigation, the reverse is true.

It is important to note, however, that a knowledge base that is logically inconsistent by definition gives contradictory advice and is therefore semantically incorrect. Likewise, a knowledge base that is logically incomplete fails to provide a solution under some circumstances, and is semantically incomplete. Logical completeness and consistency are prerequisites for semantic validation of a knowledge base. (pp. 109–110)

Decision Tree V&V

Reference 3 goes on to describe that:

A decision tree [Figure 10.9: PAMEX—Pavement Maintenance Expert System] is a set of decisions that partitions the input space into a set of disjoint regions that cover the entire input space. In a decision tree system, a sequence of decisions based on user input and other data are used to classify the input problem before going on to the rest of problem solution.

The top of the decision tree corresponds to the start of the decision process. At each interior node of a decision tree, the problem is supposed to be assigned to one and only one of the sub-

Figure 10.9 Pavement Maintenance Expert System.[3] (p. 76)

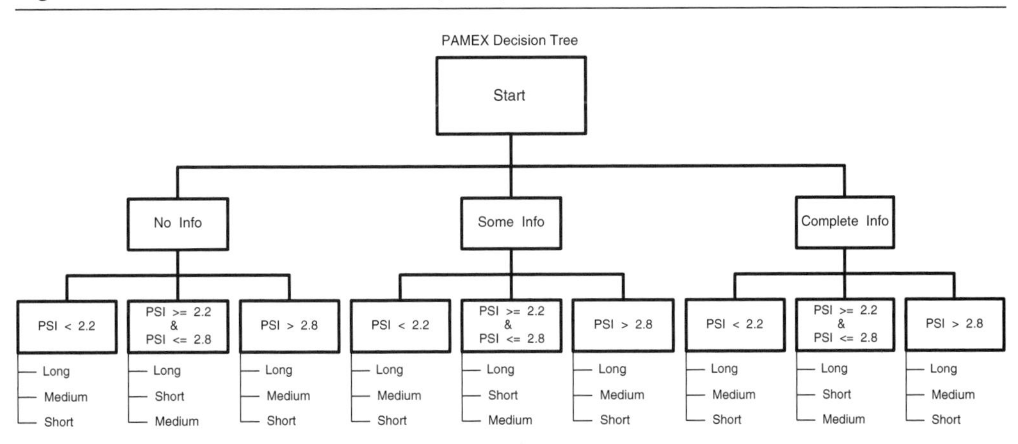

nodes. The solution of the detailed problems is often handled by specialized expert systems tailored to the specialized situations found by the decision tree.

A decision tree expert system has a structure that is described by a tree. A decision tree system has the following properties:

- Each interior node of the tree has a variable or expression assigned to it.
- Each edge to a subtree is labeled with a set of values for that variable or expression on the parent node.
- All possible values of a variable are on some edge.
- No variable value is on two different sibling edges.
- Associated with each leaf node is a subsystem or output(s).

A subsystem at a tip node *N* of a decision tree is called to solve the problems for which variables appearing in the tree have values associated with the path that leads to *N*.

Decision trees are a useful way to organize expert knowledge. Their use is indicated when the expert can describe in what order information is obtained and used to partially determine a solution. Drawing a decision tree from information the expert(s) have provided is a good way to present the knowledge engineer's conception of the information back to the domain expert for validation.

To model a KBS as a decision tree for the purpose of showing correctness, the following conditions should be satisfied:

- Each possible set of inputs should be in one and only one of the partitions generated by the decision tree.
- For each partition, there is an KBS (a subsystem of the entire system) that correctly solves problems in that partition.
- Experts validate the decision tree.
- The KBS assigns each input to the correct partition as the result of a finite computation.

To prove completeness of a KBS modeled by a decision tree, it is necessary to prove the following:

- Each possible problem in the input space is assigned to some partition of the decision tree.
- Each KBS assigned to one of the partitions computes a solution for each problem assigned to it.

To prove consistency of an KBS modeled by a decision tree, it is necessary to prove the following:

- Each possible problem in the input space is assigned to at most one partition of the decision tree.
- Each KBS assigned to one of the partitions computes at most one solution for each problem assigned to it.
- Each computed solution is internally consistent.

To prove satisfaction of a requirement of a KBS modeled by a decision tree, it needs to be shown that the requirement is satisfied for the KBS associated with each tip of the decision tree. (pp. 74–77)

KBS and Agents

One type of KBS gaining attention is agents or intelligent agents (IAs). This section on IAs is abstracted from NIST's *Reference Information for Software Verification and Validation Process.*[1]

Agents are closely related to expert systems. There are at least two approaches to defining agents... following is a list of attributes of an agent:

- autonomous behavior (e.g., periodic action, spontaneous execution, initiative)
- "personalizability" to better execute the selected tasks
- discourse or two-way communication with the agent
- risk and trust associated with delegating tasks
- low domain criticality
- graceful degradation at the domain boundary
- cooperation between user and agent
- anthropomorphism
- meets expectations enough of the time to be useful. (p. 30)

There are counter examples of agents that are missing some of these attributes, which highlights that agent technology is not well enough understood to be useful for critical domains, and therefore, are used mainly in game playing and other areas of social interaction.

The NIST[1] publication continues:

IAs have been used as assistants for enterprise integration. Each IA supports a clearly discernible task or job function, automating what it can and calling the services of other IAs, as well as human agents, when necessary. In this model, agents, both those associated with job functions and personal assistants associated with human agents, help integrate an enterprise through communication and information retrieval and synthesis. (p. 30)

It is specifically this unique part of IAs that requires unique handling from the V&V perspective. Besides the completeness and consistency elements of the KBS discussed above, IAs require the interaction of the V&V person in reviewing the human agents' potential reactions within the system.

Reference Information for Software Verification and Validation Process[1] relates that:

This model of IAs evolved from expert systems designed to better manage or integrate tasks on the factory floor. To cope with the changing demands on the factory floor, these expert systems had to be user-extensible. In [certain] models, this user-extensibility evolved into the cooperative interaction associated with IAs. These two points of departure for developing agents, factory floor controllers and social discourse, provide different criteria for evaluating agent usefulness and appropriateness for high-risk tasks. (p. 30)

Automated V&V of KBSs

This section is abstracted from Playle and Beckman's "Knowledge-Based Systems and Automated Software Validation and Verification."[2]

> The knowledge bases in most KBSs are "brittle": when the questioner moves beyond the area of expertise, the KBS simply fails, usually catastrophically rather than gracefully. In some cases, the KBS will give answers but the answers will be severely erroneous. Capturing the knowledge is difficult and tedious, almost always requiring extensive human intervention. Without a learning capability, the knowledge can become outdated as the applications change. Managing the knowledge base can range from difficult to intractable as one tries to add information to the system.
>
> Finally, without careful application of "fuzzy reasoning" or probabilistic reasoning capabilities, KBSs cannot handle the most common problems people encounter, those of compensatory reasoning. One "compensates" for particular attributes in a situation by balancing known parameters and applying rules of thumb; for example, people solve problems by saying that "in this situation, I usually...," indicating there are uncertainty and mitigating circumstances to be dealt with. Despite these problems, KBSs have application to software validation and verification....
>
> The implication for software verification and validation is that a machine-aided inspection of the specification, and design or selection of the test cases, is likely to be as accurate as human-generated selections, but much faster. Thus, if we can capture the expertise of humans in predicting software faults and in designing test cases, then reuse that knowledge in machines, we can greatly reduce the "overhead time" of specification validation, and in turn the software testing and validation. The knowledge will be embodied in studies of software faults and their generation, plus indicators of likely system segments that contain faults.
>
> The testing process involves several steps (see Figure 10.10), beginning with test planning, test case design and selection, actual execution of the test cases, and evaluation of the results. Around all these steps is the problem of managing test cases, plans, etc., as requirements and software change (configuration management and control of the test). KBSs and automation have been applied to several of these steps.
>
> [Figure 10.10] shows a conceptual view of the role KBSs could have in system specification, test, and maintenance. Either an existing system and requirement that need change, or a new requirement (usually in natural language) is the starting point. From this (traditionally), one develops a formal specification and then analyzes the specification for all the "-ilities," among which is testability. From the specification, one simultaneously develops the system, the tests, and the testbed. Once these tests are run, the results must be analyzed, reviewed, and perhaps modified, or the results may generate a change in the system requirement. If the requirement changes, one enters a feedback loop of configuration management and control. Test execution can be modified. KBSs can be central to the test process, from planning to results analysis. This expert adviser analyzes the specification and recommends test cases, areas to concentrate on testing, and changes to tests in a repository. Once the test is run, the expert adviser can quickly scan the results to ensure the testing ran as desired and the results are useful, plus search for error conditions that indicate a need for additional testing. As people review the test results, they can make changes to the tests in the repository, weight the recommendations for future KBS-aided testing cycles, and so on. Testing is costly, time-consuming, and for systems of any size, less than exhaustive. An expert adviser, used as early as the requirement or specification

Figure 10.10 Applying KBS to testing.[2] (p. 18)

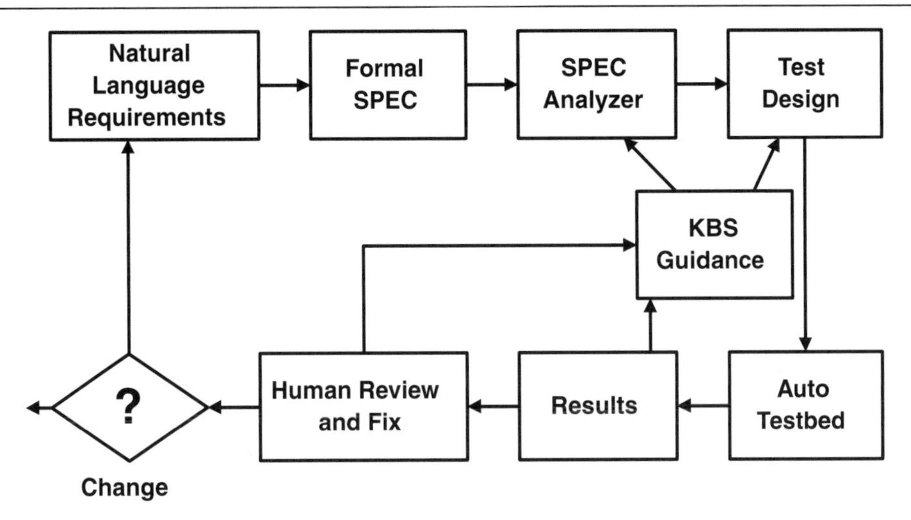

analysis phase, could search for the most cost-effective places to put early test and proof efforts, reducing overall test and life-cycle costs.

[KBSs and automated tools help an organization with their V&V] given the necessity of testing and limited time and budgets. Before trying to automate portions of the testing, an organization must have a well-defined testing process. The organization should take steps to establish and improve the testing process, then apply the automated tools to their validation process. The organization must commit to the improvement of their test and design process, providing the time, money, and staff to accomplish the effort as part of their overall capability maturity improvement. (pp. 17–19)

Summary

The key component of a KBS that distinguishes it from other types of software is its encoding of the domain model in a knowledge base. Elicitation, formulation, and encoding of this model are major steps of KBS development. It is the knowledge base component that requires special emphasis during V&V. V&V of components other than the knowledge base (e.g., the inference engine, user interface) can rely on the same techniques as conventional systems.[1]

Remember, from Janasz[7] that the V&V of KBSs poses some unique problems not typically faced with traditional software engineering. Some of the factors that may contribute to these problems include:

1. A modularized, top-down structured architecture may not be possible in all KBSs.
2. Defining testable requirements for KBSs is difficult.
3. KBSs tend to be more problem oriented than process oriented.[7]

If there are errors in the knowledge from which a knowledge base is built, there will usually be errors in the performance of the KBS as described in *Verification, Validation, and Evaluation of Expert Systems*[3] Handbook. There are several ways that the knowledge base can come to represent incorrect knowledge:

- The expert(s) provide incomplete or incorrect knowledge.
- The knowledge engineer fails to correctly understand or code the expert's knowledge.
- Formalizations of knowledge (e.g., using the range of a variable to test for some underlying condition) may fail to capture all instances of the underlying condition.[3]

When the expertise of humans in predicting software faults and in designing test cases is captured, then the "overhead time" of specification validation can be greatly reduced by reusing that knowledge in machines. From a software verification and validation perspective, a machine-aided inspection of the specification, as well as design or selection of the test cases, is likely to be as accurate as, but much faster than, human-generated selections (p. 109).

References

1 Wallace, Dolores R., Ippolito, Laura M. and Cuthill, Barbara, *Reference Information for the Software Verification and Validation Process*, NIST SP500-234, Gaithersburg, MD 20899, April, 1996.

2 Playle, Greg and Beckman, Carol, PhD, "Knowledge-Based Systems and Automated Software Validation and Verification," In *CrossTalk*, Software Technology Support Center, Ogden: Hill AFB, Vol. 9, No. 7, July 1996, pp. 17–20.

3 Wentworth, James A., Knaus, Rodger, and Aougab, Hamid, *Verification, Validation, and Evaluation of Expert Systems: An FHWA Handbook,* Version 1.2 (1st ed.), (McLean, VA: Federal Highway Administration, January 1997).

4 O'Leary, Daniel E., "Enterprise Knowledge Management," *IEEE Computer,* (© March 1998 IEEE), pp. 54–61.

5 Santos, Eugene, Ph.D., "Verifying and Validating Uncertain Knowledge Bases," Air Force Institute of Technology, Artificial Intelligence Laboratory, URL: http://www.afit.af.mil/.

6 Schmolze, Jim, Ph.D. (Tufts Univ.), *AAAI-96 Workshop on Validation & Verification of Knowledge Based Systems & Subsystems*, Thirteenth National Conference on Artificial Intelligence Call for Papers document, 1996.

7 Janusz, Paul E., "Verification and Validation of Artificial Intelligent Systems," October 27, 1995. janusz@qa.pica.army.mil.

General References

Agarwal, R., Kannan, R., & Tanniru, M. (1993) Formal Validation of a Knowledge-Based System Using a Variation of the Turing Test, *Expert Systems With Applications*, 6, p. 181–192

Bahill, A. T., (Ed.), *Verifying and Validating Person Computer-Based Expert Systems* (Englewood Cliffs, NJ: Prentice Hall, 1991).

Boose, J. and Gaines, B. R., (Eds.), *The Foundation of Knowledge Acquisition* (London: Academic Press, 1990).

Botton, N., Kusiak, A., and Raz, T. (1989) Knowledge Bases: Integration, Verification, and Partitioning, *European Journal of Operational Research*, (42), p. 111–128.

Childress, R. (1992, Feb.) AAAI'91, Part III, Knowledge-Based Systems: Verification, Validation, and Testing, *IEEE Expert*, p. 73–75

Coenen, F., Bench-Capon, T., and Kent, A. (1994) A Binary Encoded Incidence Matrix Representation to Support KBS Verification in Plant, R. T., Chair, *Validation and Verification of Knowledge-Based Systems*; 1994 Workshop Program, Seattle, July–August, 1994: Workshop Notes: American Association for Artificial Intelligence

Gupta, U. G., (Ed.), *Validating and Verifying Knowledge-Based Systems* (Los Alamitos, CA: IEEE Computer Society, 1991).

Gupta, U.G. (1993) "Validation and Verification of Knowledge-Based Systems: a Survey, *Journal of Applied Intelligence*, 3, pp. 343–363.

Harrison, P. R., and Ratcliffe, P. A. (1991) Towards Standards for the Validation of Expert Systems, *Expert Systems With Applications*, 2, p. 251–258.

Laurent, J.-P. and Ayel, M., (Eds.), *Verification, Validation and Test of KBS* (New York: John Wiley & Sons, 1991).

Liebowitz, J. and DeSalvo, D. A., (Eds.), *Structuring Expert Systems: Domain, Design and Development* (Englewood Cliffs, NJ: Yourdon Press, 1989). [URL: www.uwm.edu/~derek/kbsvvt/retbook.html].

Liu, N. K., Dillon, T. (1991) "An Approach Towards the Verification of Expert Systems Using Numerical Petri Nets," *International Journal of Intelligent Systems,* 6(3), p. 255–276.

Smith, and Kandel, A., *Verification and Validation of Rule-Based Expert Systems* (CRC Press, 1993).

Suwa, M., Scott, A., and Shortliffe, E. (1982) "An Approach to Verifying Completeness and Consistence in a Rule-Based Expert System," *AI Magazine,* (3)3, p. 16–21.

Traylor, B., Schwuttke, U. and Quan, A. (1994) "A Tool for Automatic Verification of Real-Time Expert Systems," in Plant, R. T., Chair, *Validation and Verification of Knowledge-Based Systems*; 1994

Workshop Program, Seattle, July–August, 1994: Workshop Notes: American Association for Artificial Intelligence.

CHAPTER 11

Internet and Intranet

Introduction

The humorist, Dave Barry,[1] says:

> But the point is that there is a Computer Revolution going on, and if you don't adapt to the changing climate, you will go the way of the dinosaurs, who became extinct almost overnight as a result of their inability to operate fax machines. This is similar to what is happening today, as the Information Age is rapidly turning us into a society that has two distinct and unequal classes of people: those who own personal computers, and those who have several thousand extra dollars apiece. The choice is yours! (p. 28)

Kristin Nauth, in *The Washington Post*,[2] reported that computing is undergoing its first real paradigm shift in more than two decades, since Steve Jobs and Stephen Wozniak created their famous PC prototype in a Cupertino garage in 1976. Like David bringing down Goliath, the Jobs/Wozniak innovation ended the dominance of mainframes. Power shifted to the desktop, with applications and data concentrated to each PC. In the 1980s, networks were added to the mix, bringing client/server applications to the fore (p. M11).

In the 1990s, thanks to the global reach of the Internet, network computing is introducing a whole new architecture. The "network" can be a corporate local area network (LAN), an enterprise wide area network (WAN), the Internet, or a secure intranet. Universal clients, known as web browsers—reach out over these networks and temporarily download only the software components needed by the user. PCs thus become devices for *communications*, rather than data processing and storage.

Que's Dictionary of Computer Terms[3] describes how the Internet, in its first incarnation as the ARPAnet, was designed to serve military institutions, yet its technology allows virtually any system to link to it via an electronic gateway. In this way, thousands of corporate computer systems, as well as for-profit e-mail systems such as MCI and CompuServe, have become part of the Internet. With more than 2 million host computers serving an estimated 20 million users, the Internet is exploding at the rate of a million new users each month. The Internet is a system of linked computer networks, worldwide in scope, that facilitates data communication services such as remote login, file transfer, e-mail, and newsgroups. The Internet is a way of connecting existing computer networks that greatly extends the reach of each participating system.

Robert Christensen[4] tells us that:

> many people think the intranet is simply the Internet—misspelled. But some industry experts claim that intranet business will be several times larger than the Internet. Is the intranet another technology fad—or is it a megatrend? [In other words, what is it?] Confusing intranet with Internet is natural—the technology, like the spelling, is nearly identical. Both require the same network protocol (TCP/IP) and both use e-mail and world wide web standards.
>
> The intranet is essentially a private Internet operating on your company's internal network. Intranets exploit the incredibly popular and low-cost Internet tools to gain strategic advantage over competitors, cut costs, and improve operational effectiveness. An intranet typically has three features that the Internet lacks:
>
> - Speed—broad bandwidth
> - Security—private internal network (LAN/WAN), protected from Internet users by a firewall
> - Control—Enterprise network management to ensure reliability
>
> The intranet can be viewed as an information utility for the enterprise. It does not matter whether one is using a Mac, Windows, or a UNIX workstation—just plug in to the intranet and find what you need (documents, e-mail, data, audio, and video). Corporate and department information is accessed via the standards of the Internet: e-mail (SMTP), WWW, file transfer protocol (ftp), and other similar Internet services. (p. 1)

Within the purview of the network computing within the Internet, there are further innovations that impact the manner of V&V. These include the Java language and the difficult security implications of using the Internet. This usage immediately reflects back to the development of those applications to be used on the Internet and the special care that must be taken to verify and validate the security aspects of such applications.

In *Independent Verification and Validation for Internet Multimedia Systems,*[5] it is noted that one of the challenges for V&V professionals is to continually update existing practices that can be applied to the ever-increasing number of new, emerging, and diverse technologies within the computer industry, such as multimedia, the Internet, and client/server technology. These technologies are converging in the development of powerful interactive multimedia-based applications. These applications run effectively across the Internet through the use of the Internet's World Wide Web (WWW). *Que's Dictionary of Computer Terms*[3] defines the WWW as a global hypertext system that uses the Internet as its transport mechanism. In a hypertext system, users navigate by clicking hyperlinks, which display other documents (which also contain hyperlinks). What makes the web such an exciting and useful medium is that the next document you see could be housed on a computer next door or halfway around the world. The web provides a graphical user interface (GUI) for Internet applications. The WWW was created in 1989 at the European Laboratory for Particle Physics (CERN), a research institute in Switzerland. The WWW relies upon the HyperText Transport Protocol (HTTP), an Internet standard that specifies how an application can locate and acquire resources (such as a document, sound, or graphic) stored on another computer on the Internet. HTTP provides transparent, easy-to-use access to web documents, FTP (File Transfer Protocol) file archives, Gopher menus, and even UseNet.

Continuing the discussion from *Independent Verification and Validation for Internet Multimedia Systems,*[5] as the trend toward converging multimedia, the Internet, and client/server technologies gains momentum, it becomes more and more necessary for V&V professionals to adapt and develop practices that can be applied to these new development efforts. Though standard V&V practices can be applied to Internet multimedia system development efforts, certain variations exist. To compensate for these variations, innovative V&V techniques and practices should be added to the V&V process to make them more rigorous. Identifying these variations and adding rigor to the V&V process will reduce system errors and compatibility problems.

Que's Dictionary of Computer Terms[3] defines multimedia as a computer-based method of presenting information by using more than one medium of communication, such as text, graphics, and sound, and emphasizing interactivity. In Microsoft Bookshelf, for example, one can see portraits of William Shakespeare, see a list of his works, and follow hyperlinks to related information. Advances in sound and video synchronization allow one to display moving video images within on-screen windows.

Continuing from *Independent Verification and Validation for Internet Multimedia Systems*[5] as multimedia, client/server, and Internet technologies converge and proliferate, it is critical to evaluate current V&V practices with the focus of ensuring that current practices are applicable to these new and emerging development efforts. Later in this chapter, unique variations attributable to the development of Internet multimedia applications are identified, and practices and techniques that can be applied during the development life-cycle to assist in addressing these variations are recommended.

The Java computer language was created by Sun Microsystems primarily for network computing. The idea behind Java is "write once, read anywhere:" any computer that has a piece of software called a Java Virtual Machine (JVM) can execute Java code written on any other computer. Java was originally intended to be interpreted (executed line-by-line), but there exist some JVMs which read and recomile the Java code for greater execution speed. Java code can be packaged as an application, to run by itself under the JVM, or as a much smaller "applet" which requires support from an external application like a web browser.

The Internet provided Java with a terrific initial boost; web authors used Java for everything from enhancing the appearance of their sites to providing content (information, analytical tools, etc.). Experts also propose that Java be used as a standard in appliances like cellular phones, digital cameras, televisions, and the like to improve connectivity to computers or even other similarly-enabled appliances.

When one considers the broad impact of Java applets over the Internet, the criticality of V&V is enormous. These special issues are discussed in the Contemporary V&V section in this chapter. If Java only lives up to a portion of what Sun promises, the Internet and the millions of computer users who gravitate to it will get a refreshing, helpful application tool.

The growth of the Internet means that security concerns have grown tremendously, because as one increases the ability to communicate, there is a concomitant increase in vulnerability, reports Nauth in *The Washington Post*.[2] Nauth goes on to say that network security is of urgent concern to companies eager to conduct electronic commerce. With the Internet and intranets, access management is an issue not just for the internal hierarchy of employees, but also for an enterprise's business partners, contractors, temporary employees, vendors, service organizations, clients, customers, and distributors. Privacy, access control, and intrusion detection are the three main forms of network security (p. M11).

G. Winfield Treese's "Internet Security: To Worry or Not To Worry?"[6] relates that:

> one can hardly pick up the newspaper today without reading the latest concerns about Internet security, particularly as it relates to transactions involving payment, proprietary corporate information, and personal or professional authentication. [The reasons why] the Internet is so different from other communication channels (phone, fax, letter) and demands remarkably high levels of security are:
>
> - There is a perception that the Internet is not secure.
> - Security concerns of phone, fax, and letter transmissions have been low.
> - Computers are connected.
> - The network is public.
> - The network is digital.
> - Computers collect data, whereas letters, phones, etc. do not.
> - Computers are capability of being programmed, to decode secured transmissions, whereas prior communication devices are not.
> - Computer fraud is difficult to trace.
> - Computers are not perfect replacements for humans.
> - The Internet seems anonymous and distant.
> - Information commerce is different.
> - Legal protection of security transmissions have not caught up to the technology. (pp. 16–18)

Again, Dave Barry[1] has some cogent comments about one of the most popular aspects of the Internet and intranets—e-mail:

> **Q.** How does "e-mail" work?
>
> **A.** It's very simple: Each person on the "Internet" has a unique e-mail "address" created by having a squirrel run across a computer keyboard, such as: "geekboogr2038rpm(!)rbi." When you wish to communicate with somebody, you simply put that person's address on your message, give the "send" command, and within seconds—no matter where in the world the addressee is—your message is being read by dozens of teenage "hackers," who are also using your Visa card number to purchase Hawaiian vacations. Don't try to stop them: They can also launch missiles. (p. 28)

Multidimensional Model

The Internet and intranet are technology innovations on the technology axis. These technological innovations include forces that are requiring a large increase in the knowledge base of the V&V person. Each technology increment (i.e., GUI, networks, WWW, Java, etc.) requires more knowledge from the V&V person. It is simply too much to expect a V&V person to understand all the technology increments. Shared time or teams of V&V experts need to become involved, similar to the situation described in Chapter 10 on knowledge-based systems. In that case, the split occurred between the development technology capability and the actual structure and content of the knowledge base. For the Internet/intranet situation, the major split occurs between the network-knowledgeable V&V person and the language-implementation V&V expert.

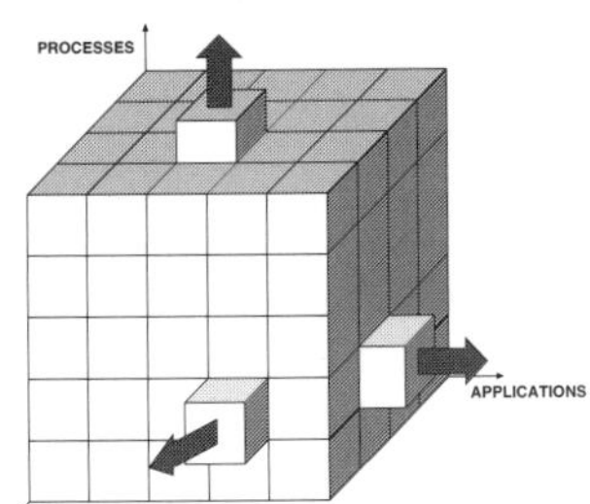

There are major process-related concepts that are relevant to V&V of Internet/intranet technology. Consider the standards and protocols that not only cover web usage, but also the list mentioned in this chapter in relation to network security (DES, Diffie-Hellman, IPSEG, SSL, SET). In this society of "instant gratification," RAD (see Chapter 7) is the most prevalent life-cycle model for Internet development.

Information services on the applications axis of the multidimensional model are primarily coincidental with Internet/intranet technology. The main thrust of the Internet/intranet is to access data or information. So, they naturally flow together. As is discovered in Chapter 12, data warehousing applications are transitioning to the intranet and the Internet.

Traditional V & V

The traditional V&V aspects include the usual intensive reviews of the requirements and design documents. A look at the code or "visual" implementation is also verified in the usual detailed method. It is when validation occurs that a divergence from the traditional methods starts. The testing at the single workstation level is very traditional; however, the use of the network comes into the test picture when V&V methods differ at the Internet/intranet level. Since most of this is relatively new ground, the Contemporary V&V section covers most of the issues involved with V&V of the Internet/intranet.

For this Traditional V&V section, first there is presented a basic survey of web security issues, then a number of traditional V&V elements are covered for the security area of the Internet/intranet. Especially pertinent is the awareness that a V&V person should have of the Systems Security Engineering (SSE) Capability Maturity Model (CMM).

From Rubin and Geer Jr.'s "A Survey of Web Security,"[7] web-specific security issues of server and host environments, mobile code, data transport, and anonymity and privacy are surveyed:

In the client/server environment, the focus is on the server side because the server is the central system and the repository of information resources. The server is thus the locus of threats, whereas the client is largely out of sight. Protecting the client side from the server side is generally not an issue, except where client privacy is a concern.

The biggest cause of security problems in the server environment is bad management. In distributed systems, the first place management affects security is in the system's configuration. A bad system configuration can mean disaster. If configuration is not controlled, it is difficult to express management policy in the system's operational characteristics. As system complexity increases, the problem becomes acute: The inability to make systems conform to policy ensures increasing disarray and the exploitable holes that result.

Host security focuses on the host system's configuration and operational practices and provides a foundation for server security. Basic threats in host system security include:

- complexity: because it is complicated to anticipate each interaction among security-sensitive and security-insensitive applications on a single machine, Webmasters typically run security-sensitive subsystems on a dedicated machinery. Also, *trusted system** formally is generally not available on the web.
- access control: Webmasters must give root-privilege access the best possible security protection. If attackers obtain superuser access, their system access is unrestricted.
- accountability: The web is an intentionally open system to a fault; components are mixed and matched from many sources. Thus, Webmasters must insist on accountability. They must check all actions of import for access authorization and keep strict records on the facts of every transaction. All such incidents must be nonmodifiable or be logged off-board.

There are two fundamentally different approaches to securing data in transit—that is, securing data transport. In the network-layer approach, the encryption and authentication is added directly into the networking stack so that traffic is protected without requiring the application to incorporate it. Traffic reaching the remote system is automatically decrypted and verified by the remote system's networking stack before the operating system passes it to the server application. In the application-level approach, the application itself is modified so that traffic is encrypted before it is submitted to the operating system and network layer. It is then decrypted by the receiving server application.

Mobile code comprises general-purpose executables that run in remote locations. That such general-purpose scripts can run on any Internet-connected computer opens up a world of possibilities for distributed applications. However, such functionality comes at a price. From a security perspective, nothing is more dangerous than a global, homogeneous, general-purpose interpreter. The fact that this interpreter is part of a browser—a large, notoriously defect-ridden software package—only increases the risks. There are basically three practical techniques to secure mobile code: sandboxing, code signing, and firewalling. The sandbox method limits the executable's privileges to a small set of operations. The code signing method checks to see if

* Trusted systems are systems designed to substitute formal proof of security in place of experimental satisfaction. Such formal evaluation criteria exist in the US Defense Department's Orange Book ("Trusted Computer System Evaluation Criteria," National Computer Security Center, DoD 5200.28-STD, December, 1985).

> the executable's source is trustworthy. The firewalling approach limits the programs a client can run based on the executable's properties.
>
> Privacy and anonymity are issues of concern in web-based security. Information about user's activity on the web is increasingly being recorded and disseminated. Thus, as web functionality increases, gains achieved in convenience are counterbalanced by privacy losses. Users are often unaware of the deficit. Web users have a data shadow, with information about what they read, where they shop, where they buy, whom they correspond with, and so on.
>
> Web security mechanisms are a collection of clever, ad hoc efforts to retrofit security into a system whose popularity overwhelmed its original design. [Rubin and Geer Jr.[7] conclude with the observation that] there is evidence that use of the web for business will inevitably result in a more serious approach to security. (pp. 34, 36, 39)

Both privacy and access control rely on encryption, as abstracted here from Kristin Nauth's article in *The Washington Post*:[2]

> Security specialists, [and consequently V&V specialist dealing with security issues], need to understand the existence of encryption standards, including Data Encryption Standard (DES), Diffie-Hellman, and public and private key cryptography, as well as Internet Protocol (IPSEG), which secures the network itself.
>
> For ensuring privacy in network transactions, especially those that involve immediate payment, a new type of software called a "merchant server" allows visitors to place orders and make payments securely. Merchant servers utilize two new protocols: Secure Socket Layer (SSL), an encryption standard, and Secure Electronic Transactions (SET), an information flow standard. Under SSL, clients and servers exchange keys (digital passwords) in a multistep process of encryption, decryption, and signing the data. SET details how payment card transactions are secured, using heavy encryption technology and keys.
>
> For controlling access, smart cards are fast gaining popularity as authentication devices. Soon, biometrics—fingerprints, retinal scans, and other biological methods—will probably become the authentication tool of choice.
>
> Intrusion detection is very similar to setting electronic tripwires and sensors in a physical building. It requires programming skills in C, C++, TCP/IP, UNIX, and Windows NT, [which leads to the need for V&V in Internet security development to ensure the adequacy of these electronic security systems]. (p. M11)

The remainder of this Traditional V&V section discusses the Systems Security Engineering (SSE) CMM extracted from Karen Ferraiolo and Victoria Thompson's "Let's Just Be Mature about Security! Using a CMM for Security Engineering:"[8]

> The SSE CMM consists of a set of practices that have been grouped into two aspects: domain and capability. This architecture was adopted from the Systems Engineering CMM. The architecture was deemed particularly applicable to the SSE CMM because it clearly separates basic characteristics of the security engineering process (domain aspect) from process management and institutionalization characteristics of the security engineering process (capability aspect).

The capability aspect consists of generic practices related to overall process management and institutionalization capability. This aspect is used during an assessment to determine how well an organization performs the practices in the domain aspect. The SSE CMM groups process capability in three tiers: capability levels, common features, and generic practices. The six capability levels indicate increasing levels of process maturity and are composed of one or more common features, as illustrated in [Figure 11.1]. Each common feature is further detailed by several generic practices. (p. 18)

[Capability levels indicate the maturity of a security engineering organization.] The domain aspect consists of base practices specific to security engineering, and is grouped by process areas. In an assessment, this aspect is used to determine what security engineering practices an organization performs. There are 21 process areas, grouped into three process categories: *engineering*, *project*, and *organization*. The security engineering process areas appear with their goals in Table 11.1. Table 11.2 lists the project and organization process areas that have been

Table 11.1 SSE CMM security *engineering* process areas.[8] (p. 17)

Engineering Process Area	Goals
Administer Security Controls	• Security controls are properly configured and used.
Assess Operational Security Risk	• An understanding of the security risk associated with operating the system within a defined environment is reached.
Attack Security	• System vulnerabilities are identified and their potential for exploitation is determined.
Build Assurance Argument	• The work products and processes clearly provide the evidence that the customer's security needs have been met.
Coordinate Security	• All members of the project team are aware of and involved with security engineering activities to the extent necessary to perform their functions. • Decisions and recommendations related to security are communicated and coordinated.
Determine Security Vulnerabilities	• An understanding of system security is reached.
Monitor System Security Posture	• Both internal and external security-related vents are detected and tracked. • Incidents are responded to in accordance with policy. • Changes to the operational security posture are identified and handled in accordance with security objectives.
Provide Security Input	• All system issues are reviewed for security implications and are resolved in accordance with security goals. • All members of the project team have an understanding of security so they can perform their functions. • The solution reflects the security input provided.
Specify Security Needs	• A common understanding of security needs is reached between all applicable parties, including the customer.
Verify and Validate Security	• Solutions meet security requirements. • Solutions meet the customer's operational security needs.

Figure 11.1 Capability levels indicate maturity of a security engineering organization.[8] (p. 18)

0 **Not Performed**	1 **Performed Informally**	2 **Planned and Tracked**	3 **Well Defined**	4 **Quantitatively Controlled**	5 **Continuously Improving**
	• Base practices are performed	• Planning performance • Disciplined performance • Tracking performance • Verifying performance	• Defining a standard process • Perform the defined process • Coordinate security practices	• Establishing measurable quality goals • Objectively managing performance	• Improving organizational capability • Improving process effectiveness

Table 11.2 SSE CMM project and organization process areas (based on SE CMM with security engineering interpretations).[8] (p. 19)

Project Process Areas	Organization Process Areas
Ensure Quality	Coordinate with Suppliers
Manage Configurations	Define Organization's Security Engineering Process
Manage Program Risk	Improve Organization's Security Engineering Processes
Monitor and Control Technical Effort	Manage Product Line Evolution
Plan Technical Effort	Manage Security Engineering Support Environment
Provide Ongoing Skills and Knowledge	

adopted from the SE CMM. In the SSE CMM model description, interpretations for security engineering are provided for each of the project and organization process areas. (p. 18)

[SSE CMM measures the security engineering capability of an organization.] Project participants predict that the SSE CMM will serve well throughout the life-cycle of an information system. They also assert that the model's use can yield benefits for a variety of organizations and functions. System developers who embrace and effectively implement the SSE CMM are expected to enjoy competitive advantage. Schedule, cost, and technical risks are likely to be reduced, and the need for extensive and expensive "reverse engineering" for security may be eliminated.... Scenarios for use of the SSE CMM are described below. (p. 19)

System Development

- Contractors use the SSE CMM to ensure the institutionalization of their security engineering processes, which will avoid reliance on heroes (the superstars that get the job done no matter what) and will control their program risk.
- System developers apply the SSE CMM to help assure customers that the system in development will meet their requirements. Their assessed security engineering capability provides the customer confidence that the developer will "do the right things." Furthermore, the customer can expect that the developer's previous security engineering successes will be repeated, since repeatable results are a hallmark of capability maturity.
- New products are easily incorporated into the system because the SSE CMM has been used to expedite their passage through evaluation. Because they have implemented the SSE CMM, product developers consistently produce appropriate evidence that the products are correctly engineered. (p. 19)

Security Assessment

- Adherence to the SSE CMM allows the developer to ensure that security requirements are appropriate before system development begins. SSE CMM capability guides the developer in the verification and validation of security requirements.
- SSE CMM process areas, such as Verify and Validate Security and Coordinate Security, guide the developer and ensure that the security requirements are met as the system is developed.
- Because the SSE CMM ensures that necessary assurance evidence was produced during the course of system development, security assessment of the developed system (e.g.,

certification and accreditation) can be accomplished quickly and easily. Evaluators need only spot-check. The security assessor may also rely on the developer's and V&V team's security engineering capability for confidence in the quality of the system's security engineering and in its integration with other engineering disciplines....

More than 40 commercial and government organizations... have applied the model to their own engineering processes with gratifying results.... The SSE CMM offers a valuable and long overdue means to mature security V&V activities and to improve the quality, cost, and availability of secure products, systems, and services. (pp. 19–20)

Contemporary V & V

Like any new paradigm, network computing changes business processes resulting in three broad categories of skills required:

1. network design, development, and management
2. web design and applications development
3. network security.[2]

For each of these developmental skills, the related V&V skills are addressed in this section.

The following information is abstracted from Nik Sargent's "VV&T of a Complex Networked-Based Telecom System."[9] Thorough V&V of large network systems is not trivial. It is further compounded when the quality and complexity of the existing system it is built upon is not known. In such circumstances, delivering a product of greater, known quality requires a planned and pragmatic use of V&V principles.

One of the key principles that must be established initially is "fitness for purpose"—that is, to determine the appropriate level of quality for the deliverable, or how much V&V to apply with the development. This is something the whole team must "buy into." Too low a level, and the customer will not be satisfied. Too high a level and the customer will be paying for effort they do not require.

[First, look at the specification and design of the new features.] Not only are these documents reviewed by software quality assurance (SQA) in the customary fashion, but separate V&V reviews are held. These V&V reviews consist of a rigorous formal inspection of documents against the requirements specification, and include prepared criteria and guidance. Experience shows that nearly 50% of all system defects are detected at these reviews. That is, when it was time to test, half the errors [are not subject to testing].

To improve the review process, all the core system components are reviewed in a single session, thereby enabling developers to resolve inconsistencies with each other immediately and ensuring that the review does not stretch out unnecessarily. [This method is particularly related to the IPT concepts covered in Chapter 15.]

This process is then followed up with inspections of the changed code, and this consistently detects nearly 100% of errors in the new functions. [Capturing inspection metrics is] essential for assessing their effectiveness.

> During development it is necessary to detect and correct existing errors, as well as avoid new ones. Static Analysis, as performed by the McCabe toolset, may prove beneficial. The McCabe toolset seems to be effective in allowing customized views of the behavior and structure of the code (important when the code is inherited), and in focusing on areas that are more error prone.... Striking correlations have been found between the code where errors are located and the tool's indication of "problem" code.
>
> Not surprisingly, implementation errors are detected and corrected more readily once testing begins. However, it is not until the latter stages of system testing that errors in the original design are usually discovered—this at a time when it is generally very difficult to correct them. Clearly, time invested in design reviews and V&V reviews is a good investment, and should be a point of focus.
>
> Automation of system testing [seems to be] a key factor to its success. Bulk call generators may be used to successfully load and stress test the system, but are not completely representative of live traffic on a system that has complex user interaction. Therefore, development of intelligent bulk testers is recommended, and their contribution to testing, by being able to accurately simulate "real" actions, cannot be underestimated.
>
> An essential feature of any system is its ability to archive its transactions. Combined with custom tools to extract, summarize, and recreate events on the platform, this forms an invaluable aid to error removal during the test phase and live service.... An automated tester may take these logs as an input, and then accurately recreate the transactions on a model system, as an aid to error removal, in much the same manner as a capture/replay tool. (p. 3)

At NASA, the FACADE project is an experiment to explore V&V methods related to the goal of Verifiable Development Techniques (VDTs). Burkhard and Cavanaugh[10] define FACADE (FAst CAse Development Environment) as "a set of tools for rapid software development that try to unify many different aspects of software development" (p. 3). Callahan and Sabolish[11] tell us that:

> initially, with VDTs, the focus is on the ability of the V&V process to find problems effectively and not on improving the capabilities of the software development process itself. However, because V&V and development are intimately related processes, a strategy has been developed* for transferring improvements to development processes based on the need for improvements in V&V. The long-term strategy is to demonstrate that changes to development are needed in cases where V&V is unable to perform its task due to inappropriate or unavailable information from development. The goal of process improvement on a development organization is to enable it to produce high-quality software, on time, and within budget. This implies that the development effort is predictable and measurable. Ultimately, this will lead to development techniques that are highly amenable to V&V activities. These development techniques are labeled VDTs to identify them as enabling effective V&V over other approaches. A VDT is comprised of many different phases that are highly amenable to V&V, [and consequently are amenable to new technologies]. For example, the requirements for a security-critical project such as credit card charges over the Internet might be expressed in specification language that is amenable to formal analysis. In a VDT, such analysis is not simply a spot check but coordinated with analyses performed in other phases.

---

* passive voice replaces personal pronouns in quote.

From a process perspective, the work in VDTs has already led to finding models where V&V can make significant impact on software development efforts.

There has been ongoing activity within the NASA V&V Cooperative Agreement to examine communication protocol design and evolution that is so important to successful networking, related from the *V&V Research Quarterly*:[10]

> As part of these activities, the Reliable Multicast Protocol (RMP) has been designed, developed, and implemented.... As memory, storage, reliability, and bandwidth increase, decentralization of data storage increases, [which] introduces new and complex issues that must be dealt with. Reliable delivery, resiliency and ordering of messages, and fault-tolerance of communications are all low-level concerns of application developers that are introduced by the decentralization of computation into distributed systems. The lack of reliable broadcast or multicast primitives has introduced a host of unnecessarily complex and inefficient schemes for providing application—specific fault tolerance, reliability, and resiliency. Although addressing the difficult issues, usually these schemes are not reusable in other applications because of the closely knit connection between the application and its communication mechanisms. In many cases these are so closely interconnected that one is not distinguishable from the other. This virtually eliminates interoperability and can seriously effect application evolution.
>
> RMP provides a totally ordered, reliable, atomic multicast service on top of an unreliable multicast service, such as IP multicasting.... [RMP uses multicast technology] instead of broadcast technology, including several extensions to provide extra functionality and changing the fault recovery model. RMP* has shown remarkable performance on LAN and WAN environments. (pp. 3, 4)

Internet Multimedia V&V

This section is abstracted from *Independent Verification and Validation for Internet Multimedia Systems*:[5]

> The WWW is the graphical multimedia interface to the Internet. The WWW requires users to utilize web browsers in order to view WWW content information. WWW content information is generally text data, graphics, images, video clips, and sound files. The web browsers act as the client software systems while the web content information is stored on a server which in essence is a database server. Thus, WWW applications utilize client/server architectures to present data in a multimedia format. WWW applications may also rely on third-party client/server database packages, such as Sybase's SQL Server, as a database back-end engine for processing/storing large data volumes.
>
> WWW application programs are often developed using a multimedia scripting language such as HTML or Java. Such languages aim to hide low-level implementation details. These languages provide mechanisms to present multimedia data and hooks to client/server database engines such as Sybase's SQL Server or Oracle's SQL Server.

---

* For more information about RMP as well as the public domain distribution of the source code, point your WWW browsers to: http://research.ivv.nasa.gov/projects/RMP/RMP.html.

...Internet multimedia development efforts involve many new technologies and thus offer many new challenges to V&V* professionals. Primarily, Internet multimedia applications differ from traditional applications in two distinct ways. Firstly, Internet multimedia applications have constraints placed on them due to bandwidth (data transfer rate) considerations and need to be taken into account when developing these applications. Internet multimedia applications that operate requiring too much bandwidth for the user-base become unusable, resulting in the application performing slowly.... These applications have a tendency to overwhelm the end-user's computer resources, causing lock-ups, system failures, and the like.

Secondly, Internet multimedia applications place a heavy emphasis on user-interface issues due to their reliance on multimedia data. Since Internet multimedia applications data are comprised of text, images, graphics, animations, video, and sound, the composition of the applications are presentation-based in nature. This shifts the emphasis in development to interface issues and away from more traditional development issues. More specifically, the following paragraphs describe variations, practices, and techniques that should be considered during Internet multimedia development efforts.

In Internet multimedia development efforts, requirements verification needs to ensure that the proper multimedia data characteristics are encapsulated. For instance, in defining graphic files that will be presented as part of the application, characteristics such as number of colors, graphic size, resolution, and file format need to be defined and verified as correct. For *video data*, frame rate, data compression, size, and positing should be verified as correct. For *sound data*, sound quality, bit sampling, and default volume should be verified as correct. Other types of multimedia data such as animations have similar but distinct characteristics that should also be defined and verified at this stage of the software development life-cycle. To complete this type of verification, V&V professionals need to develop a basic understanding of multimedia techniques and concepts.

Another aspect that needs to be verified is the relationship of the data to the client/server database back-end (if part of the application). For instance, where data will be stored, how it will be stored, and methods for data retrieval should be verified as correct. This becomes a somewhat more important requirement than the complexity of the data characteristics and the Internet data communications media the application travels across. To complete this type of verification, V&V professionals need to develop a basic understanding of client/server techniques and concepts [see Chapter 9].

Additionally, telecommunication and networking aspects need to be verified as being transcribed accurately during this phase. V&V specialists need to verify that these requirements have been properly stated and that they fit within the constraints of the intended environment. Implementation details such as transmission rates, bandwidth requirements, network topology capabilities, data transfer protocols, etc., need to be considered. For example, to verify a requirement to allow data to be transported at 10 megabytes per second, the wide-area network link, the local codex, the local cabling, and PC bus structures need to be verified as capable of meeting the data transport requirement. To complete this type of verification, V&V professionals need to develop a basic understanding of telecommunication and networking techniques and concepts.

---

* IV&V has been modified to V&V in all instances of this quote.

> During the design phase of Internet multimedia projects, V&V professionals concentrate on the content of screens [see Chapter 8] and not so much on the background software used to build them. It is important for the V&V specialist not only to evaluate whether all content is presented in a logical manner, but that the content is presented in a manner that is consistent with the interface standard prevalent on the Internet and those standards being developed by Internet standards groups. Standardization of how information is presented is important on the Internet since thousands of organizations share this medium. Information that is presented in a nonstandard way runs the risk of making the application difficult to use or unusable to the end-user.
>
> During static analysis, construction fault detection becomes somewhat more complicated. In addition to evaluating the code standard adherence, variable set-use data, syntax errors, etc., the various multimedia data and their associated characteristics need to be evaluated and examined. Data such as graphic images need to be examined to ensure they contain the correct number of colors, file compression format, and size. Video data need to be examined to ensure that the proper frame rate has been implemented, data compression has been correctly implemented, and size and positing are correct. Sound data should be examined to ensure that the sound quality, bit sampling, and default volume are correct. Examining these multimedia data characteristics will require V&V professionals to add software and hardware tools to their V&V toolset [see Chapter 3]. An example of a new tool is a graphic viewing/manipulation programs useful in analyzing graphic compositions.
>
> ...V&V specialists, then, need to increase their technical skills in the areas of multimedia, client/server, and Internet technologies in order to be capable of properly applying V&V techniques to the system development life-cycle—more of the knowledge required is discussed in the Multidimensional Model section. Additionally, V&V professionals need to consider the current Graphical User Interface standards being utilized by the Internet and place an emphasis on verifying this component during the design phase. Also, during the coding, implementation and testing phase, V&V professionals need to verify that multimedia data were presented as required; this will require V&V professionals to add new software and hardware tools to their toolsets. (p. 4)

Besides the multimedia aspect, the handling of links (such as hyperlinks) need to be understood by the V&V person. This subject is abstracted from Hermann Maurer's "Web-Based Knowledge Management:"[12]

> Creation and maintenance of links should be supported by servers, not by humans. Consider the simple case of a number of servers pointing to a document. If this document is deleted, it will introduce dangling links, which we would all like to have deleted automatically. Doing so is indeed possible, but it requires that unidirectional links with no attributes be turned into bidirectional links with attributes—[such as] author, access rights, and time of creation—whose anchors are not embedded in the documents themselves, but handled in a separate database.
>
> This type of automation would have tremendous payoffs. One could attach notes to web documents one does not own. Depending on access privileges, such annotations could be private, public for a particular group, or public to everyone. Annotations could be readily turned into structured discussions. Furthermore, links could become searchable and could be manipulated like other documents.

Implementing all the features just mentioned, in addition to adding synchronous communication facilities, workflow components (like version control), and full text indexing of arbitrary document types, would turn unmanageable spaghetti-linked web systems into surprisingly well-structured and easy to administer knowledge repositories.

The major efforts to accomplish this are:

- IRIS/Intermediate systems at Brown University [*Communications of the ACM,* Jan. 1992, pp. 197–202]
- Webcosm [http://www.webcosm.com]
- Hypermedia Object Management Environment (HOME) [http://www.cs.kuleuven.ac.be/~erikd/MANUAL/home.html]
- Hyperwave from Austria [http://www.hyperwave.com]

These developments all point to a new kind of web paradigm (called knowledge management) that could shape the future of the Internet [and its impact on the V&V person]. (p. 122)

Java V&V

Explained from the "The Java Factor:"[13]

> The Java programming language is defined as a strongly typed, object oriented language that borrows heavily from the syntax of C++ while avoiding many of the C++ language features that lead to programming errors, obfuscated code, or procedural programming.
>
> When Sun Microsystems introduced Java in 1995, the language was primarily used for developing applets—downloadable mini-applications that could be embedded inside web pages and executed in browsers. If cross-platform portability was the only advantage of Java, the language probably would have gone no further. However, since its commercial introduction, Java has emerged as a first-class programming language that is being used for everything from embedded devices to enterprise servers. The language today is seeing use in a wider range of applications than any other language, including C and C++.
>
> Java is designed to directly support OO programming. All data and functions must be encapsulated within classes, much like Smalltalk. Interfaces are first-class language constructs and are enforced by the type system. A class may be declared to implement multiple interfaces simultaneously, though it may only inherit from one implementation class. The Java run-time includes class libraries that provide high-level interfaces for GUI programming, I/O, multithreading, and networking. (p. 34)

"Platform independence in Java really takes two forms," says Paul Tyma in "Why Are We Using Java Again?"[14] He continues,

> the popular notion is that the code is written and compiled without ever having to worry about having to port it to new machines (write once, run everywhere). The more overlooked side of platform independence is Java's rather fantastic abstraction of many programming paradigms.
>
> Java's automatic memory management, operating system abstractions (through its APIs), and familiar low-level syntax (at least for C programmers) make it a curiously productive environment. Most new Java programmers are surprised at how they are able to get something (any-

thing) to work almost immediately. Before learning all there is about OO programming, multi-threading, remote method invocation, and the like, one can take a prebuilt piece of code, intuitively modify it, and get something up and running quite rapidly.

New C programmers inevitably write to some wayward pointer or commit some other fiendish memory-violating act that causes anything from "General Protection Faults" to system lockups. The guarded memory model in Java makes crashing the system much more difficult (although not impossible).

The entire interaction with memory is worry-free in Java. When one wants some memory one takes it, when one is done with it, one walks away from it. This abstraction relieves the programmer of system "details." An alternative view (and one popular with C programmers during their transition to Java) is that Java is extremely limiting in terms of memory control. Compared to C, this is certainly true. However, the word *flexibility* is often synonymous with *responsibility*. Humans inevitably make mistakes and often fail to be responsible with memory management (dangling pointers, memory leaks, and so forth). Java relies on the fact that algorithms do not make mistakes and controls memory (at the cost of some run-time performance). Most C programmers eventually embrace this productive paradigm in spite of their lost flexibility.

Java programmers need only learn one set of APIs for all operations. Writing network code is the same regardless of which platform they are using. In C and C++ environments there are a plethora of choices for networking APIs—in fact, this is a the problem. Two C programmers writing networking programs might not even be able to describe their respective projects to each other. Java programmers are always on the same level, regardless of their underlying environments. The number of APIs is vast, but if one learns them once, that is all one needs to know.

The other side of platform independence is an unexpectedly darker side. This is the "write once, run everywhere," end-all solution—that is, one executable program running on any popular architecture and operating system. A Java executable program is a set of instructions in Java bytecode. This is the machine language for the Java Virtual Machine (JVM). JVMs do not just happen to exist on every known platform; it takes serious work to create a JVM for each and every operating system. Every JVM is then expected to accept a validly compiled Java program and execute it in exactly the same way as any other JVM. This sounds like an insurmountable task, and so it is.

Platform independence at this level is not yet a total reality. There are many subtle idiosyncrasies to be found with every new operating system and a few major problems, too. For one thing, many Java programmers have quickly learned the difference between preemptive and non-preemptive multitasking operating systems. In preemptive operating systems (Windows 95/NT) processes can be stopped so that other processes have a chance to run. In other words, no single process should be able to utilize the entire CPU. In non-preemptive operating systems (Mac OS) a process only gives up the CPU when it wants to. So Java programmers can write a multithreaded program that runs well in one OS and does not run at all in another. A Java programmer can write programs to ensure they run on both types of operating systems (in fact, today it is a requirement), but it can be argued that platform independent programs should be either right or wrong (either they always run or they never run), not somewhere in between.

The worst thing about platform independence is that it keeps on going independent of the architecture—meaning that Java needs to assume the lowest common denominator of available resources. Java supported only one mouse button because Macs only have one mouse button. Java can only assume very generic things; it assumes a system has a CPU, memory, and a graphics subsystem. It also assumes the operating system is multithreaded, which negates the idea of Java on Windows 3.1 (IBM subsequently released Alphaworks, adding the required support). Joysticks, special keypads, and the like cannot be accessed from Java. Only in the latest releases are we seeing the ability to print. To get system-specific, one needs to write some (maybe just a little) C code and interface it with Java.

The problem is that if the program is even 1% C code, one can lose Java's platform independence and its solid security model. C code must be compiled for a specific machine, and the Java run time has no governing authority over what that C code can do (it might "say" it is just going to check the joystick…). There are definite applications in which C and Java fit together, but not in 100% platform-independent products.

It would seem that everybody is happy. Academics are by no means disappointed in Java. It takes the best ideas developed over the past 10 years and incorporates them into one powerful and highly supported language. Industries do not mind either; they can develop their applications in a platform-independent and robust manner. So, with all these wonderful reasons supporting its use, one would think the world would be filled with Java programs.

When the support for "Java-powdered" web pages stalled it was not necessarily bad because it evolved Java's focus into the idea of a "thin client" and the ability to make web-enabled applications. (pp. 38–41)

Continuing from Tyma's "Why Are We Using Java Again?"[14]

Many are working on improving the slow performance problems of Java. But people woke up to an interesting fact hiding behind the whole Java paradigm. The plain truth is: Java is slow. Java is not just slow, it is really slow, surprisingly slow. It is "you get to watch the buttons being drawn on your toolbar" slow. The reason for Java's speed can be simplified in one word: abstraction. To OO/high-level designers, abstraction is the goal. To the computer, any abstraction puts the code another step away from what it understands. It is also the computer's job to decode those steps down to its machine language so it can actually run the program.

Everyone in the Java industry knows about Java's addiction to abstraction, and many are trying to fix it. The compiler companies came out with their just-in-time (JIT) compilers. These programs (which are closer to assemblers than compilers) convert Java's stack-based intermediate representation (which is executable) into native machine code immediately prior to execution on a machine. That way, the Java program actually runs as a real executable program (that is, straight in machine code).

There is no argument—JIT compilers do speed up Java programs. But to be honest, after comparing Java programs that use JIT compilers to normal C and C++ applications, it is still slow. JIT compilers are also hard to make compared to interpretive environments (Java's first home), and they only exist for a few select platforms (Windows 95/NT and Mac). That hardly makes Java platform independent or fast, does it? (pp. 41–42)

Security Considerations on the Internet

In "A Flexible Security System for Using Internet Content,"[15] the authors describe FlexxGuard as:

> a flexible content interpreter that dynamically drives protection domains and uses those domains to authorize content operations. FlexxGuard derives protection domains based on a description of the content, called a *content stamp*. The authorization mechanism uses a capability-based representation of protection domains to determine whether an applet operation is granted or revoked. The major problems in developing a flexible content interpreter are deriving a "least privilege" protection domain for content and enforcing this protection domain throughout the content's execution. To derive the domain, a policy database is defined that stores the information necessary to compute a default maximal protection domain for content. This content that requires only a subset of this protection domain can be granted it automatically to enforce the protection domain. FlexxGuard determines when content is about to execute and limits it to its previously derived protection domain.
>
> Typically, users do not trust downloaded content with all their resources. In particular, users want to prevent content from reading private files, writing configuration and executable files, having uncontrolled access to the CPU, and communicating with arbitrary remote hosts. By default, a user can do all these things, but various attacks can be launched by malicious content with privileges to perform such actions: For example, viruses and Trojan horses can be implemented easily if malicious content can modify executables.
>
> The problem, then, is to define and enforce a limited protection domain for downloaded content commensurate with resource needs and the user's trust in the content manufacturers. Controlling downloaded content has three facets:
>
> 1. *Authentication* verifies security requirements (if you cannot identify the content manufacturers and content, assume the source is untrustworthy).
> 2. *Domain derivation* computes a protection domain for this content based upon manufacturer integrity, the content's quality rating, and organizational policies.
> 3. *Enforcement* uses the protection domain to limit the system access of content and its supporting routines.
>
> The FlexxGuard system [Figure 11.2] was built at IBM using Java Development Kit 1.1. The key security model components are the analysis module and the protection domain enforcer, implemented by AppletClassLoader and AppletSecurity Java classes, respectively. (pp. 53–54)

This next aspect of security for the intranet that a V&V person should be aware of is abstracted from Emily Kay's "Scared of the Web"[16] (pp. 1–3). Companies such as Cargill Inc. (a commodities-trading company with 17,000 worldwide employees) and Tufts Health Plan (a 668,000-members Waltham HMO) are considering access to a corporate data warehouse (see Chapter 12) via an intranet. Cargill Inc. says no because the nature of data warehouses as strategic data analyzers rules against providing open access to the public. Tufts Health Plan considers security as the biggest part of their requests for proposal (from their vendors). There is universal concern about unauthorized spies, hackers, and competitors wandering through the front door and snooping through business-sensitive warehouse data. Some companies are not closing that portal altogether, but they have no intention of leaving it without sufficient security.

Figure 11.2 The FlexxGuard architecture (© 1997 IEEE).[15] (p. 54)

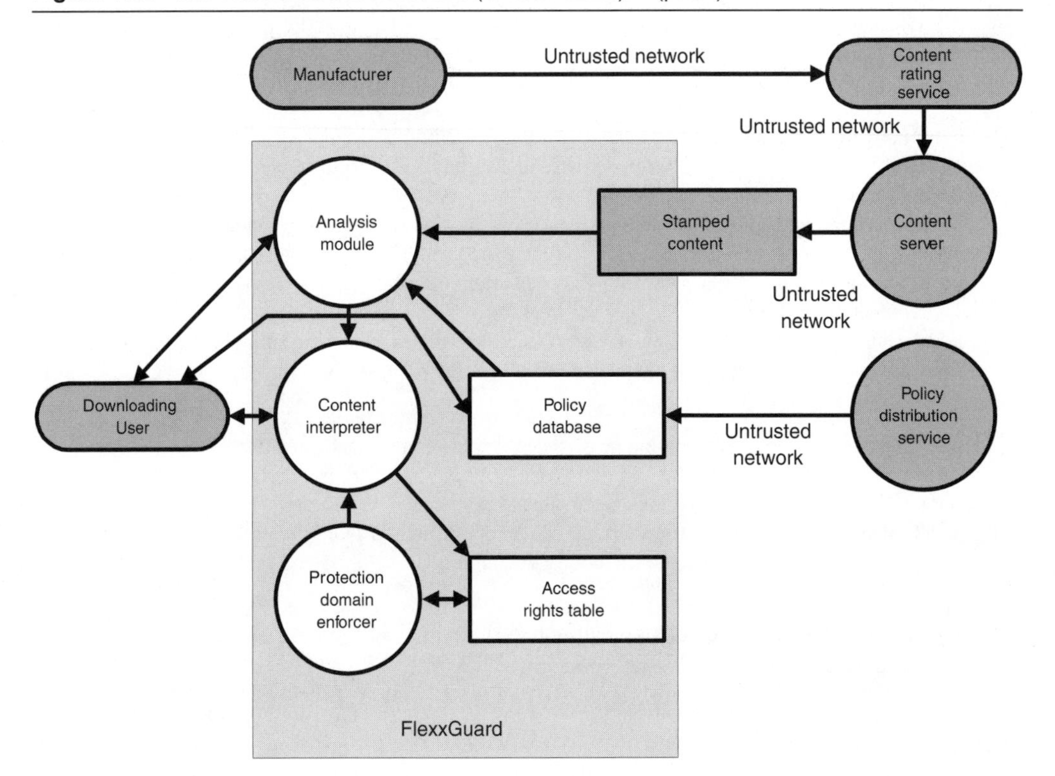

Security fears are keeping many companies from placing their data warehouses onto the web. There are so many different pieces of the security puzzle to learn, manage, and support—firewalls, data encryption, and authorization and authentication schemes among them. The threats to data safety begin long before organizations even consider allowing web access to the warehouse. Developers typically do not design security capabilities into their warehouses. The most common form of security found in data warehousing for the Internet/intranet is no security. Since the developers do not consider security for Internet/intranet projects, the security recommendations and assurance need to come from somewhere. It is this special arena that the V&V specialist may add real value to Internet/intranet software and data developments.

The lack of warehouse security may stem from the fact that limiting access is antithetical to why companies deploy warehouses in the first place—to provide more users with more access to more information. Companies want to provide their analysts with the best and most data for a comprehensive analysis, but realize when placing it on the intranet/Internet there is risk of compromise to the data.

Even when developers do build in security precautions to their data warehouses, once on the web, the warehouses are never completely safe. The fundamental lesson security experts preach is that all web-enabled data warehouses are in jeopardy. Some companies, such as American Express and America Online, only post report distribution and data dictionaries, putting all but the actual data and queries on the web.

The best an organization can do is to secure warehouses with enough obstacles to deter casual break-ins, just as they would use "The Club" to deter car thieves. If it is made sufficiently difficult, at least it may cause an intruder with bad intentions to break in elsewhere. Web-based data warehouses are never risk-free. Most authentication schemes are based on simple passwords and are subject to random attack.

V&V may help the Internet/intranet developers patch security holes and make it safer to tie databases to a web site. For instance, by building firewalls, companies can separate the Internet from the corporate intranet and keep unauthorized traffic outside. Many companies save money by implementing the firewall on the web server, but experts say the safest design is a dedicated piece of hardware that serves as the firewall between the web server and browser (see Figure 11.3). Having a data warehouse on the Internet/intranet means it is behind a firewall, so it eases security concerns by keeping non-employees out of data warehouses.

Approximately half of the companies building home pages and web sites have installed firewalls, according to a recent survey (Table 11.3) by Sentry Research Services.[16] The wide variety of products planned and in use indicates that there is a wide variety of opinions about the relative

Figure 11.3 Two views of firewall deployment.[16] (p. 2)

TWO VIEWS OF FIREWALL DEPLOYMENT
Building the firewall software as part of the Web server was the initial architecture of choice, but separating the two functions onto seperate servers is becoming prevalent in new implementations.

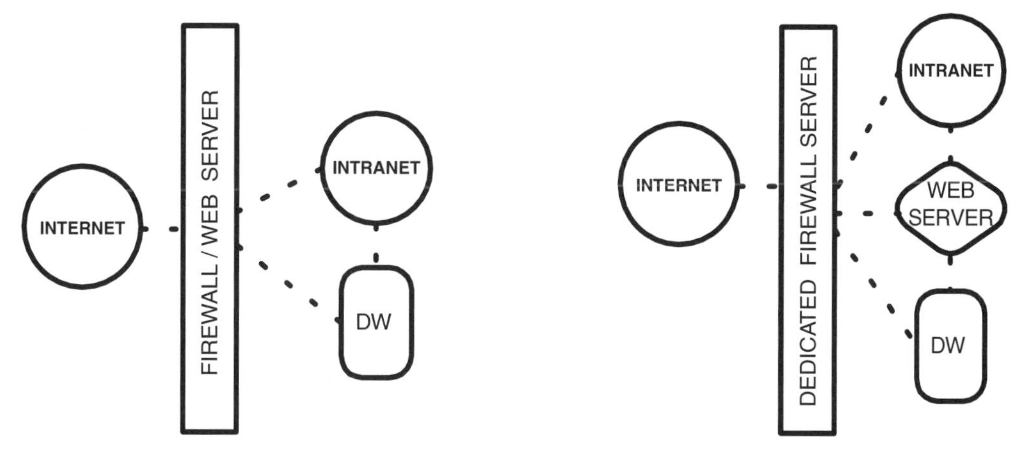

In this implementation, the firewall is on a dedicated server

In this implementation, the firewall is on a dedicated server, seperate from the Web server

Source: Sentry Research Services

Table 11.3 No clear firewall leader.[16] (p. 3)

Other	**46** 48	Microsoft	**13** 14	IBM	**13** 4	CISCO	**9** 10
Sun	**8** 8	Netscape	**7** 12	Raptor	**4** 4	**Top number = Installed** Bottom number = Planned	

Source: *1997 Software Market Survey* Percent of 1,675 respondents, January 1997

strengths and weaknesses of the various firewalls. It is believed that firewalls are just too new to be trusted to protect the data warehouse from an Internet-based break-in.

Some companies are using "digital certificate client authentication, part of the secure electronic transaction (SET) protocol that Visa and Mastercard use. Netscape and Microsoft have incorporated this security process into their web servers and browsers. The two browser vendors are leading the way to establishing de facto industry-standard status for their Internet security protocols. These standards were made for transactions over the Internet, and only by extension do they affect web-enabled data warehouses. Underneath these Internet standards are a host of proprietary security features built into most databases, as well as a variety of encryption methodologies" (p. 3).

Continuing from "Scared of the Web,"[16] Microsoft and Netscape lead the industry in the development of security standards, but there is also an Internet standard that companies can use. The key security standards are:

1. Netscape's Secure Socket Layer (SSL) and Microsoft's Secure Transaction Technology (STT), web server standards for encrypting transmissions across the network.
2. Microsoft-supported Direct Java Database Connection (JDBC), a variation on Open DBC that enables Java programs to link directly to JDBC-supported databases.
3. Secure HTTP (SHTTP), an Internet standard for sending secure transmissions. (p. 1)

Such standards will likely become more prominent in the near future as they mature and become integrated with databases, online analytical processing query tools, and warehouse extraction and transformation tools. Even then, however, securing the safety of web-enabled warehouse data will continue to require the vigilance of the V&V specialist.

The following security-related guidances from reference 8 tend to govern most projects:

1. Establish a balanced set of security needs in accordance with identified threats.
2. Transform security needs into security guidance to be integrated into the V&V activities employed on a project and into descriptions of a system configuration or operation.
3. Establish confidence in the correctness and effectiveness of security mechanisms.
4. Judge that operational impacts due to residual security vulnerabilities in a system or its operation are tolerable (i.e., acceptable security risks).
5. Integrate the efforts of all engineering disciplines and specialties (such as V&V) into a combined understanding of the trustworthiness of a system. (p. 16)

The 1990s are seeing a rapidly expanding environment for business and research with global interconnection of computer networks, dramatically increasing system vulnerabilities and the need for information system security. Continuing from Ferraiolo and Thompson:[8]

> Guidelines should apply to the product and the process. It is widely acknowledged that product and systems evaluation for security features needs some work despite the good intentions that drive these activities. Because these processes are exceptionally time-consuming and costly to the developers, trusted products and secure systems typically come to market in one of two ways: through lengthy and expensive evaluation, or without evaluation. In the former case, trusted products often reach the market long after their features are needed, and the systems deployed no longer address current threats. In the latter, buyers must rely solely on the security claims of the product or system developer. (pp. 16, 17)

To be able to do more than just rely on security claims, something must be done to aid the V&V specialist in handling network security issues. A comprehensive framework for guidance and evaluation of security engineering practice would prove helpful. Ferraiolo and Thompson[8] continue:

> More efficient processes are warranted, given the increasing cost and time required to develop secure systems and trusted products. Specifically, the following qualities need to be assured by the V&V person to produce secure systems and trusted products:
>
> - **Continuity**—a way for knowledge that has been used in previous developments or efforts to be used in the future.
> - **Repeatability**—a way to ensure that projects can repeat a successful effort.
> - **Efficiency**—a way to help both developers and evaluators work more efficiently.
> - **Assurance**—a way to obtain confidence that security needs are being addressed. (pp. 17, 18)

George Lawton, in "The Internet's Challenge to Privacy,"[17] addresses the privacy aspect of security about which the V&V person needs to be concerned. He relates that:

> Most Internet communications go across open backbones and can be intercepted or monitored via data trails. People are concerned about maintaining the privacy of their online personal information, corporate data, and financial transactions. Following are the areas of concern for privacy:
>
> - Electronic commerce:
>   - Surveys show that people are concerned about putting their financial information and shopping habits online.
>   - Businesses are concerned that a lack of trust by consumers could hurt the growth of e-commerce.
> - Online databases:
>   - People are concerned about criminals "stealing" their financial identities by accessing their social security and driver's licenses, mother's maiden name, and so on via online databases.
>   - Government and privacy:
>   - People are concerned about government agencies gaining and then abusing access to private online communications.

[V&V personnel] need to be aware that these privacy concerns are being addressed through:

- Standards:
  - The World Wide Web Consortium is promoting the Platform for Privacy Preferences, saying it would give users more control over the way their personal information is used online.
- Legal requirements:
  - The European Union has passed a Data Protection Directive that limits the use and dissemination of private information in Europe.
- Voluntary guidelines:
  - The largest U.S. private information vendors formed the Individual References Services Group and designed guidelines to address the way they handle and distribute private information.
  - Japan's Ministry of International Industry and Trade has created guidelines for the collection, use, and distribution of various types of personal data. (p. 16)

Summary

Internet multimedia applications are different than traditional software applications: First, Internet multimedia applications have constraints placed on them due to bandwidth (data transfer rate) considerations that need to be taken into account when developing these applications; Internet multimedia applications that require too much bandwidth for the user-base become unusable. Second, Internet multimedia applications place a heavy emphasis on user-interface issues due to their reliance on multimedia data. Since Internet multimedia applications are presentation-based in nature, this shifts the emphasis in development and V&V to interface issues and away from more traditional development issues.

The FACADE (FAst CAse Development Environment) experiment to explore V&V methods related to the goal of Verifiable Development Techniques (VDTs) involves a set of tools for rapid software development that try to unify many different aspects of software development. With VDTs the focus is on the ability of the V&V process to find problems effectively and not on improving the capabilities of the software development process itself. However, because V&V and development are intimately related processes, a strategy has been developed for transferring improvements to development processes based on the need for improvements in V&V.

Security fears are keeping many companies from placing their data warehouses onto the web. There are so many different pieces of the security puzzle to learn, manage, and support—firewalls, data encryption, and authorization and authentication schemes among them. These along with the following key security standards are causing great pressure on the developers and V&V personnel involved in the security aspects on intranets and the Internet:

1. Netscape's Secure Socket Layer and Microsoft's Secure Transaction Technology, web server standards for encrypting transmissions across the network

2. Microsoft-supported Direct Java Database Connection, a variation on Open DBC that enables Java programs to link directly to JBC-supported databases
3. Secure HTTP, an Internet standard for sending secure transmissions[16]

Also, the Systems Security Engineering CMM[8] provides a useful tool for the V&V specialist dealing with network security. The process areas important to the V&V specialist in security are highlighted:

Engineering Process Area	**Project Process Areas**	**Organization Process Areas**
Administer Security Controls	Ensure Quality	Coordinate with Suppliers
Assess Operational Security Risk	Manage Configurations	Define Org's Security Engrg Process
Attack Security	Manage Program Risk	Improve Org's Security Engrg Processes
Build Assurance Argument	Monitor & Control Tech Effort	Manage Product Line Evolution
Coordinate Security	Plan Technical Effort	Manage Security Engrg Support Evironment
Determine Security Vulnerabilities	Provide Ongoing Skills and Knowledge	
Monitor System Security Posture		
Provide Security Input		
Specify Security Needs		
Verify and Validate Security		

Tohru Moto-oka, Tokyo University professor and impetus behind Japan's Fifth Generation Computer Project, said, "Computers … have penetrated our daily lives and are becoming society's nervous system."[18]

References

[1] Barry, Dave, "Windows Shopping" in *The Washington Post Magazine*, p. 28, Tribune Media Services © 1995.

[2] Nauth, Kristin, "Network Computing: A Paradigm Shift," *The Washington Post*—High Tech Horizons Advertising Supplement, August 3, 1997, p. M11.

[3] *Que's Dictionary of Computer Terms*, 1996.

[4] Christensen, Robert, "Intranet: Misspelling… or Megatrend?" *Atlanta Computer Currents*, May 1996.

[5] Kline, Jeffrey S., *Independent Verification and Validation for Internet Multimedia Systems,* Copyright: MediaNet Solutions, Inc., June 1998, URL: www.MediaNetSol.com/mediaconcepts.

[6] Treese, G. Winfield, "Internet Security: To Worry or Not To Worry?" *Infobase News*, March/April 1998, pp. 16–18.

[7] Rubin, Aviel D. and Geer Jr., Daniel E., "A Survey of Web Security," *IEEE Computer* (© September 1998 IEEE), pp. 34–41.

[8] Ferraiolo, Karen and Thompson, Victoria, "Let's Just Be Mature about Security! Using a CMM for Security Engineering," In *CrossTalk*, Software Technology Support Center, Ogden: Hill AFB, Vol. 10, No. 8, August 1997, pp. 15–20.

[9] Sargent, Nik, "VV and T of a Complex Network-Based Telecom System," *SQM* issue 26, © 1995 Nik Sargent, web presentation © 1996 Tesseract Publishing, http://WWW.avnet.co.uk/tesseract/QiC/articles/Sargent/26.html.

[10] Burkhard, Bob and Cavanaugh, Rick C., *V & V Research Quarterly* Issue 2, web Curators: Bob Burkhard and Rick C. Cavanaugh on webmaster@ivv.nasa.gov, Independent Software Validation and Verification Facility, Fairmont, West Virginia, April 14, 1995.

[11] Callahan, John and Sabolish, George, "A Process Improvement Model for Software Verification and Validation," *Proceedings of 19th Annual Software Engineering Workshop* (Greenbelt: NASA Goddard Space Flight Center, November 30–December 1, 1994).

[12] Maurer, Hermann, "Web-Based Knowledge Management," *IEEE Computer,* (© March 1998 IEEE), pp. 122–123.

[13] Singhal, Sandeep and Nguyen, Binh, "The Java Factor," *Communications of the ACM* Vol. 41, No. 6, June 1998, pp. 34–37.

[14] Tyma, Paul, "Why Are We Using Java Again?" *Communications of the ACM* Vol. 41, No. 6, June 1998, pp. 38–42.

[15] Islam, Nayeem et al, "A Flexible Security System for Using Internet Content," *IEEE Software* September/(© October 1997 IEEE), pp. 52–59.

[16] Kay, Emily, "Scared of the Web," *Supplement to Software Magazine*, July 1997, pp. S9-S11. Sentry's website, WWW.sentrytech.com/dwindex.htm.

[17] Lawton, George, "The Internet's Challenge to Privacy," *IEEE Computer*, (© June 1998 IEEE), pp. 16–18.

[18] Drexler, K. Eric, *Engines of Creation* (New York: Doubleday, 1986).

General References

Arbaugh, William, Davin, James, Farber, David, and Smith, Jonathan, "Security for Virtual Private Intranets," *IEEE Computer* (© September 1998 IEEE), pp. 48–55.

Dowd, Patrick and McHenry, John, "Network Security: It's Time To Take It Seriously," *IEEE Computer* (© September 1998 IEEE), pp. 24–28.

Gong et al., "Going Beyond the Sandbox: An Overview of the New Security Architecture in the Java Development Kit 1.2," *Proceedings of USENIX Symposium Internet Technologies and Systems*, Usenix Association, Berkeley, CA, 1997, pp. 103–112.

Http://www.geonome.wi.mit.edu/WWW/faqs/www-security-faq.html.

Menezes, A., van Oorschot, P., and Vanstone, S., *Handbook of Applied Cryptography*, (Boca Raton, FL: CRC Press, 1997).

Oppenheimer, D. L., Wagner, D. A., and Crabb, M. D., *Site Security Handbook*, RFC 1244/FYI:8, IETF, 1991.

Oppliger, Rolf, "Security at the Internet Layer," *IEEE Computer* (© September 1998 IEEE), pp. 43–47.

Rubin, A. D., Geer, D., and Ranum, M. J. *Web Security Sourcebook*, (New York: John Wiley & Sons, 1997).

CHAPTER 12

Data Warehousing

Introduction

"A data warehouse is an electronic means to store a large amount of reference or historical data typically used to support the decision-making and information retrieval needs of an organization," defines Peter Joodi in "Data Warehousing Management Review."[1] He continues that:

> A data warehouse consists of three major components:
>
> - Tools to extract, transform, and load operational and external data sources...
> - A warehouse in which to store the data
> - Tools to reference and analyze the data in the warehouse.
>
> Although a data warehouse may be new for some organizations, DSS (Decision Support System) and EIS (Executive Information System) end-user computing, as aspects of KBSs [knowledge based systems—see Chapter 10], are deeply entrenched activities. Data warehousing encompasses analysis, query, and reporting capabilities that also include these DSS and EIS characteristics. DSS is a decision support system that combines relevant business data with query and presentation tools. Using a DSS, a user can analyze and query the data, produce any number of ad hoc reports, and generate decision support information to ease the decision-making process. EIS is an executive information system that consists of completed sets of reports derived from the DSS data that, in most cases, have been requested by upper management. In many organizations, these activities have taken on mission-critical status and are invaluable tools for making informed management decisions. (pp. 6–7)

Ronald Swift tells us in "Ensuring a Successful Data Warehouse"[2] that building a data warehouse takes definition, planning, thoughtful analysis, and a defined framework (Figure 12.1). V&V specialists should ensure that there is an open structure that:

- provides direction and planning
- is developed from a flexible architecture

Figure 12.1 Data warehouse view.[2] (p. 1)

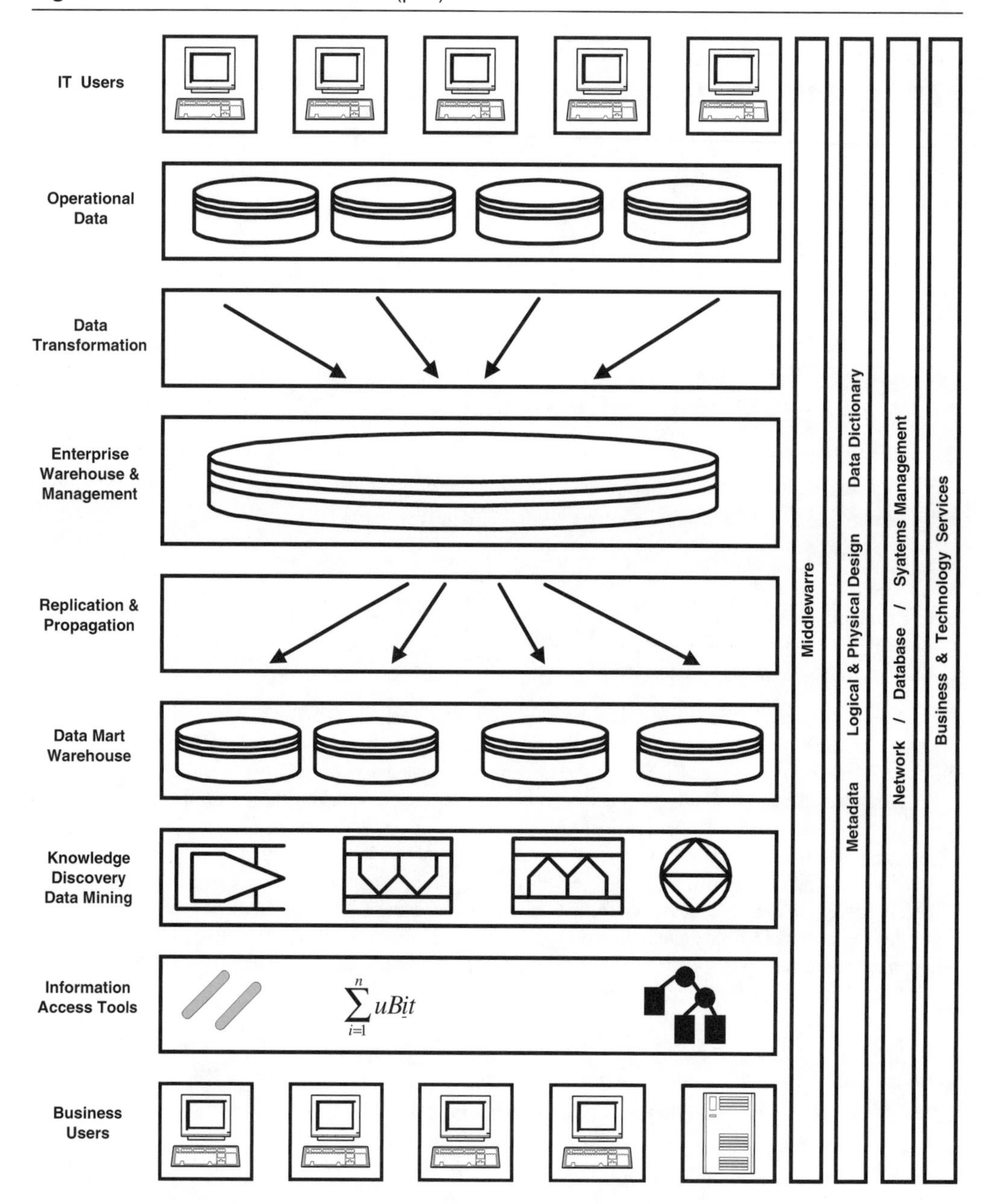

- is capable of assimilating new technologies
- allows various movements (data pathways)
- permits increasing complexity
- permits future information requirements.

As Figure 12.1 highlights, it is critically important to have a business user's view as well as an operational view. V&V should assure that the system has flow control and data flow management through middleware that are planned and changeable within the environment. It is also very useful to have centralized and distributed data mart* solutions. There are many elements shown in Figure 12.1 that are of great interest to the V&V specialist. Those elements are covered throughout this chapter.

As a general introduction to the theme of this chapter, from "Case Study: Texas Department of Public Safety,"[3] some key data warehousing problems and solutions that the V&V specialist should be aware of are covered:

> **Problem:** The shortage of skilled programmers is driving up development costs, as companies are bidding against each other for a limited pool of resources.
>
> **Solution:** [A] methodology and frameworks approach reduces the complexity of system development to the point where it can be effectively performed by low-skilled programmers and technical support staff.
>
> **Problem:** Business users have difficulty communicating their requirements to data warehouse analysts and developers. This communication gap prolongs development time and reduces the quality of the final results.
>
> **Solution:** ...Approaches, [especially ones like use case], are highly effective at involving business users in the system development process and capturing the business processes in the language of the business, so that the resulting systems accurately reflect the needs of the business and end users.
>
> **Problem:** Application developers spend too much time recreating the same basic features in each application they create instead of sharing and reusing components.
>
> **Solution:** ...Object-oriented methodology and frameworks significantly reduce the time and skill required to create sophisticated data warehouse applications. This system helps practitioners make the transition from custom built systems to software by assembly. [This is certainly a key point for V&V specialists, because they must think in terms of the building blocks approach, rather then new development.]
>
> **Problem:** Training end-users is expensive and often inconvenient.
>
> **Solution:** [There are] methodologies, [such as use case analysis, that] map directly to business processes and work procedures, which are documented in on-line procedures manuals that are easy for users to understand.

---

* Data marts target a line of business, such as the customer service application in the marketing department. Data warehouses target the business. A data mart may be highly successful with a great rate of return, but if it is tactical and not strategic, then the advantage of an Enterprise Data Warehouse may be lost.

Problem: Database security is problematic to set up and maintain.

Solution: [V&V should assure] a data security model that is simple, and yet impossible to circumvent in order to make data security a database service that is transparent to front-end applications. [It should also always return an empty data set to unauthorized users who attach to databases with a query tool.] (p. 2)

Multidimensional Model

Data warehousing exists on the application axis of the multidimensional model, and it is completely technology driven. Data warehouses exist only because there are storage methods available for billions of bytes of data, and because there are networks for easy access by users. In most cases, the process of development of data warehouse systems is approached from the perspective of integrating of many existing subsystems, so the V&V specialist needs to bring systems and software principles to assure the capabilities and usefulness of data warehouses.

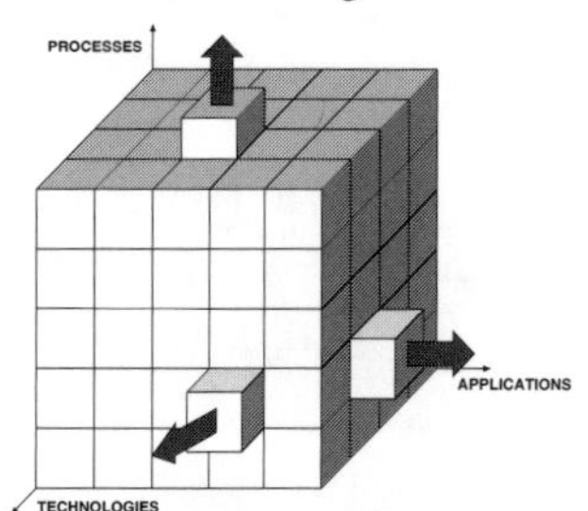

Data warehousing on the application axis intersects with the technology of data warehousing through the incremental build process. As with all large complex systems, it is advisable to achieve incremental successes of working data warehouse subsystems. This incremental subsystem approach is aided by the fact that there are many products made available from many manufacturers in this area. Since software tools change so rapidly, the Appendix to this chapter lists manufacturers, rather than tools that apply to the subsystems that comprise a data warehouse.

Traditional V & V

Although many concepts behind data warehousing, such as libraries, tape archive storage facilities, etc., have been around for some time, there is basically nothing "traditional" about data warehousing as a unified concept. It combines a database management system on a very large scale with convenient user access. For data warehousing, here are a series of management subsystems (Figure 12.2) of considerable importance to the V&V specialist:

- Service Level Management
- Data Acquisition Management
- Data Storage Management
- Metadata Management
- Data and User Security Management
- Data Access and Delivery Management

This section is adapted from a data warehouse supplement to *Software* magazine[4] of June 1997. Following is a brief discussion of each of these management areas.

Figure 12.2 Data warehouse basic architecture.[4] (p. S1)

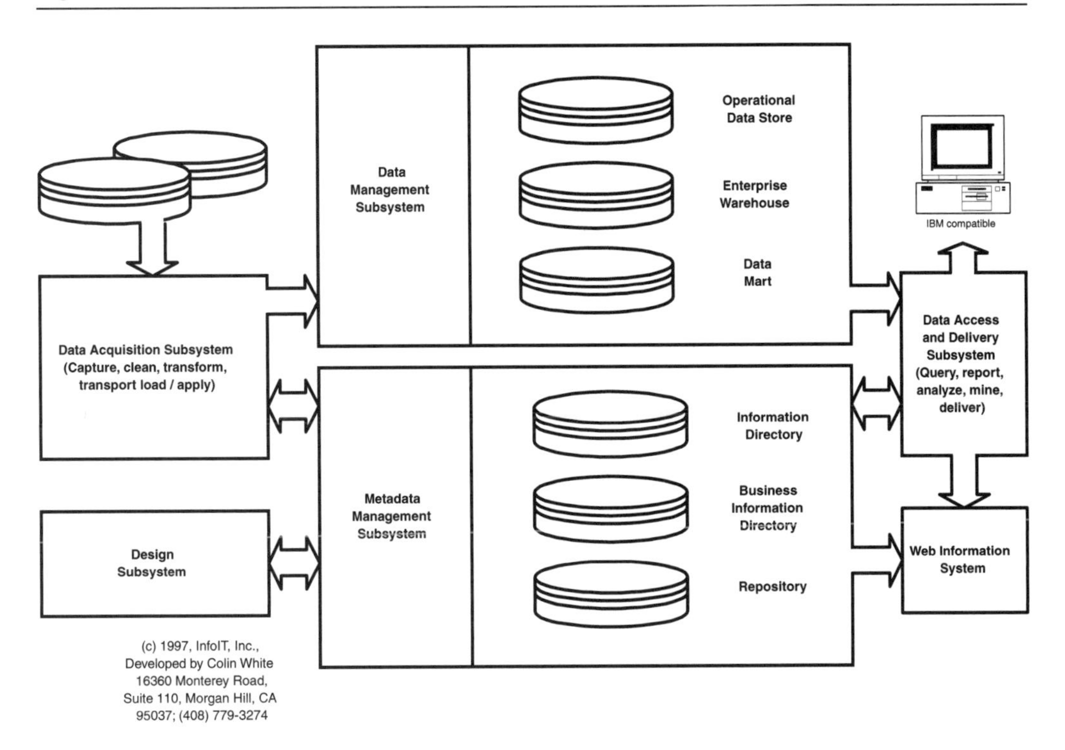

Service Level Management

V&V personnel must ensure that the expected level of service that will be provided to the users of the data warehouse is defined to a satisfactory level. Once in operation and test, V&V must ensure that the promised levels of service are delivered by the data warehousing system. From inception, as in all developments, the hardware/software requirements for the data warehouse system must be managed. All growth of these requirements also needs constant monitoring by a requirements "manager." In regard to these requirements for the system, it is a continuing responsibility of the V&V specialist to see that it is happening. The V&V person must ensure that a part of the data warehouse system includes a method for problem tracking and resolution, which should include a help desk. The problem tracking/resolution subsystem gives the users of the data warehouse a route for expressing their concerns and/or problems with the use of the data warehouse system. The help desk is a quick way to make the users comfortable with utilizing the data warehouse system (pp. S2–S3).

Data Acquisition Management

During development, the data warehouse analyst needs to have an understanding of the scheduling of data acquisition during operation. As the data warehouse goes into operation, the V&V person needs to assure that the schedules are maintained for satisfactory performance. The V&V specialist must assure the analytical work associated with the dependencies inherent in the data acquisition process. If these dependencies are not understood, data will not be delivered as required by the users. There are a number of operations associated with the data acquisition process:

- data capture
- data cleaning
- data transformation
- data transport
- data load/application

Because there are these multiple aspects to data acquisition, the V&V specialist has a major role in assuring that when these processes are run, they are properly tracked and recorded. With that type of information, the data warehouse manager can improve the operation of the data warehouse for the users. Beside data acquisition process itself, consideration of the integrity and consistency of the data in the warehouse is a constant monitoring job that the V&V specialist needs to ensure is happening. During operation and test of the data warehouse there will be data errors. The V&V specialist must ensure that a system is in place to monitor and correct any data errors uncovered (pp. S4–S5).

Data Storage Management

Because of the size of data warehouses, the prediction of the needs for a specific company is very important. V&V personnel need to ensure that the prediction made for the organization is accurate. When the data warehouse goes into operation and test, V&V should see to it that the data storage usage is tracked—in fact, it is a valuable exercise to compare the data storage predicted with the data storage used. V&V needs to ensure that the storage system is properly defined. Archiving methods of the warehouse data and associated metadata, along with the backup and recovery methods, all need to be done as part of data warehouse development. The V&V person must ensure that these activities are accomplished (pp. S6–S7).

Metadata Management

Metadata is described most simply as information-describing data. V&V must ensure that the developers identify technical, statistical, and business metadata recording and reporting requirements. Also, V&V ensures that the directory of technical metadata is appropriately maintained, monitored, and reported upon. The elements to be maintained in the information directory of business metadata are users' data views, DSS objects, data delivery subscriptions, etc. How often the metadata are updated and when and how they are reported to the user is a substantial data warehouse design factor. V&V specialists must be sure that the metadata metamodel that sits behind the data warehouse is completely and succinctly documented. Along with the metamodel, V&V must assure that the sources of the metadata are identified and documented. Expanding beyond the metadata subsystem, the V&V specialist oversees the implementation of tools and procedures for synchronizing metadata across data warehouse tools. As in any system, V&V ensures that version control is maintained over the metadata (p. S8).

Data and User Security Management

There is a significant discussion of security issues as they relate to the Internet/intranet in Chapter 11. This discussion focuses on the security aspects that deal specifically with data. First, V&V must see to it that security and authorization policies for access to the data warehouse are defined. Some initial actions associated with putting the data warehouse together include the identification of users, user groups, user data access, and user data delivery methods, as well the authorization for user access to the information directory. V&V specialists also need to ensure that these initial actions are performed. An important issue, often overlooked, is to identify the owners of the data and the metadata so that proper stewardship of that data is maintained. V&V ensures that the implementation of the following aspects of the data warehouse are sufficiently secure:

- information directory
- metadata
- data acquisition subsystem
- data management subsystem
- user data
- user authorization

Part of security V&V includes the evaluation of data encryption requirements for the data warehouse. Encryption technology itself is a rather arcane specialty, so V&V will probably have to elicit the aid of other specialists to ensure the adequacy of this area. Finally, in the security of data warehousing, V&V needs to ensure that security violations are tracked, as part of the system design (pp. S9–S10).

Data Access and Delivery Management

The basic interface of the data access and delivery subsystem is with both the data and metadata warehouses (Figure 12.2). V&V sees to it that the data access and delivery processing are completely identified. Furthermore, the design should include the tracking and recording of the data accessing and delivery processing when in operation and test. V&V makes sure that the actual data accessed through data access and delivery subsystem is kept track of, so that the system may be tweaked for optimal performance. A direct follow-up to this activity is the tuning of complex queries and analyses (involving table scans, sorts, multiway joins, data aggregations, etc.). In order for the data warehouse to meet the users' needs, V&V implements a resource controller (governor) for ad hoc queries. Without this safety feature, it is possible that the data delivery subsystem will become inoperable due to overuse (p. S10).

After this basic data warehouse architecture is in place, there are steps from Jim Murphy's "How To Build an Effective Data Warehouse: Six Key Steps to Success"[5] that a V&V person needs to assure that the IT professional consider when a data warehouse is being deployed. Ensure that business requirements are rapidly translated into a data warehouse specification that can be built incrementally, leveraging existing architecture and business processes. That there is on-going synchronization between operational and decision support data, and that decision support applications are mapped to the warehouse. That the production data and external data feeds are mapped into a data model for the data warehouse. In choosing a relational database for a data warehouse:

- verify query response time is acceptable,
- allow slack in the database to accommodate the data warehouse,
- allow for the warehouse to be larger than the raw data because it includes indices, summary tables, temporary space, etc.

Consider expansion of the data warehouse at the inception because a data warehouse is built and placed into operation incrementally. V&V must ensure for a properly designed or fully planned storage system that physically manages the movement, placement, backup and restoration of data. Ensure a start with a flexible, open systems based framework that allows the leveraging of new technologies and expertise as they become available.

Contemporary V & V

The following section concerning data quality is abstracted from "Data Quality in Context"[6] in the *Communications of the ACM:*

> Data quality problems are increasingly evident, particularly in organizational databases, [which are now ranging between 100 gigabits to 1 terabit range].* The social and economic impact of poor quality [data can be seen: for example], 50% to 80% of computerized criminal records in the U.S. were found to be inaccurate, incomplete, or ambiguous, costing billions of dollars.
>
> Organizational databases, however, reside in the larger context of information systems (IS). Within this larger context, data are collected from multiple data sources and stored in databases. From this stored data, useful information is generated for organizational decision making (For consistency, the term "data" is used throughout this article to refer to both data and information. This avoids switching between terms when there is a switch between production and use of data.)
>
> Data quality problems may arise anywhere in this larger IS context (sometimes used to mean a database or a computer system [including hardware and software], here it covers the organi-

* Meta Group, a market research company based in Westport, Connecticut.

zational processes, procedures, and roles employed in collecting, processing, distributing and using data). Thus, we argue for a conceptualization of data quality that includes this context.

Database research aims at ensuring the quality of data in databases, the key element of a data warehouse. In the data quality area, existing research investigates data quality definitions, modeling, and control. With few exceptions, however, data quality is treated as an intrinsic concept, independent of the context in which data are produced and used. This focus on intrinsic data quality problems in stored data fails to solve complex organizational problems. This failure has been attributed,* in part, to the lack of a broader data quality conceptualization. When quality problems are defined as errors in stored data, V&V professionals may not recognize, and thus solve, the most critical data quality problems in organizations.

In contrast to this intrinsic view, it is well accepted in the quality literature that quality cannot be assessed independent of consumers who choose and use products. Similarly, the quality of data cannot be assessed independent of the people who use data—data consumers. Data consumers' assessments of data quality are increasingly important because consumers now have more choices and control over their computing environment and the data they use. To solve organizational data quality problems, therefore, one must consider data quality beyond the intrinsic view. Moreover, one must move beyond stored data to include data in production and utilization processes.

Using qualitative analysis, data quality projects are examined from three cutting-edge organizations, and common patterns of quality problems are identified. (p. 103)

Definitions and Methods in Context

Continuing from "Data Quality in Context:"[6]

Production, storage, and use of data has been conceptualized as data manufacturing system. Central to this is the concept of a data production process that transforms data into information useful to data consumers. Three roles are identified within a data manufacturing system: data producers (people, groups, or other sources who generate data); data custodians (people who provide and manage computing resources for storing and processing data); and data consumers (people or groups who use data). Each role is associated with a process or task:

- data producers, associated with data-production processes
- data custodians with data storage, maintenance, and security
- data consumers with data-utilization processes, which may involve additional data aggregation and integration.

High-quality data refers to data that is fit for use by data consumers, a widely adopted criterion. This means that usefulness and usability are important aspects of quality. Using this definition, the characteristics of high-quality data (Table 12.1) consist of four categories: intrinsic, accessibility, contextual, and representational aspects. This data consumers' perspective is a broader conceptualization of data quality than the conventional intrinsic view.

* passive voice replaces personal pronouns in quote.

Table 12.1 Data quality categories and dimensions. (Strong ©1997 ACM)[6] (p. 104)

Data Quality Category	Data Quality Dimension
Intrinsic	accuracy, objectivity, believability, reputation
Accessibility	accessibility, access security
Contextual	relevancy, added value, timeliness, completeness, amount of data
Representational	interpretability, ease of understanding, concise representation, consistent representation

Table 12.2 Site characteristics. (modified from Strong ©1997 ACM)[6] (p. 104)

Site Name and Industry	Attention to data quality	IS Organization	Hardware and Software Environment
G-Air Airline	IS Development	IS is essentially a service bureau.	IBM-compatible mainframe with MS databases and MMS.
Hosp-Care	Data Quality Administrator Hospital	Centralized IS organization reporting to finance VP in a centralized, functional firm.	PC-based client/server environment with TRACE, a MUMPS-based database system.
HMO-Care HMO	Total Quality Management (TQM) Initiatives	Powerful, centralized IS organization in a decentralized, divisional firm.	Heterogeneous hardware and software across divisions.

A *data quality problem* is any difficulty encountered along one or more quality dimensions that renders data completely or largely unfit for use. A *data quality project* is defined as organizational actions taken to address a data quality problem given some recognition of poor data quality by the organization. Projects initiated for purposes other than improving data quality are intentionally included. [On one such project for] conversion of data to a client/server system, poor data quality was discovered and an improvement initiated.

…Forty-two data quality projects from three data-rich organizations are included in this analysis:

- G-Air,* an international airline
- Hosp-Care, a hospital
- HMO-Care, a Health Maintenance Organization (HMO).

In terms of industry position, attention to data quality, and information systems, these three firms are leaders, yet they exhibit sufficient variation to warrant investigating their data projects (Table 12.2). All are actively attending to significant data quality problems, in contrast to many organizations that fail to address their quality problems.

This research employed qualitative data collection and analysis techniques,… organized in terms of three problem-solving steps:

* names in article are G-Air = Golden Air, Hos-Care = Better Care, and HMO-Care = HyCare

- *problem finding:* how the organization identified a data quality problem
- *problem analysis:* what the organization determined the cause to be
- *problem resolution:* includes changing processes (changing the procedures for producing, storing, or using data) and changing data (updating the data value).

Each project was analyzed using the data quality dimensions as content analysis codes. From the coded projects, common patterns and sequences of dimensions attended to during data quality projects were identified (Table 12.3). (p. 103–105)

Table 12.3 Data Quality Patterns in Data Quality Projects (Strong ©1997 ACM)[6] (p. 104)

DQ Issue	Pattern 1: Intrinsic DQ	Pattern 2: Accessibility DQ	Pattern 3: Contextual DQ
If problem not resolved	Data not used	Barriers to accessibility	Data utilization difficulties
Subpatterns: Underlying causes of DQ problems	(1) Multiple, inconsistent data sources (2) Data production requires judgment (e.g., coding)	(1) Computing resource lacking (2) Data are confidential (3) Uninterpretable representation (4) Un-analyzable form of representation (5) Too much data, timeliness	(1) Operational data production problems: incomplete data (2) Changing needs, especially changing needs for aggregation (3) Distributed system incompatibilities
Problems and Solution Focus	Data producers, Data production processes	Technical issues, Computer systems, Data storage and maintenance	Data consumers, Data utilization processes
Context of Needed Changes	Data production processes are generating inaccurate, incomplete, or inconsistent data.	IS provides accessibility; however, data consumers view other problems (e.g., timeliness, interpretability) as accessibility problems	The basic data units, as perceived by data consumers, change over time. Databases must support this changing view of data.
Lessons and Solutions	Change both the process and supporting computer systems. Either by itself is not sufficient for long-term DQ improvements.	Understand and remedy the underlying causes of perceived poor accessibility.	Structure data around fundamental business entities so that changes in basic data units can be accommodated by actual/stored data units.

Intrinsic Data Quality Pattern

"Data Quality in Context"[6] goes on to say:

> Mismatches among sources of the same data are a common cause of intrinsic data quality concerns. Initially, data consumers do not know the source to which quality problems should be attributed; they know only that data are conflicting. Thus, these concerns initially appear as *believability** problems. Over time, information about the causes of mismatches accumulates from evaluations of the *accuracy* of different sources, which leads to a poor *reputation* of less accurate sources. (A reputation for poor quality can also develop with little factual basis.) As a *reputation* for poor-quality data becomes common knowledge, these data sources are viewed as having little *added value* for the organization, resulting in reduced use (Figure 12.3, subpattern 1).

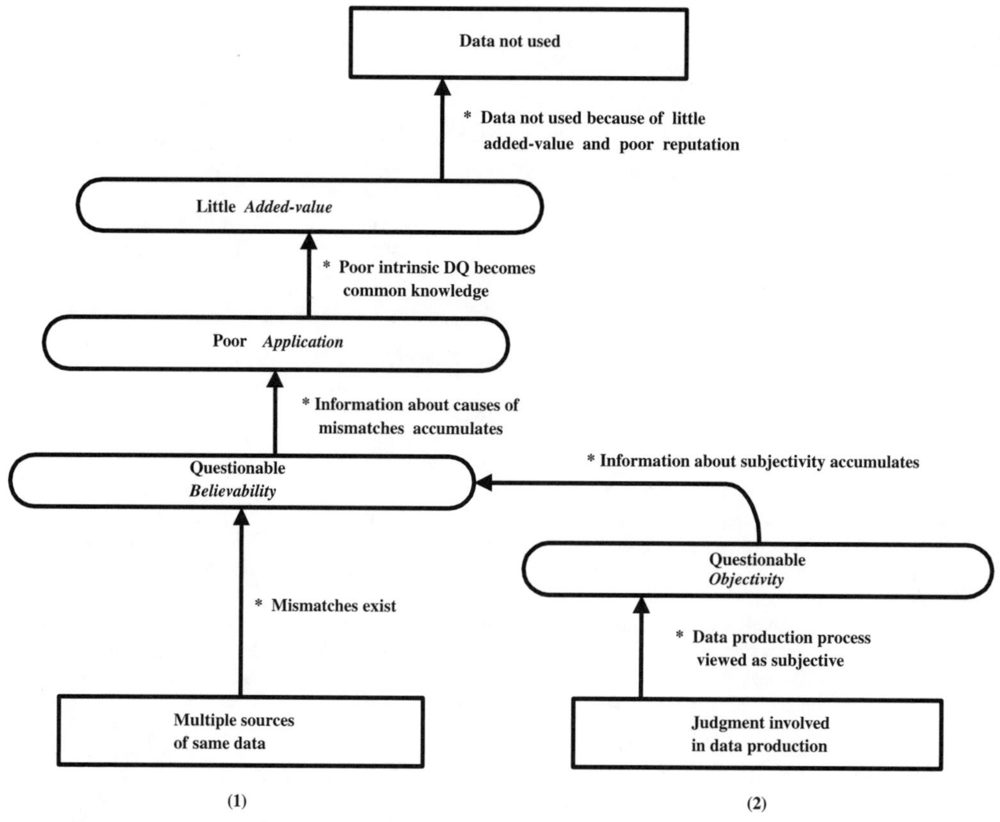

Figure 12.3 Intrinsic data quality problem pattern. (Strong ©1997 ACM)[6] (p. 105)

* The italics signifies that believability is a data quality dimension. This convention will be used to highlight the interaction of data quality project.

Judgment or subjectivity in the data production process is another common cause (subpattern 2). For example, coded or interpreted data are considered to be of lower quality than raw, uninterpreted data. Initially, only those with knowledge of data production processes are aware of these potential problems, which appear as concerns about data *objectivity.* Over time, information about the subjective nature of data production accumulates, resulting in data of questionable believability and reputation and thus of little added value to data consumers. The overall result is reduced use of this suspect data.

Intrinsic data quality (subpattern 1) was exhibited at all three research sites. G-Air has a history of mismatches between their inventory system data and physical warehouse counts. Warehouse counts serve as a standard against which to measure the accuracy of system data; that is the system data source is *inaccurate* and not believable, and is adjusted periodically to match actual warehouse counts. The system data gradually develops mismatches, however, and its reputation gradually worsens until the data is not used for decision-making.

At Hosp-Care, this subpattern occurred between TRACE and STATUS. TRACE is a database containing historical data extracted from the hospital's information and control system for use by managers making longer-term decisions and by medical researchers; STATUS is an operational system that records a snapshot of daily hospital resources. Some data, such as daily hospital bed utilization, are available from both systems. Nevertheless, the data frequently have different values. Over time, TRACE has developed a reputation as an accurate source, and the use of STATUS has declined.

At HMO-Care, inconsistent data values occur between internal HMO patient records and bills submitted by hospitals for reimbursement. For example, when the HMO is billed for coronary bypass surgery, the HMO patient record should indicate that the patient has active, serious heart problems. Mismatches occur in both directions—hospital claims without HMO records of problems, and HMO records of problems without corresponding hospital claims. Initially, HMO-Care assumed the external hospital data were wrong; HMO staff perceived their data to be more believable and have a better reputation than those of hospitals. This general sense of the quality of sources, however, was not based on factual analysis.

Subpattern 2 occurred at both Hosp-Care and HMO-Care. Using doctors' and nurses' notes about patients, Hosp-Care's medical record coders designate diagnosis and procedure codes and corresponding diagnosis-related groups (DRG) codes for billing. Although coders are highly trained, some subjectivity remains. Thus, these data are considered to be less objective than raw data.

Data-production forms also contribute to reduced objectivity of data. At HMO-Care, doctors using preprinted forms with check boxes for specifying procedure codes generated a reduced range of procedures performed, as compared to doctors using free-form input. This variance affects the believability of these data. The three organizations developed the following solutions for handling subpattern 1:

- G-Air continues their cycle of physically counting inventory and adjusting system values whenever the mismatch becomes unacceptably large.
- Hosp-Care is rewriting STATUS. They are also designating single data production points for data items and improving computerized support for data production.
- HMO-Care's analysis of the causes of mistakes between hospital and internal data found problems with both sources. They fixed an edit check problem with their internal

computer systems, fixed a data production problem in doctors' designation of active, serious problems for internal HMO records, and initiated joint data quality projects with associated hospitals.

These solutions manifest two different approaches to problem resolution: (a) changing the systems or (b) changing the production processes. G-Air focused on computer systems as the solution and ignored their data production processes. As a result, their processes continue to produce poor-quality data that increase data inaccuracies. In contrast, Hosp-Care's and HMO-Care's solutions involve both data production processes and computer systems, resulting in long-term data quality improvements.

Hosp-Care's effort to designate single data production points deserves further discussion. Systems developed for different purposes sometimes require the same data, such as an indicator of patient severity in intensive care units in both STATUS and HICS. For HICS, a specialist examines the patient immediately before intensive care. For STATUS, an intensive-care nurse observes the patient during intensive care. These two observations can be different. To designate a single source, definitions and indicators of severity were agreed upon, and both systems were changed to support this single data production source.

Hosp-Care's decision to rewrite STATUS illustrates reputation development. Like accounting systems that prohibit changes once the accounting period is closed, STATUS prohibits changes to the official daily record. STATUS's data is *consistent* across time, whereas TRACE's data is accurate because it is updated as needed. Although both systems are viewed as containing the "correct" data, TRACE developed a reputation as the system with high-quality data, whereas STATUS's data were considered to be suspect. As a result, STATUS is being rewritten with update routines. (pp. 105–106)

Accessibility Data Quality Pattern

Continuing from "Data Quality in Context:"[6]

Accessibility data quality problems were characterized by:

1. underlying concerns about technical accessibility [Figure 12.4, subpatterns 1–2],
2. data representation issues interpreted by data consumers as accessibility problems [Figure 12.4, subpatterns 3–4],
3. data volume issues interpreted as accessibility problems [Figure 12.4, subpattern 5].

G-Air provides a simple example of sub-pattern 1. When G-Air moved to its new airport, its computing operations remained at the old airport with *access* to data via unreliable data communications lines. Since reservations had priority, the unreliable lines resulted in inventory data accessibility problems. This, in turn, contributed to G-Air's inventory accuracy problems because updating took lower priority than other data-related tasks.

Hosp-Care had an accessibility data quality concern related to the confidential nature of patient records (subpattern 2). Data consumers realized the importance of access *security* for patient records, but they also perceived the permissions as barriers to accessibility, which in turn affects the overall reputation and *value* of this data. In addition, data custodians became barriers to accessibility because they could not provide data access without approval.

Figure 12.4 Accessibility data quality problem pattern. (Strong ©1997 ACM)[6] (p. 106)

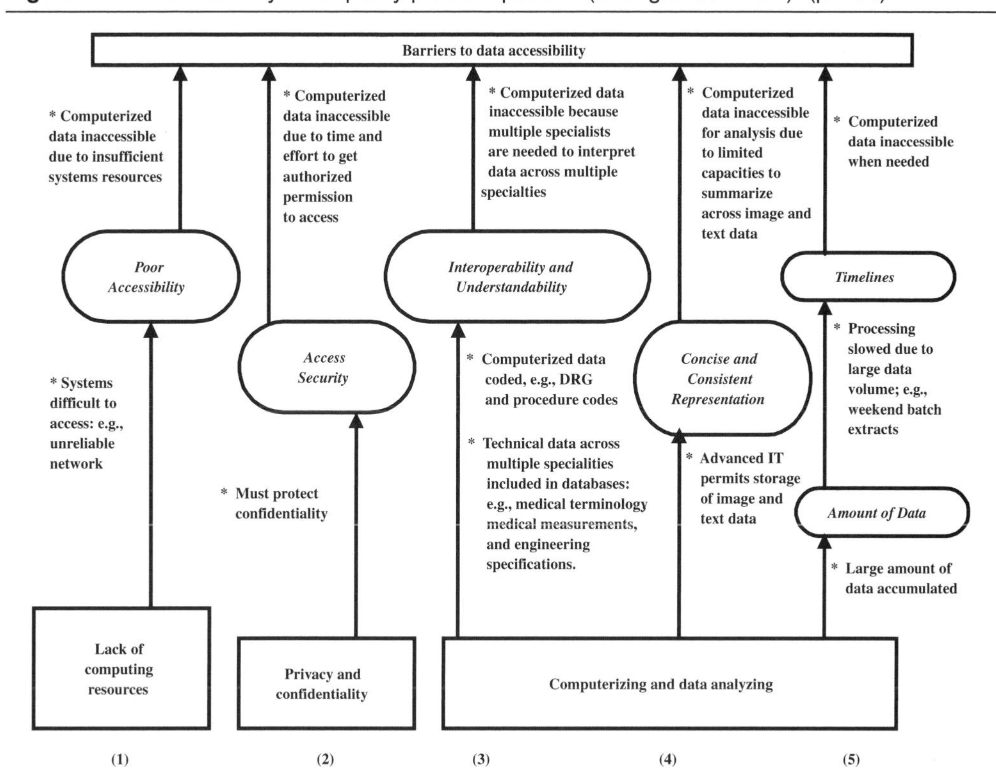

Subpattern 3 addresses concerns about *interpretability* and *understandability* of data. Coding systems for physician and hospital activities at Hosp-Care and HMO-Care are necessary for summarizing and grouping common diagnoses and procedures. The expertise required to interpret codes, however, becomes a barrier to accessibility; these codes are not understandable to most doctors and analysts. At HMO-Care, analyzing and interpreting across physician groups is a problem because they use different coding systems.

Medical data in text or image form also presents an interpretability problem (subpattern 4). Medical records include text written by doctors and nurses and images produced by medical equipment, such as X-rays and EKGs. These data are difficult to analyze across time for individual patients. Furthermore, analyzing trends across patients is difficult. Thus, data *representation* becomes a barrier to data accessibility. These data are inaccessible to data consumers because they are not in a representation that permits analysis.

Subpattern 5 addresses providing *relevant* data that add value to tasks in a timely manner. For example, HMO-Care serves hundreds of thousands of patients resulting in several million patient records tracking medical history. Analyses of patient records usually require a weekend data extraction. In addition, companies purchasing HMO options are increasingly demanding evaluations of medical practices, resulting in an increased need for these analyses at HMO-Care. This pattern of a large *amount* of *data* leading to *timeliness* problems is interpreted as accessibility problems.

Subpattern 1 has straightforward, though possibly costly, solutions. For example, G-Air is moving its computing facility to the new airport to avoid unreliable data communication lines. Subpattern 5 is also relatively easy to solve. For example, Hosp-Care's HICS generates 40GB of data per year. From this, TRACE extracts the most relevant data (totaling 5GB over 12 years) for historical and cross-patient analyses.

Subpatterns 3 and 4 are more difficult to solve. HMO-Care completely automated its medical records, including text and image data, to solve accessibility problems, but problems for individual patients and problems with analyzing data across patients persist. At Hosp-Care, data consumers and custodians believed that an automated representation of text and image data would not solve their analyzability problems; thus, they partially automated their patient records.

Contextual Data Quality Pattern

There are three underlying causes for data consumers' complaints that available data do not support their tasks:

1. missing *(incomplete)* data
2. inadequately defined or measured data
3. data that could not be appropriately aggregated.

To solve these contextual data quality problems, specific projects were initiated to provide relevant data that add value to the tasks of data consumers.

Subpattern 1 in [Figure 12.5] addresses incomplete data due to operational problems. At G-Air, incomplete data in inventory transactions contributed to inventory data accuracy problems. For example, mechanics sometimes failed to record part numbers on their work activity forms. Because transaction data were incomplete, the inventory database could not be updated, which in turn produced inaccurate records. According to one supervisor, this was tolerated because "the primary job of mechanics is to service aircraft in a timely manner, not to fill out forms."

Hosp-Care's data were incomplete by design [Figure 12.5, subpattern 2], whereas G-Air's data were incomplete due to operational problems. By design, the amount of data in Hosp-Care's TRACE database is small enough to be accessible but complete enough to be relevant and add value to data consumers' tasks. As a result, data consumers occasionally complained about incomplete data.

Subpattern 3 in [Figure 12.5] addresses problems caused by integrating data across distributed systems. At HMO-Care, data consumers complained about inconsistent definitions and data representations across divisions, like DRG codes stored with decimal points in one division and without in another. Furthermore, basic utilization measures, such as hospital days per thousand patients, were defined differently across divisions. These problems were caused by autonomous design decisions in each division.

G-Air is considering bar code readers as data input mechanisms [Figure 12.5, subpattern 1]. Hosp-Care's decision about the data to include in TRACE is reassessed as data consumers request additional data [Figure 12.5, subpattern 2], such as healthcare proxy and living will information were added.

This reassessment of TRACE data in the context of its relevance and value to data consumers goes beyond missing data. As healthcare reimbursement systems move from payments for pro-

Figure 12.5 Contextual data quality problem pattern. (Strong ©1997 ACM)[6] (p. 107)

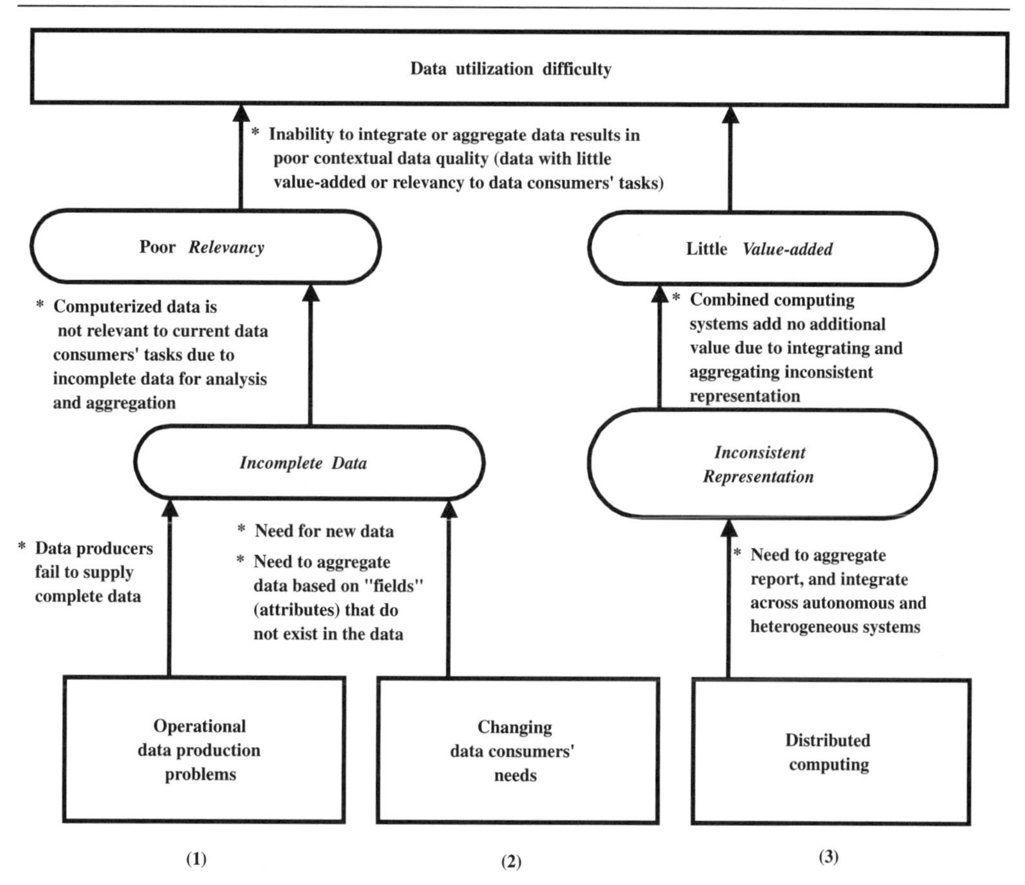

cedures performed (fee for service) to payments for diagnosed diseases (prospective payment) to possibly payments for yearly care of patients (capitated payment), the basic unit of analysis for managerial decision-making in hospitals has changed from procedures, to hospital visits, to patients. When Hosp-Care tracked data by procedures, for example, they could answer questions about costs of blood tests, but not costs of treating heart attacks. Such analyses became necessary when hospital reimbursement changed to a fixed amount for treating each disease.

TRACE was developed in response to this anticipated change to prospective payments. Such a reimbursement system began in 1983 for Medicare. At that time, TRACE had the capability to aggregate across patient visits for similar diagnoses. Currently, the ability to aggregate across all in- and out-patient medical services delivered to each patient per year is being anticipated by Hosp-Care. Thus, TRACE is being extended with out-patient data and quality indicators because management anticipates these changes. HMO-Care initiated data quality projects to develop common data definitions and representations for cross-divisional data [Figure 12.5, subpattern 3]. The comprehensive data dictionary and corresponding data warehouse are their next steps. (pp. 107–109)

Continuing from "Data Quality in Context,"[6] we now look at implications about solving intrinsic, accessibility, and contextual data quality problems that may be useful to IS professionals and V&V persons:

Implications for V&V Personnel

Conventional data quality approaches employ control techniques (like edit checks, database integrity constraints, and program control of database updates) to ensure data quality. These approaches have improved intrinsic data quality substantially, especially the accuracy dimension. Attention to accuracy alone, however, does not correspond to data consumers' broader data quality concerns. Furthermore, controls on data storage are necessary but not sufficient. [V&V personnel] need to apply process-oriented techniques, like auditing, to the processes that produce this data.

Data consumers perceive any access barriers as accessibility problems. Conventional approaches treat accessibility as a technical, computer systems issue, not a data quality concern. That is, data custodians have provided access if data is technically accessible (such as when terminals and lines are connected and available, access permission is granted, and access methods are installed). To data consumers, however, accessibility goes beyond technical accessibility; it includes the ease with which they can manipulate the data to suit their needs.

These contrasting accessibility views are evident, for example, in advanced forms of data (medical image data), which can now be stored as binary large objects (blobs). Although data custodians provide technical methods for accessing this new form of data, data consumers continue to experience data as inaccessible. They need to analyze these data like they analyze traditional record-oriented data. Other examples of differing views of accessibility include

- Data combined across autonomous systems are technically accessible, but data consumers view it as inaccessible because similar data items are defined, measured, or represented differently.
- Coded medical data are technically accessible as text, but data consumers view it as inaccessible because they cannot interpret the codes.
- Large volumes of data are technically accessible, but data consumers view it as inaccessible because of excessive access time.

IS professionals must understand the difference between the technical accessibility they supply and the broad accessibility concerns of data consumers. If V&V personnel can help to clarify this difference, then data warehouses can provide a smaller amount of more relevant data, and graphical interfaces can improve ease of access.

Data consumers evaluate data quality relative to their tasks. At any time, the same data may be needed for multiple tasks that require different quality characteristics. Furthermore, these quality characteristics will change over time as work requirements change. Therefore, providing high-quality data implies tracking an ever-moving target. Conventional approaches handle contextual data quality through techniques such as user requirements analysis and relational database query capabilities. They do not explicitly incorporate the changing nature of data consumers' task context.

Because data consumers perform many different tasks and the data requirements for these tasks change, contextual data quality means much more than good data requirements specification.

> Providing high-quality data along the dimensions of value and usefulness relative to data consumers' task contexts places a premium on designing flexible systems with data that can be easily aggregated and manipulated. The alternative is constant maintenance of data and systems to meet changing data requirements.
>
> Existing practice focuses on intrinsic aspects of data quality, which fails to address the broader concerns of data consumers. While intrinsic data quality aspects are important, organizations also initiate projects to address accessibility and contextual data quality issues. Accessibility data quality includes concerns about the ease of access and ease of understanding data. Contextual data quality includes concerns about how well data match task contexts....
>
> Some might argue [that the above] findings can be attributed to poor management or poor IS organizations at field sites.... However, these organizations are competent and address their data quality problems effectively. They are at the forefront of data quality practice. Others may agree with [the above] findings, but argue that accessibility and contextual data quality fall outside the domain. To solve organizational data quality problems, V&V personnel and IS professionals must attend to the entire range of concerns of data consumers. (pp. 109–110)

Kathy Serfin[7] relates that a V&V specialist should review the choice of data re-engineering technology to data scrubbing (intrinsic and contextual aspects of data), because a data scrubber's heavy reliance on prebuilt look-up tables limits the level of data quality attainable and restricts data clean-up. Better suited for building complex business relationships from imperfect, fragmented data, the data re-engineering process extends beyond the scope of conventional data scrubbers. The data re-engineering approach adopted by the company—while customized for its business rules and data characteristics—has a generalized and flexible technology and methodology that can be applied by any organization in any industry to make sense of "pieces and parts" buried in legacy data that collectively define customers, suppliers, products, etc.

V&V specialists should first perform a low, data-value level investigation that exposes differences between field description definitions and actual data values. From this investigation, a detailed "map" into the state of its data, showing how to best standardize, recondition and prepare the data for consolidation is obtained. Data re-engineering determines the meaning of each data "element" hidden within free-form text, gains accessible elements, and maintains relationships between entities.

Data consolidation is performed through a very flexible statistical matching engine that evaluates any or all identified data types to find matching records to a high degree of statistical certainty. Within the data re-engineering process, the low-level data investigation identifies data values that do not align with their metadata definitions and locates and consolidates all related instances of business entities hidden by spelling variations, anomalies, and the absence of common keys.

V&V specialist should follow these steps from Emily Kay[8] to monitor data quality:

1. Document data elements to be captured and maintained in operational applications.
2. Create a database of metrics for processes implemented to monitor and evaluate data quality.

3. Validate the input source, number of records to be loaded, and actual records accepted.
4. If records are rejected, research them one by one to find out why.
5. Monitor on-going data quality. Run audits when taking in a new load, and if loading data on a scheduled basis, run audits as the data is loaded. (p. S6)

A V&V specialist should provide a thorough data investigation of any legacy data to be moved into a different data warehouse. Mark Atkins[9] suggests that the V&V specialist investigate the following:

- unexamined moved data from the legacy warehouse, which will corrupt the new warehouse with missing, incorrect, and improperly consolidated data
- failure to uncover information, such as undocumented business practices and business relationships hidden in free form text fields
- limited data cleaning, standardization, and integration to domestic formats, due to the restrictions of conventional conversion utilities based on look-up tables.

Atkins[9] calls this:

> "metadata mining"—not to be confused with data mining. The latter investigates data for business trend analysis. Metadata mining, a comprehensive investigation of all data values within legacy sources, helps ensure that the warehouse data and metadata (information describing your data) are accurate and accessible for data miners and other warehouse users. Beyond surfacing missing metadata, the data investigation will:
>
> - identify missing and incorrect data values
> - point to values that stray from metadata field descriptions
> - identify entities, attributes and relationship identifies hidden within free form, text and gain access to those once un-addressable "elements".
>
> ...Metadata mining distinguishes data re-engineering from conventional data scrubbing. Organizations that re-engineer their data, rather than just scrub it, will deliver to their corporations quality information, not misinformation. (p. 17)

Internet/Intranet

Teri Robinson[10] provides the following statistics relative to the implementation of data warehousing. The access route to a data warehouse is most often (82%) through a network; this is followed by intranet access at 38%, and only 18% is associated with Internet access. It should be noted that some companies (8%) allow all three methods. The warehouse and the web come from different backgrounds, are founded on different philosophies, and speak different languages. The warehouse is fluent in Structured Query Language (SQL), while the web communicates in hypertext mark-up language (HTML). Furthermore, each has an assortment of relatives that do not often mesh (p. S4).

To access decision support information with a browser, software is needed that sits between the web server and the data warehouse. This software's sole mission is to translate the HTML of the web into the SQL of relational databases. If the data warehouse sits on top of a database that uses a different type of proprietary form of query language, translation software will have to work with that, too (p. S5).

The proliferation of the World Wide Web has provided the impetus to move data warehousing into commercial and consumer applications, Michael Saylor and Ahmed Moin[11] tell us:

> With the platform-independent web browser [Figure 12.6] providing an intuitive, interactive, and ubiquitous interface to a data warehouse, not only are costs drastically reduced for enterprise-wide deployment, but a new realm of commercial, intercompany applications is now made possible. Externally focused web-based decision support provides interactive data analysis to a wide audience.... [The V&V specialist will recognize the benefits derived on the Internet/intranet that web-based applications] are platform-independent, require few desktop resources, are easy to deploy and administer, and have upgrade cycles. [With Internet-based types of data warehouses], companies will be able to roll out decision support applications to their partners or clients over the Internet. (p. 16)

Figure 12.6 Evolution of commercial data warehouse.[11] (p. 16)

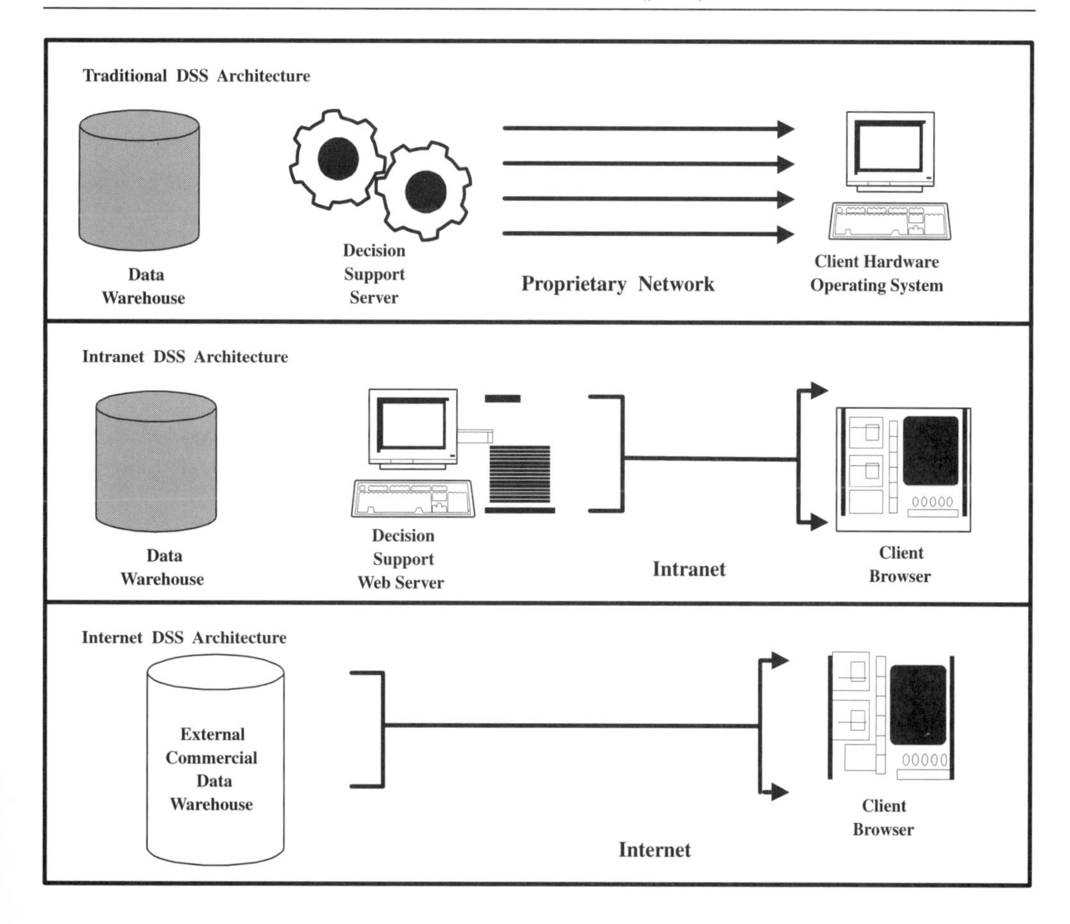

In "Putting the Data Warehouse on the Intranet"[12] Karen Drost provides software services that are critical to a successful implementation. Data warehouses employ relational database management systems (RDBMSs) that use SQL to retrieve numeric data, while unstructured content is managed as HTML documents. V&V specialists must ensure proper SQL data warehouse access from browsers running HTML. In this network environment, Drost[12] tells us V&V must see to it that four software services are provided:

- Analytic Layer—Putting structured content on intranets requires server resident analytics to generate SQL on-the-fly, perform computations, and format reports based on user requests. A structured content web format server is required to support warehouse access from an HTML browser client request. The structured content web server analytic layer lets users create reports by applying calculations based on dimensions. Without robust analytics, users are limited to simple listing of stored data.
- File Management—Analysis should be an interactive exchange of "live" information. Recipients should continue analyses initiated by an author and pursue other analysis paths from a common starting point. Users must be able to modify their copy of the logic used to create the report. A server-based file management system is required for collaboration of this level.
- Security—Data must be secured, but if too tightly controlled, the value of the warehouse will never be fully realized. Reports should not simply be stored as static text files but should include underlying logic allowing analysis and modification of reports, as well as logic. Without authorization, requests are denied. Encryption provides another layer of security.
- Agents—Agents isolate information on behalf of users and send alerts on a need-to-know basis. Agents should run continually in the background on the server, then proactively notify users of conditions that have occurred, even during a disconnect. As data warehouses grow, it is unproductive to surf through hundreds of giga-bytes looking for certain conditions. (p. S1)

Teri Robinson[10] tells us what may happen when:

> a user armed with browser and browser-based analytical tools queries a data warehouse or mart for information via the web. Queries to the warehouse via the web are interpreted by the web content server that drives the data warehouse. Web access to a data warehouse puts a heavy burden on servers. Most data warehouse operations have been small-scale (in terms of users and functionality, not actual storage size), with the burden of functionality traditionally placed on the client, so a V&V person must ensure that it has the server capacity in place to accommodate a web warehouse. An internal warehouse by today's standards usually has only a few hundred users at the most, but a web warehouse can expect tens of thousands.
>
> Even if the data warehouse technology scales nicely to web proportions, performance is bound to suffer—response times could extend well into the unacceptable. [If] one person launches a large, complex query, the rest of the network [could be locked out].... To avoid these problems, [the V&V specialist] has a handful of ways to fine-tune its web warehouse infrastructure. Prioritization parameters in the web server can go a long way to ensuring that all users get adequate response times and that the most important queries get answered first....

> Providing different users with different access parameters and tools can boost performance and take unnecessary strain off of the computing resources. Power users generally are the only group to have direct access to warehouse data because they understand it, need it, and can be trusted to interface with it directly. However, for most business users, special web on-line analytic processing (OLAP) tools offer the best view of data, as well as the best venue for manipulating it. (p. S5)

In "How to Access a Web Warehouse"[13] we are told that web-enabled OLAP uses one of three basic approaches, which are listed for the V&V specialists with their advantages and disadvantages:

Approach	Advantages	Disadvantages
Static HTML	Minimal end user training	Not very flexible
Templates	Ultra-thin client	Static reports
	Low network requirements	Not graphical
Java Applets	Enriched HTML content	Not as flexible as
	More graphics	all Java approach
	Pull-down menus	More network intensive
All Java	Most flexible	Most network intensive
	Most graphic potential	

> [The static HTML templates] let developers transform data from a warehouse into static HTML reports, which are posted on a web server. Users access these reports with a browser and can obtain other hyper-linked reports by clicking on URLs or buttons. A more sophisticated version of this strategy, based on HTML templates, lets users create "on-the-fly" charts by selecting from a list of defined measures (such as sales or returns), and filters (such as quarter, week, region, state).
>
> The second approach gives users more options about what data they view and how they view it. It uses Java applets to provide a richer GUI (including pull-down menus and windows), while maintaining the overall framework of an HTML page.
>
> The third and most complex approach is a Java-only environment (see Chapter 11). This provides a rich graphic environment and the flexibly to do ad hoc queries because it does not limit users to the restrictive structure of HTML pages.
>
> ...[It is also important for the V&V specialist to consider network usage and performance issues.] The first approach—producing static reports or templates—is that it does not require a lot of network use. Therefore, multiple users do not rack up a lot of overhead costs. This solution works well even over standard telephone lines via 28.8 kilobytes-per-second modems. The Java-only approach requires the most network use because of users downloading a lot of graphics and crunching a lot of numbers. This is not a solution for the current generation of public telephone lines, but for fiber-rich corporate networks. (pp. S13–S14)

Summary

Recall the definition provided: A data warehouse is an electronic means to store a large amount of reference or historical data typically used to support the decision-making and information retrieval needs of an organization. From the perspective of the V&V expert, many subsystems were covered in this chapter. The two elements that stand out as crucial to a successful data warehouse system are data quality and network (Internet/intranet) access and control.

High-quality data refers to data fit for use by data consumers. Therefore, usefulness and usability are important aspects of quality. The characteristics of high-quality data that the V&V person needs to look for consist of four categories: intrinsic, accessibility, contextual, and representational aspects.

Four software services of analytic layer, file management, security, and agents are essential to meet the challenge for the V&V specialist is to properly enable data warehouse access across the Internet/intranet.

References

1. Joodi, Peter, "Data Warehousing Management Review," In *CrossTalk*, Software Technology Support Center, Ogden: Hill AFB, Vol. 9, No. 10, October 1996, pp. 6–8.
2. Swift, Ronald S., "Ensuring a Successful Data Warehouse," *Data Warehousing: What Works?* Vol. 2, p. 4. [The Data Warehousing Institute, 849-J Quince Orchard Boulevard., Gaithersburg, MD 20878, 1996].
3. Kruse, Charles and Joseph, Larry, "Case Study: Texas Department of Public Safety," *Data Warehousing: What Works?* Vol. 2, pp. 68, 69. [The Data Warehousing Institute, 849-J Quince Orchard Boulevard, Gaithersburg, MD 20878, 1996].
4. Special Advertising Supplement to *Software* magazine, Sponsored by Hewlett Packard, ORACLE, Pine Cone Systems Inc., Price Waterhouse LLP, and SAS Institute, June 1997.
5. Murphy, Jim, "How to Build an Effective Data Warehouse: Six Key Steps to Success," *Data Warehousing: What Works?* Vol. 2, p. 30. [The Data Warehousing Institute, 849-J Quince Orchard Boulevard, Gaithersburg, MD 20878, 1996].
6. Strong, Diane M., Lee, Yang W. and Wang, Richard Y., "Data Quality in Context," *Communications of the ACM,* May 1997, Vol. 40, No. 5, pp. 103–110.
7. Serfin, Kathy, "Bristol-Myers Squibb Wins 'Best Practices' Award for Transforming Legacy Data Into Information Asset," *Data Warehousing: What Works?* Vol. 2, pp. 18, 19. [The Data Warehousing Institute, 849-J Quince Orchard Boulevard, Gaithersburg, MD 20878, 1996].
8. Kay, Emily. "Dirty Data Challenges Warehouses," *DW for Data Warehousing Management* (A Special Editorial Supplement to *Software* Magazine), October 1997, pp. S5–S8. [Sentry Technology Group, One Research Drive, Westborough, MA 01581].
9. Atkins, Mark E., "WARNING: Failure to Know What's in Your Legacy Data May Undermine Your Data Warehouse," *Data Warehousing: What Works?* Vol. 2, p. 17. [The Data Warehousing Institute, 849-J Quince Orchard Boulevard, Gaithersburg, MD 20878, 1996].
10. Robinson, Teri, "Warehouses and the Web: Made for Each Other," *DW for Data Warehousing Management* (A Special Editorial Supplement to *Software* Magazine), July 1997, pp. S3–S6. [Sentry Technology Group, One Research Drive, Westborough, MA 01581].
11. Saylor, Michael J. and Moin, Ahmed, "How the Web Will Enable the Revenue Generating Commercial Data Warehouse," *Data Warehousing: What Works?* Vol. 2, p. 16. [The Data Warehousing Institute, 849-J Quince Orchard Boulevard, Gaithersburg, MD 20878, 1996].

[12] Drost, Karen, "Putting the Data Warehouse on the Intranet," *Data Warehousing: What Works?* Vol. 2, p. 51. [The Data Warehousing Institute, 849-J Quince Orchard Boulevard, Gaithersburg, MD 20878, 1996].

[13] Wilson, Linda, "How to Access a Web Warehouse," *DW for Data Warehousing Management* (A Special Editorial Supplement to *Software* Magazine), July 1997, pp. S13, S14. [Sentry Technology Group, One Research Drive, Westborough, MA 01581].

[14] The Sentry Group, "Must Try Harder," *Software*, Vol. 18, No. 11, August, 1998, pp. 61–66. [Sentry Technology Group, One Research Drive, Westborough, MA 01581].

General References

Bontempo, Charles and Zagelow, George, "The IBM Data Warehouse Architecture," *Communications of the ACM*, Vol. 41, No. 9, September, 1998, pp. 38–48.

Gardner, Stephen, "Building the Data Warehouse," *Communications of the ACM*, Vol. 41, No. 9, September, 1998, pp. 52–60.

Glassey, Katherine, "Seducing the End User," *Communications of the ACM*, Vol. 41, No. 9, September, 1998, pp. 62–69.

Sen, Arun and Jacob, Varghese, "Industrial-Strength Data Warehousing," *Communications of the ACM*, Vol. 41, No. 9, September, 1998, pp. 29–31.

Sutter, James, "Project-Based Warehouses," *Communications of the ACM*, Vol. 41, No. 9, September, 1998, pp. 49–51.

Watson, Hugh and Haley, Barbara, "Mangerial Considerations," *Communications of the ACM*, Vol. 41, No. 9, September, 1998, pp. 32–37.

Appendix

The following list of manufacturers* that provide data warehousing system products is adapted from a special advertising supplement to *Software*[4] magazine. This list includes manufacturers of data warehouse-specific tools plus a representative sample of manufacturers of general management tools in the key areas of monitoring and tuning and data storage management. Manufacturers for managing tasks such as security and authorization and backup and recovery have not been included because there are few, if any, data warehouse-specific products in these categories.

Service Level Management

Manage, Monitor, and Tune a Data Warehousing System

BEZ Systems, BMC, Boole & Babbage, Candle, Computer Associates, Compuware, Digital, Hewlett-Packard, IBM, Landmark, Microsoft, Pine Cone Systems, Platinum Technology, Tivoli Systems

Data Acquisition Management

Data Quality Management and Cleanup

* Note: Manufacturing listings are not intended to be exhaustive. Manufacturers listed are representative of their respective categories.

DB, Gladstone Computer Services, Group 1, Innovative Systems,
Pine Cone Systems, Postalsoft, QDB Software, Software Search America,
Trillium Software Group, Unitech, Vality, WizSoft

Build Enterprise Data Warehouse/Operational Data Store/Data Mart

Apertus, Carleton, Constellar, Evolutionary Technologies,
Pine Cone Systems, Platinum Technology, Price Waterhouse,
Prism Solutions, SAS Institute, Software AG

Data Mart Creation

D2K, IBM, Informatica, Information Builders, Oracle,
Platinum Technology, Prism, Sagent, VMARK

Data Replication

Computer Associates, IBM, Oracle, Praxis, SAS Institute, Sybase

Data Storage Management

Data Archiving

Hewlett-Packard, IBM, Veritas Software, Platinum Technology, Sterling Software

Multidimensional Data Management (MDBMSs)

Arbor, Holistic Systems, Hyperion, Information Builders, Kenan Technologies,
Oracle, Pilot, Planning Sciences

Multidimensional Data Management (ROLAP Middleware Servers)

Information Advantage, Informix, MicroStrategy, Oracle, Platinum Technology

Relational Database Management

Computer Associates, IBM, Informix, Microsoft, NCR, Oracle, Red Brick, Tandem

Metadata Management

Manage Metadata

Enterprise Solutions, Evolutionary Technologies, Hewlett-Packard, IBM,
Information Builders, Intellidex, Metadata, Logic Works,
Manager Software Products, Platinum Technology, Prism Solutions, R&O,
SAS Institute, Software One, VIT

Data Access and Delivery Management

Deliver Warehouse Data to End-Users

DataChannel, Wayfarer, Poincast, D2K, Oracle, Sagent, SAS Institute, VIT

Manage User Access to Warehouse Data

BEZ Systems, Hewlett-Packard, Hewlett-Packard, Information Builders,
MicroStrategy, Pine Cone Systems, Precise Software Solutions,
Price Waterhouse, Sterling Software[4]

There are trends provided by The Sentry Group[14] data warehousing survey at this snap shot in time that are worth the consideration of V&V personnel who are involved in this area. The current and planned percentages of size, classification type, products in use, and refresh rate of the data are provided.

Percentage of respondents citing size of their current and planned data warehouse installations: (p. 65)

SIZE	CURRENT	PLANNED
< 100 Giga-bytes	62%	43%
100–200 Giga-bytes	19%	21%
201–500 Giga-bytes	11%	20%
501Giga-bytes–1Tera-byte	4%	9%
> 1 Tera-byte	5%	7%

Percentage of respondents citing size of current and planned sizes of data warehouse in terms of indexes contained: (p. 65)

SIZE	CURRENT	PLANNED
< 50	60%	43%
50–100	25%	29%
> 100	16%	27%

Percentage of respondents citing classification of their data warehouse installations: (p. 65)

CLASSIFICATION	CURRENT	PLANNED
Centralized enterprise warehouse	35%	54%
Data marts within an enterprise warehouse architecture	11%	21%
Distributed enterprise warehouse	8%	17%
Departmental data mart	8%	10%

Percentage of respondents citing current and planned data warehousing product types: (p. 66)

PRODUCTS	CURRENT	PLANNED
Query/data access/reporting tools	46%	78%
Systems management/backup	38%	67%
Storage systems	31%	53%
OLAP tools	22%	45%
Data replication	21%	50%
Data mining tools	15%	56%
Data cleaning tools	11%	35%

Percentage of respondents citing frequency of data refresh: (p. 66)

FREQUENCY	CURRENT	PLANNED
Daily	39%	37%
Immediately	19%	27%
Weekly	18%	14%
Monthly	12%	9%

CHAPTER 13

Project Management

Introduction

Project management for V&V of modern software-intensive systems is a wide-ranging discussion. It needs to tie together such disparate subjects as are covered in this book, such as object oriented methods, rapid application development, knowledge-based systems, data warehousing, etc.

In this introduction are discussed various V&V approaches for wide-ranging aspects of software development. Traditional aspects include a list of V&V planning documents, with a summary of V&V activities by phase and related V&V phase audits. Some scheduling management challenges for V&V are addressed. The importance of test planning is emphasized, and Microsoft's test methods are highlighted with their implications for V&V.

Contemporary aspects of V&V project management include strategies for choosing V&V techniques. Robert Lewis' work[1] is drawn upon and updated for inclusion of V&V project elements as applied to these new applications covered in this book. The Capability Maturity Model for Software project management key process areas are modified for a thought provoking way to manage V&V processes. Some very contemporary V&V project management process methods are discussed to make V&V more effective in this new application world. The Appendix to this chapter contains the table of contents from three V&V plans for another checklist of activities and products of importance to V&V. They include:

- IEEE-1013-1986 standard, *IEEE Standard for Software Verification and Validation Plans*
- FIPS PUB 101, *Guideline for Lifecycle Validation, Verification, and Testing of Computer Software*
- *Independent System Verification and Validation Plan*

Coordinated Development Management

Michael Deutsch[2] relates that:

> future directions and advances appear to be concentrated in these categories:
>
> 1. improved management approaches
> 2. improved implementation of proven technologies
> 3. evolution of present experimental techniques
>
> It... should be recognized that these areas are not necessarily mutually exclusive or discrete. In recalling the historical progression of the software project, the need for separation of system engineering, software development, and an independent test organization developed. Unfortunately, in many instances, this resulted in the deployment of separate approaches and tools by these organizations with marginal coordination. Economics and the resulting poor performance of this arrangement are bringing about its demise. A revised, more realistic approach to software development requires an overall coordinated package of tools and methodologies covering all phases of the software life-cycle. This will, of course, place more of a burden on management to achieve these results. [An important step to the achievement of this is the use of V&V specialists who are well trained in software concepts], who are committed to modern methodologies, and who will be aggressive in overcoming inertia to ensure that these approaches are implemented.
>
> What seems to have occurred is that in the compulsion to provide individual attention to verification and validation, V&V became too detached from other activities on the software project. Management must review this separation and provide a more integrated role for V&V. This would involve re-assimilating V&V, such that each area of software engineering has a synergized V&V aspect.
>
> The software development process is more accurately viewed when the technical engineering problem is considered in conjunction with the human engineering aspect of the process. The application of talented personnel should, theoretically, be sufficient requisite on which to forecast success. However, basic human fallibilities provide the possibility for errors to occur. Engineering, scientific, and management practices are frequently corrupted by human errors of inconsistency and omission. Computer automated tools have been and will continue to be developed to implement existing proven technologies that are most prone to inconsistency and omission errors if performed manually. (pp. 43, 45)

Presently, a good environment does not exist for the introduction of new V&V approaches. A consolidation of present technology is needed to fill a gap between technology and the ability of management to efficiently apply what already exists. This consolidation is a necessary step to providing a firm baseline for the introduction of advanced methodologies.

Testing is the most visible V&V activity, but not necessarily the most important. However, the notion that the traditional series of formal tests applied to software products at the end of a development constitutes effective V&V is not accurate. Such testing, in fact, has little effect on product integrity from an effectiveness/cost standpoint. Probably, the area with the greatest influence/cost ratio on product quality is V&V.

V&V and QA

A brief discussion of the differences between quality assurance (QA) and V&V is appropriate in this project management chapter. This is because the project manager needs to have the appropriate help for the right job while traveling down the road to project success. Easterbrook[3] says:

> The road metaphor is a useful one to help understand the differences between QA and IV&V. The process road needs policing, to prevent problems such as speeding (i.e., moving too fast through the requirements) and high-level design phases (i.e., faulty or missing requirements, poor choice of architecture, lack of traceability, etc. needed when accidents occur), helping to clear up the mess, and sometimes making recommendations for preventative improvements. This job is divided up as follows. QA ensures that appropriate laws ("standards and procedures" are applied, and checks for infringements of these). IV&V's job is to make sure that vehicles traveling on the road are road-worthy, are heading in the right direction, and will make it safely to their destinations. (p. 1)

Communication Difficulties

Large software projects suffer serious breakdowns in coordination and communication throughout their development life-cycle. Some of the causes for the breakdown of communication of software development projects are discussed here with recommendations of what V&V may do to help the situation. This subsection on communications difficulties is extracted from Amer Al-Rawas and Steve Easterbrook's "Communication Problems in Requirements Engineering: A Field Study:"[4]

> In many ways, software engineering methodologies are communication methodologies. Much emphasis is placed on the notations used to convey information both within the development team and with the various stakeholders. Ideally, the channels of communication between these various communities would be perfect, so that all knowledge is shared. In practice, it is expensive and time-consuming to support extensive communication between the communities, and the channels are restricted to one-way communication in the form of specification documents. Curtis et. al. [1988] observed that documentation is ineffective for communication, as it does not help resolve misunderstandings. Nevertheless, an implicit "over-the-wall" model exists in most software development projects: at each stage in the project, a specification is thrown over a wall to the next team who is waiting to proceed with the next phase. The metaphorical wall is sometimes encouraged by management practices, but more often is merely a result of the practicalities of coordinating a large team.
>
> The results of this study showed that specification documents are still the most common format in which analysts communicate requirements back to their clients for validation [see Figure 13.1, Client's Questionnaire]. The formats in which requirements are communicated. There are two standard approaches to this problem. The first emphasizes the development of better (richer) importance of contact between the development team and other stakeholders, and has given rise to practices such as end-user participation and ethnographic techniques. Each of these approaches has its own set of problems, and neither directly addresses the question of facilitating appropriate and effective communication over restricted channels. Our study showed that practitioners find it easier to adapt a compromise of the two approaches by enriching notations with natural language descriptions and by utilizing the personal contact of face-

Figure 13.1 The formats in which requirements are communicated.[4] (pp. 3, 4)

In what format do you get the analyst's interpretation of your requirements?

Natural language discussions 16%
Informal combination of documents and discussions 24%
Informal specification documents 16%
Formal specification documents 44%

> to-face discussions.... Moreover, standard software development cycles rely heavily on documentation as an exit condition in moving from stage to stage. Documents are also used as the media for communicating ideas. Consequently, a colossal amount of paperwork is generated.
>
> The nature, the domain complexity, the variety of methods and notations and the interdependency of partial requirement make it very difficult to establish total consistency. For example, we found that the recipient of the services provided by one of the end-user organizations was referred to as client, customer, applicant, candidate, and land owner by different participants who contributed to the production of the specification documents. All these names were used to describe the same entity. The names used reflected the concern of each stakeholder. (pp. 3–4)

An important consequence of this type of situation for V&V is that they must ensure that consistent terminology is used in the project documents.

Multidimensional Model

Project management of V&V is on the process axis of the multidimensional model. Because the Capability Maturity Model for Software is an important related process element, there is a good reason to bring the software CMM into focus in this chapter. The project management process is fundamental to success in any endeavor, which is why in the CMM for software it is a level 2 key process area.

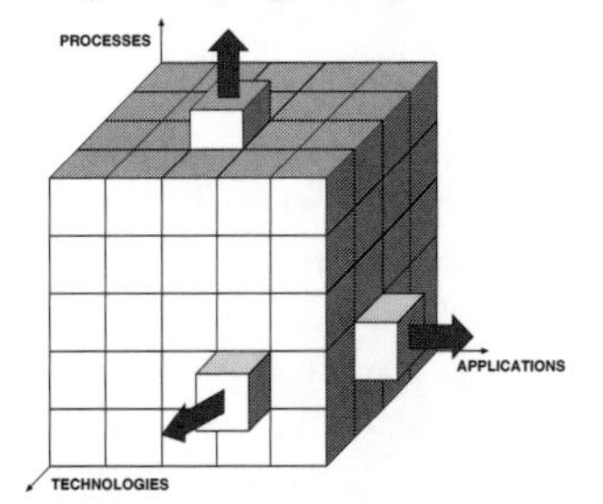

There are slightly different approaches that V&V project management may take for the various new application areas under discussion in this book. What may be applicable to rapid application development probably is not so applicable to object oriented methods used in development. With this myriad of concepts to consider, how to appropriately plan and manage a modern software-intensive V&V project is discussed in this chapter.

Technology may drive what project management process is to be used for V&V project management. One must consider whether the Internet/intranet or client/server networks are used. The graphical user interface and the CASE tools impact how to plan and manage the V&V activities.

Traditional V & V

V&V Planning

Major steps to consider in developing the V&V plan provided by Dolores Wallace and Roger Fujii[5] are to:

- define the quality and performance objectives (e.g., verify conformance to specifications, verify compliance with safety and security objectives, assess efficiency and quality of software, and assess performance across the full operating environment)
- characterize the types of problems anticipated in the system and define how they would show up in the software
- select the V&V analysis and testing techniques to effectively detect the system and software problems. (p. 6)

AverStar is the verification and validation lead for EOSDIS, a major NASA project. Extensive V&V-related planning has taken place on the EOSDIS project, and an overview of this planning is described here. On this large project, the V&V is an independent activity. The IV&V Management Plan (IVVMP)[6] provides descriptions of methodologies, techniques, and tools that AverStar employs as the IV&V prime contractor. This IVVMP also describes the management approach, organization, and resources that are applied. This plan is one of a sequence of plans that is prepared and delivered to NASA. The IVVMP and its supporting IV&V plans are:

- This IVVMP addresses IV&V at large, describing what will be done and what level of resources will be applied in total.
- The Independent System V&V Plan (see the Appendix to this chapter) addresses the development life-cycle in detail and explains how the IV&V methods, tools, and techniques can be applied to the project.
- The Integration and Certification Plan further elaborates the testing portion of the IV&V effort. IV&V testing is a mainstream activity, performed in line with the development effort, which encompasses test and integration of all principal components and certification of the end-to-end operation of the resultant system.
- An Independent Release V&V Plan provides specifics concerning the efforts that will be performed for a particular release of a project component (p. 5).

Following from the FIPS PUB 101, *Guideline for Lifecycle Validation, Verification, and Testing of Computer Software*[7] (see the Appendix in this chapter for the V&V Plan outline from this publication) is a phase-by-phase summary of V&V activities:

I. Requirements Definition and Analysis Phase
   A. Development of the project V&V* plan—During this activity, the V&V analyst will determine V&V requirements; design a V&V process; select techniques and tools; and establish schedules, responsibilities, and budgets. (V&V Activity)
   B. Generation of requirements-based test cases—A basic set of test cases is developed to clarify and to determine measurability of each software requirement. The acceptance criteria are used to develop the test cases. Input data and expected results for each test case are included in the specification. (V&V Activity, Product)
   C. Review and analysis of the requirements—Project requirements are reviewed for clarity, completeness, consistency, testability, and traceability to the problem statement. The goal of this activity is to ensure that these requirements will result in a practical, usable solution to the entire problem. (V&V Activity)
   D. Review and analysis of the draft user's manual—The user's manual is reviewed for clarity and consistency. It is checked for completeness against the requirements document. In addition, this verification activity includes ensuring that the internal specifications of the requirements document are defined sufficiently to lead to the production of the functions and interfaces described in the user's manual. (V&V Activity)

II. Design Phase
   A. Completion of V&V plan—The V&V plan specifies goals and approaches to the V&V activities. It contains the outline for a project-specific V&V process, identifies techniques and tools to be used, and specifies plans (schedules, budgets, responsibilities, etc.) for performing the V&V activities. New or revised project requirements may warrant revision of the V&V plan. The detailed design plan may indicate the need for additional testing procedures. (V&V Product)
   B. Generation of design-based test scenarios
   C. Review and analysis of the design—The design is analyzed to ensure internal consistency, completeness, correctness and clarity, and to verify that the design, when implemented, will satisfy the requirements. (V&V Activity)
      1. Preliminary design integrity check
      2. Preliminary design evolution check
   D. Development of test-support software—Development or acquisition of any support software needed for unit, integration, or system testing should be completed and installed during the detailed design phase to ensure readiness during programming and testing. (V&V Activity)

* Authors changed VV&T (validation, verification, and testing) from the FIPS PUB 101 to V&V (verification and validation), whenever referenced throughout this chapter.

III. Programming and Testing Phase

A. Completion of test-case specification—Additional test scenarios and test cases (input data and expected results) are developed to exercise and test logical and structural aspects of the design. (V&V Product)
Formal revisions and additions to the test data are made. (V&V Activity, Product)

B. Review, analysis, and testing of the program—This activity includes checking for adherence to coding standards and manual/automated analysis of the program by static, dynamic, and formal methods. (V&V Activity)
1. Code integrity check
2. Code evolution check
3. Unit test
4. Integration test
5. System test

The program is executed with the test data; actual results are compared with the expected results and are validated for satisfaction of the requirements. (V&V Activity)
The testing activities, including comparison of actual and expected results are documented. (V&V Product)
Observed problems are recorded in formal statements and may necessitate returning to a previous phase for resolution. (V&V Product)

IV. Installation Phase

A. System acceptance—Once the system is tested, the primary V&V activity centers on acceptance of the system by the customer (or principal user when the developers and users are the same). Acceptance may range from review or acknowledgment of the V&V activities during system development to detailed acceptance testing by the customer prior to formal acceptance. (V&V Activity)
A customer representative should formally sign off on a form indicating that testing has been completed and that the system is accepted. (V&V Product)

V. Operations and Maintenance Phase

A. Software evaluation—Continuous monitoring and evaluation to assess the operation of the software and to ensure continued satisfaction of user requirements occurs throughout the operation and maintenance of the software. (V&V Activity)

B. Software modification evaluation—Requested modifications to the system are evaluated in the same manner that the original software development was evaluated. If the requirements or design specifications are modified, the V&V activities appropriate to those phases should be performed. When the modifications are completed, they must be reviewed and tested to ensure that they not only fulfill the modification request, but also have not adversely affected any other part of the system. (V&V Activity)
Formal requests by V&V personnel for specific changes to the software must be submitted to those responsible for making the revisions. (V&V Product)

C. Regression testing—Test cases which a program has previously executed correctly in order to detect errors created during software modification are rerun and compared. (V&V Activity) (pp. 6–9)

Phase Audits

At the end of each phase, an audit is usually helpful. Preston Pierce[8] tells us that a review to ensure all activities specified to be completed are in fact completed and a review of defect/action items are completed from document and code reviews. This may also be a good time to review with the development team the open action items in the defect tracking system. All variances from the development plan should be documented and followed up to complete resolution.

Scheduling Management

David Myles, Jr.[9] relates that one of the challenges for V&V is to frequently evaluate the project schedule update process:

> Written management instructions and the associated threats will not ensure that the proper update processes are followed. Consequently, schedules cannot be trusted to accurately reflect the program plan or status.... Typically, higher-level schedules include component parts collected and integrated periodically from a large number of diverse technical areas. Prior to the collection process, each area is responsible for updating its schedule component with the latest planning and status information. Upon collection and review, the total schedule is recorded for official use until the process is repeated perhaps a week or two later. The collection, integration, and recording of the current schedule plans and status is called *schedule promotion*. After the schedule promotion process V&V (as part of its audit of schedule quality and sanity) must ensure that:
>
> - All component parts are submitted and are included in the higher level project schedule.
> - All component parts are compatible with one another, all project-mandated fields correctly completed, and activity identifiers adhere to a defined pattern.
> - Results from the merge action are communicated back to the individual technical areas.
> - File/data management is performed to preclude the loss of project information.
> - Historical information from previously promoted schedules is used for trend analyses. (pp. 17, 18)

Test Planning

A significant project management activity includes test planning. V&V needs to review test planning policies and policy implementation, according to "Developing a Testing Maturity Model:"[10]

> The project manager [needs to be] trained in test planning according to organizational standards, and he is responsible for negotiating commitments and assigning responsibilities to developers to develop the test plans and the test work products. [V&V ensures]... the proper development of the test plans at the unit, integration, system, and acceptance levels according to organizational standards. Each test plan should minimally contain the following:
>
> - test objectives and goals (with impact from risk analysis)
> - items to be tested (functions and features)
> - test work products, testing schedules, deadlines, and costs

- personnel and their responsibilities, resources, and tools required
- constraints and pass or fail criteria.

> [For test completeness, V&V assures]... that the project retrieves input to the test plan from requirements documents, developers, and past project history. [V&V ensures that]... there is input or consensus from users for the acceptance test plan. (p. 24)

Microsoft Testing Methods

The testing process at Microsoft abstracted from Roger Sherman's "Shipping the Right Products at the Right Time: A View of Development and Testing at Microsoft"[11] is of some interest in this project management chapter. Since Microsoft has captured a large market, at least one may learn some valuable techniques to get software to market in a salable manner, if not necessarily using the best V&V techniques. Sherman says,

> When a release is made to testing, development also publishes a Testing Release Document (TRD), which describes the scope of testing to be done for the release. The TRD specifies areas that are not ready for testing, as well as those areas that should be tested completely. The testing group performs acceptance testing to confirm that it will be able to test the areas specified in the TRD. To accept the release, the testing group must be able to test all coded features (i.e., the release must contain no "blocking bugs"), load test files, and run pre-existing automated tests against the product. Testing may reject the release if it is not testable.
>
> After acceptance, testing runs its newly developed test cases against the release, and development fixes the bugs. The bug-fix cycle continues until the test cases yield no additional bugs. The milestone is then certified, and development begins to work on the next feature set for the next milestone.
>
> After each milestone, the team holds a post-mortem with its managers. The post-mortem is a meeting where the work of the team in coding and testing the milestone is reviewed. The manager's role is to encourage honest conversation and to make sure that all necessary issues are raised. The team examines its process for the milestone, the test results, and the schedule. If necessary, the ship date is adjusted, features are cut, process is changed, or people are reassigned to tasks deemed critical to the project. This is one instance where trade-offs among the three dimensions of quality are adjusted.
>
> The last milestone of this type is called "code complete": all features are coded, there are no bugs blocking testing, and all native coding (speed optimization) is done. From code complete until release to manufacturing, development fixes bugs in releases made once or twice a week. During this period, the schedule includes a number of other milestones, such as beta testing, configuration and printer testing, and complete passes of all test cases, automated and manual.
>
> At some point, development resolves issues faster than testing can generate them. This is called "bug convergence." As the active number of issues begins to decline, one can begin to estimate with more precision when the product can be released. It is only a matter of time before development is able to make a release that resolves all active issues. This release is called the Zero Bug Release. From this point on, all changes to the code are carefully reviewed by a senior developer and a senior tester. The goal is to stabilize the product. Releases increase in frequency until they are made daily. Gradually, the bug find rate drops to less than one per day.

> Although each team may decide its own exit criteria (called Final Acceptance Test), most teams will not release the product until it has withstood five full days of testing without yielding a "must-fix" bug.
>
> After the product has shipped to customers, the entire team will hold a post-mortem to review what went well and what could be done to improve the process, tools, or work environment. The results of these post-mortems are published to the rest of the company and are a major means of sharing best practices between groups.
>
> The primary benefit of the milestone process is that it helps to maintain code stability. When a code base becomes too unstable, it will not solidify with additional testing and bug fixing. Bug fixing may actually make things worse. The best solution in this case is to throw away the code and rewrite it. Rewriting the code is very costly and is therefore a last-resort solution. Maintaining a stable code base increases the probability that testing and bug fixing will improve the product rather than destabilize it. (pp. 7–8)

So, what can V&V learn from this Microsoft methodology? After acceptance, testing runs its newly developed test cases against the release, and passes the software back to the development team which is the usual activity taken by V&V. The management lesson of most import is to hold those post-mortems after each milestone, through the "code complete" milestone. The Microsoft post-mortem when used by others needs to include the V&V person. This allows corrective action by the manager(s) and involves the V&V person in the validation of the product. The "lessons learned" post-mortem after customer delivery creates a company database of best practices, and just as importantly, a description of what did not work well. The V&V person should not do what did not work well. So, as George Santayana has said, "Those who cannot remember the past are condemned to repeat it."

Contemporary V & V

Strategies for Choosing Techniques

From the NIST Special Publication 500-234, *Reference Information for the Software Verification and Validation Process,*[12] a useful list of strategies for choosing V&V techniques to help manage a project is provided in this subsection.

> Some software V&V techniques used during software requirements V&V tasks are:
>
> - control flow analysis
> - data flow analysis
> - algorithm analysis
> - simulation.
>
> Control and data flow analysis are most applicable for real time and data-driven systems [such as data warehousing]. These flow analyses transform logic and data requirements text into graphic flows, which are easier to analyze than the text. PERT, state transition, and transaction diagrams are examples of control flow diagrams. Algorithm analysis involves rederivation of equations or evaluation of the suitability of specific numerical techniques. Simulation is used to evaluate the interactions of large, complex systems with many hard-

ware, user, and other interfacing software units. [This is especially relevant to the client/server and Internet/intranet areas.]

Some software V&V techniques used during software design V&V tasks include:

- algorithm analysis
- database analysis
- sizing and timing analysis
- simulation.

Algorithm analysis examines the correctness of the equations or numerical techniques as in the software requirements activity, but also examines truncation and round-off effects, numerical precision of word storage, and variables (e.g., single- vs. extended-precision arithmetic). Database analysis is particularly useful for programs that store and analyze data. Sizing and timing analysis is useful for real-time programs having response time requirements and constrained memory execution space requirements. [This is often implemented using object oriented methods.]

Some software V&V techniques used during code V&V tasks are:

- control flow analysis
- database analysis
- regression analysis
- sizing and timing analysis.

For large code developments, control flow diagrams showing the hierarchy of main routines and their subfunctions are useful in understanding the flow of program control. Database analysis is performed on data warehousing with significant data storage to ensure data correctness and consistency. Data integrity is enforced and no data or variable can be accidentally overwritten by overflowing data tables. Data typing and use are consistent throughout all program elements. Regression analysis is used to reevaluate software requirements and software design issues whenever any significant code change is made. This technique ensures project awareness of the original system requirements. Sizing and timing analysis is done during incremental code development and compared against predicted values. Significant deviations between actual and predicted values are possible indications of problems or the need for additional examination....

Code reading is a technique that may be used for source code verification. An expert reads through another programmer's code to detect errors. In an experiment conducted at the NASA Goddard Space Flight Center, code reading was found to be more effective than either functional testing or structural testing. The reason was attributed to the expertise of the readers who, as they read the code, were simulating its execution and were able to detect many kinds of errors.

Other techniques commonly used are walkthroughs, inspections, and reviews. These tasks occur in interactive meetings attended by a team that usually includes at least one member from the development group. Other members may belong to the development group or to other groups involved in software development. The duration of these meetings is usually no more than a few hours, in which code is examined on a line-by-line basis. In these dynamic sessions, it may be difficult to examine the code thoroughly for control logic, data flow, database errors, sizing, timing, and other features that may require considerable manual or automated effort. Advance preparation for these activities may be necessary, including code analysis techniques. The results of these techniques provide appropriate engineering information for discussion at meetings where code is evaluated. Regardless of who conducts or participates in walkthroughs and inspections, software V&V analyses may be used to support these meetings.

A comprehensive test management approach to testing recognizes the differences in strategies and in objectives for unit, software integration, and software system test. Unit test verifies the design and implementation of software units. Software integration test verifies functional requirements as the software units are integrated. Special attention is focused on software, hardware, and operator interfaces. Software system test validates the entire software program against system requirements and software performance objectives. Software system tests validate that the software executes correctly within its stated operating environment. The software's ability to deal properly with anomalies and stress conditions is emphasized. These tests are not intended to duplicate or replace the user and development group's test responsibilities, but instead supplement the development testing to test behavior not normally tested by the user or development group.

Effective testing requires a comprehensive understanding of the system. Such understanding develops from systematically analyzing the software's concept, requirements, design, and code. By knowing internal software details, software V&V testing is effective at probing for errors and weaknesses that reveal hidden faults. This is considered structural, or white-box, testing. It often finds errors for which some functional, or black-box, test cases can produce the correct output despite internal errors. Functional test cases execute part or all of the system to validate that the user requirement is satisfied; these test cases cannot always detect internal errors that will occur under special circumstances. Another software V&V test technique is to develop test cases that violate software requirements. [Usability, discussed in Chapter 8, is particularly adaptable to this technique. Remember the "monkey" tests from Microsoft covered in Chapter 3: They are a good example in the usability testing arena of tests that violate software requirements.] This approach is effective at uncovering basic design assumption errors and unusual operational use errors.

The process of planning functional test cases requires a thorough examination of the functional requirements. A [V&V] analyst who carefully develops those test cases is likely to detect errors and omissions in the software requirements. In this sense, test planning can be effective in detecting errors and can contribute to uncovering some errors before test execution. The planning process for testing must take into account the specific objectives of the software V&V for the software and the impact of different test strategies in satisfying these objectives. . . .

Criticality analysis may be used to identify software V&V techniques to address high-risk concerns [see Chapter 14]. The selection of V&V techniques for use on each critical area of the program is a method of tailoring the intensity of the software V&V against the type of risk present in each area of the software. For example, software V&V would apply algorithm analysis to critical numerical software functions, and techniques such as sizing and timing analysis, data and control flow analysis, and interface analysis to real-time executive functions. (pp. 15–17)

What strategies for verification, validation and testing (VV&T) techniques should the project employ to achieve the functionality and quality the product requires? From "Validation, Verification, and Testing: Diversity Rules,"[13] we learn that inspections are a vital part of early phase V&V activities. "Failure to identify and remove major design or specification errors early in the development process can lead to poorly structured systems with many related faults. It is not possible to test-in reliability to such systems" (p. 46).

Operational testing or inspections should be used "as part of a balanced set of VV&T techniques, selected to suit the specific requirements placed both on the product and its development process. In the current state of software engineering knowledge, human expertise is the only method of deciding an appropriate VV&T strategy" (p. 46). However, there are reasons why a mixed set of techniques is needed.

> These techniques and testing procedures include the following:
>
> - additional testing of boundary and transition conditions and of critical functions
> - design inspections and reviews to identify specification and design faults early in the development process
> - proofs for functions whose correct outcome cannot otherwise be verified
> - operational testing for those initial tests aimed at identifying the largest faults and assessing reliability. (pp. 46–49)

V&V Products and Activities

In Robert O. Lewis' book, *Independent Verification and Validation,*[1] there is a list by development phase of typical V&V products and activities. This list is useful from a V&V management perspective of preparation for a project, both for estimating the time each task takes and for ensuring that all tasks are considered. To aid in the newer technologies aspect, the list is provided in Table 13.1 with an **X**-mark indicating the relevance to the application areas discussed in this book.

Probably the most important consideration in V&V planning adapted from Lewis[1] revolves around the inherent flexibility of the methodology wherein optimization becomes the process of tailoring the approach to the unique constraints and attributes of:

- the system and its technology
- application area to be subjected to V&V (i.e., Internet, data warehousing, etc.)
- software development contractor and its maturity level
- customer and any outside organizations that may be involved (e.g., an independent test and evaluation agency, regulatory agency, or other contractors)
- facilities available, including customer-furnished equipment
- budget and schedule
- initial entry and end points of V&V in the system acquisition life-cycle (p. 241).

Table 13.1 Project Management methods applied to new V&V Applications (adapted from Lewis[1], p. 237)

Management Methods	Object Oriented(OO) Methods	Rapid ApplicationDev. (RAD)	Usability (GUI I/F)	Client/ServerNetworks	Knowledge-Based Systems (KBS)	Internet /Intranet	DataWarehousing
Requirements Phase							
System specification verification report	X		X	X		X	
Software requirements specification verification report(s)	X		X	X		X	
Requirements verification report							
• Summary of document reviews	X		X	X	X	X	
• Summary of criticality and risk assessment	X	X	X	X	X	X	X
• Review of user interface	X		X	X	X	X	X
• Review of I/O data requirements	X		X	X	X	X	X
• Review of trade studies	X			X		X	
• Review of test planning	X		X	X	X	X	X
• List of meetings and formal reviews attended	X		X	X	X	X	X
• List of problem reports produced	X	X	X	X	X	X	X
• Open / action item list	X	X	X	X	X	X	X
V&V analyst's notebook							
• Evaluation factors	X	X	X	X	X	X	X
• Independent verification studies and results	X						
• Software tools used	X	X	X	X	X	X	X
Verify the system specification	X		X	X		X	
Verify the software requirements specification	X		X	X		X	
Verify the interface requirements specification	X		X	X		X	
Verify the hardware prime item specification if required				X			
Verify the software developmnet plan and its implementation	X		X	X	X	X	X
Verify requirements tracing between documents	X		X	X	X	X	X
Perform criticality and risk assessment of requirements	X	X	X	X	X	X	X
Review user interface needs			X				
Review input and output data requirements			X	X		X	X
Review trade studies for system	X			X		X	
Review test requirements, planning and strategy	X		X	X	X	X	X
Participate in all reviews and meetings that affect the system	X	X	X	X	X	X	X
Produce problem reports	X	X	X	X	X	X	X
Design Phase							
Preliminary and detailed design V&V reports, each containing:							
• Summary of document reviews	X		X	X	X	X	X
• Verification of requirements tracing	X	X	X	X	X	X	X
• Verification of behavior	X	X	X	X	X	X	X
• Verification of algorithms	X	X	X		X		

Table 13.1 continued

Management Methods	Object Oriented(OO) Methods	Rapid ApplicationDev. (RAD)	Usability (GUI I/F)	Client/ServerNetworks	Knowledge-Based Systems (KBS)	Internet /Intranet	DataWarehousing
• Verification of database							X
• Review of user interface	X	X	X	X	X	X	X
• Review of design risks	X		X	X	X	X	X
• Review of timing, sizing and memory allocation	X		X	X	X	X	X
• Review of software development plan conformance	X		X	X	X	X	X
• List of meetings and formal reviews attended	X	X	X	X	X	X	X
• List of problem report produced	X	X	X	X	X	X	X
• Open/action item list	X	X	X	X	X	X	X
V&V analyst's notebook							
• Evaluation factors	X	X	X	X	X	X	X
• Independent verification studies and results	X						
• Software tools used	X	X	X	X	X	X	X
Verify the software design document	X		X	X		X	
Verify the interface design document	X		X	X		X	
Verify the requirements tracing into SDD for SRS	X		X	X	X	X	X
Verify data flow							X
Verify behavioral factors (especially real time systems)	X						
Verify selected algorithms	X	X	X		X		
Verify database structures and elements							X
Verify user interface			X				
Review design risks	X		X	X	X	X	X
Review timing budgets (especially real time systems)	X						
Review sizing and memory allocations (especially real time systems)	X		X	X	X	X	X
Review how well developer is following SDP	X		X	X	X	X	X
Participate in all reviews and meetings that affect the system	X	X	X	X	X	X	X
Produce problem reports	X	X	X	X	X	X	X
Coding Phase							
Results from the code to SDD comparison							
• Deficiencies and discrepancies	X		X	X	X	X	X
• Verification and data dictionary			X	X	X	X	X
• Verification of algorithms between code and SDD	X	X	X		X		
• List of problem reports produced	X	X	X	X	X	X	X
• Open/action item list	X	X	X	X	X	X	X
Review of conformance to software development plan	X		X	X	X	X	X
Results of static analysis tool and standards checking	X		X	X	X	X	
Results of auditing developer's software library, database activities and system and support software maintenance practices	X		X	X	X	X	X

Table 13.1 continued

Management Methods	**Object Oriented(OO) Methods**	**Rapid ApplicationDev. (RAD)**	**Usability (GUI I/F)**	**Client/ServerNetworks**	**Knowledge-Based Systems (KBS)**	**Internet /Intranet**	**DataWarehousing**
V&V analyst's notebook							
• Code to SDD comparison data	X		X	X	X	X	X
• Results of audits	X		X	X	X	X	X
• Independent code verification studies and results	X						
• Software tools used	X	X	X	X	X	X	X
Verify consistency between code and SDD	X		X	X	X	X	X
Verify that specified standards and practices are being followed	X	X	X	X	X	X	X
Verify that developer is using specified coding tools	X	X		X	X	X	
Verify logical structure and syntax with static analysis	X		X	X	X	X	
Verify terms between data dictionary and code	X		X	X	X	X	X
Verify sample input and output data	X		X	X	X	X	X
Verify algorithms per SDD	X	X	X		X		
Verify versions of computer, operating systems and utilities	X	X	X	X	X	X	X
Review software library and release / version control	X	X	X	X	X	X	X
Participate in all reviews and meetings that affect the system	X	X	X	X	X	X	X
Produce problem reports	X	X	X	X	X	X	X
Integration and Test Phase							
Results from the review of the developer's software test plans and descriptions	X		X	X	X	X	
Listing or network of key event tests selected for monitoring by V&V	X		X	X	X	X	
Generation of formal validation report including such things as:							
• Results from monitoring the developer's testing	X	X	X	X	X	X	X
• Results from running the V&V test tool(s) on the code	X	X	X	X	X	X	X
• Summary of pre-planned V&V tests	X	X	X	X	X	X	X
• Summary of ad hoc V&V tests that were run in response to problems that occurred during testing and investigations initiated by V&V	X	X	X	X	X	X	X
• Description of the V&V testbed and its complement of tools	X	X	X	X	X	X	X
• V&V test results (data and analysis can be referenced)	X	X	X	X	X	X	X
• List of any briefings given the customer and developer on validation activities	X	X	X	X	X	X	X
• Validation summary comparing the requirements and tests	X	X	X	X	X	X	X
• Validation of the software product specification, user's and operator's manuals	X		X	X	X	X	X
• Summary of FCA, FQR and PCA activities	X		X	X	X	X	X
• Final conclusions and recommendations for the operational or production period	X	X	X	X	X	X	X

Table 13.1 continued

Management Methods	Object Oriented(OO) Methods	Rapid ApplicationDev. (RAD)	Usability (GUI I/F)	Client/ServerNetworks	Knowledge-Based Systems (KBS)	Internet /Intranet	DataWarehousing
V&V analyst's notebook							
• Requirements-to-test comparison data	X		X	X	X	X	X
• Results of audits and reviews	X		X	X	X	X	X
• Independent validation studies and results	X						
• Software tools used	X	X	X	X	X	X	X
Evaluate software test plan and software test description for each SWCI	X		X	X	X	X	X
Evaluate developer's test program and select key event tests for data collection and monitoring	X		X	X	X	X	X
Monitor developer's testing	X	X	X	X	X	X	X
Develop V&V test strategy	X	X	X	X	X	X	X
Define and configure the V&V testbed	X	X	X	X	X	X	X
Run independent validation tests	X	X	X	X	X	X	X
Confirm validation of requirements to tests	X	X	X	X	X	X	X
Validate software product specification	X		X	X	X	X	
Validate software user's and system operator's manuals	X			X	X	X	
Track CCB actions and open item status	X			X	X	X	
Participate in all reviews, audits and meetings that affect the system	X	X	X	X	X	X	X
Produce problem reports	X	X	X	X	X	X	X

CMM for V&V Project Management

In the Software Engineering Institute's *Key Practices of the Capability Maturity Model for Software*[14], the level 2 key process areas deal with project management. Of the key process areas that are included, the most relevant for project management concepts applicable to V&V are Software Project Planning and Software Tracking and Oversight. Each of the goals and key practices relevant to V&V for Software Project Planning (Table 13.2) and Software Tracking and Oversight (Table 13.3) are revised with the appropriate V&V flavor. Since these are good basic concepts applicable to all software developments, they are, in their revised V&V form, of equal applicability to the new applications discussed in this book.

Table 13.2 Software V&V project planning.[*] (pp. L2-11–L2-28.14)

I. GOALS

1. Software V&V estimates are documented for use in planning and tracking the software V&V effort.
2. Software V&V project activities and commitments are planned and documented.
3. Affected groups and individuals agree to their commitments related to the software V&V project.

II. COMMITMENT TO PERFORM

1. A project V&V manager is designated to be responsible for negotiating commitments and developing the project's software V&V plan.
2. The project follows a written organizational policy for planning a software V&V project.

III. ABILITY TO PERFORM

1. A documented and approved statement of work exists for the software V&V project.
2. Responsibilities for developing the software V&V plan are assigned.
3. Adequate resources and funding are provided for planning the V&V project.
4. The V&V manager, V&V engineers, and other individuals involved in the V&V project planning are trained in the V&V estimating and planning procedures.

IV. ACTIVITIES PERFORMED

1. The software V&V group participates on the project proposal team.
2. Software V&V project planning is initiated in the early stages of, and in parallel with, the overall project planning.
3. The software V&V group participates with other affected groups in the overall project planning throughout the project's life.
4. Software V&V project commitments made to individuals and groups external to the organization are reviewed with senior management according to a documented procedure.
5. A software life-cycle with predefined stages of manageable size is understood and incorporated into the V&V planning.
6. The project's software V&V plan is developed according to a documented procedure.
7. The plan for the software V&V project is documented.
8. Software V&V work products that are needed to establish and maintain control of the software V&V project are identified.
9. Estimates for the size of the software V&V products (or changes to the size of software V&V work products) are derived according to a documented procedure.
10. Estimates for a software V&V project's effort and costs are derived according to a documented procedure.
11. The project's V&V software schedule is derived according to a documented procedure.
12. Plans for the project's software V&V facilities and support tools are prepared.
13. Software V&V planning data are recorded.

V. MEASUREMENT AND ANALYSIS

1. Measurements are made and used to determine the status of the software V&V planning activities.

VI. VERIFICATION IMPLEMENTATION

1. The activities for software V&V project planning are reviewed with senior management on a periodic basis.
2. The activities for software V&V project planning are reviewed with the project manager or customer on both a periodic and event-driven basis.

[*] This table is modified from *Key Practices of the Capability Maturity Model for Software.*

Table 13.3 Software V&V project tracking and oversight.* (pp. L2-11–L2-28.14)

I. GOALS

1. Actual results and performances are tracked against the software V&V plans.
2. Corrective actions are taken to closure when actual results and performance deviate significantly from the software V&V plans.
3. Changes to software V&V commitments are agreed to by affected groups and individuals.

II. COMMITMENT TO PERFORM

1. A project V&V manager is designated to be responsible for the project's software V&V activities and results.
2. The project follows a written organizational policy for managing the software V&V project.

III. ABILITY TO PERFORM

1. A software V&V plan for the software V&V project is documented and approved.
2. The project V&V manager explicitly assigns responsibility for software V&V work products and activities.
3. Adequate resources and funding are provided for tracking the software V&V project.
4. The software V&V manager is trained in managing the technical and personnel aspects of the software V&V project.
5. The software V&V manager receives orientation in the technical aspects of the software project.

IV. ACTIVITIES PERFORMED

1. A documented software V&V plan is used for tracking the software V&V activities and communicating status.
2. The project's software V&V plan is revised according to a documented procedure.
3. Software V&V project commitments and changes to commitments made to individuals and groups external to the organization are reviewed with senior management according to a documented procedure.
4. Approved changes to commitments that affect the software V&V project are communicated to the members of the software V&V group and other software-related groups.
5. The size of the software V&V products (or size of the changes to software V&V work products) are tracked, and corrective actions are taken as necessary.
6. The project's software V&V effort and costs are tracked, and corrective actions are taken as necessary.
7. The project's software V&V schedule is tracked, and corrective actions are taken as necessary.
8. Software V&V technical activities are tracked, and corrective actions are taken as necessary.
9. Actual measurement data and replanning data for the software V&V project are recorded.
10. The software V&V group conducts periodic internal reviews to track technical progress, plans, performance, and issues against the software V&V plan.

V. MEASUREMENT AND ANALYSIS

1. Measurements are made and used to determine the status of the software V&V tracking and oversight activities.

VI. VERIFICATION IMPLEMENTATION

1. The activities for software V&V project tracking and oversight are reviewed with senior management on a periodic basis.
2. The activities for software V&V project tracking and oversight are reviewed with the project manager or customer on both a periodic and event-driven basis.

* This table is modified from *Key Practices of the Capability Maturity Model for Software.*

Project Management Process Methods

As organizations move toward greater maturity in their software processes, it is incumbent upon V&V to stay abreast of the innovations affecting software. An important aspect of software process management is the management of the project artifacts that go into a process asset library (PAL) for future reuse by other projects as part of the organization's standard software process. The Software Engineering Institute's *Process Asset Library (PAL) Prototype*[15] is abstracted in this subsection:

> The PAL concept grows out of a need for organizations to develop their software process assets in order to progress toward more disciplined software engineering processes. The purposes of the PAL prototyping effort are to develop a collection of examples of software process definitions, to evolve and refine PAL concepts, and to reduce risks in process asset development and PAL design. By providing tailorable examples of assets, the process asset library can facilitate the transition to more mature software engineering processes....
>
> The process asset general form includes three representation modes:
>
> 1. Process Model: semiformal graphical representation for modeling and analyzing process information
>
>   *primary use:* engineering of processes (e.g., organizing, designing, analyzing, tailoring, etc.)
>
> 2. Process Guide
>
>   a. documentation for process enactment by software engineers and other participants
>
>   b. combination of narrative, diagrams, and tables
>
>   *primary use:* manual enactment
>
> 3. Process Asset Template
>
>   a. standard template for process information: one per object or entity
>
>   b. structured textual information in standard format
>
>   *primary use:* repository of asset information; asset exchange (p. 52)

One way to provide flexibility within these three representation modes is to have a formalized activity name assigned to a standard activity, but usable across the modes. With formalized activity names, the use with automated tools is enhanced. Just a few examples of these formalized activity names from the software quality management process and V&V process of the IEEE Standard 1074 model from reference 15 (see Chapter 2) follow:

Model from IEEE Standard 1074

IEEE Standard 1074 Activity Names	STATEMATE Model Activity Names
Software Quality Management Process (3.3)	
3. Project Management Processes	PROJ_MGMT
3.3 Software Quality Management Process	SW_QUAL_MGMT
3.3.3 Plan Software Quality Management	PLAN_SW_QUAL_MGMT
3.3.4 Define Metrics	DEFINE_METRICS

3.3.5 Manage Software Quality	MNG_SW_QUAL
3.3.6 Identify Quality Improvement Needs	ID_QUAL_IMP_NDS
Verification and Validation Process (7.1)	
7. Integral Processes	INTEGRAL
7.1 Verification and Validation Process	V_AND_V
7.1.3 Plan Verification and Validation Tasks	PLAN_V_AND_V
7.1.4 Execute Verification and Validation Tasks	EXEC_V_AND_V
7.1.5 Collect and Analyze Metric Data	ANAL_METRIC_DATA
7.1.6 Plan Testing	PLAN_TESTING
7.1.7 Develop Test Requirements	DEV_TEST_RQMTS
7.1.8 Execute the Tests	EXEC_TESTS (p. 55)

Process Variability

There is recognition among managers that the software process is an important management aspect to be reviewed by V&V. When there is a need to discover how much variability in the software process is due to random variation and how much is due to unique events or individual actions, V&V should use control charts. A control chart is simply a run chart* with statistically determined Upper Control Limit (UCL) and Lower Control Limit (LCL) lines drawn on either side of the process average. This subsection is abstracted from *The Memory Jogger: A Pocket Guide of Tools for Continuous Improvement.*[16]

These limits are calculated by running the software process untouched, taking samples, and plugging the sample averages into the appropriate formula. Then plot the sample averages onto a chart to determine whether any of the points fall between or outside of the limits or form "unnatural" patterns. If either of these happen, the software process is said to be "out of control." This awareness of an "out of control" software process is of inestimable value to the V&V specialist, because it provides a picture of where to concentrate and how to make recommendations for corrective action(s) (p. 51).

The fluctuation of the points within the limits results from variation built into the software process. These result from common causes within the system (e.g., design, choice of computer, etc.) and can only be affected by changing that system. However, points outside of the limits come from a special cause (e.g., human errors, unplanned events, freak occurrences, etc.), that is not part of the way that the software process normally operates. These special causes require exposure by the V&V personnel for elimination before the control chart can again be used as a monitoring tool. Once this is done, the software process would be "in control" and samples can be taken at regular intervals by V&V specialists to make sure that the software process does not fundamentally change (pp. 51–52).

* This helps to determine whether the software process is in statistical control (see Chapter 5).

"Control" does not necessarily mean that the finished product meets the project's needs. It only means that the process is consistent, although it may be consistently bad.

The software process is said to be "out of control" if:

1. one or more points fall outside of the control limits; **or**
2. the control chart is divided into zones as follows:

	Upper Control Limit (UCL)
Zone A	
Zone B	
Zone C	Centerline/Average
Zone C	
Zone B	
Zone A	Lower Control Limit (LCL)

Changes should be examined by the V&V person, and the process owner(s) should be advised to make a process adjustment if there are:

- two points, out of three successive points, on the same side of the centerline in Zone A or beyond.
- four points, out of five successive points, on the same side of the centerline in Zone B or beyond.
- nine successive points on one side of the centerline.
- six consecutive points increasing or decreasing.
- fourteen points in a row alternating up and down.
- fifteen points in a row within Zone C (above and below centerline).

Summary

V&V planning must be inclusive of all aspects that are relevant for the modern software-intensive systems under development. Which V&V activity and product are suitable for which new application area is given in Table 13.1.

A modified CMM for V&V (i.e., testing) is provided in this chapter to sharpen the project management capability of the V&V team. Since scheduling is critical to project success, there is coverage of the challenges for V&V to overcome in scheduling. Some test management methods employed by Microsoft Corporation include much emphasis on post-mortems to pass on project lessons learned.

There are V&V activities listed by phase with a reminder that V&V is involved at phase completion with V&V audits of the project artifacts. Those artifacts become part of the process, and the chapter discusses how that process affects V&V and how to access the artifacts in a unique manner. A suggested method for V&V to control process variability is the control chart.

References

[1] Lewis, Robert O., *Independent Verification and Validation: A Life Cycle Engineering Process for Quality Software* (New York: John Wiley & Sons, Inc., 1992). Copyright © 1992 John Wiley & Sons, Inc., Adapted by permission of John Wiley & Sons, Inc.

[2] Deutsch, Michael S., *Software Verification and Validation: Realistic Project Approaches* (Englewood Cliffs, NJ: Prentice Hall Publishing Co., 1982).

[3] Easterbrook, Steve, "The Role of Independent V&V in Upstream Software Development Processes," *Proceedings of 2nd World Conference on Integrated Design and Process Technology*, 1996, NASA/WVU Software Research Lab, NASA IV&V Facility, 100 University Drive, Fairmont, WV 26554, URL: steve@atlantis.ivv.nasa.gov.

[4] Al-Rawas, Amer and Easterbrook, Steve, "Communication Problems In Requirements Engineering: A Field Study," *Proceedings of the First Westminster Conference on Professional Awareness in Software Engineering*, Royal Society, London, February 1–2, 1996.

[5] Wallace, Dolores R. and Fujii, Roger U., *Software Verification and Validation: Its Role in Computer Assurance and Its Relationship with Software Project Management Standards*, National Institute of Standards and Technology Special Publication 500-165, May, 1989.

[6] *EOSDIS Independent Verification And Validation (V&V) Management Plan* (Deliverable 0301), Prepared by AverStar, 6301 Ivy Lane, Suite 200, Greenbelt, Maryland 20770; Prepared For: NASA Goddard Space Flight Center, EOSDIS Project, Code 505, Greenbelt, Maryland 20770; 2 December 1994.

[7] FIPS PUB 101, *Guideline for Lifecycle Validation, Verification, and Testing of Computer Software*, Federal Processing Standards Information Publication, June 6, 1983, U.S. Department of Commerce, National Bureau of Standards (now NTIS).

[8] Pierce, Preston, *Software Verification & Validation,* 1997, RELA, Inc., 6175 Longbow Drive, Boulder, CO 90301.

[9] Myles, Jr., David T., "Project Management Systems Featuring Process Enactment," In *CrossTalk*, Software Technology Support Center, Ogden: Hill AFB, Vol. 8, No. 3, March 1995, pp. 17–28.

[10] Burnstein, Ilene & Suwannasart, Taratip & Carlson, C.R., "Developing a Testing Maturity Model, Parts 1 and 2," In *CrossTalk*, Software Technology Support Center, Ogden: Hill AFB, Vol. 9, No. 8 & 9, August & September 1996, pp. 21–24 & pp. 19–26.

[11] Sherman, Roger W., "Shipping the Right Products at the Right Time: A View of Development and Testing at Microsoft," In *CrossTalk*, Software Technology Support Center, Ogden: Hill AFB, Vol. 8, No. 10, October 1995, pp. 6–9.

[12] Wallace, Dolores R., Ippolito, Laura M. and Cuthill, Barbara, *Reference Information for the Software Verification and Validation Process*, NIST SP500-234, NIST, Gaithersburg, MD 20899, April, 1996.

[13] Kitchenham, Barbara and Linkman, Steve, "Validation, Verification, and Testing: Diversity Rules," *IEEE Software*, (© July/August 1998 IEEE), pp. 46–49.

[14] *Key Practices of the Capability Maturity Model for Software*, Version 1.1, SEI-93-TR-25; and *The Capability Maturity Model for Software*, Version 1.1, SEI-93-TR-24, Carnegie Mellon University, Software Engineering Institute, Carnegie Mellon University, Software Engineering Institute, 1993.

[15] *Process Asset Library (PAL) Prototype*, Carnegie Mellon University, Software Engineering Institute, February 25, 1993 developed for the Software Technology for Adaptable, Reliable Systems (STARS) Program, developed by a joint STARS/SEI team co-located at the SEI.

[16] *The Memory Jogger: A Pocket Guide of Tools for Continuous Improvement*, Reprinted with permission from *The Memory Jogger,*™ © 1988 GOAL/QPC, 13 Branch Street, Methuen, MA 01844.

[17] IEEE-STD-1012-1986, *IEEE Standard for Software Verification and Validation Plans* (New York: IEEE, 1986)

[18] Henley, Gordon and Dennison, John, *Independent System Verification And Validation Plan (ISVVP)* (Deliverable 0302), December 15, 1994, Prepared by AverStar, 6301 Ivy Lane, Suite 200, Greenbelt, MD 20770; Prepared For: NASA Goddard Space Flight Center, EOSDIS Project, Code 505, Greenbelt, MD 20770.

General Reference

Curtis, Bill, Krasner, Herb, and Iscoe, N., "A Field Study of the Software Design Process for Large Systems," *Communications of the ACM,* Vol. 31, No. 11, 1988.

Appendix

From IEEE-1012-1986 standard, *IEEE Standard for Software Verification and Validation Plans,*[17] follows an outline of a Software V&V Plan:

Purpose
Referenced Documents
Definitions
Verification and Validation Overview
- Organization
- Master Schedule
- Resources Summary
- Responsibilities
- Tools, techniques, and Methodologies

Life-Cycle Verification and Validation
- Management of V&V
- Concept Phase V&V
  1. Verification and validation tasks
  2. Methods and criteria
  3. Inputs and outputs
  4. Schedule
  5. Resources
  6. Risks and assumptions
  7. Roles and responsibilities
- Requirements Phase V&V
  - (1) through (7) same for each phase
- Design Phase V&V
  - (1) through (7) same for each phase
- Implementation Phase V&V
  - (1) through (7) same for each phase
- Test Phase V&V
  - (1) through (7) same for each phase
- Installation and Checkout V&V
  - (1) through (7) same for each phase

Operation and Maintenance V&V
(1) through (7) same for each phase
Software Verification and Validation Reporting
Required Reports
Optional Reports
Verification and Validation Administrative Procedures
Anomaly Reporting and Resolution
Task Iteration Policy
Deviation Policy
Control Procedures
Standards, Practices, and Conventions.

Following from the FIPS PUB 101, *Guideline for Lifecycle Validation, Verification, and Testing of Computer Software*[7] is a detailed outline of a project's V&V Plan:

I. Background and Introduction

Establishes the context for the V&V document. Is brief and introductory in nature. Focuses on those aspects of the problem and/or solution which influence the V&V needs and approach.

A. Statement of problem
B. Proposed solution
C. References/related documents

II. V&V Requirements and Measurement Criteria

Presents the V&V requirements in one of several formats: the total V&V requirements, with all worksheets and phase information; a summary of requirements information; statement of project level information, with phase data presented later.

A. V&V requirements and their importance
  1. Functional
  2. Performance
  3. Reliability
  4. Other
B. Measurement criteria for each requirement
  1. General
  2. Product-specific
  3. Phase-specific
C. References/related documents

III. Phase by Phase V&V Plans

First, describes V&V approach by phases, products, and practices common to all phases. Then, presents the outline phase by phase.

A. Project background and summary information
  1. Project phases and products
  2. Major reviews (both management and technical)

B. Requirements phase V&V activities
   1. V&V activities
   2. V&V techniques and tools selected
      a. Reviews
      b. Methods of analysis
   3. Required support tools, automated & other
   4. Roles and responsibilities
   5. Schedules
   6. Budgets
   7. Personnel
C. Design phase
   1 through 7 same for each phase
D. Programming and testing phase
   1 through 7 same for each phase
E. Installation phase
   1 through 7 same for each phase
F. Operations and maintenance phase
   1 through 7 same for each phase

Appendix A: Project and Environmental Considerations

A. Technical issues
B. Project constraints
C. Computing resources

Appendix B: Technique and Tool Selection Information

A. Candidate list of techniques and tools
B. Rationale for selection of techniques and tools (p. 20).

Another outline is provided, from the EOSDIS project for an Independent* System Verification and Validation Plan:[18]

1. Introduction and Scope
   1.1 Background
   1.2 Scope
   1.3 Overview

2. Life-cycle Phase-Independent V&V Activities
   2.1 Traceability Methodology
      2.1.1 Establish Requirements Hierarchy
      2.1.2 Populate Requirements Traceability Data Base
      2.1.3 Verify and Assess Phase Linkages

---

* Independent is removed from the outline presented to make the plan more generic.

2.2 Criticality Analysis and Risk Assessment (CARA)
  2.2.1 Definition of the CARA Context
  2.2.2 Conduct of a CARA
  2.2.3 Interpretation and Use of CARA Results
2.3 Issue/Discrepancy Handling
  2.3.1 Discrepancy Assessment and Analysis
  2.3.2 Discrepancy Tracking and Reporting
2.4 Documentation/Data Configuration Control
  2.4.1 Logging and Tracking
  2.4.2 Integrity Maintenance
  2.4.3 Distribution
  2.4.4 Configuration Status Accounting
2.5 Documentation Review
  2.5.1 Objectives
  2.5.2 Documentation Review Approach
2.6 Formal Review Support
  2.6.1 Objectives
  2.6.2 Formal Review Approach
  2.6.3 Pre-Review Activities
  2.6.4 Activities During Formal Reviews
  2.6.5 Post-Review Activities and V&V Products
2.7 Analytic Studies and Impact Analyses
  2.7.1 Objective/Approach/Schedule Planning
  2.7.2 Background Investigations/Preparations
  2.7.3 Conducting the Analysis
  2.7.4 Documenting
    2.7.4.1 Recommendations
    2.7.4.2 Output/Reports

3. Life-Cycle Phase-Dependent V&V

3.1 Concept Phase
  3.1.1 Concept Evaluation
  3.1.2 Limitations/Constraints
  3.1.3 Risk Categories
  3.1.4 Concept Assessment Report
3.2 Requirements Phase
  3.2.1 Activity Flow and Methodology
    3.2.1.1 Analyze Requirements
    3.2.1.2 Assess Requirements Allocation to Releases
    3.2.1.3 Identify Problem Requirements
    3.2.1.4 Assess/Track Requirements Evolution
    3.2.1.5 Assess Potential Impacts

- 3.2.2 Outputs
- 3.2.3 Requirements Analysis Guidelines

3.3 Design Phase
- 3.3.1 Key Interface Analysis Activities
  - 3.3.1.1 Analysis of Interface Structure
  - 3.3.1.2 Evaluation of Data Content, Completeness, and Expression
  - 3.3.1.3 Assess Consistency Across Interfaces
  - 3.3.1.4 Design Impacts
  - 3.3.1.5 Development Status
- 3.3.2 Design Integrity
  - 3.3.2.1 Inputs
  - 3.3.2.2 Assessing Design Functionality
  - 3.3.2.3 Assessing Design Expression
  - 3.3.2.4 Assessing Design Compliance
  - 3.3.2.5 Documentation

3.4 Implementation Phase
- 3.4.1 Analyze Code Structure
  - 3.4.1.1 Verify Consistency With Software Design Documents
  - 3.4.1.2 Verify Consistency With The Data Dictionary
  - 3.4.1.3 Verify Compliance To Standards and Practices
  - 3.4.1.4 Code Structure Analysis Results
- 3.4.2 Assess Code and Data Base Documentation
- 3.4.3 Analyze Data Bases
  - 3.4.3.1 Verify Consistency With Data Base Design
  - 3.4.3.2 Verify Compliance to Specified Coding Standards and Practices
  - 3.4.3.3 Data Base Analysis Results
- 3.4.4 Review and Assess Test Plans and Procedures
- 3.4.5 Monitor Test Conduct
- 3.4.6 Review and Assess Test Results

3.5 Testing Phase
- 3.5.1 Certification Approach and Methods
- 3.5.2 Certification Activities
- 3.5.3 Integration and Certification Plan

3.6 Installation and Checkout Phase
- 3.6.1 Pre-Installation Activities
  - 3.6.1.1 Installation Monitoring Team
  - 3.6.1.2 Coordination Meetings
  - 3.6.1.3 Release Package Review
  - 3.6.1.4 Documentation Reviews
  - 3.6.1.5 Assessment Reports

3.6.2 Installation Activities
3.6.2.1 Installation Monitoring Activities
3.6.2.2 Certification Activities
3.6.3 Post-Installation Activities
3.6.3.1 Post-Installation Debriefing
3.6.3.2 Follow-Up Activities
3.7 Operations and Maintenance
3.7.1 Introduction
3.7.1.1 Scope
3.7.1.2 Objectives
3.7.2 Discrepancy Reports
3.7.2.1 Analysis and Evaluation
3.7.2.2 Disposition and Tracking
3.7.3 Engineering Change Proposals
3.7.3.1 Analysis and Impact Evaluation
3.7.3.2 Development Monitoring
3.7.3.3 Testing Prior to Installation
3.7.4 Emergency/Unscheduled Releases
3.7.4.1 Background
3.7.4.2 Testing
3.7.4.3 Follow-Up Documentation and Formal Release
3.7.5 System Performance and Evaluation
3.7.5.1 Data Collection
3.7.5.2 Trend Analysis
3.7.5.3 Documentation Maintenance

4. Initial V&V Tasks

4.1 V&V Project Management
4.1.1 V&V Project Management Objectives
4.1.2 V&V Management Task Scope
4.1.3 V&V Management Task Approach
4.2 Business Operations
4.2.1 Key Activities
4.2.1.1 Program Tracking
4.2.1.2 Program Status Report
4.2.1.3 Office Infrastructure Administration
4.2.1.4 Library Services
4.2.1.5 Personnel Training
4.2.1.6 Office Policies and Procedures
4.2.2 Tool Requirements for Task Accomplishment
4.2.3 Tool Requirements for Business Operations

- 4.3 V&V Planning
  - 4.3.1 Task 3 Objective
  - 4.3.2 Task 3 Approach
    - 4.3.2.1 Subtask 3.1: V&V Management Plan Development
    - 4.3.2.2 Subtask 3.2: SVVP Development
  - 4.3.3 Task 3 Milestone Schedule
- 4.4 Infrastructure and Tools
  - 4.4.1 Development of the Task 4 V&V Infrastructure
    - 4.4.1.1 Requirements
  - 4.4.2 Definition of the V&V Integrated Support Environment
  - 4.4.3 Development of the Integrated Software Environment Infrastructure
  - 4.4.4 Milestone Completion Schedule
- 4.5 Requirements Analysis and Traceability
  - 4.5.1 Subtask Structure
    - 4.5.1.1 Subtask 5.1: Preliminary Requirements Analysis and Data Base Development
    - 4.5.1.2 Subtask 5.2: Interim Release 1 Requirements Analysis
    - 4.5.1.3 Subtask 5.3: User Satisfaction Assessment
    - 4.5.1.4 Subtask 5.4: Development Monitoring
  - 4.5.2 Milestone Completion Summary
- 4.6 Interim Release 1 Development Analysis
  - 4.6.1 Subtask Structure
    - 4.6.1.1 Subtask 6.1: Independent Release V&V Plan Development
    - 4.6.1.2 Subtask 6.2: Design Verification
    - 4.6.1.3 Subtask 6.3: Implementation Verification
    - 4.6.1.4 Subtask 6.4: Testing Verification
  - 4.6.2 Summary
- 4.7 Core System Release A Development Analysis
  - 4.7.1 Subtask Structure
    - 4.7.1.1 Subtask 7.1: Release A RVVP Development
    - 4.7.1.2 Subtask 7.2: Design Verification
    - 4.7.1.3 Subtask 7.3: Implementation Verification
    - 4.7.1.4 Subtask 7.4: Testing Verification
  - 4.7.2 Summary
- 4.8 Task 8 V&V Test
  - 4.8.1 Subtask Structure
    - 4.8.1.1 Subtask 8.1: Test Planning
    - 4.8.1.2 Subtask 8.2: Test Conduct
    - 4.8.1.3 Subtask 8.3: Test Results Analysis and Reporting
  - 4.8.2 Task 8 Milestone Completion Schedule

4.9 Key Interface Analysis
4.9.1 Subtask 9.1: Key Interface Analysis Methodology
4.9.1.1 Subtask 9.1 Analysis
4.9.2 Subtask 9.2: Analysis
4.9.3 Task 9 Milestone Completion Summary
4.10 Task 10 Development
4.10.1 Task 10 Objectives
4.10.2 Task 10 Subtask Structure
4.10.2.1 Subtask 10.1: Generation
4.10.2.2 Subtask 10.2: Approach for Developing Certification Criteria.
4.10.2.3 Subtask 10.3: Maintain Design Currency.
4.10.3 Task 10 Milestone Completion Schedule
4.11 Key Interface Testing
4.11.1 Key Interface Testing
4.11.2 Release A Interface Testing
4.11.3 Overview of Milestone Completion

5. Application To Early Releases

5.1 Release A Functional Thread Analysis and Definition
5.2 Release A Major Functions (pp. i–iv).

CHAPTER 14

Risk Management

Introduction

Basically, risk management is the essence of V&V. A customer hires an independent V&V company or a prime contractor establishes an internal V&V activity to reduce risks inherent in the development process. Also, it is a reasonable extension that risk management is an element flowing from the prior chapter on project management considerations for V&V.

Risk is the perceived extent of possible loss from an undesirable or unknown situation, where the likelihood of occurrence must be considered along with the potential adverse consequences. Risk assessment helps to identify the risks; risk analysis looks at the probability of the risk occurring and the consequences if it does occur; and risk handling or mitigation helps to reduce, control, or manage the risk.

In that situation where a customer deals with a software supplier and uses an independent V&V contractor, there is a real need for understanding roles. If risk containment is a paramount concern—whether with respect to safety, reliability, even schedule—the price of assurance may be worth it. However, Dunn and Ullman[1] (p. 210) remind us that under no circumstances is the use of independent V&V an acceptable substitute for confirming that the supplier has an effective software quality process in place. The essential difference between V&V and software quality is that software quality is an inherent part of the developer's team. So, then, what about the internal V&V situation? The fundamental difference between internal V&V and software quality is that software quality focuses on standards compliance and internal V&V focuses on requirements, documentation, and test review.

The tight focus on meeting business requirements affects how tests are prioritized. The overriding principle for prioritizing conventional testing (validation) is risk. Paul Herzlich[2] (p. 3) notes that if there are limited testing resources (as is always the case), the areas of highest risk should be tested. This is not always entirely appropriate. Rationing of test resource should be guided not by risk, but by benefit. In other words, if there are limited testing resources, be sure to test those areas of the system most responsible for delivering the business benefits that justify the system's development. Sometimes, the validation priorities arrived at by applying the risk and benefit principles will coincide, but not always.

The traditional method of risk management for V&V is the use of metrics to quantify the risks for discussion with management. This chapter discusses a modified goal—question—metric (GQM) paradigm for V&V risk management in the traditional V&V section.

In the Contemporary V&V section of this chapter the methodology defined by Averstar for Criticality Analysis and Risk Assessment (CARA) is discussed in some detail. The practical application of CARA on various Averstar projects has proved its value in risk management in the modern environment. The issue of product maturity in relation to risk management is transitioned into the discussion of the risk management elements in the Capability Maturity Model for Software, and its implication to V&V. A table of risk elements from Lewis is updated to address the new applications covered in this book. Specific emphasis is placed on the V&V risk management of knowledge-based systems (KBSs).

Multidimensional Model

Risk management as a subset of project management is a process area for V&V. As in the project management chapter, the process model from the Capability Maturity Model for Software has particular relevance to risk management. There are risk management activities from the CMM for Software that are discussed in this chapter.

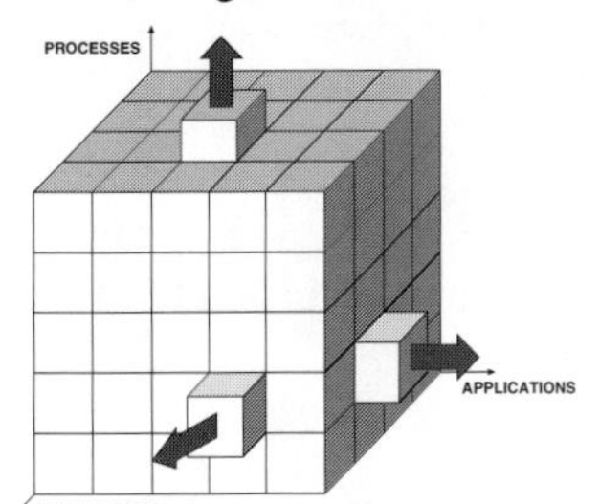

As with overall project management, the area of risk management has subtle differences for the application areas that this book covers. Those differences are highlighted in Table 14.5 later in this chapter. The V&V risks related to the Internet are much higher than an object oriented methodology, but client/server systems and knowledge-based system (KBSs) may be at the relatively same level of risk.

Technology that is pushing the state-of-the-art is going to have a significant impact on the risk of the project, so the multidimensional aspects of this risk area are particularly relevant.

Traditional V & V

Steve Easterbrook in "The Role of Independent V&V in Upstream Software Development Processes"[3] makes us think about the cost/benefit of V&V. He says:

> The main value of IV&V is the fresh perspective it offers on questions of software safety and correctness. Like a doctor providing a second opinion on a life-threatening diagnosis, IV&V provides a second opinion to counterbalance that of the developer. Questions about safety and risk then become a dialogue rather than a monologue. The cost of IV&V is typically a few percent of the entire development cost, while the benefit is a significantly reduced risk of loss of life, loss of a spacecraft, or loss of a mission. For example, IV&V for space shuttle software costs approximately $3.2 million per year. The cost of each mission is around $700 million, and the cost to replace a shuttle is estimated at $2 billion.... As well as reducing risk, IV&V

> has other benefits.... Errors are found earlier in the development process, and therefore are cheaper to fix. While this does not imply testing should be any less rigorous, savings can be made because the requirements specifications used to drive the testing process are clearer, and less effort may be needed for error-removal and re-testing. The delivered software should have fewer defects.
>
> There is strong pressure from within NASA to measure the effectiveness of IV&V, in order to ensure value for money from its contractors. Although the general benefits of IV&V are known, there is no generally accepted means of measuring the effectiveness of a specific IV&V contract. A small number of quantitative studies have been conducted over the last decade.... These have focused on the collection of metrics on the number and severity of problems identified, and have estimated the potential cost of delayed detection of these problems. Such studies appear to have established that, in general, IV&V pays for itself several times over because of early detection of problems. However, these studies were fraught with methodological difficulties, and the benefits clearly depend to a very great extent on how well IV&V is implemented. (p. 2)

Following is a measurement-based approach to calculating the risk inherent in meeting project goals. This approach leverages past project metrics and existing estimation and tracking models and is known as the V&V Goal–Questions–Metrics model (Figure 14.1). The following extensive discussion of it is abstracted from John Callahan, Tong Zhou, and Ralph Wood in *Software Risk Management Through Independent Verification and Validation:*[4]

> V&V* efforts are highly effective in early life-cycle phases if they can successfully predict the likelihood of problems based on an analysis of the current state of a project. It is difficult, however, to make such predictions with provable accuracy and show correlation between development activities and problems that arise in later life-cycle phases. Formal software development models can provide some insight based on quantified analysis of past software development efforts. While such formal models are imperfect guides to future efforts, they are far more likely to predict problems than informal methods.
>
> A V&V contractor helps identify, manage, and reduce the potential *risk of failures* to meet intended requirements in a software project at all phases of development. While some level of risk will always remain in a project,... risk can be reduced if errors and other discrepancies are found as early as possible in the software development life-cycle.

Figure 14.1 The Goal–Question–Metric (GQM) model.[4] (p. 1)

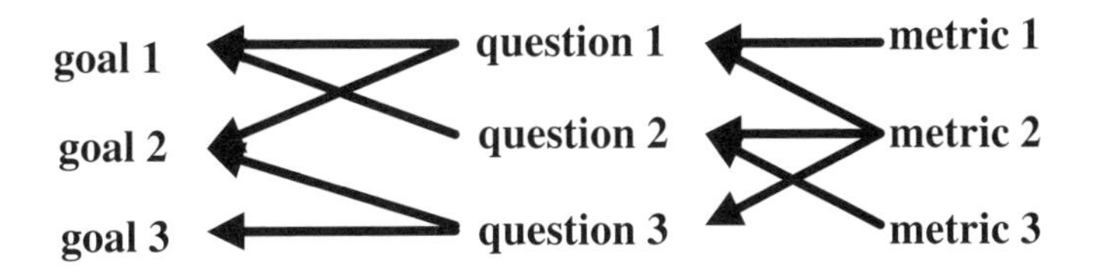

* For this abstraction "IV&V" has been replaced with "V&V."

The V&V Goal–Question–Metric method (VGQM+)[4] allows V&V* managers to monitor the level of risk in a software development project. Using VGQM, managers can use past projects as "yardsticks" against which to measure present projects. They can also assess the potential impact of their decisions about resource allocations, schedules, costs, and tradeoffs [during execution of the development effort].

The VGQM method provides *continuous* reporting of the status of a project in terms of what areas are at risk of failure. The method represents a formal interface between V&V, software development, and the customer. It summarizes the analysis work performed by V&V in terms of what project goals are at risk of failure and allows managers to make informed decisions about why problems are occurring.

Unlike other metric-based models, the VGQM method does not emphasize any specific set of metrics or functions for assessing risk. The model allows for use of other assessment models. The VGQM model is used to collect and summarize the metrics and relate them directly to project goals. Although [this] approach to V&V relies on metrics from past projects as baselines, the model can be "primed" with informal estimates or external project databases. Results from pilot projects are then used as feedback to provide continuous improvement to the model itself in order to improve predictive accuracy.

The VGQM model can incorporate several existing software estimation and tracking methods, such as the COCOMO method and Software Equation for estimating cost, size, and effort. Attempts to validate this approach use methods to reverse engineer past projects to determine if identifying risk sources early in the life-cycle could have helped prevent later problems.

The VGQM model is embedded in an automated support environment for software V&V that allows continuous analysis of a project's status. V&V is viewed as a complementary process to the software development process, and it is responsible for continuous assessment of the development process. As a software development process progresses, events are triggered in the V&V process. The V&V team must analyze changes in the development process and relate its findings to the customer in the form of an V&V report.... When a change occurs in the development process, the project measurements and risk are updated incrementally.... The risk impact of each change is assessed immediately relative to the project goals. (pp. 1–2)

VGQM Approach

A project must completely satisfy a set of goals to be implemented successfully. Goals include requirements but are much broader and can include ambiguous statements like "the system must be highly reliable." Each goal is satisfied by answering a set of related questions, which define the features needed to satisfy a particular goal.... Questions are answered true or false, but can be pararneterized with limits: for example, "Does the system have a 10,000 hour mean time between failures?" Each question is answered based on a set of quantifiable project metrics. A metric might be "lines of code" or "estimated mean time between failures" or any other discrete value. The GQM approach is used as a dialogue between customers and development organizations for agreeing on the details of a project. In this fash-

+ For this abstraction "IGQM" (Independent V&V Goal–Question–Metric) has been replaced with "VGQM."

* Passive voice replaces the personal pronoun throughout this abstract.

ion, it should be clear to the developer exactly what is expected of the final product and what the criteria are for its acceptance.

The GQM model to compute the risk of failure in a project has been augmented to satisfy the intended goals. The risk of failing to satisfy a *goal* is defined as the uncertainty of reaching that goal multiplied by the importance of that goal. Table 14.1 shows a list of goals, their importance, certainty, uncertainty, and risks for an example project. The goals G1, …, G4 might be

G1 Low cost

G2 Medium effort

G3 Use of prototyping

G4 High reliability

The questions related to each goal in the VGQM model will determine exactly what is meant by each goal. The risk values associated with each goal should change during the software development life-cycle. If we keep track of the risk at each step in the development process, we can identify high-risk goals and ensure that the overall risk is not increasing over time; that is, while risk may increase at any step, the overall risk trend is decreasing.

Risk Associated with Each Goal

To calculate the risk associated with each goal, the importance of the goal is specified explicitly by the manager, but its certainty is computed from answers to related questions in the GQM model. For each goal–questions group, a set of *certainty functions G* is employed at each step of the development life-cycle defined as

$$g_{i,\,tp} = G_{i,\,tp}\,(Q_{x,\,tq},\ Q_{y,\,tr},\ \ldots)$$

where $g_{i,\,tp} \in [0...1]$ for the *i*th goal at the process step t_p, and each $Q_{x,\,tn}$ is the probabilistic confidence answering question *x* as true at process step t_n. Thus, the certainty of satisfying each goal changes at each step in the software development process. The certainty functions may be based on the baselines of past projects or on the results of simulated models. In either case, the results of certainty functions are added to the baseline for use in future projects.

Table 14.1 Computing goal risks based on question confidence probabilities.[4] (p. 2)

Goals	Confidences				Certainty	Uncertainty	Importance+	Risk*
	Q1	Q2	Q3	Q4				
G1	1.00	0.36	0.77	0.00	0.45	0.55	0.80	0.440
G2	1.00	0.36	0.77	0.00	0.78	0.22	0.30	0.066
G3	1.00	0.36	0.77	0.00	1.00	0.00	0.90	0.00
G4	1.00	0.36	0.77	0.00	0.04	0.96	0.10	0.096

+ To calculate the risk associated with each goal, the importance of the goal is specified explicitly by the manager, but its certainty is computed from answers to related questions in the GQM model.

* The risk of failing to satisfy the goal is defined as the uncertainty of reaching that goal multiplied by the importance of that goal.

Confidence in Answers to Questions

Here is where existing estimation and tracking methods fit into the VGQM model. Each question can be answered true with a characteristic probability called its *confidence.* A false answer has a confidence value of zero. The confidence of answering a question is determined by a unique function based on collected project metrics. For each question–metrics group, a set of *confidence functions Q* is employed, defined as:

$$q_x,t_p = Qr,t_p(M_a,t_q,s_e,M_b,t_r,s_f,...)$$

where q_x,t_p [0 ... 1] for question x at the process step t_p where each M_a,t_q,s_e. is a metric a at step t_z provided by source s_e. [Table 14.2] shows a question and its related metrics from which a confidence function is defined. All metric values are the same relative to each question, but the confidence functions are *defined uniquely* for each question and process step. Metrics that are unknown at process steps can still be used because the lack of knowledge contributes to the risk calculation. Unknown measures decrease confidence in answering questions and in turn decreases the certainty of satisfying a goal. (pp. 2–3)

Predictive Functions

Callahan, Zhou, and Wood[4] continue:

The characteristic certainty and confidence functions associated with goals and questions can be based on many existing methods that have evolved from experiences on large numbers of actual projects. The VGQM model simply tries to relate the calculation of risk to the analysis these methods provide in order to help identify areas of a project that need attention and allow managers to trace problems to their sources.

For example, several methods exist for estimating the eventual number of source lines of code (SLOC) in a project. Early estimates of SLOC will be very inaccurate, but we can assess the probability of the correctness of our estimate. Consider the goal of "Small Program" in which the related questions are:

1. Are there less than 100 requirements?
2. Are there less than 50 function points?
3. Are there less than 50 modules?
4. Are there less than 10,000 SLOC?

In this example, Question 4 might be given the most weight in ultimately determining the acceptance criteria. However, in the early stages of a project, only Question 1 can be answered with a large degree of confidence, but the answer to this question will not have a large impact

Table 14.2 Computing question confidence probabilities need on project metrics.[4] (p. 2)

Questions	M1	M2	M3	M4	Confidences
Q1	34	11	88	99	1.00
Q2	34	11	88	99	0.36
Q3	34	11	88	99	0.77
Q4	34	11	88	99	0.00

on increasing the certainty of meeting the goal according to our weighting. [Figure 14.2] shows a risk profile for the different questions at this stage of development. The relatively higher slopes of the other questions illustrate a greater degree of uncertainty.

The weighting of each question confidence measure in determining goal certainty will change during the lifetime of the project; that is, the slopes will decrease and different measures will play larger roles. Eventually, confidence functions may get better with more experience and a broader database of actual projects. This will also decrease the uncertainty.

Estimating functions are highly domain-dependent. This is why it is important for each organization to institute measurement programs to improve the effectiveness of their predictions. The VGQM model can be primed with hand-picked estimates or those from external projects, but these initial estimates will be highly inaccurate. Only with time can an organization build confidence in their predictive models....

In the case of SLOC, the probability of the eventual number of lines of code exceeding the estimate can be determined. Likewise, many methods exist for cost, size, error, and effort estimation. Whereas many of these techniques are only used early in a project to construct a proposal

Figure 14.2 Confidence functions for estimated SLOC in early life-cycle phases.[4] (p. 3)

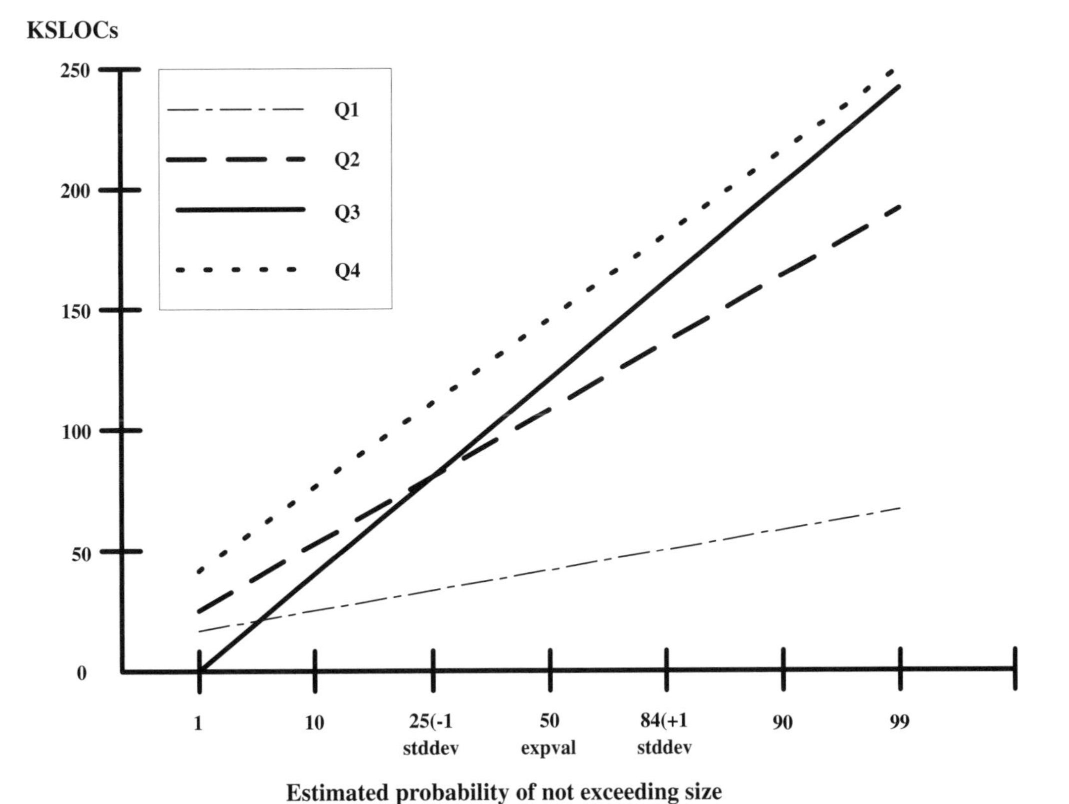

or plan, this VGQM approach allows managers to track actual measurements and compare them with estimates. As a project evolves, a manager can gain greater confidence in the estimates as they change dynamically based on actual performance.

In [Table 14.1], we can see that Goal G1 is the only goal with significant associated risk. If the confidence and certainty functions are based on methods that leverage past project data, the risk associated with Goal G1 at this process step might say something like "44% of the projects at this step with a similar goal questions profile failed to successfully satisfy this goal at time of delivery." The interpretation is based on the characteristic confidence and certainty functions related to each goal and question respectively.

Creating the certainty and confidence functions is not easy. They are based on profiles of past projects, contain coefficients that are specific to each environment or project, and must be primed initially with estimates or data from external projects. By mapping this approach to current software development and V&V practices, these estimates were "reverse" engineered from informal measures on past projects. Even though some information was not available on these projects, the information was adequate to provide working estimates. In one case, verification was made of the intuition of V&V personnel who noted problems with the delivery schedule of project milestones. In their expert opinion, the schedule was too short; and the VGQM model, based on existing methods such as COCOMO, confirmed that their intuition was correct.

Next is shown how V&V activities can be mapped to the VGQM model. Specifically, process management is related to testing to see how V&V activities contribute to project measurements and at what stages of the life-cycle. Based on this mapping, the relative effectiveness of these approaches in controlling software projects is assessed. Process management, for example, ensures that the software development team follows all process steps… and follows up on all discrepancy reports and anomalies. It monitors that the proper artifacts (i.e., documents and code) are produced on time and in their proper order. Testing, on the other hand, is usually associated with code level validation of the end-product system in a simulated environment. While it is widely believed that both of these approaches help reduce project risk, they have serious limitations in many projects, especially in large, complex systems with volatile requirements. It is possible that expensive and catastrophic errors may go undetected using traditional approaches. According to reverse-engineered projects, late life-cycle testing may find some errors but it is often too late to fix them. This fact shows up not as an increase in risk towards the end of the project, but as an inability of existing techniques to keep the risk trend from increasing and within nominal limits. Process management and testing alone are inadequate to manage risk in large, complex projects.

[Initially], a V&V team can check to make sure the software development process is followed at all steps. The goal of this task is to reduce risk by ensuring that a process is followed that increases the probability of success. The reasoning behind this task is informal: If a past task was successful using a process, then each step must be repeated to guarantee success in other projects.

The current software development practices may be cast into the VGQM risk model by asking specific questions about process steps accomplished. The metrics are Boolean values that help answer questions at each step regarding whether or not a procedure has been performed. In this fashion, the VGQM approach subsumes these current "checklist" methods and provides a metrics-based environment for formally validating whether or not generic assumptions about process effectiveness are true. Process tracking by the V&V team is necessary, but insufficient to ensure risk reduction in the development project.

Software testing has been a major focus of V&V efforts, but testing is expensive and has severe limitations. Traditional testing cannot find many problems or finds problems too late in the software development life-cycle where they are too costly to fix. In the VGQM model, the results of tests can be viewed as metrics (e.g., pass–fail). From this metrics-based perspective, early analysis of requirements and design can also be viewed as "tests," but the test results are viewed with less confidence than concrete tests at later stages of the development life-cycle. In addition, the tests can be directly associated with requirements or project goals in the VGQM model. In this case, the existence of a test is important for traceability. This approach was used to model traditional testing in the VGQM model and showed that late testing reduces risk, but that the risk trend is already too high at later phases for testing to have any significant effect.

Traditional testing does not permit early detection of problems, and it is often impossible to exercise a system with a battery of tests that completely characterize the operational environment. If major problems occur, it is often too late and expensive to fix them. As a result, the software might experience traumatic failure, the project is scrapped, it must be redone, or the customer is left dissatisfied with a partially functional system. If the customer had access to effective, predictive estimates earlier in the development process, expectations might be more realistic and the intentions better defined with the development team.

This VGQM approach depends on an intense metrics collection and archival capability to provide high levels of confidence in V&V predictions. It also depends on the continuous evolution of the predictive certainty and confidence functions. While the approach does not eliminate risk from a project, it does formalize the risk identification, management, and reduction. It makes risk management the explicit objective of the V&V process in order to deliver effective results to the customer. Moreover, the confidence of predictions can be increased as the baseline grows with each project. For [traditional] application domains, this approach will have most value based on extrapolating experiences with the VGQM model in practice. (pp. 3–5)

For contemporary application domains, such as those discussed in this book, the VGQM method may provide insight into V&V risk management when some initial data is extrapolated from existing applications and applied to these new application areas. Ultimately, results captured in the new application areas may be fed back into the VGQM model.

To provide the rigorous, disciplined methodology necessary to conduct V&V activities, it would be beneficial to formally document V&V standards and procedures. Such a documented approach to V&V, which has been developed and practiced by ADGA Group Consultants, Inc.,[5] is a top-down team approach that can be tailored to the particular requirements of a project. Of particular import to this chapter, the top-down approach focuses first on risk areas, then on technical evaluation and finally on documentation assessment. The team approach ensures that specialists skilled in the various functional and technical disciplines undertake the V&V tasks appropriate to their credentials. The output of each V&V task is a report which provides (a) an overall assessment of the product or process that was reviewed, (b) a statement as to how well it met the V&V criteria selected for the task, a description of risks and anomalies, and (c) a ranking of the criticality of these issues to the ultimate delivery of the system.

Contemporary V & V

Very often, criticality and risk go hand and hand. In these situations, the most critical functions many times represent the greatest development risk. Often, the most critical functions are implemented very late in the development cycle and consequently are poorly designed and tested. This software then produces a disproportional number of defects and requires extraordinary effort to refine it to the point where it is usable. V&V specialists should strive to do something to mitigate the risks as early as possible. The V&V analyst should record high risk items and critical functions as the specifications are being verified. But this initial discovery process is probably not focused enough to do a complete assessment, so there should be a separate review directed first at determining the high risk items, and second, at assessing their criticality.

It is helpful to understand that there are various classifications of risks. Of those numerous ways to classify risks, the following from Robert O. Lewis[6] highlights some of the major categories:

- *Management:* The challenge of directing, coordinating, and controlling the project efficiently and effectively.
- *Organization:* The risks associated with assembling the correct staff and structure to effectively run the program for the duration of the effort.
- *Facilities:* The ability to acquire or build the facility to properly match the needs of the system. Many times the facility has an important relationship with the software system (e.g., wind tunnel, a radar site, a power plant, or a factory)
- *Hardware development/availability:* The risks associated with concurrent development of special hardware to work in conjunction with the software (e.g., a missile, an automated plant process, or a toll collection system) and with the availability of sufficient prototype or production hardware to support software development and testing.
- *Software developments:* The numerous risks associated with software development—compilers, operating systems, tools, reusable components, algorithms, methodologies, environments, etc.
- *Technology:* Especially the risks associated with new technology, wherein the products or processes are being used for the first time, including high-energy lasers, neutral particle beam generators, new types of computer chips, space power systems, etc.
- *Schedule:* The risks associated with overly optimistic or erroneous scheduling, which can be impacted by virtually any other type of risk.
- *Other:* Risks peculiar to the type of system being considered. Understanding risks based upon lessons learned. (pp. 124–125)

Lewis[6] continues with two issues that form the essence of system criticality—risk and complexity:

> Risks are managed in part by a requirement-by-requirement determination of the adequacy of the automation decisions and of the software–hardware interfaces. Another part of the risk management is a judgmental evaluation of the type and degree of potential for described cat-

egories of failure contingencies. In some cases, a more formalized approach, such as the failure mode effects analysis approach, is necessary to provide additional depth to the quantification. Analysis of the effects that failures, including software errors, can have on the system often requires in-depth study. Thus, failure mode effects analysis and criticality assessments can work together to provide a good yardstick on how to get the best leverage from the V&V resources.

Complexity concerns primarily the cumulative nature of implementing multidisciplinary software requirements. That is to say, various software requirements may call for interfaces with many subsystems at the same time. There needs to be a measure to describe the degree to which a software requirement may impact the baseline system performance requirements if problems occur during program executions. That measure should reflect the concept that criticality is directly proportional to the number of connectivities to different subsystems, and that certain subsystem disciplines potentially affect the system performance more than do other disciplines.

Balancing these system-related criticality issues is a set of functional issues. These issues require analysis of the adequacy of pertinent aspects of single point control, system interlocks, error control, and man–machine interaction. Of special concern is the identification of those modules (hardware, firmware, or software) with real-time applications. In the software regime, real-time critical components are known to consist of system software (the operating system), applications software, and support software, which spans system and application software execution. (pp. 263–264)

Criticality analysis is defined and discussed by Dolores Wallace and Roger Fujii in the NIST publication, *Software Verification and Validation: Its Role in Computer Assurance and Its Relationship with Software Project Management Standards.*[7]

[It is] a method to locate and reduce high-risk problems and is performed at the beginning of a project. It identifies the functions and modules that are required to implement critical program functions or quality requirements (e.g., safety, security). The steps of criticality analysis are as follows:

- Develop a block diagram or control-flow diagram of the system and its software. Each block or control-flow box represents a system or software function (module).
- Trace each critical function or quality requirement through the block or control-flow diagram.
- Classify all traced software functions (modules) as critical either to the proper execution of critical software functions or to the quality requirements.
- Focus additional analysis on these traced software functions (modules).
- Repeat criticality analysis for each life-cycle phase to observe whether the implementation details shift the emphasis or the criticality.

The criticality analysis may be used… to identify V&V techniques to address high-risk concerns. The selection of V&V techniques to use on each critical area of the program is a method of tailoring the intensity of V&V against the type of risk present in each area of the software. For example, V&V would apply algorithm analysis to critical numerical software functions,

> and techniques such as timing analysis, data and control flow analysis, and interface analysis to real-time executive functions. (p. 9)

Criticality Analysis and Risk Assessment (CARA)

A formalized methodology for risk and criticality assessment and analysis has been devised by AverStar. The Criticality Analysis and Risk Assessment (CARA) methodology is abstracted from the referenced AverStar papers,[8, 9] as a major subsection to the Contemporary V&V section. Reference 8 defines:

> CARA is a systematic procedure for rank-ordering… program elements with respect to well-defined scoring factors associated with criticality areas and risk drivers of importance to a… project. It provides an arithmetical basis for formulating composite orderings of items with respect to multiple, possibly dissimilar rating factors. The results of a CARA are used to support decision making associated with establishing program directions, determining resource needs, and allocating resources. Because a CARA has an underlying mathematical formalism, it provides a degree of rigor not found in purely subjective decision-making paradigms. The CARA methodology can be applied to a variety of elements over the program life-cycle, including potential or actual problem areas, configuration items, functions, and applications/uses of the system. (p. 15)

The CARA process, according to reference 9, evolved from Air Force Software V&V acquisition management pamphlet 800-5, 1988, and CARA has been applied to various programs including:

- Space Shuttle Flight Software and Critical Mission Support Software
- GPS Integrated Life Cycle Support Facility
- Space Station Flight Software, and
- Earth Observing System Data and Information System (EOSDIS) covering the following domains:
  - manned space flight systems
  - command and control systems
  - high capacity and high-rate data systems
  - autonomous spacecraft
  - simulations
  - development and test facilities (p. 2).

The domains are related to the list of projects as a whole and not just EOSDIS. Additionally, CARA has also been applied to X-33 and the Checkout and Launch Control System.

Why Perform CARA?

It is not necessary or financially feasible to perform a full suite of V&V analyses on all software functions. Reference 9 continues, "CARA is a systematic method for evaluating the risk exposure for specific software functions. This risk exposure (or CARA score) is determined as the impact of a software error combined with the likelihood of occurrence. CARA results are integral to the process for V&V resource allocation, with higher scoring functions receiving enhanced levels of V&V analysis" (p. 1). CARA provides a framework for negotiating V&V plans with the customer:

- Enables V&V cost estimation and V&V scoping to a cost target
- Enables V&V breadth vs. depth tradeoffs
- Provides realism for V&V plans and personnel requirements
- Enables customer buy-in and visibility into overall project risk

Because CARA is an evaluation based upon criticality and risk, the CARA Score = (Criticality) $\times$ (Risk), where:

- Criticality (Figure 14.3) is a measure of the impact or undetected software errors on;
  - system performance and operations,
  - safety/security,
  - cost and schedule

- Risk (Figure 14.4) is a measure of the likelihood of errors based on:
  - complexity
  - maturity of technology
  - requirements definition and stability
  - testability
  - developer experience.[9] (pp. 1, 2)

Specific analysis activities for the CARA methodology are as follows: detailed design documentation, operational scenarios, requirements databases, and design repositories need to be analyzed to assess whether the design is traceable to requirements and is of high architectural quality (complete, accurate, implementable, scaleable). A detailed design analysis assessing the design in terms of requirements satisfaction, object class representation, and tool repository metrics will be performed for critical subsystems based on CARA results. A quantitative traceability analysis will be performed and documented for all subsystems verifying the existence of traces between the requirements and design elements. Software code and software development documentation (e.g., software development plans, project instructions, configuration management plans) should be analyzed for each release to assess whether the implementation is traceable to the design and is of high quality (i.e., components comply with standards, are internally consistent, do not implement unintended functionality, support desired user interaction, and do not adversely impact the expandability of the system). Results will be correlated with CARA results and previous design analysis findings, and will be used to focus V&V lifecycle activities.

Figure 14.3 CARA criticality values.[9] (p. 4)

CRITICALITY AREAS	**Catastrophic** Impact Value = 4	**Critical Moderate** Impact Value = 3	**Moderate** Impact Value = 2	**Low** Impact Value = 1
Performance and Operation	Failure could cause loss of use of system for extended time, loss of capability to perform all mission objectives. Failure is not ameliorated.	Failures could cause loss of critical function not resulting in loss of system use, lengthy maintenance downtime, or loss of multiple mission objectives. Failure is partially ameliorated.	Failure could cause loss of a single mission objective or reduction in operational capability. Failure is fully ameliorated.	Failure could cause inconvenience (e.g., rerun of programs, computer reset, manual intervention).
Safety	Failure could result in loss of life or system or cause severe personal injury	Failure could result in non disabling personal injury, serious occupational illness, or loss of emergency procedures.	Failure could result in minor injury.	No safety implications.
Development Cost/Schedule	Failure could result in cost overruns large enough to result in unachievable operational capability.	Failure could result in large cost and schedule overruns. Alternate means to implement function are not available.	Failure results in significant schedule delay. Alternate means to implement are available, but at reduced operational capability. Full operational capability delayed.	Failure results in minor impact to cost and schedule. Problems are easily corrected with insignificant impact to cost and schedule.

Figure 14.4 Sample risk driver criteria.[9] (pp. 5–6)

RISK DRIVERS	RISK CATEGORIES AND RATING CRITERIA
Complexity	**High Driver Value = 3** • Highly complex control/logic operations • Unique devices/complex interfaces • Many interrelated components • Function uses different sensor/effector set in different modes or stages. **Moderate Driver Value = 2** • Moderately complex control/logic • May be device dependent • Moderately complex interfaces • Several interrelated components • Function has different behavior in different modes or stages. • Simple control/logic • Not device dependent • Function applies to a single mode or stage
Maturity of Technology	**High Driver Value = 3** • New/unproved algorithms, languages & support environments • High probability for redesign • Little or no experience base **Moderate Driver Value = 2** • Proven on other systems with different application • Moderate experience base **Low Driver Value = 1** • Proven on other systems with same application • Mature experience
Requirements Definition & Stability	**High Driver Value = 3** • Rapidly changing, baselines not established • Many organizations required to define requirements • Much integration required • High degree of international interaction **Moderate Driver Value = 2** • Potential for some changes • Some integration required • Little interaction with international components **Low Driver Value = 1** • Solid requirements—little potential for change • Little to no integration required • No interaction with international components
Testability	**High Driver Value = 3** • Difficult to test • Requires much data analysis to determine acceptability of results • Many operational environments and inputs **Moderate Driver Value = 2** • Requires some test data analysis for acceptability of results • Moderate amount of operational environments and inputs **Low Driver Value = 1** • Acceptability of test results easily determined • Few operational environments and inputs

One of the initial steps in planning and allocating V&V resources to a release effort is to perform a CARA study. The outcome of the study allows the V&V team to assign priorities to the various release components to assure that the most critical areas receive adequate coverage.

A CARA will be performed for each release following the formal review associated with that release. Results of the release CARA need to be documented in the final version of a V&V plan.

Project risk can be reduced if errors and other discrepancies are found as early as possible in the software development life-cycle. Software project managers need tools to estimate and track project goals in a continuous fashion before, during, and after development of a system. In addition, they need an ability to compare the current project status with past project profiles to validate management intuition, identify problems, and then direct appropriate resources to the sources of problems.

Reference 8 continues,

> The general sequence of activities associated with performance of a CARA is given in [Figure 14.5]. Early activities establish the context (purpose and scope) of the particular CARA and, based on this context (which includes identification of the elements to be ranked), select the criticality areas and risk drivers for detailed evaluation. Risk drivers can include such considerations as complexity, maturity of technology base, requirements volatility (stability), testability, experience base, available resource base, suitability of tools/techniques, etc. Criticality areas include operations (mission/user), programmatics (cost/schedule), technical aspects, and safety. When setting up the CARA, each risk driver and criticality area is defined in terms of the rating criteria to be used (i.e., the guidelines for assigning a particular score). These definitions are project- and CARA context-specific and reflect program goals and objectives. Consideration is also given to other inputs, such as program documents. The next step is to have domain experts evaluate the program elements with respect to the rating factors (criticality areas and risk drivers) and record their evaluations in the scoring matrices. Scores are tabulated, a weighted composite is formed for each element being evaluated, and the results are averaged across all domain experts to produce the final CARA score. The program elements are then rank-ordered and sequenced according to the score received.
>
> [On a project], a CARA is performed as part of the V&V planning process and at other program milestones as needed. The results can be used in a number of ways to:
>
> - allocate a fixed set (given level) of resources across a set of objectives/tasks
> - assess the need for future resource requirements (i.e., to determine the V&V resources required for a certain level of coverage)
> - prioritize items for work sequencing (e.g., for determining the sequence in which a set of documents will be analyzed)
> - assess overall and relative risks (e.g., determine where to concentrate activities to maximize impact/payoff to the program)
> - establish importance levels (e.g., determine focal points/issues or establish priorities for where/what to concentrate on while engaged in V&V analyses). (p. 15)

Figure 14.5 Steps to perform CARA.[9] (pp. 3–8)

Step 1: Identify Software functions
- Collect a matrix and systems specification
- Build a matrix identifying the required software functions
- Identify system domains

Step 2: Establish Evaluation Team
- System Domain Experts
- Development Process Expert
- Management

Step 3: Develop CARA Evaluation Criteria
- If available, collect evaluation criteria from similar domains
- Develop an understanding of the mission the system is to perform
- Tailor criticality evaluation criteria in terms of what is catastrophic, critical, or of moderate impact to users, customers, and acquirers of the system
- Risk evaluation criteria is less tailored but may include additional risk drivers
- Identify Criticality Area or Risk Driver weightings if necessary
- Review criteria with the customer

Step 4: Perform Criticality Analysis and Risk Assessment
- Performed by Evaluation Team
- Perform Criticality Analysis
  - The Evaluation Team should be familiar with the system components and their interaction, failure modes and effects, and concepts of operation
  - Rate Functions according to evaluation criteria and record scoring rationale
- Perform Risk Assessment
  - Review software and system development, test, and verification plans
  - Review development plans—methods, testing approach, reuse plans, organizational interfaces, and external integration requirements
  - If available, collect program risks and risk mitigation techniques (modeling, prototyping, etc.)
  - Rate Functions according to evaluation criteria and record scoring rationale
- Calculate CARA scores

Step 5: Set V&V Analysis Level (VAL) Thresholds
- Functions with higher CARA scores receive higher VALs, in AverStar's taxonomy:

VAL	CARA Score
None:	1 < CARA < 2
Limited:	2 < CARA < 5
Focused:	5 < CARA < 8
Comprehensive:	8 < CARA < 12

- These thresholds and VALs prescribe appropriate V&V activities for the rated software functions
- VAL specific activities are summarized in Table 14.3

Step 6: Estimate software size
- Can be performed any time prior to Step 7 (Generate effort estimates)
- Size measurement is the V&V Work Point = f (number of requirements, external interfaces, output products)
- Alternatively, can use developer estimates for SLOCs

Step 7: Generate Effort Estimates with Independent V&V Effort Estimate
- V&V Productivity factors are defined for different VALs, software complexity, development types, (e.g., initial development, sustaining engineering, block updates, discrepancy analysis)
- Uses Project Schedule Data

Figure 14.5 continued

Step 8: Evaluate Effort Estimate Results

- Review results with the customer
- If prescribed VALs for software functions and associated costs are acceptable, generate the V&V Critical Functions List that defines the V&V scope
  - Each software function
  - Planned VAL

Step 9: Revise V&V Scope

- If results are not acceptable, use the independent V&V effort estimate to "re-scope" the effort
  - Breadth vs. depth tradeoffs—VAL Threshold adjustments
  - VAL selection exceptions, e.g., All Safety Criticality = 3 receives focused VAL

CARA Results

VAL thresholds based on the nominal figures in Step 5 (from Figure 14.5) on a specific project yielded approximately 140% of budgeted effort, so the VAL thresholds were adjusted to yield 100% of budgeted effort, as follows:

None:	$1 \leq \text{CARA} < 5.5$
Limited:	$5.5 \leq \text{CARA} < 7.5$, or if Safety Criticality score ≥ 3
Focused:	$7.5 \leq \text{CARA} < 10$
Comprehensive:	$10 \leq \text{CARA} \leq 12$

The reduction in effort estimates resulting from VAL threshold adjustments translate into different reductions in required skills. For example, the following skill requirements were reduced by the following amounts (where 100% = the original amount of personnel):

Skill	*Reduction*
Command and Data Handling	64%
Electrical Power Systems	76%
Environmental Control and Life Support	87%
Internal Thermal Control	71%
External Thermal Control	71%
Structures and Mechanics	98%
Guidance, Navigation, and Control	68%

Findings

The CARA process and implementation for deployed systems have had no software problems compromise mission objectives or safety. Also, no development cost over-runs resulted in the inability to deliver the operational capabilities needed to meet mission objectives. V&V problem

Table 14.3 V&V risk management activities VAL definitions for CARA Adapted from 9 (pp. 11–13)

None: 1 < CARA < 2
Limited: 2 < CARA < 5
Focused: 5 < CARA < 8
Comprehensive: 8 <= CARA <= 12

V&V ACTIVITIES INVESTIGATED FOR RISK	**L** LIMITED	**F** FOCUSED	**C** COMPREHENSIVE
Requirements Analysis Activities			
Verify documentation meets intended purpose, has appropriate detail and all necessary elements	x	x	x
Validate ability of requirements to meet system needs	x	x	x
Verify traceability to and from parent requirements	x	x	x
Analyze data/adaptation requirement	x	x	x
Analyze, Testability, Qualification requirements	x	x	x
Analyze Data Flow, Control Flow, moding and sequencing	x	x	x
Assess development metrics	x	x	x
Analyze development risks/mitigation plans	x	x	x
Analyze Timing and Sizing requirements	x	x	x
Review developer timing/sizing, loading engineering analysis		x	x
Perform engineering analysis of key algorithms		x	x
Review/use developer prototypes or dynamic models		x	x
Develop alternative static representations (diagrams, tables)		x	x
Develop prototypes or models		x	
Perform timing/sizing/loading analysis		x	
Apply formal methods		x	
Design Analysis Activities			
Verify documentation meets intended purpose, has appropriate detail and all necessary elements	x	x	x
Validate ability of design to meet system needs	x	x	x
Verify traceability to and from requirements	x	x	x
Analyze database design	x	x	x
Analyze design testability, qualification requirements	x	x	x
Analyze design data flow, control flow, moding, sequencing	x	x	x
Analyze control logic, error/exception handling design	x	x	x
Assess design development metrics	x	x	x
Analyze development risks/mitigation plans	x	x	x
Review developer timing/sizing, loading engineering analysis		x	x
Perform design analysis of select critical algorithms		x	x
Review/use developer prototypes or dynamic models		x	x
Develop alternative static representations (diagrams, tables)		x	x
Develop prototypes or models		x	
Perform timing/sizing/loading analysis		x	
Apply formal methods		x	
Code Analysis Activities			
Verify documentation meets intended purpose, has appropriate detail and all necessary elements	x	x	x
Verify traceability to and from design	x	x	x

Table 14.3 continued

	L	F	C
None: 1 < CARA < 2 Limited: 2 < CARA < 5 Focused: 5 < CARA < 8 Comprehensive: 8 <= CARA <= 12			
V&V ACTIVITIES INVESTIGATED FOR RISK	**LIMITED**	**FOCUSED**	**COMPREHENSIVE**
Verify architectural design compliance (structure, external I/O, and CSCI executive moding, sequencing and control)	x	x	x
Verify supportability and maintainability	x	x	x
Assess code static metrics	x	x	x
Verify CSU and CSC level logical structure and control flow	x	x	x
Verify internal data structures and data flow/usage	x	x	
Verify error and exception handling	x	x	
Verify code and external I/O data consistency	x	x	
Review code compilation results and syntax checking	x	x	
Verify correct adaptation data and ability to reconfigure		x	x
Verify correct operating system and run-time libraries	x	x	
For select algorithms, verify correctness and stability under full range or potential input conditions		x	
Verify code data compliance with data dictionary			x
Verify compliance with coding standards			x
Test Analysis Activities			
Analyze system-level verification requirements to verify that test definition, objectives, plans and acceptance criteria are sufficient to validate system requirements and operational needs associated with CCHR Functions	x	x	x
Perform life-cycle IV&V on test facility components including simulations, emulations, etc.	x	x	x
Verify Software Test Plan qualification testing methods and plans are sufficient to validate software requirements and operational needs	x	x	x
Verify test case: traceability and coverage of software requirements, operational needs, and capabilities	x	x	x
Verify software STD test case definition inputs, expected results, and evaluation criteria comply with STP plans and testing objectives	x	x	x
Analyze correct dispositioning of software test anomalies	x	x	x
Validate software test results compliance with test acceptance criteria	x	x	x
Verify trace and successful completion of all software test case objectives	x	x	x
Verify ability of software test environment plans and designs to meet software testing objectives	x	x	x
Verify regression tests are sufficient to determine that the software is not adversely affected by changes	x	x	x
Analyze STD procedures for test setup, execution, and data collection		x	x
Monitor execution or software testing	x	x	
Analyze select CSC test plans, procedures, and results to verify adequate logic path coverage, testing of full range of input conditions, error and exception handling, key algorithm stability, and performance in compliance with the design			x
Perform life cycle on software test environment components			x

report metrics (Table 14.4) indicate that critical problems do exist and are found in functions receiving enhanced levels of V&V analysis.

CARA establishes a structured approach to V&V by increasing customer visibility into overall program risk mitigation, and increases confidence in system integrity and reliability by answering the question "What are you going to do and why?"

CARA provides V&V project management with the capability to efficiently develop appropriate and realistic V&V plans. Criticality scoring criteria (more so than risk drivers) must be reviewed with the customer to understand what is important. The following points from reference 9 cover the recommended manner of CARA implementation:

- CARA scoring must be done by domain experts.
- CARA scoring must be done in a peer review environment.
- Project management should participate in scoring activities.
- CARA training should be done with *all* personnel present
- Automation and tools become more necessary for large projects and as the number of functions evaluated increases
- Capturing the scoring rationale is important, especially for large projects
- CARA should be repeated at least once every major development milestone
- Checklists for VAL are necessary to ensure implementation (p. 10)

Following completion of a CARA, reference 8 tells us that the results and attendant recommendations for actions and focusing of efforts is provided in report format, which contains the type of CARA performed, the factors and criteria employed in the review, and the resultant ordering of the items assessed. Recommended actions will include alternatives and priority indices to facilitate subsequent decision-making processes[8] (p. 24).

Table 14.4 V&V problem report metrics.[9] (p. 10)

VAL	Total Problems	Average Criticality	Criticality Impact			
			Catastrophic 4	Critical 3	Moderate 2	Low 1
Comprehensive	524	2.27	25 (5%)	179 (34%)	234 (45%)	86 (16%)
Focused	56	2.09	2 (4%)	17 (30%)	21 (38%)	16 (29%)
Limited	97	1.94	0	14 (14%)	63 (65%)	20 (21%)

V&V Product/Process Risk Maturity

John Nastro[10] tells us that a product maturity (see Chapter 2) may be measured from individual elements according to the following equation:

Product Maturity = PC * (PS + PR + PM)/3
where
PC = Product Capability
PS = Product Stability
PR = Product Repeatability
PM = Product Maintainability (p. 22)

Product capability is weighted more than the other elements because of its criticality. A product maturity measurement can also be used to track and compute technical risk. Useful risk models involve the probability of failure and the consequence of failure. Product maturity can be factored into both parts of the equation. As maturity increases, the probability and consequence of failure decrease. This example demonstrates how product maturity may be used in conjunction with a Level 2 SEI process maturity, specifically in the areas of project tracking and risk management (even to the extent of applying CARA). Similarly, process maturity may be used to calculate product maturity elements, such as the peer review and its impact on product maturity.

From a process maturity perspective, the Capability Maturity Model (CMM) for Software[11] addresses the areas of risk related to software in three key process areas: (a) Software Project Planning, (b) Software Project Tracking and Oversight, and (c) Integrated Software Management. The Software Project Planning key process area, Activity 13 states: "The software risks associated with the cost, resource, schedule, and technical aspects of the project are identified, assessed, and documented." The Software Project Tracking and Oversight key process area, Activity 10 states: "The software risks associated with cost, resource, schedule, and technical aspects of the project are tracked" (p. 2-30). The Integrated Software Management key process area, Activity 10 states: "The project's software risks are identified, assessed, documented, and managed according to a documented procedure" (p. 3-43).

The first two activities covered come from Level 2 of the CMM and are basic to risk management of systems or software. A more unique aspect is required in the Level 3 activity in Integrated Software Management, which is that risk management must be performed according to a documented procedure. The procedure may be project-specific, or it may be drawn from the standard process for risk management.

Risks and Contingencies

The *IEEE Standard for Software Verification and Validation Plans*[12] requires the identification of risks and the assumptions associated with the V&V tasks, including schedule, resources, or approach. Also, for each risk, a contingency plan (mitigation action) must be specified. To help identify V&V risks, there is an extensive list of potential risks throughout the project that is part of the CARA process. Table 14.5 borrows from that list, cross-referencing the new application areas discussed in this book. An indication of what potential risks are applicable to what new applications is provided by an **X**. Following the lead of the recommendations made in the *IEEE Standard for Software Verification and Validation Plans*, the V&V analyst should produce a contingency plan for all the items identified as risks.

Table 14.5 V&V risk management activities applied to new V&V applications.[Adapted from 6] (p. 11–13)

V&V ACTIVITIES INVESTIGATED FOR RISK	Object Oriented (OO) Methods	Rapid Application Dev. (RAD)	Usability (GUI I/F)	Client/Server Networks	Knowledge-Based Systems (KBS)	Internet /Intranet	DataWarehousing
Requirements Analysis Activities							
Verify documentation meets intended purpose, has appropriate detail and all necessary elements	x		x	x	x	x	x
Validate ability of requirements to meet system needs	x	x	x	x	x	x	x
Verify traceability to and from parent requirements	x	x	x	x	x	x	x
Analyze data/adaptation requirement							x
Analyze testability, qualification requirements	x	x	x	x	x	x	x
Analyze data flow, control flow, moding and sequencing	x	x	x	x	x	x	x
Assess development metrics	x			x	x	x	
Analyze development risks/mitigation plans	x	x	x	x	x	x	x
Analyze timing and sizing requirements	x	x	x	x	x	x	x
Review developer timing/sizing, loading engineering analysis	x	x	x	x	x	x	x
Perform engineering analysis of key algorithms	x		x	x	x	x	
Review/use developer prototypes or dynamic models	x		x	x	x	x	x
Develop alternative static representations (diagrams, tables)	x		x	x	x	x	x
Develop prototypes or models	x		x	x	x	x	x
Perform timing/sizing/loading analysis	x	x	x	x	x	x	x
Apply formal methods	x		x	x	x	x	
Design Analysis Activities							
Verify documentation meets intended purpose, has appropriate detail and all necessary elements	x		x	x	x	x	x
Validate ability of design to meet system needs	x	x	x	x	x	x	x
Verify traceability to and from requirements	x	x	x	x	x	x	x
Analyze database design						x	
Analyze design testability, qualification requirements	x	x	x	x	x	x	x
Analyze design data flow, control flow, moding, sequencing	x	x	x	x	x	x	x
Analyze control logic, error/exception handling design	x	x	x	x	x	x	x
Assess design development metrics	x			x	x	x	

Table 14.5 continued

V&V ACTIVITIES INVESTIGATED FOR RISK	Object Oriented (OO) Methods	Rapid Application Dev. (RAD)	Usability (GUI I/F)	Client/Server Networks	Knowledge-Based Systems (KBS)	Internet /Intranet	DataWarehousing
Analyze development risks/mitigation plans	x	x	x	x	x	x	x
Review developer timing/sizing, loading engineering analysis	x	x	x	x	x	x	x
Perform design analysis of select critical algorithms	x		x	x	x	x	
Review/use developer prototypes or dynamic models	x		x	x	x	x	x
Develop alternative static representations (diagrams, tables)	x		x	x	x	x	x
Develop prototypes or models	x		x	x	x	x	x
Perform timing/sizing/loading analysis	x	x	x	x	x	x	x
Apply formal methods	x		x	x	x	x	
Code Analysis Activities							
Verify documentation meets intended purpose, has appropriate detail and all necessary elements	x		x	x	x	x	x
Verify traceability to and from design	x	x	x	x	x	x	x
Verify architectural design compliance (structure, external I/O, and CSCI executive moding, sequencing and control)	x	x	x	x	x	x	x
Verify supportability and maintainability	x		x	x	x	x	x
Assess code static metrics	x			x	x	x	
Verify CSU and CSC level logical structure and control flow	x	x	x	x	x	x	x
Verify internal data structures and data now/usage							x
Verify error and exception handling	x		x	x	x	x	x
Verify code and external I/O data consistency	x	x	x	x	x	x	x
Review code compilation results and syntax checking	x		x	x	x	x	
Verify correct adaptation data and ability to reconfigure	x		x	x	x	x	x
Verify correct operating system and run time libraries	x	x	x	x	x	x	
For select algorithms, verify correctness and stability under full range or potential input conditions	x		x	x	x	x	
Verify code data compliance with data dictionary							x
Verify compliance with coding standards	x		x	x	x	x	
Test Analysis Activities							
Analyze system-level verification requirements to verify that test definition, objectives, plans and acceptance criteria are sufficient to validate system requirements and operational needs associated with CCHR functions	x	x	x	x	x	x	x
Perform life-cycle V&V on test facility components including simulations, emulations, etc.	x		x	x	x	x	x
Verify Software Test Plan qualification testing methods and plans are sufficient to validate software requirements and operational needs	x		x	x	x	x	x
Verify test cases traceability and coverage of software requirements, operational needs, and capabilities	x		x	x	x	x	x
Verify software STD test case definition inputs, expected results, and evaluation criteria comply with STP plans and testing objectives	x		x	x	x	x	x
Analyze correct dispositioning of software test anomalies	x		x	x	x	x	x
Validate software test results compliance with test	x		x	x	x	x	x

Table 14.5 continued

V&V ACTIVITIES INVESTIGATED FOR RISK	Object Oriented (OO) Methods	Rapid Application Dev. (RAD)	Usability (GUI I/F)	Client/Server Networks	Knowledge-Based Systems (KBS)	Internet /Intranet	DataWarehousing
acceptance criteria							
Verify trace and successful completion of all software test case objectives	x	x	x	x	x	x	x
Verify ability of software test environment plans and designs to meet software testing objectives	x		x	x	x	x	x
Verify regression tests are sufficient to determine that the software is not adversely affected by changes	x		x	x	x	x	x
Analyze STD procedures for test setup, execution, and data collection	x		x	x	x	x	x
Monitor execution of software testing	x		x	x	x	x	x
Analyze select CSC test plans, procedures, and results to verify adequate logic path coverage, testing of full range of input conditions, error and exception handling, key algorithm stability, and performance in compliance with the design	x		x	x	x	x	x
Perform life cycle on software test environment components	x		x	x	x	x	x

Expert System V&V

Before an expert system can be developed, the need has to be established, and the problem to be addressed must be clearly identified and defined. It is strongly recommended in the Federal Highway Administration's Handbook, *Verification, Validation, and Evaluation of Expert Systems,*[13] that:

> this be done in a structured manner to include the following issues:
>
> - The problem/need to be addressed and the system benefits
> - Organizational risk factors*
> - Technical risk factors
> - User risk factors
>
> Once a suitable problem domain has been defined for the expert system, the next task is to narrow the scope of the development effort by clearly defining the set of problems that the system will be expected to solve. The narrower the scope, the better the chances are that the expert system can be successfully built. Judgment must be used in establishing the scope of the system as deterministic methods are not available. In general, it is better to err on the side of too narrow a scope rather than too broad a scope. If the scope ultimately turns out to be too narrow, it may be relatively easy to

* The term risk factors is used in deference to the old adage "if it can go wrong, it will go wrong." The risk factors represent areas where it "will go wrong" if there is any deficiency in planning and common sense.

broaden the scope by adding more knowledge to the knowledge base. However, if the development tool is too limited, it will be impossible to broaden the scope of the expert system by expanding the knowledge base. This highlights the importance of selecting the proper development tool to fit the particular problem, [which is something the V&V specialist must keep in mind].

[An expected benefit of] developing an expert system will be to formalize and document the knowledge in a given problem domain, or combine and formalize the expertise from many experts in a given domain. This will result in expanded knowledge and better problem-solving techniques in the domain and will provide a mechanism for giving wide distribution of this knowledge to the users.

Under the heading of the problem/need to be addressed and system benefits, [a V&V specialist should ensure that] the following is accomplished:

- The application or the output and the use of the output is clearly defined.
- If standardization of results is desirable, the degree to which the expert system will improve standardization must be estimated.
- The use of the expert system to improve conditions by improving quality of results must be estimated.
- The expected utility of the expert system as a training tool must be described.
- End-user involvement for the duration of the development process must be assured.
- Time and money savings based on the projected use of the expert system must be estimated.

Under organizational risk factors, suggested requirements and considerations are:

- There must be a dedicated and influential advocate who wants the system to be a success.
- There must be management support for the financial support, staff, and time required to build the expert system.
- Management must have realistic expectations regarding the difficulty in developing the expert system.
- Management must have realistic expectations regarding the performance of the developed system.
- The results of the expert system must be applied without excessive management approvals being required.

Once a problem domain has been identified and the initial effort at narrowing the scope of the expert system application completed, the expert(s) whose expertise will be modeled must be selected. [V&V specialists should assure that the following] criteria be used to identify the expert(s):

1. The candidate(s) must be an expert in solving problems in the problem domain of interest and must be recognized as such by the potential user community. The need for the candidate to be an expert in the field is essential for the development of the expert system. The need for the expert to be recognized as such by the potential user community is primarily useful in selling the potential users on the viability of the given system as a useful problem solving tool for them.

2. The expert(s) must be dedicated to the successful development, testing, evaluation, and implementation of the system and be available and willing to spend the time (perhaps months) that will be required to accomplish this.

[The failure to identify such a person or persons and obtain a firm commitment means that the development project should not be undertaken.] Other useful characteristics for the domain expert(s) to have include the ability to communicate effectively, an orderly mind, patience, and the willingness to teach.

In evaluating technical risk factors, V&V analysts need to ensure that the following are included:

- There must be recognized experts in the field along with general agreement among these experts on the knowledge required to solve the problem the expert system is being developed to address.
- The development team must be identified and arrangements made to ensure their dedication to the development and follow-up processes. The availability and personal commitment of all team members must be assured.
- The availability of a manual or automated procedure to be used as a model for the development of the expert system should be considered.
- The required performance of the expert system must be defined (in terms of finding the best solution as compared to senior experts). Unrealistic expectations must be avoided.
- Ambiguity in specifications must be avoided, or if ambiguity does exist, the specifications must be modified to avoid it.
- The scope and range of problems to be addressed by the expert system must be clearly identified.
- Interaction with external programs to run algorithmic routines or for data entry, etc., must be identified.

User risk factors must be considered and resolved in the initial planning phases of the expert system development. If representative end users are not involved in the planning and development stages, the system probably will not be accepted by the user community. Issues [highlighted by the V&V expert should] include:

- The end users must want the system and have a vested interest in its success.
- The computer proficiency and other skills and interests of the end users must be accommodated.
- The environment or conditions under which the system will be operated must be accounted for. (pp. 9–11)

Summary

Risk management for V&V in this new era of software applications presents special challenges for the V&V specialists. This chapter presents the goal-question-metric paradigm as modified for use by V&V. It provides a level of confidence on the V&V choices for their focus of activities. These certainty and confidence functions applied to V&V require the coordination with existing basic V&V management concepts to achieve confidence in V&V activities.

The criticality and risk assessment (CARA) formal method is explained in some detail as the modern model for V&V as one that may be applied to new applications, as well as the old ones. CARA is a systematic method for evaluating the risk exposure (CARA score) for specific software functions, which is determined as the impact of a software error combined with the likelihood of occurrence. The sequence of 9 steps for CARA implementation are explained in this chapter.

V&V product and process maturity are viewed with emphasis on the risk elements and payoffs associated with proper handling. The CMM for software has some activities relevant to risk management which apply equally well to software and V&V. There is provided in this chapter, Table 14.5, as a cross reference of potential V&V risks versus the new application areas in this book. The table gives the reader focus for what V&V activities are required for which new application. Organizational, technical and user risks associated with the V&V of expert systems are covered.

References

1 Dunn, Robert H. and Ullman, Richard S., *TQM for Computer Software* (2nd edition) (New York: McGraw Hill Book Company, 1994), p. 210.

2 Herzlich, Paul, "A Quick Win for Testing," *SQM,* issue 25 [© 1995 Paul Herzlich, Web presentation © 1996 Tesseract Publishing, 11 March 1996, http://www.avnet.co.uk/tesseract/QiC/articles/Herzlich/25.html].

3 Easterbrook, Steve, "The Role Of Independent V&V In Upstream Software Development Processes," *Proceedings of 2nd World Conference on Integrated Design and Process Technology*, 1996. [NASA/WVU Software Research Lab, NASA IV&V Facility, 100 University Drive, Fairmont, WV 26554.

4 Callahan, John R.; Zhou, Tong C. and Wood, Ralph, "Software Risk Management Through Independent Verification and Validation," Department of Statistics & Computer Science, Concurrent Engineering Research Center, West Virginia University, 1994.

5 ADGA Group Consultants Inc., AEPOS Technologies Corp., 116 Albert Street, Suite 600, Ottawa, Ontario KIP 5G3, URL: http://www.adga.ca/ivv.htm.

6 Lewis, Robert O., *Independent Verification and Validation: A Life Cycle Engineering Process for Quality Software*, (New York: John Wiley & Sons, Inc., 1992). Copyright © 1992 John Wiley & Sons, Inc., Adapted by permission of John Wiley & Sons, Inc.

7 Wallace, Dolores R. and Fujii, Roger U., *Software Verification and Validation: Its Role in Computer Assurance and Its Relationship with Software Project Management Standards*, National Institute of Standards and Technology Special Publication 500-165, May, 1989.

8 *EOSDIS Independent Verification And Validation (V&V) Management Plan* (Deliverable 0301), Prepared By: AverStar, 6301 Ivy Lane, Suite 200, Greenbelt, Maryland 20770; Prepared For: NASA Goddard Space Flight Center, EOSDIS Project, Code 505, Greenbelt, Maryland 20770; December 2, 1994.

9 McCaugherty, Dan, *Criticality Analysis and Risk Assessment (CARA)*, AverStar, NASA/WVU IV&V Facility, 100 University Dr., Fairmont, WV 26554, (304) 367-8208, October 8, 1996.

10 Nastro, John, "A Software Product Maturity Model," In *CrossTalk*, Software Technology Support Center, Ogden: Hill AFB, Vol. 10, No. 8, August 1997, pp. 21–24.

11 *Key Practices of the Capability Maturity Model for Software*, Version 1.1, SEI-93-TR-25; and *The Capability Maturity Model for Software*, Version 1.1, SEI-93-TR-24, Carnegie Mellon University, Software Engineering Institute, Carnegie Mellon University, Software Engineering Institute, 1993.

12 IEEE-STD-1012-1986, *IEEE Standard for Software Verification and Validation Plans* (New York: IEEE, 1986).

13 Wentworth, James A., Knaus, Rodger, and Aougab, Hamid, *Verification, Validation, and Evaluation of Expert Systems: An FHWA Handbook,* Version 1.2—1st Edition (McLean, VA: Federal Highway Administration, January 1997).

CHAPTER 15

Integrated Product Teams (IPTs)

Introduction

When considering new approaches to development, the Integrated Product Team (IPT) (also known as Integrated Product Development Teams and Concurrent Engineering) introduces some interesting aspects. V&V activities can serve as a method of ensuring product quality and performance, and as a vehicle for improved synergism and communications on complex product development projects. In order to understand and utilize this interaction of V&V with IPTs, a discussion of the history and use of IPTs is provided.

In the past 25 years, the complexity of the products developed and delivered in the global marketplace has increased by an order of magnitude or more. In the military and space technology areas, the demand for the "one better" product to maintain the strategic advantage continued to up the ante in terms of requirements and performance. With the personal computer came the need to meet the insatiable appetite of the business world and more recently the home user.

Much of the burden of the increased complexity has fallen on software development for several reasons. First, although once reserved for military and space software applications, large (deliverable source code lines exceeding 100,000) software applications abound in the commercial marketplace today. Large software packages with short turnaround times to market forced increased numbers of software professionals to engage in the development of a single product. Second, the perceived flexibility (ease of change) to software drove functions previously provided by hardware to be implemented in software. Software complexity in terms of hardware–software interfaces and software–software interfaces as well as algorithm development led to increased software size and a need for enhanced communications. Third, with the ever-increasing throughput, storage, and bandwidth capabilities of the computer came the realization of integrated tool sets.

Given these increased requirements for products, the size of the development team* grew significantly since the productivity gains could not keep up with the demand. Development projects of

---

* From Katzenbach and Smith's *The Wisdom of Teams,*[1] the definition of a team is a small number of people with com-

40 to 50 people once thought to be very large became commonplace and project teams of 200 to 300 or more had to be dealt with. Traditional organizational methods left much to be desired in terms of communications and efficiency since the simplest of activities became a trial of the ability of the project to remain focused and consistent. Experiments such as the Chief Programmer Team came in vogue in the 1970s. The idea of establishing a small team led by an systems/software expert (such as a surgeon leads a team in surgery) had some success at IBM. However, it was not universally accepted, probably because of its dependence on a versatile (technical and managerial) expert.

In the late 1980s, the IPT entered the scene as a simple concept—divide the large project up and form small teams of individuals with *all* of the skills and knowledge required. Integrated product development concepts are not radically new and different. In many ways, these practices reflect the smaller, less formal organization of the past where people knew each other, communicated effectively between the various functional departments, and coordinated their activities with relatively little effort. However, since technology has advanced and become more complex, a return to that simplicity is not feasible. Integrated product development concepts represent a modern day approach to addressing the complexity and technology associated with today's new product development—in other words, what many companies had been doing for years in prototyping, research and development (R&D) and rapid application development—RAD (Chapter 7)—but in a more controlled and formal environment applied to large-scale integration.

The Institute for Defense Analyses[2] states that *concurrent engineering* is a systematic approach to the integrated, concurrent design of products and their related processes, including manufacture and support. This approach is intended to cause the developer, from the outset, to consider all elements of the product life-cycle from concept through disposal, including quality control, cost, scheduling, and user requirements. This is what IPTs do. They enhance communications of the total product requirements rather than compartmentalizing and "throwing the information over the wall." The emphasis on integrating the necessary disciplines has resulted in numerous studies and research groups, a plethora of articles and internet files. The Society of Concurrent Engineering (SOCE), whose prime mission is to disseminate knowledge and develop an understanding of concurrent engineering and integrated product development concepts and processes, is a prime example of such a research group.

This discussion on the structure of IPTs is derived from Kenneth Crow's "Building Effective Product Development Teams."[3] The structure of IPTs is not significantly different from the organization of projects. Generic IPT organizational structure (Figure 15.1) depicts the basic IPT organizational framework for the formation of project-specific IPTs. A program management team (program office) is formed that has the overall responsibility for the project development in terms of cost and schedule as well as ensuring that the product meets the requirements. The program office is the primary interface to the end-user (external customer). In the past, a systems design group had responsibility for the definition of the system in terms of allocation of requirements, sys-

---

plementary skills who are committed to a common purpose, performance goals, and approach for which they hold themselves mutually accountable.

Figure 15.1 Generic IPT organizational structure.

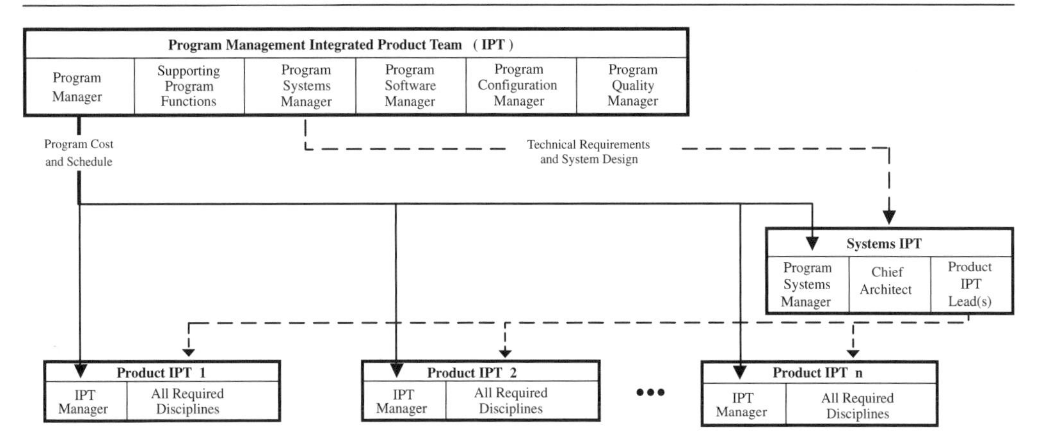

tem architecture definition and testing of the product at the system level against requirements. This is true for the IPT approach as well, except that the systems organization is an IPT of itself and has members from the supporting IPTs. At this point the similarities stop.

In the past, the development teams represented functional disciplines such as software, hardware, logistics, and manufacturing. This aspect of non-IPT approaches caused many of the problems as communications broke down in large project organizations. The early solutions were to hold interdisciplinary group meetings on a regular basis to exchange information and resolve issues. The limitations of these meetings were that:

1. The size of the meeting became unwieldy and the usefulness diminished.
2. Critical functional area concerns and events often caused attendance to be less than that needed for a fully productive meeting.
3. Program office commitment was required and often found difficult due to the demands of the customer.

The breakdown of the communications and coordination of the project disciplines led to multiple problems and tremendous amounts of rework. Design reviews, system documentation, detailed documentation, and other aspects of the system design were often found inconsistent despite requirements allocation and tracing since the details of interfaces and functionality were not available to all members of the project team.

As shown in Figure 15.1, product IPTs executing in conjunction with the systems IPT provide a viable solution to this problem. Product IPTs are formed that contain all of the project disciplines required to facilitate the design and implementation of the product required. Resources (including funding, facilities and personnel) are allocated to the product IPT, and the IPT assumes full responsibility for its success in terms of cost, schedule and performance. Cross-functional product development teams are a way to break down this organizational complexity and put together the necessary skills and resources to support more effective product and process development. By breaking the very large project down into multiple smaller projects, the ability to communicate and coordinate is greatly enhanced. This structure of itself does not solve the total problem—how do projects ensure that the constituent parts are consistent?

This aspect of the IPT organization is addressed through the participation of the product IPT leads (technical experts) on the systems IPT. Regular systems IPT meetings are held to provide inter-IPT communications and coordination. Similar to the interdisciplinary group meetings discussed in the traditional project approach, these meetings require the commitment of the total project team to succeed. In this case, however, the responsibility lies within the charter of the systems IPT to manage requirements and to ensure that the detailed design and interfaces are consistent.

A final introductory note on IPT structure and organization is that when a team is formed, it is extremely valuable to collocate the team into a project area. This physical proximity of the team members provides a number of benefits. It allows interpersonal relationships to develop more quickly leading to more effective and timely communication of information. This proximity provides a greater opportunity for feedback and discussion of the design requirements and design issues.

Multidimensional Model

The IPT is on the process axis of the multidimensional model. The IPT process has a significant effect on the applications dimension under development. It is also a subset of the project management dimension and has great impact on the risk management process dimension. Because it is a way of managing the project under development, it is used for the large projects for the reasons discussed throughout this chapter. For these large projects, IPTs have significant impact on helping to reduce risk. The ability to break up large problems into manageable pieces has been known for a long time to facilitate more competent handling of the problem. This is exactly what IPTs do for the large project.

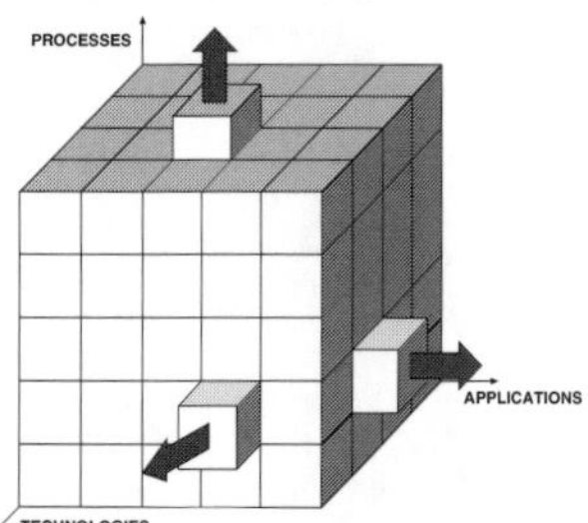

The technology dimension that includes items such as PCs, architectures, Internet/intranet, etc. only has an effect on the IPT process dimension to the extent that these technologies provide the underpinning of the large projects. An example of client/server networks that the authors are aware of exist in a government agency that connects over 8,000 workstations. To define and build that size network requires an IPT approach to make it manageable for the program manager.

An application dimension example involves a major data warehouse system. The IPT process may be implemented by breaking the project into subsystems that combine database, client/server, and Knowledge-Based System (KBS) personnel as IPT members. As usual with an IPT, these product IPTs need architectural leadership by a systems IPT.

V&V Aspects of IPTs

This section covers how to improve basic teamwork, so that the IPT can function most effectively. This is followed by examining how to establish an effective IPT specifically. Then, how IPTs operate on large projects is discussed, followed by specific V&V considerations in an IPT project environment. Most of this section deals with the multiple pieces that make up an effective IPT, that is presented analogous to constructing a picture puzzle, where each of the pieces represents a program element and how it fits together to produce an effective project utilizing IPTs.

Effective Teams

To start a project using IPTs, Watts Humphrey's[4] launch methodology based on the Team Software Process project launch, leads teams through the following steps:

- Review project objectives with management and agree on and document team goals.
- Establish team roles.
- Define the team's development process.
- Make a quality plan and set quality targets.
- Plan for the needed support facilities.
- Produce an overall development strategy.
- Make a development plan for the entire project.
- Make detailed plans for each developer for the next phase.
- Merge the individual plans into a team plan.
- Rebalance team workload to achieve a minimum overall schedule.
- Assess project risks and assign tracking responsibility for each key risk. (p. 15)

Once established, teams need guides to perform effectively and how to overcome barriers for proper performance as a team. Clear aims, assertive leadership, effective management processes, positive climate, appropriate structure, developed individuals, and effective teamwork are attributes that McGibbon[5] tells us help a team perform more effectively.

The commitment to using teams has gained a strong foothold in corporate management. The surveys and common barriers to teams that follows is extracted from "Improving Team Effectiveness:"[6]

> Organizations that find teams to be an effective way to get work done are facing new challenges: They have discovered that organizing, coaching, and aligning the efforts of many different teams requires new methods and systems.... Effective teams depend on a delicate balance of management, team, and individual commitments, plus a combination of knowledge, skills, and methods [such as listed above] that allow team members to accomplish their work. Experience has driven the development of various tools and methods that help organizations assess their strengths and weaknesses and identify ways to improve their use of teams.... As an organization assembles more and more teams, it becomes increasingly important that it assess its use of teams from a macro level. One way to do this is to have managers, team leaders, and the organization give feedback on key factors [an example of a rating questionnaire is shown in Figure 15.2]. (pp. 43–44)

One such major survey that included more than 40 teams identified major system-wide barriers to team progress, which management could then address. The major categories of barriers are shown in Figure 15.3. To further refine this, Table 15.1 captures the common barriers to team progress.

Figure 15.2 Team effectiveness questionnaire.[6] (p. 45)

	Not at all 1	2	3	4	Very much 5
Management actively supports and reviews the team.	☐	☐	☐	☐	☐
There is a management sponsor/champion who will secure needed resources and grease the wheels.	☐	☐	☐	☐	☐
Project scope or work function is manageable, not too large.	☐	☐	☐	☐	☐
Problem/work is important to organization's business success.	☐	☐	☐	☐	☐
The team has a clear mission.	☐	☐	☐	☐	☐
The team knows how to measure success.	☐	☐	☐	☐	☐
The team is not too large or too small (recommend four to six members).	☐	☐	☐	☐	☐
Team members have been trained in communication skills (listening, feedback).	☐	☐	☐	☐	☐
The team knows how to study and analyze processes (through data collection, creation of flowcharts, etc.)	☐	☐	☐	☐	☐
The organization's culture supports and rewards teamwork.	☐	☐	☐	☐	☐
There are mechanisms in place to maintain the gains made by the team (e.g., ongoing monitoring and reviews, documentation used for training, etc.)	☐	☐	☐	☐	☐
The team has methods for getting its work done (e.g., planning, improvement methods).	☐	☐	☐	☐	☐

Figure 15.3 One organization's barriers to team progress.[6] (p. 46)

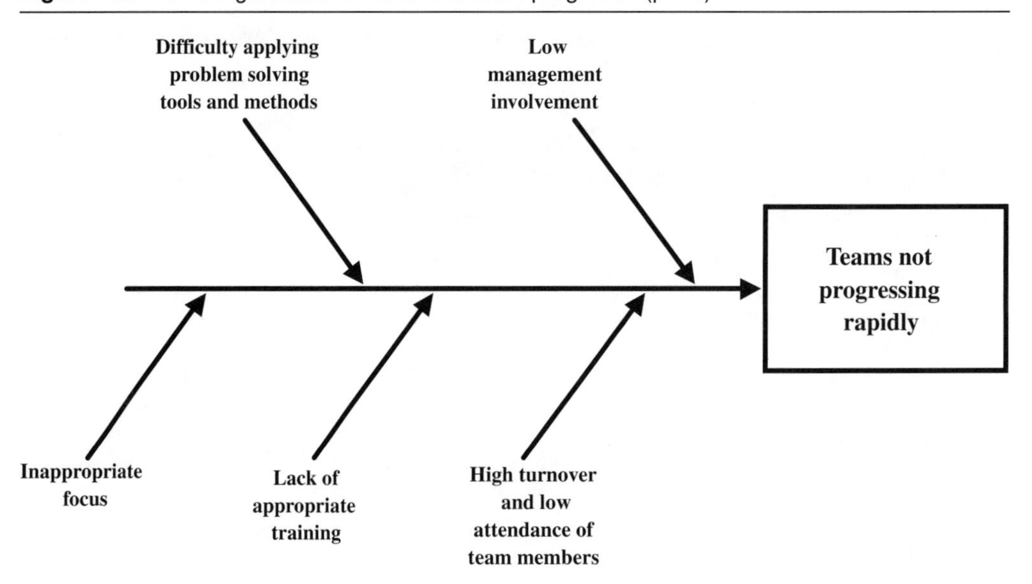

Table 15.1 Common barriers to team progress.[6] (p. 47)

Barrier / *Contributing factors*
Teams not supported by management
Organization lacks either commitment to team support and/or methods for making it happen.
Project scope too large
The team and organization are not clear on what is reasonable, or management is abdicating its responsibility to guide the team.
Project objectives not significant
Management has not defined what role teams will play in the organization.
No clear measures of success
Team is not clear about its charter and goals.
Team too large
Organization lacks methods for involving people in ways other than team membership.
No time to do improvement work
Values and benefits of the organization are incompatible with team's work.
Team not trained
Organization is not aware of which skills are needed to help teams operate more effectively or has not made training a priority.
Team not aligned within itself or with organization
The organization is not clear about its priorities for the team and how the team's charter supports its business goals and objectives.
Data not readily available
Management information systems are not adequate.

In summary, points have been provided from "Improving Team Effectiveness"[6] on how to successfully launch a team, how to run and maintain an effective team, and potential barriers to team effectiveness. By understanding these barriers, a team can better cope with the barriers, and in fact, can overcome the barriers. Now, why one should take the team approach as IPTs on projects is addressed.

Procedures from a major electronics corporation[7] state that program organizations are influenced by items such as:

- program dollar value
- complexity of program
- schedule
- organization's contract responsibility (prime, major subcontractor, lower tier subcontractor)
- deliverables
- specific program phase
- security requirements
- joint venture partners

Taking these program drivers into consideration could lead to the use of IPTs on a project. Many of the elements to force that decision are covered in the introduction. Once made, the procedures[7] relate that:

> IPTs provide a flexible organizational framework to make the right decisions while ensuring clear product responsibility, accountability and authority throughout the entire program life-cycle. The integrated product development philosophy systematically employs a teaming of disciplines to integrate processes to produce an effective and efficient product that satisfies the customer's requirements. The program manager, together with the program team, defines the roles and responsibilities of the program team members and develops integrated schedules that include performance objectives, spending allocation, and flowing-down requirements to the IPTs. [To operate most effectively], each IPT should be a member of the program team.... The IPT philosophy provides the framework to make effective and efficient common-sense decisions. The goal is to bring resources together, at the right time, to make integrated and timely decisions....
>
> The IPT is responsible for an integrated product evolution, which includes design and procurement, manufacturing, integration and test, delivery, post delivery support, and associated support functions (cost, schedule, configuration, etc.). (p. 1)

The procedures[7] continue with an IPT philosophy and the expected benefits from using IPTs on projects:

> The IPT philosophy embodies nine key tenets:
>
> 1. up-front planning
> 2. cultural change
> 3. product focus
> 4. right people, right place, right time
> 5. teamwork and communications
> 6. teamwork and recognition
> 7. empowerment
> 8. seamless management tools
> 9. integration throughout the life-cycle (p. 3)

Using these key tenets to support IPTs on a project, the procedures[7] say often results in the following significant benefits:

- reduced overall time to provide a product to the customer
- reduced product cost
- improved quality
- improved communication and decision making
- clear focus on risk. (p. 4)

Effective Teams

The information for this subsection is abstracted from two DoD documents: *DoD Guide to Integrated Product and Process Development*[8] and *Rules of the Road: A Guide For Leading Successful Integrated Product Teams*.[9] Each abstraction is appropriately referenced by footnote. IPTs operate under the following broad principles:

1. Open discussions with no secrets
2. Qualified, empowered team members
3. Consistent, success-oriented, proactive participation
4. Continuous "up-the-line" communications
5. Reasoned disagreement
6. Early identification and resolution of issues[9] (p. 4)

The ground rules for implementing IPTs are:

- *Open discussions with no secrets*—Cooperation is essential. Teams must have full and open discussions with no secrets. All facts must be on the table for each team member to understand and assess. Each member brings unique expertise to the team that needs to be recognized by all. Because of that expertise, each person's views are important in developing a successful program, and these views need to be heard. Full and open discussion does not mean that each view must be acted on by the team.
- *Qualified, empowered team members*—Empowerment is critical to making and keeping the agreements essential to effective IPTs. All representatives assigned to IPTs at all levels must be empowered by their leadership. They must be able to speak for their superiors, the "principals," in the decision-making process.
- *Consistent, success-oriented, proactive participation*—IPTs should be organized to allow all stakeholders to participate. There should be no attempt to limit membership.
- *Continuous, "up-the-line" communications*—IPT members are expected to ensure that their leadership is in agreement with what the IPT is doing. When issues arise that exceed the limits of empowerment, the project manager or IPT leader must allow members adequate time to coordinate issues and positions with their principals.
- *Reasoned disagreement*—The team is not searching for "lowest common denominator" consensus. There can be disagreement on how to approach a particular issue, but that disagreement must be reasoned disagreement based on an alternative plan of action rather than unyielding opposition.
- *Early identification and resolution of issues*—The agreements essential to IPT success will be founded on the early identification and resolution of issues. When an issue cannot be resolved by an IPT, the project manager should raise the issue as quickly as possible to a decision-making level where resolution can be achieved.[9] (pp. 9, 11)

Situations can develop throughout the process that can impede IPT implementation or its effective use, much like that discussed for the team in general. Like most barriers of this nature, careful planning and vigilance can identify these problems and mitigate them as they arise. A description from reference 8 for the V&V person on an IPT to recognize some of the more common barriers with suggested recommendations for solution follows:

Barrier

Recommendation

Lack of sustained top management commitment

Obtain a written commitment from senior management to the principles of IPTs and their application to the project at issue before embarking on this effort.

Cultural change required

Do not underestimate the forces of resistance to change. Spend what may seem like an inordinate effort on cultural change management.

Functional organization not fully integrated into the IPT process

With the implementation of IPTs, the role of the functional organization changes from controlling the work of the program to the care and development of the resources available to the team. These include people, information systems, libraries, models, education and training, public and financial recognition, and often operational processes and capital equipment.

Lack of planning

(1) Up-front planning that includes all functions, customers, and suppliers must be accomplished at the start of any team activity. This allows the program activities and work to be defined and the early identification and management of risk. (2) The integrated master plan must be consistent with the project/organization objectives and it must be constantly reevaluated and modified to meet current team needs and capabilities. (3) Resist temptation to take short cuts because it will cost more later.

Insufficient education/training

Include IPT education/training as an integral part of the comprehensive up-front planning. In order to optimize the effect of training, it should be done immediately before the particular skill is required.

Lessons learned and good practices not shared across programs

A formalized, documented process for exchanging information related to IPT implementation should be created and used.

Not invented here

The key concept that must be stressed is the idea of teamwork where all individuals are working together for a common goal.

Contractors promise more than they can deliver in implementing IPTs

It is important that the customer become familiar with successful IPT techniques/methods and what can realistically be done, perform a thorough technical evaluation of each proposal, and look closely at contractor past performance in IPT implementation.

Over-extended reviews

Setting a specific agenda for meetings and reviews should create a structure that allows for the discussion of issues. This structured agenda should not allow the discussion to be dominated by any one specific point. Time limits, however, should only be stressed by the meeting facilitator or chairperson when the discussion becomes repetitive, or a consensus cannot be reached.[8] (pp. 2-10–2-12)

The DoD Guide[8] continues:

The [IPT] approach to teaming differs from traditional program organizations, which usually focus on single-function disciplines. IPTs are responsible not only for designing the product and its associated processes, but also for planning, tracking, and managing their own work and the processes by which they do their work. Successful application of IPTs rests heavily on the ability to form, align, empower, and lead these cross-functional teams. By transitioning from the traditional use of mandated decisions to a style of leadership that operates through coaching and empowering, an open environment of rapid and honest communication and effective, timely decision making required by IPTs can be created....

IPTs can be applied at various levels ranging from the overall structure of an organization to informal groups functioning across existing units. IPTs can be formally chartered or natural working groups. Implementation of IPTs, therefore, does not mean that an organization needs to restructure. However, virtually all successful, sustained implementations in industry have eventually entailed reorganizations of organizations. These reorganizations are generally undertaken after IPT implementation has been initiated and experience has indicated a need to realign functions. The IPTs are created for the specific purpose of delivering a product and its processes or managing a process for the customer(s).

[The V&V person should be aware that] an IPT structure can be optimized for the product/customer requirements. The number of teams, functional disciplines, and full/part-time members required to support the product development may be different for every program. In addition, team membership, including team leadership, may change throughout the product development cycle. The core members of the team, who are generally assigned full-time, provide continuity from one development phase to another.

IPT members should have complementary skills and be committed to a common purpose, performance objectives, and approach for which they hold themselves mutually accountable. Members of an IPT represent technical, manufacturing, business, and support functions and organizations that are critical to developing, procuring, and supporting the product. Having these functions represented concurrently permits teams to consider more and broader alternatives quickly, and in a broader context, enables faster and better decisions. Once on a team, the role of an IPT member changes from that of a member of a particular functional organization, who focuses on a given discipline, to that of an IPT team member, who focuses on a product and its associated processes. Each individual should offer his or her expertise to the team as well as understand and respect the expertise available from other members of the team. Team members work together to achieve the team's objectives.

Critical to the formation of a successful IPT are:

1. All functional disciplines influencing the product throughout its lifetime should be represented on the team.

2. A clear understanding of the team's goals, responsibilities, and authority should be established among the business unit manager, program and functional managers, as well as the IPT.

3. ...Resource requirements such as staffing, funding, and facilities [need to be identified]. The above can be defined in a team charter which provides guidance. (pp. 1-7–1-9)

Some guidelines from the *DoD Rules of the Road*[9] for meeting management were presented above for the general team meeting; here the emphasis is on IPT meetings specifically:

> An IPT* must have a clear focus or reason for being. The IPT leader or project manager, as appropriate, must clearly articulate the IPT's focus at the outset of the process. Examples of a specific focus may be to prepare for a decision milestone, to develop and reach agreement on a proposed acquisition strategy, or to resolve a specific issue or set of issues.
>
> To ensure that all IPT members have a common understanding of the program, the project manager should provide a program overview briefing at the first meeting. Before the first IPT meeting, the project manager... and her staff will develop a proposed program strategy, documentation requirements and IPT structure.... The IPT members will discuss and agree to a meeting management approach, to include the following items.... To ensure productive meetings, detailed agendas with timelines for topics and supporting material must be distributed at least three business days before the IPT meeting—definitely not during the meeting. Every effort should be made to use electronic media for distribution. It may prove useful for the project manager and the IPT leader to jointly prepare the agenda to ensure that all concerns are addressed.... Once established, IPTs may meet as often as necessary to understand and build program strategies and to resolve issues or to produce a specified product. With that focus, the IPT will only meet for a particular purpose at a scheduled time. It should not meet regularly or continuously in an "update" or oversight role. Advance notice of an IPT meeting should be provided as soon as the date is known, but *at least* two weeks before the initial or kick-off meeting and *at least* three business days before a meeting of an ongoing IPT. Subsequent meetings should be scheduled in association with product completion dates and the resolution of action items from an earlier meeting.... Good [IPT] meeting summaries will be brief and will preclude revisiting previous agreements and wasting the time and resources of the team members. Meeting summaries should:
>
> - Record attendance
> - Document any decisions or agreements reached by the IPT
> - Document action items and suspenses
> - Set the agenda for the next meeting
> - Frame issues for higher-level resolution
>
> Draft meeting summaries should be provided to IPT members within one working day of a meeting. The final summary should be provided to all members within two working days after the deadline for the receipt of comments. (p. 12)

* IPT has been substituted throughout quote for xIPT, where x represents various descriptions.

The formalization and structure of IPTs may seem burdensome; however, V&V personnel who have actively participated on successful IPTs know that the burden has pay-offs. The expected benefits of IPTs from the *DoD Guide*[8] are:

1. reduced overall time to deliver an operational product
2. reduced system (product) cost
3. reduced risk
4. improved quality (pp. 1-10, 1-11).

IPTs for Large Projects

When considering the construction of IPTs in large-scale projects, two scenarios typically unfold: (a) the large-scale software development and (b) the large-scale product development. The differentiation here between software and product is that the product is not only software, but hardware, manufacturing, and support elements as well. This product development is used as the example since software is a subset of the product development, and IPTs for software may be formed within the product organizational structure. At the end of the overall discussion of the IPT operation, consideration of the need for a consistent, defined, and repeatable software process across the IPTs is discussed in the context of the Software Engineering Institute's (SEI) Capability Maturity Model (CMM).

One good example of a large-scale product development is a country-wide radar network and operations center. Numerous systems like this have been built over the past two decades to support domestic and foreign commercial aviation and military applications. The top-level system requirements include radar sites with associated data links and protocols, voice communications, operator consoles and displays, large screen situation displays, and the operations center data integration system. Systems of this type generally contain 500,000 to 1,000,000 lines of code or more, and the complexity of the systems is staggering. In order to address the scope of these systems, product IPTs are formed that generally align to physical entities. There are typically four fundamental product IPTs defined as follows:

1. Communications
2. Consoles and Displays
3. Radar Systems
4. Air Space Command and Control

These IPTs could be further subdivided into the following sub-IPTs formed based on the scope of effort:

1. Communications
   a. Voice Communications
   b. Data Communications

2. Consoles and Displays
   a. Operator Console Displays (Large Screen Displays)
   b. Command Center Displays (Very Large Screen Displays)
3. Radar Systems
   a. Radar Sensor System Type 1
   b. Radar Sensor System Type 2
4. Air Space Command and Control
   a. Man–Machine Interface
   b. Air Space Management
   c. Surveillance and Tracking
   d. Crosstell
   e. Operator Position Assignment
   f. Switchover and Failover Operations (Fault Tolerance)

Although many of these subprocesses and products are each fairly large, most approaches to these systems are only decomposed into the original four to keep the organization as horizontal as possible to reduce overhead. In either case, the application of IPTs and the associated effects on the V&V process are essentially the same. Typical membership in the product IPTs is:

1. Communications
   a. Systems (with specialists in communications protocols and human factors)
   b. Software Development
   c. Hardware Design
   d. Quality Assurance
   e. Configuration Management
   f. Test
   g. Manufacturing
2. Consoles and Displays
   a. Systems (with specialists in human factors/usability (Chapter 8))
   b. Software Development
   c. Hardware Design
   d. Quality Assurance
   e. Configuration Management
   f. Test
   g. Manufacturing
3. Radar Systems
   a. Systems (with specialists in data link protocols and algorithm development)
   b. Software Development
   c. Hardware Design
   d. Quality Assurance

   e. Configuration Management
   f. Test
   g. Manufacturing
4. Air Space Command and Control
   a. Systems (with specialists in crosstell protocols and human factors)
   b. Software Development
   c. Quality Assurance
   d. Configuration Management
   e. Test

The number of members in each IPT varies dependent on the scope of the effort. In general, each IPT has a QA and a CM function being performed at the product IPT level and another CM function being performed at the systems IPT level to control the configuration of the system builds, subcontractor deliverables, and total requirements. In some cases, the QA and CM resources are shared to reduce the overhead costs, when the total scope of the effort in each IPT does not warrant the application of full time personnel.

V&V Considerations in the IPT Environment

Several aspects of V&V are discussed prior to launching into how the pieces of the IPT puzzle connect together. Some points are for clarification, and others are to dispel some misconceptions of the roles and responsibilities of V&V.

First, a point of clarification that has been previously explained in this book, but often needs repeating to ensure appropriate emphasis: Verification and Validation are so often thought of as a single concept that one forgets that there is a conceptual difference between them. Both connote traceability to the problem being solved. Verification accomplishes this by assuring that the process of solution evolves step by step (although possibly iteratively); validation by providing direct traceability to customer requirements without concern of how the solution was derived.

Dunn and Ullman[10] tell us that V&V is not used exclusively in the sense of a team of inspectors coming in and passing judgment on the work, even though many companies like to use independent verifiers and validators. Rather, the processes of V&V that are referred to must lie either within or without the general process of software development. In that sense, peer reviews may accomplish many of the purposes of V&V. Customer involvement in prototype evaluation, test planning, and technical reviews is a form of verification. However performed, V&V can find early evidence to confirm that projects are on the right course to meet customer needs. V&V can range from documentation reviews to formal inspections to peer walkthroughs to test. The earlier V&V can occur, the higher the probability that the product will achieve its performance objectives within cost and schedule constraints (pp. 147–148).

Another point calls for clarification, which most would assume, but some forget: V&V must be planned, scheduled, staffed, and funded (Chapter 13). As the roles of the IPT members in the V&V process are discussed, allocating personnel time (integrating schedules and events) is a difficult task in order to achieve the most effective use of the IPT structure.

Next is a point that deviates from some traditional views of V&V. In the traditional view, as Roger Pressman[11] (p. 633) relates, V&V encompasses a wide array of QA activities that include formal technical reviews, quality and configuration audits, performance monitoring, simulation, feasibility study, documentation review, database review, algorithm analysis, development testing, qualification testing, and installation testing. The key deviation from tradition is the assignment of roles to QA, to other members of the IPT, and to other IPTs. QA personnel can perform the roles of reviewer and auditor, but the key added value of IPT V&V is that the other disciplines provide the critical review of the products under inspection. The key to quality products that meet cost, schedule, and performance objectives is not in the independence of the organization but in the capability of the reviewers to:

1. take ownership of the process and product
2. be directly impacted by the success or failure of the product
3. understand the technical aspects of the product so as to contribute to the design
4. effectively evaluate the consistency of the product to other products within the total program.

In an IPT structure, the participants of the reviews have technical knowledge and expertise not only to review for consistency, but also for technical correctness and adequacy; thus the power of the reviews is amplified several times.

The IPT Puzzle

Pieces of the program puzzle, shown in Figure 15.4, need to be coordinated to show the strength of IPT usage on projects. Each of the parts must be integrated to form a complete picture and vision of the product. The strengths of each part provide for a powerful and effective V&V operation within an IPT. The elements of the program puzzle are:

Figure 15.4 Pieces of the program puzzle to be coordinated.

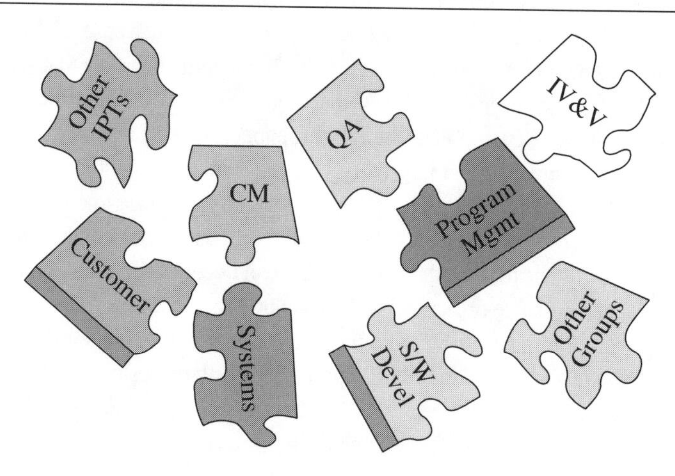

1. Customer
2. Systems
3. Software Development
4. Program Management
5. Quality Assurance (QA)
6. Configuration Management (CM)
7. Verification and Validation (V&V)
8. Other Groups (within an IPT)
9. Other IPTs

The Customer

The customer is the critical element of all successful projects. Customers may be internal (such as system test, field engineering, or logistics) or external (end-users or agents for the end-users). In this case, it is the external customer. It is highly desirable for the customer to be involved in the development process at each and every step of the development. This means participation as a member of the IPT and as participants in the internal inspections and reviews. Often customers employ IV&V (independent V&V) agents to represent the customer's interest where the customer lacks the technical expertise to appropriately and adequately assess the product development, quality, and performance. When IV&V agents are employed, then these agents should be a part of the development process from beginning to end.

Historically it has been shown that the total team approach that includes the customer results in the highest degree of success for the program. The strengths of such an approach include the following considerations:

1. An early understanding and agreement on the requirements is achieved, leading to stable requirements—a critical aspect of program management. The SEI CMM calls for such an understanding in the Requirements Management key process area as a Level 2 capability[12] (p. 126). For those unfamiliar with the key process areas and levels of the SEI CMM, Level 2 is the first level of software process beyond essentially uncontrolled development.
2. Customer buy-in to the results of each of the phases reduces the chance of rework and enhances customer satisfaction.
3. Incremental customer participation alleviates the need for formal, large-scale, event-driven reviews such as Preliminary Design Review (PDR) and Critical Design Review (CDR) in most cases. The most recent DoD and government standards (MIL-STD-498 and IEEE/EIA 12207 series) encourage incremental reviews with customer participation in lieu of formal reviews. As most individuals who have been involved in the formal review process already know, PDRs and CDRs have numerous drawbacks, such as (a) disrupting the normal development work flow to produce formal deliveries and presentations, (b) inundating reviewers with data that cannot reasonably be assimilated in the

timeline provided, and (c) becoming a "dog and pony show" instead of a communication and agreement on product performance and capability.

Unfortunately, customer participation in the development process is not without risk on the part of the developer. Customers who lack the sophistication to enter the process with an objective of total team success can bring the program to a grinding halt with constant confrontations and unnecessary alarms. Errors and misinterpretations are inevitable, but through early detection and removal, the probability of program success is maximized. Disruptive behavior (acting as an auditor instead of a team member) destroys the team process (see team barriers discussed above).

Therefore, in an IPT environment, the customer plays a key role in the verification process, while actively participating in the development process. With proper attitude and a total team attitude, the first and critical piece of the puzzle falls into place.

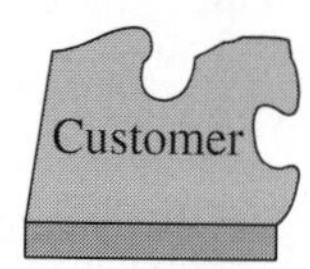

Systems

The systems IPT serves the critical role of focal point and coordinator for the system requirements allocation and system architecture across the product IPTs. In addition, the systems IPT is responsible for the system integration test planning and execution, wherein the systems IPT takes on the validation role for the project.

The systems IPT has the responsibility for system requirements allocation to the product IPTs and for the creation, maintenance, and communication of the system architecture and design. For most projects, the person responsible for requirements management (a requirements manager is recommended) resides within the systems IPT and reports to the systems manager. As mentioned above with the customer, the SEI CMM Requirements Management key process area defines a critical role in successful software development to be the requirements manager[12] (p. 126).

The systems IPT typically has responsibility for the systems integration and test on the project. As part of the requirements allocation process, the requirements are evaluated for testability. This evaluation includes clarity, feasibility of test, completeness, and understandability of the requirements. Such historically indefinite requirements as "user-friendly" and "rapid response" without the proper definition and understanding become issues later in the test process and during customer acceptance. This understanding is reached between the systems IPT and the customer (especially if the customer is a member of the IPT process) using the requirements manager, systems integration, and test team to facilitate the necessary understanding. The system test plan is formulated early in the system requirements analysis and allocation process. The system test plan defines the overall approach to the validation of the requirements by the project. This validation process may be independent of the customer validation (acceptance) or may be integrated with the customer V&V program. The latter approach is recommended, since time and effort are optimized with no reduction in product quality or performance.

In some project IPT structures, the V&V organization is a separate IPT that works closely with the systems IPT and the product IPTs. Such structures are generally specified by contract requirements for independence of the test organization. Generally, these "independent" test IPTs are not very efficient and the value added is difficult to measure, if there is any value at all. The major problem is that the V&V IPT must either have the systems knowledge (requirements and design) or must garner this knowledge from the systems IPT either by intensive training, mentoring, or participation in the systems requirements allocation and design process. In most of these cases, the difficulty is resolved by splintering off a group specifically for test that has the systems knowledge.

In the verification process, the systems IPT plays an active role in the review of the work products of the product IPT. In an IPT environment, the systems IPT plays the key role in the validation process and also contributes to the verification process by actively participating in the development process. With the systems IPT, the second piece of the puzzle falls into place.

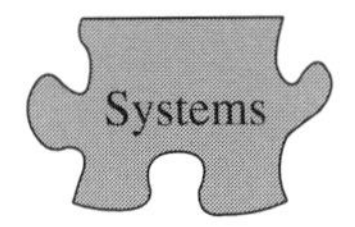

Software Development

In the modern world, software is the center of the universe. Once a support process to control complex hardware-intensive systems, software development now commands center stage. Software affects every aspect of our everyday lives from surfing the Net, to PC banking, to airline reservations, to operating our cars, to teaching our children, to operating and controlling sophisticated military systems. Software process controls and product quality are no longer concepts for military and space applications but rather are integral to the banking industry, PC computing systems, and manufacturing automation. Even the computer games industry has critical practices and controls that coordinate product teams, with each team focused on a particular aspect of the game's performance (such as graphics, sound, algorithms and user interface navigation).

Again, this discussion will focus on the large-scale project defined earlier. The software development effort is performed within the product IPT(s) as part of a tightly coupled organization focused on product performance and quality. Two serious issues must be addressed in this environment of separate product teams, each with its own software development activity and team. First, how is the software development process maintained consistent across IPTs such that the end product (system) is fully integrated, consistent, documented, and maintainable? Second, what is the optimal approach to V&V that maximizes return on investment, optimizes product quality, and ensures product performance to requirements?

Although some might argue that the road to software process was built of necessity to control a seemingly uncontrolled discipline (an art, not a science some would argue), software processes and controls are now perhaps the most mature and documented process in modern industry. In 1987, the SEI was founded to address software "catastrophes" in the military community. Product complexity was increasing, while productivity and quality of the products were decreasing. The CMM was created through the contributions of defense contractors, commercial industry, and the U.S. government to establish a framework for good, efficient, and practical software development practices. Built into this framework was a fundamental concept for V&V of software products through reviews and inspections. Also included in the SEI CMM is the need for Intergroup Coordination, which is the primary concept behind the formation of IPTs. Therefore, the implementation of IPTs is fully consistent with and supportive of the concepts and principals of the SEI CMM. To emphasize the importance and impact of the SEI CMM, since its inception and application into practice, numerous other CMMs have been or are being developed, including the Systems Engineering CMM, Software Acquisition CMM, and Integrated Product Development (IPD) CMM, which is directly applicable to the discussions herein.

Arthur Pyster[13] relates that the IPD CMM architecture is composed of three major areas: product life-cycle capability, process enabling, and integration enabling. The area of specific import to this discussion is integration enabling, because it contains the team maintenance base practices that describes how to establish and maintain an effective team:

- establish and maintain the team's charter that defines its responsibility and authority
- provide necessary skills and knowledge to the team to accomplish its goals
- document and maintain the team's operating procedures to achieve its responsibilities
- define and periodically update the roles and responsibilities of each team member
- establish and use methods for communicating and sharing data within the team.

So, for an integrated product development in an IPT environment, software V&V activities performed by the software developers include:

1. peer reviews and inspections
2. design reviews and technical interchange meetings
3. software development practices definition in a Software Development Plan (SDP)

The SDP describes methods and tools, checklists of requirements for work products, and standards for design and coding, as well as the methods for reviews, inspections, and interchange meetings. Most of the practices deal with the operation of the processes as a team activity with participation by members of IPTs. However, the application of checklists and standards is often performed by the actual software developer prior to the group review or inspection process as a self inspection. This self-inspection process applies the Japanese "poka-yoke"[14] concepts (p. 92). These concepts are espoused and a practical approach defined in the book *Zero Defect Software,*[15] which provides a framework for effective use of self- and successive inspections optimizing the effects of V&V activities (p. 133–146).

System V&V activities performed by the software group include:

1. analysis of requirements allocated to software by the systems IPT for adequacy, correctness, and understanding
2. participation in reviews and inspections of hardware designs (focused on interfaces to software)
3. participation in reviews and inspections of system architecture and design (focused on interfaces and functionality of the software)
4. participation in reviews and inspections of system "ility" considerations such as reliability, maintainability, safety, usability, etc.
5. participation in reviews and inspections of system integration and test plans and procedures
6. participation in reviews and inspections of formal acceptance test plans and procedures
7. participation in reviews and inspections of facilities and tools for use across the IPT and program.

The participation of software developers in the systems and hardware design and test activities enhances the developer's understanding of the total system product. It may certainly be said that good software developers are hard to find and harder to keep. But perhaps more importantly in today's complex systems, a good systems software developer is hard to develop and must be kept.

Software development is the third key element to be correctly located in the program puzzle as a total V&V approach to effective product development is formed.

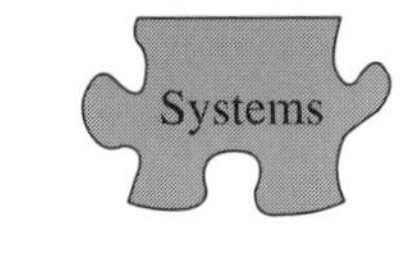

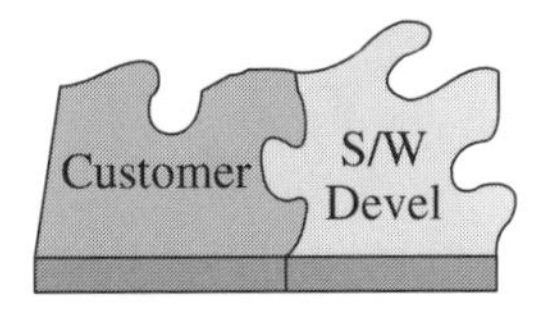

Quality Assurance

As touched on briefly in the introductory comments to IPTs, the role of QA deviates from some traditional views of V&V in effective IPT operations. Remember, from Pressman,[11] that V&V encompasses a wide array of QA activities.

QA operates in effective IPT implementations as a participating member contributing to the total value of the product. In practice to date, there is a fine line between the traditional role of QA in providing independent and objective assessment of products and the ability of the QA personnel to add value as a contributing member of the IPT. One recent occurrence at a major company caused quite an uproar, and the ramifications have not yet been resolved. In this case, a software quality person was participating in the IPT process and was essentially performing the role of auditor and independent assessor. However, since the process was so participative, the software quality person had failed to "write up" the discrepancies noted in reviews and inspections, but rather had made comments during the meetings. These comments were merely documented in the review meeting minutes with all of the other observations and hence, when it came time for formal audits, there were no findings by the software quality person to report. The auditing agency filed a "complaint" that the company was violating the contract requirements by having no findings; and that was not possible based on historical information. The question to be addressed is: How does a participating member that adds value also act as an objective and independent auditor?

The answer is quite simple and goes back to the discussion of customer roles in the IPT. Just as was the case with the customer playing a key role in the verification when applying a total team attitude, QA personnel must also be permitted to operate in that same environment. Clearly in a participative customer environment, there will be fewer action items and problem reports generated by the customer when issues are resolved as a team. But just as clearly, if an issue arises such that the customer and developer cannot agree then the issue is elevated and resolved in much the same fashion as past practices. Similarly, QA can operate in a participative process and still be empowered to act independently if the organizational structure of the IPT is properly formulated and implemented. The issue is more cultural than technical or organizational.

QA must continue to assess the quality of the products and can perform activities that are difficult for the developers to handle themselves. Consistency of terms and usage, flowdown and traceability, product and test readiness, tools certification, etc. are all activities that are best performed by a group that is not too close to the product. However, in an IPT structure, the staffing needs of the QA organization can be reduced dramatically by off-loading certain activities to the other members of the V&V process through reviews and inspections. The QA role in IPT programs is just as necessary as in traditional programs, but the role is now focused on added value and distributing the load to the most qualified personnel for the job. With QA comes the fourth piece of the program puzzle.

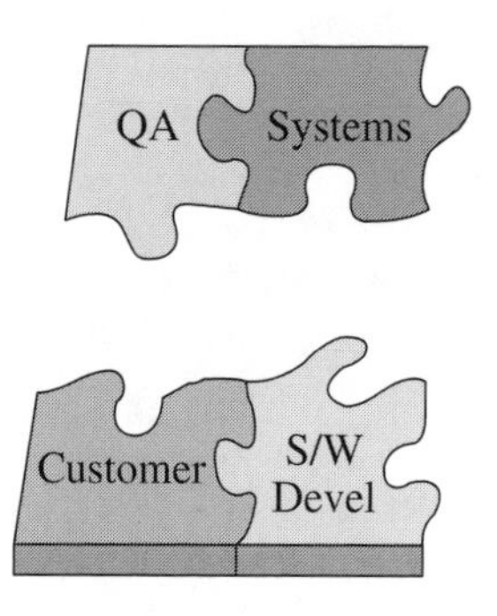

Program Management

The V&V puzzle now transitions from the high-profile elements that make the major contributions to the lower-profile elements that are necessary for the success of the V&V effort from a software standpoint. These organizations operate in more of a supporting role, making contributions to specific aspects of the product development. Program management's role in effective IPTs is primarily as a facilitator, mediator, and when absolutely required, final decision maker. In practice to date, program management has the overall responsibility for the cost, schedule, and performance of the system. However, the systems IPT performs the day-to-day systems functions of technical definition and allocation. Program management provides the funding resources and defines the schedules under which the systems IPT and product IPT must operate.

Program management operates as a facilitator and mediator by defining the IPT operations in terms of reporting responsibility, periodicity, and roles of inter-IPT meetings; coordination with the customer; and issue resolution when an impasse is reached. This operational concept for the program is typically defined in an IPT operations plan. From a V&V perspective, program management serves as the final decision maker in issue resolution, whether it be adequacy of test approach, adequacy of requirements definition, or test results assessment. In all of these cases, program management interfaces and obtains concurrence with the customer in order to assure that the process continues without significant risk of rework. Hence, program management's piece of the program puzzle is important to the V&V process, since without adequate resources and funding and an effective interface to the customer for issue resolution, the success of the V&V effort, as well as the program, is threatened.

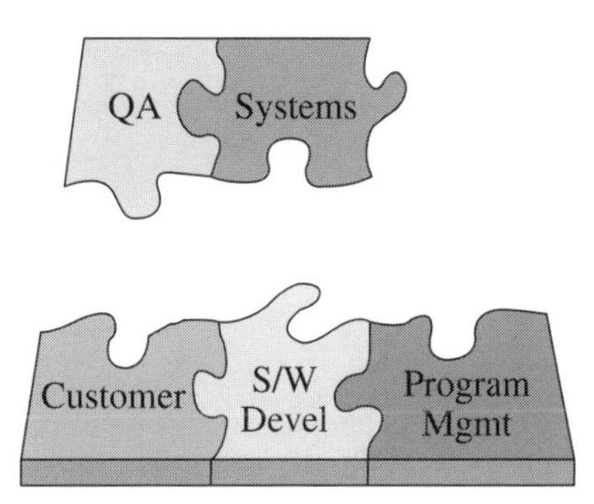

Other Groups

For this discussion, other groups are defined as other disciplines within a product IPT that make contributions to the total product. As discussed above, in a large-scale development program, the product IPTs may well be as large as some complete program teams. For product IPTs that encompass hardware and software, the IPT may consist of elements of systems, software, hardware, QA, CM, logistics, etc. Therefore, even when programs utilize IPTs, the interrelationship of product disciplines must be addressed. The concepts discussed here also apply to a single product program using IPTs.

With multidiscipline product IPTs, the contributions of the various disciplines to the V&V effort center around the work product inspections and reviews focused on interfaces and system performance. Hardware design groups support the systems design and requirements allocation process through inspection participation, providing key insight into design-to-cost trade studies and overall system effectiveness evaluations. Along with manufacturing operations, there are considerations of life-cycle costs, mean time to repair (MTTR), mean time between failures (MTBF), spares and logistics, and other considerations of the total life-cycle of the product. These support a total system approach to maximize system performance and customer satisfaction with the delivered product. Although in software-intensive systems the role of these other groups is greatly diminished, even there the role must exist at some level.

These other groups also utilize software and systems for their own inspections, and the cross training of personnel in the total system leads to increased productivity and improved verification processes that make the product integration and validation process smoother and more effective. Other functional disciplines within the IPT add yet another piece of the program puzzle.

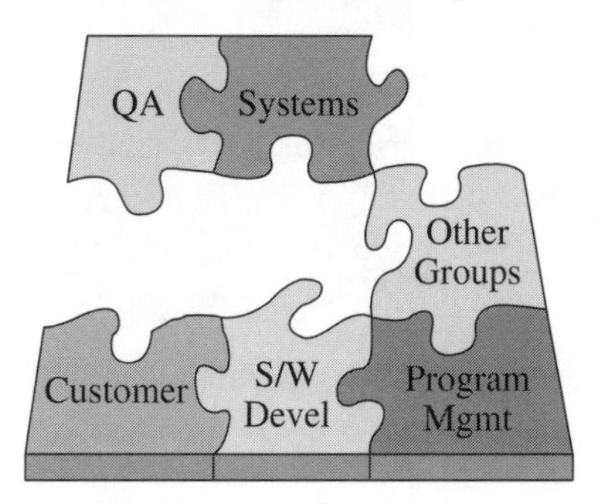

Other IPTs

Other IPTs make similar contributions to the total product as other groups within a product IPT. In a large-scale development program, multiple product IPTs are employed. Going back to the discussion of the multidimensional model and the Air Defense System example, the IPTs consist of software-intensive activities, such as the command and control functions, and hardware-intensive efforts, such as the communications systems. In order for the total system to operate as a cohesive product, participation of IPT members at other IPT reviews and inspections is critical to verify that the interface designs, timing models, ergonomics, facilities (power, weight cooling, etc.), and other aspects of the system that cross the product boundaries are coordinated and consistent. Planning for the integration and validation of the total system must also be coordinated and planned, with critical path analysis being performed and monitored by the program management IPT as well as the individual product IPTs. As stated previously, the systems IPT serves the critical coordination role across the IPTs for technical and performance issues and often is the V&V agent when an independent V&V team is not utilized. Other IPTs assist in the V&V process through participation in reviews and critical path analysis for integration of the total system product, thus supplying another piece of the program puzzle.

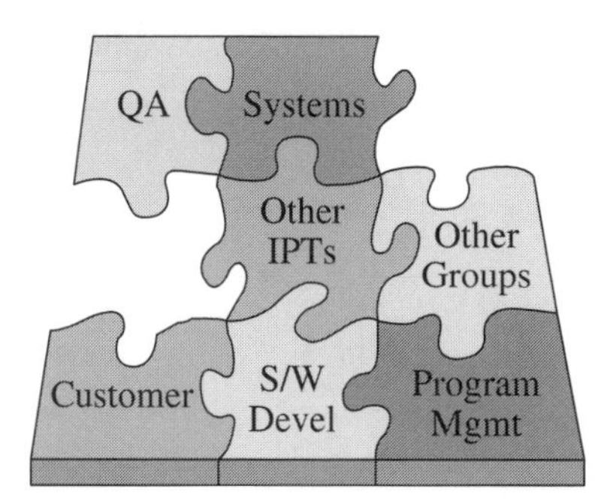

Configuration Management

Although addressed late in this discussion of IPTs and contributions to the V&V process in this environment, the role of configuration management (CM) is critical to the V&V process in a support role. The role in an IPT environment is not different than in the typical V&V program, but does potentially have some unique considerations in the case of the large-scale system.

Just as in the case of a traditional CM approach, the fundamental role of CM is to maintain control of the versions and configurations of the products as they progress through the development lifecycle. This is generally achieved through an automated CM tool that captures product baselines and protects information from unauthorized modification. This information is typically stored in a development library or vault structure, and once a product is baselined, that baseline is placed under configuration control. Configuration control is most often implemented by a Change Control Board (CCB) that reviews and approves all changes to configured work products.

There is no industry standard timeline for the initiation of configuration management of the work products. Dependent on the maturity of the organization and the use of the products in the verification process, controls may be imposed as early as the initial inspection or review of a work products or as late as the configuration identification for acceptance test.

One area where CM plays the lead role is in the preparation for final acceptance and delivery of the products. Military and government standards call for a Functional Configuration Audit (FCA), which checks that the requirements have been validated, and a Physical Configuration Audit (PCA), which ensures that the documentation matches the part. In commercial developments these audits are often referred to as First Article Inspection (FAI) and Performance Verification (PV). Regardless of the nomenclature applied, the fundamental objective of these audits is to perform the final V&V step prior to delivery of the product to the customer.

In an IPT environment, one unique application of CM may be noteworthy. In many cases, each product IPT has a self-contained CM organization to control and audit the IPT product, while there is also a system-level CM group that ensures that the total product is configured and controlled. The system-level organization is concerned with the system-level testing and verification to assure that the individual products are ready for test.

CM provides an essential piece of the program puzzle, although it is not as visible in the development process life-cycle. Without the CM function, V&V activities would be chaotic and probably could never be achieved.

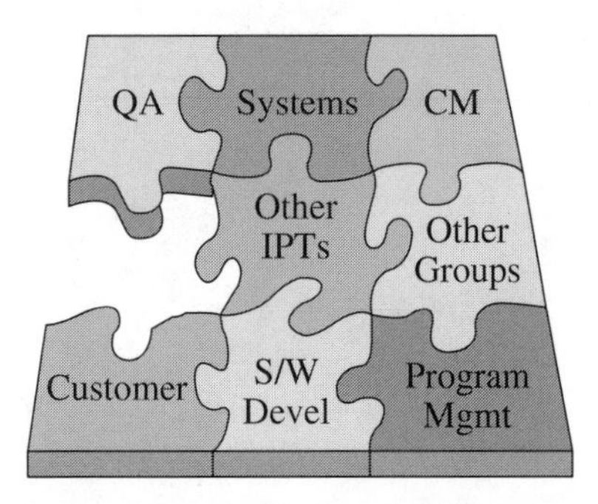

Independent Verification and Validation (IV&V)

It is now time to add the final program puzzle piece that completes the picture of V&V in an IPT implementation. Although truly an implementation strategy for V&V used by many customers to assure that the product delivered meets the requirements, IV&V can be implemented without outside intervention in an IPT environment.

For most programs, IV&V consists of a customer-provided independent agent. In traditional approaches, these agents are given information and perform independent verification and validation by executing a series of reviews and tests that have been created by the agents themselves. Often these agents are treated as outsiders and are provided little insight into the details of the development processes and internal work products. In a true IPT application, the IV&V agents are participating members of the IPTs and are provided information readily so that the process can be maximally effected. A certain risk is assumed by the developer. Clearly, the more information available, the more "errors" can be found. It is how the IV&V agent deals with the information that makes or breaks the process.

In a recent large-scale development program, the IV&V agents were afforded open access to all meetings within the IPTs. All internal reviews and inspections were open to these agents. The risk assumed was not trivial, but the value to be gained was of equal or greater proportion. In this particular case, the IV&V agents made several critical observations that improved the product design without raising the red flag when the information was presented. A solid working relationship was formed, and the end result was a superior product at lower cost.

Unfortunately, the same success cannot be said to be universal. In another program running at the same time, another group of IV&V agents were afforded the same access to information and meetings but chose to report all findings to higher management as a problem for immediate review and corrective action. This approach to participation quickly closed all lines of effective communications between the developer and the customer and resulted in schedule slips, poor customer relations, and cost overruns. As is typically the case when good practice fails, the issue is more cultural than technical or organizational.

There is another approach in the application of IPTs that defines an internal IV&V activity as a separate IPT. The IPT acts independently and reports directly to the program manager. The operation of the IV&V IPT mimics the activities of the IV&V agent approach but is far less threatening. The IV&V IPT often takes on the role of the integration test group and generates the plans and procedures for the system test and acceptance test. The IV&V IPT participates from the program's onset as a participating member of the product and systems IPTs and uses the information and knowledge from this participation to formulate the test plans and procedures. This approach to independent V&V has been very successfully applied throughout industry.

And so the final piece of the program puzzle falls into place. V&V applied to the IPT approach to product development utilizes all of the development disciplines to enhance and improve the product as well as to verify its performance and validate that it meets the requirements.

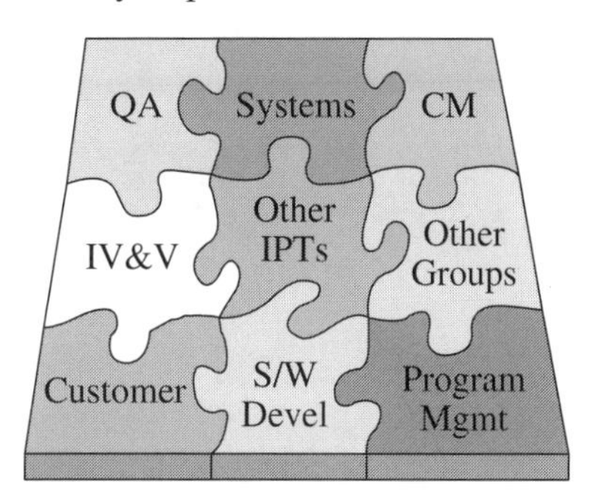

Summary

The use of IPTs can greatly enhance the V&V activities through the contributions of a more knowledgeable staff of personnel with a broader range of experience. In addition, the cross-training of project personnel provides for a more flexible staff that can operate more effectively. Each contributing organization plays a role in the total product performance and quality. Several aspects of V&V have been discussed.

First, verification assures that the development process evolves step by step according to the development plans, while validation provides direct traceability to customer requirements without concern of how the solution was derived. V&V is not used exclusively in the sense of a team of inspectors coming in and passing judgment on the work, even though many companies like to use independent verifiers and validators. Rather, the processes of V&V must lie within the general process of software development. In that sense, peer reviews (inspections) accomplish many of the purposes of V&V. Customer involvement in prototype evaluation, test planning, and technical reviews is a form of verification.

Second, V&V must be planned, scheduled, staffed, and funded (Chapter 13). As the roles of the IPT members in the V&V process are defined, allocating personnel time (integrating schedules and events) is a difficult task in order to achieve the most effective use of the IPT structure.

Third, V&V in modern IPT environments deviates from some traditional views of V&V. In the traditional view, V&V encompasses a wide array of QA activities. In an IPT, the key deviation from tradition is the assignment of roles to QA, other members of the IPT, and other IPTs. QA can perform the roles of reviewer and auditor, but the key added value of IPT V&V is that the other disciplines provide the critical review of the products under inspection. The key to quality products that meet cost, schedule, and performance objectives is not in the independence of the organization but in the capability of the reviewers to:

1. take ownership of the process and product
2. be directly impacted by the success or failure of the product
3. understand the technical aspects of the product such as to contribute to the design
4. effectively evaluate the consistency of the product to other products within the total program.

IPTs address the need to establish simpler communication patterns within the software development project. The key features that Michael Deutsch[16] notes that distinguish IPT practices from the individual effort are:

- continuous V&V
- simpler communication paths
- limited number of elements controlled by any leader
- continuous inspection/review environment
- insurance against loss of team member
- better integration of individual efforts (pp. 259–262).

In an IPT structure where the participants of the reviews have technical knowledge and expertise to review not only for consistency, but also for technical correctness and adequacy, the power of the reviews is amplified several times.

Although not specifically addressing the IPT concept, Microsoft's Jim McCarthy[17] posits a theoretical equation relevant to this V&V book, that TEAM = SOFTWARE. He means that software expresses the team that created it. Anything that is needed to know about the team can be discovered by examining the software. The words and behavior of the team are really too confusing at any given moment to diagnose, but the software that the team created does not lie. The software will eventually express every weakness and strength, every gift and curse, every unconscious ailment and top-of-the-mind brilliance the team possesses. Without the software itself there is no second side to the equation TEAM = SOFTWARE (pp. 50–52).

The basic principle is, if one is having a hard time understanding something about the team, one can look to the software. If the team and the software both tell the same thing, one can act on it with some degree of confidence. Conversely, if the software has not reached the desired state, the way to fix it is to analyze the genesis of the problem in the team. One may easily expand this unique thought to this chapter by contemplating the theoretical equation IPT = PRODUCT.

References

[1] Katzenbach, Jon and Smith, Douglas, *The Wisdom of Teams*, (Boston, MA: Harvard Business School Press, 1993).

[2] Society of Concurrent Engineering (SOCE), www.soce.org, March, 1998.

[3] Crow, Kenneth A., *Building Effective Product Development Teams*, © 1994 DRM Associates. kcrow@aol.com, (310) 377-5569.

[4] Humphrey, Watts S., "Three Dimensions of Process Improvement: Part III: The Team Process," In *CrossTalk*, Software Technology Support Center, Ogden: Hill AFB, Vol. 11, No. 4, April 1998, pp. 14–17.

[5] McGibbon, Barry, "High Performance Through Team Building," *Object Magazine*, November 1997, pp. 57–59.[SIGS Publications, Inc., 71 W. 23rd Street, New York, NY 10010], pp. 57–59.

[6] Snee, Ronald D. et al, "Improving Team Effectiveness," *Quality Progress*, May 1998, pp. 43–48.

[7] Northrop Grumman ESSD, *Program Organization*, ESSD Command Media No. D130, February 20, 1998.

[8] *DoD Guide to Integrated Product and Process Development* (Version 1.0), Office of the Under Secretary Of Defense (Acquisition and Technology), Washington, DC 20301-3000, February 5, 1996.

[9] *Rules of the Road: A Guide For Leading Successful Integrated Product Teams*, Under Secretary of Defense for Acquisition and Technology, Assistant Secretary of Defense for Command, Control, Communications & Intelligence (C3I), November 1995.

[10] Dunn Robert H. and Ullman, Richard S., *TQM for Computer Software* (2nd edition) (New York: McGraw Hill Book Company, 1994).

[11] Pressman, Roger S., *Software Engineering: A Practitioner's Approach* (3rd edition) (New York: McGraw Hill Book Company, 1992).

[12] *Key Practices of the Capability Maturity Model for Software*, Version 1.1, SEI-93-TR-25; and *The Capability Maturity Model for Software*, Version 1.1, SEI-93-TR-24, Carnegie Mellon University, Software Engineering Institute, Carnegie Mellon University, Software Engineering Institute, 1993.

[13] Pyster, Arthur, "Integrated Product Development CMM," Software Productivity Consortium, *WWRRT-TYY Conference Proceedings*, October 1996, pp. 176–191.

[14] Shingo, Shigeo, *Zero Quality Control: Source Inspection and the Poka-Yoke System* (Andrew P. Dillon, Trans.) (Cambridge, MA: Productivity Press, 1986) Published with permission.

[15] Schulmeyer, G. Gordon, *Zero Defect Software* (New York: McGraw Hill Book Company, 1990).

[16] Deutsch, Michael S., *Software Verification and Validation: Realistic Project Approaches* (Englewood Cliffs, NJ: Prentice Hall Publishing Co., 1982).

[17] McCarthy, Jim, *Dynamics of Software Development* (Redmond, WA: Microsoft Press, 1995).

General References

Holden, James, Stevens, Paul, Schulmeyer, Gordon, and Zetlmeisl, Bernard, "Large Software Project Control: How Much is Enough," *Defense Electronics*, Vol. 26, No. 6, June 1994, pp. 40–42.

IEEE/EIA 12207.0-1996, *Software Life Cycle Processes*, March 1998.

IEEE/EIA P12207.1 (Draft) Guide for Information Technology: *Software Life Cycle Processes, Life Cycle Data*, February 11, 1997.

IEEE/EIA 12207.2-1997, *Software Life Cycle Processes—Implementation Considerations*, April 1998.

U.S. Dept. of Defense, MIL-STD-498, *Software Development and Documentation*, December 5, 1994.

CHAPTER 16

Conclusion/Future Trends

Introduction

Remember from Chapter 1 the definitions of verification and validation from the Air Force Instruction 16-1001, *Verification, Validation and Accreditation:*[1] "Verification is the process of determining that a [system] accurately represents the developer's conceptual description and specifications. This is accomplished by identifying and eliminating mistakes in logic, mathematics, or programming. This process establishes that the [system's] code and logic correctly perform the intended functions, and to what extent the... development activities conform to state-of-the-practice software engineering techniques" (p. 3). Validation is the process of determining the degree to which a system accurately represents the user's requirements.

These definitions are applicable to the modern software-intensive systems discussed throughout this book. The multidimensional model presented throughout the book ties the elements of technologies, applications, and processes together for V&V of each of the modern methods discussed. An attempt was made to clarify the implications of V&V with each of these modern systems by analyzing the elements of each of the modern methods.

In this final chapter there are sections that highlight what needs to be done for improvement and what the future directions of V&V are taking:

- effectiveness of V&V
- Testing Maturity Model
- maturity levels applied to V&V
- performance assurance and continuous improvement
- process improvement model for V&V
- using Knowledge-Based Systems (KBS) to perform V&V activities
- V&V provides future safety for the Food and Drug Administration (FDA)
- V&V matrix for the future.

How has software process improvement affected V&V? What is in store for the V&V specialists of the future? What are the impacts now and in the future for V&V of the new applications? This chapter focuses on responses to these and related future-oriented implications to V&V.

Conclusions/Trends

Effectiveness of V&V

This subsection is abstracted from Wallace and Fujii's NIST publication, *Software Verification and Validation: Its Role in Computer Assurance and Its Relationship with Software Project Management Standards*.[2]

> Two studies to evaluate the effectiveness of V&V at an independent organization used different data and reported on different factors. [Although the studies are rather old (early 1980s), the relevant elements for V&V of modern software-intensive systems are covered.] While no direct comparison of results is possible, insights on V&V effectiveness may be gained from the highlights of the results of each study.
>
> Three flight dynamics projects ranging in size from 10K to 50K lines of code were selected in the first study. V&V was involved in requirements and design verification, separate system testing, and validation of consistency from start to finish. The V&V effort lasted 18 months and used [between 1 and 3 staff persons. Relevant] results follow:
>
> - Productivity of the development teams was the lowest of any previously monitored similar project (due to the V&V interface).
> - Rates of uncovering errors early in the development cycle were better.
> - V&V found 2.3 errors per thousand lines of code.
> - Cost rate to fix all discovered errors was no less than in any other [similar] project.
> - Reliability of the software (error rate during acceptance and maintenance and operations) was no different from other [similar] projects.
>
> [It seems that on these three small projects V&V was not very effective.]
>
> [The other study] reported V&V effectiveness results for four large IV&V projects ranging from 90K to 176K lines of code. The projects were real-time command and control, missile tracking, and avionics programs and a time-critical batch trajectory computation program. The projects varied from 2.5 to 4 years to develop. Two projects started V&V at the requirements phase, one at the code phase, and one at testing. The V&V organization used 5 to 12 staff persons per project. Relevant results were:
>
> - Errors were detected early in the development—50% to 89% detected before development testing began.
> - Large number of discrepancies were reported (total 1,259) on an average of over 300 per program.
> - V&V found an average of 5.5 errors per thousand lines of code.
> - Over 85% of the errors affected reliability and maintainability.

- Effect on programmer productivity was positive; that is, hours of programmer time saved by the programmers not having to find the error, minus the time required to evaluate the V&V error report—total savings per error of 1.3 to 6.1 hours of programmer time and over 7 minutes of computer time.
- For the two projects beginning at the code phase, early error detection savings amounted to 20%–28% of V&V costs; for the two projects beginning at the requirements phase, early error detection savings amounted to 92%–180% of V&V costs. (p. 15)

Table 16.1 depicts some positive and negative effects of V&V on a software project based on these studies. Wallace and Fujii[2] continue:

> Some steps can be taken to minimize the negative effects and to maximize the positive effects of V&V. To recover many of the V&V costs, V&V is started early in the software requirements phase to allow the earliest error detection when correction costs are lowest. The interface activities for documentation, data, and software deliveries between developer and V&V groups should be considered as an inherently necessary step required to evaluate intermediate development products....
>
> To offset unnecessary costs, V&V must organize its activities to focus on critical areas of the software so that it uncovers critical errors for the development group and thereby results in significant cost savings to the development process. To do this, V&V must use its criticality analysis [see Chapter 14] to identify critical areas....
>
> To eliminate the need to have development personnel train the V&V staff, it is imperative that V&V select personnel who are experienced and knowledgeable about the software and its

Table 16.1 V&V positive and negative effects.[2] (p. 16)

V&V Positive Effects	V&V Negative Effects
Better quality (e.g., complete, consistent, readable, testable) and more stable requirements.	Additional project cost of V&V (10%—30% extra)
More rigorous development planning at least to interface with the V&V organization.	Additional interface involving the development team, user, and V&V organization (e.g., attendance at V&V status meeting, anomaly resolution meeting)
Better adherence by the development organization to programming language and development standards and configuration management practices.	Lower development staff productivity if programmers and engineers spend time explaining the system to V&V analysts and resolving invalid anomaly reports
Early error detection and reduced false starts	Additional documentation requirements, beyond the deliverable products, if V&V is receiving incremental program and documentation releases
Better schedule compliance and progress monitoring	Need to share computing facilities with and to provide access to classified data for the V&V organization
Greater project management visibility into interim technical quality and progress	Increased paperwork to provide written responses to V&V error reports and other V&V data requirements (e.g., notices of formal review and audit meetings. updates to software release schedule,
Better criteria and results for decision making at formal reviews and audits.	

> application—an aspect often stated in this book. When V&V [personnel] and computer scientists reconstruct the specific details and idiosyncrasies of the software as a method of reconfirming the correctness of development assumptions, they often find subtle errors. They gain detailed insight into the development process and an ability to spot critical errors early. The cost of the development interface is minimal, and at times nonexistent, when the V&V assessment is independent.
>
> Finally, the number of discrepancies detected in software and the improvement in documentation quality resulting from error correction suggests that V&V costs are offset by having more reliable and maintainable software.... Failure of the system, loss of data, and release of or tampering with sensitive information may cause serious work disruptions and serious financial impact. The costs of V&V are offset in many application areas by increased reliability during operation and reduced costs of maintenance. (pp. 15–17)

A quantitative cost model for V&V is needed to demonstrate the effectiveness of V&V: (a) higher quality, (b) higher reliability, and (c) lower maintenance costs. Research defining a Return on Investment model for V&V is underway at the NASA V&V Research Facility at Fairmont, West Virginia.

Testing Maturity Model (TMM)

Because of the importance of software systems, quality issues that relate to both the software development process and the software product must be addressed. The Testing Maturity Model (TMM), which is a complement to the CMM, is described earlier in this book. That initial introduction to a particular new application area sets the stage for this further explanation of the TMM and why it will provide help for validation concepts in the future for the V&V specialist. It is designed to help software development organizations evaluate and improve their testing processes. Testing is used in its broadest sense to encompass review and execution-based testing activities; that is, validation. Improving the testing process through application of the TMM maturity criteria will have a positive impact on software quality.

As an aid to V&V of the future, the proposed TMM creates value similar to the CMM for Software. This TMM gives the V&V specialist modern, unique methods for performing V&V of the future. This subsection, abstracted from "Developing a Testing Maturity Model"[3] covers the approach to developing the TMM, the model framework (Figure 16.1), the behavioral characteristics of the five TMM levels, and its internal framework. Required support from CMM key process areas are also described.

Burnstein et al.[3] define the following characteristics of a mature testing process:

> *A set of defined testing policies.* There is a set of well-defined and documented testing policies that is applied throughout the organization. The testing policies are supported by upper management, institutionalized, and integrated into the organizational culture.
>
> *A test planning process.* There is a well-defined and documented test planning process used throughout the organization that allows for the specification of test objectives and goals, test

Figure 16.1 Testing Maturity Model (TMM) (Redrawn from Burnstein et al. in 3) (p. 19)

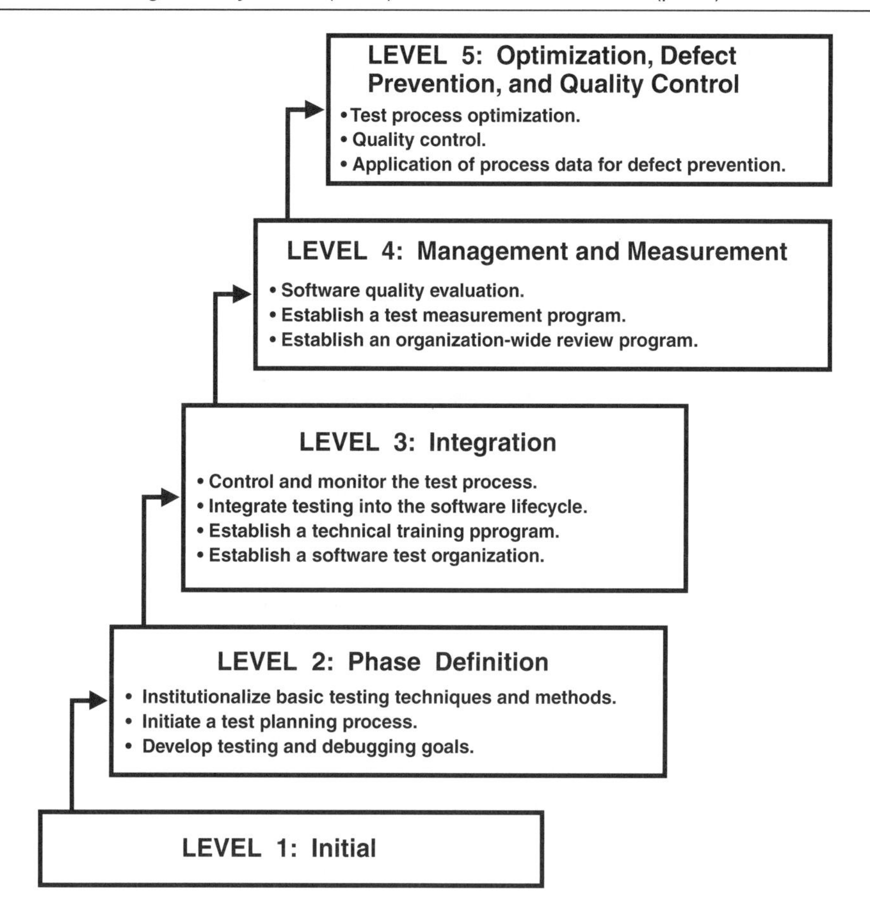

resource allocation, test designs, test cases, test schedules, test costs, and test tasks. Test plans reflect the risks of failures; time and resources are allocated accordingly.

A test life-cycle. The test process is broad-based and includes activities in addition to execution-based testing. There is a well-defined test life-cycle with a set of phases and activities that is integrated into the software life-cycle. The test life-cycle encompasses all broad-based testing activities, for example, test planning, test plan reviews, test design, implementation of test-related software, and maintenance of test work products. It is applied to all projects.

A test group. There is an independent testing group. The position of tester is defined and supported by upper management. Instruction and training opportunities exist to educate and motivate the test staff.

A test process improvement group. There is a group devoted to test process improvement. They can be a part of a general process improvement group, a software quality assurance group, the V&V personnel, or a component of the test group. Since the test process is well defined and measured, the test improvement group can exert leadership to fine-tune the process, apply incremental improvement techniques, and evaluate their impact.

A set of test-related metrics. The organization has a measurement program. A set of test-related metrics is defined; data are collected and analyzed with automated support. The metrics are used to support the appropriate actions needed for test process improvement.

Tools and equipment. Appropriate tools are available to assist the testing group with testing tasks and to collect and analyze test-related data. The test process improvement group provides the leadership to evaluate potential tools and oversees the technology transfer issues associated with integrating the tools into the organizational environment.

Controlling and tracking. The test process is monitored and controlled by the test managers to track progress, take actions when problems occur, and evaluate performance and capability. Quantitative techniques are used to analyze the testing process and to determine test process capability and effectiveness.

Product quality control. Statistical methods are used for testing to meet quality standards. "Stop testing" criteria are quantitative to be used judiciously by V&V and/or software quality assurance. Product quality is monitored, defects are tracked, and causal analysis is applied for defect prevention. (p. 22)

A mature testing process requires a broadening of the traditional definition of what is considered to be a testing activity. The expanded definition of testing includes reviews, audits, walk-throughs, and inspections activities considered to be a part of V&V processes. It also requires integration of all these activities into the software life-cycle. This allows quality to be built into the software with the aid of V&V from the beginning of the software life-cycle. (p. 22)

The TMM [Figure 16.1][3] is characterized by five testing maturity levels within a framework of goals, subgoals, activities, tasks, and responsibilities. Each level implies a specific testing maturity. With the exception of Level 1, several maturity goals, which identify key process areas, are indicated at each level. The maturity goals identify testing improvement goals that must be addressed to achieve maturity at that level. To be placed at a level, an organization must satisfy the maturity goals at that level. Each maturity goal is supported by one or more maturity subgoals. The maturity subgoals specify less abstract objectives, and they define the scope, boundaries, and needed accomplishments for a particular level.

The maturity subgoals are achieved through a group of activities and tasks with responsibilities. The activities and tasks with responsibilities address implementation and organizational adaptation issues at a specific level. Activities and tasks are defined in terms of actions that must be performed at a given level to improve testing capability; they are linked to organizational commitments. Responsibilities are assigned for these activities and tasks to three groups that we believe represent the key participants in the testing process: managers, developers and testers, and users and clients. In the model they are referred to as "the three critical views." Definition of their roles is essential in developing a maturity framework. The manager's view involves commitment and ability to perform activities and tasks related to improving testing capability. The developer and tester's view encompasses technical activities and tasks that, when applied, constitute mature testing practices. The users and client's view is defined as a cooperating or supporting view. The developers and testers work with client and user groups on quality-related activities and tasks that concern user-oriented needs. The focus is on soliciting client/user support, consensus, and participation in activities such as requirements analysis, usability testing [Chapter 8], and acceptance test planning. (pp. 22–24)

Burnstein et al.[3] give the following definitions of the five TMM levels:

Level 1—Initial

Testing is a chaotic process; it is ill-defined and not distinguished from debugging. Tests are developed in an ad hoc way after coding is done. Testing and debugging are interleaved to get the errors out of the software. The objective of testing is to show that the software works. Software products are released without quality assurance or V&V. There is a lack of resources, tools, and properly trained staff. This type of organization would be on Level 1 of the CMM developed by the Software Engineering Institute. There are no maturity goals at this level.

Level 2—Phase Definition

Testing is separated from debugging and is defined as a phase that follows coding. It is a planned activity; however, test planning at Level 2 may occur after coding for reasons related to the immaturity of the test process. For example, at Level 2 there is the perception that all testing is execution-based and dependent on the code, and therefore it should be planned only when the code is complete.

The primary goal of testing at this level of maturity is to show that the software meets its specifications. Basic testing techniques and methods are in place. Many quality problems at this TMM level occur because test planning occurs late in the software life-cycle. In addition, defects propagate into the code from the requirements and design phases, as there are no review programs that address this important issue. Post-code, execution-based testing is still considered the primary testing activity.

Level 3—Integration

Testing is no longer a phase that follows coding; it is integrated into the entire software life-cycle. Organizations can build on the test planning skills they have acquired at Level 2. Unlike Level 2, planning for testing at TMM Level 3 begins at the requirements phase and continues throughout the life-cycle. Test objectives are established with respect to the requirements based on user and client needs and are used for test case design and success criteria. There is a test organization, and testing is recognized as a professional activity. There is a technical training organization with a testing focus. Basic tools support key testing activities. Although organizations at this level begin to realize the important role of reviews in quality control, there is no formal review program, and reviews do not yet take place across the life-cycle. A test measurement program has not yet been established to qualify process and product attributes.

Level 4—Management and Measurement

Testing is a measured and quantified process. Reviews at all phases of the development process are now recognized as testing and quality control activities. Software products are tested for quality attributes such as reliability, usability, and maintainability. Test cases from all projects are collected and recorded in a test case database to test case reuse and regression testing. Defects are logged and given a severity level. Deficiencies in the test process are now often due to the lack of a defect prevention philosophy and the porosity of automated support for the collection, analysis, and dissemination of test-related metrics.

Level 5—Optimization, Defect Prevention, and Quality Control

Because of the infrastructure provided by the attainment of maturity goals at Levels 1 through 4 of the TMM, the testing process is now said to be defined and managed, its cost and effectiveness can be monitored. At Level 5, there are mechanisms that fine-tune and continuously improve testing. Defect prevention, quality control, and V&V are practiced. The testing process is driven by statistical sampling, measurements of confidence levels, trustworthiness, and reliability. There is an established procedure to select and evaluate testing tools. Automated tools totally support the running and rerunning of test cases, providing support for test case design, maintenance of test-related items, defect collection and analysis, and the collection, analysis, and application of test-related metrics. (pp. 19–20)

Maturity Levels Applied to V&V

This subsection is paraphrased from Lewis:[4]

The application of V&V to an effort in which the developer is at CMM Level 1 is going to have so much uncertainty that the outcome becomes somewhat unpredictable. Major concerns about the project center on the inability to effectively plan and consequently execute the process, the project's tendency to be crisis-managed, and large amounts of wasted effort from rework and throwaway designs and code. These factors invariably result in:

- cost overruns
- schedule slips
- poor design
- inadequate testing
- all sorts of defects
- general user dissatisfaction.

If the developer does not know where he is going, V&V cannot plan its own methodology, select tools, or estimate the size or complexity of the software and will spend an inordinate amount of time working on management issues. V&V seldom has enough force or weight to change the course of the project. Sometimes the developer may be bootstrapped to a Level 2 by the concerted efforts of the customer and V&V team. The key is to understand the development process enough to investigate essential controls and direction. Sometimes it may be as simple as finding the right manager, which assumes that the staff is willing to be taught a better way. It usually requires the following steps to get out of Level 1:

- management awareness and a strong desire for improvement
- willingness to provide training to virtually the whole staff
- recognition and definition of an acceptable development process for the type of products involved (usually with the assistance from the outside)
- willingness to institutionalize the essential things like project management, configuration management, and quality assurance

- willingness to provide a stable and adequate development environment, which includes appropriate computer(s) and support software (compilers, debuggers, editors, utilities, operating system, etc.)
- willingness to begin a systematic acquisition of appropriate software tools, staged to support the worst problem area first.

As can be seen, most of the decisions are managerial, not technical. Most organizations follow the attitudes and beliefs of their leaders.

Once CMM Level 2 is reached and the development process is defined and most essentials are in place, V&V becomes much more predictable in its behavior and can anticipate and plan its effort. Because the process still may be shaky and the tools and methods not optimized, V&V will find itself doing some unplanned ad hoc analyses and evaluations. These can include the following:

- evaluating and benchmarking competing operating systems and compilers
- helping to write sample sections of specifications
- evaluating CASE tools
- advising on hardware configurations and features
- helping to select communications protocols and network configurations
- a myriad of other things normally done by the developer.

In addition, V&V will likely spend some of its time and resources on management-related things like determining project status, auditing configuration management records, tracking things that the developer normally would, evaluating how well the developer is following the software development plan, and participating more than normally would be expected in meetings and reviews. It is estimated that up to 25% of the V&V program budget will be spent on nontechnical issues when the developer is at Level 2. As the levels get better, the amount of nontechnical V&V effort continues to shrink; however, it should never reach zero because there are still some management-related activities required no matter how efficient the software development process becomes.

Level 3 is considered the minimum threshold to qualify for some DoD procurements; therefore, all U.S. Department of Defense contractors should consider this achievement as the ground floor and seek to improve beyond that point as soon as is reasonable. Other government agencies are requiring a minimum CMM Level 2 now, with a not-too-distant future prospect of requiring Level 3. When the development contractor is at Level 3, chances are that the use of metrics and other management and technical performance indicators is either absent or is not widespread. In addition, the mechanisms to define and collect the appropriate data are probably lacking. V&V will usually need to support the customer in quantifying the key pre-code products (requirement and design specifications) so that an objective measure of percent complete can be established. Next there are usually some noticeable deficiencies in the area of CASE tools. Sometimes obsolete practices and tools are being used, or the tools do not cover the entire process adequately. Here, V&V can fill noticeable gaps, but the developer will eventually have to improve the application of tools to advance to the next level. Another area that often represents a weakness in Level 3 involves the organization and how much continuous training is provided to keep the staff current and to enhance the overall skill level. Over specification in specific software skills is not always a good thing, and cross-training is very beneficial, espe-

> cially if staff turnover is a problem. Loss of key personnel with critical kills can quickly reduce the maturity level of the process. Very often, Level 3 contractors do not benefit much from lessons learned on previous projects and continue to do a poor job at estimating and detailed planning for each new project. There is a tendency to collect data at the wrong levels and not know how to recognize and react to adverse trends or pinpoint faults.
>
> Level 4 developers have identified and collected data on the detailed factors through which their development process is controlled and managed. Through the use of metrics and other performance indicators, this level effectively quantifies the development process, enabling much better understanding of cause-and-effect relationships, greatly improving estimating and planning, and enabling corrective actions to be applied efficiently. Level 4 developers will typically recognize the critical paths in the software project and will focus resources based on known organizational capabilities—skills, experience, productivity rates, and other measurable data. Extensive use of automated tools can be expected based on cost-effectiveness analysis and return on investment, not individual programmer preference. Level 4 will include an active training program, wherein all levels of the organization are kept abreast of the current technology and development trends. Thus, Level 4 will have an active program to assess and replace aging technology on a periodic basis. V&V personnel will find that working with a Level 4 developer allows a strong concentration on the technical issues together with expectations of good quality specifications, design, and code. Even when working with a Level 4 developer, however, V&V personnel can expect to continue to find deficiencies in requirements and design, poorly expressed algorithms, errors in the code, and testing shortcomings. The development process, no matter how well understood or refined, is a human-intensive activity and thus prone to errors, interpretations, and misunderstandings.
>
> Level 5 developers spend a good bit of energy using and exploiting the data collected and processed at Level 4. The goal at this level is to continuously improve and adapt the process to each new development effort in an optimal manner. This requires a focus on continuous training and infusion of the latest technology that suits the development process. This means that tool selection is based on key factors that pertain to the developer's type of business and software products. The Level 5 developer is able to use the data collected at Level 4 to initiate preventive actions directed at the known problem areas. Perhaps the greatest challenge at Level 5 is staying there. It requires continuous effort on behalf of the entire staff, graceful introduction of new methods and tools, and a strong desire at all levels to continue to become more efficient and skilled by handling the day-to-day activities. V&V can still expect to find plenty of technical issues simply because the process cannot do it all. There will be errors and deficiencies as long as people develop software. Tools are only as good as the input, so V&V will be needed even for the Level 5 developers. (pp. 296–300)

Performance Assurance and Continuous Improvement

AverStar's Continuous Improvement Program is important to a project's V&V methodology. This is discussed here based on the *EOSDIS Independent Verification and Validation Management Plan*.[5]

> Performance-assurance collected metrics on [V&V] performance can be used to mold and improve [V&V] methods, tools, and procedures. Metrics that address overall performance in terms of time and accuracy are [useful] during internal self-assessments to determine areas of improvement and means for streamlining the [V&V] process and enhancing its responsiveness.

> The performance assurance function provides a customer perspective when assessing [V&V] performance. Performance assurance can also identify training programs and materials that would be valuable for correcting any deficiencies in [V&V] performance, or for enabling [V&V] to stay abreast of changes in the technology base. These recommendations are provided to the [project's V&V] program manager and will be used to ensure the program staff stays current. (p. 27)

In *The Role of Independent V&V in Upstream Software Development Processes*[6] Easterbrook in his conclusions states the following:

> This paper has examined the role of IV&V* in the software development process, concentrating especially on its role in requirements and design processes. IV&V provides an independent assessment of both developmental and operational risk. It helps to identify safety, reliability and performance concerns early in the software life-cycle, and has generally been demonstrated to save money through early identification of errors.
>
> The role of IV&V is complementary to that of QA. Where QA focuses on checking that appropriate standards and process models are applied, IV&V focuses on the technical integrity of the software, through analysis of specifications, designs, code, and other documentation. Hence, IV&V will ensure that the requirements are complete, that a proposed system architecture will meet the requirements, and that traceability is demonstrated among requirements, designs and test cases.
>
> An interesting emergent property of the IV&V process is that the IV&V agent can play a role as a process improvement agent, for a number of reasons. First, the recommendations made by IV&V in response to errors often address ways to prevent similar errors occurring in the future. Second the IV&V team have some flexibility to apply new techniques and tools, especially where these plug perceived gaps in the analysis performed by the developer. If these new techniques and tools demonstrate their value in identifying errors, the development team may choose to adopt them themselves. Finally, the presence of an IV&V contractor provides an incentive for the developers to improve their own internal V&V practices, in order to catch errors before the IV&V contractor does.
>
> Within the process model described for IV&V, there are still a number of problems. Some of these arise from the constraints imposed on the IV&V process. For example, the IV&V team need to devote resources to analyzing documents as soon as they are released, without necessarily knowing ahead of time what types of analysis will be needed. Other problems are due to the inherent conflicts between the goals of the developer and the IV&V contractor. For example, the developer may be reluctant to release draft documents to the IV&V team, for fear that the IV&V contractor will make them look bad by reporting large numbers of problems to the customer.
>
> Although IV&V has been generally shown to have strong benefits, it is difficult to ensure that any particular IV&V effort will be effective. While an understanding of the processes involved is an important step, the biggest factor determining the effectiveness of an IV&V contract is the nature of the organizational relationship between the developer, customer and

* The authors believe that Easterbrook's remarks apply not only just to IV&V, but equally to V&V.

> IV&V agent. Although the developer may be contractually obliged to work with the IV&V agent, this does not ensure a constructive relationship. Nor does it ensure that the customer will listen to the IV&V agent when the news is bad....
>
> Our research to date has concentrated on observing the IV&V process, and identifying problem areas, as described in this paper. We are now focusing on potential solutions to the coordination problems illustrated by our scenarios. These problems are a result of the size of the documentation. and the fact that it continues to evolve. Tracing the effects of any small change to a specification is especially difficult. Where the IV&V contractor creates alternative representations for the developer's specifications, it can be difficult to ensure the alternative representations are faithful to the original. Furthermore, the models created by the IV&V team need to be updated whenever the documents on which they are based evolve. There is always a tension between the need to analyze drafts of the specifications in order to detect errors as early as possible, and the volatile nature of these early drafts.
>
> We are also investigating the use of lightweight formal methods for checking properties of partial specifications. The majority of work on formal methods assumes a commitment to the development of a complete and consistent formal specification. In contrast, when we use formal methods in the IV&V process, we are interested in developing just enough of a formal model to test particular properties. Problems here include the maintenance of fidelity between formal and informal representations of the same specification. Existing work on consistency checking does not help here, it generally assumes that consistency checks are being applied within a well-defined method, rather than between methods.... We are currently pursuing techniques based on behavioral analysis of formal specifications using model checkers. (p. 8)

Process Improvement Model for V&V

This subsection is derived from "A Process Improvement Model for Software Verification and Validation,"[7] by John Callahan and George Sabolish who state:

> Verification involves analyzing software products after each major development stage to ensure that the product agrees with the specification established prior to that stage. Validation involves ensuring that the products after each stage agree with the original specifications. Although validation is traditionally performed only at later stages (i.e., testing with respect to requirements), we employ the broader definition. (p. 1)

Callahan and Sabolish define three dimensions for characterizing a specific application of V&V:

1. *Orientation:* V&V activities can focus on either the software development process or the products produced by that process. Most V&V activities, however, perform a combination of both process-oriented and product-oriented analysis as mentioned above.
2. *Scope:* The scope of V&V activities can range from being comprehensive across all development phases, to being limited to specific subsystems and process stages.
3. *Independence:* V&V activities can be embedded within or independent of a development effort. Independence can vary over levels of technical, managerial, and financial control (p. 1).

They state:

> Regardless of its organization, however, all V&V organizations are charged with detecting (and sometimes correcting) errors in software products and processes as early as possible in the development life-cycle. This implies that effective techniques must be employed that help find the most critical problems in early phases. Clear correlation must be established between these early errors and their consequences later in the development life-cycle. Otherwise, such problems can be dismissed as false warnings or noncritical.... [The] effort involves establishing a framework for iterative measurement and ongoing improvement of a V&V organization's ability to find critical errors early and more accurately estimate costs and benefits of V&V. (p. 1)

The Callahan and Sabolish process improvement model for V&V organizations (Figure 16.2) has the following objectives:

- To establish criteria for measuring V&V activities
- Measure ongoing V&V projects
- Suggest incremental improvements to both product analysis and a V&V process.

The process improvement model for V&V, based on measurement of products and processes from both development and V&V, generally iterates over the following steps:

1. Measure the current process.
2. Analyze strengths and weaknesses.
3. Improve the process by developing and introducing new technologies to addresses weaknesses.
4. Measure the process to determine the effectiveness of the improvement.
5. Repeat steps 2, 3, 4 (p. 2).

> Can V&V help predict problems? The status of a project is more than the analysis of its parts. While the individual product errors may not be severe in a project, their cumulative effect can be serious. V&V efforts will yield analysis in the form of metrics on development processes and products. These metrics can be used by a V&V organization to predict trends that may result in schedule slippage, increased errors, costs, and other composite effects. It is necessary for a V&V organization to spot process problems early in the life-cycle and to have effective means to predict them. [The] model relies on the cyclic phases of development to allow identification of trends in software processes based on the analysis of correlation to find leading indicators in a project that foreshadow potential problems. (p. 2)

Callahan and Sabolish note that once these indicators are identified and validated, they can also increase the accuracy of estimates and confidence in V&V assessments. V&V has also been shown to have an influence on software reliability and maintenance. Existing models are being modified to incorporate the ability to estimate the impact of V&V on reliability and maintainability. These qualities are very difficult to quantify and are only meaningful in the context of a project's goals. Methods of quantifying such qualities are under exploration, so that the full value of

Figure 16.2 An overview of the V&V process improvement model[7] (p. 2).

Goals:	V&V	Increase software quality
	V&V improvements	Identify and develop new tools and techniques
	Software development	Develop and maintain quality software
Approach:	Apply tools and techniques to catch errors as early as possible and increase software longevity	
Methods:	Empirical data and problem areas	
	New tools and techniques	
	Guidelines and standards	
	Research results	
	Life-cycle software development	
	Errors and corrections	
	Process events and software products	
	Process improvement relationship	

V&V on a project can be assessed. As improved V&V measurements and techniques are identified, new methods will be introduced into the V&V life-cycle. Again, the cyclic nature of the associated projects allows for the incorporation of changes at strategic points in the process. These ongoing measurements will allow assessment of the impact of such changes on the effectiveness of V&V (p. 3).

> How much and what types of V&V are required on a project? It is necessary to improve the ability of V&V to find problems in a software development project and focus analysis on the most critical aspects of development products and processes. The framework analyzes the success and failure of existing V&V techniques to detect specific errors by auditing errors (i.e., V&V discrepancy reports) backward in the V&V process. Auditing these problems should help identify gaps in the V&V processes. For example, errors can be missed due to several problems in the V&V process, including:
>
> - **Omission.** The problem was caused by an error that could have been caught by the V&V process, but was overlooked due to the lack of V&V personnel expertise or the difficulty in applying the analysis.
> - **Incompleteness.** The problem could have been avoided via existing techniques, but the lack of information from the development process prevented its application.
> - **Lack of Resources.** The problem could have been found but there was insufficient time or personnel to find it.
> - **Lack of Capability.** The problem was caused by an error that could not have been caught by the V&V process because of the inadequacy of the methods and tools involved or the inherent complexity of the error.
>
> This is not a complete list of reasons why errors are missed, but they are typical of the way in which errors can be classified in order to help improve detection of errors in earlier life-cycle phases. Analysis of classified V&V errors can lead to discovery of common types of errors that may suggest new methods, specifications, or processes.

The need to change V&V methods as part of an ongoing improvement program will impact the development process. For this and other reasons, much debate has surrounded the need for V&V. Some argue that it is more important to improve the quality of the development organization.... V&V should not simply assess the status of a development effort, but should provide feedback for improvement of the development process itself. In other words, V&V can act as a process improvement organization for development.

Initially, [the focus is] on the ability of the V&V process to find problems effectively and not on improving the capabilities of the software development process itself. However, because V&V and development are intimately related processes, [a strategy has been developed] for transferring improvements to development processes based on the need for improvements in V&V. [The] strategy is to demonstrate that changes to development are needed in cases where V&V is unable to perform its task due to inappropriate or unavailable information from development. The goal of process improvement on a development organization is to enable it to produce high-quality software, on time, and within budget. This implies that the development effort is predictable and measurable. Ultimately, this will lead to development techniques that are highly amenable to V&V activities. [These are labeled] *verifiable development techniques* (VDTs) to identify them as enabling effective V&V over other approaches. A [VDT] is comprised of many different phases that are highly amenable to V&V. For example, the requirements for a safety-critical project might be expressed in specification language that is amenable to formal analysis. In a VDT, such analysis is not simply a spot check but is coordinated with analyses performed in other phases.

Current research activates are focused on the short-term task to construct the V&V process improvement framework. The framework is needed to form the basis of any future improvements in the area of V&V. While it is true that V&V activities have been conducted on projects for many years, industry has yet to define and document V&V processes involved with any degree of consistency. Working with real projects using real project data [provides] the unique ability to define a baseline set of processes that can then be improved through use of a structured improvement process. Many metrics, models, techniques, and processes exist that can be incorporated into [the V&V] framework. [Those that currently exist must be identified and an attempt be made] to formulate the characteristics of new approaches. The tasks include: (p. 4)

Calahan and Sobolish review some of these tasks:

- **Metrics.** Some metrics are highly effective in predicting the potential occurrence of problems in software projects, with emphasis on existing metric "success" stories and studies. In addition, the "Hawthorne effect" in software development that occurs when a V&V organization is employed is being examined.
- **Processes.** V&V processes are being mapped to existing development processes. V&V as related to nonstandard development processes are being examined, particularly in large-scale projects where requirements change dramatically during development.
- **Classification.** Because V&V cannot be applied uniformly across all phases and products due to resource limitations, means are being devised to classify software products according to their impact on system failure. Such classification schemes will help tailor V&V processes to direct their attention to appropriate problems.

- **Testing.** This traditional role of V&V cannot be ignored; "testing" is being moved to earlier stages in the software development life-cycle, as related in the TMM. For instance, a "test" of the requirements specifications can be posed as a challenge to be disputed by some analysis on the project requirements. Work in these areas will help establish the criteria for validating the framework employed on ongoing projects. They are needed to establish a means of assessing the cost estimates and error detection methods at all phases of the development and V&V life-cycles (p. 4).

Their paper concludes:

> [This] process improvement model for V&V can benefit both V&V and development efforts. Many barriers still remain to conducting research on software development and V&V efforts:
>
> - Many vendors are reluctant to provide measurements because it will expose them to criticism.
> - Visibility into proprietary techniques and processes may harm their competitive advantage.
> - Measurements provided by the measured project will always tend to be skewed optimistically.
>
> [These barriers are under attack] through memoranda of understanding and other contractual mechanisms. On large software efforts, several agencies of the U.S. government, including NASA, have invested heavily in independent V&V as insurance against catastrophic errors. As development methods evolve, V&V processes must also improve. Since V&V is a complementary process, its improvement will drive improvements in development. This relationship will be mutually beneficial in achieving high-quality software. (p. 5)

Using KBS to Perform the V&V Activities

Remember from Chapter 10 on knowledge-based systems (KBS) from Playle and Beckman[8] that:

> The implication of using KBSs for software V&V is that a machine-aided inspection of the specification, and design or selection of the test cases, is likely to be as accurate as human-generated selections but much faster. Thus, if we can capture the expertise of humans in predicting software faults and in designing test cases, then reuse that knowledge in machines, we can greatly reduce the "overhead time" of specification validation, and in turn the software testing and validation.
>
> With greater mainstreaming of knowledge-based techniques, new software development techniques such as object oriented development [Chapter 6], reusable knowledge-based testing, and automatic test suite generation may be expected to increase.
>
> The testing process involves several steps [Figure 16.3], beginning with test planning, test case design and selection, actual execution of the test cases, and evaluation of the results. Around all these steps is the problem of managing test cases, plans, etc., as requirements and software change (configuration management and control of the test). KBSs and automation have been applied to several of these steps. (p. 17)

NIST's publication, *Reference Information for the Software Verification and Validation Process,*[9] mentions a specific KBS for V&V (KADS) that emphasizes the development of models

Figure 16.3 Potential testing flow[8] (p. 18).

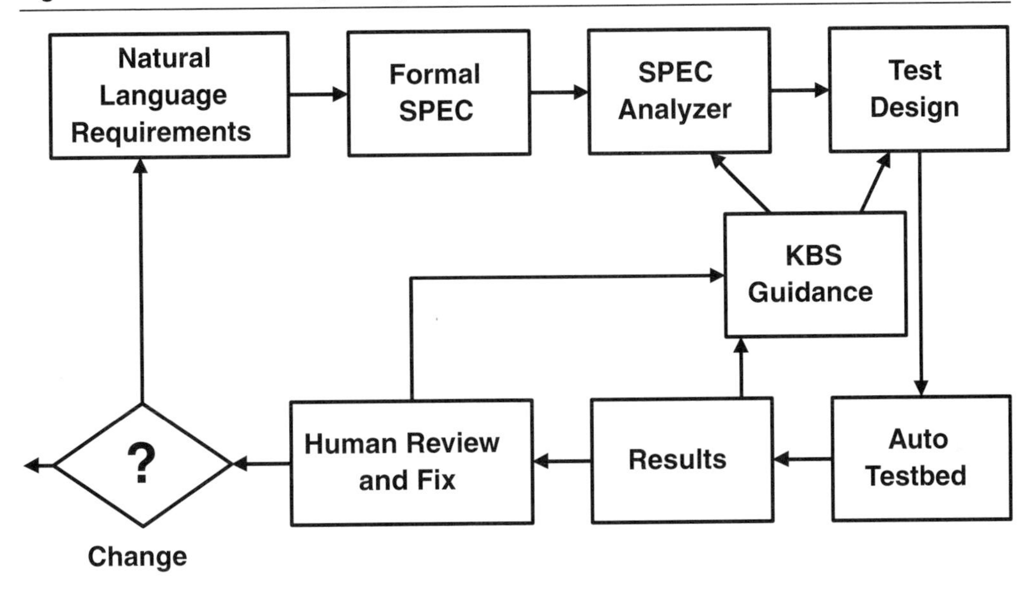

through the requirements analysis and design activities. Table 16.2 lists the activities, tasks, and products of that KBS development process.

Playle and Beckman continue:

> Given the necessity of testing and limited time and budgets, can KBSs and automated tools help an organization? Before trying to automate portions of the testing, an organization must have a well-defined testing process. The organizations should take steps to establish and improve the testing process, then apply the automated tools.
>
> 1. The organization must commit to the improvement of their test and design process, providing the time, money, and staff to accomplish the effort as part of their overall capability maturity improvement.
> 2. They can begin capturing the extant knowledge in the organization on test practices, formalizing and documenting the process, and turning the tests and their use into a quantifiable, improvable process.

Table 16.2 KBS activities, tasks, and products[9] (p. 32)

Activity	Tasks	Models/Products
Requirements Analysis	Process Analysis	Cooperation Analysis
Expertise Analysis	Constraints Analysis	System Overview
Process Model	Cooperation Model	Expertise Model
Constraints	Model System	Overview Document
Design Global	Design KBS	Design Global System Architecture
KBS Functional Design	KBS Behavioral Design	KBS Physical Design

3. They can include testing as part of the initial project design and specification, making the tests themselves reusable artifacts.
4. They can get and explore such tools as ATPS.
5. They can build a "repository" of tests, past results (before and after) tools, etc., using almost a CASE-like approach to testing.
6. The organization can automate these processes as much as possible, building a system that captures and reuses the knowledge that people have built up, forming continuity of knowledge and allowing improvement over time. (pp. 19–20)

V&V Provides Future Safety for FDA

Preston Pierce[10] points out that "V&V is required by the Food and Drug Administration (FDA)"* (p. 4). He goes on to say that "the rigor of the V&V depends on the level of concern: minor, moderate or major.... It [may be] tempting just to develop software in the usual way and then try to assure that the finished product is safe. This approach is akin to relying on downstream protection systems—the cost can be exorbitant and the assurance limited. The most practical and effective way to enhance software system safety is to... apply safety-enhancing techniques throughout software development and maintenance" (p. 4). The FDA safety program has a significant focus on V&V for software developments. Pierce continues,

> Verification testing verifies that requirements for a subsystem have been met. Validation tests a finished device to the original requirements to ensure they have been met. Appropriately applied V&V decreases the cost of software development. V&V can make a significant contribution in making the final product safe and effective. Software changes can be more easily and safely made when the development process is controlled and documented....
>
> The FDA requires evidence that V&V is included in the product development process. The emphasis is on appropriately applied V&V. A software development process that produces on-time, defect-free code, meets all of its requirements, and has intrinsic V&V identifying defects as early as possible, is a very cost-efficient process, regardless of industry. (p. 4)

V&V Matrix for the Future

Table 16.3 provides a cross reference between the future trends for V&V and the items of concern to modern V&V, which are chapters in this book. Basically, all the future trends have some effect on the V&V of the elements listed across the top of the matrix. However, the prime relationship has been highlighted with an **X** to denote a strong relationship.

Of major consequence will be V&V tools for shortening and strengthening the process, which include V&V management tools, V&V costing tools, V&V technical aids for formal proofs, V&V metrics automation, and tools related to KBSs for V&V use. Another area of major conse-

* See the FDA "Reviewer Guidance for Computer Controlled Medical Devices Undergoing 510(k) Review" for details. Also see the Safe Medical Devices Act of 1990, Sec 18 (e) which adds the requirement of "pre-production design validation."

Table 16.3 V&V trends for the future.

FUTURE TRENDS	Standards, Processes and Models	Tools and Methodologies	Documentation	Metrics	Object Oriented (OO) Methods	Rapid Application Development (RAD)	Usability (GUI I/F)	Client/Server Networks	Knowledge Based Systems (KBS)	Internet /Intranet	Data Warehousing	Project Management	Risk Management	Integrated Product Teams (IPTs)
V&V standards	X	X	X	X								X	X	X
V&V formalized automated process definition	X	X										X	X	X
V&V Maturity Model	X	X	X	X								X	X	X
V&V tools integration		X	X	X	X	X	X	X	X	X	X	X		
Methods for V&V costing		X		X								X		
Methods for V&V technical implementation more integrated with the development team		X										X		X
Formal automated documentation evaluation of software development documents		X	X	X	X	X	X	X	X	X	X		X	
Document templates for the V&V project documents (e.g., V&V Plan)			X									X		
System/software documents produced as an output of tools, so V&V can reproduce and monitor the outputs		X	X		X	X	X	X	X	X	X			
Metrics that are proof of the pay-off of V&V				X								X	X	
V&V metrics that tie in with a V&V Maturity Model	X			X								X	X	
Accurate, automated methods for measuring the acceptability of system/software work products		X	X	X	X	X	X	X	X	X	X			
Efficient V&V for RAD, so that it is not slowed down	X					X								
V&V acceptance of RAD for the customer						X						X		
Usability methods for V&V		X					X					X		
Automation for V&V to do usability testing		X					X					X		
Ease of access for V&V to client/server networks		X						X					X	
Tools for V&V to use in checking network protocols		X						X		X			X	

Table 16.3 (continued)

FUTURE TRENDS	V&V AREAS OF INTEREST: Standards, Processes and Models	Tools and Methodologies	Documentation	Metrics	Object Oriented (OO) Methods	Rapid Application Development (RAD)	Usability (GUI I/F)	Client/Server Networks	Knowledge Based Systems (KBS)	Internet /Intranet	Data Warehousing	Project Management	Risk Management	Integrated Product Teams (IPTs)
V&V network check capability that is non-interferring to the users		X						X		X			X	
Access to automated expert databases for V&V verification		X							X				X	
Decision support systems for V&V decision making		X							X				X	
Use of KBSs for V&V		X							X			X	X	
Ease of access for V&V to intranets		X								X			X	
V&V access to a truly “fast” internet response		X								X			X	
Statistical methods for V&V use to satisfy data completeness and accuracy		X		X							X			
Provide non-interferring access to V&V to the data warehouse		X									X			
Institute a data warehouse for V&V access for future use		X									X			
Make V&V an integral part of the developer’s company, just as SQA generally is now	X	X										X	X	X
Automated tools that produce the V&V douments required for a project	X	X	X		X	X	X	X	X	X	X	X	X	X
V&V risk management tools that quickly and accurately calculate project risks		X		X	X	X	X	X	X	X	X	X	X	
Application of risk management methods to V&V itself, not just to the devlopment underway		X		X	X	X	X	X	X	X	X	X	X	
V&V involvement in virtual IPTs	X				X	X	X	X	X	X	X	X	X	X

quence is expert systems coordinated with data warehouses for the V&V specialist's use. Historical lessons learned coupled with extensive project V&V data will have enormous positive influence on V&V in the future.

V&V, just like software quality assurance, needs to maintain its objectivity. This may be accomplished, as it often is now, with an independent organization. However, the optimal way in the future would be an integrated team of developers, V&V, and software quality assurance (SQA). The closeness of this arrangement (maybe an IPT—Chapter 15) gives added strength to the project. Varying knowledgeable personnel can help to produce the correct work products the first time. All may share project resources for optimal benefit from limited resources. All should result in cost and schedule reduction, while enhancing product quality (conformance to requirements).

Summary

This book has focused on V&V of modern software-intensive systems. How to apply V&V to these modern applications with new technology and related processes has been discussed. Hopefully, the goal of providing V&V-related thought-provoking fodder for your imagination is provided, and not just provoking concepts. One of those thought-provokers from the FDA in this chapter is: Verification testing verifies that requirements for a subsystem have been met. Validation tests a finished device to the original requirements to ensure they have been met.

An element that is pervasive is the continual appearance throughout many of the chapters of the capability maturity model and its descendants (Testing Maturity Model, Software Documentation Review Levels, System Security Engineering, V&V Project Management Model, and Integrated Product Development). It is clear that the CMM is positively impacting the development of software. That success has given impetus to many others related to software development to produce a model that uses a similar framework because it has proven effective. There will soon be a V&V Maturity Model (V&VMM) flowing from some of the work covered in this chapter. That will provide a structure to the V&V team for continuous process improvement of V&V. There is hope for the future of V&V!

References

1 Air Force Instruction 16-1001, *Verification, Validation and Accreditation (VV&A)*, June 1, 1996.

2 Wallace, Dolores R. and Fujii, Roger U., *Software Verification and Validation: Its Role in Computer Assurance and Its Relationship with Software Project Management Standards*, National Institute of Standards and Technology Special Publication 500-165, May, 1989.

3 Burnstein, Ilene & Suwannasart, Taratip & Carlson, C.R., "Developing a Testing Maturity Model, Parts 1 and 2," In *CrossTalk*, Software Technology Support Center, Ogden: Hill AFB, Vol. 9, No. 8 & 9, August & September 1996, pp. 21–24 & pp. 19–26.

4 Lewis, Robert O., *Independent Verification and Validation: A Life Cycle Engineering Process for Quality Software* (New York: John Wiley & Sons, Inc., 1992). Copyright © 1992 John Wiley & Sons, Inc., Adapted by permission of John Wiley & Sons, Inc.

[5] *EOSDIS Independent Verification And Validation (V&V) Management Plan* (Deliverable 0301), Prepared By: AverStar, 6301 Ivy Lane, Suite 200, Greenbelt, Maryland 20770; Prepared For: NASA Goddard Space Flight Center, EOSDIS Project, Code 505, Greenbelt, Maryland 20770; December 2, 1994.

[6] Easterbrook, Steve, "The Role of Independent V&V in Upstream Software Development Processes," *Proceedings of 2nd World Conference on Integrated Design and Process Technology*, 1996, NASA/WVU Software Research Lab, NASA IV&V Facility, 100 University Drive, Fairmont, WV 26554, URL: steve@atlantis.ivv.nasa.gov.

[7] Callahan, John and Sabolish, George, *A Process Improvement Model for Software Verification and Validation*, NASA Software IV&V Facility West Virginia University, In *Proceedings of 19th Annual Software Engineering Workshop*, NASA Goddard Space Flight Center, Greenbelt, MD, November 30–December 1, 1994.

[8] Playle, Greg and Dr. Beckman, Carol, "Knowledge-Based Systems and Automated Software Validation and Verification," In *CrossTalk*, Software Technology Support Center, Ogden: Hill AFB, Vol. 9, No. 7, July 1996, pp. 17–20.

[9] Wallace, Dolores R., Ippolito, Laura M. and Cuthill, Barbara, *Reference Information for the Software Verification and Validation Process*, NIST SP500-234, NIST, Gaithersburg, MD 20899, April, 1996.

[10] Pierce, Preston, *Software Verification & Validation,* 1997, RELA, Inc., 6175 Longbow Drive, Boulder, CO 80301, (303) 530-2626.

APPENDIX A

Case Studies

Introduction

This appendix presents two case studies that illustrate many of the V&V concepts and issues that are discussed in this book.

The first case study—the MAPS information system—is derived from *Practical Software Measurement, A Foundation for Objective Project Management*[1] (pp. 6-3–6-27). While the focus is on measurement and metrics, the problems encountered in migrating from a legacy mainframe system to a distributed client/server architecture are typical V&V challenges. This study is primarily quoted from the original with modifications made to remove the names of personnel and military bases and to emphasize those areas that are particularly relevant to V&V.

The second case study, "Formal Methods for Verification and Validation of Partial Specifications: A Case Study,"[2] is a report directly from the NASA/West Virginia University Software Research Laboratory. It discusses several state-of-the-art techniques in the use of formal specifications and associated models and tools for independent V&V.

Case Study 1: MAPS Information System

Project Overview

This [case study] introduces the information system project scenario and illustrates the technical and management aspects of the development effort. The project scenario describes the implementation of a measurement process on an existing project. Special consideration is given to using software measurement data that are readily available within an established software and project management processes. The example project is representative of a typical information system project under development to meet business process reengineering objectives....

[In 1993, the Air Force started an initiative to reengineer the Air Force's administrative business processes.] The reengineering plan included service-wide initiatives to modernize information system hardware, software, and communications interfaces at both the base and headquarters levels. Existing mainframes and terminals were to be replaced by client/server architectures, and new capabilities were to be implemented by adapting existing databases and integrating them with newly developed applications software. [Military Automated Personnel System (MAPS) represented the Air Force's "next generation" military personnel information system.] MAPS was an important link in this business system modernization effort, since it was the first part of the overall system to be developed and delivered. MAPS was scheduled to be deployed at a number of Air Force bases during 1997....

In 1995, MAPS had been under development for two years. During that time, the MAPS's software development group had tried to keep current with changing DoD acquisition policy and related software initiatives. These included the definition of open systems architectures, the integration of commercial-off-the-shelf (COTS) software components, and the use of advanced programming languages and tools.

In November 1995, a new program manager was assigned to the MAPS project.... The program manager's assignment to the MAPS project did not come under the best of circumstances. At the time of his arrival, MAPS had just undergone an unsuccessful review by the DoD's oversight committee for major information systems. MAPS had failed to receive a Milestone III approval for system production and deployment. This was largely a result of problems with the software, especially with respect to the amount of completed functionality and the overall quality of the existing code. The [oversight committee] report indicated that there was little confidence in the cost and schedule estimates and a lack of available data to show how the key MAPS software development issues were being addressed....

The program manager's first task was to review the overall technical and management characteristics of the project and identifying the key software issues and problems that needed to be addressed.

In reviewing the MAPS project history with the MAPS's development team, the program manager learned exactly how MAPS fit into the Air Force Business Process Modernization Initiative. MAPS was the first application to be developed and was intended to reengineer the existing military personnel information system currently in use throughout the Air Force. Subsequent applications that were to be integrated as part of the initiative included revised supply, finance and accounting, medical, payroll, and base-level maintenance functions. The scope of the initiative was significant. In addition to the upgrade of the base-level business functions, the new applications were required to support a seamless interface at the headquarters level. Thus, almost all key Air Force information systems would be impacted in one way or another.

The program manager noted several key features of the Air Force Business Process Modernization Initiative:

- Client/Server Architecture: The existing mainframe computers and associated video display terminals were to be replaced by client/server architectures at each base and at each command headquarters.
- Open Systems: The current dependence on vendor-specific, proprietary operating systems and database management systems was to be replaced by open system standards-based archi-

tectures. A POSIX-compliant operating system had been selected as part of the software architecture for MAPS and the other Air Force information systems that were to be reengineered.

- Standard Data Elements: The efficient flow of data from one DoD information system to another was an important objective of the initiative. In order to achieve a high level of interoperability, the revised Air Force systems, including MAPS, had to adhere to a standard set of data definitions.
- Process Modeling: All of the business processes that fell under the modernization initiative were required to be modeled using the ICAM definition language (IDEF). This modeling effort was important to ensure the efficiency and interoperability of the various information systems that would be reengineered as part of the initiative.
- Integrated Databases: An important aspect of the modernization initiative was the intent to move away from "stove-piped" business applications, each with its own database and unique application characteristics. Therefore, MAPS had to include an integrated database that could be accessed by the various user applications using a common data interface. The intent was for any given data element to be entered only once at the point of origination. The data would then be made available to other applications. Development and control of the logical and physical data models rested with Defense Information Systems Agency (DISA), and again the MAPS design had to comply with higher-level requirements.
- Maximum use of COTS Software Components: The use of commercial software packages was strongly encouraged. As part of the modernization initiative, special waivers had to be obtained to develop unique software applications if a commercial counterpart that met the defined requirements was available.
- Technical Architecture Framework for Information Management (TAFIM): All of the revised information systems that comprised the modernization initiative, including MAPS, were required to be designed and implemented in accordance with the DoD TAFIM. They were required to demonstrate Level-3 compliance with the Defense Information Infrastructure Common Operating Environment.

[The system and software requirements, and high-level design were defined during 1993, the first year of the MAPS development.]... In November 1995, a briefing was given to the DoD... oversight group to support a Milestone III decision. Serious concerns were voiced by the members of the group during the briefing. The major issues focused on the development of the MAPS software and included the following:

1. The original software development schedule had been slipping on an incremental basis.
2. The revised "get well" schedule presented by the previous program manager appeared to be unrealistic, and could not be substantiated based upon the development performance to date.
3. Similar to the schedule issue, there was no credible basis for the cost projections presented to the [oversight committee].

4. It appeared to the oversight committee that the cost of the software was driven by the number of development personnel available, not by the size and capability of the software that had to be developed.

The original MAPS development plan called for two incremental deliveries. When the program manager arrived on the MAPS project in November 1995, the software for the first incremental release was under development.

MAPS began under a tailored MIL-STD-7935A[3] software process and was transitioning to MIL-STD-498.[4] The software development languages included both Ada 95 and C. Development tools included a state-of-the-art Ada programming support environment, a screen generator, and a report generator. A COTS relational database was also an integral part of the design.

The MAPS software design included 24 functionally defined Configuration Items (CIs). Thirteen of these were allocated to Increment 1 of the development and nine were allocated to Increment 2. The remaining two CIs were data conversion software. For each of these CIs, access to the database was to be implemented using SQL. User access and interface were designed to be implemented using predefined, "user friendly" screens. Site operators had additional access using SQL. The user interface was to be developed using X-Windows and was designed to be MOTIF compliant.

To better understand the goal of the MAPS project, the technical implications of migrating the architecture and functionality of the current military personnel system to the new MAPS requirements and specifications are explained.

Figure A.1 shows the hardware architecture for the current personnel system, which is actually two separate information systems. One resides at the base level and the other at command headquarters. Both the base level and the headquarters implementations were based on the use of mainframe computers and video display terminals. The applications for both legacy systems were written in COBOL and included hierarchical databases. Both incorporated character-oriented, non-graphical user interfaces.

The operating concept of the current system included periodic data transactions from the base-level system to the headquarters-level system. Selected data were uploaded to headquarters every 24 hours. As with many legacy information systems, the current military personnel implementation had experienced a significant number of problems with respect to inconsistent edits between the two systems. Part of this was attributable to the base-level system requiring very loose edits, while the edits for the headquarters system were much more constrained. Consequently, there was a large rejection rate for data that were uploaded to the headquarters system. As such, data were often lost in the transaction process.

To access data at the base level from the headquarters database, users had to log in and connect to the system over standard phone lines. This access approach had proven to be unreliable and added to the problems associated with transferring data.

The hardware architecture for MAPS is shown in Figure A.2. MAPS is designed as a single integrated personnel system that incorporates real-time data updates and access between the base-

Figure A.1 Existing personnel information system (p. 6-8).

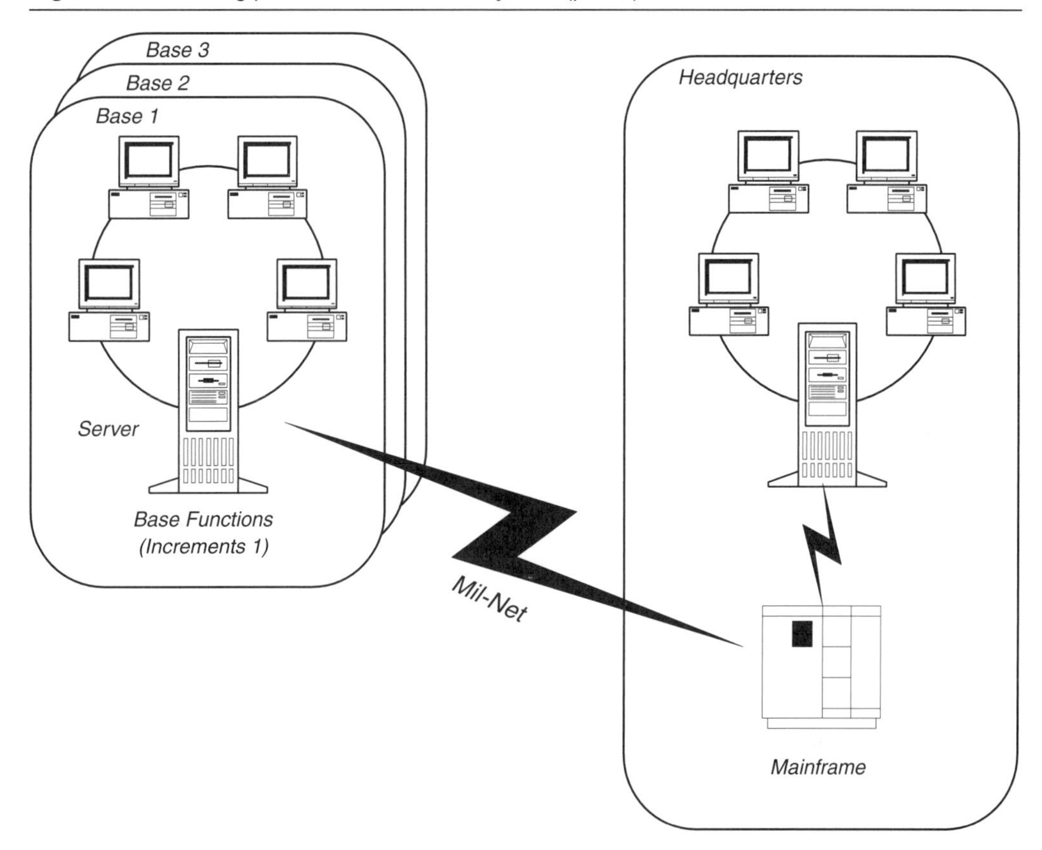

and headquarters-level system implementations. The headquarters portion of the system incorporates a mainframe computer that is used only for data storage. It is part of the headquarters local area network (LAN). MAPS incorporates a client/server design at both the base and headquarters levels. Data transfer between the levels is provided by a designated [military network] interface.

The MAPS client/server architecture integrates Graphical User Interface (GUI) and display functions on individual PCs, while the shared application functions reside on a UNIX-based server. This design is applicable at both the base and headquarters levels.

When MAPS is initially fielded at each Air Force base, it will be required to interface with the existing base-level information systems. These systems will gradually disappear as the Business Process Modernization Initiative progresses. As each existing information system is reengineered and integrated into the overall information system structure, all base-level applications will transition to a common enterprise architecture with access to a common database. As with MAPS, all interaction between applications will then occur through the shared database.

Figure A.2 MAPS system architecture (p. 6-9).

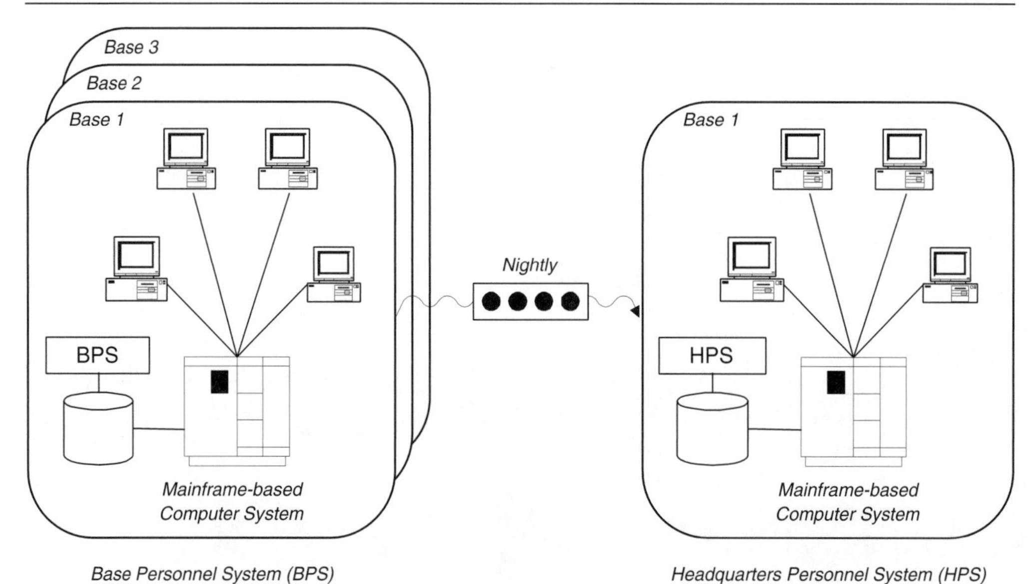

The MAPS design incorporates two functional subsystems. As expected, these include the base-level functional subsystem and the headquarters-level functional subsystem. The base-level subsystem includes those standard functions that support the military personnel assigned to individual bases, or to commands, such as individual aircraft squadrons, that are resident on base. The type of personnel data that must be available from MAPS at the base level includes individual information on each officer and enlisted person assigned to the base. These data include age, rank, skill level, training history, individual personnel assignment and promotion history, and information pertinent to past performance evaluations. The base-level MAPS subsystem also contains personnel information at the command level, such as squadron mobilization personnel requirements, casualty data, skill profiles, and personnel replacement priority information.

The MAPS headquarters subsystem includes military personnel functions that generally support higher-level information requirements than those needed at the base level. The headquarters subsystem provides information that supports overall force mobilization, strategic planning, and analysis of force manpower requirements. For example, if a senior Air Force commander wants to deploy an offensive air superiority fighter such as the F15-E, the headquarters subsystem can provide information about the location of each F15-E squadron, and the availability and training history of the pilots, maintenance personnel, and other support crew. If the Air Force needed to plan for night air sorties into mountainous terrain, MAPS would help identify those squadrons with the appropriate qualifications.

The overall MAPS development plan called for the subsystems to be developed and delivered in separate increments. Increment 1 would include the base-level functions, and Increment 2 would include the headquarters functions. In addition to development of the respective increment functionality, MAPS required that the data from the current military personnel information system be converted and entered into the redesigned MAPS data structures. As such, the MAPS software development effort included the development of data conversion software for both the base-level and the headquarters-level databases.

Getting the Project Under Control

...A detailed review of the software development and management processes revealed that the project was essentially being run with milestone schedules and viewgraphs. By mid-1995, the software development schedule milestones had begun to slip on a regular basis. Although this was evident in the milestone charts, no action was being taken to identify and correct the underlying causes. An analysis of the problem report data in the configuration management database showed that many more software problem reports were being opened than were being closed. All of the available personnel seemed to be assigned to implementing and testing the code to meet the defined schedule for Increment 1. There was not enough time to keep up with the problem fixes at this stage of the development.

[Two key issues had to be addressed to gain control over the MAPS software.] The primary issue was the software development schedule and progress. The feasibility of the current schedule had to be assessed, and a determination made as to why performance against the schedule was lagging. Second, the overall product quality of the developed software products had to be addressed. Based upon past experience, it was recognized that the software defects represented in the open problem report backlog had a lot to do with the schedule pressures. The schedule had also limited the time spent resolving and closing problems.

...[It was clear that better and more detailed information was needed to manage the critical software issues. A member of the project staff was assigned as the MAPS software measurement lead. The measurement lead had previous experience with implementing a measurement process, but this would be the first time she had to tailor and apply measurement for an existing project. The measurement lead and the program manager identified and prioritized the major software issues to be addressed by the measurement effort. The measurement activities were given a high priority to help get the project back on track, and also to show senior management how the project was progressing. There was enough basic measurement information to start to address the key issues, so these data were reviewed on a weekly basis.]

As one major step in gaining control of the MAPS development, the program manager put together an Integrated Product Team (IPT) consisting of representatives of a number of organizations associated with MAPS. These included the base-level and headquarters user communities, the designers, the test and integration organization, quality assurance, and installation personnel. [The measurement lead] was also a member of the IPT. The IPT's task was to identify and prioritize the risks to the project.

The major risk that the IPT identified was in converting the existing databases to the shared relational database that would be accessed not only by MAPS but by future applications as well.

One concern was that the existing data would be so error-prone that it would make the conversion process labor-intensive and would result in a schedule slippage. They estimated the probability of this occurring at 0.5, with impact on effort as well as schedule. Without more information, they viewed their probability estimate as a guess more than anything else. They also could not come up with a precise impact estimate.

[The other risk that the IPT identified] was that the process of data standardization that was necessary to make the shared data concept a reality would get bogged down in organizational battles. They estimated the probability that this would happen as 0.70. There was high-level support within the Air Force for data standardization. Their concern was that this could change with personnel changes in the future. They estimated the impact on MAPS as minor. The real impact would be on the Air Force vision of data sharing and interoperability.

The IPT... recommended two risk mitigation strategies to the program manager. To handle the error-prone data, they suggested that very close attention be paid to the first few data conversion efforts. The IPT felt that this would give them a much better sense of the extent of the problem and they could replan for more manual effort in the conversion phase if necessary. For the risk related to the data standardization effort, they suggested that the MAPS project take a proactive approach to working with other Air Force organizations... in identifying shared data and in reaching a consensus on the data model and data elements. They also identified a middleware package to use in translating between the MAPS data and the other databases if it turned out to be necessary.

[The program manager] gave the IPT the go-ahead to implement these recommendations. [He asked the measurement lead] to develop a means to quantify the extent of any problems related to data conversion. This quantitative data would be used as an objective basis to change the plan, if that proved to be necessary.

Evaluating the Software Development Plan

When [the program manager] reviewed the MAPS development plan, he tried to identify how the original schedules and staffing requirements had been established. The most detailed schedule information that was available was in the form of Gantt charts showing major project milestones and dates. There was little detail with respect to the low-level MAPS software development activities and associated CI development tasks. There was a project Work Breakdown Structure (WBS), but it seemed to apply only loosely to the current tasks. It appeared that the overall development schedule was driven by the required delivery date of the system. Key development activities were scheduled very optimistically to meet the delivery date.

There was no MAPS staffing plan that allocated personnel resources to specific software development tasks. A total of 40 software personnel were assigned full time to the MAPS project. All were available through the planned delivery date for Increment 2. The people were being applied to the project on a level of effort basis. The first question the program manager had to answer was whether or not the original MAPS software schedule was realistic, given the projected level of staffing and the overall performance of the development team to date.

[The program manager asked the measurement lead] to generate an independent schedule estimate based upon the size of the software and the expected software productivity. Although this sounded like a straightforward request, the measurement lead understood that the characteristics of the project required two separate sets of analysis. There were two different "types" of software development taking place, each described by distinct development approaches:

1. Development of the application software for both incremental deliveries. This development effort was based on the use of a commercial database, SQL, Ada, and screen-generation and report-generation tools.
2. Development of the data conversion software. This development effort could best be described as a "typical" support software development effort using a high order language with minimal process requirements.

[The measurement lead] needed to estimate the size of the software to be developed in order to generate a new estimate of the MAPS development schedule.... She decided to use function points as the basic size measure for the Increment 1 and 2 application software because of the mix of languages (Ada, SQL, code generators). The measurement lead used two methods to calculate the required productivity figures. In addition to a simple functional size-to-effort ratio, the measurement lead used a software cost model that accepted function points as data input. The model also took into account the productivity impact of language type and reused code.

For the data conversion software, [the measurement lead] decided to use lines of code to estimate the size of the software. In this case, lines of code seemed a better choice because she was not readily able to convert the sizing information to function points.

[The measurement lead] spent several weeks with the development team to arrive at the function point counts and the lines of code estimates. The function point counts were based upon the methodology defined in the Function Point Counting Practices Manual from the International Function Point Users Group (IFPUG). Estimates of source lines of code were generated for each of the application functions by the responsible team leaders....

[The measurement lead's] projections indicated the following:

- The minimum schedule to develop both functional increments would be four months longer than the current planned development schedule based on the MAPS software size indicator.
- In order to meet even the extended schedule, the MAPS development staffing levels would have to be significantly increased.

Although these analysis results were expected, they indicated that [the program manager] would have to replan the remainder of the MAPS project to define a more realistic development plan.

Revising the Software Development Plan

...The revised schedule began with the completed activities. The system requirements and high-level design activities were ongoing from July 1994 through May 1995. Top level requirements and design were completed early in the development effort for the entire system. With these activities complete, the revised schedule called for the independent development of the application software in two parallel increments as previously defined. The development of each increment included detailed design, coding, and integration and test.

The detailed design for Increment 1 was completed in November of 1995. Increment 1 was to be fielded by the end of 1996. Detailed design for Increment 2 was scheduled to begin in early 1996. Increment 2 was scheduled for delivery in mid 1997. The data conversion software was scheduled for parallel development with the respective functional increments. Data conversion and installation were scheduled to occur over a ten-month period for Increment 1 and a one-month period for Increment 2.

[The program manager] identified two major development activities on the critical path. These were the Personnel Information CI for the base-level subsystem and the data conversion software for both functional increments. The "Personnel Information" CI was critical because it had to be completed before the other CIs could be integrated and tested. The data conversion software was critical because it was needed to convert the existing databases at each base and at headquarters. The data conversion effort had already been identified as a high-risk item by the IPT. The data conversion software had to be completed, and had to work properly, before the MAPS increments could be fielded. The program manager decided to track these critical-path items closely. The results of the productivity analysis were also used as the basis for the revised MAPS staffing plan....

[When the program manager] looked at the total system effort profile that aggregated the individual effort requirements, several things became apparent. It was clear that the number of people currently assigned to the development team was not adequate to meet the peak staffing requirements that would occur in 1996. Even more important, the level staffing profile of 40 people did not meet the needs of the project. The development had been inefficiently overstaffed through 1995, and was then projected to experience staffing shortfalls as both Increments 1 and 2 were under development in 1996....

Tracking Performance Against the Revised Plan

Once the new schedule and staffing plans were in place, [the program manager's] concerns shifted from evaluating the feasibility of the plans to assessing performance against the plans. Although the milestone data continued to be useful in addressing the schedule and progress issues, more detailed information was required to track the degree of completion of the key development activities and products. The milestone schedule indicated that detailed design for Increment 1 had been completed, and software implementation was well underway. Based on the schedule, about two thirds of the time allocated for coding had already elapsed. This did not mean, however, that two thirds of the Increment 1 software had been coded. To get the information about the degree of activity and product completion that they needed, the team decided to implement several work unit progress measures.

Work unit progress measures compare the actual completion of associated work units for software products and activities against a pre-established plan. If objective completion criteria for each type of work unit are defined and adhered to, work unit progress measures provide for a clear determination of software development progress. For each of the MAPS CIs, the measurement lead recommended that the project use counts of the number of design units implemented as the measure of work unit progress. The design units represented the lowest practical level of measurement, and the data could easily be collected from the configuration management system. In this case, an implemented design unit was defined as passing unit test and being entered into the project library.

To generate the CI work unit progress indicators, [the measurement lead] first defined the planned rate of unit completion. Without detailed planning data available, the measurement lead generated a straight-line completion plan beginning with CDR and ending with the scheduled completion of the Increment 1 coding activity. In the measurement lead's previous experience with work unit progress measures, she had found that the more accurate plans for the cumulative number of work units completed over time often looked more like an S-shaped curve than a straight line. This was due to the fact that the first few units tended to be completed slowly, followed by a faster rate of completion rate as the activity progressed. Nearing the end of the software activity, the completion rates tended to slow again as the more difficult units tended to be completed last. For the MAPS work unit progress measures, the straight-line plan was not perfect, but was seen as a useful approximation. Everyone understood that they would not be too alarmed if progress lagged behind the straight-line plan at the beginning of the development activity.

Once [the measurement lead] had established the plan, she accessed the configuration management library to obtain a count of units completed to date. Specifically, she counted the number of units that had been entered into the library each week over the course of Increment 1 implementation.

[The measurement lead] knew that [the program manager] wanted to emphasize software measures related to the schedule and progress issue. As such, she decided to track progress for the two items on the critical path very closely. These were the development of the Personnel Information CI and the development of the data conversion software. The Personnel Information CI was scheduled to be completed by March 1996. The measurement lead constructed a plan to track work unit progress for the single CI the same way she did it for the aggregate of the CIs in Increment 1. Again, the plan was derived by drawing a straight line between CDR and the scheduled end of the coding activity. When the actual number of design units were compared to the plan, it became immediately clear that progress on this critical CI was lagging significantly.

[The measurement lead] then decided to try to identify the source of the progress problem in the Personnel Information CI. She defined two new work unit progress indicators using a somewhat different perspective. She graphed the development progress data for the screens and reports separately from the units that performed internal processing. The screens and reports were being implemented using a 4GL, while the internal processing code was being written in Ada.

...The measurement data showed that the screen and report development was on track and indicated that the problem was confined to the Ada code. When the program manager investigated, he found out that the Ada developers were having difficulty with interfacing their respective CIs to the COTS relational database. The problem was not critical from a technical perspective, but the workarounds were taking quite a bit of time to implement using SQL. The program manager did several things to correct the interface problems. The first thing that he did was to bring in representatives from the COTS vendors to work on-site with the Ada developers to provide real-time support in resolving interface problems. Secondly, he had the development team conduct a one-time, in-depth inspection of the CI's design and completed code. This inspection identified some design structures that were inefficient, but could be corrected. [The program manager] also assigned several of his most experienced Ada programmers to work on the Personnel Information CI in an attempt to correct the problem.

The other portion of the Increment 1 work that was on the critical path was the data conversion software for the base-level databases. In tracking work unit progress for this software, [the measurement lead] decided to count the lines of code that had been entered into the configuration management library rather than counting the number of completed units.

She decided that completed lines of code was a better measure of progress than a count of units because the data conversion software was divided up into relatively few units and they varied drastically in size. The units were not equivalent, and using them to track progress would have been misleading....

Evaluating Readiness for Test

During 1996, the MAPS measurement process was effective in helping to manage software development effort. Progress against the revised plan was sufficient to allow for the resolution of the problem reports that were previously backlogged. The additional personnel allowed for the concurrent development of both the base and headquarters level MAPS increments. The progress measures showed that Increment 1 was nearing the completion of integration and test, and some system level testing had already been conducted. The primary issue had shifted from schedule and progress to the quality of the software. The key question was the readiness of the software for Operational Test and Evaluation.

As the initial 1997 delivery dates grew closer, [the program manager] wanted to know if Increment 1 was ready to begin Operational Test. To help answer this question [the measurement lead] defined a set of related indicators. When the measurement lead first joined the MAPS project, the project had not been collecting effort data at the level of detail required to show how much effort was being applied to software rework. To get the data that she needed, [the measurement lead] asked one of the programmers to modify the problem reporting system to collect the "re-development" and "retesting" effort data related to software rework on a problem-by-problem basis. The change in the process was briefed to the developers, and [the measurement lead] began to collect the data she needed to compare the amount of effort spent in rework vs. new development....

[The measurement lead] combined the rework effort data with a work unit progress graph for cumulative problem reports and a graph of the number of problem reports being opened on a weekly basis. She also included a graph of test case progress. This combination of measurement indicators suggested that Increment 1 was not yet ready to begin Operational Test. [The program manager] wanted to see the open and closed problem report trends converging, the number of new problems being discovered declining, the number of test cases passed equal to the number planned, and the amount of effort being applied for rework decreasing. The results indicated that the development staff was increasingly spending time correcting new Increment 1 problems. This was of concern because they should have been transitioning to the development of the code for Increment 2. He met with [the measurement lead] and asked her for more information in order to identify what needed to be done to improve the situation. Specifically, he wanted information about the types of problems that were being reported. He was hoping that there was a common type of problem that could be effectively managed.

[The measurement lead] spent the better part of a week with several of the testing personnel reviewing the problem reports and classifying them as being related to performance, logic, interfaces, or other. She decided to implement this classification scheme as a permanent part of the problem reporting system so that the information would be readily available to support future analysis. The results of the classification effort were graphed. By far, the greatest number of the Increment 1 problems were related to performance deficiencies. [The measurement lead] further classified the performance problems according to their sources. The most common type of performance problem was due to the incorrect use of SQL by the developers.

[It was discovered]... and pointed out that the MAPS development represented the first time that many of the people on the development team had used a relational database and SQL. The staff's previous experience had been with hierarchical databases and COBOL. This probably should not have been a surprise since the SQL issue was part of the reason for the previous Personnel Information CI development problems. The program manager again decided to bring in some additional expertise to address the SQL issue. Although it may not have been the best approach this late in the project, the problems needed to be fixed quickly.

Increment 2 was scheduled for delivery early in 1997. According to the development schedule, Increment 2 should have been nearing the completion of system test by the end of February 1997. To assess the Increment 2 readiness for test status, [the measurement lead] generated the same combination of graphs using the same indicators as she had done for Increment 1.

This time the situation was much more encouraging. The trends for open and closed problem reports were converging, the discovery rate for new problems was declining rapidly, and the amount of rework was relatively low and stable. In addition, a comparison between the number of test cases planned, executed, and passed provided further evidence that testing was being completed in accordance with the schedule. [The measurement lead] wondered why the number of newly discovered problems was declining so rapidly, and asked the following questions:

- Was the software that much better?

- Were discovered problems not being reported?
- Had the testing stopped?

The test progress results helped [the measurement lead] answer part of her question. Since testing was proceeding as scheduled, the lower number of new problem reports were not a result of reduced testing efforts. [The measurement lead] looked into the reporting process and found that the identified problems were still being consistently documented.

[The measurement lead] continued to track the classes of reported problems. In contrast to the results for Increment 1, which had a high proportion of problems related to performance, the problems for Increment 2 were much more evenly distributed. The measurement data for Increment 2 indicated that the issues and problems that were experienced in Increment 1 had been successfully addressed....

With the development of the MAPS software proceeding according to plan, [the program manager] asked [the measurement lead] to extend the measurement process to track the progress of the fielding of the Increment 1 base-level systems at the various bases. This was scheduled to occur throughout 1997, from January through October, with delivery of the systems occurring at a relatively constant rate.

Installation and Software Support

To support the installation process, a total of ten people were assigned and divided into five teams. Each team was scheduled to spend two weeks installing MAPS at each of the 100 base-level sites. The work during the two-week installation period included data conversion, software installation, user training, and user support. After installation, the MAPS development team would provide support via a 24-hour help line. The plan called for each site to run the existing military personnel system concurrently with the newly installed MAPS for one week before shutting down the old system completely. The 100 base-level sites included all Air Force bases in the United States and overseas, Air Force Reserve commands, and selected Air National Guard units.

To address the installation progress question, [the measurement lead] defined and graphed a simple work unit progress indicator.... Since data conversion was one of the major risks identified by the IPT, she wanted to have the earliest possible warning of any problems.

It was clear from the graph that the installations were behind schedule almost from the start. [The measurement lead] investigated and contacted each of the installation teams to try to identify the causes for the delays. She heard a consistent story. The old base-level system that MAPS was replacing had very loose edit requirements. It would accept almost any personnel data that were entered. The result was that the data conversion software that was written to the MAPS data specifications kept rejecting data that were in a different format from what was expected. This was not an easy problem to fix because each of the existing base-level databases was different from the others.

[The measurement lead] showed [the program manager] a linear extrapolation of the actual installation data points.... Based on the actual rate of progress, a total of fifteen months would be required to complete the installations, not ten months as originally planned. The rate of base installation was limited by the availability of teams. Based on the projection, [the program manager] decided to extend the installation schedule. He also asked [the measurement lead] to provide an update to the projection as more data became available....

By November of 1997, 68 of the 100 base-level sites had been installed. As part of the measurement process, [the measurement lead] had been tracking and categorizing problem reports from the field. Given the previous problems on the project, it was important to... address the user's concerns.

At the highest level, [the measurement lead] classified the problem reports as being related to hardware, software, or user error. She analyzed the software-related problem reports in more detail by focusing on those that were the result of defects in the design or the code. She classified the problems as related to performance, logic, interfaces with other systems, and other. The data coming in from the field showed that the most frequent type of problem was related to logic defects....

[The measurement lead] also decided to classify the problems according to their source by identifying the CI that had to be changed in order to correct the problem. She graphed the ratio of problem reports to function points for each CI. The measurement lead found that the Unit Mobilization CI accounted for a disproportionate number of the logic defects....

[The measurement lead] was asked to compare how much effort was being applied to correcting the problems with what it would cost to redesign and redevelop the Unit Mobilization CI. The measurement lead noted that the Unit Mobilization CI required the equivalent of three full-time staff members to support problem resolution.... She was surprised that there continued to be such a high rate of newly discovered problems, particularly considering that the Unit Mobilization CI had been in operational use for almost a year. In talking with the lead programmer responsible for maintaining the CI, she found that as existing problems were corrected, new ones were being introduced. She decided to compare the cost of continuing to maintain the CI as currently implemented over a projected ten-year period with the cost of reengineering and maintaining a more reliable version of the CI. The screen and report generation functions did not need to be changed....

[The measurement lead] estimated that the cost of reengineering would be $1.2 million over a 10-month period, with estimated software support costs of $800K over the remaining nine-year period. This $2.0 million was compared to an estimated $3.0 million cost to maintain the existing CI over the same ten year time frame. This comparison was based on an average $100K cost per person year. [The program manager] decided to redesign the Unit Mobilization CI and planned to release it in the next MAPS update scheduled for late 1998.

Epilogue

The MAPS development turned out to be a good example of implementing a measurement process on an existing project. As the project progressed, the data required to manage the key issues was identified, collected, and analyzed. The measurement activity was focused on the primary software issues of schedule and progress, and product quality....

Case Study 2:*[2]
Formal Methods for Verification and Validation of Partial Specifications

Introduction

Requirements engineering methods typically provide a set of notations for expressing software specifications, together with tools for checking properties of specifications, such as completeness and consistency. In general, such methods demand a full commitment. It is assumed that the method will be used to construct a complete specification, which will then act as a baseline for subsequent development phases. However, to validate and verify large specifications for safety-critical real-time systems, it is sensible to apply a number of different methods, to overcome weaknesses and biases of each individual method. For example, a formal method might be used to model a critical portion of an informal specification, to check safety and liveness properties of that portion. In order to manage the application of multiple methods, it is necessary to develop and maintain alternative representations of partial specifications, and to express the relationships between them.

This paper describes a case study of the use of formal specification as a tool for Independent Verification and Validation (IV&V). Our intention is to use formal methods not as a part of the development process itself, but as a 'shadow' activity, performed by an independent team of experts. Our long-term expectation is that this approach will turn out to be a less painful way of introducing formal methods into well-established, large-scale software development processes.

There are a number of questions that need to be addressed before formal methods can be used in this way. Most published case studies of formal methods have focused on the use of a formal specification as a baseline from which design and code can be verified.[1] In contrast, we have been applying formal methods for intermittent "spot checks" to test for errors as the requirements evolve. The term "lightweight formal methods" has been used to describe this approach.[2] In this context, the formal specification may be dispensable—what is important is the insight gained from *the process of* formalizing partial views of the requirements and from validating properties of the resulting models. However, it is still necessary to demonstrate fidelity between the original (informal) specification, and the formal model. Furthermore, iterative application of this approach can be greatly facilitated if the relationships between the partial views are captured.[3]

The context for this work is the development of software for the International Space Station (ISS) project. Boeing Space and Defense Group Houston (Prime) is responsible for supervising the overall development and integration of 2 International Space Station software. There are three Product Groups (PGs), McDonnell Douglas Aerospace, Rockwell Aerospace - Rocketdyne and Boeing Space and Defense Group Huntsville, who are developing several key Computer Software Configuration Items (CSCIs). There are also several International Partners (IPs)

* Directly quoted from the NASA-IVV-97-010 Report.

including Russia, Japan, Canada, and the European Space Agency, who are developing software that will need to be incorporated into ISS. With over 45 flight computers and an estimated 1.1 million source line of flight code, the potential problems are considerable. Software IV&V is being performed by Intermetrics. The Intermetrics team is based at Fairmont, W.Va., with personnel stationed in Houston and Huntsville in order to interact with the development teams.

In section 2, we outline the IV&V process, and discuss the aspects of this process that hinder effective IV&V. The remainder of the paper focuses on the use of methods and tools within this process. The study made use of a combination of AND/OR tables,[4] the Software Cost Reduction (SCR) approach,[5] and the SPIN model checker.[6] Application of formal methods in this context was not always easy. The informal specification from which we derived our models did not permit an easy translation into a state-based model. We encountered problems in demonstrating fidelity, and providing traceability between the two. Section 4 discusses the issues involved in maintaining multiple representations of requirements, and the use of consistency checking to increase fidelity.

We conclude that in an IV&V context, the analytical benefits offered by formal methods have to be weighed against the effort needed to maintain fidelity between a formal model and the informal specification used by the development team. An IV&V team needs to be able to perform partial analyses on partial specifications, without being tied to any one formalism. The analysis carried out must be sufficient to reveal important problems, as opposed to surface defects. Further analysis is a waste of effort until these problems have been fixed. This conclusion implies a change of perspective for the use of formal methods: while the specification is still evolving it is important to identify quickly any major defects; it is not necessary to perform a complete analysis. Tools that are geared towards finding and characterizing such problems (e.g. SCR*,[5] Nitpick,[7] etc.) are more useful than tools geared towards proving correctness (e.g. theorem provers).

Context: The IV&V Process

For *Independent* Verification and Validation (IV&V), the software customer hires a separate contractor to analyze the products and process of the software development contractor. This analysis is performed in parallel with the development process, throughout the software lifecycle, and in no way replaces in-house verification and validation. IV&V is applied in high-cost and safety-critical projects to overcome analysis bias and reduce development risk. The customer relies on the IV&V contractor as an informed, unbiased advocate to assess the status of a project's schedule, cost, and the viability of its product during development. Most importantly, the IV&V contractor should be engaged as early as possible in the project: studies have shown that IV&V has the biggest impact in the early phases, especially in the requirements phase.[8]

As an example IV&V activity, consider the analysis of specifications on the Space Station project. The relevant development contractor writes a Software Requirements Specification (SRS) for each Software Configuration Item (CSCI). These specifications are written in natural language, and follow the format of DOD-STD-2167A. The IV&V contractor periodically receives copies of the SRS documents, in various stages of completion. The IV&V contractor analyzes these for technical integrity, in order to identify any requirements problems and risks. The kind of analysis performed will vary according to the level and the type of specification, and will cover issues such as clarity, testability, traceability, consistency and completeness. If problems are identified, the IV&V contractor may recommend that either the requirements be rewritten, or the problem be tracked through subsequent phases.

Performing IV&V on large projects is far from straightforward. Problems faced by the IV&V contractor include:

Resource allocation—A complete, detailed analysis of the entire system is infeasible. Effort has to be allocated so as to maximize effectiveness. A criticality and risk analysis may be performed to determine which components need the most scrutiny. Timing is also a factor; effort needs to be allocated at the right points in the development of a product (e.g. a document), so that the product is mature enough to be analyzed, but not so mature that it cannot be changed.

Short timescales—To be most effective, IV&V reports are needed as quickly as possible. There is always a delay between the delivery of an interim product to the IV&V team, and the completion of analysis of that product. During this time, the development process continues. Hence, if IV&V analysis takes too long, the results might be available too late to be useful. In general, the earlier an error is reported, the cheaper it is to correct.

Lack of access—Contact between the development team and the IV&V team is difficult to manage. The IV&V team needs to maintain independence, whilst ensuring they obtain enough information from the developers to do their job. From the developers' point of view, interaction with the IV&V team represents a cost overhead, which can interfere with project deadlines. Inevitably, the IV&V contractor has less access to the development team than is ideal.

Evolving products—Documentation from the development team is usually made available to the IV&V contractor in draft form, to facilitate early analysis. The drawback is that documents may be revised while the IV&V team is analyzing them, making the results of the analysis irrelevant before it is finished.

Reporting the right problems—The IV&V contractor has, by necessity, considerable discretion over the kinds of analysis to perform on different products. It also has discretion over which problems to report. It is vital to the effective use of IV&V that the IV&V contractor prioritizes the problems it identifies. If too many trivial problems are reported, this may swamp the communication channels with the developer and the customer.

Lack of voice—The IV&V contractor may have difficulty in getting its message across, especially when the development contractor disputes IV&V's assessment. Often, problems found by IV&V have cost and schedule implications, and in such circumstances the customer may be more willing to listen to assurances from the developer. The effectiveness of IV&V then depends on having a high-placed advocate within the customer organization.

Despite these problems, IV&V has been shown to be a cost-effective means of improving the quality of the software product, and providing extra assurance for high-cost, safety-critical projects.[9, 10] In addition to providing analysis of project artifacts (e.g. requirements, code, test plans), the presence of IV&V in the lifecycle also has a positive effect on the quality of the software. Our work suggests that the interaction between the IV&V and development teams drives improvements in both products and processes.[11, 12] This effect, however, is difficult to capture and quantify.

In this paper we report our work in the evaluation and adaptation of tools and methods for IV&V, and in particular the potential of formal methods to address the problems we have described. The choice of the right methods and tools is important to the success of IV&V. Ideally, an IV&V contractor will have access to all the tools used by the development team, including the ability to share all project databases. However, the IV&V team also needs to supplement these with additional methods and tools, to address any gaps or weaknesses in the coverage of the developer's tools. These additional tools need to complement the developer's tools, so that interoperability does not become a problem. The use of these additional tools is an important factor in ensuring that IV&V is truly independent.

It is often the case that the use of a particular method or tool by the IV&V team leads to the adoption of that method or tool by the developers. In part this is due to the 'watchdog effect': if the developers know that their product will be analyzed in a particular way, it is in their interest to perform the analysis themselves before releasing it. If this seems to be a rather negative reason to adopt a technique, there is also a positive aspect. Because the IV&V team is out of the critical path for the software development effort, they have more scope for experimentation with new techniques than the developers.[13] Hence, in some ways the IV&V team can play a role as a proving ground for new techniques, and can come to be an agent of process improvement. For these reasons, we believe that IV&V offers a practical route through which formal methods may be introduced into projects that would otherwise not be able to adopt them.

There are still problems to be overcome whenever the IV&V team adopts a tool that is not used by the developers. If the IV&V team uses a formal specification tool, the informal specification delivered by the developers will need to be translated into the formal specification language not just once, but each time the developers produce a new draft. Any problems identified by using the tool must be traced back to the informal specification, before they can be reported. There must be a reasonable assurance that the formal specification remains faithful to the original, otherwise any analysis performed on it is worthless. Hence, keeping track of the relationship between the formal and informal specifications is vital.

Lightweight formal methods seems to offer an ideal tools for IV&V. We use the term 'lightweight' to indicate that the methods can be used to perform partial analysis on partial specifications, without a commitment to developing and baselining complete, consistent formal spec-

```
(2.16.3.f) While acting as the bus controller, the C&C MDM CSCI shall
set the e,c,w, indicator identified in Table 3.2.16-II for the corre-
sponding RT to "failed" and set the failure status to "failed" for all
RT's on the bus upon detection of transaction errors of selected mes-
sages to RTs whose 1553 FDIR is not inhibited in two consecutive pro-
cessing frames within 100 millisec of detection of the second
transaction error if; a backup BC is available, the BC has been
switched in the last 20 sec, the SPD card reset capability is inhib-
ited, or the SPD card has been reset in the last 10 major (10-second)
frames, and either:

1. the transaction errors are from multiple RT's, the current channel
has been reset within the last major frame, or

2. the transaction errors are from multiple RT's, the bus channel's
reset capability is inhibited, and the current channel has not been
reset within the last major frame.
```

Figure 1. An example of a level 3 requirement for Bus FDIR. This requirement specifies the circumstances under which all remote terminals (RTs) on the bus should be switched to their backups.

ifications. The formal methods are used to model critical chunks of an informal specification, to check that key properties hold. Application of the methods is driven by the needs of the project, and is used as a modeling tool to answer questions that arise during verification and validation. In the remainder of the paper we describe a case study that investigated the applicability of lightweight formal methods to an IV&V effort.

The Case Study

The purpose of this case study was to analyze the detailed Fault Detection, Isolation and Recovery (FDIR) requirements associated with the bus controller for the main 1553 communications bus on the space station. The study was conducted at the request of the Independent Verification and Validation (IV&V) team. The IV&V team was having particular difficulty validating the bus FDIR requirements, as they were hard to read, and some of the properties they wished to test could not be established using existing informal methods. The study was conducted by the authors, as part of a larger study of the use of formal methods in the V&V process.[14]

The requirements for Bus FDIR had been expressed in natural language, with a supporting flowchart showing the processing steps involved. The flowchart did not have the status of a requirement, but was merely provided for guidance; the intention was that the prose completely expressed the requirements. The prose contained a number of long complicated sentences, expressing complex conjunctions and disjunctions of conditions (E.g. see figure 1). The IV&V team had recommended that to improve clarity, the requirements should be re-written in a tabular form (specifically, as truth tables similar to those used by Heimdahl & Leveson[4]). This recommendation had been rejected because of the cost involved in re-writing them all. The IV&V team was the faced with the problem of how to validate the informal statement of the requirements, given that this informal statement would act as the baseline. Hence, the IV&V team generated their own tabular versions, in order to facilitate the kinds of analysis they wished to perform.

Approach

Our approach to the application of formal methods in an IV&V context follows a simple four step process as follows:

1. restate the requirements in a clear, precise and unambiguous format;
2. identify & correct internal inconsistencies;
3. test the requirements by proving statements about expected behavior;
4. feed the results back to the requirements authors.

In some cases step 1 involves the use of an intermediate representation, as abstractions introduced in the formalization do not necessarily have any natural correspondences in the original requirements statements. In such cases, intermediate representations help to ease the translation process, and help to provide a traceability path between the informal and formal statements.

For this case study, the four step approach was applied as follows. Each individual requirement was restated as a truth table, to clarify the logic. These were then combined into a single state-machine model, using SCR.[5] The SCR model was checked for consistency using the SCR toolset. Properties of the model were then tested in two ways. Firstly, static properties of the state model, such as disjointness and coverage, were tested using the built-in checker in the SCR tool. Secondly, dynamic properties of the model were tested by translating the SCR state machine model into PROMELA,[6] and applying the SPIN model checker to explore its behavior. This allowed us to explore timing properties that could not be validated in SCR. The results were fed back to the development team through the normal IV&V reporting process.

The choices of method and notation to use in the study were entirely pragmatic. In each case, the choice was made only after the previous step was underway, and the decision was driven by a need to test certain properties. The initial truth table representation was chosen as it was precise, easy to read, and represented approximately the same abstraction as the original informal requirements (See table 1). These tables are modeled on the AND/OR tables adopted by Leveson during the development of the RSML specifications for TCAS II.[4]

SCR was chosen as it offered a tabular notation that corresponded well to the truth tables that the IV&V team had already adopted, and it provided tool support for checking consistency of state models. The consistency checking in SCR is sufficiently sophisticated that it allowed us to express some of the validation properties as consistency checks. Specifically, we wanted to establish that each failure mode in the model was disjoint (i.e. that there was no condition in which two different failure modes would be diagnosed simultaneously), and that together the failure modes covered all possible combinations of failure conditions. By expressing the failure modes as a mode transition table in SCR, we could test these properties automatically. Most importantly, the tool did not require us to define the complete state model in order to test these properties. A further advantage of SCR was that the consistency checker in the SCR tool provides a counter-example whenever an inconsistency is found. The provision of counter-examples is important in tracing problems back to the informal specification, and in convincing the development team that there really is a problem.

The SPIN model checker was adopted for the final part of the study,* as it allowed us to explore dynamic aspects of the state model, including the ability to simulate different types of error condition. Properties of interest were expressed as "never clauses", so that the model checker would report any reachable state where the property was satisfied. Interesting error conditions, such as intermittent and repeating faults, were simulated by including a test harness in the PROMELA model, to set and reset the inputs to the fault detection model. Strictly speaking this test harness was unnecessary, as it merely produced a specialization of the original model. However, we found it useful as a way of reducing the search space, and observing certain key behaviors directly, rather than searching for them in the model.

			OR		
	C&C MDM acting as the bus controller	T	T	T	T
	Detection of transaction errors in two consecutive processing frames	T	T	T	T
	errors are on selected messages	T	T	T	T
	the RT's 1553 FDIR is not inhibited	T	T	T	T
	A backup BC is available	T	T	T	T
A	The BC has been switched in the last 20 seconds	T	T	T	T
N	The SPD card reset capability is inhibited	T	T	o	o
D	The SPD card has been reset in the last 10 major (10 second) frames	o	o	T	T
	The transaction errors are from multiple RTs	T	T	T	T
	The current channel has been reset within the last major frame	T	F	T	F
	The bus channel's reset capability is inhibited	o	T	o	T

Table 1: The truth table version of the requirement shown in figure 1, showing the four conditions (the four columns) under which the action should be carried out. A "o" indicates "don't care".

* Note: since this case study was conducted, the spin model checker has been incorporated into the SCR toolset.[15]

Procedure

The generation of a tabular interpretation of each individual requirement proved to be hard, as there are a number of ambiguities in the prose requirements. These ambiguities concern the associativity of 'and' and 'or' in English, and the correct binding of subclauses of long sentences. For example, in figure 1, it is not clear what the phrase "in two consecutive processing frames" refers to. To confirm the existence of such ambiguities, the requirement shown in Figure 1 was given to four different people, for translation into tabular form. Four semantically different tables resulted. By comparing these different interpretations, an extensive list of ambiguities was compiled. The ambiguities were resolved through detailed reading of the documentation, and questioning the original authors. This process also revealed some inconsistencies in the way in which terminology was used.

Current Mode	Conditions											Next Mode
	errors in two cons. frames	bus swch'd last frame	bus switch inhibit	bus swch'd this avail.	backup BC 20 sec.	BC swch'd in last inhibit	card reset frames	card reset last 10 RTs	errors from mult. frame	channel reset last frame	channel reset inhibit	
Normal	@T	—	—	F	—	—	—	—	—	—	—	switch buses
	@T	—	T	F	—	—	—	—	—	—	F	reset the channel
	@T	T	—	F	—	—	—	—	—	—	F	
	@T	—	—	—	—	—	F	F	T	T	—	reset the card
	@T	—	—	—	—	—	F	F	T	F	T	
	@T	T	—	—	—	—	—	—	F	T	—	switch RT to backup
	@T	F	T	—	—	—	—	—	F	T	—	
	@T	T	—	—	—	—	—	—	F	F	T	
	@T	F	T	—	—	—	—	—	F	F	T	
	@T	—	—	—	T	F	T	—	T	T	—	switch BC to backup
	@T	—	—	—	T	F	T	—	T	F	T	
	@T	—	—	—	T	F	—	T	T	T	—	
	@T	—	—	—	T	F	—	T	T	F	T	
	@T	—	—	—	T	T	T	—	T	T	—	switch all RTs
	@T	—	—	—	T	T	T	—	T	F	T	
	@T	—	—	—	T	T	—	T	T	T	—	
	@T	—	—	—	T	T	—	T	T	F	T	

Table 2: An SCR Mode transition table. Each of the central columns represents a condition, showing whether it should be true or false; "—" means "don't care"; "@T" indicates a trigger condition for the mode transition. The four columns of table 1 correspond to the last four rows of this table. The semantics of SCR require this table to represent a function, so that the disjunction of all the rows covers all possible conditions (coverage), and the conjunction of any two rows is false (disjointness).

Merging the individual AND/OR tables to produce the SCR model (Table 2) was not straightforward. Although there were a number of conditions common to several of the tables, the wording varied, and it was not always obvious whether similar sounding phrases actually referred to the same condition, due to inconsistencies in the use of terminology. For example the condition "the bus has been switched in the major (10-second) frame" appeared in one paragraph, and "the bus has been switched in the last major frame" appeared in another. We initially assumed these to be equivalent. However, this led to an inconsistency in the table. In fact the former refers to the current frame, while the latter refers to the previous frame. There were numerous places where we had to make assumptions to proceed, and we carefully recorded these as annotations to the original text, to be checked with the developers.

Having obtained a clearer statement of the requirements, the next step was to explore some of the properties that ought to be true of these requirements. Example properties are "for each combination of failure conditions, there is an FDIR response specified" and "for each combination of failure conditions there is at most one FDIR response specified". These properties correspond to checks for coverage and completeness of a mode table in SCR. By constructing a state-based model in which each of the requirements represented a transition from the "normal" mode to a unique failure mode, the coverage and disjointness tests in the SCR tool would test these properties Note that the failure modes are not identified explicitly in the original specification. In Table 2, we have named them after the corrective action rather than the type of failure, to preserve traceability to the informal specification. A number of disjointness problems were identified at this stage, which are described below.

The final part of this study was to explore the dynamic properties of the model. For example, some of the requirements express conditions that test whether various recovery actions have already been tried. In order to validate these conditions, it was necessary to explore the dynamic behavior of the specified system in the face of multiple failures, and recurring failures. To do this we needed a way to exhaustively search the state space for safety and liveness properties. We needed to add non-determinism to the model, to simulate possible occurrences of faults, as inputs to the system being modeled. The state-based model expressed in SCR was translated into PROMELA, and the model checker SPIN was used to explore the behaviors.

The PROMELA model consisted of a number of concurrent processes. The main process modeled the failure diagnosis model, and was translated more or less directly from the SCR mode table. Figure 2 shows a portion of this process, and can be compared with the mode table shown in table 2. Additional processes were added for: the state space of inputs to the system, a timer to model timeout behavior, and a simulation of the state of each of the devices that the FDIR system interacts with.

Experimentation with this model in SPIN indicated some inconsistencies in the timing constraints that had not been revealed in the SCR model. Once these were fixed, the model checker was used to verify properties such as "if an error persists after all recovery actions have been tried, the bus FDIR will eventually report failure of itself to a higher level FDIR domain". Figure 3 shows how a claim such as this is translated into a Linear Temporal Logic (LTL) formula, to be used by the model checker.

```
proctype FDIR_mode_pc ()
{
mtype mode = normal;

end:
   do :: new_frame?true ->
      if
         :: (errors == false || FDIR_inhibit_RT == true) -> mode = normal
         :: else -> if
            :: /* [branches here for each failure mode] */
            ::
            :: (((backup_BC_avail == true) && (BC_switched_20_sec == false)
      && ((cd_reset_inhibit == true) || (cd_reset == true))
      && (((errors_mult_RTs == true) && (ch_reset_last == true))
      || ((errors_mult_RTs == true) && (ch_reset_inhibit == true)
      && (ch_reset_last == false)))) && mode == error1) ->
      atomic{ mode = fm_BC_failure;
              BC_switch_count = BC_SWITCH_TIMEOUT };
                   BC_switcher!true

         :: else -> assert(false) /* This is a coverage error */
         fi
      fi; new_frame!false
   od
}
```

Figure 2: Excerpt from the promela model. The inner if loop contains branches for each of the failure modes shown in table 2. Only the code for the failure mode "Switch BC to backup" is shown here. This branch corresponds to four rows in Table 2.

```
#define p (errors==true)
#define q (mode==fm_BC_failure)
[](p -> <>(!p \/ q))
```

Figure 3: A sample proof claim for the SPIN model. The symbols [] and <> are the usual temporal operators 'always' and 'eventually'. The claim is "whenever an error occurs, eventually a state will be reached in which the error is cleared or the b us controller will report failure of itself to a higher level FDIR domain". This claim failed, leading to finding 4 described in section 3.3

Findings

In addition to a number of minor problems with inconsistent use of terminology, the following major problems were reported:

1. There were significant ambiguities in the prose requirements, as a result of the complex sentence structure. Some of these ambiguities could be resolved by studying the higher

level FDIR requirements, and the specifications for the bus architecture. The ambiguities that arose from the combination of 'ands' and 'ors' in the same sentence could not be resolved in this way, and could lead to mistakes in the design. These ambiguities were detected in the initial reformulation of the requirements as truth tables

2. There was one missing requirement to test the value of the Bus Switch Inhibit Flag before attempting to switch to the backup bus. This was detected during the test for disjointness in the SCR specification.
3. The prose requirements were missing a number of preconditions that enforce the ordering in which the inference rules should be applied. The accompanying flowchart for these requirements implied a sequence for these rules. An attempt had been made in the prose requirements to express this sequence as a set of preconditions for each rule, to ensure that all the earlier rules have been tested and have failed. The preconditions did not completely capture the precedences implied by flowchart. This corresponded with an informal observation made by the IV&V team that the ordering of the requirements should be made explicit. This problem was found during the test for disjointness in the SCR specification.
4. The timing constraints expressed in the requirements were incorrect. Several of the failure isolation tests referred to testing whether certain FDIR actions had already been tried "in the previous processing frame". However, as each FDIR recovery action is followed by a time-out in order for the action to take effect, and as further FDIR intervention is only initiated on occurrence of errors in two consecutive processing frames, these tests can never be true. This was discovered during model checking of the PROMELA model.

Observations

The study analyzed 15 pages of level 3 requirements, and was conducted over a period of four months, by one person working part time. The total effort was approximately 1.5 person months. The main effort was in formalizing the requirements. Translation from the SCR model to PROMELA was relatively straightforward, and took two days effort. Once a formal model was obtained, testing of the properties was straightforward, as both the SCR tool and the SPIN model checker provided facilities for automated checking of these properties, and provided counter-examples when the tests failed. Although problems were found both during formalization and the property checking, the latter problems were more serious. It is unlikely that they would have been discovered in this phase without the use of formal methods.

A major difficulty during this study was the volatility of the requirements. New drafts of the requirements document were being released approximately every two months. This meant that in at least one case (finding 3 above), the problem had already been fixed by the time it was discovered in this study. This particular finding had already been observed informally and reported by the IV&V team, and had been addressed by reducing the complexity of this section of the requirements. We mitigated the problem of fluctuating requirements by only doing the minimum amount of modeling necessary to test the properties that were of interest. For example, the SCR model is not a complete state model, as it models only a subset of the state transitions expressed in the requirements. The transitions for returning to the normal state have not been modeled. This partial model was sufficient to perform the coverage and disjointness analysis.

It should also be noted that in order to perform the analysis in this study, the SCR notation was slightly misused. The modes shown in figure 4 do not represent true modes in the SCR sense – a more correct representation would express these as output events from the FDIR system. However, defining them as modes permitted the use of coverage and disjointness tests on the transitions. This reflects our pragmatic approach in which the formal method is applied in whatever way gives the most benefit, without necessarily following the original intent of the method

Discussion

This paper presented a case study on the use of formal methods for IV&V. The results are very encouraging: the translation process was extremely valuable in identifying ambiguities and improving our understanding of the specification. In this process, a number of errors were found. Analysis of a partial formal specification demonstrated several important errors in the specification, and appears to be a powerful means of gaining maximal results from minimal effort. We constructed just enough of a model to test the properties we were interested in, without any further commitment to the method.

The study described in this paper differs from other studies in the literature in several ways. The majority of published case studies of the use of formal methods are post hoc application of formal method to on-going or finished projects. Such studies are demonstrate what formal methods can do, and help to refine the methods, but they do not help to answer questions of how such methods can be integrated with existing practices on large projects. A few notable exceptions have used formal methods 'live' during the development of real systems.[1, 4, 16, 17] However, in all these cases, the emphasis was on the use of formal notations as a part of the baseline specifications, from which varying degrees of formal verification of the resulting design and implementation are possible. In contrast, we applied formal methods as a means of performing V&V on an informal baseline specification. Rather than treating formal specification as an end product of the requirements phase, we used it to answer questions and improve the quality of the existing specifications.

The introduction of formal methods as an IV&V technique for large projects offers a low risk approach to technology transfer. This approach allows us to be flexible and pragmatic. The amount of formal modeling performed can be varied according to the project needs. In particular, the case study indicates that significant results can be obtained from the use of formal methods using partial validation of partial specifications. For an IV&V team, the formal methods provide an additional tool to be used on highly critical sections of a specification, or to test certain key properties, where existing techniques cannot help.

There are two potential pitfalls with this approach: it is hard to guarantee fidelity between informal and formal specifications, and it is hard to manage consistency between partial specifications expressed in different notations. These problems arise from the need to maintain both informal and formal specifications of the same requirements.

The fidelity issue is more of a problem in IV&V than in development. A formal model developed by the IV&V team cannot replace the informal specification. The IV&V team must therefore either persuade the developers to adopt formal notations themselves, or take care to maintain fidelity between the developers' informal specifications and their own formal models. The formal models are only useful for checking the developer's specifications if they are accurate representations of the developer's specifications. Also, when analysis of the formal models reveals problems in the specifications, these problems must be traced back to the informal specification before they can be reported.

Although the fidelity problem can affect the utility of any formal analysis performed by the IV&V team, we should point out that it does not affect all the benefits of formal specification. The process of translating pieces of the informal specification into a formal notation has benefit not just for the analysis that it leads to, but also for the removal of ambiguities and for improved understanding. For this benefit, it is the process of formalization, rather than the end product that is important. In particular, we observed that the IV&V analysts had a much better understanding of the requirements after conducting the translation exercise than they would normally obtain.

The fidelity problem is really a special case of a more general problem: management of consistency between partial specifications expressed in different notations.[3] For instance, the AND/OR tables have a clear relationship with the SCR mode tables, but if we make a correction to one of the AND/OR tables, it is fairly tedious to identify the corresponding correction in the SCR tables. Similarly, each time the developers issue a new informal specification, we need to update our tabular representations. Although it may seem that the use of both AND/OR tables and SCR models together would compound this problem, the opposite is true. The AND/OR tables mapped clearly onto the textual requirements, while the relationship between the AND/OR tables and the SCR model was relatively straightforward. Therefore, the use of AND/OR tables as an intermediate representation reduced the traceability gap, and made it easier to keep the formal model up to date. There remains, however, a significant bookkeeping problem.

There is a growing body of work on managing consistency in specifications. Our previous work demonstrated how to delay the resolution of inconsistency, and provided a generic framework for expressing consistency relationships.[3] Other work has taken consistency checking further, making use of semantic models underlying a method to determine what consistency rules are needed and how to operationalize them. For example, Heitmeyer's work with consistency checking in SCR[5] uses the semantics of SCR to define a series of consistency rules ranging from simple syntactic checks (e.g. that all names are unique) to sophisticated properties of tables (e.g. coverage and disjointness). Similarly, Leveson's work on consistency checking in RSML[4] uses the semantics of the statechart formalism to determine a set of consistency rules that can be tested, tractably, using a high level abstract model. In both these approaches, the completeness of the formal specifications is important, and consistency checking is seen as part of the process of obtaining a complete, consistent specification.

Unfortunately, these approaches do not help with consistency checking between partial specifications expressed in different notations. Because the IV&V process is concurrent with and complementary to the development process, there is an unusually large amount of flexibility in how a formal method can be used. There is no need to make a commitment to any one formal notation, just as there is no need to develop complete specifications. In fact, the aim of the IV&V agent is not to perform complete analyses, but to do just enough analysis to check specific aspects of the software. Development of complete formal models is therefore unnecessary and may be counter-productive. For example, in our second experiment, the limited analysis we performed on a partial model was sufficient to reveal a major problem; the existence of this problem meant that any further effort to complete the model would have been wasted.

While the use of partial specifications offers greater flexibility in the use of methods and tools, it also means that we do not have a well-defined method from which to generate a set of consistency relationships. There are implicit consistency relationships between the assorted partial specifications drawn from different methods, but there is no overall 'method' to tell us what these relationships are. Actually, there is a method: the problem is that the method is implicit, and to some extent is generated on the fly. For example, there is a method for generating SCR mode tables from the AND/OR tables, but the method was not defined before we did it. With some effort, we could formalize this method, and define semantic relationships between the two types of table. However, this effort will only be worthwhile if we intend to re-use the method extensively. In the meantime, we would like to have tools to help us keep track of consistency relationships in our opportunistic use of partial specifications.

In our previous work defining consistency relationships between viewpoints, we assumed that the majority of such rules are defined by the method.[18] The viewpoints framework explicitly supports the process of method definition, in which, among other things, the inter-viewpoint relationships are defined. Hence the general problem of defining arbitrary relationships between any two notations is avoided. However, we also recognized that some consistency relationships could not be defined in this way, and gave the example of a user-defined synonym relationship between two different labels. We outlined an approach to discovering such relationships through low level process monitoring. We now regard this type of consistency relationship as vital to any approach involving partial specifications.

Conclusions

This paper has described our initial work in the use of formal methods in an IV&V project. We have discussed how the demands placed on methods and tools in IV&V are different from their use in a development context. We have also discussed how IV&V can act as a process improvement agent, and hence can be a fruitful way of introducing formal methods into large projects.

As with all potential uses of a new method, any extra effort needed to use the method must be more than offset by the benefits it brings. Use of a method in IV&V is no different. We can divide the benefits of using formal methods in IV&V into three areas:

- The process of translating portions of a specification into formal notations helps to detect ambiguities and increase readability, even if the translation is only partial. The process can also be used to catch misunderstandings, thus increasing the confidence that the IV&V team is interpreting the specification correctly. The process of having several analysts produce their own tabular translations was particularly useful in this respect. Differences in the tables they produced allowed us to pinpoint exactly where the ambiguities were.
- The partial formal models can be analyzed for internal consistency, to help establish the technical integrity of the original, informal specification. This step also helps to check that the models are faithful to the original.
- The partial formal models can be tested against key domain properties, to validate the original requirements. In our study, this included both static and dynamic properties of the state-based model. Such properties are particularly hard to analyze from the informal specifications. Most importantly, this analysis can be conducted without the need to build complete models.

From this study, we conclude that lightweight formal methods are an ideal tool for an IV&V agent. They address many of the problems we identified in section 2:

Limited resources: Lightweight formal methods can be applied to selected portions of specifications. The amount of modeling and analysis can be adjusted to fit resource constraints.

Short timescales: Partial analysis can generate preliminary results quickly, as the analysis can proceed even without a full model.

Lack of access: The case study demonstrated that a formal modeling effort can be based almost exclusively on informal documents. Interaction with the development team was only necessary to check assumptions, and to discuss the analysis results.

Evolving Products: Small, partial models can be generated quickly, and updated as the specification evolves. The investment in each model is small enough that they can be discarded if the specification changes significantly.

Avoiding trivial/obvious problems: Formal analysis can reveal subtle problems that escape the notice of informal, inspection-based methods. In particular, it is a powerful way of detecting timing and safety-related problems. The formal analysis also allowed us to explore the significance of potential errors before reporting them.

Lack of voice: Formal methods can help the IV&V agent to strengthen their case when they report issues back to the customer and developer. Animation of formal models provides a powerful was of demonstrating errors, and helps to provide a more precise characterization of each problem.

The problems we encountered in applying formal methods were as follows:

- The process of translating into a formal notation is error-prone. Only by duplicating the translation effort were we able to discover just how much scope there is for misinterpretation. Luckily, our chosen formal notations were very readable. Therefore it is much easier to compare different tables than it is to compare different versions of the informal specification.
- For IV&V, fidelity and traceability between the informal and formal specifications is difficult to guarantee. The value of any analysis carried out by IV&V on the formal model is entirely dependent on how faithful the formal model is to the developer's informal specification. The IV&V's formal model can not be used in place of the informal specifications produced by the developers.
- Opportunistic use of partial specifications means that there is not a well-defined method from which to derive consistency rules. Maintenance of consistency in our partial specifications became a real problem.

The problem of consistency checking in partial specifications written in different notations is important enough to warrant more attention. We plan to study the problem in more detail by developing a set of tools based on the ViewPoints framework, which will allow us to model relationships between partial specifications written by different people. We are also exploring how this problem relates to that of linking test case scenarios to requirements.[19]

Acknowledgments

Our thanks are due to Chuck Neppach and Dan McCaugherty for many interesting discussions of the work presented here, and to Frank Schneider, Edward Addy, John Hinkle, George Sabolish, Todd Montgomery and Butch Neal for detailed comments on earlier drafts of this paper. This work was supported by NASA Cooperative Research Agreement NCCW-0040.

Notes

1 D. Craigen, S. L. Gerhart, and T. Ralston, "Formal Methods Reality Check: Industrial Usage," IEEE Transactions on Software Engineering, vol. 21, pp. 90–98, 1995.

2 H. Saiedain, J. P. Bowen, R. W. Butler, D. L. Dill, R. L. Glass, A. Hall, M. G. Hinchey, C. M. Holloway, D. Jackson, C. B. Jones, M. J. Lutz, D. L. Parnas, J. Rushby, J. Wing, and P. Zave, "An Invitation to Formal Methods," IEEE Computer, vol. 29, pp. 16–30, 1996.

3 S. M. Easterbrook and B. Nuseibeh, "Using ViewPoints for Inconsistency Management," Software Engineering Journal, vol. 11, pp. 31–43, 1996.

4 M. Heimdahl and N. Leveson, "Completeness and Consistency Analysis of State-Based Requirements," IEEE Transactions on Software Engineering, vol. 22, pp. 363–377, 1996.

[5] C. L. Heitmeyer, B. Labaw, and D. Kiskis, "Consistency Checking of SCR-Style Requirements Specifications," Second IEEE Symposium on Requirements Engineering, York, UK, March 27–29, 1995.

[6] G. J. Holtzmann, Design and Validation of Computer Protocols: Prentice Hall, 1991.

[7] D. Jackson and C. A. Damon, "Elements of Style: Analysing a software design with a counter-example detector," International Symposium on Software Testing and Analysis (ISSTA'96), San Diego, CA, 8-10 January 1996.

[8] R. O. Lewis, Independent Verification and Validation: A Lifecycle Engineering Process for Quality Software: J. Wiley & Sons, 1992.

[9] Jet Propulsion Lab, "Cost-effectiveness of Software Independent Verification and Validation," NASA JPL, Pasadena, CA, NASA RTOP report 1985.

[10] J. D. Arthur, M. K. Groener, S. Gupta, M. Cannon, and Z. Khan, "Reducing the Mean Time to Remove Faults Through Early Error Detection: An Experiment in Independent Verification and Validation," 18th Minnowbrook Workshop on Software Engineering, Blue Mountain Lake, NY.

[11] J. Callahan and G. Sabolish, "A Process Improvement Model for Software Verification and Validation," Journal of the Quality Assurance Institute, vol. 10, pp. 24–32, 1996.

[12] S. M. Easterbrook, "The Role of Independent V&V in Upstream Software Development Processes," Second World Conference on Integrated Design and Process Technology (IDPT-96), Austin, TX, Dec 1996.

[13] V. Basili, "The Experience Factory and its relationship to other improvement paradigms," Proceedings of the 4th European Software Engineering Conference (ESEC'93), Garmish-Partenkirchen, Germany, September 1993.

[14] R. W. Butler, J. L. Caldwell, V. A. Carreno, C. M. Holloway, P. S. Miner, and B. L. Di Vito, "NASA Langley's Research and Technology Transfer Program in Formal Methods," Tenth Annual Conference on Computer Assurance (COMPASS 95), Gaithersburg, MD, June 1995.

[15] R. Bharadwaj and C. L. Heitmeyer, "Verifying SCR Requirements Specifications using State Exploration," Proceedings of First ACM SIGPLAN Workshop on Automatic Analysis of Software, Paris, France, January 14, 1997.

[16] A. Hall, "Using formal methods to develop an ATC Information System," IEEE Software, vol. 13, pp. 66–76, 1996.

[17] R. A. Kemmerer, "Integrating Formal Methods into the Development Process," IEEE Software, vol. 7, pp. 37– 50, 1990.

[18] S. M. Easterbrook and B. A. Nuseibeh, "Managing Inconsistencies in an Evolving Specification," Second IEEE Symposium on Requirements Engineering, York, UK.

[19] J. R. Callahan and T. L. Montgomery, "An Approach to Verification and Validation of a Reliable Multicasting Protocol," International Symposium on Software Testing and Analysis (ISSTA'96), San Diego, CA, 8–10 January 1996.

References

[1] Practical Software Measurement, A Foundation for Objective Project Management,1 section 6.b, Version 3.1, April 17, 1998, Office of the Under Secretary of Defense for Acquisition and Technology.

[2] Easterbrook, Steve and Callahan, John, "Formal Methods for Verification and Validation of Partial Specifications: A Case Study," NASA–IVV–97–010 (1997). Article also appeared in *Journal of Systems and Software,* Vol. 40, Issue 3, March 1998. Reprinted with permission from Elsevier Science.

[3] MIL-STD-7935A, DoD Automated Information System (AIS) Documentation Standards, October 31, 1988.

[4] MIL-STD-498, Software Development and Documentation, December 5, 1994.

APPENDIX B

Acronyms

4GL fourth generation language
4GT fourth generation techniques

A

ADS advanced distributed simulation
AFB Air Force base
AFLCP Air Force Logistics Command Pamphlet
AFSC Air Force Systems Command
AI artificial intelligence
ANS artificial neural system
ANSI American National Standards Institute
API application programming interface
ASD Aeronautical Systems Division of the Air Force Systems Command
ASIC application-specific integrated circuit
ASQ American Society for Quality
ATPS tool for knowledge based systems
AVAL Automated VALidation
AVS automated verification system

B

BDD binary decision diagram
blobs binary large objects

C

C&A construction and assembly
CAD computer aided design
CARA criticality analysis and risk assessment
CASE computer aided software engineering
CAST Computer aided software test
CCB configuration control board
CCS calculus of communicating systems
CD compact disk
CD-ROM compact disk—read only memory
CDR critical design review
CERN European Laboratory for Particle Physics
CM configuration management
CMM capability maturity model
CNUCE interactor model
CORBA common object request broker architecture
COCOMO constructive cost model
COM component object model
COTS commercial-off-the-shelf
CPU central processing unit
CQI continuous quality improvement
CSC computer software component
CSCI computer software configuration item
CSP communicating sequential processes

D

DBC database connection
DBMS database management system
DCOM distributed component object module
DDP defect detection process
DES data encryption standard
DoD Department of Defense
DPP defect prevention process
DRG diagnosis-related groups

DRUM	diagnostic recorder for usability measurement
DSDM	dynamic systems development method
DSMC	Defense System Management College
DSS	decision support system

E

EIA	Electronics Industry Association
EIS	executive information system
EJB	Enterprise JavaBeans
email	electronic mail
ENS	exterior nodal system
EOSDIS	Earth Observing System Data and Information System
ESPRIT	European Commission, information technology program
ESSD	Electronic Sensors and Systems Division

F

FACADE	FAst CAse development environment
FAI	first article inspection
FAT	factory acceptance test
FCA	functional configuration audit
FD	fault days number
FDA	Food and Drug Administration
FHWA	Federal HighWay Administration
FIBSPUB	Federal Information Processing Publication
FQT	formal qualification test
FTP	file transfer protocol

G

GIOP	general inter-ORB protocol
GPS	global positioning system
GQM	goal / question / metric
GUI	graphical user interface

H

H/W	hardware
HCI	human computer interface
HMO	health maintenance organization
HTML	hypertext mark-up language
HTTP	hypertext transport protocol

I

I&T	integration and test
I/F	interface
I/O	input / output
IA	intelligent agent
IC	integrated circuit
ICO	interactive cooperative objects
IDL	interface definition language
IEC	International Electrotechnical Commission
IEEE	Institute of Electrical and Electronics Engineers
IGQM	integrated goal / question / metric
IIOP	Internat inter-ORB protocol
IIR	integrated information repository
IM&M	information movement and management
IOR	interoperable object reference
IP	Internet protocol
IPD	integrated product development
IPSEG	Internet protocol SEGmentation reassembly
IPT	integrated product team
IPX	Internet packet exchange
IS	information systems
ISE	integrated support environment
ISO	international organization for standardization
IT	information technology
ITU-T	(former CCITT)
IV&V	independent verification and validation
IVVMP	IV&V management plan

J

JAD	joint application development
JDBC	Java database connectivity
JIT	just-in-time
JPL	Jet Propulsion Laboratory
JVM	Java Virtual Machine

K

KADS	specific KBS for V&V
KB	knowledge base
KBS	knowledge based system
KPA	key process area
KSLOC	number of source lines of executable code in thousands

KSLOD source lines of design statements in thousands

L

LAN local area network
Larch property-based notations for sequential systems
LCL lower control limit
LOC line of code
LOTOS process algebra, a property-based notation with behavioral capabilities

M

M&S models and simulations
MAN metropolitan area network
MCCR mission critical computer resources
MELAS extends a conventional debugging system with additional commands for formal verification, normal and symbolic testing, and rapid prototyping using executable specifications
MOE measure of effectiveness
MOP measure of performance
MSC message sequence chart
MTBF mean time between failures
MTTF mean time to failure
MTTR mean time to repair
MUSiC measuring usability of systems in context

N

NASA National Aeronautical and Space Administration
NBS National Bureau of Standards
NIST National Institute of Standards and Technology
NT Microsoft Windows operating system

O

OBJ property-based notations for sequential systems
OLAP on-line analytic processing
OLE object linking and embedding
OMG Object Management Group
OMT object modeling technique
OO object oriented
OOD object oriented design
ORB object request broker
OS operating system
OSI open systems interconnect
OVID object view interaction design

P

PAL process asset library
PAMEX pavement maintenance expert system
PC personal computer
PCA physical configuration audit
PDA personal digital assistant
PDR preliminary design review
PDDD post-development design document
PDLC prototype development life cycle
PERT program evaluation and review technique
PV performance verification

Q

QA quality assurance
QFD quality function deployment

R

R&D research and development
RAD rapid application development
RAID reporting and information database
RAM random access memory
RDBMS relational database management system
RVM requirements verification matrix
RMP reliable multicast protocol
RVVP release V&V plan

S

S/W software
SADT structured analysis and design technique
SAM software analyst's manual
SAN system area network
SANe toolkit which derives predictive analytic usability measures
SDD software design document
SDF software development file
SDL specification and description language
SDP software development plan
SE systems engineering
SEI Software Engineering Institute

SEMP systems engineering management plan
SEPG software engineering process group
SET secure electronic transaction
SHTTP secure hypertext transfer protocol
SLM source library manager
SLOC source lines of code
SMART susceptibility model assessment and range test
SME subject matter expert
SMTP simple mail transfer protocol
SOCE Society of Concurrent Engineering
SOW statement of work
SPC statistical process control
SPICE Software Process Improvement Capability dEtermination
SPM software programmer's manual
SQA software quality assurance
SQL structured query language
SREM software requirements engineering methodology
SSE systems security engineering
SSL secure socket layer
STD software test description
STP software test plan
STS Space Transportation Systems
STT secure transaction technology
SUM software user's manual
SUMI software usability measurement inventory
SUMISCO software tool used to evaluate software usability measurement inventory
SVVP systems V&V plan

T

T&E test and evaluation
TAE transportable applications environment
TBD to be determined
TCP transmission control protocol
TCP / IP transmission control protocol / Internet protocol
TMM test maturity model
TM strongly typed functional database language used for specification of OO database schemas
TQM total quality management
TRD testing release document

U

UCA usability context analysis
UCL upper control limit
UML unified modeling language
URL uniform resource locator
UsAGE user action graphing effort

V

V&V verification and validation
V&VMM V&V maturity model
VAL V&V analysis level
VBA visual Basic for applications
VDM model-based notations for sequential systems
VDT verifiable development technique
VGQM V&V goal / question / metric
VHDL very high density language
VHSIC Very high scale integrated circuit
VLSI very large scale integration
VOCAL method based around life cycle set of test process perspectives, guiding expertise, and test identification
VRML virtual reality mark-up language
VV&A verification, validation and accreditation

W

WAN wide area network
WISE web-integrated software environment
WP work package
WWW world wide web

Z

Z (pronounced "Zed") model-based notations for sequential systems

INDEX

A
Abilene Paradox, xi, xii
access control, 290, 292, 293
ADS (*see* advanced distributed simulations)
advanced distributed simulations, 196, 255–258
advantages of rapid application development, 175
AI (*see* artificial intelligence)
analysis
  context *a*, xiv, 209, 226–229
  criticality *a*, 352, 383–393, 399, 400, 433
  defect *a*, 20, 54
  dynamic *a*, 4, 81, 82, 185–187, 347
  object oriented *a*, 11
  static *a*, 4, 81, 185–187, 254, 298, 301, 347
API (*see* Application Programming Interface)
applets, 289, 302, 305, 335
Application Programming Interface, 78, 211, 212, 241, 302, 303
applications, 8–15, 95, 119, 131–140, 173–179, 238–249, 252–254, 258–267, 282–292, 297–310, 315–320, 331–341, 357, 374, 381–384, 395–397, 399–404, 413, 431–432, 454–459
architecture of data warehousing, 313, 316–320
  data access and delivery management, 316, 319, 320, 338
  data acquisition management, 316, 318, 337, 338
  data and user security management, 316, 319
  data storage management, 316, 318, 338
  metadata management, 316, 318, 319, 338
  service level management, 316, 317, 337
artificial intelligence, xiv, 264
audits, xv, xvi, 7, 152, 341, 348, 362, 415, 416, 422, 425, 436
automated V&V of knowledge-based systems, 282, 283
Automated VALidation, xiii, 150, 151, 162
AVAL (*see* Automated VALidation)
AverStar, 71, 114, 345, 374, 440, 469

B
bar graph, 130
barriers to teams, 406, 407, 410, 411
basic proof method for knowledge-based systems, 267–278
beta testing, 79, 212, 213, 349
Boehm, Barry W., 98, 100, 102, 105, 115, 181
Boeing STS, 20–22, 48
Bootstrap, 20
build life-cycle model, xii, 32, 33

C
caching, xiv, 251, 252
Callahan, John, xvii, 134, 177, 298, 375, 378, 442, 443, 445
Capability Maturity Model, xii, xv, xvi, 20–22, 27–29, 40–42, 48, 64, 80, 120, 293–297, 311, 357, 362, 413, 418, 420, 434, 437–440, 451
CARA (*see* criticality and risk assessment)
CASE (*see* computer aided software engineering)
case study
  Formal Methods for Verification and Validation of Partial Specifications, 468–483
  MAPS Information System, 453–467
  V&V, 453–483
CAST (*see* computer-aided software test)
categories of tools, 51, 52
characteristics metrics, 121
client, 237, 242, 243, 244, 248, 249, 251
client/server, xi, xiv, 1, 143–151, 166, 172, 174, 207, 237–262, 287–289, 299, 300, 322, 344, 351, 374, 404, 405
  attributes, 238, 239
  communications, 240, 241
  multitiered architecture, 241–243
  OSI layers, 242
  points of failure, 247
  rules of thumb, 246, 247
CM (*see* configuration management)
CMM (*see* Capability Maturity Model)
CMM Level 5, 20–22, 27, 440
COBRA protocol, 61, 62, 145–147, 166, 243
cognitive walkthrough, 213–215
COM protocol, 147, 166, 167, 172, 243, 254
commercial off-the-shelf software, 77, 454–456, 464
communications difficulties, 343, 344
completeness, xiii, xiv, 98–100, 107, 110, 113, 115, 121–124, 128, 132, 140, 265, 268, 272–274, 278, 280, 281, 418, 468, 470, 476, 480
Component Object Model protocol, 147, 166, 167, 172, 243, 254
computer-aided software test, 58, 59, 91
computer-aided software engineering, 10, 56, 58, 61, 93, 96, 115, 116, 172, 178, 193, 194, 226, 344, 439, 448
concurrent engineering (*see* integrated product team)
confidence function, xv, 378–381, 399
configuration management, xvi, 4, 5, 14, 15, 183, 190, 194, 195, 385, 414–417, 425, 426, 433, 438, 439, 446
consistency, xiii, xiv, 55, 61–76, 87–90, 98–101, 113, 115, 133, 139, 154, 219, 252, 265, 268, 275–281, 318, 346, 351, 368, 416, 428, 442, 445, 468–483
context analysis, xiv, 209, 226, 228–230
context of use, 202–204, 223–225, 228–231, 234
continuous improvement program, xvi, 64, 431, 440–442
control charts, 129, 130, 361, 362
correctness verification, xiv, 110
cost, 2–27, 49, 58, 64–80, 99–103, 108, 122–131, 139, 197, 219, 233, 244, 260, 329, 346, 374–376, 385–391, 407, 408, 428, 433, 438, 443, 453–483
COTS (*see* commercial off-the-shelf software)
coverage metric, 128
criticality analysis, 382–384, 433
criticality and risk assessment, xv, 374, 384–393, 399, 400
  steps, 389, 390
customer, xv, 93–105, 169–171, 175, 191, 209, 294–297, 344, 350–358, 373–376, 385, 389, 393, 402, 417–427, 438–441, 469, 470, 482
cyclomatic complexity metric, 126

D
data acquisition and storage, xv, 316, 318, 335, 337, 338
data management, 5, 316–319, 338
data mart, 314, 315
data quality, xv, 78, 79, 320–332, 336
data warehousing, xi, xii, xv, 148, 245, 306, 307, 313–341, 350–353, 404, 449, 450
  architecture, 314, 316–320
    data access and delivery management, 316, 319, 320
    data acquisition management, 316, 318

data and user security management, 316, 319
data storage management, 316, 318
metadata management, 316, 318, 319
service level management, 316, 317
definition, 313–314
survey, 339–340
database management system, xiv, 258, 259, 334
DBMS (*see* database management system)
DDP (*see* defect detection process)
decision tree, 279–281
defect age metric, 127
defect analysis and prevention, 20, 155
defect density metric, 125
defect detection process, 17, 27, 28
defect prevention process, 17, 27, 28
defect removal efficiency metric, 127
definition of data warehousing, 313–315
design specification, 96–106, 115, 132, 133
design specification tools, 85
design verification, 3, 4, 46, 250, 251
determinates of usability, 202
Deutsch, Michael S., xvii, 342, 428
development of knowledge-based systems, 264, 265
differences and similarities of knowledge-based systems, 265–267
disadvantages of rapid application development, 176
distributed component platforms, 254, 255
document development tasks, 95
document metrics, 132–134
document reviews, xiii, 113–115, 291
documentation, xiii, 6, 15, 77, 79, 93–116, 172, 277, 278, 373, 381, 385, 403, 406, 412, 425, 475
documentation process, 94–98
documentation review levels, xiii, 112–116
documentation review methods, 110, 111, 115
documentation system characteristics, 93
DPP (*see* defect prevention process)
DSDM (*see* dynamic systems development method)
dynamic analysis tool, 4, 81–90, 112, 185–187, 347
dynamic systems development method, xiv, 177, 180–189, 197, 198
dynamic verification, xiii, 141, 157, 158, 163

E
Earth Observing System Data and Information System, 51, 71, 113, 114, 345, 366, 384, 440
Easterbrook, Steve, 96, 177, 343, 374, 441
effectiveness of teams, xvi, 402, 404–411
effectiveness of V&V, 432–434
EOSDIS (*see* Earth Observing System Data and Information System)
Esprit Project, xiii, xiv, 150, 162, 202, 226
excuses for not implementing a process, 19, 20
expert system, xiv, xv, 110, 111, 263, 268, 272, 277, 279, 282, 397–400, 451
experts, 110, 210, 229, 263, 264, 277–280, 284, 398, 404, 468

F
FACADE project, xv, 77, 298, 299, 310
failure rate metric, 128
fault days metric, 124
fault density metric, 127
feasibility, xiii, 102
firewall, 288, 292, 306–309
formal methods, 61, 84–86, 108–111, 154, 155, 219–228, 269–278, 347, 468, 478, 480–484
Formal Methods for Verification and Validation of Partial Specifications case study, 468–484
formal proofs, 74, 75, 269–278
formal specification, 73–75, 170, 446–448, 453, 468–483
formal usability inspections, 213, 216, 217
formality of methods and tools, 70
fourth-generation life-cycle model, xii, 36, 37
fourth generation techniques, 173
function points metric, 124, 461
functional specification, 106–113, 115, 132, 133
future trends, xvi, 431, 432, 446–451

G
goal/question/metric, xiii, xv, 134–136, 375–381
GQM (*see* goal/question/metric)
graphical user interface, xi, xii, xiv, 137–140, 147, 160, 161, 172, 173, 187, 201–235, 242, 249, 258, 259, 288, 291, 301, 355, 344, 456, 457
GUI (*see* graphical user interface)
Guidelines for Lifecycle Validation, Verification and Testing of Computer Software, 341, 345, 365

H
heuristic evaluations, 214–215

I
IBM, 63, 64, 180, 224, 304, 402
IDL (*see* interface definition language)
IEEE Standard for Software Verification and Validation Plans, 341, 364, 394
implementation verification, 3, 4
Independent Release V&V Plan, 345
Independent Systems Verification and Validation Plan, 341, 345, 366
Information Mapping, 22, 23
inspections, xii, xvi, 7, 62–64, 68, 69, 81, 172, 253, 297, 351, 352, 420–428, 436, 464, 482
integrated product development, xvi, 402–404, 419–421
integrated product development team (*see* integrated product team)
integrated product team, xv, 14, 16, 297, 401–429, 449–451, 459, 460, 466
configuration management, 425, 426
customer, 417, 418
independent verification and validation, 426, 427
other groups,423, 424
other IPTs, 424
philosophy, 408
program management, 423
quality assurance, 421, 422
software development, 419–421
structure, 402–404, 413
systems, 418, 419
integrated support environment, 71, 72
Integration and Certification Plan, 345
intelligent agent, 230, 231, 263, 281
interface definition language, 145, 146
Internet, xii, 93, 173, 287–289, 291, 292, 300–305, 332–334
Internet/intranet, xi, xv, 136–139, 147, 172, 287–312, 332–335, 344, 351, 354–357, 395–397, 449, 450
intranet, 1, 93, 288, 291, 308–311
IPD (*see* integrated product development)
IPT (*see* integrated product team)
ISE (*see* integrated support environment)
ISO 12207 life-cycle model, xii, 34, 35
iterative DSDM life-cycle model, 187, 189

J
JAD (*see* joint application development)
Java, xv, 147, 166, 167, 174, 259, 289, 299, 302–305, 335, 348
JavaBeans, 167, 254, 255
joint application development, 172, 175–177
just in time inspections, xiv, 172, 177

K
KBS (*see* knowledge-based systems)
knowledge-based systems, xi, xii, xiv, xvi, 120, 137–140, 148, 263–285, 313, 374, 404, 449, 450
automated V&V of, 282, 283
basic proof method, 267–278
development, 266
differences and similarities, 265–267
knowledge-based systems to perform V&V activities, 446–450

L
LAN (*see* local area network)
launching of teams, 402, 410
Lewis, Robert O., xvii, 1, 3, 16, 132, 136, 140, 170, 176, 196, 255, 353, 363, 374, 382, 438
life-cycle, 25, 76, 94, 102, 112, 113, 163, 175, 189, 216, 266, 289, 296–301, 345, 353, 358, 364–367, 375, 383, 388, 392, 435
life-cycle models, xii, 8, 17, 18, 29–39, 41, 48, 119, 186, 187, 264, 291
build, xii, 33, 34
fourth-generation, xii, 36, 37
ISO 12207, xii, 34, 35
iterative DSDM, 187, 189
model-based, xii, 36, 249, 250, 264, 266

modified waterfall, xii, 32, 33
spiral, xii, 35, 36
waterfall, xii, 29–32, 42, 186, 187
lines of code metric, 126, 135, 461
load testing, xiv, 245, 252, 253
local area network, 241–245, 249, 287, 299, 353

M
maintenance, 107, 133, 279–281, 347, 421, 437, 438, 444, 448
management metrics, 120
MAPS Information System case study, 453–467
mean time to failure (MTTF) metric, 128, 135, 424
measurement, xiii, 64, 120–135, 375, 379, 439, 444, 446, 453–467
measurement validation, 121
Measuring Usability of Systems in Context, xiv, 202, 208, 209, 226–228
MELAS system, 158, 163
methodology, 52–82, 163, 172, 315, 342, 353, 374, 407, 438
methods for V&V, 54–56
metric
coverage, 128
cyclomatic complexity, 126
defect age, 127
defect density, 125
defect removal efficiency, 127
failure rate, 128
fault days, 124
fault density, 127
function points, 124, 461
lines of code, 126, 135, 461
mean time to failure (MTTF), 128, 135, 424
primitive fault, 125
primitive size, 122–125
software science, 126
staff hours per major defect, 125
test coverage, 125, 126
usability, 211, 224, 227
metrics, xiii, 20, 54, 64, 119–140, 211, 224, 225, 382–393, 453–483
characteristics, 121
document, 132–134
management, 120
primitive, 121–125
quality, 127, 128
risk, 374–381
Microsoft Corporation, x, xiii, 78–80, 144, 166, 167, 177, 205, 212, 243–245, 254, 289, 290, 308, 311, 352
Microsoft test methods, 347, 349, 350, 362
model-based development approach, 206
model-based life-cycle model, xii, 36, 249, 250, 264, 266
modeling a process, 40, 41
models, 17, 28–46, 48, 375, 447, 451–460, 476–482
Models and Simulations Master Plan, 190–195
modified waterfall life-cycle model, xii, 32, 33
multidimensional model, xii, xvi, 7–11, 17, 18, 56, 94, 119, 147, 148, 172, 205, 206, 245, 264, 291, 316, 344, 374, 404, 431, 438
multimedia, 288, 289, 299–302, 310
MUSiC (*see* Measuring Usability of Systems in Context)

N
NASA, xv, 1, 8, 74, 75, 162, 298, 299, 345, 351, 453
network partitioning, 258

O
Object Modeling Technique, 18, 76, 161, 179
object oriented, xii, xiii, 137–139, 141–167, 172, 245, 302, 303, 341, 344, 351, 449, 450
benefits, 141, 143, 147
definitions, 142
problems and preventions, 148, 149
object oriented analysis, 11
object oriented database verification, 154, 155
object oriented design, xiv
object oriented project management, 163, 164
object request broker, 146, 147, 166, 167
Object View Interaction Design, xiii, 141, 158–161, 163
ObjectGEODE, xiv, 177, 179, 180, 198
OLAP (*see* on-line analytic processing)
OMT (*see* Object Modeling Technique)
on-line analytic processing, 339
OOA (*see* object oriented analysis)
OOD (*see* object oriented design)
ORB (*see* object request broker)
output validation, 192
OVID (*see* Object View Interaction Design)

P
packaging a process, 23, 24
Pareto charts, xiii, 125, 130, 131
Pareto diagram, 130, 131
PDLC (*see* prototype development life-cycle)
peer reviews, xiii, 65–69, 81, 212, 351, 393, 420, 424, 427, 428, 436
code reading review, 66, 67
inspections, 68, 69, 351
round-robin review, 67
walkthrough, 68, 351, 436
perspective-based techniques, 214, 217
predictive function, 378–381
Pressman, Roger S., 105, 169, 170, 416, 421
primitive fault metric, 125
primitive metrics, 121–125
primitive size metric, 122–125
privacy, 290–293, 309, 310
process, 8–12, 17–28, 48, 94, 119, 172, 173, 253, 266, 283, 291–310, 344, 360–362, 374, 394, 400, 418–421, 431–440, 442–446, 453–483
defect detection *p*, 17, 27, 28
defect prevention *p*, 17, 27, 28
documentation *p*, 94–98
excuses for not implementing, 19, 20
modeling a *p*, 40, 41
packaging, 23, 24
project management *p* methods, 344, 360–362
purpose, 22
Systems Engineering, 23, 25–27
process improvement model of V&V, 431, 442–446
process paralysis, 20
process variability, xv, 361, 362
Product Maturity Model, xii, 41–44, 48, 394
product risk maturity, 374, 394, 400
product V&V, 44–46
program verification, xiii, 60–62
project management, xv, 341–371, 373–376, 383, 393, 404, 432, 433, 438, 451, 453–467
project management process methods, 344, 360–362
protocol
COM (*see* Component Object Model)
Component Object Model, 147, 166, 167, 172, 243, 245, 254
CORBA, 61, 62, 145–147, 166, 243
protocols, 8, 61, 62, 241, 246, 287, 288, 299, 413, 439
prototype development life-cycle, 175–178, 188
prototyping, 55, 59, 81, 136, 169–200, 220, 253, 266, 377, 389, 402
graphical user interface, 173–178
purpose of a process, 22

Q
QA (*see* quality assurance)
QFD (*see* quality function deployment)
quality assurance, xvi, 16, 62, 253, 297, 343, 421–423, 428, 441, 451
quality function deployment, 175
quality metrics, 127, 128
quality of use, 204, 223–225, 230

R
RAD (*see* rapid application development)
Rakitin, Steven R., 63, 64, 175, 250
rapid application development, xiv, 137–139, 148, 169–200, 291, 341, 344, 402
advantages, 175
disadvantages, 176
rapid prototyping, 4, 169, 170, 253, 266
Raytheon, 27
regression method, xiii
regression testing, xiii, 59, 60, 79
relationship to other groups of V&V, 6
release method, xiii, 345, 349, 350, 371
requirement, 1–6, 15–17, 25–27, 29–32, 44–48, 53–57, 70–76, 81–90,

96–109, 128–135, 169–172, 175–177, 182–192, 195–198, 267, 281–283, 291–300, 305, 310, 346, 401–408, 411–427, 431–451, 455–463, 468–483
requirements specification, 98–106, 115, 132, 133
requirements specification tools, 84
requirements verification, 3, 4
requirements verification matrix, 44, 45
response time, 252, 253
reviews, xvi, 3–7, 81, 96, 113–116, 134, 152, 250–254, 291–298,346–353, 403–406, 415–428, 433–437, 451, 454, 459–461
risk, xiii, xv, 3, 14, 15, 26, 38, 103, 104, 134–136, 218, 271–276, 281, 296, 352, 360, 373–400, 410, 416, 435, 441, 459, 460, 466, 469, 479
risk assessment, xv, 373
risk categories, 387
risk management, xv, 373–400, 404
risk metrics, 374–381
risk mitigation, 373, 394, 396
RVM (*see* requirements verification matrix)

S

safety, xvi, 5, 74, 77, 95, 104, 305, 308, 320, 345, 373, 385, 421, 431, 441, 448, 468, 469, 471, 476, 482
scalability, xiv, 253, 254
scatter diagram, 131
schedule, xv, 95, 169, 178, 318, 346–359, 364, 371–385, 402–412, 427–434, 444, 451, 454, 467–470
security, xv, 288–298, 305–311, 316, 319, 321, 326, 334, 336, 345, 383, 385, 407, 451
SEI (*see* Software Engineering Institute)
server, 237, 246–250, 291, 292, 299, 308
simulation, 4, 55, 59, 73, 76, 87, 90, 169–180, 191–198, 350, 351, 384, 416, 476
simulation and modeling, 4, 177, 190–193, 198
  accreditation process challenges, 193
  validation process challenges, 192, 193
  verification process challenges, 192
simulations
  advanced distributed, 196, 197
SMART (*see* Susceptibility Model Assessment and Range Test)
social user interface, 205, 230
software development, xiii, xv, xvi, 2, 3, 17, 18, 52–64, 93, 140–163, 171–174, 182, 198, 298–310, 341–347, 352–357, 375, 385, 401, 413–428, 434–471
software engineering environments, 71–73
Software Engineering Institute, xii, xv, xvi, 20–22, 27–29, 64, 80, 120, 357, 360, 394, 413–420, 437
software maintenance, xvi, 432–448, 454, 458, 483
software quality, ix, 5, 17, 40, 253, 297, 422, 434, 436, 444, 451
software reliability, 128, 131, 132, 373, 424, 443
software science metric, 126
Software Usability Measurement Inventory, xiv, 208, 209, 226, 227
software V&V project planning, 358
software V&V project tracking and oversight, 359
SPC (*see* statistical process control)
specification
  design *s*, 98–106, 115, 132, 133
  formal *s*, 73–75, 170, 446–448, 453, 468–483
  functional *s*, 106–113, 115, 132, 133
  requirements *s*, 98–106, 115, 132, 133
  test *s*, 106–113, 115, 132, 133
specifications, xiii, 17, 265–278, 345–347, 375, 382, 399, 431–446, 453, 456, 466–483
SPICE, 20
spiral life-cycle model, xii, 35, 36
SSE (*see* Systems Security Engineering)
staff hours per major defect metric, 125
standards, xv, 8, 17, 18, 46–48, 95, 115, 147, 288–297, 301–311, 345, 348, 373, 381, 388, 394, 433, 436, 441, 444, 454
  registration, 48
standards list for V&V, 46–48
static analysis tool, 4, 81–90, 186, 187, 254, 298, 299, 347
statistical process control, xiii, 120, 128–131, 361, 362
  bar graph, 130
  control charts, 129, 130, 361, 362
  Pareto diagram, 130, 131
  scatter diagram, 131
SUMI (*see* Software Usability Measurement Inventory)
survey of data warehousing, 339, 340
Susceptibility Model Assessment and Range Test, xiv, 177, 190, 192–195
syntactical checking tool, 160–162
Systems Engineering process, 23, 25–27
Systems Security Engineering (SSE), 291, 293–297, 311, 451

T

T&E (*see* test and evaluation)
teams, 401–428
  barriers, 406, 407, 410, 411
  effectiveness, xvi, 402, 406–411
  launching, 402, 410
technology, xvi, 9–11, 94,120, 147, 172, 245, 264, 265,287–299, 308, 316, 344, 353, 374–387, 403–406, 436, 440, 441, 451, 479
tenets of V&V, 11–16
test and evaluation, 257
test coverage metric, 125, 126
test specification, 106–113, 115, 132, 133
testability, xiii, 99, 104–106, 133, 385–388, 470
tester's workbench, 53, 54
testing, xiii, 4–6, 78, 79, 112, 127, 148–154, 175–189, 209–213, 217–219, 349, 350, 373–389, 398–416, 425–448, 459, 464–466, 478
  beta *t*, 79, 212, 213, 349
  load *t*, xiv, 245, 252, 253
  regression *t*, xiii, 59, 60, 79
  usability *t*, 155, 209–213, 217–219, 349, 437
Testing Maturity Model, xvi, 80, 81, 119, 133, 134, 431, 434–438, 451
thin client, 243, 244, 304
throughput, 249, 251, 401
time boxing, xiv, 184, 185
TM language, 154, 155, 163
TMM (*see* Testing Maturity Model)
tool
  dynamic analysis, 4, 81, 82, 84–90, 112, 185–187, 347
  static analysis, 4, 81, 84–90, 186, 187, 254, 298, 299, 347
  syntactical checking, 160–162
tool and method keywords, 87–90
tool categories, 51, 52
tools, 4, 313–319, 334–349, 358–370, 382–393, 420–471, 481–483
tools and methodologies, xii, xiii, 7, 18, 51–92, 439
  formality of, 70
tools and methods selection, 52, 53, 84–90, 441
traceability, xiii, 70, 71, 94, 99–102, 121, 132, 343, 346, 366, 370–385, 415–427, 441, 469–483

U

UML (*see* Unified Modeling Language)
Unified Modeling language, 143, 144, 162
usability, xiv, 201–235
  determinates of, 202
  metrics of views, 201
usability and quality, 203, 209, 223–229
usability in web sites, 2, 29, 229–235
usability inspections, xiv, 210–219, 230
  cognitive walkthrough, 215
  formal usability inspections, 216, 217
  heuristic evaluations, 214, 215
  perspective-based techniques, 217
  usability testing, 214, 217–219
usability metric, 211, 224, 227
usability testing, 155, 209–213, 217–219, 349, 437
  usability inspections, 210, 212–219
user, 106, 159, 173–187, 201–218, 223–230, 316–319, 335–352, 370, 385, 388, 397–438, 455–467, 481
user interface correctness, 210, 219–222, 230
user interface design, 160
User Validation Plan, 206

V

V&V
  case studies, 453–484

effectiveness, 432–434
methods, 54–56
process improvement model, 431, 442–446
product, 44–46
relationship to other groups, 6
standards list, 46–48
tenets, 11–16
V&V activities by phase, 341, 342, 353–357
V&V activities performed by knowledge-based systems, 431, 446–448
V&V management methods, 352–357
V&V Management Plan, 113, 345, 440
V&V maturity levels, 431, 438–440
V&V phase audits, 341, 348, 362
V&V planning, 341, 345–347, 353, 357, 358, 362, 388, 420
V&V scheduling management, 341, 348, 362
V&V techniques, 341, 350–353
V&V test planning, 341, 348, 349, 362
V&V Tool Management Plan, xiii, 56, 57, 71, 72
validating underlying knowledge, 278, 279
validation, 3, 4
validation tests, 176, 177, 255–258
VDT (*see* verifiable development technique)
verifiable development technique, xv, 77, 298, 299, 310, 445
verification tests, 176, 177, 256, 257, 451
verification, validation, and accreditation, xiv, 2, 177, 190–198, 255–257, 431
VOCAL, 141, 155–157, 163
VV&A (*see* verification, validation and accreditation)

W

Wallace, Dolores R., 5, 120, 345, 383, 432
WAN (*see* wide area network)
waterfall life-cycle model, xii, 186, 187
web-based client/server, 258, 259
wide area network, 241–245, 249, 253, 287, 299
World Wide Web, xiv, 166, 235, 258, 288, 291, 299, 302, 333
WWW (*see* World Wide Web)

Z

Z notation, 162, 220–222